Here's What People Say
About Bestselling Author Tom Swan

S0-BBZ-805

"Tom's writing style makes even dense programming issues crystal clear."

— Brett Salter, The Periscope Company

"Everything that's done by Tom Swan is satisfaction guaranteed."

— Albert Lee, Indonesia

"Tom Swan is an excellent author who makes learning a programming language a clear, concise process."

— Jason Major, Canada

"A brilliant approach to teaching."

— Paul Dugas, Richford, VT

"Tom Swan makes learning simple and easy."

— Brian Mayfield, Silverdale, CT

"I couldn't put his book down. A 'must-use' for programmers."

— Martin Little, US Army

"One of the best books on programming I have come across."

— Philip Rezk, Ridgefield, CT

"An easy-to-follow progression from basic to complex topics with thorough explanation of each topic."

— Michael Mills, Boca Raton, FL

FOUNDATIONS™ *of*

Delphi™

DEVELOPMENT FOR

WINDOWS® 95

TOM SWAN

Internationally Acclaimed Bestselling Computer Programming Author

Foundations™ of Delphi™ Development for Windows® 95

Published by
IDG Books Worldwide, Inc.
An International Data Group Company
919 East Hillsdale Boulevard, Suite 400
Foster City, CA 94404

Copyright © 1995 by Tom Swan. All rights reserved. No part of this book (including interior design, cover design, and illustrations) may be reproduced or transmitted in any form, by any means, (electronic, photocopying, recording, or otherwise) without the prior written permission of the publisher. For authorization to photocopy items for internal corporate use, personal use, or for educational and/or classroom use, please contact: Copyright Clearance Center, 222 Rosewood Drive, Danvers, MA 01923 USA, Fax 508-750-4470.

Library of Congress Catalog Card No.: 95-077587

ISBN 1-56884-347-X

Printed in the United States of America

First Printing, September, 1995
10 9 8 7 6 5 4 3 2 1

Distributed in the United States by IDG Books Worldwide, Inc.

Limit of Liability/Disclaimer of Warranty: The author and publisher of this book have used their best efforts in preparing this book. IDG Books Worldwide, Inc., International Data Group, Inc., and the author make no representation or warranties with respect to the accuracy or completeness of the contents of this book or the material on the CD-ROM included with this book, and specifically disclaim any implied warranties of merchantability or fitness for any particular purpose, and shall in no event be liable for any loss of profit or any other commercial damage, including but not limited to special, incidental, consequential or other damages.

Trademarks: All brand names and product names used in this book are trademarks, registered trademarks, or trade names of their respective holders. IDG Books Worldwide, Inc., is not associated with any product or vendor mentioned in this book.

 Published in the United States

FROM THE PUBLISHER

The *Foundations* series is designed, written, and edited by working programmers for working programmers. We asked you what you needed from a book to become productive using a programming tool, technique, or language. You told us to publish a book that:

- Is written from the perspective of a professional programmer
- Provides great coding examples that can be readily applied to your programs
- Serves as a tutorial that facilitates mastery of complex techniques, features, and concepts
- Serves as a comprehensive reference, achieving "dog-eared" status on your short-shelf of must-have books
- Provides a comprehensive index (programmers always go to the index first!)
- Includes either a fully indexed and linked electronic reference for quick and portable reference or valuable software that helps you get your job done better.

Our goal is to deliver all of this and more. We offer no gimmicks; no promise of instant proficiency through repetition or oversimplification. Sure, it's okay to learn the basics of driving a car doing 20 MPH with your dad in an empty parking lot. But if you're competing the next day in the Indy 500, you need entirely different preparation. You need to know the capabilities of your machine, the idiosyncrasies of the course, and how to translate that knowledge into a competitive advantage.

Like all Programmers Press books, this book is written by professionals. It is meticulously edited for technical accuracy, completeness, and readability. It is a book you will come to trust and rely on.

Thank you for choosing our product.

Christopher J. Williams

Christopher J. Williams
Group Publisher and Vice President

ABOUT IDG BOOKS WORLDWIDE

Welcome to the world of IDG Books Worldwide.

IDG Books Worldwide, Inc. is a subsidiary of International Data Group, the world's largest publisher of computer-related information and the leading global provider of information services on information technology. IDG was founded more than 25 years ago and now employs more than 7,500 people worldwide. IDG publishes more than 235 computer publications in 67 countries (see listing below). More than fifty million people read one or more IDG publications each month.

Launched in 1990, IDG Books Worldwide is today the #1 publisher of best-selling computer books in the United States. We are proud to have received 3 awards from the Computer Press Association in recognition of editorial excellence, and our best-selling ...For Dummies™ series has more than 18 million copies in print with translations in 24 languages. IDG Books, through a recent joint venture with IDG's Hi-Tech Beijing, became the first U.S. publisher to publish a computer book in the People's Republic of China. In record time, IDG Books has become the first choice for millions of readers around the world who want to learn how to better manage their businesses.

Our mission is simple: Every IDG book is designed to bring extra value and skill-building instructions to the reader. Our books are written by experts who understand and care about our readers. The knowledge base of our editorial staff comes from years of experience in publishing, education, and journalism — experience which we use to produce books for the '90s. In short, we care about books, so we attract the best people. We devote special attention to details such as audience, interior design, use of icons, and illustrations. And because we use an efficient process of authoring, editing, and desktop publishing our books electronically, we can spend more time ensuring superior content and spend less time on the technicalities of making books.

You can count on our commitment to deliver high-quality books at competitive prices on topics consumers want to read about. At IDG, we value quality, and we have been delivering quality for more than 25 years. You'll find no better book on a subject than an IDG book.

John J. Kilcullen

John Kilcullen
President and CEO
IDG Books Worldwide, Inc.

IDG Books Worldwide, Inc. is a subsidiary of International Data Group, the world's largest publisher of computer-related information and the leading global provider of information services on information technology. International Data Group publishes over 235 computer publications in 67 countries. More than fifty million people read one or more International Data Group publications each month. The officers are Patrick J. McGovern, Founder and Board Chairman; Kelly Conlin, President; Jim Casella, Chief Operating Officer. International Data Group's publications include: **ARGENTINA'S** Computerworld Argentina, Infoworld Argentina; **AUSTRALIA'S** Computerworld Australia, Computer Living, Australian PC World, Australian Macworld, Network World, Mobile Business Australia, Publish!, Reseller, IDG Sources; **AUSTRIA'S** Computerwelt Oesterreich, PC Test; **BELGIUM'S** Data News (CW); **BOLIVIA'S** Computerworld; **BRAZIL'S** Computerworld, Connections, Game Power, Mundo Unix, PC World, Publish, Super Game; **BULGARIA'S** Computerworld Bulgaria, PC & Mac World Bulgaria, Network World Bulgaria; **CANADA'S** CIO Canada, Computerworld Canada, Info-Canada, Network World Canada, Reseller; **CHILE'S** Computerworld Chile, Informatica; **COLOMBIA'S** Computerworld Colombia, PC World; **COSTA RICA'S** PC World; **CZECH REPUBLIC'S** Computerworld, Elektronika, PC World; **DENMARK'S** Communications World, Computerworld Danmark, Computerworld Focus, Macintosh Produktkatalog, Macworld Danmark, PC World Danmark, PC Produktguide, Tech World, Windows World; **ECUADOR'S** PC World Ecuador; **EGYPT'S** Computerworld (CW) Middle East, PC World Middle East; **FINLAND'S** MikroPC, Tietoviikko, Tietoverkko; **FRANCE'S** Distributique, GOLDEN MAC, InfoPC, Le Guide du Monde Informatique, Le Monde Informatique, Telecoms & Reseaux; **GERMANY'S** Computerwoche, Computerwoche Focus, Computerwoche Extra, Electronic Entertainment, Gamepro, Information Management, Macwelt, Netzwelt, PC Welt, Publish, Publish; **GREECE'S** Publish & Macworld; **HONG KONG'S** Computerworld Hong Kong, PC World Hong Kong; **HUNGARY'S** Computerworld SZT, PC World; **INDIA'S** Computers & Communications; **INDONESIA'S** Info Komputer; **IRELAND'S** ComputerScope; **ISRAEL'S** Beyond Windows, Computerworld Israel, Multimedia, PC World Israel; **ITALY'S** Computerworld Italia, Lotus Magazine, Macworld Italia, Networking Italia, PC Shopping Italy, PC World Italia; **JAPAN'S** Computerworld Today, Information Systems World, Macworld Japan, Nikkei Personal Computing, SunWorld Japan, Windows World; **KENYA'S** East African Computer News; **KOREA'S** Computerworld Korea, Macworld Korea, PC World Korea; **LATIN AMERICA'S** GamePro; **MALAYSIA'S** Computerworld Malaysia, PC World Malaysia; **MEXICO'S** Compu Edicion, Compu Manufactura, Computacion/Punto de Venta, Computerworld Mexico, MacWorld, Mundo Unix, PC World, Windows; **THE NETHERLANDS'** Computer! Totaal, Computable (CW), LAN Magazine, Lotus Magazine, MacWorld; **NEW ZEALAND'S** Computer Buyer, Computerworld New Zealand, Network World, New Zealand PC World; **NIGERIA'S** PC World Africa; **NORWAY'S** Computerworld Norge, Lotusworld Norge, Macworld Norge, Maxi Data, Networld, PC World Ekspress, PC World Nettverk, PC World Norge, PC World's Produktguide, Publish& Multimedia World, Student Data, Unix World, Windowsworld; **PAKISTAN'S** PC World Pakistan; **PANAMA'S** PC World Panama; **PERU'S** Computerworld Peru, PC World; **PEOPLE'S REPUBLIC OF CHINA'S** China Computerworld, China Infoworld, China PC Info Magazine, Computer Fan, PC World China, Electronics International, Electronics Today/Multimedia World, Electronic Product World, China Network World, Software World Magazine, Telecom Product World; **PHILIPPINES'** Computerworld Philippines, PC Digest (PCW); **POLAND'S** Computerworld Poland, Computerworld Special Report, Networld, PC World/Komputer, Sunworld; **PORTUGAL'S** Cerebro/PC World, Correio Informatico/Computerworld, MacIn; **ROMANIA'S** Computerworld, PC World, Telecom Romania; **RUSSIA'S** Computerworld-Moscow, Mir - PK (PCW), Sety (Networks); **SINGAPORE'S** Computerworld Southeast Asia, PC World Singapore; **SLOVENIA'S** Monitor Magazine; **SOUTH AFRICA'S** Computer Mail (CIO), Computing S.A., Network World S.A., Software World; **SPAIN'S** Advanced Systems, Amiga World, Computerworld Espana, Communicaciones World, Macworld Espana, NeXTWORLD, Super Juegos Magazine (GamePro), PC World Espana, Publish; **SWEDEN'S** Attack, ComputerSweden, Corporate Computing, Macworld, Mikrodatorn, Natverk & Kommunikation, PC World, CAP & Design, Datalngenjoren, Maxi Data, Windows World; **SWITZERLAND'S** Computerworld Schweiz, Macworld Schweiz, PC Tip; **TAIWAN'S** Computerworld Taiwan, PC World Taiwan; **THAILAND'S** Thai Computerworld; **TURKEY'S** Computerworld Monitor, Macworld Turkiye, PC World Turkiye; **UKRAINE'S** Computerworld, Computers+Software Magazine; **UNITED KINGDOM'S** Computing /Computerworld, Connexion/Network World, Lotus Magazine, Macworld, Open Computing/Sunworld; **UNITED STATES'** Advanced Systems, Amiga-World, Cable in the Classroom, CD Review, CIO, Computerworld, Computerworld Client/Server Journal, Digital Video, DOS World, Electronic Entertainment Magazine (E2), Federal Computer Week, Game Hits, GamePro, IDG Books, Infoworld, Laser Event, Macworld, Maximize, Multimedia World, Network World, PC Letter, PC World, Publish, SWATPro, Video Event; **URUGUAY'S** PC World Uruguay; **VENEZUELA'S** Computerworld Venezuela, PC World; **VIETNAM'S** PC World Vietnam.

For More Information...

For general information on IDG Books in the U.S., including information on discounts and premiums, contact IDG Books at 800-434-3422.

For information on where to purchase IDG's books outside the U.S., contact Christina Turner at 415-655-3022.

For information on translations, contact Marc Jeffrey Mikulich, Foreign Rights Manager, at IDG Books Worldwide; fax number: 415-655-3295.

For sales inquiries and special prices for bulk quantities, contact Tony Real at 800-434-3422 or 415-655-3048.

For information on using IDG's books in the classroom and ordering examination copies, contact Jim Kelly at 800-434-2086.

Foundations of Delphi Development for Windows 95 is distributed in Canada by Macmillan of Canada, a Division of Canada Publishing Corporation; by Computer and Technical Books in Miami, Florida, for South America and the Caribbean; by Longman Singapore in Singapore, Malaysia, Thailand, and Korea; by Toppan Co. Ltd. in Japan; by Asia Computerworld in Hong Kong; by Woodslane Pty. Ltd. in Australia and New Zealand; and by Transword Publishers Ltd. in the U.K. and Europe.

Credits

Group Publisher and Vice President
Christopher J. Williams

Publishing Director
John Osborn

Senior Acquisitions Manager
Amorette Pedersen

Editorial Director
Anne Marie Walker

Editorial Assistant
Tracy Brown

Production Director
Beth A. Roberts

Project Editors
Mary Ann Faughnan
Denise Peters

Manuscript Editor
John Pont

Technical Editor
Danny Thorpe

Composition and Layout
Ronnie Bucci
Dusty Parsons

Proofreader
Phyllis Coyne

Indexer
Ted Laux

CD-ROM Production
The Komando Corporation

Cover Design
Draper and Liew Inc.

Cover Photo
Mark Tomalty/Masterfile

About the Author

Tom Swan has written more than 30 computer books and editions including *Type and Learn C, Type and Learn Windows Programming with WinScope, Mastering Borland C++,* and *Mastering Turbo Assembler.* Over 250,000 copies of the author's best-selling classic, *Mastering Turbo Pascal,* are in print. Many of Swan's books have been translated into several foreign languages and are favorite selections in classrooms.

The author has also published hundreds of articles on programming techniques, and he is a former contributing editor for *PC World, Dr. Dobb's Journal,* and *PC Techniques.*

Tom Swan lives in Key West, Florida. When not writing and programming, he spends his time sailing, diving, and exploring the Florida Keys. The existence of this book is proof that Tom has still managed not to drop his laptop overboard, one of his proudest accomplishments to date.

Dedication

To Larry Weeldreyer

Acknowledgments

Thanks are due all IDG editors and employees who worked hard to bring this book to you, most especially Amy Pedersen and Anne Marie Walker. Also, a huge thank you to Danny Thorpe for a superb technical review. To John Pont for a careful edit. To Ted Laux for an expertly crafted index. To Larry for tea and company. To my brother David Swan for helping with the database chapter. To my agents, Bill Gladstone and Margot Maley, and all at Waterside Productions, for taking care of business. To Jerry Bever and Lynne Goewey of Key West Office Center, for a great place to work. And as always, to Anne Swan for reading and formatting the manuscript, but mostly for being there.

The publisher would like to give special thanks to Patrick J. McGovern, without whom this book would not have been possible.

Contents Overview

Add common file-selection, font, color, and find-and-replace dialogs to applications. Also learn how to use Delphi's paged components to create complex, multiple page, dialog windows.

PART III   THE APPLICATION 439

Every application is different, of course, but most applications fall into one of the categories covered here. Learn how to use Delphi's components to construct graphics, printer, MDI, DDE, OLE, and database applications.

Use Delphi's Canvas property to control your program's graphical output. The Canvas puts an object-oriented face on the Windows graphical device interface (GDI).

Implement text and graphics printing with Delphi's TPrinter class. You'll also learn how to create a print-preview command by "printing" to a bitmap.

Construct Multiple Document Interface (MDI) applications with Delphi forms. Learn to create same- and different-type document child windows.

Pass data to and from the Windows clipboard, and establish conversations between applications using the Windows dynamic data exchange (DDE) protocols. Also learn how to build OLE container applications using Delphi components.

Delphi's extensive database capabilities open the world of database development to every programmer. Learn how to construct database entry screens and how to access and create Paradox, dBase, and ODBC-compliant database tables.

Table of Contents

Preface

Sometimes it seems only the gods could comprehend all that's required to develop a Windows application. For many developers, languages such as C++, while highly capable, may be as difficult to learn as classical Greek. Isn't there a less painful method to write quality Windows software?

Yes, there is. With Borland's Delphi, you don't need thunderbolts and teams of programmers in winged chariots to develop for Windows. Called a *Rapid Application Development* system, or RAD, Delphi is a smart code generator, a visual application designer, and a database tool in a superb interface that's simple to learn, yet powerful to use. Programming with Delphi is even a bit scary. I swear this thing can read my mind.

Foundations of Delphi Development provides a complete guide to Windows software development with Delphi. You don't need a degree in computer science to read this book, but if you know Pascal, C, C++, or Visual Basic, you'll be way ahead of the pack. Numerous step-by-step instructions demonstrate the ins and outs of visual components and the Object Pascal language. You'll learn how to create snazzy user interfaces for a variety of applications using graphics, printing, DDE, OLE, databases and more. Dozens of sample applications, all provided on the included CD-ROM, light the way.

On a personal note, I cut my programming teeth on Pascal, and it's been great fun to rediscover this highly capable language. In Delphi, Object Pascal proves its value as the perfect partner in a visual-programming environment. There's never been a product quite like Delphi, and I hope you enjoy learning about it as much as I have. Good luck!

Tom Swan
Key West, Florida

I Introduction

*I*f you're just getting started in Windows software development, you've come to the right place to begin. As you will learn, with Delphi's help, you can develop complex applications in short order, regardless of your programming experience.

If you already know your way around Delphi, or you're an experienced programmer, you can read the three chapters in Part 1 quickly. But do read them. They introduce the book's format and contain information that you need to know before you'll be ready to tackle more advanced topics.

Part 1 Chapters

- Chapter 1, *Introducing Delphi*
- Chapter 2, *Introducing Visual Components*
- Chapter 3, *Introducing Forms*

1

Introducing Delphi

*G*etting started is always the hardest part of learning to use a new software development tool. (For me, just getting up in the morning is difficult enough.) With Delphi, however, you'll create your first application in just minutes. In this chapter, I'll introduce the book's layout, and I'll highlight key features of Delphi's visual programming environment.

About This Book

Foundations of Delphi Development covers Delphi's commands, features, and techniques in four parts:

- Part I, "Introductions." Chapters in this part introduce Delphi's environment, and explain many of its commands and features. You'll learn how to use visual components, forms, properties, and events to create practical Windows applications.

- Part II, "The User Interface." Chapters in this part explain how to create user interfaces with Delphi's *Visual Component Library* (VCL). You'll learn how to build user interfaces with objects such as menus, buttons, toolbars, status panels, scroll bars, and dialog boxes.

- Part III, "The Application." Chapters in this part cover application development topics and explain how to use Delphi's advanced visual components. You'll learn how to program applications for graphics, printer output, multiple-document interface (MDI), object-linking and embedding (OLE), dynamic data exchange (DDE), and database systems.

- Part IV, "Advanced Techniques." Chapters in this part present topics of interest to advanced Delphi developers. You'll learn how to use exceptions for error handling, how to construct custom components, plus other techniques such as how to use file streams and how to use components in a dynamic link library (DLL).

 Parts II and III cover most Delphi visual components. To find references to specific components, look them up the subject index at the back of the book. Also refer to the online visual component reference on the CD-ROM.

REQUIREMENTS

In addition to this book, you need a copy of Delphi's Desktop or Client/Server editions installed on your PC. You also need to install Windows 3.1, Windows NT, or Windows 95. All applications and step-by-step tutorials in this book make full use of Delphi's visual environment running in Windows. To create and test the programs for this book, I used at various times Windows 3.1, Windows 3.11, and a prerelease copy of Windows 95.

Delphi's Desktop edition requires a minimum of 6MB of system memory. The Client/Server edition requires 8MB. You may use either edition with this book. A full Delphi installation and associated tools occupy approximately 60MB to 80MB of hard disk space. You do not need the visual component source code files provided with the Client/Server edition (also available separately from Borland); however, advanced developers should eventually acquire these files.

Any PC with an 80386, 80486, or Pentium processor, at least 8MB to 12MB of memory, a VGA display, and a 200MB or larger hard disk makes an excellent Delphi development system. You'll need a printer for Chapter 14. A good supply of munchies and a case of your favorite beverage are optional, but highly recommended.

NOTE ►   Although Windows 3.1 can run on PCs with 80286 processors, Delphi requires an 80386 processor or later model. Delphi *applications*, however, can run in Windows Standard mode on 80286-based computers. Also on the subject of CPUs, Delphi automatically generates corrected code for Pentium processors with the infamous floating-point-division bug. To enable this feature, select the *Options|Project* command, click the *Compiler* page tab at the bottom of the resulting dialog box, and switch on the *Pentium-safe FDIV* check box.

I assume in this book that you know how to use Windows, and that you have a mouse (or that you know the equivalent keyboard commands). I will not waste your time or mine explaining topics such as how to select menu commands, click buttons, and switch among windows. If you need help using Windows, consult one of the many excellent tutorials on the market, or refer to the references and guides that come with the Windows operating system.

If you are truly getting started, install Windows first, and then install Delphi, following the instructions provided with each product. If you can successfully install and run Delphi, you are ready to begin. Refer to Appendix A for instructions on using the accompanying CD-ROM, which contains an online edition of this book plus all application project files.

NOTE ►   Of course, I never make a mistake (you believe that, right?), but if you discover an error in this book, drop me a note in care of the publisher, or send e-mail to my CompuServe ID: 73627,3241. *Keep it short and please do not send large files electronically.* For a reply via mail, please include a self-addressed, stamped envelope.

CHAPTERS

Each chapter is small enough to read in a single session. If you finish one or two chapters a day, you should be able to master Delphi in about two weeks. Stay with it for another week or so, and you'll be a certified guru.

I recognize, however, that there aren't enough hours in the day for everyone to read every word in a large book such as this. To help you find what you need quickly — and especially so you don't waste time studying what you already know — most chapters end with four sections:

- *Summary* — Read this point-by-point summary to refresh your memory of the chapter's contents. You might also scan the summaries to find chapters that cover specific topics.

- *Projects* — To test your comprehension of the chapter's contents, try your hand at the suggested projects at the end of each chapter. The book's CD-ROM contains any files mentioned in this section.

- *Expert-User Tips* — Browse these additional tips to enhance your understanding of the chapter's topic, and to pick up additional programming lore, tricks, tidbits, and techniques.

- *Coming Up* — Read this description for a look ahead to the next chapter's contents.

Throughout the text, you'll find additional Notes, Tips, and Warnings that explain dozens of Delphi techniques. These sections can also help you find specific topics when browsing. Here's a sample:

If you already know Pascal, or if you are familiar with Delphi, first skim a chapter's summary, projects, and expert-user tips to help you decide whether you should read the chapter.

Delphi Application Development

As with most software, the best way to learn your way around Delphi is by using it. In this section, you'll try out Delphi's visual environment. Start or switch to Delphi now. Figure 1-1a shows Delphi running in Windows 95. Figure 1-1b shows Delphi in Windows 3.1. If your screen does not resemble one of the figures, select the *File|New Project* command.

Speed buttons   Component palette

Menu bar   Minimize, Maximize, Close buttons

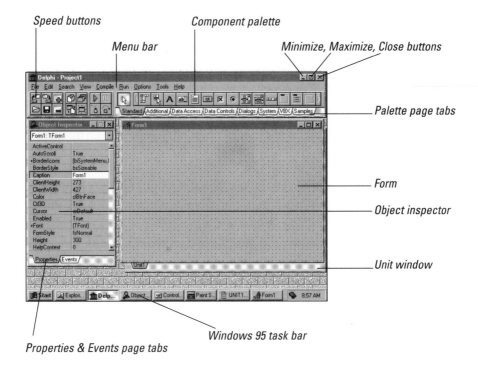

Palette page tabs

Form

Object inspector

Unit window

Properties & Events page tabs   Windows 95 task bar

Figure 1-1a
Delphi running in Windows 95.

Some buttons and windows may differ depending on your software version, operating system, and installation options. To prepare most screen illustrations in this book, I used Delphi's Client/Server edition, version 1.0, with the copyright date 1983-95, running under Windows 95. You may use Delphi's Client/Server or Desktop editions with all projects in this book. Depending on your Windows version, many title bars, borders, buttons, and other objects will differ from those shown here. These differences are largely cosmetic, and except where I've indicated otherwise, they do not affect the information in this book.

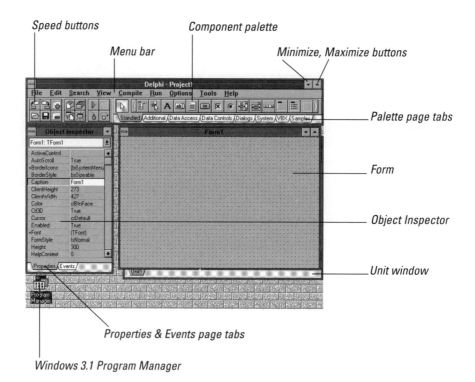

Figure 1-1b
Delphi running in Windows 3.1.

There are several main elements in Delphi's integrated development environment (IDE). Starting in the upper-left corner in Figure 1-1a or 1-1b and proceeding clockwise, these elements are:

■ *Speed buttons* — These are point-and-click buttons for selected menu commands. As in the component palette, you can learn what a button does by positioning the mouse cursor over it (don't click) and waiting a moment to see a hint box with the button's name. Get used to using Delphi's speed buttons, which in the long run will save you hours of development time, especially if you are handy with a mouse. For example, although there are other ways to run programs, the fastest method is to click the Run speed button (the right-pointing triangle).

- *Menu bar* — This is a standard Windows-style menu. Scan through Delphi's menus now to become familiar with them.

- *Component palette* — This palette contains icons that represent components in the VCL. Click a palette button to select a visual component, and then click the mouse inside the form window to insert a component *object*. Position the mouse cursor over any component button but don't click the mouse button. After a moment, Delphi displays a hint box with the component's name. Move the mouse to view other component hint boxes. *Use this method to locate specific components mentioned in this book.*

- *Palette page tabs* — To view other component categories, click one of the page tabs below the VCL palette. For example, click the *Dialogs* page tab to display Delphi's dialog-box components.

- *Form* — In most applications, a form is a visual representation of the program's main window. However, a form can also represent other windows — for example, a dialog box or a child window in multiple-document interface (MDI) software. Simple programs may have just one form; complex applications can have dozens. The dotted grid helps you align components inserted into the form window. This grid does not appear in the final application.

- *Object Inspector* — This window shows all of the properties and events for one or more selected components or forms. In time, you and this window will become fond friends; despite its apparent simplicity, the Object Inspector window is one of Delphi's most important programming tools.

- *Unit window* — This window shows the Pascal programming text associated with each form in the application. Delphi automatically creates this programming, to which you can add Pascal statements that perform actions for events such as menu commands and button clicks. You can also use this window to edit other Pascal modules and text files. Select among opened files by clicking the page tabs along the bottom of the unit window.

- *Properties and Events page tabs* — Click one of these two page tabs at the bottom of the Object Inspector window to switch between a component or form's properties and events. A *property* represents a component's attribute, such as a button's size or a text label's font. An *event* represents an action, such as a mouse click or a key press.

You'll learn more about each of Delphi's windows, commands, and other capabilities as you try out this book's sample applications. You'll also meet many other windows, such as the Project Manager, the Object Browser, the Integrated Debugger, the Code Editor, the Bitmap Editor, and the Menu Designer. Until you become familiar with Delphi, however, you should arrange your display so it resembles Figure 1-1a or 1-1b.

By the way, if you are running Windows 95, the taskbar at the bottom of the screen makes switching among Delphi's many windows quick and painless. The operating system, not Delphi, provides this taskbar, and the Windows 3.1 desktop lacks this feature.

Important: Before continuing, select the *Options | Environment* command, and choose the *Preferences* page tab at the bottom of the dialog window. Enable the check box, *Use on New Form.* Disable the other check box, *Use on New Project.* (These are the default installation values.) When enabled, the two options present *gallery dialogs* for selecting project and form templates, which make it easy to choose among standard applications and windows such as MDI child windows and multipage dialogs. (You'll meet all of these items eventually.)

PREPARING A NEW APPLICATION

The first step after beginning a new application is to give it a name. I like to do this immediately after selecting *File | New Project.* Naming a new project as soon as possible prevents Delphi from saving the project in its own directories under default filenames, which wastes disk space and can cause trouble because of the way Delphi uses a module's filename to create programming statements and declarations. (Delphi does not support long filenames under Windows 95 and Windows NT. Delphi *applications,* however, can support long filenames.)

A typical Delphi project consists of several types of files. Some files contain text, others contain binary values, bitmaps, and code. Because each application consists of many files, it's a good idea to create a separate directory on your hard disk for each new project. That way, you can easily copy an application's files to a floppy disk or a network drive for safekeeping, and you can delete old applications simply by removing their directories.

To follow along and create your first Delphi application, perform these steps now:

1. Use the Windows File Manager to create a new directory, C:\Projects, for storing this book's projects. In Windows 95, use the Explorer to create a new folder. (Windows 95 folders are equivalent to directories in DOS and Windows 3.1.) Select the directory or folder, and create a subdirectory named Hello. This creates the path, C:\Projects\Hello, for holding the project's files.

2. Select *File|New Project.* If another project has already been loaded and modified, Delphi gives you a chance to save the project or discard it. If you see the *Confirm* dialog, choose *Yes* to save the old project or *No* to discard it.

3. Select *File|Save Project.* In the resulting file-save dialog, change to the C:\Projects\Hello directory that you created in step 1, and type Main in the dialog's *File Name* input box. To save the form in a text file named Main.Pas, click the *OK* button or press Enter. Delphi automatically supplies the .Pas filename extension, which indicates the file contains Pascal programming.

4. Delphi next requests a project name in another file-save dialog. Type Hello for the *File Name*, and select *OK* or press Enter. This creates the main project file, Hello.Dpr. Delphi automatically supplies the .Dpr filename extension, which stands for *Delphi Project.*

If Delphi does not request a project name in step 4, you may have mistakenly selected the *File|Save File* command, which saves only a single file. If this happens, repeat steps 3 and 4 and be sure to select the *File|Save Project* command (the third one in the *File* menu).

Saving the project in a separate directory before adding any programming helps keep the application's modules well organized. *For best results, never store multiple projects in the same directory.*

The CD-ROM inside the back cover contains all the sample projects described in this book. Copy the files from any CD-ROM directory to an empty directory on your hard disk, and then open the copied project with Delphi's *File|Open Project* command. *Do not copy multiple projects to the same directory — create a new, blank directory for each project.* You can use the prepared files to examine how the sample applications work, but to gain experience with Delphi, you should try to create some or all of the projects by following the book's step-by-step instructions. Refer to the supplied files if you get stuck, or, if you dislike typing, copy sections of programming from the CD-ROM to your own modules.

To develop more of your first Delphi application, continue with the instructions in the next section.

SETTING THE WINDOW CAPTION

By default, Delphi sets the sample Hello project's form-window caption to *Form1*. The caption appears in the title bar under the window's top border. Follow these steps to change the caption to the program's title:

1. At the bottom of the Object Inspector window (refer back to Figure 1-1), click the *Properties* page tab to display properties for the program's form.

2. Select the Caption property. (It may already be selected by default.)

3. To modify a property, simply type or select a new value in the column to the right of the property's name. For example, change the Caption's value from *Form1* to *Hello Delphi Programmer!* Just start typing — you don't have to highlight the text beforehand. You also don't have to press Enter after typing. If you do press Enter, however, the field is simply rehighlighted. Notice that the form's window caption changes as you type.

4. Save the project by selecting the *File | Save Project* command. Because you have already supplied filenames, Delphi executes the command immediately — that is, it does not display the file-save dialog. (Every time you add a new form to a project, you'll see this dialog again when you save the project.)

You can save a project by clicking the *Save project* speed button. If you are handy with a mouse, this is usually faster than selecting the *File | Save Project* command.

To finish your first application, continue with the instructions in the next section.

RUNNING THE APPLICATION

Believe it or not, you have just finished programming your first Delphi application! To complete the development process and run the program, follow these steps:

1. Press F9, or select the *Run* command from the *Run* menu. Or, click the *Run* speed button. Try to run your application frequently during its development to test new programming. *You do not have to finish a project before running it.*

2. Your computer's gears whirl, the disk turns, smoke pours out of the floppy bays (well, I *thought* I saw a puff), and after a few seconds, your first application's window appears on screen. Figure 1-2 shows Hello's display in Windows 95. The program's appearance may differ depending on your Windows operating system.

3. To quit the application, double-click the system-menu button in the window's upper-left corner, or single-click the button and select *Close* from the system menu. If you prefer to use the keyboard, press Alt+F4 to close the application and return to Delphi. If you are running Windows 95, click the window-close button in the upper-right corner.

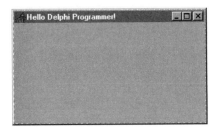

Figure 1-2
The Hello application's display.

TIP   After running applications from inside Delphi, always close them to return to programming mode. If you accidentally leave an application open, you will not be able to select many of Delphi's commands. If Delphi becomes recalcitrant, the cause may be a running application that you forgot to close.

Press F9 to rerun Hello. Notice that this time, the application window appears more quickly than when you first ran the program. Delphi knows that you made no changes to the project, so it simply reloads the application's code file. Close the Hello program window now.

You can also use the Windows File Manager or the Windows 95 Explorer to run a Delphi application. For example, open the File Manager or the Explorer, and select the C:\Projects\Hello directory. Double-click Hello.Exe, or highlight that filename and press Enter. Remember to close the program before continuing.

Use the File Manager or the Windows 95 Explorer to run multiple instances of an application. For example, try running two or more copies of Hello. You can run only one program instance from Delphi. To run multiple instances, you must use the File Manager or the Explorer. Close all instances of Hello before continuing.

A Delphi application is a full-fledged Windows program — you run it the same way you run other applications. You can click and drag an application's code file to a Program Manager window and then double-click the resulting icon, or you can use the File and Program Manager *File|Run* commands and enter the code file's path name. Under Windows 95, you can drag the program's code file to a taskbar folder, or create a shortcut entry for it.

COMPILING AND LINKING THE CODE

When you run an application by pressing F9, Delphi *compiles and links* the program to create an executable code file. Two key actions occur. First, the Delphi compiler translates the program's text into binary code. Then, the linker combines that code with other modules required for various start-up chores and other tasks. The result of *compiling and linking* a Delphi project is a complete, executable code file, which has the same name as the project, but the filename ends with the extension .Exe.

Unlike other visual programming systems, Delphi generates *true native code*, which means that finished programs do not require a run-time interpreter. A Delphi .Exe code file is 100% complete. *This is the only file you must provide to your program's users.*

To compile and link an application, but *not* run it, press Ctrl+F9 or select the *Compile|Syntax Check* command. You might use these methods to verify that the program is free of errors such as minor typing mistakes.

Programming with Components

Before continuing with this chapter, let's pause for a quick review. You now know three essential Delphi techniques:

- How to create and save a new project.
- How to modify a property such as a Caption in a Delphi form.
- How to compile, link, and run an application by pressing F9.

You will use these techniques in every application you write. Of course, programs that do nothing but display a title aren't going to burn up the best-seller charts. To give the Hello application something to do, you can insert a *visual component* in the program's window, as explained in the following section.

INSERTING VISUAL COMPONENTS

Follow these steps to insert a visual component object into the Hello program's window:

1. Close the running Hello program if necessary to return to Delphi. Select *File|Open Project* or click the *Open project* speed button. (Do this for experience even if Hello is already open.) When the *Open Project* dialog appears, change directories if necessary and select Hello.Dpr. Press Enter or click *OK* to open the project. (You'll use this same method to open other projects mentioned in this book. If you need to pause for a breather midway through a chapter, save the project and then reload it when you are ready to continue.)

2. Click the *Standard* page tab below the Component palette, and then select the Button component labeled *Ok*.

3. Move the mouse cursor into the form, and click once to insert a Button object in the window. The location doesn't matter.

4. Make sure the Button object is selected — you should see square handles around it. If the object is not selected, click it once now. By default, Delphi names the object Button1. For a more meaningful name, select the Name property in the Object Inspector (it may already be selected), and type CloseButton. That's one word, not two — don't type any spaces in it. Press Enter.

5. Notice that the Caption property and the button's text also change to CloseButton. This is normal, but in many cases, you will want a component object's Name and Caption properties to differ. In this case, for example, select the Caption property, and type Close. Your form window should resemble Figure 1-3.

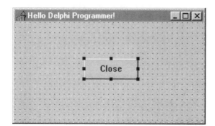

Figure 1-3
Hello's form window in Delphi.

6. Single-click the CloseButton object if necessary to select it. Select the *Events* page tab at the bottom of the Object Inspector window, which lists the actions that the button can perform. Double-click the blank space to the right of the OnClick event. Main.Pas appears in the unit window, and Delphi positions the flashing cursor between the keywords *begin* and *end*. Type the following statement:

```
Close;
```

7. You have just programmed a procedure called an *event handler* for the button's OnClick event. *Be sure to end the statement with a semicolon.* Make sure the text in your window matches Listing 1-1.

8. Save the project, and then run it by pressing F9. You can now click the *OK* button to close the window. Because this is the program's main window, closing it also ends the application.

Listing 1-1
The CloseButton object's OnClick event handler.

```
procedure TForm1.CloseButtonClick(Sender: TObject);
begin
  Close;
end;
```

The *File|Open File* command opens individual files. To load a complete Delphi application, always use *File|Open Project* or click the *Open project* speed button.

The preceding steps demonstrate three important aspects of programming with Delphi:

- You inserted a Button *component object* into a form window.

- You modified the object's *properties* to change its program Name and Caption values.

- You programmed one of the object's *events* to perform a runtime action in response to the button's selection.

Delphi's interface and all components except VBX controls were written using Delphi. This is powerful proof of what you can accomplish with this remarkable development system.

DEBUGGING PROGRAM STATEMENTS

Programmers hate debugging as much as gardeners hate weeding. Who wouldn't rather design new code than waste time squashing bugs? Delphi can't prevent bugs, of course, but it can help you avoid many common errors by giving you a smart visual environment that automatically creates much of your application. Unfortunately, there's still plenty of room for error, and I would be fibbing if I promised that programming with Delphi will always be pest free.

When the critters start chewing up your code, use Delphi's debugging commands to run your applications one step at a time and view the values of objects and variables. By slowing a program's usual breakneck speed, the cause of a problem will often become obvious. Get used to Delphi's debugging commands now so you'll know how to use them when you need them — trust me, you *will* need them!

Delphi's debugging commands are also useful for investigating how a program works. Use them frequently to examine the sample programs in this book as well as those in Delphi's Demos directory. Follow these steps to learn how to use some of Delphi's debugging features:

1. Open the Hello project if necessary.

2. If you did not insert a Close button into the form, do so now by following the instructions in the preceding section.

3. Locate the TForm1.CloseButtonClick procedure in the Main.Pas unit window. Insert a statement above Close to display a message. The two lines between *begin* and *end* should look like this:

```
ShowMessage('Ready to close application');
Close;
```

4. Normally, you press F9 to compile, link, and run a program. This time, however, press F8 to select Delphi's *Step Over* command. When the main window appears, click the Close button. Instead of ending the program, Delphi pauses it inside the CloseButtonClick procedure. This is an example of *single-stepping*, one of the most important investigation tools you will use during a program's development.

5. Press F8 two more times to step to the ShowMessage statement and execute it. A box with an OK button appears on screen. Click this button. Again, because you pressed F8, Delphi pauses the program at the next statement to execute, Close.

6. Press F9 to execute the Close statement and run the program to completion. After pressing F8 to single-step one or more statements, you will usually continue to run a program this way by pressing F9.

Another way to step through a program is by setting a *breakpoint*. When the program reaches the marked statement, Delphi halts the application before that statement executes. Follow these steps to set a breakpoint and step through the program:

1. Move the flashing cursor to the ShowMessage statement in Main.Pas, and select *Run |Add Breakpoint*. Click the *New* button in the resulting dialog, or just press Enter. The marked statement is now highlighted in red (dark gray on monochrome monitors).

2. Press F9 to run the program. When you click the Close button, Delphi halts the code at the marked statement. Press F8 to single-step that statement and display a message. Close the message dialog by clicking its OK button, and press F9 to run the program to completion.

3. Try step 2 again, but this time, press Alt+F4 to end the program. Because this does not execute the CloseButtonClick procedure, the program ends without stopping at the breakpoint. (Hint: If you see a stop-sign icon when you move the cursor over a program's window, you know the program is paused. If this happens, switch back to Delphi, and press F9 to continue running the program.)

4. Always try to run a program to completion. If you can't do that, select *Run |Program Reset* and start over. This may skip termination routines that delete various resources from memory, causing a gradual loss of available memory that eventually requires you to exit and restart Windows. Such is the software developer's life, but fortunately, this problem is rare.

5. To toggle a breakpoint on or off, move the mouse cursor to the extreme left of a marked statement and click the left button once. This is the easiest way to set and remove a breakpoint. You can also use the *View |Breakpoints* command to add, delete, disable, and perform other operations on breakpoints. Select this command and click the right mouse button in the *Breakpoint list* window for a list of available commands. Remove the breakpoint from the ShowMessage statement now.

NOTE
I'll explain how to use other Delphi debugging commands at the appropriate times. However, don't wait for me to suggest single-stepping a program's statements by pressing F8 and by setting breakpoints. Use Delphi's debugging features often to investigate this book's sample applications. You'll be amazed at what you can learn just by slowing down the code and examining the program's state at strategic locations.

Files and Filename Extensions

The following sections describe the contents of files that Delphi creates for an application and lists their filename extensions. I'll also explain which files you may safely delete from a project directory.

SOURCE CODE FILES

When you insert components into a form, and when you modify form and component properties and events, Delphi writes the text of your program in Object Pascal. This text is called the program's *source code*. At any time while developing an application, you can view the program's source code files, and you can print them for paper backups.

Experienced Pascal programmers may be tempted to modify their applications' source code. Regardless of your experience, however, you should enter new programming only with extreme care. Delphi's code generator is smart, but it can't understand every change you make. For best results, follow this book's suggestions for creating applications. In time, the rules for what you can and cannot change will become obvious.

Follow these steps to examine the source code for the sample Hello application and to become more familiar with the programming that Delphi generates:

1. Select *File | Open Project* to open a fresh copy of the Hello.Dpr project file. You don't have to save the changes you made.

2. Select *View | Units* or click the *Select unit from list* speed button, and choose *Main* from the resulting dialog's list of modules. Press Enter or click *OK* to close the dialog and switch to the unit window. Listing 1-2 shows the text you see on screen. This same text is stored on disk as Main.Pas in the Hello subdirectory.

3. Select *View | Units* again but this time choose the *Hello* module. The unit window now shows two files — select between them by clicking a page tab at the bottom of the window. Listing 1-3 shows the project file's text, which is stored on disk as Hello.Dpr.

Listing 1-2
Hello\Main.Pas

```
unit Main;

interface

uses
   SysUtils, WinTypes, WinProcs, Messages, Classes, Graphics, Controls,
   Forms, Dialogs, StdCtrls;

type
  TForm1 = class(TForm)
    CloseButton: TButton;
    procedure CloseButtonClick(Sender: TObject);
  private
    { Private declarations }
  public
    { Public declarations }
  end;

var
  Form1: TForm1;

implementation

{$R *.DFM}

procedure TForm1.CloseButtonClick(Sender: TObject);
begin
  Close;
end;

end.
```

Closes the main window and ends the program.

Listing 1-3

Hello\Hello.Dpr

```
program Hello;

uses
  Forms,
  Main in 'MAIN.PAS' {Form1};

{$R *.RES}

begin
  Application.CreateForm(TForm1, Form1);
  Application.Run;
end.
```

 To close individual files in the unit window, press Alt+F3, or click the right mouse button and choose *Close Page*.

A Delphi project's source code is stored in at least two text files — in this case, Main.Pas and Hello.Dpr. The Main.Pas file in Listing 1-2 is an example of a *unit*, a module that represents the Hello program's main-window form. All applications in this book have at least one unit, but complex projects may have multiple modules, each stored in a separate .Pas file.

The second source code file in a typical Delphi application represents the entire project. For example, Hello.Dpr in Listing 1-3 shows the source code for the Hello project. Every application has one and only one project file.

To print the currently selected file in the unit window, select *File|Print*. You can choose from a variety of options in the resulting *Print Selection* dialog. For example, enable *Line numbers* to number each programming line, or enable the *Header/page number* option for a finished appearance. Enable the *Syntax print* option to print keywords in bold and to use italics and underlining for other program elements. Disable *Syntax print* for faster printing on slow, dot-matrix printers or if you prefer a relatively plain appearance in listings.

UNIT FILES

The first line in Main.Pas, Listing 1-2, states the unit's name — in this case, Main. Delphi gives the unit the same name that you specify when saving the project's unit file.

Next comes an interface directive, which makes the items that follow available to other modules that use this unit. The interface contains the unit's public declarations. Items not in the interface are hidden from other modules.

Units may — and usually do — use other units. For example, Main uses many different units, all of which are listed in the module's *uses* directive. Units such as WinTypes and WinProcs provide data and code for the Windows API, or *application programming interface*. Other units, such as Classes, Graphics, and Controls, provide data and code for the program's form, components, and other elements.

Next in Main.Pas comes a *type declaration* section, identified by the keyword *type*. A type — also called a *data type* — describes the nature of an item that can be created in memory. For example, an Integer is a data type that represents whole numbers. To use Integers, you must create one or more *variables* of that type that can store specific values such as 123 or --96. Other Pascal data types include characters, strings, records, and floating-point values. I'll explain more about these and other types as you meet examples of them in this book's sample applications.

A data type can also be a *class*, an object-oriented structure used extensively in Delphi applications. A class *encapsulates* related code and data, which are collectively known as class *members*. Classes can *inherit* the members of other classes. For example, the TForm1 class in Main.Pas inherits TForm's members, a class that Delphi provides for creating forms. Because of its inheritance, the TForm1 class is called a *descendant* of TForm.

The TForm1 class in Main.Pas declares two additional members to those it inherits. The first member is a TButton object, named CloseButton. The second member of TForm1 is a *procedure*, a subroutine that performs an action. In this case, the CloseButtonClick procedure ends the program when you click the program's *Close* button.

Classes may have additional declarations, some of which might be private (for use only in the class's unit) or public (available also to statements in other units). In this case, there are no private and public declarations. Two *comments* surrounded by opening and closing curly braces indicate where these types of declarations can go:

```
private
  { Private declarations }
public
  { Public declarations }
```

Comments have no runtime effects. They are merely notes that describe an aspect of the program. A comment might explain a tricky statement, or it can identify the program's author, revision number, and other sundry facts. You may type anything you want between the braces except another closing brace. Comments can also extend over more than one line. Here's an example of a multiline comment:

```
{ This multiline comment occupies three lines. It
begins with an opening brace on the first line,
and ends with a closing brace. }
```

Instead of curly braces, you may use the double-character symbols (* and *) — leftovers from the early days of Pascal when many keyboards and terminals lacked curly brace characters. For example, this is a perfectly acceptable comment:

```
(* Program author: Your name goes here *)
```

You may mix different comment styles in the same program, but if you begin a comment with an opening brace, you must end it with a closing brace. Likewise, if you begin a comment with (*, you must end it with *).

Finally in the unit's interface section are one or more *variables*, preceded by the keyword *var*. Units may have zero, one, or more variables. In this example, there is only one variable:

```
var
  Form1: TForm1;
```

The declaration creates a variable named Form1 of the TForm1 class. In other words, Form1 is an *object of a class* that occupies space in memory. The object in this example represents the Hello program's main window, which contains a button and an event handler that performs the button's action.

A class object is similar to a variable of a data type such as an Integer. You may create one or more actual objects of any class, just as you can create multiple Integer variables.

Following its interface section is the unit's *implementation*, where Delphi creates statements to perform runtime actions. You can also type statements into a unit's implementation. For example, locate the procedure in which you typed the Close; statement. Here it is again for reference:

```
procedure TForm1.CloseButtonClick(Sender: TObject);
begin
  Close;
end;
```

Just prior to that procedure, you find this strange-looking directive:

```
{$R *.DFM}
```

Although it looks like a comment, the dollar sign immediately following the opening brace tells Delphi that this line is a special directive that opens and reads a file ending with the filename extension .Dfm (short for *Delphi Form*). The asterisk tells Delphi to look for a file named the same as the project, but ending with the filename extension .Dfm. This file contains the form's properties entered with the Object Inspector.

On the last line of Main.Pas is an *end* keyword followed by a period. Technically, the *end* keyword designates the end of the unit *module*, and the period signifies the end of the *file*. However, this is a relatively unimportant distinction. Just remember that only the final *end* in a unit ends with a period.

PROJECT FILES

Pascal experts in the audience will recognize Hello.Dpr as a Pascal program (refer back to Listing 1-3). As with the Main unit, Delphi creates this text automatically. *A Delphi project is actually a Pascal program.* A project has two main purposes — to declare the application's unit modules and to run the program.

The first line in Hello.Dpr specifies the project name in a *program declaration* — in this case, *Hello*. Next, a *uses* declaration specifies other units that the program uses.

In this case, there are two such units. First is a standard unit, Forms, that provides the capabilities for Delphi forms. Second is the Main unit in the file Main.Pas. The second line of the *uses* declaration indicates that unit Main is located in file Main.Pas, and that Form1 is the name of the form object in that unit.

The command {$R *.RES} binds a binary resource file into the compiled .Exe code file. Typically, resource files contain only the program's system icon, but they can have other types of resources. However, you won't use resource files as extensively in Delphi as you might with other development systems such as C and C++.

Finally in the project are two statements between *begin* and *end* keywords, followed by a period that marks the end of the file. The first statement creates the application's form object in memory. The second statement runs the application.

Delphi automatically creates and maintains the source code for the Hello.Dpr project file. You will rarely need to modify this file's statements, and for that reason, chapters in this book do not list most application project files.

FILENAME EXTENSIONS

A Delphi application consists of many different types of files. Each filename ends with an extension that identifies the file's contents. The following list describes the files that Delphi creates and their filename extensions. I've also indicated which files you may safely delete, in case you are short on disk space or — like me — you frequently clean house by getting rid of deadwood files.

Here are the files that Delphi creates:

- *.~* files* — Files with names ending in .~* (for example, Hello.~dp) are backup copies of modified and saved files. You may safely delete these files at any time, although you might want to keep them for recovering lost or damaged programming, or to return to a previous revision.

- *.Dcr files* — Delphi Component Resource files contain a component's icon as it appears on the VCL palette. You will use .Dcr files only when constructing custom components. You should not delete these files. If you do, Delphi will substitute a stock icon for the component when you install it into the palette.

- *.Dcu files* — These files contain compiled code and data for a program's units. For example, Main.Dcu contains the code and data declared in the Main.Pas source file. You may safely delete a project's .Dcu files because Delphi recreates them when you compile the application.

- *.Dfm files* — These files contain binary values representing form properties as well as the properties of any components inserted into the form. Relationships between events and event handlers are also stored in .Dfm files. Delphi copies this information into the finished .Exe code file. *Never delete .Dfm files.* Treat them with the same care as you do source code files.

- *.Dsm files* — These files are undocumented, but they appear to contain intermediate code or symbols. I have successfully deleted them with no harmful effects, but I suggest copying them to a temporary directory and deleting them only after you successfully compile your application.

- *.Dll files* — These files contain code for dynamic link libraries. Although you may safely delete .Dll files for which you have the source code, some third-party DLLs are provided only in binary form. Don't delete a .Dll file unless you wrote it or you are sure of its origin.

- *.Dpr files* — Short for Delphi Project, .Dpr files are actually Pascal source code files in disguise. In most cases, you should not modify .Dpr files, although experienced Pascal programmers may do so. Delphi creates a .Dpr file when you first save a new application project. *Never delete .Dpr files.*

- *.Dsk files* — These files store the application's desktop configuration, but only if you selected the *Desktop Autosave* option with the *Options|Environment* command. You may delete .Dsk files if you don't want to preserve the arrangement of Delphi's windows, or if you want to return to a default layout. However, desktop files also store project pathnames, so if you move your projects to other locations, or if you store project modules in multiple directories, you should not delete .Dsk files.

- *.Exe files* — As you probably know, files ending in .Exe are executable code files. As I mentioned, Delphi creates a *complete* .Exe code file, which is the only one you must distribute to your application's users. You may safely delete a project's .Exe file because Delphi recreates it when you compile the application.

- *.Opt files* — In these files, Delphi stores options selected with the *Options|Project* command. There are numerous choices in the resulting dialog, but until you become more familiar with Delphi, the default settings are probably more than adequate. If you delete .Opt files, Delphi recreates them using default options. This may cause problems for applications that depend on nonstandard options, so you should delete .Opt files only with extreme care.

- *.Pas files* — These files contain Pascal source code. In a typical Delphi application, there is one .Pas file for each form's associated unit, although experienced Pascal developers may store other programming in .Pas files. You may edit .Pas files using Delphi's unit window, or with any ASCII text editor. *Never delete .Pas files.*

- *.Res files* — Files with names ending in .Res contain binary resources such as the program's system icon and other bitmaps. Resource files figure more prominently in nonvisual Windows programming with Borland Pascal, C, or C++ than they do with Delphi. In Delphi, use the Image Editor in the *Tools* menu to create and modify .Res files. Never make changes to the project's resource file, named the same as the project but ending with the filename extension .Res. When Delphi regenerates this file, any resources you added will be permanently lost.

Never delete files with names ending in .Dfm, .Dpr, or .Pas, unless of course, you want to throw away a project. These files contain the application's properties and source code. When backing up an application under development, these are the critical files to save.

Summary

- Delphi is a rapid application development system, suitable for creating Windows prototypes and finished applications that rival or exceed the speed and efficiency of programs written in C, C++, Borland Pascal 7.0, and Visual Basic, as well as programs created by any other means.

- This book explains all you need for creating Windows applications with Delphi. Numerous hands-on tutorials and examples fully explain all commands and features, as well as all components in the VCL (visual component library).

- Chapters in this book also cover advanced application topics such as printing, graphics, multiple document interfaces, DDE, OLE, and databases. Advanced chapters explain how to use exceptions for error handling, how to write and use units and DLLs, and how to create custom components.

- Delphi is based on Borland's Object Pascal, but you don't need to be a Pascal programmer to use this book. You can learn what you need to know about Pascal by following this book's step-by-step tutorials. As you design your application visually, Delphi automatically creates the program's Object Pascal statements.

- A Delphi application consists of one or more form windows into which you place visual components. You can modify component and form properties, such as their Names and Captions, and you can create Pascal procedures to perform actions for events such as mouse clicks.

- When you run an application, Delphi compiles and links source code and other modules to create a finished .Exe code file. This is the only file you need to distribute to your program's users.

Projects to Try

1-1: Open the Hello project and select the form window's Close button. Change that button's Default property to True. Press F9 to compile, link, and run the modified program. To end the program, you can now press Enter, which selects the default control in a window. Back in Delphi, set the Close button's Cancel property to True. Now when you run the program, you can also press Esc to end. In general, only one component in a form should have its Default or Cancel property set to True.

1-2: Try adding other components to Hello, or create a new test application. A few minutes spent playing around will help you become more comfortable with Delphi's layout. View the properties and events for various components. Click and drag components in the form window, and run your applications — it doesn't matter whether you provide any events or new properties. A Delphi application is *always* ready to run, regardless of its current state of completion.

1-3: Select the *Options|Environment* command to customize Delphi's environment. Use the *Editor display* and *Editor colors* page tabs to modify text editor features, and to select syntax-highlighting colors. Delphi can display keywords and other elements in source code files in bold, different colors, italic text, and so on. Syntax highlighting is not just for show — a good selection of colors and text features can help make programs clearer by highlighting statements, keywords, comments, and other elements.

1-4: For added safety, select the *Options|Environment* command, click the *Preferences* tab, and enable the two *Autosave options*. The first option, *Editor files*, automatically saves all files in a project when you compile and run it, or when you exit Delphi. The second option, *Desktop*, preserves the arrangements of Delphi's windows. With this option, when you restart Delphi, you can pick up where you left off during the previous session.

If you run a lot of short trial programs to test Delphi features, you may want to disable the *Autosave Editor files* option to reduce disk activity. When developing a major application with many different files, however, this option may prevent the accidental loss of a critical file.

Expert-User Tips

- If you receive an "out of resources" error during installation of Delphi, the likely cause is an out-of-date or nonstandard video driver. Use the Windows Setup utility to change the driver to Standard VGA. This should permit you to install Delphi. Contact your VGA vendor for an updated driver.

- You will frequently toggle back and forth between form and unit windows, but they often hide each other and may be difficult to find. For easier switching, click the *Toggle Form/Unit* button in Delphi's Speedbar. Or, press F12 if your keyboard has this function key.

- Delphi's hint boxes, displayed when you rest the cursor on a component icon or speed button, appear only if one of Delphi's windows is active. Hint boxes do not appear if another application or icon is active — a fact that is not always obvious due to Delphi's unconfined window arrangement. If you don't see a hint box after a sufficient wait, click the mouse cursor on Delphi's title bar or on another window such as the Object Inspector, and then try again.

- For a progress report while compiling and linking, choose the *Options|Environment* command, select the *Preferences* page tab, and enable *Show compiler progress*. When you next compile and link a program, Delphi displays a status report dialog that shows the file and the number of lines compiled or linked. This information isn't particularly valuable to most developers, but it verifies that something is happening during compilation. Displaying the dialog steals time from the compiler, and if you write a lot of small applications, it might take longer to display the dialog than to compile your programs.

- Double-click form or unit windows to expand them to full screen. If this hides Delphi's menus and buttons, press Alt to make Delphi's main window reappear. Press Alt again to return to the expanded window. Normally, Delphi displays an expanded unit window below the VCL palette. To expand the window to cover the entire screen, select *Options|Environment,* choose the *Editor display* page tab, and switch on *Zoom to full screen*.

- You may use the unit window to edit any Pascal module (usually ending with the filename extension .Pas) or a text file (usually ending with .Txt). Choose the *File|Open File* command, or click the *Open file* speed button. To close a file, *do not close the Unit window.* Instead, press Atl+F3, select *File|Close File*, or click the right mouse button in the window and select *Close Page*.

- By convention, statements between the *begin* and *end* keywords — technically called a *block* — are indented by two spaces (refer to Listings 1-1 and 1-2). Indentation is not required, but it helps keep programs understandable by showing which statements go together. By convention, statements indented to the same level are in some way associated.

- On a 640-by-480 display, choose *Options|Environment*, and select the *Editor display* page tab. Set the Editor font to *Courier New* and specify a *Size* of 9 points. This setting, which is useful on laptops, will display most of a program's source code in the default-sized unit window without requiring horizontal scrolling. If your eyes are better than mine, try 8 points to see even more text. You might also want to experiment with this dialog's *Keystroke mappings* option, which configures the editor's keyboard commands. Select *Default* if you are an expert Windows user, *Classic* if you are familiar with Borland Pascal or C++ environments, or *Brief* or *Epsilon* if you know these editors.

- To test multiple running applications, start the first instance in Delphi, and use the File Manager or the Windows 95 Explorer to start the second. Or, to test the second or subsequent instances, start the first ones with the File Manager or the Explorer, and then run the final instance from Delphi. Use the *Run* menu's debugging commands to step through the programming statements for the instance that you started with Delphi.

- Properties and event relationships are stored in .Dfm files. These are not text files — they are binary data files — and you should never use a text editor to modify them. However, if you open a .Dfm file using *File | Open File*, Delphi displays it as text. Pascal programmers will recognize this text as object-type declarations that specify component properties and event relationships. To save a printable copy of this data, choose *File | Save File As*, and rename the file with a .Txt filename extension. You can also do the reverse — open the text file, modify it, and save it with a .Dfm filename extension to convert the text back to binary.

Only expert Pascal programmers should attempt to modify form properties and event relationships as text. For best results, you should open project files as suggested in this book, and use the Object Inspector window to modify properties and events for components and forms.

Coming Up

In the next chapter, "Introducing Visual Components," you learn more about how to insert components into an application's forms. The chapter introduces Delphi's component categories with sample applications that demonstrate many properties and events found in visual components.

2 Introducing Visual Components

*P*rogramming with visual components is easier than shooting fish in a barrel. You can make a big splash with very little effort, and best of all, you don't even have to get wet.

A visual component is an object such as a button or a text memo that you insert into a form window. Actually, a form is also a component — one that can hold other component objects. As you develop Delphi applications, you will spend most of your time inserting and modifying visual component objects, so it's important to understand them thoroughly. Visual components are literally the building blocks on which your code's foundation rests.

The Visual Component Library

With Delphi's Visual Component Library (VCL), you can create useful applications with only a dash of programming. But don't take my word for it; try the sample applications in this chapter for hands-on demonstrations of rapid application development with Delphi.

 After mastering the basics of visual components in this chapter, you can find more information on specific components in Parts II and III.

VISUAL COMPONENT CATEGORIES

To choose a component category, click a page tab such as *Dialogs* below Delphi's Component palette (see Figure 2-1). Table 2-1 lists and describes all Delphi visual component categories. The order and number of categories on your screen may differ depending on installation options, whether you have installed additional components, or if you have used *Options|Environment* to arrange palette icons.

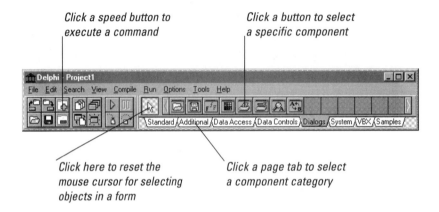

Click a speed button to execute a command

Click a button to select a specific component

Click here to reset the mouse cursor for selecting objects in a form

Click a page tab to select a component category

Figure 2-1
Delphi's visual component palette provides page tabs that organize components into categories.

Table 2-1
Delphi's Visual Component Categories

Category	Description
Standard	Standard Windows controls, such as buttons, labels, input boxes, lists, check boxes, and scroll bars.
Additional	Custom controls, such as bit buttons with graphic images (called glyphs), toolbar speed buttons, spreadsheet grids, outlines, bitmap images, and graphics shapes.
Data Access	Components for accessing databases through tables and SQL queries, and for creating reports with Borland's ReportSmith application, which is included with Delphi.
Data Controls	Data-aware components for working with database information using controls such as navigators, edit boxes, memos, pictures, check boxes, and lists.

Category	Description
Dialogs	Common dialog boxes for such tasks as selecting files and directories, choosing fonts and colors, setting up print jobs, and finding or replacing data in documents.
System	Miscellaneous components for creating timers, paint areas, disk directory tools, and multimedia applications, as well as for data sharing with OLE and DDE.
VBX	Components that serve as interfaces to Visual BASIC Extended (VBX) controls. Any VBX control — not just those supplied with Delphi — can be a visual component.
Samples	Sample components for which the source code programming is provided in Delphi's Source\Samples directory. These components are mostly intended as guides for creating your own components, but you may find them useful in applications.

SAMPLE APPLICATIONS IN THIS CHAPTER

The sample applications in this chapter perform useful jobs while demonstrating techniques you will typically need in Delphi programming. The MemoPad application demonstrates menu and file handling. The BitView application demonstrates how to use graphics and dialog boxes. The DClock application demonstrates how to use a Timer component to create background processes.

I urge you to create these applications on your own by following the hints and suggestions in this chapter — it's a great way to learn Delphi's techniques. *Don't merely run the sample programs — you won't learn anything that way.* Of course, this book's CD-ROM provides all applications and their source code files. Copy selected project directories from the CD-ROM to your hard drive (see Appendix A: How to Use the CD), and then use *File|Load Project* to load any .Dpr project file. Press F9 to compile and run the application. You can also use the supplied files as guides if you get stuck while creating your own programs.

Table 2-2 lists this chapter's sample applications, which are stored in directories that match the application names. For example, you'll find the MemoPad application's files in the Memopad directory. The table also shows the component categories that each application uses.

Table 2-2

Visual Component Sample Applications.

Application	Category	Description
MemoPad	Standard	Memo pad text file editor. Demonstrates how to program main- and pop-up-menu commands, and how to read and write text files.
BitView	Standard, Additional, Dialogs	Bitmap file viewer. Opens and displays any Windows bitmap file. Demonstrates graphical and dialog component programming.
DClock	Standard, System	Digital clock. Shows how to program a timer component that runs concurrently with other tasks.

Standard Components

With Standard components, you can create Windows control objects and common interface elements such as buttons, check boxes, and menus. Because Standard components are relatively simple to use, they also make a good introduction to visual component programming.

DESIGNING APPLICATIONS WITH COMPONENT OBJECTS

If Delphi is not running, start it now. If an application is already loaded, use *File | New Project* to prepare a fresh form window. Click the *Standard* page tab under the Component palette to display component icons in this category (refer back to Figure 2-1).

Select a component icon. For example, click the button labeled with a capital A, which represents the Label component. Move the cursor into the form window and click the left mouse button to insert a Label component *object* into the form. The exact location doesn't matter. *Don't drag the component into the form; instead, click the component icon, move the mouse pointer into the form, and click again to insert the object.*

To avoid potential ambiguities in this book, the term *component* refers to an icon in the VCL palette; a *component object* is an instance of a component inserted into a form. If an intruction in this book tells you to click an *object* or a *component object*, select it in the form window.

Add a few other component objects to the form by selecting them from the Standard palette and clicking the mouse in the form window. After you insert several objects (the exact number and types don't matter), try the following experiments to become familiar with component arrangement commands:

- To move and resize a component, first select it with the mouse. (Delphi automatically selects newly inserted components.) This surrounds the component with small boxes called *handles*. To alter the selected component's size, click and drag a handle. To move the object on the form, click inside the component and drag the mouse.

- Click and drag the mouse in the form background to surround multiple component objects with a rubberband outline. Release the mouse to select the outlined objects. You can then click and drag inside the selected objects to move them en masse. Delphi displays dim handles around all selected component objects. You can't use these handles to size multiple objects — you can size only individual component objects, one at a time.

- Here's another way to select multiple objects. Click the first one to select it, and hold down the Shift key while clicking the mouse pointer on others. Choose *Edit|Select All* if you want to select all component objects in a form.

- With several objects selected, shift-click any one to deselect it. In some cases, to select a large set of objects, it's easier to select them all and then deselect the ones you don't want.

- To deselect objects, click the mouse on the form's background. Or, with the form window active, press Esc (this is a good method to use when one or more component objects completely fill a form, making it difficult or impossible to click the window's background). You know all component objects are deselected when no handles are visible. It's important to recognize this state because you can modify a form's properties and events only when no component objects are selected.

- To align multiple component objects, select them and choose the *Edit|Align* command, which displays a dialog box. Use the buttons in this dialog to align edges, to space controls equally within their conglomerate space, and to perform other rearrangements. Try several of the dialog's options to become familiar with alignment commands.

- When one component object covers another, use *Edit|Bring to Front* and *Edit|Send to Back* to change the objects' relative display order. To try out these commands, insert a few CheckBox objects into a form, and then insert a GroupBox, an example of a *container component*. If you move the GroupBox over the buttons, it covers them. To make the buttons reappear, select the GroupBox and choose *Edit|Send to Back* to shove it behind the buttons. (If nothing seems to happen, the reason might be that you selected the buttons *and* the GroupBox. To select only the GroupBox, first deselect all objects, and then click the GroupBox.)

- At runtime, users can press the Tab key to shift the input focus from one control to another. (The *input focus* refers to the current control that will receive any keyboard activity.) To set the tab order, select some or all component objects and choose the *Edit|Tab* Order command. This brings up a dialog box that you can use to specify the order in which each control becomes active in response to Tab key presses. The dialog's commands are intuitive — simply click and drag component object names to rearrange them or select a name and click the dialog's up and down buttons.

 When you select two or more component objects, the Object Inspector window shows their shared properties and events. Any changes to those values affect all selected objects. For example, to change the text style for a set of check boxes, first select them all and then enter your settings into the shared Font property. Tip: You know you are viewing shared properties and events when the Object Inspector's drop-down list is blank.

Sample Application: MemoPad

This section's sample application, MemoPad, shows how to use standard Label and Memo components. The program also demonstrates how to create a simple menu bar of commands. Figure 2-2 shows MemoPad's display.

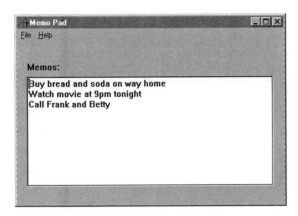

Figure 2-2
MemoPad demonstrates Label and Memo components.

To run the MemoPad application now, choose *File | Open Project*, and open Memopad.Dpr. Press F9 to compile, link, and run the program. Type a few notes, then quit MemoPad and return to Delphi so you can inspect the application's form and components.

Choose MemoPad's *File | Save* command to save your memos in a text file named Memos.Txt in the current directory. MemoPad always uses this filename. Choose *File | Exit* to end MemoPad, which also saves your memos automatically. (You can also use any other method to quit the program.) Choosing *Help | About* displays the *message dialog box* shown in Figure 2-3, which identifies the application.

Figure 2-3
MemoPad's message dialog box displayed when you select the program's Help | About command.

Two of the sample program's menu commands have correspond-ing *accelerator keys* that users can press to select menu commands without using the mouse. Press F2 to save your memos. Press F1 to display the message dialog box. In addition, menu commands have underlined *hot keys*. For example, press Alt+F X to select *File|Exit*.

NOTE Delphi somewhat incorrectly terms all keyboard aliases *shortcut keys*. Technically speaking, an *accelerator key* is a combination of one or more Ctrl, Alt, or other function keys assigned to a menu command and shown to its immediate right in the menu's pop-up window. A shortcut key is an underlined letter in a menu or a menu command. This isn't an important problem — just be aware that a menu command's underlined keys such as Alt+F X are different from accelerator keys such as F1 or Ctrl+X. Any menu command can have either or both kinds of shortcut assignments.

The MemoPad program also uses a PopupMenu component to pro-vide yet another alternative for executing commands. Move the mouse pointer anywhere inside MemoPad's window — but not on the menu bar — and click the *right* mouse button. As Figure 2-4 shows, this opens a small floating pop-up menu that works like a main menu but appears at the mouse position. To close this menu window, click the right mouse button outside of the pop-up menu, or select a command (or press Esc).

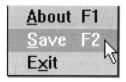

Figure 2-4
MemoPad's floating pop-up menu pops into view when you click the right mouse button.

TIP Always give users several different methods for executing common commands. That way, beginners can select commands from the applica-tion's menus (which are relatively simple to learn how to use), but experts can memorize shortcut keys and use floating pop-up menus to execute commands quickly.

HANDS-ON TUTORIAL

After you become familiar with the MemoPad application, use Delphi to inspect the program's form and components. Exit MemoPad now to get back to Delphi. Select each of the program's component objects in the form window with single mouse clicks, and view their properties and events in the Object Inspector window.

Get in the habit of single-clicking component objects in form windows. For most components, if you double-click their objects, Delphi creates a procedure in the program's source code for the default event, usually OnClick. If this happens by accident, select *Edit|Undo* to recover (or press Ctrl+Z or Alt+Backspace). To undo changes since the last save, reopen the project and answer No if Delphi suggests saving your changes. However, if you accidentally create an event handler that you don't want, don't worry about it — as long as you didn't add any statements or comments to the procedure, Delphi will remove it automatically the next time you compile the project.

Also view the statements in the Main unit (the window captioned MAIN.PAS). If you can't find this window, bring it up with *View|Units* or click the *Toggle Form/Unit* speed button. Main.Pas contains Object Pascal source code, which Delphi synchronizes with the form and its visual component objects. While developing an application, you will often switch between a form and its associated unit window.

It's helpful to think of a form and its corresponding unit as offering different *views* of the same objects. The form shows the visual appearance of a window and its controls. The unit shows the Object Pascal commands that perform component activities such as responding to a button click or saving data in a file.

Don't be concerned about understanding all of the programming in MemoPad's Main.Pas file, shown here in Listing 2-1. The file and others in this book are listed purely for reference. Because Delphi creates most of the program text automatically, you don't have to type the listing.

Listing 2-1
Memopad\Main.Pas

```
unit Main;

interface

uses
  SysUtils, WinTypes, WinProcs, Messages, Classes, Graphics, Controls,
  Forms, Dialogs, Menus, StdCtrls;

type
  TMainForm = class(TForm)
    MainMenu1: TMainMenu;
    PopupMenu1: TPopupMenu;
    File1: TMenuItem;
    Save1: TMenuItem;
    Exit1: TMenuItem;
    Help1: TMenuItem;
    About1: TMenuItem;
    About2: TMenuItem;
    Save2: TMenuItem;
    Exit2: TMenuItem;
    MemoLabel: TLabel;
    Memo1: TMemo;
    procedure Save1Click(Sender: TObject);
    procedure Exit1Click(Sender: TObject);
    procedure About1Click(Sender: TObject);
    procedure FormActivate(Sender: TObject);
    procedure FormClose(Sender: TObject; var Action: TCloseAction);
  private
    { Private declarations }
  public
    { Public declarations }
  end;

var
  MainForm: TMainForm;

implementation

{$R *.DFM}

procedure TMainForm.Save1Click(Sender: TObject);
begin
  Memo1.Lines.SaveToFile('memos.txt');
end;

procedure TMainForm.Exit1Click(Sender: TObject);
begin
  Close;
end;
```

This closes the main window and ends the program.

```
procedure TMainForm.About1Click(Sender: TObject);
begin
  MessageDlg('Memo Pad'#13#10'© 1995 by Tom Swan'#13#10'Version 1.00',
    mtInformation, [mbOk], 0);
end;

procedure TMainForm.FormActivate(Sender: TObject);
begin
  if FileExists('memos.txt')
    then Memo1.Lines.LoadFromFile('memos.txt')
    else Memo1.Lines.SaveToFile('memos.txt');
end;

procedure TMainForm.FormClose(Sender: TObject; var Action: TCloseAction);
begin
  Memo1.Lines.SaveToFile('memos.txt');
end;

end.
```

Carriage return and line feed control codes.

1
2

Now, try to recreate the MemoPad application on your own. If you get stuck, use the files on the CD-ROM as guides, or refer to Listing 2-1. Follow these step-by-step instructions:

1. Use the Windows File Manager to create a directory such as C:\Projects\Memopad to save your application's files. If you don't want to save the application, you can store files in a directory named Temp and delete them later.

2. Start a new project. Click inside the form to select it, and change the Caption property in the Object Inspector window to *Memo Pad*. From now on, when I suggest changing a property, first select the component or form, and if necessary, click the *Properties* tab in the Object Inspector window. Then, select the property and change its value, shown to the right of the property.

3. Change the form's Name property to MainForm. That's one word with no spaces. If you type illegal characters into a Name property, Delphi displays an error message. Names must begin with a letter or under-score, and they may contain only letters, digits, and underscores.

4. Choose *File | Save Project* or click the *Save project* speed button to create the project's files. You could wait until later to save the project, but doing so now creates filenames that Delphi uses to create various elements in the program's text. I strongly urge you to save a project as soon as possible after you name its main-window form.

5. Delphi presents you with two file dialogs, one after the other. In the first dialog, titled *Save Unit1 As*, change to the directory from step 1, and type Main in the *File Name* box. Press Enter or click OK. In the second dialog, labeled *Save Project1 As*, type Memopad for the filename. Press Enter or click OK. You have just created two files: Main.Pas and Memopad.Dpr. Delphi appends the .Pas and .Dpr extensions to your filenames.

6. Insert a MainMenu component into the form. Also insert a Popup-Menu component. In this example, you will use the default Names, MainMenu1 and PopupMenu1, to identify the objects. Because they are relatively complex components, Delphi displays them in the form window as icons that represent their final appearances (see Figure 2-5). The icons are invisible at runtime. Move both icons to the upper-left corner of the form. The exact locations don't matter.

 MainMenu component

 PopupMenu component

Figure 2-5
MainMenu and PopupMenu component icons show only at design time — they do not appear in the running program's window.

7. To create the menu's commands, double-click the MainMenu1 component object, which opens Delphi's Menu Designer, as shown in Figure 2-6. To create the File menu, type &File, and press Enter to change the Caption property for this menu object. Precede a letter with an ampersand (&) to designate the command's Alt shortcut key.

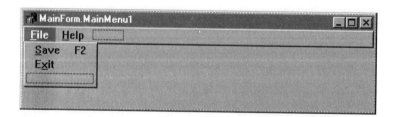

Figure 2-6
Delphi's Menu Designer showing the commands in MemoPad's MainMenu object.

8. The Menu Designer now highlights the next place to insert a command, in this case, below the File menu. Enter &Save to create the Save command. Don't press Enter (if you did, use the up-arrow key to rehighlight the command). Select the ShortCut property, click its down arrow, and select the F2 accelerator shortcut key for this command. Hint: I think it's faster just to type F and 2 and press Enter than it is to search for keys using this property's lengthy drop-down list.

9. Click the blank space below the Save command in the Menu Designer, and select the Caption property. Enter E&xit to create the Exit key and designate the letter *x* as the command's Alt shortcut key. (Note: When entering new menu commands, always select the Caption property before you type the command's text.)

10. Using similar methods, enter the Help menu and its About command. Designate F1 as the accelerator shortcut key for the command the same way you designated F2 for Save.

11. Close the Menu Designer window to view your menu in the form window. You may inspect this menu, but for the time being, don't select a command, which creates an event handler in the unit module. (There's no harm done if you do this by accident. Just make the form window active before continuing.)

12. Double-click the PopupMenu component to reopen the Menu Designer, which this time displays a simpler style for floating pop-up menus (see Figure 2-7). Enter the About, Save, and Exit commands into this menu. Precede underlined letters with ampersands. Use each command's ShortCut property to assign accelerator shortcut keys such as F1 and F2.

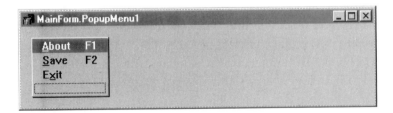

Figure 2-7
Delphi's Menu Designer showing the commands in MemoPad's PopupMenu object.

13. It's not enough just to create a PopupMenu object — you must also tell the form to use it. Close the Menu Designer window, and then click inside the form's background to deselect any components. You should see *MainForm: TMainForm* in the Object Inspector's drop-down list. Change the form's PopupMenu property to PopupMenu1. You can type this name or select it from the property's drop-down list. This programs the form to display the PopupMenu1 object when the user clicks the right mouse button.

14. Press F9 to compile and run the application, which at this stage, is unfinished. I usually do this immediately after creating a program's commands so I can test their appearance. Try out the program's menu commands (none of which work at this point), and click the right mouse button to display the floating pop-up menu, which is also inoperative. To return to Delphi, either press Alt+F4, double-click the system-menu button, or click the Windows 95 close button.

You have now completed stage one of MemoPad's programming. If you want to take a breather, have lunch, or finish college, this is a good place to pause. After you are refreshed, load the MemoPad project if necessary, and follow these steps to complete the application:

1. Insert a Label component into the form window, and change its Name property to MemoLabel. Press Enter and notice that Delphi sets the object's Caption to the same text.

2. Often, it is not desirable for a component object to show its internal name. To change the label's displayed text, select MemoLabel and change its Caption property to Memos:.

3. Also insert a Memo component object into the form. This time, you may leave the object's Name property set to the default, Memo1. However, delete all characters from the Lines property so the input area is blank. To do that, select Memo1's Lines property, and click the ellipsis button at right. This opens Delphi's *String list editor,* which you can use to delete the line *Memo1* (press backspace repeatedly or highlight that text and press Del). Press Enter or select the editor's OK button to make the change stick.

4. Resize Memo1 and arrange all components to make your display match Figure 2-8. At this point, you might want to save the project, and compile and run it to view the application's final appearance. *Tip: Don't wait for me to suggest trying out your applications. You can press F9 to compile and run a program at nearly any stage in its development.*

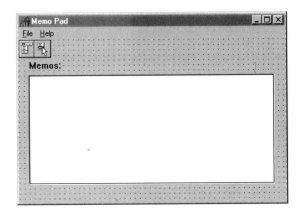

Figure 2-8
Use this image of the MemoPad form window in Delphi as a guide when you create the application.

5. To program MemoPad's commands, in the form window, select the program's *File|Save* command. *(Do not select the command in the running application — select it in Delphi's form window.)* Selecting this menu command inserts a procedure, called an *event handler*, into the program's text, and positions the cursor where you can type a *statement* to perform the command's actions. Enter the following statement between *begin* and *end*. The text inside the parentheses should be enclosed with single quotation marks. *Don't use double quotes.* Refer to Memopad\Main.pas if you get stuck.

```
Memo1.Lines.SaveToFile('memos.txt');
```

6. In English, the statement you just entered saves Memo1's lines in a file named Memos.Txt. Lines is an *object* that Memo1 owns. SaveToFile is a *method* that Lines can perform. The periods, called *dot notation*, specify that Memo1, Lines, and SaveToFile are associated. The *string*

'memos.txt' represents a filename. The statement *passes* the string in parentheses to the SaveToFile method. The statement ends with a semicolon. Technically speaking, in Pascal, a semicolon separates one statement from another. In this case, because there is no subsequent statement, you can leave out the semicolon; however, it does no harm to insert it anyway.

7. Complete the other MemoPad commands. Select *File | Exit* in the form. Enter Close; between the *begin* and *end* keywords (refer to procedure TMainForm.Exit1Click in Main.Pas). As you learned in the preceding chapter, the Close procedure, one of hundreds you can call, closes a window. If, as in this example, that is the program's main window, Close also ends the program.

8. Return to the form window and select *Help | About*. Enter the following statement between *begin* and *end*. Carefully type each character exactly as shown, or if you want to cheat, copy and paste the statement from the Main.Pas file. (I always advocate cheating to meet deadlines, so please don't hesitate to copy sample programming from these pages or from the accompanying CD-ROM. *You do not need special permission to use this book's source code in your own work.*)

```
MessageDlg('Memo Pad'#13#10'© 1995 by Tom Swan'#13#10'Version 1.00',
  mtInformation, [mbOk], 0);
```

9. The statement creates a message dialog that displays MemoPad's copyright notice and version number. To the MessageDlg procedure, the program passes four arguments in parentheses, separated by commas. The first argument is a string, delimited with quotation marks. In this string, the notation #13#10 inserts carriage return and line feed *ASCII control codes* that start subsequent text on new lines. To enter the copyright symbol, use the Windows Character Map utility, or cut and paste the character from the sample files on the CD-ROM. (Or, just type C.) The mtInformation argument selects from several dialog styles. The [mbOk] argument is a set, which in this example, has only one member, mbOk, that specifies a dialog box style with an *OK* button. The 0 argument is a placeholder for the dialog's *help context*, which MemoPad doesn't use. Once again, a semicolon ends the statement. (For more information on these argument values, look up MessageDlg in Delphi's on-line help.)

10. To program the pop-up menu's commands, double-click the Popup-Menu1 object (the one with the arrow) that you inserted into the form. This reopens the Menu Designer window. Click the *Events* page tab in the Object Inspector window. Select the About command in the Menu Designer, and set the OnClick event to About1Click. You can enter this event handler's name, or select it from the OnClick's drop-down menu. Set the *Save* command's OnClick event to Save1Click. Set the *Exit* command's OnClick event to Exit1Click. These are the same event handlers that you programmed for the main menu — a demonstration of how two or more events can share the same code.

11. Close the Menu Designer window. Click inside the form's background, and if necessary, select the *Events* page tab in the Object Inspector window. Double-click the blank space to the right of the OnActivate event, and enter the following *if-then-else* statement between *begin* and *end*. The statement reads the designated file's text into the component's Lines object:

```
if FileExists('memos.txt')
   then Memo1.Lines.LoadFromFile('memos.txt')
   else Memo1.Lines.SaveToFile('memos.txt');
```

12. The preceding statement calls a function FileExists, which returns True if the stated file is on disk, or False if not. If the file exists, the statement reads the file into Memo1's Lines. If the file does not exist, the statement saves Lines to a new file. *Because the object's Lines property is empty at this point, calling its SaveToFile method creates a blank, new file.* Although it may appear that many operations are taking place, the entire *if-then-else* construction is actually a *single* statement, and therefore only one semicolon is needed to separate this statement from another. As before, because there is no subsequent statement, the semicolon isn't strictly required.

13. Select the form (it is probably already selected), and double-click the space to the right of the event OnClose. Delphi inserts a procedure for this event, which occurs when you close the program's window. Enter the following statement between *begin* and *end* to save the component's Lines in a stated file:

```
Memo1.Lines.SaveToFile('memos.txt');
```

14. Press F9 to compile, link, and run the completed program. Try out the commands and return to Delphi. Compare your program's Main.Pas file with the sample file of the same name on the book's CD-ROM. Some of the procedures may be in different orders, but the statements and general layout should be the same.

Additional and Dialog Components

In this section, you'll develop a bitmap viewer application that uses visual components from two other Delphi categories, Additional and Dialog. Select those page tabs and use Delphi's hint boxes to locate the components mentioned here. (Reminder: Point the mouse cursor at a component icon and wait for the hint box to appear.)

Among other items, the Additional category provides graphics components that you can use to create bitmap images and GDI shapes such as rectangles, circles, and lines. The Windows GDI, or *Graphics Device Interface*, provides a device-independent method for drawing and printing graphics. You access the GDI by inserting component objects into a form window.

The Dialog category provides components that interface with common Windows dialog boxes. Although these are all Delphi components, Windows provides the actual appearance and code for the resulting dialog boxes. Using common dialog boxes gives users familiar ways to navigate disk directories and choose filenames, select fonts and colors, and search or replace values in documents.

USING THE IMAGE COMPONENT

To create a bitmap in a form, insert an object of the Image component from the Additional category. Try it now. First choose *File|New Project* to clear Delphi's workspaces, and then insert an Image object into a blank form. Because the Image component doesn't have a runtime shape — in other words, a bitmap's *content* defines its appearance — Delphi displays the Image as a dashed outline, which does not appear in the finished program.

With the Image object outline selected, highlight the Picture property in the Object Inspector window, and click the ellipsis button to open Delphi's Picture Editor. Or, you can simply double-click the component object. Use the Picture Editor to import any bitmap image into the application. First click the *Load* button, and then choose a file that ends with the extension .Bmp (bitmap), .Ico (icon), or .Wmf (Windows metafile). You can then click *Save* to copy the file to another disk file, *Clear* to erase a previously loaded image, *Cancel* to perform no operation, or *OK* to load the image into the Image component object.

If you are following along, use the Picture Editor's *Load* button to switch to the Data directory, from the CD-ROM. Open the Sample.Ico icon file, and click *OK*. The file's icon appears in the form's Image component, and the Picture property changes to TIcon. Or, to insert a bitmap, select the Sample.Bmp file. You can also load other images if you have some bitmaps stored on disk.

 You can resize a bitmap's image loaded into an Image component object, but an icon's image always remains a fixed size.

SAMPLE APPLICATION: BITVIEW

The application described in this section combines Standard, Additional, and Dialog components to create a bitmap file viewer. To try the application, open the Bitview.Dpr project file in the Bitview subdirectory, and press F9. Select any .Bmp bitmap file. There's a sample file if you need it in the Data directory. Figure 2-9 shows BitView displaying the Winlogo.Bmp bitmap file in the C:\Windows directory.

In the next section, you create your own BitView application. If you ran BitView, exit the program now before continuing.

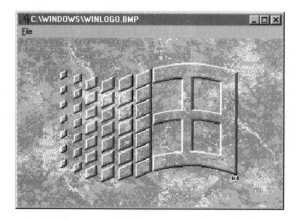

Figure 2-9
BitView's display showing the Windows logo file, Winlogo.Bmp.

Hands-On Tutorial

Listing 2-2 shows the BitView application's Main.Pas source code. Use this file as a guide when you create the application by following the step-by-step instructions after the listing.

Listing 2-2
Bitview\Main.Pas

```
unit Main;

interface

uses
   SysUtils, WinTypes, WinProcs, Messages, Classes, Graphics, Controls,
   Forms, Dialogs, Menus, ExtCtrls;

type
   TMainForm = class(TForm)
     BitImage: TImage;
     MainMenu1: TMainMenu;
     File1: TMenuItem;
     Open1: TMenuItem;
     Exit1: TMenuItem;
     OpenDialog1: TOpenDialog;
     procedure Open1Click(Sender: TObject);
     procedure Exit1Click(Sender: TObject);
```

```
    private
      { Private declarations }
    public
      { Public declarations }
    end;

var
  MainForm: TMainForm;

implementation

{$R *.DFM}

procedure TMainForm.Open1Click(Sender: TObject);
begin
  if OpenDialog1.Execute then
  begin
    BitImage.Picture.LoadFromFile(OpenDialog1.Filename);
    Caption := OpenDialog1.Filename;
  end;
end;

procedure TMainForm.Exit1Click(Sender: TObject);
begin
  Close;
end;

end.
```

Displays are open-file dialog.

To create your own BitView application, first choose *File | New Project* to clear any currently loaded project. You should be getting used to these start-up steps by now, so in future hands-on tutorials, I won't repeat them. I'll also abbreviate some of the following steps such as how to save a project. If you completed the previous application successfully, you should have no trouble with this one:

1. Change the form's Caption property to *Bitmap Viewer.* Change its Name property to MainForm.

2. Use the Windows File Manager or Windows 95 Explorer to create a directory such as C:\Projects\Bitview to hold the project's files. Return to Delphi, and save the project. Change to the directory you just created. Specify Main for the unit's filename; specify Bitview for the project's filename.

3. Change the form's WindowState property from wsNormal to wsMaximized by selecting that value from the property's drop-down list. This displays BitView's window in full-screen mode. The other values select different window states — wsMinimized displays a window as an icon; wsNormal displays the window in its designed size at a position that Windows determines.

4. Select the Additional component category, and insert an Image component into the form. Change the object's Name property to BitImage. The object's exact location and size are unimportant.

5. With the BitImage object still selected, change its Align property to alClient. This automatically resizes the component object to the same size as the form's client area, which is the space inside the window's borders.

6. To make the bitmap *inside* the component object also fit within the client area requires one more change. Highlight the BitImage component's Stretch property, and double-click the property value to toggle it from False to True. (You can also type or select True or False from the property's drop-down list, but double-clicking a True/False property is the easiest way to toggle its value.) With Stretch set to True, the program displays the bitmap within the component's space. Because the component object is automatically sized to the window, so is the bitmap image. This also demonstrates how a component object and its data, though related, can sometimes require separate programming.

7. Insert a Standard MainMenu component into the form. The default Name, MainMenu1, is descriptive enough, and you don't have to change it. Double-click the menu object's icon, and create a menu named File with two commands, Open and Exit. Remember to type an ampersand ahead of an underlined shortcut key — &File, for example. If you have trouble creating the program's menu, review the steps for MemoPad. You don't have to assign accelerator shortcut keys, but you may do so if you want. Close the Menu Designer window when you are done.

8. From the Dialog component palette, insert an OpenDialog component into the form. As it does for menus, Delphi represents dialogs

as icons that are invisible when the program runs. You can position the MainMenu1 and OpenDialog1 objects anywhere you like. Your display should resemble Figure 2-10, which shows BitView's form window under development in Delphi.

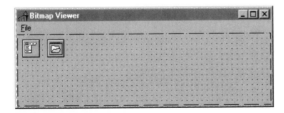

Figure 2-10
Use this image of BitView's form window in Delphi as a guide when you create the application.

9. Select the OpenDialog1 component object, and click the ellipsis button next to the Filter property's value. This opens Delphi's Filter Editor, which you can use to specify *filename filters*. For example, you can specify the filter *.Bmp to show only bitmap files. Enter two filters, one for .Bmp files and one for All files, using Figure 2-11 as a guide. Click the dialog's *OK* button to save your filters.

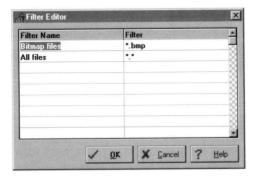

Figure 2-11
Delphi's filename Filter Editor simplifies entering filename filters.

10. All components are now in place, and you might want to save, compile, link, and run the application. Quit the program to return to Delphi. (Menu commands are still unfinished, and you can't use *File|Exit* to quit.)

11. In the form window — *not in the running program* — select *File|Open* to create a procedure for this command. In between the procedure's *begin* and *end* keywords, insert the following programming (refer to Bitview\Main.Pas as a guide, or open that file in the Windows Notepad and copy the statements):

```
if OpenDialog1.Execute then
begin
  BitImage.Picture.LoadFromFile(OpenDialog1.Filename);
  Caption := OpenDialog1.Filename;
end;
```

12. The preceding *if* statement activates OpenDialog1 by calling the object's Execute function. If that function returns True, the user closed the dialog by selecting its *OK* button. In that case, the program executes the following two statements inside a second set of *begin* and *end* keywords. The first statement calls the LoadFromFile method for the Picture object to load the file named by the dialog's Filename property. The second statement assigns this same filename to the form's caption, thus changing the window title to the bitmap's path. The := symbol is Pascal's *assignment operator,* which copies the value at right to the object at left.

13. Return to the form window, select *File|Exit,* and insert the statement Close; between *begin* and *end* in the event-handler procedure that Delphi creates for the command.

14. Save the completed project, and press F9 to compile, link, and run. Load any bitmap file. Click the double-arrow button on BitView's upper-right border to shrink the window to its normal size. Resize the window with your mouse, and notice that the bitmap shrinks or expands to fit inside the window. This can make some images look weird, but at least they fit. See Project 2-4 at the end of this chapter for a suggested change to this feature.

System Components

System components provide an assortment of objects for accessing system hardware and software. Components in this category include a Timer for background processing, a PaintBox for general-purpose graphics, and disk file and directory boxes for custom disk navigation tools. Others include a MediaPlayer component for multimedia applications, and OLE and DDE components for data sharing.

Eventually, you'll meet examples of all these components. In this section, you'll use a Timer to create a digital 24-hour clock, which also demonstrates how to perform background processes.

USING THE TIMER COMPONENT

The Timer component is one of Delphi's simplest. It has only a few properties and a single event. You can program one or more timers to perform jobs that run concurrently with other applications, or that run in the background.

To create a Timer component, select it from the Component palette's System category. Insert the component object into a blank form, change its Name property if you wish, and set the Interval to the desired event frequency in milliseconds from 1 to 65535. A value of 1000 creates a one-second timer; a value of 100 creates a 1/10-second timer. (Delphi permits you to set a timer's interval to zero, but there's no good reason to do so.)

The Timer component offers only one event, OnTimer. Double-click the event value and insert statements between *begin* and *end* to perform at the Timer's frequency.

SAMPLE APPLICATION: DCLOCK

Figure 2-12 shows DClock's display. Unlike in MemoPad, the clock window does not have minimize and maximize buttons, and it has no menu or commands. The following hands-on tutorial demonstrates how to create a fixed-sized window, which is often useful when there are no benefits in permitting users to adjust the window size.

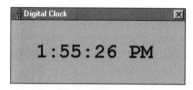

Figure 2-12
DClock's display demonstrates background processing using a Timer object.

HANDS-ON TUTORIAL

Open the Dclock.Dpr file now and inspect the form's component objects. Scan the program's Main.Pas source code in Listing 2-3. When you are done looking around, close the application and try to create your own digital clock by following the instructions after the listing.

Listing 2-3
Dclock\Main.Pas

```
unit Main;

interface

uses
  SysUtils, WinTypes, WinProcs, Messages, Classes, Graphics, Controls,
  Forms, Dialogs, ExtCtrls, StdCtrls;

type
  TMainForm = class(TForm)
    TimeLabel: TLabel;
    Timer1: TTimer;
    procedure Timer1Timer(Sender: TObject);
  private
    { Private declarations }
  public
    { Public declarations }
  end;

var
  MainForm: TMainForm;

implementation
```

```
{$R *.DFM}

procedure TMainForm.Timer1Timer(Sender: TObject);
begin
  TimeLabel.Caption := TimeToStr(Time);
end;

end.
```

Displays the time as a label's caption.

1. Start a new project. Change the form's Caption property to *Digital Clock* and set its Name to MainForm. Create a directory such as C:\Projects\Dclock to store the application files, and save the project. Name the unit file Main and the project file Dclock.

2. To eliminate the window's minimize and maximize buttons, select the form (click inside its window) and double-click the BorderIcons property. (Position the mouse over the property name at left, not on its value at right.) Notice the small plus sign to the left of the property name, which changes to a minus after double-clicking. The plus sign tells you this property has one or more hidden subvalues. A minus sign indicates that the subvalues are displayed. In this case, there are three such values. Set biSystemMenu to True (its default value), and set biMinimize and biMaximize to False. Despite this change, the form in Delphi still shows minimize and maximize buttons. This is normal — you must run the program to view the window's actual appearance.

3. Also change the window to a fixed size so that users cannot resize it. To do this, select the form's BorderStyle property, and select bsSingle from the drop-down list. You see the effect of this change only when you run the program.

4. Insert a Standard Label component into the form. Change the object's Name property to TimeLabel, and change its Caption to 00:00:00 AM. This ensures that the label is the proper size for the time digits inserted at runtime.

5. Select TimeLabel's Font property. Click the ellipsis button to open a font-selection dialog. Choose a font, a size, and a style for your clock. I specified Bold Courier New with a size of 24 points.

6. Add a System Timer component to the form window. Because this is the program's only timer object, the default Name, Timer1, is adequate.

7. Select the Timer1 object, and click the Object Inspector's *Events* page tab. You should see only one event, OnTimer. Double-click the value to the right of the event to create a procedure in the program's source code. Enter the following line above the *begin* keyword:

```
TimeLabel.Caption := TimeToStr(Time);
```

8. The preceding line converts the current time to a string and assigns the result to the label's Caption. This displays the time on screen.

9. Resize the form window for a comfortable fit. (Use *View*|*Form* to find the window if it is hidden.) Your window should resemble Figure 2-13, which shows DClock's form in Delphi. The Timer1 object's icon is not visible at runtime, and you can move it to any convenient location.

10. Press F9 to compile, link, and run the application. In a few seconds, you should see a digital clock ticking the time away. Press Alt+F4 or use the System menu's *Close* command (or click the Windows 95 close button) to quit and return to Delphi.

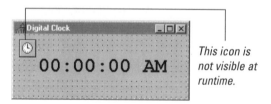

This icon is not visible at runtime.

Figure 2-13
Use this image of DClock's form window in Delphi as a guide when you create the application.

Summary

- Visual components simplify Windows programming. To create a Delphi application, you simply insert component objects into a form, and you select and modify object properties and events.

- Choose among Delphi's component categories by selecting one of the page tabs under the Component palette. Click the icon of the component you want, move the mouse cursor into the form, and click again to insert a component object at that location.

- Selecting a component displays handles around it that you can use to resize the object. You can also click and drag components to position them in the form. Select a component by single-clicking it, or choose it by name from the Object Inspector's drop-down list. You can also select multiple components by clicking and dragging an outline around them.

- Properties are values that specify component characteristics. For example, components such as buttons and labels have a Font property for selecting a text font name, point size, and style.

- Events represent a component's runtime actions. Double-clicking an event value inserts an event-handler procedure into the program's source code. To program the event, insert one or more Pascal statements between the procedure's *begin* and *end* keywords that Delphi automatically inserts.

- When you select two or more components, the Object Inspector window displays their shared properties and events. Any changes you make to these values affect all selected components.

- Delphi maintains a visual representation of your application in the form window, and an Object Pascal source code representation in a unit window. The two representations are synchronized so that changes in one window reflect in the other.

- A small plus sign to the left of a property indicates that the property has subvalues. Double-click the property value field to list and unlist these values.

- An ellipsis button to the right of a property's value indicates that double-clicking the value, or single-clicking the button, opens a dialog box for changing this property's setting. Some properties have both subvalues and dialog boxes.

Projects to Try

2-1: Change various properties of MemoPad's component objects. For example, assign a different *Font* for the Memo1 object. Change the style of the MemoLabel component, and try out its Color property.

2-2: When you start the DClock application, it first displays *00:00:00 AM* before showing the current time. To improve the display and show the time as soon as the program's window appears, create an event handler for the form's OnCreate event. Click the form background to select the form, and then choose the *Events* page tab in the Object Inspector. Click the down-arrow to the right of the OnCreate event, and select Timer1Timer. This is the same event handler you programmed for the Timer1 component. When you run the program, it initializes TimeLabel by calling the Timer1Timer procedure, which sets the label to the current time before the window becomes visible.

2-3: Open the BitView project and select its OpenDialog1 component object. Change the Ctl3D property to False, and press F9 to compile, link, and run. When you select the program's *File | Open* command, you see a standard Windows dialog box, probably with a white background and a relatively plain appearance. To return to a 3D effect, change the Ctl3D property back to True.

 The Ctrl3D property has no effect under Windows 95, which provides 3D controls by default.

2-4: Open the BitView project, and select the BitImage component. Set the image's Stretch property to False, and press F9 to compile, link, and run. Open a bitmap file. It displays more quickly because adjusting image sizes takes time. Unfortunately, however, displaying full-size images may cut off areas that extend beyond the window borders. In the next chapter, you'll insert scroll bars into the window to solve this problem. Also refer to Chapter 10 for more information about scrolling.

Expert-User Tips

- In most cases, after inserting a component into a form, you should give the object a Name that reflects its purpose. The usual exception to this rule is when you insert only one type of component object. For example, if your program has only one main menu, the default name — MainMenu1 — is probably adequate.

- Use descriptive Names such as CloseButton, AgeLabel, and NameEdit. Some programmers like to use short names — for example, B1, B2, and B3 for buttons — but if you do that, you may not recognize your objects next year or next month — or, if your memory is no better than mine, by noon tomorrow.

- As a rule of thumb, your programs will be easier to understand and maintain if you append component names to the end of Name property values. For example, NoteMemo is probably a better name for a Memo object than NoteArea. The former name reminds you of the object's component type; the latter hides this important fact.

- Names must begin with a letter or underscore, and they may contain only letters, digits, and underscores. Label10 is a legal name; 10Label is not. Names may not have embedded spaces. Use capital letters to clarify long Names — for example, MainSysMenu is more readable than mainsysmenu. A Name may contain embedded underscores as in My_Main_Menu. Underscores are hard to see on screen, however, and I don't recommend using them. Names may be from 1 to 63 characters long and must adhere to Pascal identifier syntax.

- Unlike Names, Captions and other text-value properties may have any characters that you can type or cut and paste, in any order, including spaces and punctuation. The length of a Caption is technically limited to 255 characters, but in practice, a component object's size limits its Caption length.

- When a form becomes full of component objects, or when one or more objects cover the window's client area, you may have trouble selecting the form. In that case, use the Object Inspector's drop-down list to select the form by name. For example, to select the main-window form in most of this book's applications, choose MainForm from the Object Inspector list. You can also use this method to select any component object inserted into a form.

- To align multiple components, first move one component to its proper position. *Select this component first, and then select the others.* The *Edit|Align* command aligns component objects relative to the first one you select.

- In the Menu Designer, press Ctrl+Ins to insert a menu command between two others. Press Ctrl+Del to delete a command. Type a single dash in a command's Caption property to insert a separator between two other commands.

- Select *Edit | Lock Controls* to enable this menu option (a check mark appears next to it). When enabled, this option prevents moving or resizing component objects, but you can still modify control properties and events. After you program a form just the way you want it, use this command to prevent accidental rearrangements of your carefully positioned objects.

- If you cannot move or resize selected component objects, check whether *Lock Controls* from the preceding tip is enabled.

- Newcomers to Pascal typically worry about semicolon placement, but don't be overly concerned. If you type a semicolon in the wrong place, Delphi displays an *Error in statement* message. In C and C++, semicolons terminate statements. In Pascal, semicolons separate statements from one another. For example, you may not insert a semicolon after an *if* statement's *else* clause because, unlike in C and C++, Pascal's *if-then-else* is a single statement. Refer to this book's listings for examples of correct semicolon placement.

- For a faster way to insert component objects into a form, double-click any component icon in Delphi's palette. This inserts an object of that component in the center of the current form. Use this method to insert multiple component objects — a set of check boxes, for example. Each object exactly overlays the preceding ones, and you should click and drag them to their final resting spots before doing anything else.

- After inserting a component object into a form, double-click the object to create an event handler for its default event. This is always the first event listed in the Object Inspector window. Some components don't work this way. For example, double-clicking a MainMenu component object opens the Menu Designer window.

- To locate an existing event handler, double-click it in the Object Inspector window's Events page. This displays the form's unit window, and positions the cursor inside the event handler. Delphi creates a new event handler only if one does not already exist.

- Set a Label component object's AutoSize property to True to have the control automatically adjust its size to fit its Caption data. Set this property to False if you want the component to remain a fixed size at all times. You must use a fixed size if you set WordWrap True to display multiline labels.

- Editing lengthy window captions and other single-line strings can be difficult because of the Object Inspector's small size. For easier editing, enter the text into the Windows Notepad or another text editor. Highlight the text, press Ctrl+Ins to copy it to the Windows clipboard, switch back to the Object Inspector, highlight the target property such as Caption, and press Ctrl+Ins.

Coming Up

In the next chapter, you'll investigate more about forms, properties, and events. You'll also learn how to respond to mouse actions, how to add scroll bars to a form window, how to make a window stay on top, and how to create an opening splash screen.

3 Introducing Forms

*T*he word *form* can mean many things. On a construction site, a form is a box that shapes wet cement. We say that healthy individuals are in good form. You can form a corporation, and you can march the troops into formation, but nobody loves a tax form.

In Delphi, every project has at least one *form object* that represents the program's main window. Projects can also have multiple forms for child windows, dialog boxes, and data-entry screens. Although a form's main purpose is to hold other components such as buttons and check boxes, a form can also perform actions in response to events such as key presses and mouse clicks.

Forms are among Delphi's most versatile objects, and you will use them extensively to develop applications. In this chapter, you'll learn key features of forms and their properties and events.

Forms as Components

A form represents a window's visual appearance, but a form is not just another pretty window. A form is actually a Delphi component with its own set of properties and events. Unlike other components, however, a form doesn't appear on the Component palette.

You create a form object in one of two ways: by starting a new project or by selecting the *File | New Form* command. Use the first method to create your application's main window form. Use the second method for additional forms — to create an About dialog, for example, or to display a start-up splash screen. (More on these subjects later.)

FORMS AND UNITS

When you create a new form, Delphi adds two windows to the programming environment. The *form window* shows the form's visual representation as it will appear in the finished application. The *unit window* lists the form's Object Pascal programming. Figure 3-1 shows the form and unit windows for the DClock application from Chapter 2. Internally, the form is an *object* in the unit, which is also sometimes called a *module*.

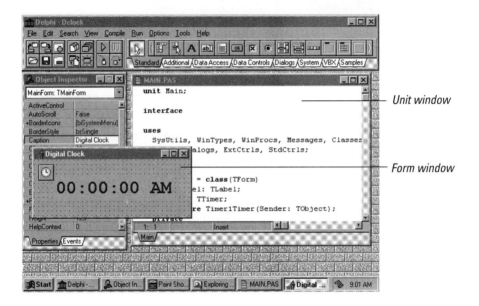

Unit window

Form window

Figure 3-1

Delphi maintains a form window (labeled Digital Clock) and its associated programming in a unit window (labeled Main.Pas).

Delphi automatically creates an Object Pascal unit for each new form you insert into an application. It is not possible or desirable to insert multiple form objects into one unit. Every form must have a corresponding unit. However, all units do not have forms. Some units merely provide code for other modules to use.

Expert Pascal programmers beware! Attempting to insert multiple forms into a unit may cause Delphi to lose its marbles. Inserting multiple form objects into a unit can disrupt Delphi's visual programming and automatic code generation capabilities. For best results, adhere to the one-form-one-unit rule. Delphi will never insert multiple forms into a unit, so the only way you'll experience this error is by writing units from scratch or by attempting to combine two form units into one. Don't do that.

SAVING FORMS IN PROJECTS

When saving a new project, never set a form's Name property and unit filename the same. For example, if you set a form's Name property to MainForm, *do not save the form unit as Mainform.Pas* (I suggest using Main.Pas instead). Because the unit's internal name equals its filename minus the .Pas extension, using the same name for the form and the unit results in a name conflict.

To experience this error so you can avoid it in the future, follow these steps:

1. Start a new project and change the form's Name property to Main.

2. Save the project, and enter Main for the unit filename. Delphi automatically adds the .Pas extension to create the actual filename, Main.Pas.

3. Click the file-save dialog's OK button or press Enter. Because of the naming conflict, instead of saving the file, Delphi displays the error message, [this] *project already contains a form or module named Main.*

4. Fix the problem by changing the form's Name property to any text that is different from the filename — for example, MainForm. You can now repeat step 2 and save the unit as Main.Pas.

To prevent this type of name conflict, which may be frequent until you become familiar with Delphi's naming rules, follow these suggestions for choosing Name properties and unit filenames:

- Append the word *Form* to every form's Name property. Examples of good form Names are MainForm for the program's main window, AboutForm for an About dialog, and EntryForm for a data-entry screen.

- Save the unit modules using their Name properties *minus* Form. For example, when you save the project, specify the file names Main for the MainForm module, About for AboutForm, and Entry for Entry-Form. This creates the three files Main.Pas, About.Pas, and Entry.Pas.

SELECTED FORM PROPERTIES

Specific examples throughout this book demonstrate many properties of form objects. Many properties have obvious purposes, and I won't explain them further here. (It doesn't take a genius to understand the purpose of a form's Height and Width properties.) Also, you have already met many form properties such as Caption, Name, and Border-Style. The following notes describe less obvious properties that you can view and edit in the object inspector window.

- *ActiveControl*— Set this to any component object Name to give that object the *input focus* when the form window first becomes visible. The input focus is not permanent, and users can still press Tab to move the focus to other components.

- *AutoScroll*— Set to True to have scroll bars automatically appear and disappear in a window depending on whether more information extends beyond the window borders. Also affects form scaling. If False, both the form's client area and the window rectangle will be scaled; if True, only the form client area is scaled. Usually, with scaled forms, you should set AutoScroll to False. For more information about using scroll bars, see "Form Frameworks" in this chapter.

- *Cursor*—Specifies a cursor shape to display when the mouse cursor moves into the window's client area. Select one of the values from this property's drop-down list.

- *Enabled* — Normally set to True to have the form respond to mouse, timer, or keyboard events. Set to False to disable event handling.

Don't do this for main-window forms. Set this property to False only for forms that the program manages. (The splash-screen method explained in this chapter uses this feature.)

- *HorzScrollBar* — Sets a horizontal scroll bar's values. The scroll bar appears only if the subvalue Visible is True and if Range is greater than ClientWidth. Double-click the property name (not its value) to open these subvalues.

- *Icon* — Selects an associated icon to represent the form window. If the form is the program's main window, the Icon property specifies the system icon that Windows displays when you minimize the window.

- *KeyPreview* — Set to True if you want the form to receive most keyboard events *before* they go to the focused control. If False, all keyboard events go to the selected control. Regardless of KeyPreview's setting, the form never receives navigation key events such as generated by pressing the Tab, BackTab, and cursor arrow keys, *unless* the current control (an input box, for example) processes those keys.

- *Menu* — Specifies which MainMenu component to use for the form's menu bar. Delphi normally sets this property to the form's first MainMenu object, but you can change it to another menu. See Chapter 5 for more information.

- *ObjectMenuItem* — Used with OLE applications. See Chapter 16 for more information.

- *PixelsPerInch* — Designates how the application creates a form window scaled to pixels per inch. Use with Scaled to create forms that appear similar in size in different screen resolutions. If Scaled is False, PixelsPerInch has no effect. This property's name is somewhat misleading because its value does not equal the number of pixels in one inch. Instead, Delphi determines PixelsPerInch based on the system font size, and then uses this value to scale the form window.

- *Position* — Determines the method for calculating a form's size and position. The default setting, poDefault, displays the window in its designed size and position; poDefaultPosOnly positions the window as designed, but calculates its size at runtime; (Windows determines the initial size of the runtime form); poDefaultSizeOnly sizes the window as designed, but positions it at runtime (Windows determines where the window appears); and poScreenCenter centers the window in the display.

- Scaled — Set to True to use the PixelsPerInch property and create a form that automatically scales to the same apparent size regardless of display resolution. Set to False to not scale a form.

- Tag — No preset meaning. Use Tag to store any integer (whole number) value you wish — for example, a version number, or a code or count that the program inspects at runtime.

- VertScrollBar — Same as HorzScrollBar, but configures the form's vertical scroll bar subproperties.

- Visible —Set to True to make a component visible; False to hide it until the program calls the component object's Show method. A form's Visible property is normally False because applications automatically make their forms visible at the proper times. For a form used as a child window or dialog box, however, Visible might set Visible False to hide the window until needed.

- WindowMenu — In multiple-document interface (MDI) applications, designates the menu to display titles of opened windows. Set this property to any menu item (usually Captioned *Window*) in the form's MainMenu object.

 See Chapter 15 for more information about MDI applications and on using forms to create child windows.

Selected Form Events

As with form properties, examples throughout this book demonstrate many form events; others — for example, such as OnClick and OnDblClick — are self-evident. Following are less obvious events displayed in a selected form's Object Inspector window:

- OnActivate — Called when the program activates the form — that is, when it *first* receives the input focus as when, for example, you switch back to the program from another application. See also OnDeactivate.

3

- OnClose — Called when the form closes. See also OnDestroy.

- OnCloseQuery — Called just *before* the form closes, usually when the application calls the Close procedure. You can use this event to prevent data loss by prompting users to save changed files before the application ends, or to prevent a form from closing. See "Closing a Window" in this chapter for more information.

- OnCreate — Called once when the program creates a form object in memory. Use this event to perform one-time initializations.

- OnDeactivate — Called when the user switches away from the application. See also OnActivate.

- OnDestroy — Called just before a form object's destruction. Use this event to release any system-held resources or to perform critical cleanup chores. If the form is the program's main window, OnDestroy is your last best opportunity to perform actions before the program terminates.

- OnDonner, OnBlitzen — Called in response to jingling bells heard on the rooftop. (Just checking whether you're still paying attention.)

- OnDragDrop, OnDragOver — Part of Delphi's drag-and-drop services. See Chapter 16 for more information on data transfers, DDE, and OLE.

- OnHide — Used to perform actions when a form is hidden. For example, an OnHide event handler could release memory or other resources when a form is not visible.

- OnKeyDown — Called when the user presses any key, including function and special keys. Use this event to interpret multikey activity, such as pressing the Alt and Shift keys, perhaps in combination with a function key. It is possible for a program to receive multiple OnKeyDown events without receiving intervening OnKeyUp events. Usually set KeyPreview to True when using this event.

- OnKeyPress — Called when the user presses a single ASCII or control key, but not a function or other special key. Use this event to detect character keypresses. This event occurs after OnKeyDown but before OnKeyUp. Usually set KeyPreview to True when using this event.

- OnKeyUp — Called when the user releases any key, including function and special keys. There is always one OnKeyUp event to match every OnKeyDown event. Use this event along with OnKeyDown to fine-tune control over keyboard activity — for example, in a game that performs activities (perhaps via a Timer component) *while* the user holds down a certain key combination. An OnKeyUp event occurs for every OnKeyDown event, but not necessarily in strict down-up-down-up order. Usually set KeyPreview to True when using this event.

- OnMouseDown — Called when the user clicks any mouse button and the mouse cursor is positioned over the form's client area. Delphi calls the Windows API GetCapture for an OnMouseDown event to ensure that the object will receive subsequent OnMouse-Move and OnMouseUp events. This feature is controlled by the csCaptureMouse flag in the TControl class's ControlState property.

- OnMouseMove — Called when the user moves the mouse cursor within the form's client area. You can also determine whether the user has pressed the Shift, Alt, or Ctrl keys while moving the mouse.

- OnMouseUp — Called when the user releases a mouse button that previously generated an OnMouseDown event, regardless of the mouse cursor's position.

- OnPaint — Called when the form's contents require updating — for example, after the user moves another window aside. For more information on graphics programming, see Chapter 14.

- OnResize — Called after the window changes size. This can be in reponse to dragging the window's size button, and minimizing or maximizing the window. Note that the window has already been resized when your application receives this event.

- OnShow — Called just before a window becomes visible. Use this event to perform initializations before the window appears.

When processing Tab keystrokes in OnKeyDown events, always check the Shift flags. If the user presses Alt+Tab to switch away from the application, the OnKeyDown event will receive that key combination. If you do not check for the Alt key in the Shift flags, your program will interfere with the operation of Windows.

Form Templates

You can construct your own forms from scratch, or you can select from one of several preprogrammed *form templates* supplied with Delphi. The templates are easy to use and modify, and they are especially valuable for quickly getting prototypes up and running.

As demonstrated in the following sections, you can also create your own form templates to provide a common base for new programs, standard data-entry screens, custom dialog boxes, and many other applications.

USING FORM TEMPLATES

Try the following steps to create an About dialog using a form template that displays a copyright notice and other information about your application.

Before starting, select *Options|Environment* and enable the *Gallery* option, *Use on New Form*. This option is selected by default for a new Delphi installation.

1. Begin a new project, and create a directory such as C:\Projects\Aboutex for its files. Change the form's Name to MainForm and its Caption to *About Box Example*. Save the project in the directory you created. Name the unit Main and the project Aboutex.

2. To add a second form to the project, select *File|New Form* or click the *New form* speed button. As shown in Figure 3-2, this brings up the *Browse Gallery dialog* which lists form templates. Click the Templates page tab if your screen doesn't resemble the figure. Table 3-1 describes the form templates in the *Browse Gallery* dialog.

3. Choose the *About box* template with the mouse or by pressing Tab or arrow keys. Press Enter or click OK to insert this form into the application and close the *Browse Gallery* dialog.

4. You should see the blank About dialog window illustrated in Figure 3-3. By default, the form's Name property is set to AboutBox. Change this Name to AboutForm. (Reminder: I strongly suggest

including the component name, such as Form, in its Name property.) Also change AboutForm's Caption to *About This Program*, or
to any other text.

Table 3-1

Form Templates

Gallery Form	Description
Blank form	General-purpose form. Use it to create a program's main window, child windows, and custom dialog boxes.
About box	Displays a copyright notice, version number, and other program information. Usually displayed in response to a *Help|About* command.
Dual list box	Two interactive lists, with buttons for transferring selected items from one list to the other. Useful for selecting among options, files, and other information sets.
Multi-page dialog	Standard dialog box with *OK, Cancel,* and *Help* buttons, a Group Box area that can hold other components, and a set of page tabs displayed at bottom. Useful for complex dialogs that have too many controls to fit on one screen. Users can select page tabs to view other parts of the dialog. See also Tabbed notebook dialog.
Standard dialog box (buttons at bottom)	Same as a blank form, but with *OK, Cancel,* and *Help* buttons placed along the bottom. Useful for many different kinds of diaog boxes.
Standard dialog box (buttons at right)	Same as the preceding standard dialog box, but with buttons placed along the right edge.
Password dialog	Small dialog with an input box, *OK,* and *Cancel* buttons. Use it to request a password from users. The password is not visible while typing.
Tabbed notebook dialog	For complex dialogs with too many controls to fit on one screen. Each page of the dialog looks like a file-folder, with an identifying tab at top. See also Multi-page dialog.

5. Save the project, and when Delphi presents the file-save dialog, enter
About for the AboutForm unit filename. This creates a new Object Pascal module, About.Pas, in the current directory. The project now has
two forms — one for the program's main window (MainForm) and
one for an About dialog (AboutForm). Each form has an associated
Object Pascal module: Main.Pas for MainForm and About.Pas for
AboutForm. In addition, the file Main.Dfm stores MainForm's proper-

ties; About.Dfm stores AboutForm's properties. You might want to view the project's filenames with the Windows File Manager at this stage.

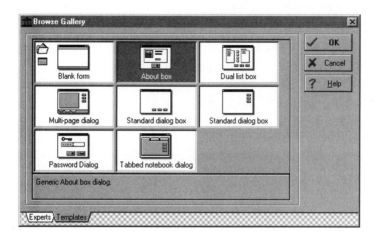

Figure 3-2
Delphi's Browse Gallery of form templates.

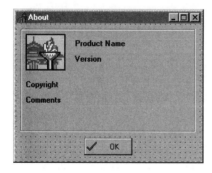

Figure 3-3
The unmodified AboutBox form window.

6. Modify AboutForm's Label component objects as you wish. Insert your program's name, a copyright notice, and any other text you want. You can also insert additional components into AboutForm's window. Any changes you make affect only this application — the form template remains unblemished for future uses. Figure 3-4 shows a sample finished AboutForm dialog.

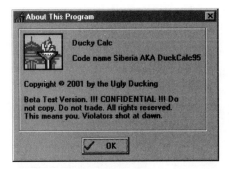

Figure 3-4

The finished AboutForm from the AboutEx application.

7. If you compile and run the program at this stage, it displays only a blank window. Although MainForm automatically becomes visible, the AboutForm dialog hides until needed. To display the dialog, first add a Button component to MainForm. Keep the default Name, Button1, and change the Caption to *Click Me!*, or to any other text. Size the button and MainForm window as you wish. Double-click the Button1 object in the form to create an OnClick event handler, and enter this statement between *begin* and *end*:

```
AboutForm.ShowModal;
```

8. The preceding statement calls AboutForm's ShowModal function. This displays a *modal dialog*, which you must close before continuing to use the application. A *modeless dialog* permits menus and other commands to operate normally while the dialog remains open. Chapter 12 explains more about modal and modeless dialogs.

9. The preceding statement will not compile because the Main unit module doesn't yet recognize the AboutForm object in the About module. To import AboutForm, press Ctrl+F12 and select Main from the *View Unit* dialog. Locate the uses directive at the top of Main, which lists other modules used by this one. Between the last module name and semicolon, type a comma and the word About. Make sure the directive still ends with a semicolon. For example, your uses directive might look like the following, but the exact order and

number of modules may differ depending on the changes you made
to the AboutForm window:

```
uses
   SysUtils, WinTypes, WinProcs, Messages, Classes, Graphics, Controls,
   Forms, Dialogs, About;
```

10. Press F9 to compile, link, and run the application. When its main
window appears, click the button to display the AboutForm dialog.
Close the dialog and the program to return to Delphi.

You can use similar steps to program a menu command that displays
AboutForm. Instead of a Button, insert a MainMenu component into
MainForm, and double-click the object to create the menu's commands.
Select a command such as *Help|About* in the form window to create an
event handler, and enter the same statement you typed for Button1's
OnClick event.

When you first save a project with multiple forms, Delphi presents a
gaggle of file-save-as dialogs, one for each unnamed module. At best,
this can be confusing. At worst, it can cause even skilled programmers
to run screaming for the nearest watering hole. To guard against accidentally misnaming module files, create each new form, enter a Name
and Caption, and then select *File|Save Project* or click the *Save project*
speed button. It takes a little more time to save each new form as you
create it, but this method is potentially less disorienting than saving
multiple forms all at once.

CREATING FORM TEMPLATES

Creating your own form templates is a great way to share programming or
to develop software shells. For example, if your program's users require
several data-entry screens that differ in minor ways, you can save time by
creating templates for commonly shared elements. Programming teams
can also save time and effort by developing templates for new projects,
demos, and prototypes.

You can save any form as a template. Either create the new form
from scratch, or choose *File|New Form* and select an existing template on

which to base your form. Insert component objects, modify properties, and create event handlers. To test your form, write a project similar to AboutEx with a button or menu command that displays the form. Or, you can simply design your form as the test program's main window. When you are satisfied with your design, use the following steps to convert your form into a template.

The book's CD-ROM does not include files for the following tutorial. Use these steps to convert your own forms into templates.

1. Bring up your target form's window (press Shift+F12, if necessary, or choose the *View|Form* command).

2. Press Alt+F10 or single-click the right mouse button with the mouse cursor inside the target form's window. Choose *Save As Template* from the floating pop-up menu that's displayed.

3. In the resulting *Save Form Template* dialog, the template filename is set by default to the unit name under which you saved the form. Change this filename only if necessary. Enter a Title and Description to display in the Browse Gallery dialog.

4. Optionally click *Browse* and choose a bitmap for the template. Use the Windows PaintBrush or Delphi's Image Editor to create a 60-pixels-wide by 40-pixels-tall, 16-color bitmap file for this purpose. You'll find a sample file, Gallery.Bmp, in the correct format on this book's CD-ROM in the Data directory.

5. When you are done specifying the template's parameters and bitmap, press Enter or click OK to close the *Save Form Template* dialog.

When you next select *File|New Form*, the Browse Gallery dialog lists your form. Delphi stores the form's .Pas and .Dfm files in the Gallery subdirectory. You may save or discard your original development files, but you should probably keep them for future updates.

To modify a form template for which you don't have the original source code files, first insert the form into a project with *File|New Form*. Make your changes, and then repeat the preceding steps. Saving a modified form inserted into a project preserves only that specific use of the form. To update the template, you must again save the form *as* a template.

DELETING FORM TEMPLATES

Follow these steps to delete a form template from Delphi's gallery. For demonstration purposes, I assume that you have created a form template named AnyForm, and that you have saved the form's unit module as Any.Pas. (The accompanying CD-ROM does not include these hypothetical files.)

1. Select *Options|Gallery*. This opens the *Gallery Options* dialog, which you can use to configure Delphi's form and project templates.

2. Click the *Form Templates* page tab to display the current list of existing form templates.

3. Select the template you want to discard, and click the Delete button. (You cannot delete the *Blank form* entry.) Answer Yes to the resulting *Confirm* dialog to delete the form from the gallery.

4. Close the *Gallery Options* dialog by pressing Enter or clicking *OK*. Delphi doesn't actually delete the form template until you complete this step. If you change your mind, press Esc or click *Cancel* to close the dialog and make no changes.

Deleting a form does not erase its files, which remain in Delphi's Gallery subdirectory. To restore a deleted form template, close the current project or start a new one, and select *File|Open File*. Change to the Gallery directory, and open the form's unit file (Anyform.Pas in this demonstration). You can then resave the inserted form as a template.

To permanently remove a template and its files, follow the preceding numbered steps, and then use the Windows File Manager to delete the form's .Pas and .Dfm files from Delphi's Gallery subdirectory. For example, to exterminate the demonstration template, delete Any.Pas and Any.Dfm. *After you delete these files, Delphi cannot recover the form template.*

You may delete Delphi's standard form templates, but these are highly useful objects and you should not remove them from disk without good reason. Some of the sample applications in this book assume that one or more standard templates are available.

Using a Dialog for a Main Window Form

In some cases, you might want to change the main window to a different form. For example, it's often useful to use a dialog box as an application window. The resulting interface is simple and clean, and it doesn't require a menu bar. Users run the program by clicking buttons and selecting other controls in the dialog window.

Follow these steps to change an application's main window to another form or template:

1. Start a new project.

2. Select *File|New Form* or click the *New form* speed button, and choose a form template such as *Tabbed notebook dialog.* Press Enter or click OK to close the *Browse Gallery* dialog. Or, if your mouse-aim is on target, simply double-click the form template you want.

3. Choose *View|Project* to open Delphi's Project Manager window, which is shown in Figure 3-5. Highlight the form you created in the preceding step (if you are following along, select *Unit2 TabbedNotebookDlg).* If you accidentally double-clicked the mouse, return to the Project Manager window. Click the *Options* button — alternatively, press Alt+T or click the right mouse button and select Options from the pop-up menu. At the top of the resulting *Project Options dialog,* change *Main form* to the selected form's Name from the drop-down list (choose TabbedNotebookDlg if you are following along).

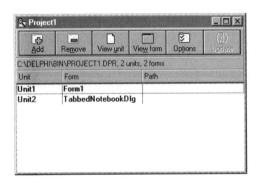

Figure 3-5
Delphi's Project Manager window.

4. Press Enter or select the OK button to close the *Project Options* dialog. Highlight *Unit1 Form1* in the Project Manager window, and press Del to delete it. Answer No when Delphi prompts you to save Unit1.pas. You are discarding the project's default form and unit, so there's no reason to save this module.

5. Close the Project Manager window. Save the project, and as usual, name the unit Main and the project Test (the exact names are unimportant).

6. Compile, link, and run the application by pressing F9. Figure 3-6 shows the program's main window — a tabbed, notebook-style dialog box. Because you didn't supply any event handlers for the dialog's buttons, the dialog's buttons don't do anything. To return to Delphi, press Alt+F4, double-click the system-menu button, or click the Windows 95 close button.

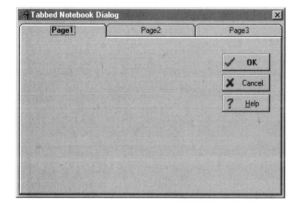

Figure 3-6
A Tabbed notebook used as a main window.

Closing a Window

Why is it we close things *up* but shut them *down?* I don't know, but whichever way you like to travel, closing a window correctly is as important as getting one up and running.

As you have learned, you close any Delphi form window by calling its Close procedure. If the window is the application's main one, closing it also ends the program. For example, insert a Button object into a form, and create an event handler by double-clicking the object, and entering Close; between the procedure's *begin* and *end* key-words:

```
begin
  Close;    { <-- insert this statement here }
end;
```

Calling Close sets several behind-the-scenes actions into motion. You don't have to program these activities — they are automatic. Internally, Close calls another function, CloseQuery, which returns True if it is okay for the window to close. If CloseQuery returns False, the call to Close is canceled and the window does not close. If CloseQuery returns True, the program activates the OnClose event handler (if there is one) for this form.

Delphi's closure sequence provides several good opportunities to perform actions when forms close. Internally, CloseQuery activates the OnCloseQuery event handler, which you can use to determine whether it is safe to close the form window. For example, OnCloseQuery might check whether the user saved critical data. If not, the program can display a warning, or it can cancel the request to close the window. Figure 3-7 illustrates the actions that occur when you call Close.

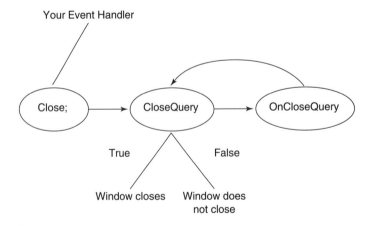

Figure 3-7
Delphi performs these actions when a program calls a window's Close event.

A simple example demonstrates how to use OnCloseQuery to confirm a user's intention to end a program by closing its main window. Start a new project (you don't have to save this one), and follow these steps:

1. Insert a Button component into the form. Double-click the Button and enter Close; between the resulting event-handler's *begin* and *end* keywords.

2. Press F9 to compile, link, and run the program. Click the Button object to exit and return to Delphi. This demonstrates normal form closure. By tapping into the Close sequence, you can add a confirmation box that permits users to change their minds about ending the program.

3. Back in Delphi, select the form by clicking in its background. Be sure the Button1 object is not selected. Go to the Events page in the Object Inspector window, and double-click the mouse cursor in the value field to the right of the OnCloseQuery event. Enter the programming in Listing 3-1. (For reference, the listing shows the entire event handler — enter only the statements between the *begin* and *end* keywords.) The programming displays a message dialog with *Yes* and *No* buttons. If the user chooses *Yes*, MessageDlg returns the value mrYes, and the *if* statement sets CanClose to True. If the user chooses *No*, the program sets CanClose to False.

4. Press F9 to run the program. This time, when you click the window's button, the message dialog requests confirmation as shown in Figure 3-8. Choose Yes to end. Choose No to cancel the close request.

 Carefully enter the programming in Listing 3-1 exactly as shown. There is a mix of square brackets and parentheses in this code, which may look similar on the printed page.

Listing 3-1
An OnCloseQuery event handler

```
procedure TForm1.FormCloseQuery(Sender: TObject; var CanClose: Boolean);
begin
  if MessageDlg('End the program?',
    mtConfirmation, [mbYes, mbNo], 0) = mrYes
    then CanClose := True
    else CanClose := False;
end;
```

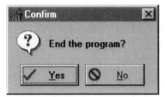

Figure 3-8
Confirmation message dialog.

Form Frameworks

The following sections describe some other neat things you can do with forms, such as attaching scroll bars, making a window stay on top of other windows, and creating a start-up splash screen.

QUICK-AND-DIRTY SCROLL BARS

A *scroll* is one of the most ancient known devices for viewing information in a relatively small space. Today, *scrolling* has become one of modern computing's most accepted display tricks for viewing large documents on small screens. Besides being a useful interface tool, a *scroll bar* is literally a link to the past.

As you probably know, a scroll bar is a Windows control that you click, drag, and poke to scroll information in a window. Click a scroll bar's buttons to browse at slow speed (a line at a time, for example), or click inside the shaded bar to page through data more quickly. The scroll bar's *thumb box* indicates the relative position of the window's view. Drag the thumb box for another view. For example, to move to the document's midpoint, drag the thumb box to the center of the bar.

In Windows 95, scroll bar thumb boxes grow to indicate how much information is *not* displayed in a window — a large thumb box indicates that very little information is out of view, while a small thumb box indicates there's a lot of off-screen information. You don't have to perform any special programming to take advantage of this feature.

It's easy to add scroll bars to a form, but there are several refinements you can make for smoother scrolling. Follow these steps to add scroll bars to the BitView application from Chapter 2.

1. Copy the BitView sample application from Chapter 2 to a new directory named Mybits (or another name). Copy only the Bitview.Dpr, Main.Dfm, and Main.Pas files. *Do not copy any other files, especially those such as desktop files ending in .Dsk which may contain pathnames to the original Bitview directory.* For reference, this tutorial's finished files are in the Bitview2 directory on the CD-ROM.

2. Open the BitView project (be sure to change to the directory you created from step 1). Single-click inside the outlined BitImage component object, which fills the form's client area. (Alternatively, select BitImage from the Object Inspector's drop-down list.) In the Object Inspector's Properties page, double-click the bitmap's Stretch property to change True to False. With Stretch disabled, the program no longer adjusts bitmaps to fit BitImage's size, and therefore, you need to add scroll bars to view pictures larger than the window.

3. Set MainForm's WindowState property to wsNormal so the window displays in its designed size rather than full screen. (Select MainForm from the Object Inspector's drop-down list.) Also, change MainForm's Caption to *Bitmap Viewer With Scroll Bars*.

4. To add a horizontal scroll bar to the form, double-click the form's HorzScrollBar property to open its five subvalues. *Click the property name, not its value.* Set Range to 1000 and make sure that Visible is True (the default value). When you press Enter or move to another Property, a horizontal scroll bar appears in the form window. If not, specify a larger Range.

5. To add a vertical scroll bar to the form, repeat the preceding step for MainForm's VertScrollBar property. The final form window now shows horizontal and vertical scroll bars.

6. Press F9 to run the modified application. Open any bitmap file such as Sample.Bmp in the Data directory. Resize the window, and use its scroll bars to move the image up, down, left, and right.

In general, you can use similar steps to add scroll bars to any informational component aligned to the window's client area. For each scroll bar property, make sure that:

- The subvalue Visible is True.
- The subvalue Range is greater than the form's ClientWidth property. A value from 1000 to 2000 is usually adequate.

Quick-and-dirty scroll bars are useful for prototypes and for testing scrolling operations; however, for smoother scrolling, you will want to make several refinements to finished applications.

FINE-TUNING SCROLL BARS

Experienced Windows users expect scroll bars to perform as though choreographed in a ballet. Following are some of the dance steps, that if not followed exactly, will bring jeers from your program's users:

- Scroll bars should not appear until the user opens a document in the window.
- The appearance of a scroll bar should indicate that more information is available by scrolling. For example, in a text window, a vertical scroll bar indicates there are more lines in the document than the window can show.
- Resizing the window, or loading another document, should display or remove scroll bars as necessary. For example, if maximizing a window causes the entire document to come into view, scroll bars should disappear. If you load a large document, scroll bars should come back into view if necessary.
- The scroll bar's thumb position should indicate the relative viewing location in the document — or, to state that in technical terms, *scroll bar ranges should mirror the document's size.*

In the following tutorial, you make all of the preceding improvements to the BitView application. Listing 3-2 shows the final Main.Pas form unit file from the Bitview2 directory on disk.

Listing 3-2
Bitview2\Main.Pas

```
unit Main;

interface

uses
  SysUtils, WinTypes, WinProcs, Messages, Classes, Graphics, Controls,
  Forms, Dialogs, Menus, ExtCtrls;

type
  TMainForm = class(TForm)
    BitImage: TImage;
    MainMenu1: TMainMenu;
    File1: TMenuItem;
    Open1: TMenuItem;
    Exit1: TMenuItem;
    OpenDialog1: TOpenDialog;
    procedure Open1Click(Sender: TObject);
    procedure Exit1Click(Sender: TObject);
    procedure FormResize(Sender: TObject);
  private
    { Private declarations }
  public
    { Public declarations }
  end;

var
  MainForm: TMainForm;

implementation

{$R *.DFM}

procedure TMainForm.Open1Click(Sender: TObject);
begin
  if OpenDialog1.Execute then
  begin
    BitImage.Picture.LoadFromFile(OpenDialog1.Filename);
    Caption := OpenDialog1.Filename;
    FormResize(Sender);
  end;
end;
```

Adjusts scroll bars when opening a file.

```
procedure TMainForm.Exit1Click(Sender: TObject);
begin
  Close;
end;

procedure TMainForm.FormResize(Sender: TObject);
begin
  HorzScrollBar.Range := BitImage.Picture.Width;
  VertScrollBar.Range := BitImage.Picture.Height;
end;

end.
```

These statements adjust scroll bars when the winbdow's size changes.

Open the modified BitView project file from the preceding section, or start with fresh copies of the project's .Dpr, .Dfm, and .Pas files. Then, follow these steps:

1. Double-click MainForm's HorzScrollBar and VertScrollBar properties, and set the Range subvalues for each property back to 0. This removes the scroll bars from the form and ensures that they do not appear until the user opens a bitmap file.

2. Click MainForm's Events page tab in the Object Inspector. Double-click the value field next to the OnResize event to create an event-handler procedure named FormResize. The program calls this procedure whenever the window size changes, regardless of how that action occurs. Enter the following two statements between *begin* and *end* (also refer to Listing 3-2 if you need more help):

```
HorzScrollBar.Range := BitImage.Picture.Width;
VertScrollBar.Range := BitImage.Picture.Height;
```

3. The preceding statements set the Range properties in the form's horizontal and vertical scroll bar objects equal to the width and height of the BitImage object's Picture. With these changes, scroll bars automatically mirror the image size. As you will discover, however, these changes alone are not enough to ensure smooth scrolling.

4. Press F9 to compile, link, and run the application. Open a bitmap file. At this stage, no scroll bars appear until *after* you resize the window. To display scroll bars upon opening a new file requires modifying the *File | Open* event handler. Quit the program now to return to Delphi.

5. To locate the correct event handler, select *File | Open* from the form window. Because a procedure already exists for this command, Delphi positions the cursor at the first statement in the event handler. Insert the following line after the statement that assigns a filename to the form's Caption property. This is inside the innermost *begin* and *end* keywords. (Refer to Listing 3-2 if you need help positioning the statement.)

```
FormResize(Sender);
```

6. Press F9 to compile, link, and run the application. Open a bitmap file. Scroll bars automatically appear if the image doesn't fit inside the program's window. Change the window's size if necessary, and try out the scroll bar operations.

The statement you added in step 5 calls an existing event handler from inside another procedure. In earlier examples, you learned how to set two or more events to the same handler, thus sharing existing code among multiple processes. Here, you are using another code-sharing technique, but in this case, you *called* an event-handler procedure from inside another one that performs additional actions — in this case, loading a bitmap file from disk.

As a result of the new statement, when you load a bitmap document, the program automatically adjusts scroll bar ranges, which causes the scroll bars to appear or disappear as necessary.

When calculating an image's size, be sure to use the correct Height and Width properties. For example, the expression *BitImage.Picture.Height* obtains the height of the bitmap loaded into the BitImage component. The expression *BitImage.Height* refers to the *component object's* height, not to the height of the data in that object, which is the value you probably want.

QUICK-AND-DIRTY LISTBOX SCROLL BARS

Here's an even simpler way to add scroll bars to a window. The technique is especially useful for displaying lengthy lists. Try these steps:

1. Start a new project and insert a ListBox component object into the form. You don't have to save the project.

2. Double-click the ListBox object's Items property value to open Delphi's string editor. Enter 20 or so lines of text (or copy some lines from a text file). Close the editor.

3. Set the ListBox's Align property to alClient. This expands the ListBox object to fill the form window.

4. Press F9 to compile, link, and run. A vertical scroll bar automatically appears when the window is too short to display all lines of text.

The preceding steps add only vertical scroll bars to ListBox component objects. To create a horizontal scroll bar, insert the following statement in an event handler — a Form's OnActivate event, for example:

```
ListBox1.Perform(LB_SETHORIZONTALEXTENT, 1000, 0);
```

The statement calls the VCL-internal Perform procedure, inherited components such as ListBox from the TControl class. Perform sends a Windows message, in this case LB_SETHORIZONTALEXTENT, to the control for which the component serves as an interface. The value 1000 is the width of the data in the list box in pixels — an approximation in this case. The zero is a meaningless placeholder.

WHO'S ON TOP?

Some programs — for example, clocks, system resource utilities, and toolbars — are easier to use if they remain on top of other windows. Here's how to make a form window always stay on top of things. Now, if I could just figure out how to make my *pen* do that on my *actual* desktop, I'd really be thrilled.

 The following tutorial's files are stored in the Ontop directory.

1. Start a new project. Name the form MainForm and set its Caption to *On Top Demo*. Save the project in a directory such as C:\Projects\Ontop. Name MainForm's unit Main and the project file Ontop.

2. Insert a MainMenu object into MainForm. Double-click the object icon and create a menu named Demo with two commands: *Stay on top* and *Exit*. Close the Menu Designer.

3. Back in the form window, select the Exit command and enter Close; between the *begin* and *end* keywords. Select the *Stay on top* command and enter the programming shown in Listing 3-3. After the last step of this tutorial, I'll explain how this programming works.

4. Press F9 to run the completed program. Select the *Stay on top* command to cause the window to stay on top of other application windows. Notice that selecting the command adds a check mark to it. Select the command again to delete the check mark.

Listing 3-3

Stay on top demonstration.

```
procedure TMainForm.Stayontop1Click(Sender: TObject);
begin
  with Sender as TMenuItem do
  begin
    Checked := not Checked;
    if Checked
      then FormStyle := fsStayOnTop
      else FormStyle := fsNormal;
  end;
end;
```

Command object that user selected.

Toggles the command's checkmark on and off.

The procedure in Listing 3-3 demonstrates two techniques. The Sender parameter to this procedure represents the command object that the user selected. However, the parameter's type is TObject, on which all Delphi objects are based. Thus, any object descendent of TObject can be passed to the procedure. To use the object, though, requires telling Delphi what it is.

That's done here in a *with* statement which tells Delphi to treat Sender as a TMenuItem object. This gives the program access to the menu command's properties, one of which is *Checked*. Setting this parameter to its opposite value with the expression *not Checked* inserts and removes a check mark from the menu.

The second technique that Listing 3-3 demonstrates is in the *if* statement that sets the form's FormStyle to one of two values — fsStayOnTop or fsNormal. The same FormStyle property is available in the Object Inspector window, but to have a window stay on top in response to a user command as shown here, the program itself must assign the property value at runtime.

This brings up an important point. You can assign most property values at runtime. For example, create a procedure for an event handler, or insert a button object and double-click it. Insert an assignment such as the following between *begin* and *end*:

```
Caption := 'A New Window Title!';
```

When you run the program, click the button to change the form's title. Notice that the statement should *not* be:

```
MainForm.Caption := 'A New Window Title!';  { ??? }
```

Although that works, it refers directly to the MainForm object, making the resulting code less generally useful. The former statement could change the caption of *any* window; the latter can change only MainForm's caption.

CREATING A START-UP SPLASH SCREEN

Well-written Windows programs display a start-up notice, sometimes called a *splash screen*. With a little splishin' and splashin', you can add a significant *flash factor* to your program's display.

Because the project itself creates the program's main window, and because the splash screen must appear before that happens, the project itself has to create its own splash. This means you must modify the source code in the project file, which is usually not necessary in Delphi programming.

The following tutorial's files are in the Splashin subdirectory. Figure 3-9 shows the program's splash screen, which appears as a borderless, fixed-size window with no title bar, system menu, or buttons.

Figure 3-9
A start-up splash screen.

1. Start a new project. Name the form MainForm and set its Caption to *Splashin Demo*. Save the project in a directory such as C:\Projects\ Splashin. Name MainForm's unit Main and the project file Splashin.

2. Insert a Button component into MainForm. Change the Button's Name property to ExitButton and its Caption to Exit. (Hint: Type E&xit in the Caption to designate the letter x as a shortcut key. Users can then press Alt+X to select the button.) Just for fun, enlarge the button and resize the form window as shown in Figure 3-10. Create a handler for ExitButton's OnClick event (you can simply double-click the button object), and insert the statement Close; between the procedure's *begin* and *end* keywords

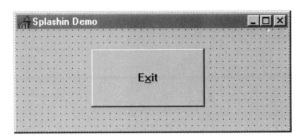

Figure 3-10
SplashIn's MainForm window in Delphi.

3. Select the *File|New Form* command or click the *New form* speed
   button. This brings up the *Browse Gallery* dialog, which presents
   several preprogrammed forms. (If you don't see the dialog, use
   Options|Environment to enable the *Use on New Form* check box
   under the *Gallery* label.) Choose the *Blank form* template and press
   Enter or click OK to close the Browse Gallery dialog.

4. You have just added a second form to the application. Change this
   form's Name property to SplashForm. Delete its Caption. Also, change
   its BorderStyle property to bsNone and set the three subvalues under
   BorderIcons to False. Some of these values are optional, and you might
   want to experiment with different window styles after you finish the
   tutorial. Figure 3-11 shows the sample SplashForm window in Delphi
   that you'll create in the next several steps (the exact contents of the
   window, however, are up to you).

Figure 3-11
SplashIn's SplashForm window in Delphi.

5. Save the project. When Delphi prompts you for a unit filename, be sure the correct directory is current (C:\Projects\Splashin if you are following along). Enter Splash for SplashForm's unit filename.

6. Set SplashForm's Enabled property to False. This is one of the rare times when you don't want users to be able to give keyboard and mouse commands to a window. In this case, we want the program to have total control over SplashForm's display.

7. Resize the SpashForm window. Because the window has no outline, insert a Bevel component object from the Additional category. This will help define the window's edges. Set Bevel1's Align property to alClient. Also, change the object's Shape to bsFrame and its Style to bsRaised. These values are up to you — try different settings after you finish the tutorial.

8. Insert Image and Label component objects into SplashForm. You can insert any graphical items you want to display during the program's start-up. However, don't insert any buttons or other interactive controls. The application itself displays and removes the splash dialog.

9. This is an optional step. Set the SplashForm's FormStyle property to fsStayOnTop, and change Position to poScreenCenter. Here again, the settings depend on your preferences, but it's probably a good idea to center a splash screen and to have its window always stay on top of others.

10. Select *View|Project Manager,* and click the *Options* button. Select the Forms page tab at the bottom of the resulting *Project Options* dialog. Notice that MainForm and SplashForm are in the *Auto-create forms* list. Highlight SplashForm and click the right-arrow button to move this form to *Available forms.* All Delphi forms are automatically created in memory by default, which consumes memory and system resources. In cases such as this one, where the program will create a form at runtime, you should remove that form from the auto-create list. Close the Project Manager window.

11. Next, modify the project's source code to display the splash dialog before the main window becomes visible. This is one of the rare cases in which you need to insert statements into the project file. To

do that, select the *View | Project Source* command. Modify the statements between *begin* and *end* to match the Splash.Dpr project file in Listing 3-4. I'll explain more about this programming after these steps.

12. If you compile and run the program at this stage, it will display and remove the start-up splash dialog so quickly you might not have the chance to see it. To force the dialog to remain visible for a few seconds, select the program's MainForm (the one with the big button). Create a handler for the form's OnCreate command. Preceding the *begin* keyword, add a longInt variable named currentTime. Between *begin* and *end*, insert two statements that call the Windows GetTickCount function to set currentTime to the number of seconds that Windows has been running and to use a *while* statement that delays for an additonal 4 seconds. (GetTickCount returns the number of milliseconds that Windows has been running. Dividing this value by 1000 converts it to seconds.) Refer to Listing 3-5, Main.Pas, for these statements.

13. Press F9 to compile, link, and run. The program displays the start-up splash dialog, waits a few seconds, removes the dialog, and displays the main window.

Listing 3-4
Splashin/Splashin.Dpr

```
program Splash;

uses
  Forms,
  Main in 'MAIN.PAS' {MainForm},
  Start in 'START.PAS' {SplashForm};

{$R *.RES}

begin
  SplashForm := TSplashForm.Create(Application);
  SplashForm.Show;
  SplashForm.Update;
  Application.CreateForm(TMainForm, MainForm);
  SplashForm.Hide;
  SplashForm.Free;
  Application.Run;
end.
```

This creates the splash screen form object.

This disposes of the form object from memory.

Listing 3-5

Splashin/Main.Pas

```pascal
unit Main;

interface

uses
  SysUtils, WinTypes, WinProcs, Messages, Classes, Graphics, Controls,
  Forms, Dialogs, StdCtrls;

type
  TMainForm = class(TForm)
    ExitButton: TButton;
    procedure ExitButtonClick(Sender: TObject);
    procedure FormCreate(Sender: TObject);
  private
    { Private declarations }
  public
    { Public declarations }
  end;

var
  MainForm: TMainForm;

implementation

{$R *.DFM}

procedure TMainForm.ExitButtonClick(Sender: TObject);
begin
  Close;
end;


procedure TMainForm.FormCreate(Sender: TObject);
var
  CurrentTime: LongInt;
begin
  CurrentTime := GetTickCount div 1000;
  while ( (GetTickCount div 1000) < (CurrentTime + 4) ) do
    { nothing };
end;

end.
```

This procedure pauses for a few seconds so the Splash dialog remains visible for a predetermined length of time.

This function returns the number of elapsed milliseconds since Windows was started.

Listing 3-4, Splashin.Dpr, demonstrates how a program can create a form object at runtime. To do that, call the Create method in the object's class, as this statement demonstrates:

```
SplashForm := TSplashForm.Create(Application);
```

That statement creates the object, and assigns it to SplashForm, which is defined in the Splash.Pas module. The object now exists in memory, but it is not yet visible. To make it appear and to update its contents, call the object's Show and Update methods:

```
SplashForm.Show;
SplashForm.Update;
```

You can use similar steps to create and display any form at runtime. Be sure, however, that the form is not auto-created (use the Project Manager's Options button to check).

After you are done using a form object, hide it from display and then delete the memory it occupies. The freed memory is then available for other objects. For example, after creating the main window (which in this case pauses for several seconds so you can see the splash window), the demonstration program uses these statements to get rid of the splashy dialog:

```
SplashForm.Hide;
SplashForm.Free;
```

Listing 3-5 also demonstrates some useful techniques for MainForm's OnCreate event. First, the procedure calls GetTickTime, a Windows function that returns the number of milliseconds that have passed since Windows was started. This value divided by 1000 equals the number of elapsed seconds.

To pause for a few seconds, the program assigns the divided value to CurrentTime, a variable of the LongInt type. A *while* loop then uses a complex-looking expression to test whether GetTickTime (again divided by 1000) is less than the previously saved time plus four. The *while* loop performs no other actions. After about four seconds, the *while* loop's expression is no longer true, and the procedure ends. This proves that time indeed passes despite our best efforts to slow it down — if this trick fails, the universe is okay, but your computer's clock is probably busted.

TIP

The demonstration program pauses only because it has nothing else to do. If your program's OnCreate event performs many initializations, you may not need to insert an artificial pause. However, computers are becoming faster every day, and instructions that take four seconds today might zip by in the future. For safety, call GetTickCount to test whether *at least* a certain amount of time has passed before ending your splash form's OnCreate event handler.

Summary

- Every project has at least one form object that represents the program's main window. However, projects may have multiple forms.

- A form is a component, but it doesn't appear on the Component palette. Create a form by starting a new project or by selecting *File | New Form*.

- Every form has a corresponding unit module that lists the form's programming. *The form's Name property and its unit filename must differ.* (Hint: Use a Name such as EntryForm and a filename such as Entry.Pas.)

- A form is more than a representation of the program's window. Forms also have properties and events that you can program to select window characteristics and to perform actions.

- Form templates are useful for creating common screens, prototypes, and demos. You can select from several supplied form templates, or you can create your own.

- You may designate any form as an application's main window. For example, you can use a dialog box for a simple and clean application interface that doesn't require a menu bar.

- The OnCloseQuery event confirms or cancels a window's closure. Use this event to help prevent data loss.

- Scroll bars enable windows to display more information than fits in the window's borders. It's easy to add quick-and-dirty scroll bars to windows, but in finished applications, you should make several refinements to your windows' scroll bars as explained in this chapter.

- Assign a form's FormStyle property to fsStayOnTop to have that window stay on top of other application windows. You may assign this value in the Object Inspector, or at runtime.

- A project may have multiple forms as the Splashin program demonstrates. Delphi normally creates form objects at runtime, a fact that may have consequences on memory and other resources in large applications. To create a form object under program control, select the Project Manager's Options button and in the Forms page, remove the form from the Auto-create forms list. The form object will no longer be created automatically.

Projects to Try

3-1: Design and add a system icon to the sample BitView application. Use the Windows Paintbrush or Delphi's Image Editor to create an icon file with the filename extension .Ico. Or, copy an existing icon file from a network, shareware, or public domain disk. Select MainForm, and double-click its Icon property. Use the resulting dialog to open your icon file. Delphi copies the icon image into the finished .Exe code file — you do not have to distribute the .Ico file to your program's users.

3-2: Customize Delphi's About-box form template. Insert your copyright, company name, and other common information. You might also want to customize the About-box template to display a company logo (use an Image component).

3-3: Create a form template for obtaining Yes and No answers to various prompts. For example, the dialog might display a question and have *Yes* and *No* buttons. If you get stuck, refer to the YesNo project on the book's CD-ROM. Open the project and follow this chapter's instructions to insert the YesNoDlg form into the Browse Gallery. Name the form unit Yesno.Pas.

3-4: *Advanced.* Write your own text-file lister using BitView2 as a guide. In place of the Image component, use Memo. You do not have to add scroll bars to the form window, although you may do so if you wish. However, it's easier to select the form's Memo component and set its ScrollBar property to ssBoth. If you get stuck, refer to the List-Text project on this book's CD-ROM.

Expert-User Tips

- When designing form templates, it is probably best to keep separate copies of your original development files. At this point in Delphi's young life, it isn't clear whether future versions will preserve your own templates inserted into the Browse Gallery, or what will happen when name conflicts occur during updates. To prevent accidental deletions, save your development files and projects so you can always reinstall them as templates.

- At times, Delphi may report that an event handler is referenced but not available, and request permission to delete the event. Usually, when this happens, you should answer Yes, especially if the event is one that you have been trying to kill. But if the event is one that you think should not be deleted, you may have accidentally erased an event handler's assignment. Answer No in that case, and double-click the event (or select a handler from the drop-down list) to recover the procedure.

- Use *File | Open File* to open a form's .Pas unit file to inspect a form and its programming. This command does not add the form to the current project. To do that, select *File | Add* to add it to the project. The form does not appear automatically. To make it visible, choose *View | Form*. To bring up the form's unit, choose *View | Unit*.

- If you are familiar with other text editors that display files in separate windows, you may be tempted to close Delphi's editor window before editing another module. *Resist this temptation*. Delphi uses a *single* editor window for all unit modules in a project, and closing this window closes all opened modules. To switch to another module, use *View | Unit* or select the module from the editor window's page tabs. Because of Delphi's single-window text editor, you can open all of a project's units without cluttering the display with dozens of windows, so you may as well leave them all open.

- If you prefer to have multiple edit windows, select *View | New Edit Window*.

- Normally, new projects use a blank form for the main window. To designate a different window such as a dialog box for the default main-window form, select *Options | Gallery* and click the *Form*

Templates page tab in the *Gallery Options* dialog. Highlight the form template you want to use, and click the *Default Main Form* button. If you make this change, you may have trouble following this book's step-by-step tutorials. Select *Blank form* to restore Delphi's default setting.

- Scroll bar properties have additional subvalues that you might use in special circumstances. To view these values, double-click a form's HorzScrollBar or VertScrollBar property. The Increment value determines how many units the thumb box moves when you click a scroll bar's arrow buttons. The Margin determines how far the scroll bar sits from the form's edge. The Position represents the current location of the thumb box.

- If two or more windows are set to stay on top, they revert to normal overlapping windows. There's nothing you can do about this. Everybody — that is, every window — can't be on top all the time.

Coming Up

In the next chapter, you'll begin learning how to use Delphi components and forms to design attractive user interfaces. You'll also learn how to program two of the computer's most important input devices: the keyboard and the mouse.

II

The User Interface

*C*reating an efficient user interface isn't easy. Of course, anybody with an ounce of brains and a suitable laboratory can sew together check boxes, buttons, input fields, and menus to conceive a monster that looks like a Windows application. But it takes hard work and careful planning to build handsome interfaces that attract users rather than scare the wits out of them.

The chapters in this part cover Delphi components and techniques for assembling practical and friendly application interfaces. You'll learn the gory details about creating graphical user interfaces and using component objects such as menus, buttons, toolbars, status panels, lists, scrollbars, dialog boxes, plus other application body parts.

Part 2 Chapters

- Chapter 4, *Programming the Keyboard and Mouse*
- Chapter 5, *Constructing Menus*

- Chapter 6, *Attaching Buttons and Check Boxes*
- Chapter 7, *Creating Toolbars and Status Panels*
- Chapter 8, *Making Lists*
- Chapter 9, *Working with Single Line Strings*
- Chapter 10, *Working with Multiple-Line Text*
- Chapter 11, *Navigating Files and Directories*
- Chapter 12, *Communicating with Dialog Boxes*

4

Programming the Keyboard and Mouse

Some day — let's hope it's soon — talking to a computer will seem as natural as gossiping with the neighbors. But until voice-recognition hardware undergoes major improvements, the keyboard and the mouse are likely to remain the primary input tools for conversing with software applications. Computers can talk fairly well, but they just don't know how to listen.

As experienced developers know, an application's input capabilities literally define its ease of use. Even one needless keystroke or mouse command is enough to aggravate expert users who don't want to type and click more than absolutely necessary. Because ease of input is crucial to a program's success, the subjects of keyboard and mouse handling are appropriate places to begin Part II's investigations into the development of application user interfaces with Delphi's visual component library.

About Parts II and III

Part II of this book covers user-interface design techniques using Delphi components such as menus, buttons, and other interface-related objects. Part III explains application-specific topics such as graphics and data sharing, and covers advanced objects in the visual component library. To make the most of this information, you should know how to perform the following tasks:

- Start a new Delphi project.

- Assign Name and Caption properties to a form.

- Save the project and assign filenames.

- Insert component objects into a form.

- Insert a new form into an application.

- Modify form and component object properties.

- Create procedures for form and component events.

If you are unfamiliar with any of the preceding items, all of which were introduced in Part I, read the preceding three chapters and complete one or more of the step-by-step tutorials. If you are pressed for time, you don't have to memorize every word. Just be sure you understand how to do the preceding tasks before continuing.

COMPONENTS COVERED

Except for this introduction, the chapters in Parts II and III begin with a list and brief descriptions of covered components and related classes. Most chapters also refer to other components in hands-on tutorials and sample applications.

Near the end of each chapter (except this one) are summaries of the topics covered in the chapter. At the end of each chapter, you'll also find suggested projects to try and several expert-user tips.

For the complete story on a specific component, look it up in the table of contents and the subject index. Also consult the online visual component reference on the CD-ROM.

TUTORIALS AND PROPERTY TABLES

To shorten step-by-step instructions, and to avoid restating the obvious (such as how to save unit and project files), upcoming hands-on tutorials are more abbreviated than in Part I. In addition, some tutorials list property values in tables. Table 4-0 demonstrates the property-table format used throughout the rest of this book.

Table 4-0

Sample Property-Table Format

Component	Name	Property	Value
Form	MainForm	Caption	Window Demo
Label	XCoordLabel	Caption	X Coordinate
		Alignment	taRightJustify
		Font.Name	Arial
		Font.Size	24
Edit	Edit1	Text	

The first line of a property table lists the form that holds subsequent component objects. For example, Table 4-0 indicates that you should change the Name property of the program's default form to MainForm, and set its Caption to *Window Demo.* You should then insert the other listed objects into MainForm's window.

Except where noted otherwise, all sample main-window forms in this book are named MainForm. On the CD-ROM, MainForm's unit module, Main.Pas, is stored in a subdirectory that matches the project name. Other form modules are similarly named. For example, NextForm's unit module would be named Next.Pas.

The second line of Table 4-0 indicates that you should insert into Main-Form a Label component object and change its Name to XCoordLabel. Set this object's Caption to *X Coordinate,* and change its Alignment and Font properties to the indicated values. For object placement and size, refer to figures in the book, and to the supplied files.

A period separates a property and its subvalue. For example, the *Property* column of Table 4-0 indicates that you should set the Font property's Name subvalue to Arial and its Size subvalue to 24 points.

The final line of Table 4-0 tells you to insert an Edit component object into MainForm, but to leave the object's Name set to the default value, Edit1. The blank last column indicates that you should clear the object's Text property by highlighting and deleting this value.

Property tables do not include noncritical or obvious settings such as window width and height values. The tables also do not list window dressing such as the Bevels used in the KeyInfo project to organize the window's display. (Peek ahead to Figure 4-1.) I'll explain many of these extra goodies throughout this book, but I don't want to waste space documenting obvious matters at the expense of more important information.

By convention, in this book, most component Name properties end with the component's identifier. For example, you know that XCoord-Label in Table 4-0 is a Label component object. The usual exception to this rule is a default name such as Edit1, which Delphi assigns.

On the Keyboard

Delphi applications can use two fundamental methods for receiving keyboard input. The first, and easiest, is to use a component object, such as Edit, that automatically responds to keypresses. For more general-purpose keyboard handling, however, you can create procedures in a form that handle any combination of three events:

- OnKeyDown — Called when you press any key, including function keys and special keys such as Shift, Alt, and Ctrl.

- OnKeyPress — Called when you press an ASCII character-generating key, including control keys.

- OnKeyUp — Called when you release any key.

Each of these events receives at least one parameter, named Key, that represents a pressed key. In the OnKeyDown and OnKeyUp events, Key is an unsigned (that is, positive only) Word value that represents a Windows *virtual key code*. In the OnKeyPress event, Key is a Char value that represents an ASCII character. Even though both variables are named Key, they represent different keyboard information. All ASCII characters have corresponding virtual key codes, but the reverse is not true — there are many virtual keys with no ASCII counterparts.

Windows represents keystrokes with virtual key code symbols prefaced with vk_. For example, vk_alt is the virtual key code for the Alt key. For a list of virtual key codes, search for that topic in Delphi's on-line help.

RESPONDING TO KEYBOARD EVENTS

A sample application, KeyInfo, demonstrates how to program a form's three keyboard events. Figure 4-1 shows KeyInfo's display. Locate and run this program by loading its project file from the Keyinfo directory and pressing F9. Press various keys — including function, Ctrl, Shift, and Alt — and observe the values displayed to the right of the window's labels:

- *Keypress character* shows ASCII characters. For keys with no visible symbol, an empty box is displayed.

- *Key down value* shows the key's numeric value. When you press a multiple key combination such as Shift+Alt+A, this box shows the value of the last key pressed (A in this example).

- *Key down shift* shows the current shift state. For example, when you press the Alt and Ctrl keys together, the program displays Alt+Ctrl, and the Key down value shows the numeric value of the key last pressed (Ctrl in this case).

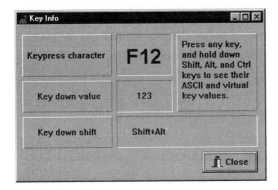

Figure 4-1
Keyinfo's display.

Even though KeyInfo shows information for most keypresses, the program continues to respond to standard keyboard commands. For example, pressing Enter selects the Close button and ends the program. Pressing F10 selects the system menu icon, after which you can press the spacebar or Enter to open the menu, or press Esc to return to normal operation.

Follow the numbered steps in this section to recreate the KeyInfo sample application. Table 4-1 shows significant component and form property values.

The instructions assume that you have created a new project, changed its main-window form Name to MainForm, and saved the unit module as Main and the project as Keyinfo.

Table 4-1
KeyInfo's Properties

Component	Name	Property	Value
Form	MainForm	Caption	Key Info
Label	CharLabel	Caption	
		Alignment	taCenter
		AutoSize	False
		Font:Name	Arial
		Font:Size	24
		Font:Style	[fsBold]
Label	ValueLabel	Alignment	taCenter
		AutoSize	False
Label	ShiftLabel	Alignment	taLeftJustify
		AutoSize	False

1. Insert Bevels and Labels into a form to organize the window as shown in Figure 4-1. The exact placement of these items is unimportant. Use Delphi's default property Names for all of them.

2. Insert a BitBtn component from the Additional category. Change its Kind to bkClose and its Name to CloseBitBtn.

3. Insert three Label components into the center indented Bevels shown in Figure 4-1. Name them CharLabel, ValueLabel, and ShiftLabel respectively, and delete their Captions. Refer to Table 4-1 for other property values. Adjust the Font properties for a pleasing display — for example, you might want to make the CharLabel Font large and bold.

4. Select MainForm, and create event handlers for OnKeyDown, OnKey-Press, and OnKeyUp. Insert the programming shown in Listing 4-1 for these three procedures. I'll explain how the statements work after the listing.

5. Press F9 to compile, link, and run.

Listing 4-1

Keyinfo\Main.Pas

```pascal
unit Main;

interface

uses
  SysUtils, WinTypes, WinProcs, Messages, Classes, Graphics, Controls,
  Forms, Dialogs, Buttons, StdCtrls, ExtCtrls;

type
  TMainForm = class(TForm)
    Label2: TLabel;
    CharLabel: TLabel;
    Label3: TLabel;
    Label4: TLabel;
    ValueLabel: TLabel;
    ShiftLabel: TLabel;
    Bevel1: TBevel;
    Bevel2: TBevel;
    Bevel3: TBevel;
    Label1: TLabel;
    Bevel4: TBevel;
    Bevel5: TBevel;
    Bevel6: TBevel;
    Bevel7: TBevel;
    CloseButton: TBitBtn;
    procedure FormKeyDown(Sender: TObject; var Key: Word;
      Shift: TShiftState);
    procedure FormKeyPress(Sender: TObject; var Key: Char);
    procedure FormKeyUp(Sender: TObject; var Key: Word;
      Shift: TShiftState);
  private
    { Private declarations }
  public
    { Public declarations }
  end;

var
  MainForm: TMainForm;

implementation

{$R *.DFM}

const
  ctrl_A = 1;     { ASCII value for Ctrl+A }
  ctrl_Z = 26;    { ASCII value for Ctrl+Z }

  FunctionKeys: array [vk_f1 .. vk_f12] of string[3] =
    ('F1', 'F2', 'F3', 'F4', 'F5', 'F6', 'F7', 'F8',
     'F9', 'F10', 'F11', 'F12');
```

Typed constant array of strings for displaying function key labels.

■ ■

4

```
procedure TMainForm.FormKeyDown(Sender: TObject; var Key: Word;
  Shift: TShiftState);
var
  s: string;
begin
{- Show integer Key value }
  ValueLabel.Caption := IntToStr(Key);
{- Show Key shift state }
  s := '';
  if ssShift in Shift then s := s + 'Shift+';
  if ssAlt   in Shift then s := s + 'Alt+';
  if ssCtrl  in Shift then s := s + 'Ctrl+';
  if Length(s) > 0 then
    Delete(s, Length(s), 1); { Delete final '+' }
  ShiftLabel.Caption := s;
{- Do function key labels }
  if Key in [vk_f1 .. vk_f12] then
    CharLabel.Caption := FunctionKeys[Key]
  else
    CharLabel.Caption := '';   { Erase old character label }
{- Disable Spacebar to prevent selecting Close button }
  if Key = vk_space then
    Key := 0;
end;

procedure TMainForm.FormKeyPress(Sender: TObject; var Key: Char);
begin
  if Ord(Key) in [ctrl_A .. ctrl_Z] then
    CharLabel.Caption := Chr(Ord(Key) + Ord('A') - 1)
  else
    CharLabel.Caption := Key;
  ValueLabel.Caption := IntToStr(Ord(Key));
end;

procedure TMainForm.FormKeyUp(Sender: TObject; var Key: Word;
  Shift: TShiftState);
begin
{- Erase the three labels when user releases key(s) }
  CharLabel.Caption := '';
  ValueLabel.Caption := '';
  ShiftLabel.Caption := '';
end;

end.
```

These expressions detect Shift, Alt, and Ctrl key presses.

Displays function key label

Setting key to zero disables the key press, here if user types space.

INSIDE KEYINFO

Two constants, ctrl_A and ctrl_Z in the Main unit's implementation section, declare the ASCII values for Ctrl+A and Ctrl+Z keys. The program uses these values to define a range of control keys so that, when you press Ctrl+Q, for example, the Keypress character label shows that value.

A third constant defines function key strings such as F1 and F2, also for display in the Keypress character label. This *typed constant* array is automatically initialized to the values shown in parentheses, and in this case, is indexed with the virtual key codes vk_f1 through vk_f12. Given a string variable named FunctionS, the following statement sets the string equal to F3:

```
FunctionS := FunctionKeys[vk_f3];  { Assign F3 key to FunctionS }
```

The keyboard event handler, FormKeyDown, receives a Key value equal to the virtual key code for a pressed key. First, the procedure assigns the Key value to the ValueLabel object's Caption property in order to display that value under the *Key down value* label in the window. Because a Captain is a string, however, you cannot assign Key directly to it. This would *not* work:

```
ValueLabel.Caption := Key;  { ??? }
```

Throughout this book, I use three question marks in comment braces, { ??? }, to indicate a questionable practice or a faulty statement that you should avoid using in your own programs.

Instead, you have to convert Key to a string value. In this case, you can do that by passing Key to Delphi's IntToStr function, which accepts a Word argument and returns a string:

```
ValueLabel.Caption := IntToStr(Key);
```

The next statement in FormKeyDown assigns the *null string* to s. This initializes the string for the upcoming *if* statements:

```
s := '';
```

To create a null string, type two single quotation marks (apostrophes) with no space between them. Assigning a null string to a string variable with the := operator erases the string's characters.

Three *if* statements build the string s to show combination key values such as Shift+Ctrl. The statements use the Shift parameter, of type

TShiftState, passed to the procedure. Delphi declares the TShiftState data type as:

```
TShiftState =
   set of (ssShift, ssAlt, ssCtrl, ssRight, ssLeft,
   ssMiddle, ssDouble);
```

A variable such as Shift — a *set* of TShiftState values — can hold zero, one, or more values. For example, you could assign this set to Shift to represent the Shift and Ctrl keys:

```
Shift := [ssShift, ssCtrl];
```

Pascal represents the set using single bits, so this is an efficient method for storing multiple items in a very small space.

A series of *if* statements determines which of the possible values (if any) are in the Shift set. Examine the first of these statements:

```
if ssShift in Shift then s := s + 'Shift+';
```

In English, this states that if the value ssShift is in the Shift set, the program appends the string *Shift+* to the end of the string variable s. Similar statements check for other set values, and append additional strings onto s.

After forming the string, the variable s is either empty or it lists the names of various special keys, separated with plus signs. If the string is *not* empty, it ends with an extra plus sign, which this statement deletes:

```
if Length(s) > 0 then
   Delete(s, Length(s), 1);
```

Pascal's Length procedure returns the length in characters of any string. If that length is greater than zero, the *if* statement here calls Delete to erase the final character. To Delete, you pass the string, the position at which the deletion is to begin, and the number of characters to delete from that location. Because the first character in a string is in position 1 — in other words, at the string index 1 — passing the string's length to Delete's second parameter deletes the last character in the string.

To display the completed string, the program assigns it to the ShiftLabel component's Caption property:

```
ShiftLabel.Caption := s;
```

To handle function keys, another *if* statement tests whether Key is in the set of virtual key codes vk_f1 through vk_f12. If so, the program assigns one of the unit's constant strings from the FunctionKeys array to CharLabel's Caption. Otherwise, the program sets this field to the null string, erasing any text shown in this area.

The FormKeyDown procedure also assigns a null string to Char-Label.Caption to erase any character displayed in that field:

```
CharLabel.Caption := '';
```

Finally in FormKeyDown, an *if* statement tests whether Key equals vk_space. I added this statement because pressing the spacebar selects the current control object — in this case, CloseButton. Notice that the Key variable in FormKeyDown's header (its first line) is preceded by *var.* This means the parameter is *variable,* and assigning a value to it passes that value back to FormKeyDown's caller. Thus, setting Key equal to zero disables this key (because zero represents no particular key):

```
if Key = vk_space then
   Key := 0;  { Disable SpaceBar }
```

The other two procedures are relatively easy to understand. FormKeyUp assigns null strings to the Caption properties in Char-Label, ValueLabel, and ShiftLabel; this erases these labels when you release a key.

FormKeyPress, receives a Key value equal to an ASCII character. If the ordinal value of Key is in the set of values defined by the range of control-code constants, ctrl_A through ctrl_Z, then the program sets CharLabel's Caption to 'A', 'B', and so on. This is necessary because a control code has no associated visible symbol.

The *else* clause handles noncontrol characters, merely assigning Key directly to CharLabel's Caption. Note that you can assign a Char variable such as Key to a string such as Caption — one of the few areas in which Pascal bends its usual strong type-checking rules.

Finally, the program sets ValueLabel's Caption field to the string equivalent of Key's ordinal value. When you press Q, for example, this statement assigns the *string* 81 to Caption.

PREVIEWING KEYPRESSES

In the preceding section, you inserted event handlers into a form to respond to keypresses. Many components also respond to keyboard activity, and it's often necessary to decide whether a component or the form should be first to receive a specific keyboard event.

Windows uses the *input focus* to determine where to send keyboard events. For example, the currently selected component in a form has the input focus, and therefore, it receives all keyboard events. If the component doesn't handle the event — for example, because it is not programmed to use a certain key such as Esc or Ctrl — that event is passed to the component's owner, which is usually the form. Figure 4-2 shows this relationship between a component, a form, and the input focus.

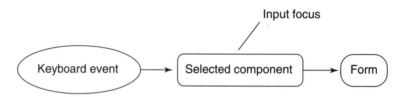

Figure 4-2
Keyboard events normally go to the selected component, and then to the form.

To send keyboard events to the form before the selected component receives those events, set the form's KeyPreview property to True. For example, you might do this to modify certain keys or to prevent users from typing unwanted characters such as digits or punctuation symbols. Figure 4-3 illustrates the relationship between a component, the form, and the input focus when KeyPreview is True.

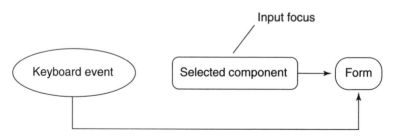

Figure 4-3
Set KeyPreview to True to receive keyboard events in the form before the selected component receives those events.

A simple experiment demonstrates the value of the KeyPreview property, which you can use to restrict input in text-editing components. Start a new project, and follow these steps:

1. Insert an Edit component into the form. You don't have to change its Name or other properties.

2. Change the form's KeyPreview property from False to True by double-clicking its value.

3. Change to the Events page in the Object Inspector, and double-click the form's OnKeypress event to create a handler. *Be sure to do this for the form, not for the Edit1 object.* Type the following statement between *begin* and *end* to convert lowercase characters to uppercase:

```
Key := Upcase(Key);
```

4. Press F9 to compile and run the program. If Delphi displays file-save dialogs, save the unit and the project under the default names in a temporary directory.

5. Type some text into Edit1. The program automatically converts lowercase letters to uppercase whether or not you press Caps Lock or shift.

6. Exit the program, set KeyPreview to False, and then press F9 to compile and run. The program no longer converts characters to uppercase. This happens because the control that has the input focus — rather than the form — receives keyboard events first.

This technique is also useful for limiting the kinds of characters that users can enter. For example, to prevent users from typing digit keys into an Edit component, add this statement to the form's OnKeypress event handler and set KeyPreview to True:

```
if Key in ['0' .. '9'] then
  Key := Chr(0);
```

This *if* statement checks whether the Key parameter passed to the event handler is in the set of characters from '0' to '9'. If so, the second line of the statement assigns the character value of 0 to Key. Because a zero ASCII character value has no meaning, this prevents any input into the Edit component when it receives the modified Key.

The preceding *if* statement uses some valuable Pascal techniques that may be new to you. The expression '0' .. '9' is called a *range*. It is composed of two values separated by a two-dot ellipsis. Pascal interprets this expression as equivalent to the series of characters:

```
'0', '1', '2', '3', '4', '5', '6', '7', '8', '9'
```

NOTE You may also compose ranges of integer values. For example, the range 5 .. 8 is equivalent to the series of values 5, 6, 7, 8. Be sure to understand, however, that ASCII characters and integer values are not equivalent. The range '0' .. '9' equals the series of *ASCII* digit characters. The range 0 .. 9 (without quotation marks) equals the series of *integer* values from zero to nine. You can only stuff ordinal values (those represented by integer values) into a set. You cannot, for example, create a set of strings, because Pascal can't represent string values with single bits. An array is the appropriate data type for collections of complex values such as strings, records, and class objects.

The preceding *if* statement also shows how to assign a specific ASCII value to a variable of the type Char. Because it is impossible to type a character with the ASCII value 0, another method is needed to assign this value to Key. Because the Key parameter is a Char variable, you can assign any character to it with a statement such as:

```
Key := 'Q';
```

However, you cannot assign an ASCII *value* directly to a Char variable. This does not work:

```
Key := 81;   { ??? }
```

The value 81 is not a character, even though it happens to be the ASCII value for Q. You can't assign zero directly to Key:

```
Key := 0;   { ??? }
```

Pascal is finicky about such assignments — the assigned value must match the variable's type. The solution is to *convert* the value to the proper data type, which you can do here by using the Chr function.

The following statements show three logically equivalent methods for assigning the Q character to Key:

```
Key := Chr(81);  { Calls Pascal Chr to convert 81 to a Char }
Key := Char(81); { "Casts" the value 81 to the type Char }
Key := 'Q';      { Directly assigns the character Q to Key }
```

CREATING A WHILE-KEY EVENT

Some programs need to perform actions *while* users hold down a key. For example, a graphics design system could use the technique to adjust a color shade from light to dark while you hold down an arrow key. A game might shoot a weapon while you hold down the spacebar. The technique's possibilities are endless, and as the following hands-on tutorial demonstrates, the programming isn't difficult. Although the sample program, KeyCount, has no practical value — it merely increments and decrements an integer value while you press and hold the up- or down-arrow keys — it demonstrates the necessary basics for creating while-key events.

Compile and run KeyCount. Press and hold the up- or down-arrow keys to increment or decrement the integer value in the center of the program's window. Press Alt+F4 to end. Figure 4-4 shows the program's display. Listing 4-2 lists the program's Main.Pas unit.

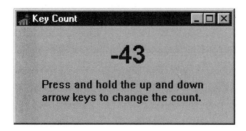

Figure 4-4
KeyCount's display.

Listing 4-2
Keycount\Main.Pas

```pascal
unit Main;

interface

uses
  SysUtils, WinTypes, WinProcs, Messages, Classes, Graphics, Controls,
  Forms, Dialogs, ExtCtrls, StdCtrls;

type
  TMainForm = class(TForm)
    Label1: TLabel;
    Label2: TLabel;
    Timer1: TTimer;
    procedure FormCreate(Sender: TObject);
    procedure FormKeyDown(Sender: TObject; var Key: Word;
      Shift: TShiftState);
    procedure FormKeyUp(Sender: TObject; var Key: Word;
      Shift: TShiftState);
    procedure Timer1Timer(Sender: TObject);
  private
    { Private declarations }
  public
    { Public declarations }
  end;

var
  MainForm: TMainForm;
  Count: Integer;
  KeyPressed: Word;

implementation

{$R *.DFM}

procedure TMainForm.FormCreate(Sender: TObject);
begin
  Count := 0;
end;

procedure TMainForm.FormKeyDown(Sender: TObject; var Key: Word;
  Shift: TShiftState);
begin
  if ((Key = vk_up) or (Key = vk_down)) then
  begin
    KeyPressed := Key;
    Timer1.Enabled := True;
  end;
end;
```

Starts timer events

```
procedure TMainForm.FormKeyUp(Sender: TObject; var Key: Word;
  Shift: TShiftState);
begin
  Timer1.Enabled := False;                          ─────────→  Stops timer events.
end;

procedure TMainForm.Timer1Timer(Sender: TObject);
begin
  if KeyPressed = vk_up then
    Inc(Count)
  else if KeyPressed = vk_down then
    Dec(Count);                                              Called repeatedly at
  Label1.Caption := IntToStr(Count);                         the timer's frequency.
end;


end.
```

The following step-by-step tutorial shows you how to create the KeyCount application and how to program a *while-key* event. Table 4-2 shows the program's significant property values.

Table 4-2

KeyCount Properties

Component	Name	Property	Value
Form	MainForm	Caption	Key Count
Label	Label1	Caption	0
		Font:Name	Arial
		Font:Size	24
		Font:Style	[fsBold]
Label	Label2	Caption	(see Figure 4-4)
		WordWrap	True
		AutoSize	False
Timer	Timer1	Interval	100

1. To create the text at the bottom of the program's window, insert a Label component (Label2 in Table 4-2), and change its WordWrap property to True and its AutoSize property to False. Adjust the object's size, and then select the Caption property. Don't press Enter as you type. Instead, allow the lines to wrap around automatically within the component and window boundaries.

2. Create two *global* variables, so named because they are available globally to all parts of a unit module. The first variable, named Count, of type Integer, holds the current counter value, displayed at the center of the window. The second variable, named KeyPressed, of type Word, holds a virtual key value. Declare these variables by switching to the program's Main.Pas unit window, and enter these lines after the *var* keyword (use Listing 4-2 as a placement guide):

```
Count: Integer;
KeyPressed: Word;
```

3. To initialize Count to zero when the program runs, double-click the form's OnActivate event value and enter this assignment between *begin* and *end*:

```
Count := 0;
```

4. The program needs two other event handlers — one for a keypress and another for the key's release. Double-click the form's OnKeyDown event and enter the programming from Listing 4-2 between *begin* and *end*. Study this programming carefully. If the Key value is vk_up or vk_down (representing the up- and down-arrow keys) then the program saves the Key value in the global KeyPressed variable. The program also engages the Timer1 component with the following statement. After this statement, the timer begins calling its OnTimer event handler:

```
Timer1.Enabled := True;
```

5. Create another handler for the form's OnKeyUp event. This event disables the timer by setting its Enabled property to False. After this statement, the timer no longer calls its OnTimer handler:

```
Timer1.Enabled := False;
```

6. Finally, select the Timer1 object and create a handler for its OnTimer event (the only one that Timers have). The programming for this event increments or decrements Count depending on whether KeyPressed equals vk_up or vk_down. The timer event displays the current count by converting Count to a string with the standard IntToStr procedure and assigning the result to Label1's Caption.

Integer variables can store negative and positive values from -32,768 to 32,767. Word variables can store only positive values from 0 to 65,535. Variables of either data type can represent only whole numbers, not fractions.

When you need to add or subtract 1 from an ordinal value, use Pascal's Inc and Dec functions as the Timer1Timer procedure demonstrates. For example, if Count is an Integer variable, instead of statements such as these:

```
Count := Count + 1;  { ??? }
Count := Count - 1;  { ??? }
```

you can write

```
Inc(Count);
Dec(Count);
```

However, you can't use Inc and Dec on properties, and the procedures have little if any positive effect on runtime performance.

CHANGING ENTER TO TAB

Although Windows expects users to press the Tab key to move from one input field to another, many computer users naturally press Enter for this purpose. Unfortunately, pressing Enter usually selects an OK button, which closes the window or saves current entries before you have the chance to complete them all. This can be highly frustrating.

For a simple solution to this problem, follow these steps to reprogram the keyboard so that pressing Enter works similarly to pressing Tab:

1. Insert three or more Edit components into a form. The default Names are adequate, but you can change them if you wish.

2. Insert a BitBtn object and change its Kind to bkClose.

3. Set the form's KeyPreview property to True.

4. Change the form's ActiveControl to Edit1 (or to the Name of any Edit component object).

5. Create a handler for the form's OnKeyPress event. Enter the programming shown in Listing 4-3. Press F9 to compile and run, and

then try pressing Tab and Enter. The window closes on pressing Enter only when the Close button is selected.

Listing 4-3

Making Enter behave like Tab.

```
procedure TForm1.FormKeyPress(Sender: TObject; var Key: Char);
begin
  if Key = #13 then
  begin
    Key := #0;
    SelectNext(ActiveControl, True, True);
  end;
end;
```

The *if* statement in Listing 4-3 checks whether Key represents the Enter key, which has the ASCII value 13 in decimal. The expression #13 is another way to represent an ASCII character value in Pascal. If Key equals Enter, an assignment statement sets Key to null. This effectively disables Enter.

SelectNext is a method of the TWinControl class, a base class for all visible controls that can receive the input focus. Call SelectNext to advance or retard the focus to the next control. The method is defined as:

```
procedure SelectNext(CurControl: TWinControl;
  GoForward, CheckTabStop: Boolean);
```

- CurControl — Usually, this should equal the form's ActiveControl. However, you may specify a different control object to move the focus starting from a control other than the current one — for example, to select the first edit field in a data entry form.

- GoForward — Set this parameter True to move the focus to the next control. Set it False to move the focus to the previous control.

- CheckTabStop — Set this parameter True to move the focus to the next or previous control in tab order. Set it False to move the focus to the next or previous control regardless of whether the control's TabStop property is True.

POSTING MESSAGES

Instead of calling SelectNext, you may also post a Windows message to change the focus to another control. For example, in Listing 4-3, you may replace the call to SelectNext with the following statement, which demonstrates how to post a message:

```
PostMessage(Handle, WM_NEXTDLGCTL, 0, 0);
```

The statement posts the Windows message WM_NEXTDLGCTL, which changes the focus to the next control in the tab-order lineup. The Handle argument represents the form's window — a value that various Windows procedures need in order to know which window should receive a certain message. The two zero arguments are unused.

Although this technique works, posting messages this way risks making your code nonportable, and is less object-oriented than calling the SelectNext class method. There's nothing technically wrong with posting Windows messages to controls and other windows, but when a method exists to perform an operation, it is always preferable to call the method.

Mouse Traps

Some users motor a computer mouse like a Porsche racing down a mountain switch-back. Others delicately pedal a mouse as though it needed training wheels. But whether you love 'em or hate 'em, computer mice are here to stay, and the success of your software may depend on how well you program your application's mouse events, as I'll explain next.

SINGLE- AND DOUBLE-CLICKING

You have already used mouse-click events to perform various actions. For example, to take an action if the user clicks the right mouse button, you can simply program an OnClick event handler for any form or most components. To respond to a double-click, use the OnDblClick event.

You can program either or both events for the same form or component. The events occur for the default mouse button, usually the left one. Remember, however, that users can change the default button with the Windows Control Panel.

The OnClick and OnDblClick events are adequate for many, if not most, mouse chores. But for finer control over mousing around, you can create handlers for these three events, which are available to forms and most components:

- OnMouseDown — Called when the user presses any mouse button.

- OnMouseMove — Called when the user moves the mouse cursor.

- OnMouseUp — Called when the user releases a mouse button.

Procedures for these events receive additional information about mouse activity — for example, which button the user pressed, and the mouse cursor's location. To inspect some of this information, start a new project and create empty event handlers for each of the three events. Examine the procedure declarations. For example, here's the declaration for the OnMouseDown event:

```
procedure TForm1.FormMouseDown(
  Sender: TObject;
  Button: TMouseButton;
  Shift: TShiftState;
  X, Y: Integer);
```

- Sender — Represents the object that received this event. If two or more components share the same event handler, you can use Sender to determine which object was clicked. (More on this later.)

- Button — One of three values: mbRight, mbLeft, or mbMiddle. Use this parameter to determine which mouse button the user pressed.

- Shift — A set of zero or more values: ssShift, ssAlt, ssCtrl, ssRight, ssLeft, ssMiddle, and ssDouble. Use this parameter to determine whether the user was pressing the Shift, Alt, or Ctrl keys (or a combination of those keys) while clicking the mouse. You can also use this parameter to determine which mouse button the user clicked.

- X, Y — The form or component pixel location of the mouse cursor's hot spot. Use these values to select objects in windows, to draw graphics, and to begin a click-and-drag operation. (Some copies of Borland's documentation incorrectly state that these values are relative to the screen. They are actually relative to the window's client area, with the coordinate 0,0 at the upper-left corner.)

It's best not to require the use of a middle mouse button, except in special circumstances when you can be certain that a third mouse button is available. Most PCs have a two-button mouse .

The OnMouseUp event handler declares the same parameters as OnMouseDown, but is called when the user releases the mouse button. The OnMouseMove event handler also receives the same parameters except for Button.

To distinguish between the left and right mouse buttons, you should normally use the Button parameter. For example, to sound a beep when the user presses the right or middle mouse buttons — which you might do to indicate that the program does not recognize them — insert an event handler for a form's OnMouseDown event and insert the following statement:

```
if (Button = mbRight) or (Button = mbMiddle)
  then MessageBeep(0);
```

Use the Shift parameter to determine whether the user also pressed a key while clicking the mouse. For example, to beep the speaker if the user clicks the left mouse button while also pressing the Ctrl key, you can use this statement:

```
if (Button = mbLeft) and (ssCtrl in Shift)
  then MessageBeep(0);
```

The first part of the expression is true if Button *equals* mbLeft, indicating a left button click. The second part tests whether ssCtrl or another possible value is in the *set* of Shift values passed to the procedure.

You can also use the Shift parameter to determine which button the user clicked. For example, the following statement produces the identical result as the preceding, but checks whether ssLeft is in the Shift set of values:

```
if (ssLeft in Shift) and (ssCtrl in Shift)
  then MessageBeep(0);
```

You can extend this method to test for other keys such as Alt:

```
if (ssLeft in Shift) and
   (ssCtrl in Shift) and
   (ssAlt  in Shift)
  then MessageBeep(0);
```

In such cases, it is often easier to define the possible key values as a literal set in brackets, and compare it to Shift:

```
if [ssLeft, ssCtrl, ssAlt] = Shift
  then MessageBeep(0);
```

However, the two techniques are not exactly equivalent. The former method beeps the speaker if ssLeft, ssCtrl, and ssAlt are in Shift *regardless of whether other values are also in the set*. The latter method beeps the speaker if *only* the three stated values are in Shift. For example, the first technique would allow users to also hold down a shift key; the second method would not. As this indicates, sets are handy, but you have to think carefully about what you are trying to achieve.

Don't mistake the Shift parameter for the *Shift key*. To determine whether a Shift key was held down during a mouse event, use a statement such as *if (ssShift in Shift) then...*

Use the X and Y parameters to determine the location of the mouse cursor's hot spot during a mouse up, down, or move event. For example, to display mouse coordinates when the user clicks the mouse button, insert two Label components into a form, and create a handler for the form's OnMouseDown event. (Be sure to select the form event.) Insert these statements between *begin* and *end*:

```
Label1.Caption := IntToStr(X);
Label2.Caption := IntToStr(Y);
```

Run the program and click the mouse inside the window. The two labels show the mouse cursor position relative to the window's client area.

RETURN TO SENDER

I promised earlier in this chapter to explain how to use the Sender parameter passed to many event handlers such as OnMouseDown. When several objects share an event handler, you can use Sender to determine which object received the event.

For an example of this useful technique, follow these steps:

1. In a form window, insert three buttons named by default Button1, Button2, and Button3. (Tip: Insert one button, press Ctrl+C to copy it to the clipboard, and then press Ctrl+V twice to paste two more objects. This is faster than inserting multiple objects one by one, but you must also modify the button Captions or they will all be labeled *Button1*.)

2. Click and drag a rubberband outline to select the three buttons. You should see dim handles around them. The Object Inspector window now shows the buttons' shared properties and events.

3. Select the Object Inspector's Events page, and double-click the OnMouseDown event value. This creates an event handler that the three buttons share. In other words, clicking any one button at runtime calls this *same* procedure.

4. Obviously, the shared procedure needs a method to determine which button you clicked, and this is where Sender comes in. In the OnMouseDown procedure, enter the variable declaration and statements in Listing 4-4.

5. Press F9 to run the program. When you click a button, a message confirms which button object you selected.

Listing 4-4
Sender example.

```
procedure TForm1.Button1MouseDown(Sender: TObject; Button: TMouseButton;
  Shift: TShiftState; X, Y: Integer);
var
  s : string;
begin
  if Sender = Button1 then
    s := 'Button1'
  else if Sender = Button2 then
    s := 'Button2'
  else if Sender = Button3 then
    s := 'Button3'
  else s := 'Unknown Object';
  ShowMessage('You clicked ' + s);
end;
```

Sender refers to the Button object for which this procedure was called.

In Listing 4-4, a nested *if-then-else* statement compares Sender to Button1, Button2, and Button3. Depending on Sender's value, the program sets a string variable to the appropriate button name. A final *else* clause sets the variable to *Unknown Object* just in case Sender doesn't match one of our three buttons.

The final statement in Listing 4-4 calls ShowMessage to display a note about the button you selected. You can pass any string to ShowMessage. Notice how a plus sign adds the string assigned by the preceding *if-then-else* statement to the literal string *"You clicked"*.

The nested *if-then-else* statement in Listing 4-4 is *one* statement, not several. It is therefore separated from the next statement by one semicolon.

When using Sender, you often need to tell Delphi what type of object the parameter represents. You can then assign values to the Sender's properties. For example, to change each button's Caption after it is selected, the following does *not* work:

```
Sender.Caption := 'Clicked';  { ??? }
```

You cannot do this because Sender is of type TObject, from which all Delphi components descend. In other words, all components are TObjects just as oaks, spruces, and maples in a forest are all trees. To access the button Caption properties, use a *with-do* statement to tell Delphi that Sender is actually a TButton object. Insert this statement into the procedure in Listing 4-4:

```
with Sender as TButton do
  Caption := 'Clicked';
```

The *with* expression tells Delphi to treat Sender as a TButton object, which has a Caption property. When you run the modified program, each button's label now changes to *Clicked* after you select it. Using *as* does not convert Sender to a TButton component — it merely views Sender as the specified type of object. It is your responsibility to ensure that Sender really is the type of object you specify. You can't use *as* to change an object into another of a different type.

MOUSE CURSORS

You can specify one of several stock cursor shapes for any form or component. For example, start a new project and change the form's Cursor property from crDefault to crCross. Press F9 to compile and run, and move the mouse cursor over and away from the program's window. The cursor automatically changes to a cross, then back to an arrow when you move it away from the window's client area.

Components may also have associated cursor shapes that indicate the types of operations users can select or perform. For example, add a GroupBox component to the form and set its Cursor property to crHSplit. Press F9 to compile and run. When you move the mouse pointer into the GroupBox, the cross hair changes to a split-cursor shape, which typically indicates that clicking and dragging the mouse changes the relative sizes of a split window.

CUSTOM MOUSE CURSORS

You can also create your own cursor shapes for any form or component. This is not difficult to do, but requires some extra work and a little programming. Run Delphi's Image Editor from the Tools menu to create or modify a cursor image, usually a 2-color, 32-by-32 pixel bitmap. Save your image in a file with the extension .Cur. You can also find numerous cursor files on bulletin boards or public domain and shareware disks. Also check out the files in Images\Cursors in Delphi's directory.

 If you didn't install Delphi's cursor files and you don't have time to create one, use the Sample.Cur file in the Data subdirectory on this book's CD-ROM.

You next have to import the cursor as a *resource* into a Delphi application. Resources are stored inside the program's compiled .Exe code file, but during development, it's more convenient to store them separately in .Res files. Compiling and linking the program binds the .Res file data into the finished code file — you don't have to distribute .Res files to end users.

Use Delphi's Image Editor to create a resource file, perhaps named Cursor.Res. Select the Cursors tab in the resource list window, and click

New to create a new cursor with the default name CURSOR_1. You may change this name if you want. Save the resource file, and copy it to a temporary directory.

You can use the Image Editor to create a cursor image file, as well as other types of images such as bitmaps. As a resource, however, a cursor has a *resource name* to which a program can refer — plain cursor images are unnamed. The cursor resource is also bound directly into the program's compiled .Exe code file.

To use the cursor resource, the program must carry out three steps:

- Combine the resource into the program's compiled code file.
- Load the resource into memory at runtime.
- Save a handle to the resource for use in the program.

Delphi takes care of the first step when you compile and link the program. You perform the other two steps by adding instructions and statements to the program. Start a new project, and in the Pascal unit source code file, insert this command after the keyword *implementation,* following the similar-looking command that reads the program's .Dfm form file:

```
{$R CURSOR.RES}
```

You can also specify a path to a directory in which you store your resource files:

```
{$R C:\tswan\delphi\source\data\CURSOR.RES}
```

Change the filename, Cursor.Res, if necessary. (You could also enter Cursor without a filename extension.) The command tells the linker to read the resource file, which may contain multiple resources, and insert the resources into the finished .Exe code file. You can import any resource from a .Res file using this same type of command, and you may insert as many such commands as needed into a Pascal unit file. For example, you could use Borland's Resource Workshop from Borland Pascal 7.0 or Borland C++ to create resources and import them into a Delphi application.

NOTE ➤ The {$R filename} command executes during compilation and linking, not at runtime. You do not have to supply the .Res file with the finished application.

Next, insert program code to load the cursor image from the .Exe file into memory at runtime. For example, to load and enable the cursor before the form window becomes visible, create a handler for the form's OnCreate event. Declare an integer constant to identify the cursor. For example, insert these lines before the *begin* keyword:

```
const
  newCursorID = 2;
```

You may use any positive integer value not already used for another cursor. If you have multiple cursors (or other resources), declare integer constants for each. Finish the OnCreate event handler by adding programming to load the cursor resource into memory. Listing 4-5 shows the final procedure.

Listing 4-5
Loading a cursor resource.

```
procedure TForm1.FormCreate(Sender: TObject);
const
  newCursorID = 2;
begin
  Screen.Cursors[newCursorID] :=
    LoadCursor(HInstance, 'CURSOR_1');
  Cursor := newCursorID;
end;
```

Loads a cursor image from the program's resources.

The two statements in Listing 4-5 demonstrate the proper way to load a cursor resource and use it in a form or other component. The Screen variable, of type TScreen, represents various display aspects, and serves as a kind of parent to the application. (Look up the TScreen in Delphi's on-line help for more information about this extensive data type.) Screen.Cursors provides a list of cursor images, and is technically called an *array property*. To assign a value to Cursors, use the Windows LoadCursor function as shown here to load into memory the cursor resource, named here 'CURSOR_1'. (This string is not case sensitive —

you can enter resource names in upper- or lowercase.) The HInstance argument refers to the current task, or instance, of the program. Windows uses HInstance to find the proper .Exe code file that contains the specified cursor resource.

Assign the result of LoadCursor to the Cursors array property, and specify the constant identifier in brackets. To enable the cursor for the form, assign the constant identifier also to the Cursor member of the form or other component. (Note: The *singular* Cursor specifies the currently assigned cursor; the *plural* Cursors refers to the array property that lists all available cursors.) When you compile and run the program, move the mouse cursor into the window to see the new cursor shape.

NOTE ▸ You may question the validity of the assignment to Cursors in Listing 4-5. Despite appearances, Cursors is not a Pascal array. It is an *array property*. As such, references to Cursors actually call read and write procedures that return and insert cursor resources. A reference to Cursors[X] initiates a search for a cursor identified as X. An assignment to Cursors[X] deletes any cursor identified as X before inserting a new cursor into the property. Behind the scenes, Cursors is implemented as a linked list and is technically a *sparse associated array,* but this is a fact that TScreen conveniently hides.

SKETCHING WITH THE MOUSE

Using the mouse techniques you have learned in this chapter, you can program *click-and-drag* operations for a variety of purposes. The next sample application, Sketch, demonstrates the necessary basics for clicking and dragging. Locate this project in the Sketch directory. (There's a similar program in Delphi's directories — use the one supplied with this book's CD-ROM.) Run Sketch, and click and drag the mouse inside the application's window to draw simple shapes. Double-click the mouse cursor in the window to erase the display. Listing 4-6 shows the program's source code.

Listing 4-6

Sketch\Main.Pas

```
unit Main;

interface

uses
  SysUtils, WinTypes, WinProcs, Messages, Classes, Graphics, Controls,
  Forms, Dialogs, Menus;

type
  TMainForm = class(TForm)
    MainMenu1: TMainMenu;
    Demo1: TMenuItem;
    Erase1: TMenuItem;
    Exit1: TMenuItem;
    N1: TMenuItem;
    procedure FormMouseDown(Sender: TObject; Button: TMouseButton;
      Shift: TShiftState; X, Y: Integer);
    procedure FormMouseMove(Sender: TObject; Shift: TShiftState; X,
      Y: Integer);
    procedure FormMouseUp(Sender: TObject; Button: TMouseButton;
      Shift: TShiftState; X, Y: Integer);
    procedure FormDblClick(Sender: TObject);
    procedure Erase1Click(Sender: TObject);
    procedure Exit1Click(Sender: TObject);
    procedure FormCreate(Sender: TObject);
  private
    { Private declarations }
  public
    { Public declarations }
    Dragging: Boolean;
  end;

var
  MainForm: TMainForm;

implementation

{$R *.DFM}

procedure TMainForm.FormCreate(Sender: TObject);
begin
  Dragging := False;
end;

procedure TMainForm.FormMouseDown(Sender: TObject; Button: TMouseButton;
  Shift: TShiftState; X, Y: Integer);
begin
  Dragging := True;
  Canvas.MoveTo(X, Y);
end;
```

Positions the pen for the next line to statement.

```
procedure TMainForm.FormMouseMove(Sender: TObject; Shift: TShiftState; X,
  Y: Integer);
begin
  if Dragging then
    Canvas.LineTo(X, Y);
end;
```

Draws a line from the pen position.

```
procedure TMainForm.FormMouseUp(Sender: TObject; Button: TMouseButton;
  Shift: TShiftState; X, Y: Integer);
begin
  Dragging := False;
end;

procedure TMainForm.FormDblClick(Sender: TObject);
begin
  Erase1Click(Sender);
end;

procedure TMainForm.Erase1Click(Sender: TObject);
begin
  Canvas.Brush := Brush; { Assign form's brush to Canvas }
  Canvas.FillRect(MainForm.ClientRect); { Repaint form background }
end;

procedure TMainForm.Exit1Click(Sender: TObject);
begin
  Close;
end;

end.
```

Erases the background by filling the window's client area.

Follow these steps to recreate the Sketch application and to learn how to implement click-and-drag mouse operations:

1. Go to the unit window, and in the TMainForm class's public section, declare a variable Dragging, of type Boolean. (See Listing 4-6.) The program sets this variable to True to indicate that a click-and-drag operation is in effect. When False, Dragging indicates normal mouse operation.

2. Initialize the Dragging variable to False by inserting a procedure for the form's OnCreate event. Insert this statement into the procedure:

```
Dragging := False;
```

3. To implement the clicking-and-dragging operation, insert procedures for each of the three form events, OnMouseDown, OnMouseMove, and OnMouseUp. Insert the programming from Listing 4-6 into the event handlers. I'll explain this programming after the last step in this tutorial.

4. Add a menu component, and insert commands for erasing the display and exiting the application. The erase command can use statements such as the following to fill the window's client area with the current background color. First, assign the form's Brush property to the drawing Canvas's Brush, and then call FillRect to fill the Canvas with that color (Chapter 13 explains more about Canvases and graphics):

```
Canvas.Brush := Brush;
Canvas.FillRect(MainForm.ClientRect);
```

5. Specify your Erase procedure for the form's OnDblClick event. You can now select the menu command or double-click the mouse to erase the window's contents.

6. Compile, link, and run the application by pressing F9.

When you click the mouse, OnMouseDown sets the Dragging flag True, and calls the MoveTo procedure in the form's Canvas to set the current graphics position to the mouse coordinates. Any visible drawing takes place at this location. When you release the mouse, OnMouseUp sets Dragging False, canceling the click-and-drag operation.

When you move the mouse, OnMouseMove checks whether Dragging is True — if so, it calls the Canvas's LineTo procedure to draw a visible line from the most recent current graphics position to the new mouse position, which becomes the graphics position for the next drawing operation. If Dragging is False, OnMouseMove performs no actions.

The Sketch application merely demonstrates clicking and dragging — it doesn't preserve your drawings. Also, covering Sketch's display with another window erases any drawing. Chapter 13 explains methods for creating more practical graphics applications.

Summary

- There are two ways to add keyboard handling to applications: use Edit or other input-aware components, or insert procedures for a form's OnKeyDown, OnKeyPress, or OnKeyUp events.

- OnKeyDown and OnKeyUp events represent keys using *virtual key codes* such as vk_up and vk_shift. OnKeyPress events represent keys as ASCII characters.

- Windows uses the input focus to determine where to send keyboard events. Normally, keyboard input goes first to the currently selected component. Set a form's KeyPreview property to True to redirect any keyboard activity destined for the current component object first to the form's keyboard events.

- Use a Timer component to create a while-key event, which is useful for performing actions repeatedly while the user holds down a specified key.

- Use the OnKeyPress event to modify key values. For example, use the technique in this chapter to change Tab keys to Enter so that users can press Enter to move the input focus from one input control to another.

- The OnClick and OnDblClick mouse events are adequate for most mouse-handling chores. For finer control over mouse activity, insert procedures for the OnMouseDown, OnMouseMove, and OnMouseUp events. These events receive additional information such as whether a key is pressed and the mouse cursor location.

- Use the Sender parameter passed to most event handlers to determine which object received an event. This method is most useful when multiple objects share the same event handler.

- Change a form or component's Cursor property to display a different cursor shape when the mouse moves over the form or component. You can select from a number of supplied cursors.

- You can also design and load a custom cursor as a resource in a .RES file. Use an {$R filename} directive to combine the resource file data into the compiled .EXE code file. For an event such as OnCreate, call the Windows LoadCursor function and assign the result to the form or component's Cursors (plural) array using an integer constant index. Assign the index to the Cursor property (singular) to enable the custom cursor image.

Projects to Try

4-1: Create a keyboard version of the Sketch program. You'll need a couple of Integer variables to represent the current drawing position. Program event handlers for incrementing and decrementing the current position when the user presses the keyboard's arrow keys, and call the form Canvas MoveTo and LineTo methods to draw lines.

4-2: Write a test program that displays a message or beeps the speaker (the exact response doesn't matter) when *both* mouse keys are clicked. You'll need a Boolean flag that, when True, indicates the first mouse button was clicked but not released. The event handler for the second button can check whether the flag is True, and in that way, program the two buttons to work similarly to Ctrl and Alt keys.

4-3: Add a custom pen-shaped cursor to the sample Sketch application.

4-4: *Advanced.* Add menu commands to select among different cursors for the Sketch application. Hint: Load each cursor resource, identified by a unique constant, and in the menu command procedures, assign the selected constant to the form's Cursor property.

Expert-User Tips

- KeyCount's FormKeyDown procedure assigns the current key value to KeyPressed *before* enabling the timer. Reversing the order of these two statements would be an error because timers begin ticking as soon as you set their Enabled property to True. Never do that until after preparing any and all conditions required by a Timer component's OnTimer event.

- You may use a third-party resource editor, or Borland's Resource Workshop, to create .RES files for use in Delphi applications. Combine the resource file into the finished code file by inserting the directive {$R filename.res} following a unit's *implementation* key word.

- Experienced programmers use upper- and lowercase to help distinguish among a program's identifiers. By convention, constant identifiers such as newCursorId begin with lowercase letters; variables such as Count begin with uppercase letters. Procedures such as LoadCursor also begin with uppercase letters. These are not rigid rules, and you can adopt another convention if you want. Just be sure to follow *some* convention to keep your code as understandable as possible.

- Programming the Tab key is often difficult because of the way Windows uses this key to shift the focus from one control to another. To recognize Tab-key events in Delphi applications, insert programming into an OnKeyUp event. (The OnKeyDown and OnKeyPress events do not receive Tab keypresses.) For example, insert the programming from Listing 4-7 into a form's OnKeyUp event handler to display a message when you press Tab or Shift-Tab.

Listing 4-7

Receiving Tab and Shift-Tab Keypresses in a Form's OnKeyUp Event Handler.

```
procedure TForm1.FormKeyUp(Sender: TObject; var Key: Word;
  Shift: TShiftState);
var
  S: string;
begin
  if Key = vk_Tab then                          Detects tab
  begin
    S := 'Tab Key Pressed';
    if ssShift in Shift then
      S := 'Shift-' + S;                        Detects shift
    ShowMessage(S);
  end;
end;
```

Coming Up

One of the most recognizable user-interface features in most Windows applications is the menu bar. Although programming menu bars is easy with Delphi's Menu Designer, there are a number of options you can use in your program's menus such as check marks, icons, and dynamic menus, as I'll explain in the next chapter.

5

Constructing Menus

*T*he word *menu* comes from the Latin for *minute,* meaning very small or detailed. As every Windows user knows, a *pop-up menu* is a detailed list of commands such as *Open* and *Exit.* In most applications, a *menu bar* lists the names of one or more pop-up menus. You can also create *floating pop-up menus* that appear when you click the right mouse button.

Browsing a cleverly designed menu is like slipping on a favorite sweater, and you can't spend too much effort making your application's menus comfortable to use. As this chapter explains, Delphi provides two menu components and a number of related techniques for constructing easy-to-use menus with sophisticated features that users will appreciate.

Components

- MainMenu — Use this component to create a window's menu bar, which is always displayed below the top border and caption. To create dynamic menus — those that change at runtime according to various program operations such as opening a new form window — you can insert multiple MainMenu objects into forms and follow instructions in this chapter to merge the menus' commands. Palette: Standard.

- PopupMenu — Use this component to create floating pop-up menus, which appear when the user clicks the right mouse button with the mouse cursor over the window's client area. You can also define other ways to display a floating pop-up menu at any screen location. Palette: Standard.

- MenuItem — Each item in a pop-up or a floating pop-up menu is an object of the TMenuItem class. The MenuItem component, however, does not appear on the VCL palette. Although it's usually easiest to create these objects with Delphi's Menu Designer, as this chapter explains, you can also use program statements or resource scripts to create menu items. (Although TMenuItem is the class name, I'll refer to this component as MenuItem from now on to be consistent with other component names.) Pallette: None.

Delphi prefaces a component's Pascal class name with the letter T, meaning *data type*. For example, TMainMenu is the class name for the MainMenu component. In this book, I use class names only when necessary — for example, in a variable declaration that requires a component's class name.

Pop-Up Menus

Technically speaking, a *pop-up menu* is the window you see when you open an item on a window's menu bar. A *floating pop-up menu* can appear anywhere on screen. The two types of menus are otherwise the same. This section explains programming techniques that apply to both types of pop-up menus. Use the MainMenu component to create pop-up menus on a window's menu bar. Use the PopupMenu component to create floating pop-up menus.

MAIN MENUS

Most Windows programs have a main menu, which you can create using a MainMenu component. As you have learned from other examples in this book, you create a main menu by inserting a MainMenu object into the program's main-window form. Double-click the object to open Delphi's Menu Designer, and enter your program's commands.

There are three main steps in creating a program's main menu:

1. Choose *Options|Project*, select the *Forms* page tab, and set *Main form* to the program's main-window form.

2. Insert a MainMenu object into the main-window form.

3. Set the form's Menu property to the MainMenu object's name.

Although there can be only one main menu in an application, except for two restrictions, any form, even a dialog box, can have a menu bar. Simply insert a MainMenu object into the form. The form's BorderStyle property may not equal bsDialog, and its FormStyle may not equal fsMDIChild. (MDI child windows may own MainMenu objects, but as Chapter 15 explains, these menus are merged into the main window's menu bar.)

FLOATING POP-UP MENUS

To create a floating pop-up menu that appears when users click the right mouse button, follow these steps (also see the main section, "Floating Pop-up Menus," later in this chapter):

1. Insert a PopupMenu object into a form. Delphi names the object PopupMenu1 by default.

2. Double-click the PopupMenu1 object and use the Menu Designer to enter the menu's commands.

3. Assign PopupMenu1 to the form's PopupMenu property.

MENU ITEMS

Every item in a menu is an object of the TMenuItem class. Delphi automatically creates these objects when you design your menus with the Menu Designer. You may, however, create MenuItem objects with program statements, and you'll often refer to these objects in statements. For example, to add a check mark to a menu command, assign True to a MenuItem object's Checked property. You can also perform operations on all MenuItems contained in a MainMenu or PopupMenu object by referring to the Items array in that object.

As with all objects, adopting a good naming convention is the key to creating maintainable menus. Delphi automatically chooses MenuItem names such as File1, Open1, and Save2, which are adequate only for quick tests and demos. I change these names using this scheme:

- For menu-bar labels, I append the word Menu to MenuItem object names — for example, FileMenu for the File menu object, and EditMenu for the Edit menu.

- For commands in pop-up menus, I preface the command with the menu-bar label. For example, MenuItem command objects in the *File* menu are named FileOpen, FileSave, and FileSaveAs. Objects in the *Edit* menu have names such as EditCut, EditCopy, and EditPaste.

Objects such as FileMenu (representing the *File* menu) and OpenFile (representing the *Open* command in the *File* menu) are objects of the same TMenuItem class, as are all menu items — even separator bars that divide commands into categories.

Set the MenuItem's Caption property to the text you want to display in the menu bar or a command. When designing a new menu, I find it easiest to type in all my menu Captions, and then change the default MenuItem object Names, but you can enter these values in any order.

You can also assign values to MenuItem objects at runtime to create dynamic menus that insert and delete commands according to the program's needs. For example, try these steps:

1. Insert a MainMenu object into a form, and double-click it to open the Menu Designer.

2. Create a *File* menu with an *Exit* command (type *&File* and *E&xit* to underline the *F* and *x* shortcut keys).

3. Select each menu item either in the Menu Designer or in the form. Change the property name File1 to FileMenu. Change Exit1 to FileExit.

You now have a MainMenu object that owns two MenuItem objects, FileMenu and FileExit. You can enter statements to program these menu items for a variety of purposes. For example, add a button to the form and double-click it to create an event handler. Then, insert this statement between *begin* and *end:*

```
with FileExit do
  Visible := not Visible;
```

Also, insert a Close; statement for the *File|Exit* command's procedure. Run the program and click the button to toggle the Exit command on and off. Using the Visible property is an effective way to create dynamic menus with commands that appear and disappear according to various program conditions.

Alternatively, you can disable a menu item by setting its Enabled property True or False. For example, change the preceding code to:

```
with FileExit do
  Enabled := not Enabled;
```

COMMAND SIMULATIONS

To simulate selecting a command, call any MenuItem's Click method. This can be useful, for example, when you want an event handler to perform the same task as a pop-up menu command. If that command object is OptionsProject, you can execute the command's event handler with the following statement:

```
OptionsProject.Click;  { Simulate selecting Options|Project }
```

 Click has no effect on a MenuItem object that labels a menu in a window's menu bar. However, the MenuItem still receives the OnClick event for any user activity such as clicking the mouse on the menu item's name. You could use this event to perform actions such as changing the names of commands in a menu, or inserting check marks.

THE ITEMS PROPERTY

You can also get to MenuItem objects by using the Items property, which is an element of MainMenu, PopupMenu, and MenuItem components. Items is a TMenuItem object, which you can use to call methods such as Items.Insert, or as an array in expressions such as MyMenu.Items[N]. In a MainMenu object, the Items property contains the menu bar's pop-up menu items. For example, in a program with three pop-up menus — *File, Edit,* and *Help* — the following statements change the first menu's name to *Presto-Chango,* disable the *Edit* menu, and make the *Help* menu invisible:

```
with MainMenu1 do
begin
  Items[0].Caption := 'Presto-Chango';
  Items[1].Enabled := False;
  Items[2].Visible := False;
end;
```

Each MenuItem object also has an Items property, which you can use to access menu commands. For example, to disable the *File|Exit* command, assuming this is the only command in the menu, you can use this statement

```
FileMenu.Items[0].Enabled := False;
```

This has the same effect as the following statement, which is probably simpler in most cases:

```
FileExit.Enabled := False;
```

As a general rule, to perform tasks for individual MenuItem objects, it's easiest to refer to their object names, as in the preceding example. To set multiple properties, however, it may be more convenient to use the Items property. Either technique accesses the same MenuItem objects, so use whichever makes sense. For example, the following statement uses an Integer variable in a *for* loop to disable all commands in the FileMenu:

```
for I := 0 to FileMenu.Count - 1 do
  FileMenu.Items[I].Enabled := False;
```

By the way, because the preceding statement refers to FileMenu twice, you can simplify the code by using a *with* statement. Even though the result has one more line, it is logically more efficient:

```
with FileMenu do
  for I := 0 to Count - 1 do
    Items[I].Enabled := False;
```

The *with* statement tells Delphi to use FileMenu's Count and Items, eliminating the need to preface those names with FileMenu and a period. This saves typing, and can help the compiler produce more efficient code. Try to use *with* as often as you can.

FileMenu's Count property equals the number of MenuItem objects in the Items array. Because the first array index is 0, the last object index equals Count − 1. Always consider this fact when writing loops to process the Items property as an array.

MULTIWAY MENUS

Any item in a pop-up menu can have an attached submenu. As Figure 5-1 shows, you can carry this idea to extremes, but it's best not to go too far overboard. Although multiway menus are useful for organizing complex command structures, they can be difficult to use. (Windows 95 simplifies menu selection by not requiring users to click the mouse button multiple times. This makes multiway menus easier to use than in past Windows versions. However, it's still wise to limit the amount of nesting to two levels. Three levels is almost always too many.)

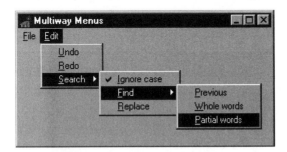

Figure 5-1

Multiway menus nest complex command structures, and are easier to use in Windows 95 than in Windows 3.1. This display is from the MultiMen program on the book's CD-ROM.

To create submenus in the Menu Designer, create a menu command such as *Search* (see Figure 5-1). Highlight the command and press Ctrl+right-arrow. This creates a submenu that you can edit as you do other pop-up menu windows. Repeat these steps to create additional nesting levels.

Multiway menus require no special programming. You create event handlers for their commands the same as you do for single-level pop-up menus. In other words, menu nesting is purely visual. Therefore, regardless of nesting level, all MenuItem objects in a MainMenu or PopupMenu object must have unique Name properties.

MENU ITEM SHORTCUT KEYS

There are two types of shortcut key assignments you can make for menu commands. You can preface a letter with & to designate an Alt key. For example, if you set a MenuItem's Caption to &Configure, users can press Alt+C to open the *Configure* menu.

A second type of shortcut key is called an *accelerator*. Usually, accelerator keys are combinations of alphanumeric, Ctrl, Shift, arrow, and function keys. They are called accelerators because users can press them to select commands without having to open a menu window.

Do not enter shortcut key labels in MenuItem Captions. Delphi automatically appends the key names. For example, enter E&xit for the File-Exit object's Caption, and set that object's ShortCut key to Alt+X. Delphi automatically displays the command as *Exit Alt+X* in the pop-up menu.

You can select ShortCut keys from that property's drop-down list. However, because this list has so many entries, I find it easier to enter the key label as text. For example, instead of pressing Alt+X, I type the five characters A L T + X into the ShortCut property and press Enter. You must do this to assign keys such as Enter which are not in the drop-down list — type E N T E R, for example. You can also create character shortcuts by entering A, B, C, 1, 9 or any other key you can type.

Table 5-1 lists some standard accelerator ShortCut key assignments for common menu items. Windows 95 applications more closely follow these standards than in past Windows versions, and it's a good idea to use them in your applications. These aren't strictly rigid rules, and key usage depends on the application — for example, you might use the Ins key to insert a field rather than toggle an editor's insert/overtype switch. (I disagree with Alt+F4 as the official standard *File|Exit* key. Everybody and their aunts and uncles know that *Alt+X* is the standard program-exit accelerator.)

Table 5-1

Standard Accelerator ShortCut Keys

Command	*Menu*	*ShortCut*
Cascade	Window	Shift+F5
Collapse all	Tree	Ctrl+* (keypad)
Collapse item	Tree	– (keypad)
Copy	Edit	Ctrl+C
Cut	Edit	Ctrl+X
Delete	Edit	Del
Exit	File	Alt+X (officially Alt+F4)
Expand all	Tree	* (keypad)
Expand item	Tree	+ (keypad)
Expand/Collapse	Tree	Enter
Find	Edit	Ctrl+F
Find next	Edit	F3
Insert/Overtype	Edit	Ins
New	File	Ctrl+N
Open	File	Ctrl+O
Paste	Edit	Ctrl+V
Print	File	Ctrl+P
Replace	Edit	Ctrl+H
Save	File	Ctrl+S
Search	Help	F1
Select all	Edit	Ctrl+A
Tile	Window	Shift+F4
Undo	Edit	Ctrl+Z

CHECK MARKS

Adding and removing check marks from menu commands couldn't be easier. Simply set any MenuItem's Checked property True to display a check mark, or False to erase one. You can do this at design time or at runtime using a statement such as:

```
EditInsert.Checked := True;
```

In designing your program's user interface, think carefully whether to make a checkmarked command operate as a toggle, or as a selection from a group of related commands. For example, a game's *Level* menu might list difficulty levels, only one of which can be selected at a time. However, an *Insert* command in an Edit menu should probably be an on/off toggle.

Create a toggle by using Pascal's *not* operator as in this statement, which you might enter into the MenuItem's OnClick event handler:

```
with EditInsert do
  Checked := not Checked;
```

Elsewhere in the program, use Checked in an *if* statement to select an action:

```
if EditInsert.Checked then
  ... { do something if menu item is checked }
```

Run the Checks application and try the Level menu. The program uses check marks in two ways: to select among nine levels, and to toggle an Insert command on and off. Click the window's button to display the current level settings. Figure 5-2 shows the program's window. Listing 5-1 shows the form's source code.

Listing 5-1 shows how a series of menu commands can share the same event handler. To create the LevelClick procedure, declare it as shown in the TMainForm class, and enter the procedure's statements in the unit's implementation section. The procedure turns off check marks for commands Level1 through Level9, and then sets the Sender's Checked property to True. The expression TMenuItem(Sender) *casts* Sender as a TMenuItem object. To use the LevelClick procedure, assign it to the OnClick event for each MenuItem, Level1 through Level9.

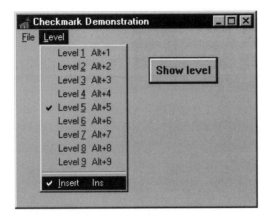

Figure 5-2
The Checks application demonstrates how to use check marks as toggles and to select one of a set of commands, such as the nine levels shown here.

Listing 5-1
Checks\Main.Pas

```
unit Main;

interface

uses
  SysUtils, WinTypes, WinProcs, Messages, Classes, Graphics, Controls,
  Forms, Dialogs, Menus, StdCtrls;

type
  TMainForm = class(TForm)
    MainMenu1: TMainMenu;
    FileMenu: TMenuItem;
    FileExit: TMenuItem;
    LevelMenu: TMenuItem;
    Level1: TMenuItem;
    Level2: TMenuItem;
    Level3: TMenuItem;
    Level4: TMenuItem;
    Level5: TMenuItem;
    Level6: TMenuItem;
    Level7: TMenuItem;
    Level8: TMenuItem;
    Level9: TMenuItem;
    ShowButton: TButton;
    N1: TMenuItem;
    LevelInsert: TMenuItem;
```

```
    procedure FileExitClick(Sender: TObject);
    procedure LevelClick(Sender: TObject);
    procedure ShowButtonClick(Sender: TObject);
    procedure LevelInsertClick(Sender: TObject);
  private
    { Private declarations }
    function GetLevel: Integer;
  public
    { Public declarations }
  end;

var
  MainForm: TMainForm;

implementation

{$R *.DFM}

const
  highLevel = 9;    { Highest level command }

procedure TMainForm.FileExitClick(Sender: TObject);
begin
  Close;
end;

procedure TMainForm.LevelClick(Sender: TObject);
var
  I: Integer;
begin
  with LevelMenu do
    for I := 0 to highLevel - 1 do
      Items[I].Checked := False;
    TMenuItem(Sender).Checked := True;
end;

function TMainForm.GetLevel: Integer;
var
  I: Integer;
begin
  GetLevel := -1;
  with LevelMenu do
    for I := 0 to highLevel - 1 do
      if Items[I].Checked then
        GetLevel := I + 1;
end;

procedure TMainForm.ShowButtonClick(Sender: TObject);
var
  S: string;
begin
  S := 'Level = ' + IntToStr(GetLevel) + ' -- Insert:';
```

This for-loup removes all check marks.

This assignment adds a check mark to the selected command.

Casts Sender for use as a TMenuItem.

```
      if LevelInsert.Checked
        then S := S + 'ON'
        else S := S + 'OFF';
      ShowMessage(S);
    end;

    procedure TMainForm.LevelInsertClick(Sender: TObject);
    begin
      with Sender as TMenuItem do
        Checked := not Checked;
    end;

    end.
```

Function GetLevel shows how to interrogate MenuItem objects through the Items array to determine which command has a check mark. The function returns –1 if no command is checked, or it returns the level, 1 through 9.

When you click the button, ShowButtonClick creates a string that shows the current level (by calling the GetLevel function) and the current setting of the Insert toggle. Delphi's handy ShowMessage procedure displays the final result.

Floating Pop-up Menus

As they say in the real estate business, there are only three important differences between floating and nonfloating pop-up menus: location, location, and location. You program PopupMenu objects the same as MainMenu objects, but instead of appearing in a menu bar, a floating pop-up menu can appear at any screen location. The MemoPad application from Chapter 2 demonstrates how to create and use floating pop-up menus.

To create a floating pop-up menu, simply insert a PopupMenu component into a form, double-click the object, and enter its commands using the Menu Designer the same way you do for MainMenu components. Assign the PopupMenu object to the form's PopupMenu property, and you're done.

Most often, floating pop-up menu commands share the same event handlers as a window's main menu, but this isn't a rule. You can program separate event handlers for floating pop-up menus if you want.

THE RIGHT MOUSE BUTTON

To program right mouse-button clicks to display a floating pop-up menu, assign the PopupMenu object's name to a form's PopupMenu property. The menu appears when users click the right mouse button in the form window.

You can also assign PopupMenu objects at runtime, which you might do to change between two or more floating pop-up menus depending on various program conditions. In a button's event handler, or in a procedure for a menu command, use a statement such as this to assign a PopupMenu object to a form's PopupMenu property:

```
PopupMenu := PopupMenu2;  { Assign PopupMenu2 to PopupMenu }
```

OTHER WAYS TO FLOAT

Call the PopupMenu component's Popup method to display a floating popup menu in response to events other than a right mouse button click. Pass screen x- and y-coordinates to Popup as in this statement:

```
PopupMenu1.Popup(100, 100);
```

Popup's x- and y-coordinates are relative to the Windows screen, with (0,0) at the upper-left corner.

When passing mouse-click coordinates to Popup, because those values are relative to the active window, call the ClientToScreen function to convert to screen-relative coordinates. First declare a variable of type TPoint:

```
var
  Pt: TPoint;
```

Then, in a form's MouseDown event handler, enter these statements:

```
Pt.X := X;
Pt.Y := Y;
Pt := ClientToScreen(Pt);
PopupMenu1.Popup(Pt.X, Pt.Y);
```

The first two lines assign the mouse coordinates X and Y passed to the event handler to the TPoint variable. The third line calls ClientToScreen in the TControl class, which is one of TForm's distant ancestors. This converts Pt from window-client-relative coordinates to screen-relative values. The last line passes the converted X and Y values to PopupMenu's Popup method.

Dynamic Menus

Delphi provides several techniques for creating menus that change dynamically at runtime. You can change a window's entire menu bar, you can insert and delete pop-up menus, you can add and remove commands, and you can merge menu objects. The following sections explain these techniques and more.

CHANGING MENUS

The easiest way to change a window's menu is to assign a different MainMenu object to a form's Menu property. First, insert two or more MainMenu objects into the form, and use the Menu Designer to enter their commands. Then, perhaps in a command or a button event handler, enter a statement such as:

```
Menu := MainMenu2;
```

When you run the program, the menu bar changes from its design-time assignment to MainMenu2. The menu bar automatically changes its visual appearance when the program executes the preceding assignment statement.

INSERTING AND DELETING MENUS

You can merge menu objects (see "Merging MainMenu Objects," later in this chapter) but there's a much simpler method you can use to insert and delete entire pop-up menus in a window's menu bar. To try this technique, insert a single MainMenu object into a form, double-click the object, and use the Menu Designer to enter menus and commands.

Next, create a handler for the form's OnCreate event. Insert statements such as the following to make selected pop-up menus invisible:

```
OptionMenu.Visible := False;
WindowMenu.Visible := False;
```

Finally, in response to a button click or a menu command (or any other event), set a menu item's Visible property True. The menu automatically appears. This is a good method for programming a quick-and-dirty *Advanced Menus* command that expands menus to their full regalia. Invisible menu items remain active, however, and still receive OnClick events. If those menu items have associated shortcut keys, users can still select them even if the commands are not visible.

CHANGING MENU ITEMS

To change a command's text, simply assign a new Caption to any MenuItem object. For example, you might program an *Undo* command to inform users what can be undone:

```
EditUndo.Caption := '&Undo deletion';
```

ADDING, INSERTING, AND DELETING MENU ITEMS

You can add, insert, and delete commands from any pop-up menu object of the TMenuItem class. For example, you can append filenames to the end of a *File* menu's FileMenu object. Or, you can use the technique to modify a pop-up menu's commands at runtime.

The first step in adding or inserting a menu item is to create a TMenuItem object. First, declare a variable like this in an event handler:

```
var
  MI: TMenuItem;
begin
  ...
end;
```

In the procedure body, create a new TMenuItem object by calling the Create method, and pass the parent object, which is usually the parent menu for the new command item:

```
MI := TMenuItem.Create(FileMenu);
```

You now have a new menu object referenced as MI. Assign the object's caption and other properties using statements such as the following:

```
MI.Caption := '&New command';
MI.Visible := True;
MI.ShortCut := ShortCut(vk_F1);
```

When you are done configuring the new menu item, add it to the bottom of a pop-up menu by calling Add:

```
FileMenu.Add(MI);  { Add menu item to bottom of File menu }
```

At this point, the FileMenu object assumes ownership of MI, and will delete that object at the proper time. You do not have to delete the memory allocated to MI by Create.

You may use MI again to create another menu item, but for each one, you *must* call the Create method as shown here. For example, you cannot simply assign a different caption to MI and add it to the menu. For experienced Pascal programmers: MI is actually a pointer to a dynamically allocated object. In programs, you do not have to dereference this pointer — simply use it as you would a variable of the addressed type.

Alternatively, you can insert a menu item between others. Suppose you have a separator line object named FileSep. To insert MI above that line, first locate the separator's index and assign it to an Integer variable:

```
Index := FileMenu.IndexOf(FileSep);
```

Then, instead of calling Add, insert MI by calling the Insert method and passing it the Index value and the new menu object:

```
FileMenu.Insert(Index, MI);  { Insert menu item at Index }
```

You can also delete menu items by index value. Call TMenuItem's Delete method:

```
FileMenu.Delete(Index);
```

Or, you can delete a menu item object by calling Remove. For example, this deletes the Exit command from the File menu:

```
FileMenu.Remove(FileExit);
```

You can modify the contents of a popup or main menu through the Items property. Use Items as an array of TMenuItem objects. For example, MyMenu.Items[I] refers to the TMenuItem object at index I in MyMenu.

ASSIGNING CODE TO MENU ITEMS

When you create a new menu item, you should also assign it an event handler to perform an action when users select the command. This takes three steps:

1. Declare the event handler procedure in the form's class.

2. Implement the procedure in the unit's implementation section.

3. Assign the procedure to the menu item's OnClick event.

For example, add the following declaration to the TForm1 class (usually just before the *private* keyword):

```
procedure NewCommandClick(Sender: TObject);
```

Next, implement the procedure anywhere in the unit's implementation section:

```
procedure TForm1.NewCommandClick(Sender: TObject);
begin
  ShowMessage('New command executed!');
end;
```

Finally, declare a TMenuItem variable such as MI, create the object, assign the properties you want, and assign the event handler to the OnClick event:

```
MI := TMenuItem.Create(FileMenu);
MI.Caption := '&New command';
MI.OnClick := NewCommandClick;
```

Insert or add the new object into a menu. When users select it, the program calls NewCommandClick.

 Of course, you can assign an existing menu-command event handler to a new menu item's OnClick event. Just use the final line from the preceding example, and change NewCommandClick to the existing procedure's name.

ADDING FILENAMES TO A FILE MENU

MenuItem objects do not have to be commands. They can also be informational — for example, the names of recently opened files. You can use Add, Insert, and Delete to manage this list — just create TMenuItem objects and assign filenames to the Caption properties. However, I find it's easier to insert dummy commands into the File menu, and assign filenames to them as users open new files.

The FileMenu sample application on the book's CD-ROM shows the necessary code. Figure 5-3 shows the program's *File* menu with four recently opened files. You can select these names like any other command, and each has an Alt+*N* key, where *N* is the underlined number. The code to manage the filename list is a bit tricky, as Listing 5-2 shows.

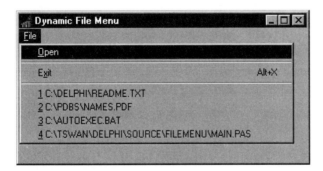

Figure 5-3
A common interface technique lists recently opened files in the File menu, but the programming can be tricky, as the FileMenu application demonstrates.

Listing 5-2

Filemenu\Main.Pas

```pascal
unit Main;

interface

uses
  SysUtils, WinTypes, WinProcs, Messages, Classes, Graphics, Controls,
  Forms, Dialogs, StdCtrls, Menus;

type
  TMainForm = class(TForm)
    MainMenu1: TMainMenu;
    FileMenu: TMenuItem;
    FileExit: TMenuItem;
    OpenButton: TButton;
    OpenDialog: TOpenDialog;
    FileOpen: TMenuItem;
    FileSep1: TMenuItem;
    FileSep2: TMenuItem;
    FileName1: TMenuItem;
    FileName2: TMenuItem;
    FileName3: TMenuItem;
    FileName4: TMenuItem;
    procedure FileExitClick(Sender: TObject);
    procedure OpenButtonClick(Sender: TObject);
    procedure FileName1Click(Sender: TObject);
  private
    { Private declarations }
  public
    { Public declarations }
  end;

var
  MainForm: TMainForm;

implementation

{$R *.DFM}

procedure TMainForm.FileExitClick(Sender: TObject);
begin
  Close;
end;

{- Prompt for filename and add name to File menu }
procedure TMainForm.OpenButtonClick(Sender: TObject);
var
  S: string;
  I, K: Integer;
```

```
begin
  if OpenDialog.Execute then with FileMenu do
  begin
    if not FileSep2.Visible then
      FileSep2.Visible := True;  { Make separator visible }
    K := IndexOf(FileName1);
    for I := Count - 1 downto K + 1 do
    begin  { Move current filenames down one position }
      S := Items[I - 1].Caption;
      S[2] := Chr(Ord('0') + (I - K + 1));  { Alt-Shortcut }
      Items[I].Caption := S;
      Items[I].Visible := Items[I - 1].Visible;
    end;
    FileName1.Caption := '&1 ' + OpenDialog.Filename;
    FileName1.Visible := True;
  end;
end;

{- Get filename selected from File menu }
procedure TMainForm.FileName1Click(Sender: TObject);
var
  Filename: string;
begin
  with Sender as TMenuItem do
  begin
    Filename := Caption;
    System.Delete(Filename, 1, 2);
  end;
  ShowMessage('Filename = ' + Filename);
end;

end.
```

Follow these steps to create a File menu and add recently opened filenames to the bottom of the menu window:

1. Insert a MainMenu component into a form, and use the Menu Designer to create a File menu with a separator (enter a hyphen in the Caption property) and four dummy filename menu items. See Figure 5-4 for an example. Name the menu FileMenu, and the dummies FileName1, File-Name2, FileName3, and FileName4. Name the separators FileSep1 and FileSep2. Table 5-2 lists significant component names and properties.

2. Set Visible to False for the separator and all dummy menu items. The program will make them visible as users open new files.

Figure 5-4

The FileMenu application's menu opened in Delphi's Menu Designer, with four dummy filename items.

3. Create an event handler for the first dummy entry by selecting it in the Menu Designer. See FileName1Click in the sample listing, which simply displays the selected filename. Assign this same event handler to the other dummy items.

4. Insert an OpenDialog object into the form.

5. Create an event handler for an Open command or button, and insert the programming from the demonstration's OpenButtonClick procedure.

Table 5-2

FileMenu Application Component Properties

Component	Name	Property	Value
Form	MainForm	Caption	Dynamic File Menu
Button	OpenButton	Caption	Open file
BitBtn	BitBtn1	Kind	bkClose
OpenDialog	OpenDialog	Filter	All files (*.*)I*.*
MainMenu	MainMenu1		
MenuItem	FileOpen	Caption	&Open
MenuItem	FileExit	Caption	E&xit
MenuItem	FileSep1	Caption	-

II

5

Component	Name	Property	Value
MenuItem	FileSep2	Caption	-
		Visible	False
MenuItem	FileName1	Caption	&1 name
		Visible	False
MenuItem	FileName2	Caption	&2 name
		Visible	False
MenuItem	FileName3	Caption	&3 name
		Visible	False .
MenuItem	FileName4	Caption	&4 name
		Visible	False

TIP

Procedure FileName1Click in Listing 5-2 shows how to resolve a common conflict that may give you trouble from time to time. The procedure calls the Pascal Delete procedure to remove the underlined Alt-key labels added to each filename. However, the preceding *with* statement tells Delphi to use TMenuItem members, one of which is also named Delete. I resolved this name conflict by prefacing Delete with System and a period, which tells the compiler to use the Delete string procedure found in the System unit, not the TMenuItem method of the same name. Other commonly used generic names that you may need to qualify include Insert, Text, Assign, and Close.

Using Shortcut Keys

Delphi's Menus unit, added to any program with a MainMenu or PopupMenu object, provides four subroutines that are useful for assigning and using accelerator shortcut keys. To follow along, insert a MainMenu object into a form, and use the Menu Designer to create a menu with at least one item named *Demo*. I'll use the default Name Demo1 here.

Use the ShortCut function to assign an accelerator key to a menu item. Delphi defines the function as follows:

```
function ShortCut(Key: Word; Shift: TShiftState): TShortCut;
```

Using ShortCut, you can assign F9 to Demo1's ShortCut key property (to follow along, add this statement to a button's event handler):

```
Demo1.ShortCut := ShortCut(vk_F9, []);
```

Delphi automatically displays shortcut keys in the pop-up menu to the right of the Demo command. You don't have to modify the menu item's caption.

The empty brackets specify a null set of shift keys. To assign Alt+F9, specify a TShiftState value in brackets:

```
Demo1.ShortCut := ShortCut(vk_F9, [ssAlt]);
```

Because the shift state is a Pascal set, you can specify multiple values separated by commas. For example, this statement assigns Ctrl+Shift+A as the shortcut (the order of values in the set doesn't matter):

```
Demo1.ShortCut := ShortCut(Ord('A'), [ssCtrl, ssShift]);
```

You cannot specify the A key using the virtual key code vk_A, even though this and other alphanumeric codes are listed in Delphi's on-line help. Use Pascal's Ord function and a literal character in single quotation marks to specify ASCII character keys.

To break apart a shortcut key into its separate values, call ShortCut-ToKey, which is defined as follows:

```
procedure ShortCutToKey(ShortCut: TShortCut;
  var Key: Word; var Shift: TShiftState);
```

Pass a menu item's ShortCut property to the first parameter. The procedure assigns the ShortCut's virtual key code to Key and its set of shift-state values to Shift.

Another function, TextToShortCut, interprets a string value as a shortcut key assignment. For example, specify Alt+X as a string with this statement:

```
Demo1.ShortCut := TextToShortCut('Alt+X');
```

You can use this method to prompt users to enter a shortcut key value, perhaps in a configuration utility that lets users program their own menu commands:

```
var
  S: string;
begin
  S := InputBox('Input Dialog', 'Enter shortcut key', '');
  if Length(S) > 0 then
    Demo1.ShortCut := TextToShortCut(S);
end;
```

The InputBox function is especially handy for prompting users for string values. The first string is the dialog's caption, the second is a prompt displayed in the dialog window, and the third (null here) is the default string value returned if the user does not enter a string value.

Perform the reverse operation with ShortCutToText, which is defined as follows:

```
function ShortCutToText(ShortCut: TShortCut): string;
```

For example, you can display a menu item's shortcut key as a string in a dialog box:

```
ShowMessage('Demo1 shortcut = ' +
  ShortCutToText(Demo1.ShortCut));
```

ENABLING AND DISABLING COMMANDS

I already explained in this chapter how to enable and disable menu items by setting the Enabled property to True or False. When Enabled is False, the menu item's caption is dimmed in the pop-up menu window, and users cannot select it.

In practice, it takes careful planning to dim the proper commands at the correct times. The easiest approach is to write a procedure that configures an entire menu according to global flags and other values. For example, define a Boolean FileIsOpen variable, and write a procedure to enable or disable a *File* menu's *Open, Save,* and other commands according to the variable's value.

The ToDo application on this book's CD-ROM shows how to do this for a common *File* menu. The program's form class, TMainForm, declares a procedure named EnableMenu:

```
procedure EnableMenu;
```

The program implements the procedure as shown in Listing 5-3. The statements enable and disable the commands in the program's *File* menu according to the program's file-open and file-saved states.

Listing 5-3

Procedure EnableMenu from the ToDo sample application.

```
procedure TMainForm.EnableMenu;
var
  I: Integer;
begin
  with FileMenu do
  begin
    for I := 0 to Count - 1 do          { Enable all File commands }
      Items[I].Enabled := True;
    if not FileDirty then
    begin   {- No edits }
      FileSave.Enabled := False;        { Must use Save as }
      if Length(Filename) = 0 then      { i.e. file not named }
      begin   {- No edits; no name }
        FileSaveAs.Enabled := False;    { Nothing to save }
        FilePrint.Enabled := False;     { Nothing to print }
      end;
    end;
  end;
end;
```

The ToDo program uses a flag, FileDirty, to indicate whether changes have been made to an opened file. Procedure EnableMenu uses this flag to enable the menu's *Save* command, which remains dim (and therefore unselectable) if the file data is unchanged. The procedure also enables and disables other commands such as *Save as* and *Print*.

To use EnableMenu, create a handler for FileMenu's OnClick event, and call the procedure. As a result, the menu's commands are configured before the pop-up menu window becomes visible. For example, here's the OnClick event handler from ToDo:

```
procedure TMainForm.FileMenuClick(Sender: TObject);
begin
  EnableMenu;   { Enable/disable commands before menu opens }
end;
```

In a more complex application, it might be best to write a menu-enabling procedure for each of the program's menus, *File, Edit, Window,* and so forth. Call the procedures from OnClick event handlers for each

MainMenu item. However, this does not prevent users from selecting commands by pressing shortcut keys. The safest course is for each command to perform its own validation. For example, a *File*|*Save* command could simply exit without taking any action if there is no file open, and therefore, nothing to save.

MERGING MAINMENU OBJECTS

Any form can have multiple MainMenu objects that you can merge into one another to create dynamic menus. This technique is especially useful in programs with two or more forms. When the program displays a secondary form, its MainMenu commands automatically merge with the program's main window. For example, a configuration dialog could use this technique to merge a new set of commands into the menu bar. When the user closes the dialog, the merged commands automatically disappear.

The key element in merging menus is the GroupIndex byte value in the TMenuItem class. This value, which may range from 0 to 255, determines the effect of the merge. Use equal GroupIndex values to replace one menu with another. Use lesser values to insert menus to the left. Use higher values to insert menus to the right.

Assign GroupIndex values in multiples of 10 to make it easier to insert new menus between existing ones. However, in OLE applications (see Chapter 16), Windows requires you to use specific GroupIndex values to enable menu merging for in-place editing.

Follow these steps to merge two MainMenu objects in the same form and experiment with the technique:

1. Insert two MainMenu objects into a form window. I'll use the default object names MainMenu1 and MainMenu2, but you could change these names if you want.

2. Double-click MainMenu1 and use the Menu Designer to create a Demo menu with a command *Advanced*. Delphi names the menu item Demo1 by default. Select Demo1 in the Object Inspector window, and set Demo1's GroupIndex value to 0 (the default value).

3. Double-click MainMenu2, and create an *Extra* menu with a command *Exit*. Delphi names the menu item Extra1 by default. Select Extra1 in the Object Inspector window, and set Extra1's GroupIndex value to 1.

4. Create an event handler for the Advanced command by selecting it in the form or in the Menu Designer, and insert the following statement between *begin* and *end:*

```
MainMenu1.Merge(MainMenu2);
```

5. Create an event handler for the Exit command. (Because MainMenu2 is not shown in the form, you must use the Menu Designer to select the command.) Insert a Close statement for this command's procedure.

6. Press F9 to run the program. Select the *Demo|Advanced* command to merge the secondary menu, and make the *Exit* command available.

Try other GroupIndex values. For example, set GroupIndex to 1 for both Demo1 and Exit1. Selecting the *Advanced* command then causes the *Extra* menu to replace *Demo.* Or, set the GroupIndex to a higher value in Demo1 than in Exit1. The *Advanced* command now inserts the *Extra* menu to the left of *Demo.*

UNMERGING MAINMENU OBJECTS

Undo the effect of a menu merge by calling the UnMerge method for any MainMenu object. For example, insert a button into the form window and use the following statement in the button's OnClick event handler. Clicking the button removes MainMenu2 from MainMenu1:

```
MainMenu1.UnMerge(MainMenu2);
```

MERGING MAINMENU OBJECTS IN MULTIPLE FORMS

When merging MainMenu objects in two or more forms, use the AutoMerge property to determine whether merging is automatic or occurs under program control. Try these steps to experiment with multiple-form menu merging:

1. Insert a MainMenu object into a form, double-click it, and use the Menu Designer to create a *Demo* menu with a command, *Show*

form. Delphi names the menu Demo1 by default. Select this object in the Object Inspector and make sure that GroupIndex equals 0 (the default value).

2. Add a new form to the project by clicking the *New form* speed button, or by selecting Delphi's *File|New Form* command. Select the *Standard dialog box* from the *Browse Gallery* dialog. This creates a second form named BtnBottomDlg.

3. Insert a MainMenu object into the BtnBottomDlg form, and set this object's AutoMerge property to True. Double-click the MainMenu1 object and create an *Advanced* menu with a *Close* command. Select this command and insert a Close statement in the event handler. Adjust the size of the window so the buttons at the bottom are visible. (Although the dialog shows a menu bar, the menu will actually appear in the main window's menu bar.)

4. Using the Menu Designer, single-click the *Advanced* menu item, and set its GroupIndex property to 1. Double-click *Advanced* and enter this statement in its event handler:

```
BtnBottomDlg.Show;
```

5. Locate Unit1's *uses* declaration, and add Unit2 to the list of unit names. Separate multiple names with commas, and end with a semicolon.

6. Locate Unit2's *implementation* keyword, and below it, add this *uses* declaration for Unit1:

```
uses
   Unit1;
```

7. Finally, create an event handler for the dialog form's OnClose event. Insert this statement:

```
Form1.MainMenu1.UnMerge(MainMenu1);
```

8. Press F9 to run the program. Select the *Demo|Show form* command, and move the resulting dialog aside to view the main window's menu, which now has an *Advanced* menu item. Select this menu's *Close* command which closes the dialog and removes the merged menu.

The preceding steps may seem a bit complex the first time you do them. When merging MainMenu objects in multiple forms, keep these tips in mind:

- Insert one MainMenu object into each form. Set AutoMerge to False for the main window's object. Set AutoMerge to True for all other MainMenu objects. If you don't want automatic merging, set AutoMerge to False for all menus, and call Merge to perform menu merges as you did for single-form merging.

- Add the secondary unit module names (Unit2, Unit3, and so on) to Unit1's *uses* declaration. This tells the main module to use the secondary ones.

- Add the main module unit name (for example, Unit1) to a new *uses* declaration in each secondary module, below the *implementation keyword*. You cannot do this in the secondary units' *interface* sections because that would create a circular unit reference error (two or more units may not publicly use one another).

- Call UnMerge for the main form's MainMenu object to remove a menu automatically when the secondary form closes. See step 7 in the preceding tutorial for sample code. Despite the AutoMerge setting, unmerging is never automatic when a form closes (though perhaps it should be).

- Call Show to display a secondary form window as a child or modeless dialog of the main window parent.

- Delphi names each MainMenu object MainMenu1 in each form. For a clearer program, select better names for these objects such as MyMainMenu and DialogMenu.

 MDI and OLE applications require different menu merging techniques. See chapters 15 and 16 for more information on MDI and OLE programming.

MODIFYING THE SYSTEM MENU

The system menu appears when you click the Close button in the upper-left window border for Windows 3.1 programs, or when you click the program icon in Windows 95 applications. Most applications shouldn't need to add commands to this menu — also, Delphi autmomatically handles the menu's standard commands. However, if you need to modify the system menu for a special application, here's how.

There are two basic problems to solve. First, the system menu is owned by Windows, not the application. Therefore, you cannot use a MainMenu object to access the system menu. Second, there are actually two system menus in a Delphi application — one for a form window, and one for the Application object, which is normally hidden except when the application window is minimized. You must modify *both* menus in order to display your command in the application's normal window, and in its desktop minimized icon.

To add the command, call the Windows AppendMenu function. To respond to the command's selection, add a message-handler procedure to the form's class. Follow these steps to try out the technique and add an *About...* command to the system menu:

1. Create a handler for the main-window form's OnCreate event. Insert the programming for procedure FormCreate from Listing 5-4.

2. Declare a constant to represent the new command. Use any small value such as hexadecimal $00A0 (100 decimal). Windows uses the low four bits of this value for command flags, which should be zero. The easiest way to satisfy this requirement is to assign values in hexadecimal with the last digit equal to 0. For example, add this declaration above the unit's *type* declaration:

```
const
  cm_About = $00A0;
```

3. In the form's class (TForm1 by default), insert the following message-handler declaration in the class's private section. The first line declares the procedure, which must have the single TWMSysCommand variable parameter as shown. The second line tells Delphi to call this procedure when the form receives a wm_Syscommand message from Windows. This message indicates that the user has selected a system-menu command:

```
procedure WMSysCommand(var Message: TWMSysCommand);
  message wm_SysCommand;
```

4. Implement the WMSysCommand procedure as shown in Listing 5-4. Run the program and select the system menu's *About...* command to display a message dialog. Minimize the program to an icon and select the system menu command, which performs the same task. There are actually two system menus at work, though there appears to be only one.

Listing 5-4
Adding commands to an application's system menu.

```
procedure TForm1.WMSysCommand(var Message: TWMSysCommand);
begin
  case Message.CmdType of
    cm_About: ShowMessage('About command selected!');
  else
    inherited; { Default processing }
  end;
end;
```

This calls the inherited method to process all other system-menu commands.

```
procedure TForm1.FormCreate(Sender: TObject);
var
  MenuH: HMenu;
begin
  MenuH := GetSystemMenu(Handle, False);
  AppendMenu(MenuH, mf_String, cm_About, 'About...');
  MenuH := GetSystemMenu(Application.Handle, False);
  AppendMenu(MenuH, mf_String, cm_About, 'About...');
end;
```

Add the command to the form and the application windows.

NOTE When you minimize an application in Windows 95, it appears as a button on the taskbar rather than an icon as in Windows 3.1. Clicking the taskbar with the left mouse button reopens the application. Clicking the taskbar with the right mouse button opens the system menu. The preceding technique works for both Windows 95 and Windows 3.1 system menus.

In Listing 5-4, the WMSysCommand procedure demonstrates how to handle a message in a form class. The procedure receives a TWmSysCommand variable that describes a message's contents. In this variable, field CmdType represents the value of a selected command. If that value equals our cm_About constant, a *case* statement calls ShowMessage to display a dialog box. To perform default processing for other system menu commands, the procedure calls *inherited* for unhandled CmdType values.

The form's OnCreate event handler demonstrates how to get the window handle for a system menu. The procedure stores this handle in a variable, MenuH, of type HMenu (handle to a menu). First, GetSystem-Menu returns the menu handle for the form window — the Handle argument in this statement belongs to the form. The Windows Append-Menu function adds the *About...* command to this menu.

Next, the OnCreate event handler repeats the preceding two steps, but this time, the program passes the Handle from the Application object to GetSystemMenu. This is necessary to modify the system menu for a minimized application, for which the form window is hidden from view.

Portable Menus

Many application menus have similar commands, and you can save time by developing portable menus for sharing among multiple programs. There are two basic tools for creating portable menus: templates and resources.

Menu Templates

Delphi has several built-in menu templates that you can import into MainMenu and PopupMenu objects. Simply insert one of those objects into a form, and double-click it to open the Menu Designer. Click the right mouse button or press Alt+F10 to open a floating pop-up menu, and select *Insert From Template*. Choose your menu poison (a stock *File* menu, for example).

After inserting a menu template, it's a good idea to rename all the menu item objects. This takes only a few moments, but greatly con-tributes to readable code. *Always do this before writing statements that refer to objects by name.*

If you import a menu template into a PopupMenu object, Delphi creates a nested menu as though the floating pop-up menu were a menu bar turned on its side. Try this! It's a good interface technique that's not often used.

You can also save any menu as a template. Use the Menu Designer's *Save as Template* command to store your favorite menus with stock templates. Delphi stores menu templates in the Delphi.Dmt file, located in the C:\Delphi\Bin directory. It is not clear at this point in Delphi's young life what will happen to custom templates in future Delphi revisions, but we'll all cross that bridge when Borland builds it. (Just between you and me, I'd like to have Delphi store custom menu and other templates in a Template subdirectory for easier preservation during future reinstallations.)

Name properties and event handlers are not stored with menu templates because these will likely be different in each application. Menu templates are strictly MenuItem objects. They don't contain any code. If you need to save code with your menu templates, create a test program for each menu, and then after importing the template into a new application, copy and paste statements from the test module.

MENU RESOURCE SCRIPTS

Another way to create portable menus is to design them the "old-fashioned way," using resource script commands. You can also use this technique to import menus from other applications — those developed in C or C++, for example.

Listings 5-5 and 5-6 show a sample menu script. Multimen.Inc is an include file that defines constants to represent menu items. Multimen.Mnu is a resource script that declares the menu's text and layout. You can find both files in the Multimenu subdirectory on this book's CD-ROM.

Listing 5-5
Multimen.Inc

```
const
    id_Menu     = 100;
    cm_FileMenu = 101;
    cm_FileExit = 102;
```

To use the Multimen.Mnu script, insert a MainMenu or PopupMenu object into a form. Double-click the object to open the Menu Designer, and select the *Insert From Resource* command. Open the .Mnu script file.

(By the way, this is how I created the nested menu for the MultiMen application in this chapter.)

After importing a menu script into a Delphi application, use the Menu Designer to modify your menu's commands. You cannot easily modify the original script and merge it back into the application.

Delphi's menu script loader is nonstandard in one way. All menu items on a menu bar *must* have at least one command item. Windows, however, permits a menu item with no commands on a menu bar. Selecting the command-less item does not open a menu window but immediately executes the item as a command.

Listing 5-6
Multimen.Mnu

```
#include multimen.inc

id_Menu MENU
BEGIN
  POPUP "&File"
  BEGIN
    MENUITEM "E&xit", cm_FileExit
  END
  POPUP "&Edit"
  BEGIN
    MENUITEM "&Undo", 201
    MENUITEM "&Redo", 202
    POPUP "&Search"
    BEGIN
      MENUITEM "&Ignore case", 301, CHECKED
      POPUP "&Find"
      BEGIN
        MENUITEM "&Previous", 401
        MENUITEM "&Whole words", 402
        MENUITEM "&Partial words", 403
      END
      MENUITEM "&Replace", 303
    END
  END
END
```

Because Delphi does not permit command-less menus, a resource script cannot have two POPUP commands in succession, as in this example:

```
POPUP "&Demo"
POPUP "&Help"
```

Menus with no commands are unusual, and this problem is a minor one. However, Borland Pascal 7.0 and most C and C++ development systems support command-less menus, and you may find an occasional resource script that Delphi cannot read.

Menu Designer Tips

Delphi's Menu Designer has an intuitive interface that's easy to master. However, following are a few tips that may be less than obvious:

- Press Ins to insert a blank menu item ahead of the currently high-lighted one. Highlight a menu bar item and press Ins to insert a new pop-up menu in the menu bar.

- Press Del to delete a menu item. *Be careful when pressing Del — you cannot undo a menu deletion.*

- Enter a single hyphen into a menu item's Caption to display a separator line. This line appears in the correct size in the form and in the runtime window, but in the Menu Designer, the separator is as tall as a normal menu command so you can select and edit it as any other menu item.

- To create a nested menu, highlight any menu item and press Ctrl+right-arrow. Press Esc to return to a previous level, or use the mouse and the arrow keys to navigate through the menu.

- Drag and drop menu items to rearrange them. Try this with a sample menu; it's the easiest way to perform major surgery on a menu's layout.

Summary

- Use the MainMenu object to create main-window menu bars.

- Use the PopupMenu object to create floating pop-up menus that appear when users click the right mouse button. You can also call the Popup method to display floating pop-up menus at any screen location.

■ All items in MainMenu and PopupMenu objects are objects of the TMenuItem class. Assign values to CheckMark, Visible, and Enable properties (and others) in TMenuItem objects to create dynamic menus.

■ Use the Items property in MainMenu, PopupMenu, and MenuItem objects to access any MenuItem objects that the three types of menu objects contain. Limit array index values to the range 0 to Count - 1. Items is a TMenuItem, which has an array property; thus you may call methods such as Insert for Items, or you can use it as an array.

■ Use standard accelerator ShortCut keys when possible. You may assign just about any key combination as an accelerator shortcut. For fine-tuning shortcut key assignments at runtime, use the ShortCut, ShortCutToKey, TextToShortCut, and ShortCutToText functions described in this chapter.

■ The easiest way to create dynamic menus is to insert multiple Main-Menu objects in a form and assign them at runtime to the Menu property. You can also assign PopupMenu objects to a form's Popup-Menu property.

■ Another easy method for creating dynamic menus is to set the Visible property in MenuItem objects True and False. This makes menu items — or even entire menus on the menu bar — appear and disappear under program control.

■ Use the Add, Delete, Insert, and Remove methods to modify menu items at runtime. For example, you can use these procedures to insert filenames at the bottom of a *File* menu. However, I find it easier to create dummy menu items for this purpose and set their Visible properties to True as users open new files.

■ You may create new TMenuItem objects at runtime. Call the Create method to create each object, and use Add or Insert to inject the item into a menu. Assign an event handler procedure to the item's OnClick event.

■ Merge multiple MainMenu objects by setting MenuItem GroupIndex values and AutoMerge properties as described in this chapter. You may merge MainMenu objects in the same form, or in different forms. MDI and OLE applications use different menu merging techniques.

- It's tricky to do, but you can add commands to an application's system menu. Because of the way Delphi constructs forms, however, you must add commands to the main-form's window and to the application, which Windows displays when the application is minimized on the desktop or on the Windows 95 taskbar.

- Use menu templates and resource scripts to create portable menus for sharing among multiple applications. You can also create your own menu templates.

Projects to Try

5-1: Write a program for a standard File menu template. Add code from this chapter to implement *Open, Save, Save as,* and other commands. Also add code from the FileMenu sample application to append file-names to the bottom of the menu. Save the result as a shell for beginning new file-related projects (very useful for prototypes).

5-2: Modify the FileMenu sample application to permit users to specify the number of displayed names in the *File* menu.

5-3: *Advanced.* Write a program that lets users build a new menu at run-time. Include commands for entering accelerator shortcut keys.

5-4: Advanced. Using your code from project 5-3, write menus in resource script form for importing into Delphi applications.

Expert-User Tips

- Although MenuItems are components, you cannot select them all in the form window to program shared properties and events. To create a shared event for multiple MenuItem objects, write one procedure for the first or any other item, and assign it to the other objects one by one in the Object Inspector window. There doesn't seem to be any easier way to do this. Alternatively, you can assign procedures to the objects' OnClick event at runtime — perhaps in the form's OnCreate handler.

- Increment MenuItem Tag fields in the object's OnClick event handlers. Print these values before the program terminates for a report on menu command usage. Use this data to better organize menu items — putting more frequently used commands on top, for example.

- Insert a *copy* of a selected menu command into the top of a menu. As users select commands, they tend to appear nearer the top of the menu window. You might use this technique to make frequently selected commands more readily accessible — font names, for example.

- In the Menu Designer, set a MenuItem object's Break property to mbBarBreak (vertical separator) or to mbBreak (no separator) to create horizontally-segmented pop-up menus. View the resulting menu in the form — you see no visible change in the Menu Designer. These features are rarely used in Windows software, but are handy for building some types of complex menus, especially those with numerous commands that cause the menu window to extend far beyond the window's bottom border.

- Use the Alignment property in PopupMenu objects to alter the location of the menu window relative to the mouse cursor. For example, set Alignment to paCenter to center the top of the window at the mouse cursor. Alignment works only with floating pop-up menus assigned to a form's PopupMenu property.

Coming Up

Delphi makes a science out of the lowly Windows button control, as you'll discover in the next chapter. Of course, you can use Delphi components to create standard issue buttons, check boxes, and radio buttons. For a more modern user interface, Delphi provides a RadioGroup object that simplifies radio-button organization, and a SpinButton with up- and down-arrow controls. You can select from several BitBtn objects that use colorful *glyphs* to add icons to button faces. You can even animate button gylphs for a truly fancy display.

6 Attaching Buttons and Check Boxes

*B*uttons and check boxes are the nuts and bolts of a graphical user interface, and Delphi provides a virtual toolchest of pushbuttons, radio buttons, check boxes, speed buttons, and bitmap-buttons. You can assemble groups of button objects, and you can use organizational components such as bevels and panels to arrange a busy window full of buttons and other controls.

In this chapter, I'll explain how to use Delphi's button objects and related components such as GroupBox, RadioGroup, SpinEdit, and Spin-Button. I'll also explain how to create and use colorful bitmap images, called *glyphs,* that appear on BitBtn and SpeedButton components. You can also display glyphs in SpinButton controls.

 This chapter introduces the SpeedButton and Panel components. See the next chapter for more information on using these components to construct toolbars and status panels.

Components

- Bevel — This purely visual component looks like a rectangular indentation in a window. A Bevel can also display horizontal and vertical lines — affectionately known to interface designers as *speed bumps* and *dips* — that are useful for dividing a window into sections. Palette: Additional.

- BitBtn — You might call this component "a pushbutton with flair." A BitBtn works like a Button component, but can display a colorful icon, called a glyph, that visually represents the button's action. Palette: Additional.

- Button — This is a standard Windows button control encapsulated in a Delphi component. I'll explain about Buttons in this chapter, but you'll probably want to use BitBtns instead. Palette: Standard.

- CheckBox — This also is a standard Windows control, composed of a label with a box that users can check on and off. It's highly useful for designing dialog boxes with sets of program options. Palette: Standard.

- GroupBox — Another standard Windows control, this component logically groups multiple RadioButtons and other objects. Users can press Tab to move among multiple GroupBoxes, and then press the arrow keys to select from the grouped controls. Also see the RadioGroup component, which simplifies grouping RadioButton objects. Palette: Standard.

- Panel — This component provides a platform for segmenting a busy window and for creating toolbars and status panels (discussed in the next chapter). A Panel object can appear as a raised surface, or it can look indented and have a variety of beveled borders. Panels never receive the input focus. They are purely visual, and serve as containers for other controls. Palette: Panel.

- RadioButton — You can insert multiple RadioButton objects into a GroupBox or Panel component, but in most cases, you'll find the RadioGroup object easier to use for creating RadioButton sets. You can also insert sets of RadioButtons directly into forms. Palette: Standard.

- RadioGroup — This component is similar to a GroupBox, but is easier to use for grouping multiple RadioButton objects. Simply enter strings into a RadioGroup's Items property to create your buttons. Palette: RadioGroup.

- SpeedButton — Usually, you'll use SpeedButtons to create toolbars, as the next chapter explains. However, you can insert individual SpeedButtons in forms. This chapter's Calc32 application — a 32-bit programmer's calculator provided on the book's CD-ROM — uses SpeedButtons this way. Palette: Additional.

- SpinEdit — Located on the Samples VCL palette, this component demonstrates custom component design, but it is also useful in its own right. I'll also explain in this chapter how to use the related SpinButton component. Palette: Samples.

Basic Buttons

Windows offers three standard types of buttons, which Delphi encapsulates in components. The three buttons and their corresponding components are:

- Push buttons — Button
- Check boxes — CheckBox component.
- Radio buttons — RadioButton component

The three types of components recognize similar events. For example, insert statements into an OnClick event handler to perform actions when users select a button, a check box, or a radio button. For finer control over button selection, use the OnMouseDown or OnKeyDown events. You can also program actions for a button's release by creating a procedure for an OnMouseUp event.

Preface any character in a button Caption property with an ampersand to designate an Alt-shortcut accelerator key. For example, users can press Alt+C to select a button with the caption **&Close**. As in menu items, the accelerator key can be any letter in the Caption property. For example, the Caption **E&xit** designates Alt+X as the button's shortcut key.

PUSHBUTTONS

Pushbuttons are easy to use. Just insert a Button object into a form, and assign a string to the Caption property for the button's label. As you have seen in several other examples, to perform actions when users click a button, create an event handler for the button's OnClick event, and insert statements between *begin* and *end*.

For a default button, change the Default property to True. Only one button in a form (usually labeled OK) should be the default, which users can select by pressing Enter. To associate a button (usually labeled Cancel) with the Esc key, set the button's Cancel property to True. Regardless of the Cancel and Default settings, however, you still have to create event handlers for the buttons.

Buttons and other controls assume the form's Font. For a pleasing display, change the form's Font to a TrueType font such as Arial. However, when doing this, be sure to choose a font that is available on all Windows installations. Table 6-1 lists the fonts available on a virgin Windows 95 installation. You can also select different fonts for individual buttons and other controls.

Table 6-1

Windows 95 Installed Fonts. (TrueType fonts are scalable in size; bitmap fonts are also scalable, but look best in their listed point sizes.)

Font	TrueType
Arial	•
Arial Bold	•
Arial Bold Italic	•
Arial Italic	•
Courier 10,12,15	
Courier New	•
Courier New Bold	•
Courier New Bold Italic	•
Courier New Italic	•
Modern	
MS Sans Serif 8,10,12,14,18,24	
MS Serif 8,10,12,14,18,24	
Roman	
Script	
Small Fonts	
Symbol	•
Symbol 8,10,12,14,18,24	
Times New Roman	•
Times New Roman Bold	•
Times New Roman Bold Italic	•
Times New Roman Italic	•
WingDings	•

On rare occasions, you might want to force users to select a particular push button — an OK button, for example. You can't do this by setting the button's Default property to True because users can still press Tab to shift the focus to another button such as Cancel. This can be confusing, especially to novice computer users who, until they gain experience, may fail to notice the faint outline around the focused control.

One solution to this problem is to disable all buttons and other objects on a form by setting their Enabled properties False. To do that, declare an Integer variable I, and use code such as the following:

```
for I := 0 to ComponentCount - 1 do
  if Components[I] is TWinControl then
    TWinControl(Components[I]).Enabled := False;
```

The preceding code accesses the Components array in a form to set the Enabled properties of all control objects to False. An *if* statement tests whether the object *is* a TWinControl (the grandparent class from which control objects such as buttons are derived). If so, the program sets the control's Enabled property False by casting Components[I] to a TWinControl object. The cast is necessary because the Components array's contents are of the general type, TComponent, which doesn't have an Enabled property.

After executing the preceding code, all controls on the form are disabled and displayed in a dim style. To finish the programming, enable one button and change the focus to that button. This is the only button that users can select:

```
OKButton.Enabled := True;    { Enable button and set the focus }
OKButton.SetFocus;           { so pressing Enter selects it. }
```

CHECK BOXES

CheckBox components are among Windows' simplest, but most useful, interface-design tools. Insert a CheckBox object into a form, and set its Checked property True to display a checkmark in the box, or False for no check mark. At runtime, you can detect whether a CheckBox is on or off using code such as this:

```
if MyCheckBox.Checked
  then {do something};
```

A CheckBox is usually an on-and-off toggle, but it can also be a three-way switch that is either on, disabled, or off. A disabled CheckBox has a grayed check mark in its box. To create a three-way CheckBox, set its AllowGrayed property True, and then set State to one of three initial values: cbChecked, cbGrayed, or chUnchecked (the default). Users can now select the CheckBox to turn it on or off, or to disable it.

NOTE

If AllowGrayed is False and State is cbGrayed, a disabled check mark appears in the CheckBox control. Users can select the control to switch it on and off, but they cannot return the check box to its disabled state.

You may color a CheckBox's background by selecting a value for the Color property. For example, set Color to clBtnShadow to color a CheckBox control the same as the system setting for button shadows. Or, select a fixed color such as clOlive from the Color property's drop-down list.

NOTE

You cannot color a Button object as you can a CheckBox. This is a Windows limitation. For more colorful buttons, use BitBtn instead of Button components.

In many cases, you'll create multiple CheckBoxes. I find it's easiest to do this by first inserting one CheckBox object, pressing Ctrl+C to copy it to the clipboard, and then pressing Ctrl+V repeatedly to paste new objects into the form window. (These keys may differ depending on your *Environment* Options — open the *Edit* menu to check.) I then select each object, change its Name and Caption properties, and move each object to its final position.

Radio Buttons

The third and final standard Windows control is a radio button, which Delphi encapsulates in the RadioButton component. Radio buttons are like potato chips — one is never enough, and you will always use at least two RadioButton objects. (A CheckBox is more appropriate than a RadioButton for an individual on/off control.) You can color RadioButton objects as you can CheckBoxes.

When a form contains multiple RadioButton objects, users can toggle only one button at a time on or off. But when you insert multiple *sets* of radio buttons, they function as a single set, which is probably not what you want. The solution is to *group* each set of controls so that users may select one button from each set, and press Tab to shift the focus from one set to another (and to other controls). i'll explain more about grouping control objects in the section "Button Groups," later in this chapter. Also, see "Using Radio Groups" for an alternate radio-button-grouping technique.

RadioButton objects provide a double-click event that is not available for pushbuttons and check boxes. Double-click the OnDblClick event value in the Object Inspector to create the event handler. Users can then single-click the radio button control, or they can double-click the object to perform a different action.

Colorful Buttons

For a more eye-catching display, use a BitBtn object instead of a standard Windows Button. The BitBtn component works like a pushbutton, but it can display a colorful bitmap, called a *glyph,* that reminds users what the button does. Looks may be deceiving, but a little makeup goes a long way, and glyphs can help dress up an otherwise drab window. You can select glyphs from a library of stock images, or you can create your own. You can also choose from several predefined BitBtn objects with default glyphs that represent standard operations such as Yes, No, Close, Help, Ignore, and Retry.

Delphi also provides the SpeedButton component, which is similar to a BitBtn with a glyph bitmap and, usually, no Caption. As the next chapter explains, you can use SpeedButtons and Panels to create toolbars, but you also can insert independent SpeedButtons into a form window. This chapter's Calc32 application — a 32-bit programmer's integer calculator — demonstrates how to use SpeedButtons as individual controls.

BITMAP BUTTONS

The BitBtn component is the first one on the *Additional* VCL palette. The easiest way to use this component is to insert it into a form, and then set its Kind property to one of the values shown in Figure 6-1 —

for example, bkHelp. Set Kind to bkCustom to display your own glyph image or none. If you don't display a glyph on a BitBtn, however, you may as well use a Button component.

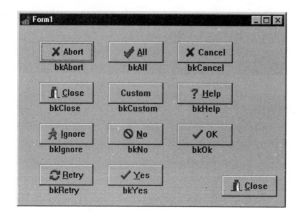

Figure 6-1

A sample form with each type of BitBtn object. Labels show the values inserted into the objects' Kind properties.

If you set a BitBtn's Kind property to bkClose, users can select the button to close its form window. The button does this by internally setting ModalResult to a value such as mrOk. You do not have to write your own code to do this. However, if you do *not* want a Close BitBtn to close the window, first set Kind to bkClose and then change it to bkCustom. The button label and glyph will stay the same, but you can now assign your own event handler to the object's OnClick event.

You may assign an image to a BitBtn object. Double-click the object's Glyph property value to open the Picture Editor. Select *Load* and specify a bitmap file. You'll find a bunch of sample files in Delphi's Images\Buttons directory. After loading a bitmap, select *Save* to copy the image to a new file. Select *OK* to copy the bitmap image to the BitBtn object. These steps also work for SpeedButtons.

You do not have to supply the bitmap file with your application's code file. However, you may want to copy Delphi's bitmap and other files to your development directories in order to build a complete set of source files for your application.

To adjust the location of a BitBtn's glyph relative to its caption, set the Layout property to blGlyphBottom, blGlyphLeft, blGlyphRight, or blGlyph-Top. Try these on sample BitBtn objects to see their effects. For a standard appearance, use the default value blGlyphLeft, which places the glyph to the left of the button caption. Also adjust the Margin property to separate images from button borders — 0 for no separation, 1 for a single pixel space, 2 for two pixels, and so on. To center a glyph, set Margin to –1.

NOTE For more information on glyph bitmaps, see "More About Glyphs," after the next section on SpeedButtons.

Another BitBtn property selects a display style based on the Windows version number. Select one of the following three values (the resulting effects are subtle — if you don't know which value to use, select bsAutoDetect, the default):

- bsAutoDetect — Automatically uses the bsNew style for Windows 95 and the bsWin31 style for Windows 3.1.

- bsNew — Always uses the new Windows 95 button style, with thinner shadow effects on the bottom and right edges.

- bsWin31 — Always uses the Windows 3.1 button style, with denser shadows on the bottom and right edges.

SPEEDBUTTONS

SpeedButton objects usually appear on toolbars, but you can also create individual SpeedButtons as I'll explain here. See the next chapter for more information on using SpeedButtons and Panels to create toolbars.

In general, you program SpeedButton events as you do pushbuttons, but SpeedButtons recognize only five events. Use OnClick and OnDblClick to perform actions for mouse clicks and double-clicks. Use OnMouse-Down, OnMouseMove, and OnMouseUp for finer control over button selection — for example, inspecting the OnMouseDown Shift parameter to determine whether a key was pressed. (See Chapter 4 for information on this parameter's TShiftState data type.)

A SpeedButton's primary advantage over other button types is its capability to function in two manners: as an on/off toggle or as a "sticky" button that stays down when you push it. These characteristics made SpeedButtons the ideal choice for my 32-bit programmer's calculator, which you can find on this book's CD-ROM in the Calc32 directory. Figure 6-2 shows Calc32's display.

Another reason to use SpeedButtons concerns resources. SpeedButtons do not have window handles and associated structures internal to Windows, so a form with a dozen SpeedButtons will use less memory than a dozen standard buttons. SpeedButton objects also display more quickly than standard controls.

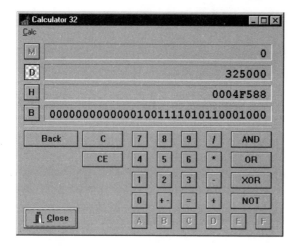

Figure 6-2

To create the Calc32 programmer's calculator, I used SpeedButton objects, which can function as on/off toggles (such as the digit entry keys) and "sticky" buttons that stay down when you click them (such as the Memory, Decimal, Hexadecimal, and Binary buttons under the Calc menu item).

Calc32 is a 32-bit integer calculator, suitable for programming tasks such as figuring out bit patterns and converting between hexadecimal, binary, and decimal. Calc32 is intuitively simple to use. Click the D, H, or B buttons to select decimal, hexadecimal, or binary input. Enter values using the keyboard or by clicking buttons. The display fields near the top of the window always show values in three radices regardless of input mode. Values stored in the memory field (M) are always decimal. Calc32 does not support floating-point values.

Calc32's source code is too long to list entirely here; of course, all source files are on the CD-ROM. I'll refer to sections of the code from time to time. To examine the module, open the Calc32.Dpr project file in the Calc32 directory.

Calc32 demonstrates that SpeedButtons do not have to display glyph images to be useful. To create the program's buttons, I simply entered Captions such as 1, 2, 3, C, and CE, and I set Glyph to None (the default value).

I chose SpeedButtons for Calc32 rather than standard Button components because two or more SpeedButtons can operate like a group of RadioButtons. Assign GroupIndex values to define SpeedButton groups. If GroupIndex equals 0 (the default value), a SpeedButton works like a spring-loaded on/off switch. Other positive GroupIndex values create groups of SpeedButton objects. For example, set a series of SpeedButton GroupIndexes to 3. Users may then select only one SpeedButton in that group, and selecting one button automatically toggles off the currently selected control.

In Calc32, the memory (M), decimal (D), hexadecimal (H), and binary (B) SpeedButtons all have GroupIndex values equal to 1. Selecting one of these buttons pops up one of the others. The selected button stays down until you select another in the group.

One of the problems I had writing Calc32 was assigning event handlers for groups of SpeedButton objects. I wanted to use my own procedure names rather than the ones that Delphi assigns by default. To do that, I performed the following steps:

1. First, I chose one object of the group — for example, the hexadecimal A button.

2. I double-clicked the object to create an event handler named by default, ButtonAClick.

3. Next, I used Delphi's *Search |Replace* command to rename every occurrence of ButtonAClick to DigitButtonClick, which more accurately describes what the procedure does.

4. Finally, I selected all of the buttons in the group, including the original button from step 1. Using the Object Inspector's Events page tab, I set the shared OnClick event to DigitButtonClick.

MORE ABOUT GLYPHS

A glyph is a Windows bitmap displayed on a BitBtn or SpeedButton object. Although there's no restriction on glyph size, the standard image is 16-by-16 pixels, in 16 living colors. In a component, a Glyph property is an object of the TBitmap type.

As shown in Figure 6-3, glyphs may contain from one to four separate images, stored side by side in the bitmap file. Delphi displays each image to represent a different button state:

1. Button state = up (normal display)

2. Button state = Disabled (dimmed; Enabled = False)

3. Button state = Down (shifted and possibly dimmed)

4. Button state = Stay down (SpeedButtons only)

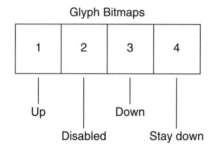

Figure 6-3

Glyph bitmaps may have from one to four side-by-side images, each of which must be equal in width and height (usually 16-by-16 pixels). Each separate image has a different purpose. For example, Delphi uses the second image to display a disabled button.

To display a button in its normal state, Delphi uses the first image. To display a button in its pushed state, Delphi displays the glyph's third image. If the glyph doesn't have a third image, Delphi instead shifts the bitmap down and to the right. Figure 6-4 shows expanded and normal views of the Alarmrng.Bmp file supplied with Delphi. As in this sample image, most glyphs have only two bitmaps. However, you can supply images 3 and 4 to animate a BitBtn or SpeedButton when it's selected.

Figure 6-4
The Alarmrng.Bmp file contains a two-part glyph. Delphi uses the first image for normal, unpushed buttons, and the second image for disabled buttons. Because the bitmap lacks third and fourth images, Delphi shifts the glyph's bits down and to the right to represent pushed button states.

When loading a glyph bitmap, set the NumGlyphs property to the number of images it contains. This must be a value from 1 to 4. Normally, Delphi figures out the correct value from the bitmap's size. For example, Delphi assumes that a 32-bit-wide by 16-bit-tall bitmap contains two 16-by-16 glyphs.

You can assign glyph images when you design a form, or you can load bitmap files at runtime, perhaps to animate a BitBtn or SpeedButton object, or simply to change its appearance based on an external condition. To load a glyph at runtime, insert a BitBtn object into a form, double-click it, and insert these statements into the OnClick event handler:

```
BitBtn1.Glyph.LoadFromFile(
  'c:\delphi\images\buttons\alarm.bmp');  { Or use another file }
BitBtn1.NumGlyphs := 2;                    { Important step! }
```

The first statement calls the LoadFromFile procedure for the Glyph object to load the Alarm.Bmp file supplied with Delphi. The second statement sets the number of glyphs to 2.

Always set NumGlyphs to the proper value when loading glyph bitmaps at runtime. Delphi automatically calculates the number of glyphs in a bitmap file only at design time.

You can also assign any TBitMap object to a BitBtn's or SpeedButton's Glyph property. However, it's important to understand that Delphi makes a copy of the bitmap to insert into the button object. *It is your responsibility to delete from memory any original TBitMap objects that you create.* When loading bitmaps from disk files and assigning the resulting bitmap directly to a Glyph property, you do not have to delete anything because the image is copied directly into the object. However, suppose you define a separate TBitMap object, perhaps because you want to use it for more than one purpose. First, declare the TBitMap object, referenced here as MyImage:

```
var
  MyImage: TBitMap;
```

Create the bitmap object in memory by calling the TBitMap class's Create method:

```
MyImage := TBitMap.Create;  { Create MyImage object }
```

You now have an object in memory, referenced by MyImage, into which you can load a bitmap file. You can then assign the object to a BitBtn or a SpeedButton's Glyph property. You can also use MyImage for other purposes. Here's the rest of the code:

```
MyImage.LoadFromFile('c:\delphi\images\buttons\alarm.bmp');
BitBtn1.Glyph := MyImage;
{ ... insert other uses for MyImage here }
MyImage.Free;
```

The first statement calls LoadFromFile for MyImage. The second statement copies the object to a BitBtn's Glyph property. Insert other uses for MyImage where the comment indicates. When you are done using the TBitmap object, free its memory by calling Free. This last step is essential; if you forget to free a TBitmap that you create, portions of it will remain in memory even after the program terminates. Delphi applications automatically free any objects owned by another parent object; however, the program must free any other structures such as bitmap pixels associated with an object. If the program doesn't free such structures, *the only way to recover the lost memory is to exit and restart Windows.*

A glyph's background color equals the color of the single pixel in the lower-left corner. All other pixels in the glyph of that same color are considered to be transparent — in other words, whatever the user selects as the background color for buttons *replaces* the glyph's designated background pixels. If users color their buttons fire-engine red, your glyph backgrounds will be equally red-faced, but at least they'll still appear to float on the button surface. Unfortunately, however, any fixed red pixels will blend in with the button's red color, effectively disappearing. The most effective way to guard against this problem is by using as many different colors as possible in your glyph images. That way, your glyphs will still look right even to users who actually *like* Windows' "Hotdog Stand" desktop color scheme.

HOW TO ANIMATE A GLYPH

You can animate glyph bitmaps to display different images when, for example, users click a BitBtn object. Follow these steps to try out the technique:

1. Insert a BitBtn object into a form. I'll use the default name BitBtn1 here.

2. Select BitBtn1's Glyph property, click the ellipsis button, and load the bitmap file Dooropen.Bmp from Delphi's Images\Buttons directory.

3. Insert the following declarations into the TForm1 class's public section (they could also go in the private section):

```
DoorShutBmp: TBitmap;
DoorOpenBmp: TBitmap;
```

4. Initialize the bitmap objects and load images into them by inserting these statements into the form's OnCreate event:

```
DoorShutBmp := TBitmap.Create;
DoorOpenBmp := TBitmap.Create;
DoorShutBmp.LoadFromFile('c:\delphi\images\buttons\doorshut.bmp');
DoorOpenBmp.LoadFromFile('c:\delphi\images\buttons\dooropen.bmp');
```

5. Free the images by inserting these statements into the form's OnDestroy event handler:

```
DoorShutBmp.Free;
DoorOpenBmp.Free;
```

6. Create a handler for BitBtn1's OnMouseDown event (be sure to select the button object, not the form). Insert this statement into the procedure:

```
BitBtn1.Glyph := DoorShutBmp;
```

7. Create another handler for BitBtn1's OnMouseUp event, and insert this statement into the procedure:

```
BitBtn1.Glyph := DoorOpenBmp;
```

8. Press F9 to run the program. When you click the BitBtn1 object, the door shuts. When you release the mouse, the door opens.

Another way to animate a glyph is by creating one bitmap containing separate images for the button's up and down states. For example, you could combine the Dooropen.Bmp and Doorshut.Bmp bitmap files, and assign the resulting four-part glyph to a BitBtn object. This way, you eliminate the need to load and free individual bitmap objects at runtime.

Button Groups

In busy windows — configuration dialogs, for example — it's a good idea to categorize multiple buttons into groups. There are three general ways to organize button object groups:

- Use Bevel and Panel objects to create sections in a form that appear indented or raised. Insert buttons into these objects.
- Insert buttons into a GroupBox component.
- Create a RadioGroup object, which can automatically generate multiple RadioButtons. Simply enter button labels into the RadioGroup's Items array (more on this later).

USING BEVELS AND PANELS

Bevels and Panels are visual aids that can help you produce an attractive display. The Bevel component is on the *Additional* VCL palette; the Panel component is on the *Standard* palette.

 Panel objects can respond to events such as OnClick and OnMouse-Down. In fact, Panels are akin to simple buttons that don't appear pushed when you click them. The Bevel component is purely visual, and recognizes no events. Panels are also useful for creating toolbars and status panels, as the next chapter explains.

Figure 6-5 shows a default form with a Panel object and a Bevel object. The Panel has a default caption (Panel1 in the figure), but you can delete the Caption property value to display a blank surface.

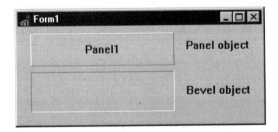

Figure 6-5
A default form with Panel and Bevel objects, which are useful for organizing a busy display into visual sections.

Adjust the BevelOuter, BevelWidth, BorderStyle, and BorderWidth properties for different Panel appearances. Adjust the Shape property to alter Bevel object appearances. (It may seem confusing that Panels use *Bevelxxx* properties to set their appearances, but this is just a naming oddity of no significance. Panels and Bevels are separate types of components.)

Bevels don't have to be boxy. You can also use them to create dividing lines, which some programmers imaginatively call *speed bumps* and *speed dips* because they resemble the traffic control barriers in a supermarket parking lot. For example, set a Bevel object's Shape property to bsBottomLine to display a horizontal speed dip, which is useful for carving a window into top and bottom sections. Use bsLeftLine or bsRightLine to create vertical barriers. Change Style to bsRaised to create speed bumps.

USING GROUP BOXES

A GroupBox is a standard Windows control that Delphi encapsulates in a component. Use GroupBoxes to create sets of check boxes, radio buttons, and other controls. Users can press Tab to move from one GroupBox to another, and they can press arrow keys and the spacebar to select among grouped controls.

GroupBoxes are mostly useful for organizing radio buttons into logical sets. For example, you can insert several radio buttons into each of two GroupBox objects. Users can then select one button from either set. If you don't insert RadioButtons into GroupBoxes, users will be able to select only one of all buttons in the window.

Figure 6-6 shows a default form with two GroupBox objects, each with three RadioButtons. To create this window, insert the two Group-Box components first, and then insert RadioButtons into the GroupBox objects. Clicking the mouse pointer inside the GroupBox to insert a RadioButton (or other control) tells Delphi to associate the inserted object with the GroupBox.

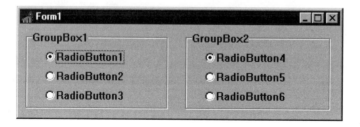

Figure 6-6

To create this window, insert two GroupBox objects into a form, and then insert three RadioButtons into each GroupBox object. This tells Delphi to associate the RadioButtons with their respective groups.

For tabbing to work correctly, at least one RadioButton of each group must be selected. Set the Checked property to True for one RadioButton object in each GroupBox. This is a Windows restriction on grouped radio button controls.

If you insert RadioButtons *before* you create their GroupBoxes, the buttons will not operate as distinct groups. Dragging the RadioButtons into a GroupBox is no help — the objects remain associated with the component in which they were initially dropped (the form or another container control). If you experience this problem, select the RadioButtons, cut them to the clipboard, select the intended GroupBox, and paste the RadioButtons from the clipboard into the selected container. You can also delete the buttons and reinsert them from the VCL palette directly into a GroupBox object, but then you lose whatever property changes you've made to the controls.

To group RadioButton or other control objects at runtime, set the button object's Parent property to a target GroupBox. (You can do this only at runtime because the Parent property is not available in the Object Inspector window.) For example, to associate three RadioButton objects with GroupBox1, use statements such as these, perhaps in a form's OnCreate event handler:

```
RadioButton1.Parent := GroupBox1;
RadioButton2.Parent := GroupBox1;
RadioButton3.Parent := GroupBox1;
RadioButton1.Checked := True;  { Select one grouped button }
```

A good way to tell if RadioButtons are properly grouped is to drag the GroupBox object. If the RadioButtons follow along like ducks behind their mother, they are associated with that group. If not, the buttons are probably associated with the form. Cut and paste the buttons to fix the problem.

You can also group CheckBox objects, but because these controls operate individually, there's usually no good reason to group them. In most cases, it's probably just as well to use Panel or Bevel objects to visually organize sets of CheckBox objects.

To get radio button groups working as you want when users press the Tab key, you'll probably have to fuss with your form's tabbing order. After creating the GroupBox objects and inserting RadioButton controls, select the form and choose *Edit|Tab Order* to set the order in which users can press Tab to move among the groups. Next, select each GroupBox object, and again use *Edit|Tab Order*, but this time, to affect the tab order of the grouped RadioButton objects.

USING RADIO GROUPS

Most developers soon realize that GroupBoxes and RadioButtons are as ornery as bulls in a ring. For a less painful way to create radio button groups, insert a RadioGroup component into a form. *Do not insert RadioButton objects into the RadioGroup.* Instead, select the RadioGroup's Items property, and double-click its value or click the ellipsis button to open Delphi's String list editor. Enter labels for each radio button in the order you want them to appear. That's all you have to do to create sets of RadioButton controls in a RadioGroup object.

Optionally set the RadioGroup's Columns property to the number of columns for displaying RadioButtons. Figure 6-7 shows four radio buttons in a RadioGroup with Columns equal to 1. Figure 6-8 shows the same RadioGroup object with Columns set to 2.

Figure 6-7

Four radio buttons in a RadioGroup with Columns equal to 1.

Figure 6-8

The same buttons from Figure 6-7, but with Columns equal to 2.

Use the ItemIndex property to detect the currently selected button. Set ItemIndex to –1 (the default value) to deselect all buttons in the group. Set it to 0 to select the first button, 1 to select the second button, and so on.

You can also create radio buttons in RadioGroup objects at runtime. For example, use this variable and procedure to let users enter new radio buttons into a group:

```
var
  S: string;
begin
  if InputQuery('Input', 'Enter Radio Button', S) then
    RadioGroup1.Items.Add(S);
end;
```

The Items array is a string list of type TStrings. Call the list's Add method to insert a new string, which also causes the RadioGroup to create a new RadioButton object using the string as a label. The Items Count property equals the number of strings in the Strings property, and therefore, also equals the number of RadioButtons owned by the RadioGroup. ItemIndex equals the currently selected button's index. Use these values to iterate through button labels, as in the following sample statement, which calls AnyProcedure (not shown):

```
for I := 0 to RadioGroup1.Items.Count - 1 do
  AnyProcedure(RadioGroup1.Items.Strings[I]);
```

Alternatively, use a *with* statement to make the preceding code more understandable, and to reduce the two references to RadioGroup1 to one reference:

```
with RadioGroup1, Items do
  for I := 0 to Count - 1 do
    AnyProcedure(Strings[I]);
```

Notice the special syntax for *with,* using commas to separate multiple identifiers. The first line in the preceding example is equivalent to:

```
with RadioGroup1 do with Items do
```

Use ItemIndex to determine the selected button. For example, an *if* statement can take an action for a particular button identified by its label:

```
with RadioGroup1, Items do
  if Strings[ItemIndex] = 'Button2' then...
```

Always set one button to its *on* state for each RadioGroup object; otherwise, users will not be able to press Tab to shift the focus to the group (a Windows oddity). Either set ItemIndex to 0 when you design the RadioGroup object, or insert the following code into the form's OnCreate event handler:

```
with RadioGroup1, Items do
if Count > 0 then
  ItemIndex := 0
else
  ItemIndex := -1;
```

You can also use this code in another event handler for RadioGroups that the program builds at runtime; in which case you must allow for the possibility that the group will have no buttons. In that case, you should set ItemIndex to –1 as demonstrated here.

> **NOTE** The TRadioGroup class descends from TCustomGroupBox, which is the immediate ancestor of TGroupBox. GroupBox rules and regulations therefore apply equally to RadioGroup objects. For example, to enable tabbing between groups, preselect one button in each group by setting ItemIndex to a value from 0 to Items.Count – 1.

RadioGroup objects contain two lists that represent the grouped RadioButtons. The Items array contains a string list of button labels, and is available at design time and at runtime. The Components array, which is available only at runtime, contains references to the actual RadioGroup objects.

To investigate the Components array and related items, insert a RadioGroup object into a form, and enter several button labels into the Item's string list. Insert a Button object and create an OnClick event handler with these statements:

```
with RadioGroup1 do
if ItemIndex >= 0 then
  ShowMessage('You selected ' + Items.Strings[ItemIndex]);
```

Run the program and click the button to display the currently selected radio button's label. Quit and return to Delphi, and then set a debugger breakpoint on the *with* statement. To do that, single-click the mouse cursor at the extreme left of the line, or move the flashing keyboard cursor to the line and select *Run|Add Breakpoint*. Either way, Delphi colors the statement stop-sign red, which indicates that the program will halt just before this statement executes.

Run the program again, and click the button. The program halts at the breakpoint. Move the flashing cursor to anywhere in the RadioButton1 identifier, and press Ctrl+F7 to open the debugger's *Evaluate/Modify* dialog. You should see RadioGroup1 in the *Expression* field and a list of property values in the *Result* box. If not, enter *RadioGroup1* in the *Expression* field. This is a useful technique listing members of objects that are not publicly available through the Object Inspector window.

Lengthy lists of values in objects and records are difficult to decipher in the *Evaluate/Modify* dialog. To display each property by name along with its value, enter ",R" (don't type the quotes) after the identifier in the *Expression* field. For example, if you are following along, type the expression *RadioGroup1,R* and press Enter.

You should now see the following values, plus lots of others, in the *Evaluate/Modify* dialog. The property name is followed by its associated class method. For example, here are the first two lines from the *Result* field:

```
Components:<GetComponent>;
ComponentCount:<GetComponentCount>;
```

The Components array contains the RadioButton objects that belong to the RadioGroup. ComponentCount equals the number of those objects. Use these two values to access individual RadioButtons in the RadioGroup object. For example, to set the Checked property to False for all RadioButtons in a group, you can use a *for* loop such as this:

```
with RadioGroup1 do
for I := 0 to ComponentCount - 1 do
  TRadioButton(Components[I]).Checked := False;
```

Or, to switch on a particular button, use this statement:

```
with RadioGroup1 do
  TRadioButton(Components[2]).Checked := True;
```

When referring to the Components array, you must tell the compiler what type of objects the array contains. Do that by using the class name (TRadioButton here) as though it were a function that returns an object of the specified type. Pass the indexed Components reference to this *type cast* construction. You can then access object properties such as Checked.

If you are following along, get back to Delphi, and press F9 to continue running the program, which is paused at the breakpoint. Quit the program to return to Delphi's design mode. You can then remove the breakpoint or start a new project.

RadioGroups are also useful for designing opinion-survey, option, and multiple-choice forms. Create several RadioGroup objects, and enter blank spaces, punctuation marks, digits or any other characters into the Items array. In this case, you probably don't want full labels — you just want to display the RadioButton control's circles. Set the Columns property equal to the number of buttons, and shrink the RadioGroup object as small as possible. Figure 6-9 shows a hypothetical example that uses RadioGroups for a pychological profile inspired by a psychologist friend who hands out similar tests at parties.

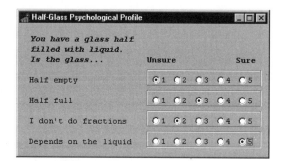

Figure 6-9
RadioGroups are useful for creating multiple choice quizzes and opinion surveys as in this hypothetical profile.

Delphi's documentation states that you can put other types of controls (other than radio buttons) into a TRadioGroup object. This is incorrect. You can insert only radio buttons into a RadioGroup object.

OTHER KINDS OF RADIO GROUPS

As you may know, you can insert RadioButton objects directly into form windows. If you need only one set of RadioButtons, you don't have to insert them into a GroupBox and you don't need to use a RadioGroup object. Just insert as many RadioButtons as you need into any form.

Although it's not widely known (but not exactly a big secret), you can also group multiple RadioButton objects in Panel components. Try this: Insert two Panels into a form, and then insert several RadioButtons into each panel. Set the Checked property of one RadioButton in each group to True. Run the program. As this experiment shows, there's no operational difference between a GroupBox and a Panel — at least in terms of their capability for grouping together multiple RadioButtons. A GroupBox caption, however, appears on its top border — a Panel displays its caption inside, and you'll probably have to erase it to make room for RadioButtons and other controls.

One advantage in using Panels as group boxes is the Panel component's 3D graphics capability, which the GroupBox lacks. As Figure 6-10 illustrates, you can use Panels to create fancy RadioButton sets. The Fancy application, which has no significant code, is in the Fancy directory.

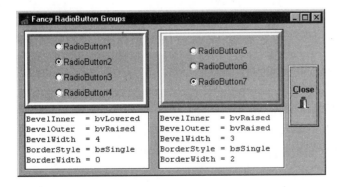

Figure 6-10

The Fancy sample application demonstrates how to use Panel objects to create 3D RadioButton groups. The text below each set of RadioButtons shows the property values that produce the illustrated 3D effects.

It's also possible to insert objects of *different* types into GroupBox and Panel components. For example, a Panel might contain three RadioButtons and two CheckBoxes. Users can press Tab to move among the groups, and the end result might be useful in programs that are largely keyboard driven. Because users select CheckBoxes individually, however, inserting them into GroupBox and Panel components isn't usually advantageous.

Spin Buttons

The *Samples* page tab on the VCL palette provides two extra button components that come in handy in many applications. The two components are:

- SpinButton — A double component with up and down buttons. Clicking one of the buttons calls the OnDownClick or OnUpClick event handler.
- SpinEdit — A SpinButton attached to an edit field. Clicking the button's up or down arrows increases or decreases an integer value in the edit field. Users can also enter values into this field, which also recognizes cut, copy, and paste commands.

USING SPINBUTTON COMPONENTS

Insert a SpinButton component into a form and insert code into its OnDownClick and OnUpClick event handlers. To follow along, also insert a Label object into the form, and declare the following variable in the TForm1 class's private section:

```
private
  Count: Integer;
```

Create a handler for the form's OnCreate event and initialize Count to zero:

```
Count := 0;
```

Next, create event handlers for the SpinButton's OnDownClick and OnUpClick events. Use the programming in Listing 6-1 to increment and decrement Count, and to display Count's value in the label.

Listing 6-1

Use a SpinButton component and this programming in the OnDownClick and OnUpClick events to increment and decrement a Count variable and display it in a Label object.

```
procedure TForm1.SpinButton1DownClick(Sender: TObject);
begin
  Dec(Count);
  Label1.Caption := IntToStr(Count);
end;

procedure TForm1.SpinButton1UpClick(Sender: TObject);
begin
  Inc(Count);
  Label1.Caption := IntToStr(Count);
end;
```

Converts an integer to a string.

Use the UpGlyph and DownGlyph properties in the SpinButton component to display glyphs for the object's up and down buttons. Either select from Delphi's stock arrow bitmaps, or create your own glyphs.

SpinButton glyphs may not contain multiple images, and therefore, to use Delphi's supplied bitmaps (which all contain double images) you must convert them to single-image glyphs. Do that by copying the files you want to another directory — the Arrow1d.Bmp and Arrow1u.Bmp files, for example, from Delphi's Images\Buttons directory. Open these files in the Image Editor from the *Tools* menu. For each file, select *Image|Attributes*, change *Width* from 32 to 16 (or make it equal to *Height*), and deselect *Scale image to fit.* You can then save the converted image. This is the easiest way I've found to chop down a multi-image glyph to a single-image bitmap.

Of course, you can also create your own glyphs using any bitmap editor. Either way, you can now insert your glyphs into a SpinButton object. For example, try these steps:

1. Insert a SpinButton object from the *Samples* page tab on the VCL Palette. Be sure to select the SpinButton component, not SpinEdit.

2. Click the DownGlyph property's ellipsis to open the Image Editor. Load a modified down-arrow image file such as Arrow1d.Bmp.

3. Repeat step 2 for the UpGlyph property to load the modified Arrow1u.Bmp.

4. Depending on the glyph bitmap sizes, you may have to adjust the SpinButton object's dimensions to show the glyphs in full.

USING SPINEDIT COMPONENTS

The SpinEdit component combines a SpinButton with an Edit input field to create a spin button with full editing capabilities, including cut, copy, and paste commands. Figure 6-11 shows sample SpinEdit and SpinButton objects from the SpinButt application. Listing 6-2 shows the application's source code.

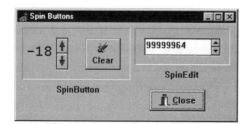

Figure 6-11

The SpinButt sample application shows SpinEdit and SpinButton objects.

Listing 6-2

Spinbutt\Main.Pas

```
unit Main;

interface

uses
    SysUtils, WinTypes, WinProcs, Messages, Classes, Graphics, Controls,
    Forms, Dialogs, Spin, StdCtrls, ExtCtrls, Buttons;
```

```
type
  TMainForm = class(TForm)
    SpinButton1: TSpinButton;
    Label1: TLabel;
    SpinEdit1: TSpinEdit;
    SpinEdit: TLabel;
    SpinLabel: TLabel;
    BitBtn1: TBitBtn;
    Bevel1: TBevel;
    Bevel2: TBevel;
    BitBtn2: TBitBtn;
    procedure FormCreate(Sender: TObject);
    procedure SpinButton1DownClick(Sender: TObject);
    procedure SpinButton1UpClick(Sender: TObject);
    procedure BitBtn1Click(Sender: TObject);
    procedure SetSpinButtonCaption;
  private
    { Private declarations }
    Count: Integer;
  public
    { Public declarations }
  end;

var
  MainForm: TMainForm;

implementation

{$R *.DFM}

const
  minCount = -99;
  maxCount = 99;

procedure TMainForm.SetSpinButtonCaption;
begin
  SpinLabel.Caption := IntToStr(Count);
end;

procedure TMainForm.FormCreate(Sender: TObject);
begin
  Count := 0;
end;

procedure TMainForm.SpinButton1DownClick(Sender: TObject);
begin
  if Count > minCount then Dec(Count);
  SetSpinButtonCaption;
end;
```

```
procedure TMainForm.SpinButton1UpClick(Sender: TObject);
begin
  if Count < maxCount then Inc(Count);
  SetSpinButtonCaption;
end;

procedure TMainForm.BitBtn1Click(Sender: TObject);
begin
  Count := 0;
  SetSpinButtonCaption;
end;

end.
```

The SpinEdit component has an internal Button object of the Spin-Button type. (The name Button is an unfortunate choice — it is *not* a Button component, but rather a SpinButton object *named* Button.) Use a SpinEdit's Button as you do a stand-alone SpinButton. For example, to assign up and down glyph images of type TBitmap, you can insert statements such as these:

```
SpinEdit1.Button.UpGlyph := NewUpGlyph;
SpinEdit2.Button.DownGlyph := NewDownGlyph;
```

Summary

- Windows provides three types of standard buttons — pushbuttons, check boxes, and radio buttons. Delphi encapsulates these standard controls into Button, CheckBox and RadioButton components.

- Use the form's Components array to access all objects — for example, to disable all but one button control in a window.

- CheckBoxes normally operate as on/off toggles, but they can also be three-way switches by setting AllowGrayed True. Users can then check the box to enable, disable, and gray its check mark.

- You may color CheckBox and RadioButton controls, but due to a limitation in Windows, you may not color Button objects. For a more colorful button, use the BitBtn component instead.

- BitBtn and SpeedButton components can display bitmap glyphs that represent a control's purpose. A glyph is a Windows bitmap, represented as a TBitmap object, and is usually 16-by-16-pixels in 16 colors. However, there are no restrictions on a glyph's size. A glyph may have from one to four separate images that represent a button's various states.

- SpeedButton objects normally appear in toolbars (see the next chapter), but as this chapter's Calc32 application demonstrates, you also can use SpeedButtons as stand-alone objects.

- Use the GroupBox component to logically group multiple controls. GroupBoxes usually contain RadioButton objects, but they may contain other controls. Users can press Tab to move the focus from one GroupBox to another.

- Use the RadioGroup component for a simpler method of creating sets of RadioButtons. Enter button labels into the RadioGroup's Items property.

- Panel and Bevel objects are purely visual components, but they are useful for organizing a busy display full of buttons and other controls.

- The *Samples* page tab on the VCL palette provides two additional button controls, SpinButton and SpinEdit. Assign your own glyphs to these objects' DownGlyph and UpGlyph properties to display custom up and down arrows or other shapes.

Projects to Try

6-1: Write a program that displays Bevel and Panel objects in many possible configurations. You'll find this useful as a guide to creating new Bevels and Panels in applications. Your program should allow users to input object properties and instantly see their effects.

6-2: Modify Calc32 to use double-precision 64-bit integer values. Hint: Use the Comp data type.

6-3: Create glyphs for Calc32's SpeedButtons and generally spruce up the calculator's user interface.

6-4: Try the animation technique suggested in this chapter. First, combine the Doorshut.Bmp and Dooropen.Bmp files using Delphi's Image editor. The resulting file should contain four separate glyph images, each of the size 16-by-16 pixels. Assign the modified glyph to a BitBtn object and run the program — the door will shut when you click the button. You might want to start a library of animated glyph images.

6-5: Write a glyph catalog program (GlyphCat) that displays all the glyph patterns in Delphi's Images\Buttons directory.

6-6: Write a program that displays four SpeedButton objects showing the four possible states of its glyph bitmap (use the AllowAllUp, Down, and Enabled properties). To the SpeedButtons, assign a glyph bitmap at runtime, perhaps selected from a file directory.

6-7: *Advanced.* Write a floating-point calculator, using Calc32 as a guide. Use the Double (8-byte) or Extended (10-byte) data types to store values internally.

Expert-User Tips

▪ A GroupBox can have a PopupMenu separate from a form's PopupMenu. Assign any PopupMenu object to a GroupBox's PopupMenu property, similar to the way you designate a form's PopupMenu. Using multiple GroupBox objects in a form is a good way to design multiple floating pop-up menus that depend on where users click the right mouse button.

▪ To create buttons that appear and disappear in response to commands or various program conditions, set a button's Visible property to True or False. You may do this for any of the components described in this chapter, as well as most other Delphi components.

▪ Enter text into a SpeedButton's Hint property, and set ShowHint to True. Users will then see a small hint box when they rest the mouse cursor on the button.

▪ Use a BitBtn's Spacing property to adjust the amount of space between a glyph image and the button's caption. The default value is 4. Use –1 to center the text between the image and the button edge. Set Spacing to 0 if you want no extra pixels between the image and the text. The SpeedButton component, which has no Caption, also has a Spacing property that you can use to adjust glyph placement.

- Although Panels are most useful as purely visual objects, you may create event handlers for them. For example, create an OnClick handler to perform an action when users click a Panel object. Another highly useful event is OnResize, typically used for Panels aligned to a window's client area. When users resize the window, the Panel's OnResize event handler can adjust the positions of controls inside its window.

- The SpinButton component described in this chapter uses an object of the undocumented TTimerSpeedButton class. Based on TSpeedButton, a TTimerSpeedButton creates a Timer object that repeatedly simulates a button click while you hold down the mouse. The component does this by calling its own Click method, which simulates an OnClick event. See the Spin.Pas file in Delphi's Source\Samples directory for the source code to the TTimerSpeedButton class.

- Any container control can group radio buttons, check boxes, and other component objects. For example, if you want two radio button groups without borders, use TPanels as the containers and turn off their borders.

Coming Up

The next chapter explains how to use SpeedButton and Panel components to create toolbars and status panels — two interface elements that practically every Windows application should have.

7 Creating Toolbars and Status Panels

O ne of the hallmarks of a well-written Windows program is a *toolbar* of speed buttons for quickly selecting commands with a mouse. Toolbar buttons are to the mouse what hot keys are to the keyboard — shortcuts for power users who don't want to waste time opening menus to select commands.

A related interface element is a *status panel,* which usually appears at the bottom of a window, and is often divided into multiple sections. For example, a text editor's status panel might display the line and column numbers for the current cursor position. Or, a panel can display the date and time to remind clock-watchers how late they are on their deadlines.

This chapter explains how to create toolbars and status panels with the Panel and SpeedButton components introduced in the preceding chapter. I'll also explain how to use the Header component, which is not well documented in Delphi's printed manuals.

Components

- Header — Similar to a plain raised Panel, a Header is a multisectional object suitable for status panels. You and your program's users can resize a Header's sections by clicking and dragging with the mouse. You can also build new sections into a Header object when you design the program, or at run-time. Palette: Additional.

- Panel — Use this component to create a platform for building tool-bars and status panels. You can alter the platform's 3D appearance to make it look like an indented crater or a raised plateau. A Panel is a *container object.* When used as a toolbar, a Panel holds Speed-Button objects. Panel objects may also contain other panels and text to build sectional display areas. Palette: Standard.

- SpeedButton — This chapter explains how to use SpeedButtons to build toolbars. See the preceding chapter for more information on this component's properties and events. Palette: Additional.

Toolbars

Figure 7-1 shows a sample toolbar for the Tabs application on the CD-ROM. Although the program's source code is too lengthy to list entirely here, all source files are on the CD-ROM. Open the Tabs.Dpr project file to inspect the modules.

The Tabs application inserts and removes tab control codes from text files, and can also convert files with different tab settings. For example, Tabs can convert a file that uses four-space tabs to one that uses standard eight-space tabs. To use the program, select the Convert, Remove, or Insert SpeedButtons, then click the Open button to open a file. Answer Yes to process the file. *Always keep a separate backup copy of processed source code files.* Use the Options commands and buttons to configure the program. By the way, I originally wrote Tabs in Turbo Vision for DOS using Turbo Pascal. It took only a few hours work to convert the program for Delphi. All of the user-interface programming is new, but the tab-processing procedures and functions are largely unchanged.

CREATING A TOOLBAR

A toolbar consists of a Panel object and one or more SpeedButtons. To create a toolbar, first insert a Panel component into a form. The default Panel Height value is 41. I prefer 25, but you can use any value you want. Assign an appropriate Name to the Panel such as ToolbarPanel. This is the name that Tabs uses.

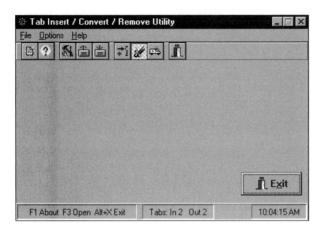

Figure 7-1

The Tabs application removes and inserts tab control codes in text files, and can also convert tab interval settings. This chapter uses Tabs to demonstrate toolbar and status panel techniques.

Set the ToolbarPanel's Align property to alBottom or alTop, depending on whether you want the toolbar to appear at the top or bottom of the window. You can also design toolbars to appear at the left (alLeft) or right (alRight) borders, although the standard location is at the top of the window's client area, just below the window's menu bar.

For a toolbar with two or more rows of SpeedButtons, insert multiple panels into a form and set their Align properties to alTop. This stacks the panels like appliances under a countertop. You can then insert SpeedButtons into the Panel objects.

After creating the Panel, delete its Caption and insert as many SpeedButton objects as you need. I name my SpeedButtons OpenSB and ConfigSB, which reminds me of the object component types. Create OnClick event handlers for them. Or, share handlers with menu commands and buttons. That's all you need to do to create a toolbar of SpeedButtons. Simple, no?

However, there's more to toolbar management than meets the eye. You'll probably want to add Hint text. Type a brief description in each SpeedButton's Hint property, and set ShowHint to True. A small information box will then pop into view when the mouse cursor rests on the button for about a second. Always add hints to your toolbar buttons — they go a long way toward making programs easy to use.

Panels also respond to their own events. For example, you can create an OnClick event handler for a Panel object to perform an action when the user clicks inside the Panel. Later in this chapter, I'll explain how to use this feature to create a floating toolbar that users can click and drag around the window. In general, however, it's probably best *not* to handle events for Panels — users intuitively know that they can click buttons in toolbars, but providing a clickable toolbar might be more confusing than helpful.

SPEEDBUTTON OPERATIONS

When designing a toolbar, consider whether you need spring-loaded buttons that pop back up as soon as you release the mouse button, or a set of objects that operate like radio buttons. For example, you can create a "sticky" SpeedButton that stays down when pushed; and you can also create SpeedButton sets in which clicking one button deselects another.

A spring-loaded SpeedButton is the easiest to create. Just insert a SpeedButton object into a toolbar Panel, and create a handler for its OnClick event. (See the preceding chapter for more information on programming SpeedButtons, assigning them glyph bitmaps, and animating button images.) Spring-loaded buttons are useful for operations such as opening a file, printing, and other tasks that commence immediately.

Alternatively, you can create an on/off SpeedButton that stays down when you click it, and then pops up when you click it again. This type of sticky toolbar button is useful for options that select program features. In a word processor, for example, a sticky SpeedButton might choose text styles such as bold face, italics, and underlining. Click the button once to convert selected text to bold; click the button again to return text to normal.

Follow these steps to create a sticky on/off SpeedButton:

1. Set the SpeedButton's GroupIndex to any nonzero value that no other control in the toolbar uses.

2. Set the SpeedButton's AllowAllUp property to True.

3. Optionally set the SpeedButton's Down property to True to display the button initially in its pressed state.

A sample application, Toolbar1, demonstrates spring-loaded and sticky SpeedButtons. Figure 7-2 shows the program's display. The left SpeedButton is sticky; it stays down when you click it. Do that now and select Close, which prompts you for confirmation before ending the program, as shown in Figure 7-3. Release the left SpeedButton to exit normally without displaying a message dialog. Listing 7-1 shows the program's source code.

Figure 7-2
The Toolbar1 demonstration uses two SpeedButtons in a simple toolbar. The left button is a sticky SpeedButton that stays down when you click it. When that button is down, clicking an exit button displays the message dialog in Figure 7-3.

Figure 7-3
When the toolbar's leftmost SpeedButton is down, Toolbar1 requests confirmation before ending.

Listing 7-1

Toolbar1\Main.Pas

```pascal
unit Main;

interface

uses
  SysUtils, WinTypes, WinProcs, Messages, Classes, Graphics, Controls,
  Forms, Dialogs, StdCtrls, Buttons, ExtCtrls;

type
  TMainForm = class(TForm)
    Panel1: TPanel;
    PromptSB: TSpeedButton;
    ExitSB: TSpeedButton;
    CloseBitBtn: TBitBtn;
    Label1: TLabel;
    Bevel1: TBevel;
    procedure ExitSBClick(Sender: TObject);
    procedure FormActivate(Sender: TObject);
  private
    { Private declarations }
  public
    { Public declarations }
  end;

var
  MainForm: TMainForm;

implementation

{$R *.DFM}

procedure TMainForm.ExitSBClick(Sender: TObject);
begin
  if not PromptSB.Down then
    Close
  else if MessageDlg('Exit program?',mtConfirmation,
    [mbYes, mbNo], 0) = mrYes then
    Close;
end;

procedure TMainForm.FormActivate(Sender: TObject);
begin
  ExitSB.Glyph := CloseBitBtn.Glyph;
end;

end.
```

True if the PromptSB SpeedButton is pressed.

"Steal" the Close BitBtn's bitmap glyph for the ExitSB SpeedButton.

Toolbar1's Main.Pas module demonstrates two interesting techniques for working with SpeedButtons. For a sticky button, you can use an *if* statement to detect whether the button is down. For example, see the first line in procedure ExitSBClick, which executes a statement if the PromptSB button is *not* down:

```
if not promptSB.Down then ...
```

Secondly, the module shows how to steal a glyph from another object for displaying on a SpeedButton's face. Notice in Figure 7-2 that the SpeedButton on the right and the Close pushbutton have the same glyph. The SpeedButton steals this image at runtime by executing the following statement in the form's OnActivate event handler:

```
ExitSB.Glyph := CloseBitBtn.Glyph;
```

SpeedButton Groups

To create a set of sticky SpeedButtons that operate like radio buttons, select all buttons in the group and set their GroupIndex properties to any nonzero value that is not used by any other toolbar control. With this setup, clicking an unselected button causes the currently selected button to pop back up.

Initially, all buttons may be in the up state. Once users click a button, however, at least one button will always be down. If you want users to be able to deselect *all* buttons in a group, set the AllowAllUp property to True for each button allowed to return to an up state.

At design time, you may set a SpeedButton's Down property to True to initially display it in a down state. For this to work, however, you must set the button's GroupIndex to a nonzero value. Use a unique value among all buttons unless you intend to group them as you would a set of radio buttons.

If a SpeedButton's Down property refuses to change to True, set the button's GroupIndex property to any unused nonzero value. If the SpeedButton gets stuck in the down position — that is, if Down refuses to change back to False — set AllowAllUp to True. You can then reset Down to pop up the button.

The Tabs program (refer back to Figure 7-1) demonstrates how to program a group of toolbar SpeedButtons to operate like radio buttons. Run Tabs and select the *Insert, Remove,* and *Convert* buttons to select the operation you want to perform on a text file. One of these three buttons is always in the down state. The other toolbar buttons in Tabs operate as spring-loaded pushbuttons.

DYNAMIC TOOLBARS

By using a combination of MouseDown, MouseUp, and OnClick events, you can create dynamic toolbars that users can configure at runtime. The sample application Toolbar2, shown in Figure 7-4, demonstrates these techniques. Run the program and click the Speed-Button objects in the form to move them into the toolbar. After moving a button into the toolbar, click the button to perform an action such as displaying a calendar (See Figure 7-5). Click the Calendar button again to remove the calendar. You must move the Exit SpeedButton into the toolbar before you can click it to end the program. Listing 7-2 shows the program's source code.

Figure 7-4
Click the SpeedButtons in Toolbar2's form to move them into the toolbar. You can then click the buttons to perform their actions.

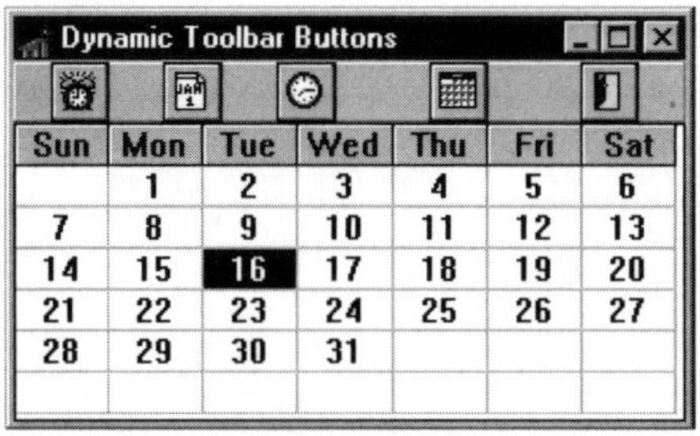

Figure 7-5
After moving Toolbar2's SpeedButtons into the toolbar, click the Calendar button to display a monthly calendar.

Listing 7-2
Toolbar2\Main.Pas

```
unit Main;

interface

uses
  SysUtils, WinTypes, WinProcs, Messages, Classes, Graphics, Controls,
  Forms, Dialogs, ExtCtrls, StdCtrls, Buttons, Grids, Calendar;

type
  TMainForm = class(TForm)
    ToolbarPanel: TPanel;
    RingSB: TSpeedButton;
    DateSB: TSpeedButton;
    TimeSB: TSpeedButton;
    CalendarSB: TSpeedButton;
    ExitSB: TSpeedButton;
    Label1: TLabel;
    Label2: TLabel;
    Label3: TLabel;
    Label4: TLabel;
    Label5: TLabel;
    Label6: TLabel;
    Bevel1: TBevel;
    Calendar1: TCalendar;
    procedure SBMouseDown(Sender: TObject; Button: TMouseButton;
      Shift: TShiftState; X, Y: Integer);
    procedure SBMouseUp(Sender: TObject; Button: TMouseButton;
      Shift: TShiftState; X, Y: Integer);
    procedure RingSBClick(Sender: TObject);
    procedure DateSBClick(Sender: TObject);
    procedure TimeSBClick(Sender: TObject);
```

```
    procedure CalendarSBClick(Sender: TObject);
    procedure ExitSBClick(Sender: TObject);
  private
    { Private declarations }
    function InToolbar(Sender: TObject): Boolean;
  public
    { Public declarations }
  end;

var
  MainForm: TMainForm;

implementation

{$R *.DFM}

const
  isNotInToolbar = 0;      { SpeedButton Tag flag }
  isInToolbar    = 1;      { SpeedButton Tag flag }

{- Returns True if Sender is in the toolbar }
function TMainForm.InToolbar(Sender: TObject): Boolean;
begin
  with Sender as TSpeedButton do
  if Tag = isNotInToolbar then
  begin
    Tag := isInToolbar;    { Set Tag flag }
    Result := False;       { Return function result = False }
  end else
    Result := True;        { Return function result = True }
end;

{- Assign OnClick event handlers for buttons not in toolbar }
procedure TMainForm.SBMouseDown(Sender: TObject; Button: TMouseButton;
  Shift: TShiftState; X, Y: Integer);
begin
  with Sender as TSpeedButton do
  if Tag = isNotInToolbar then
  begin { Assign OnClick event handler to a button }
    if Sender = RingSB then
      RingSB.OnClick := RingSBClick
    else if Sender = DateSB then
      DateSB.OnClick := DateSBClick
    else if Sender = TimeSB then
      TimeSB.OnClick := TimeSBClick
    else if Sender = CalendarSB then
      CalendarSB.OnClick := CalendarSBClick
    else if Sender = ExitSB then
      ExitSB.OnClick := ExitSBClick;
  end;
end;
```

The object's Tag property indicates whether the button was moved into the toolbar. The use of Tag is up to you.

These statements demonstrate how to assign event handlers at run time.

```
{- Move buttons into the toolbar }
procedure TMainForm.SBMouseUp(Sender: TObject; Button: TMouseButton;
  Shift: TShiftState; X, Y: Integer);
begin
  with Sender as TSpeedButton do
  if Tag = isNotInToolbar then
  begin  { Move button into the toolbar }
    Parent := ToolbarPanel;  { Toolbar now owns the button }
    Top := 0;                { Reposition button }
  end;
end;
```

Assigns the button's Parent field to the ToolbarPanel.

```
{- Respond to Ring button click }
procedure TMainForm.RingSBClick(Sender: TObject);
begin
  if InToolbar(Sender) then
    MessageBeep(0);
end;
```

Use this expression to convert the current date to a string.

```
{- Respond to Date button click }
procedure TMainForm.DateSBClick(Sender: TObject);
begin
  if InToolbar(Sender) then
    ShowMessage('The date is ' + DateToStr(Date));
end;
```

```
{- Respond to Time button click }
procedure TMainForm.TimeSBClick(Sender: TObject);
begin
  if InToolbar(Sender) then
    ShowMessage('The time is ' + TimeToStr(Time));
end;
```

Use this expression to convert the current time to a string.

```
{- Respond to Calendar button click }
procedure TMainForm.CalendarSBClick(Sender: TObject);
begin
  if InToolbar(Sender) then
  with Calendar1 do
  begin
    Align := alClient;
    Visible := not Visible;
  end;
end;
```

Toggles the Calendar object on and off.

```
{- Respond to Exit button click }
procedure TMainForm.ExitSBClick(Sender: TObject);
begin
  if InToolbar(Sender) then
    Close;
end;

end.
```

II

7

To create Toolbar2, insert a Panel and several SpeedButton objects into the form. Create OnClick event handlers such as RingSBClick and DateSBClick for each button. Then, in the Object Inspector, highlight each OnClick event handler and press Del to delete it. This leaves the procedure in the source module, but decouples it from the button object — necessary because the first time users click the button the program moves it into the toolbar rather than perform an action.

To indicate whether a button is in the toolbar, the program inspects the button's Tag field, which can equal one of the two constants isNotInToolbar or isInToolbar. The program defines these constants just after the implementation keyword in the unit module. Function InToolbar returns True or False depending on Tag's value and changes that value to isInToolbar.

You can use an object's Tag field for any integer value. A typical use is a flag that indicates some fact about the object's state.

Each of the SpeedButtons shares the same MouseDown and MouseUp event handlers. In procedure SBMouseDown, an *if* statement checks whether Tag equals isNotInToolbar, in which case we can assume the user has clicked a button to move it into the toolbar. To ensure that the next use of that button executes an action, SBMouseDown reattaches the button's OnClick event handler, which was decoupled earlier.

On releasing the mouse, procedure SBMouseUp again checks whether Tag equals isNotInToolbar. If so, the procedure moves the button into the toolbar by setting the SpeedButton object's Parent property to the toolbar Panel, and setting the button's Top property to 0, which repositions the button relative to the Panel's border. These two statements perform the necessary actions:

```
Parent := ToolbarPanel;
Top := 0;
```

Each OnClick event calls the InToolbar function to detect whether the button has been moved to the toolbar. If InToolbar returns True, the event handler performs the button's action. By the way, take a look at how the CalendarSBClick procedure switches the calendar object on and off simply by toggling its Visible property with the statement:

```
Visible := not Visible;
```

FLOATING TOOLBARS

Toolbar Panels do not have to be cemented in place. You can also create toolbars that users can click and drag to any location inside a form window. The Toolbar3 sample application, shown in Figure 7-6, explores this useful technique. The program's source code in Listing 7-3 explains the details of creating a draggable Panel object. After the listing, I'll explain how the program works.

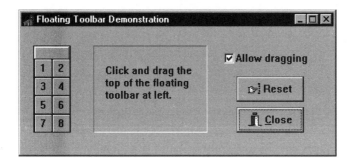

Figure 7-6
Toolbar3 demonstrates how to create a floating toolbar of SpeedButtons. Run the program, and click and drag the toolbar's top border. Select any button, which simply confirms your choice. Turn off the checkbox to fix the toolbar in place. Click Reset to return the toolbar to its startup location.

Listing 7-3
Toolbar3\Main.Pas

```
unit Main;

interface

uses
  SysUtils, WinTypes, WinProcs, Messages, Classes, Graphics, Controls,
  Forms, Dialogs, Buttons, ExtCtrls, StdCtrls;

type
  TMainForm = class(TForm)
    FloatingToolbar: TPanel;
    SpeedButton1: TSpeedButton;
    SpeedButton2: TSpeedButton;
    SpeedButton3: TSpeedButton;
    SpeedButton4: TSpeedButton;
```

```
        SpeedButton5: TSpeedButton;
        SpeedButton6: TSpeedButton;
        SpeedButton7: TSpeedButton;
        SpeedButton8: TSpeedButton;
        BitBtn1: TBitBtn;
        Label1: TLabel;
        Bevel1: TBevel;
        AllowDraggingCB: TCheckBox;
        ResetBitBtn: TBitBtn;
        procedure FormCreate(Sender: TObject);
        procedure SpeedButton1Click(Sender: TObject);
        procedure FloatingToolbarMouseDown(Sender: TObject;
          Button: TMouseButton; Shift: TShiftState; X, Y: Integer);
        procedure FormMouseUp(Sender: TObject; Button: TMouseButton;
          Shift: TShiftState; X, Y: Integer);
        procedure FormMouseMove(Sender: TObject; Shift: TShiftState; X,
          Y: Integer);
        procedure ResetBitBtnClick(Sender: TObject);
        procedure AllowDraggingCBClick(Sender: TObject);
      private
        { Private declarations }
        Dragging: Boolean;
        XOffset, YOffset: Integer;
        procedure MoveToolbar(X, Y: Integer);
      public
        { Public declarations }
      end;

var
  MainForm: TMainForm;

implementation

{$R *.DFM}

{- Initialize }
procedure TMainForm.FormCreate(Sender: TObject);
begin
  Dragging := False;
end;

{- Display number of selected SpeedButton in toolbar }
procedure TMainForm.SpeedButton1Click(Sender: TObject);
begin
  ShowMessage('You selected button number ' +
    IntToStr(TSpeedButton(Sender).Tag));
end;

{- Start dragging operation on clicking in toolbar }
procedure TMainForm.FloatingToolbarMouseDown(Sender: TObject;
  Button: TMouseButton; Shift: TShiftState; X, Y: Integer);
begin
  if AllowDraggingCB.Checked then
```

```
begin
  Dragging := True;      { Dragging operation in effect }
  SetCapture(Handle);    { Send all mouse messages to form }
  XOffset := X;          { Save mouse coordinates to compute }
  YOffset := Y;          { offset from top-left corner }
  end;
end;
```

Captures all mouse activity for this form window.

```
{- End dragging operation on releasing mouse button }
procedure TMainForm.FormMouseUp(Sender: TObject; Button: TMouseButton;
  Shift: TShiftState; X, Y: Integer);
begin
  if Dragging then       { Ignore if not dragging }
  begin
    MoveToolbar(X, Y);   { Move toolbar to final location }
    Dragging := False;   { End dragging operation }
    ReleaseCapture;      { Return mouse message handling to normal }
  end;
end;
```

Returns mouse activity to normal.

```
{- Move toolbar if dragging operation in progress }
procedure TMainForm.FormMouseMove(Sender: TObject; Shift:
  TShiftState; X, Y: Integer);
begin
  if Dragging then       { Ignore if not dragging }
    MoveToolbar(X, Y);   { Move toolbar to mouse location }
end;

{- Move the toolbar to mouse location X and Y }
procedure TMainForm.MoveToolbar(X, Y: Integer);
begin
  FloatingToolbar.Left := X - XOffset;   { Adjust for location of }
  FloatingToolbar.Top  := Y - YOffset;   { panel's top-left corner }
end;

{- Reset toolbar to startup location }
procedure TMainForm.ResetBitBtnClick(Sender: TObject);
begin
  with FloatingToolbar do
  begin
    Left := 24;
    Top := 24;
  end;
  AllowDraggingCB.Checked := True;
end;

procedure TMainForm.AllowDraggingCBClick(Sender: TObject);
begin
  with Label1 do
    Enabled := not Enabled;
end;

end.
```

Setting the toolbar's left and top properties moves the toolbar to the mouse cursor position.

To create a floating toolbar, insert a Panel object into a form window and assign it an appropriate Name. In Toolbar3, I used the name Floating-Toolbar, and I changed the object's width to 50 — exactly twice the width of a SpeedButton. The toolbar's Height is less critical. Make it tall enough to hold your buttons plus a little at the top for a border. Users can click and drag in this area to move the toolbar to another location.

The sample toolbar's BevelInner and BevelOuter properties are both set to bvRaised, but you may want to experiment with other Panel styles and settings. The SpeedButtons in the Panel are standard issue. Simply insert as many buttons as you need.

To manage dragging requires three variables, declared in TMain-Form's private section. These variables are:

- Dragging — A Boolean variable that, when True, indicates that a dragging operation is in progress.

- Xoffset — The number of pixels between the left edge of the toolbar Panel and the mouse's X-coordinate. This makes dragging more realistic by allowing users to click the mouse anywhere in the Panel's visible surface.

- Yoffset — The number of pixels between the top of the toolbar Panel and the mouse's Y-coordinate.

In addition to these variables, the class declares one private procedure, MoveToolbar. Pass the X- and Y-coordinates of the mouse location (from a MouseMove event, for example) to move the toolbar to this location.

Write an OnCreate event handler for the form and set the Dragging variable to False. This is the only required initialization.

Next, create an OnMouseDown event for the FloatingToolbar object. Be sure to do this for the Panel object, not for the form. Toolbar3 checks whether the *Allow dragging* checkbox is on — if not, the procedure ends, which effectively prevents the toolbar from moving.

Four statements begin a dragging operation (refer to the MouseDown event handler in the listing). First, the program sets Dragging to True so that other procedures can detect that a dragging operation is in progress. SetCapture, a Windows API function, sends all mouse messages to the active window — thus, while dragging, users cannot use the mouse to shift to other tasks. Finally, two assignments initialize XOffset and YOffset to the mouse coordinates, which are relative to the Panel object for which the MouseDown event occurred.

When you release the mouse button, the form's MouseUp event takes over. Do not create this event for the Panel — you *must* create the MouseUp event for the form, even though the dragging operation began for the Panel.

When creating any kind of draggable object, the MouseUp event must be for the form, despite the fact that the MouseDown event is for the object. The reason for this is because SetCapture, called in the MouseDown event handler, causes all mouse messages to be sent to the active window. Thus, during a SetCapture, the Panel will never receive MouseMove and MouseUp events.

The MouseUp event first checks whether Dragging is True. If so, MoveToolbar shifts the toolbar to its final position at the mouse coordinates X and Y adjusted for the panel's offset. The procedure sets Dragging to False, canceling the dragging operation, and calls ReleaseCapture to return mouse messages to their normal traffic patterns.

Always pair every call to SetCapture with ReleaseCapture, or your program's customers will lose mouse control. If this happens, *you* will probably lose your customers.

The final wrinkle in creating a floating toolbar is the form's Mouse-Move event. Again, because of the call to SetCapture, you must create this handler for the form's event, not the toolbar's. The procedure checks whether Dragging is True, indicating that a click-and-drag operation is underway, and if so, calls MoveToolbar to move the toolbar Panel to the mouse location. Because the toolbar owns its SpeedButton objects, those objects follow along automatically — you don't have to reposition them; you have to move only the Panel object.

The other procedures in Toolbar3 have obvious purposes. Move-Toolbar relocates the FloatingToolbar object by assigning new values to its Left and Top properties. Subtracting the mouse offset values from X and Y allows users to click the mouse anywhere in the Panel's visible surface. (Try assigning X and Y without subtracting the offsets to see why this step is necessary.)

Procedure ResetBitBtnClick, called when you click the Reset button, returns the floating toolbar to its start-up location. It is always a good idea to include this capability in case users lose track of the toolbar, which can easily happen when resizing the program's window.

Status Panels

A status panel resembles a toolbar, but usually displays text rather than SpeedButton objects. Status panels typically appear at the bottom of a window, and may have subsections that make them easier to read. For example, Microsoft Word, which I used to write this book, displays the current page number, line and column values, the time (yikes, I'm late again!), and keyboard indicators in subdivided status panels.

You might also display on-line help or error messages in a status panel. Delphi makes it easy to create sectional status panels, but there are a few gotchas to learn about so they don't getcha.

CREATING A STATUS PANEL

First, insert a Panel object into a form window to serve as the base for each panel subsection. Give this main Panel a Name such as StatusPanel, and change the Height property to 25. You can use a smaller value, but remember, not all computer users are 18 years old with 20-20 vision, so don't make your panels too small.

For a nice 3D effect, set the Panel's BevelInner property to bvLowered, and set BevelOuter to bvRaised (the default value). Also, set BorderWidth to 0 (the default value). Delete the Caption. To affix the Panel to the window's bottom border, change Align to alBottom. Of course, you are free to use other styles.

Many successful Windows programs use 8-point MS Sans Serif font for a status panel's text. With this font, you can pack nearly 100 characters into a maximized window's status panel on a standard 640-by-480 display.

Figure 7-7 shows the status panel from the Tabs program, introduced at the beginning of this chapter. Each subsection in the panel is itself a separate Panel object.

| F1 About F3 Open Alt+X Exit | Tabs: In 2 Out 2 | 12:59:59 pm |

Figure 7-7
The Tabs program displays a sectional status panel at the bottom of the window's border. The panel shows function and Alt keys, the current input and output tab-width settings, and the current time.

SECTIONING A STATUS PANEL

To divide a status panel into sections, insert additional Panel objects into StatusPanel (the main Panel object). Choose easy-to-remember names for each subpanel. For example, Tabs names its subpanels KeyPanel, Tab-Panel, and TimePanel. Use the same 3D settings as for the main Panel, but set BevelOuter to None. To automatically align subpanels, change their Align properties to alLeft or alRight.

When you set Align to alLeft or alRight, each subpanel jumps to abut any other panels in the main status bar. After you do this, set Align to alNone. You can then click and drag the subpanel to another location — to increase the amount of space between sections, for example. This is how I created the raised spaces between the subpanels in the Tabs application (see Figure 7-7).

Table 7-1 lists significant properties for the StatusPanel and subpanel objects in the Tabs application. You might find this information useful in constructing your own subdivided status panels.

Table 7-1
Tabs Status Panel Object Properties

Component	Name	Property	Value
Panel	StatusPanel	Align	alBottom
		BevelInner	bvLowered
		BevelOuter	bvRaised
		Height	25
Panel	KeyPanel	Align	alLeft
		BevelInner	bvLowered
		BevelOuter	bvNone
		Font:Name	MS Sans Serif
		Font:Size	8
Panel	TabPanel	Align	alNone
Panel	TimePanel	Align	alRight

UPDATING A STATUS PANEL

To change the text in a status panel, simply assign strings to Caption properties. For example, to display the time, Tabs executes this statement in a Timer object's OnTimer event handler:

```
TimePanel.Caption := TimeToStr(Time);
```

This causes the time to advance automatically. The Timer's Interval is set to 1000 milliseconds (one second). Assign literal strings for those that don't change, or set their Caption properties in the Object Inspector.

Avoid the urge to poke individual characters into subpanel Captions. For example, it is a futile exercise to assign individual hour, minute, and second digits into the TimePanel Caption. It's a whole lot easier, and probably more efficient, to reassign the entire Caption string every second, even though this may seem wasteful.

You might find it necessary on occasion to display text on top of a status panel's subdivisions. For example, you could display an on-line hint or an error message. Temporarily, you'll want to overwrite the subpanels to display the message, and then, when the user presses a key or uses the mouse, you can restore the status panel to normal.

The technique is easy to implement. Set the main panel's Alignment to taLeftJustify, and hide the subpanels when you want to display the message. Assign a string to the main panel's Caption property. Finally, reverse these steps to restore the status panel to normal.

For example, the Tabs program might display an error message using code similar to the following. First, hide the two subpanels that display function key labels and the tab-width settings (the time subpanel at the extreme right isn't in the way, and it can remain visible):

```
KeyPanel.Visible := False;
TabPanel.Visible := False;
```

Next, set the main StatusPanel's Alignment, and assign text to the Caption property:

```
with StatusPanel do
begin
  Alignment := taLeftJustify;
  Caption := 'Error #45: Now look what you''ve done!';
end;
```

Type two single quote marks to enter a quote mark character into a string. See the preceding Caption assignment statement for an example.

You can also set the Alignment property at design time with the Object Inspector, in which case you can simply assign a string to Caption. To restore the status panel to normal — after a Timer expires, for example, or on receipt of keyboard or mouse events — assign a null string to the main panel, and set the subpanel Visible properties to True. For example, execute this code:

```
StatusPanel.Caption := '';
KeyPanel.Visible := True;
TabPanel.Visible := True;
```

USING THE FORMAT FUNCTION

Delphi's Format function is especially helpful for preparing strings to display in status panels, but you can use this utility function for other string-formatting purposes. You might want to look up Format in Delphi's on-line help before reading the following notes and suggestions. If you know C or C++, you'll recognize Format as Pascal's equivalent to the sprintf( ) function.

Pass to Format two or more arguments, and assign the function result to a string variable or pass it directly to a non-var string parameter in a procedure or function. Delphi defines Format as follows:

```
function Format(const Format: string; const Args: array of const): string;
```

- *Format* — a literal or variable string that contains format *specifiers* that the Format function uses to create the output string.

- *Args* — an open array of one or more arguments — such as integers, floating-point variables, characters, and strings — to be inserted into the output string. There must be one argument for each format specifier in the Format string. Enclose arguments in brackets and separate multiple arguments with commas.

Pascal permits a procedure or function name to be the same as a parameter, thus the Format function's first parameter is named Format. In a function, however, assigning a value to the function name is ambiguous if a parameter uses that same name. In that case, you can assign the function result to the reserved *result* keyword.

Format is useful for inserting one string into another. For example, declare a string variable such as the following (if you want to follow along, insert a Button and a Label component into a form and enter the following code in the Button's Onclick event handler, before the *begin* keyword):

```
var
   Proc: string;
```

Assign a string to Proc and then use Format to insert that string into another (insert this code between *begin* and *end*):

```
Proc := 'Pentium';
Label1.Caption := Format('I wish my PC had a %s CPU', [Proc]);
```

The first line assigns a literal string to Proc. The second line uses Format to insert Proc into a literal string, replacing the format specifier %s with Proc's value. Notice that Proc is encased in brackets because the second argument passed to Format is an *open array,* which resembles a Pascal set in useage, but is actually a variable list of parameters that can be of any types. The final result is the label:

```
I wish my PC had a Pentium CPU
```

You can also use Format to insert numeric values into strings. For example, declare a floating-point, double-precision variable:

```
var
   Balance: double;
```

Assign a value to Balance, and insert it into a string using the Format specifier %8.2f, which converts the value to a string in eight columns and two decimal places:

```
Balance := 159.72;
Label2.Caption := Format('Your balance is $%8.2f', [Balance]);
```

Executing those two statements sets Label2's Caption to the following string (notice that the eight columns *include* the decimal point):

```
Your balance is $  159.72
```

Format specifiers begin with a percent sign followed by a letter, called the *type,* that represents the type of information to insert into the string. For example, %d indicates a decimal value, %x indicates a hexadecimal value, %s is a Pascal or null-terminated string, and %f or %g indicate floating-point values. It is your responsibility to supply a value in Args for each format specifier. It is also your responsibility to supply values of the indicated types.

In between *type* and % may be several other types of information, such as a left-justification indicator (-), a column-width value, and a precision (preceded by a decimal point). For example, the specifier %6.3f formats a floating-point value in six columns and three decimal places. The specifier %-8x left-justifies an integer value in hexadecimal within eight columns.

A few more examples will help you to use and understand Format. First, define some typed constants (which are similar to variables, but have declared data types and default values):

```
const
  XInt: Integer = 123;
  XLongInt: Longint = 12345678;
  XChar: Char = '@';
  XString: string = 'My dog has knees';
  XSingle: Single = 3.14159;
  XDouble: Double =  9.8695877281;
  XExtended: Extended = 9.51413;
```

Insert Label objects into a form to display each of these values. In a Button or other event handler, insert the following statements (your Label object Names may differ from mine):

```
Label3.Caption  := Format('XInt (dec) = %d', [XInt]);
Label4.Caption  := Format('XInt (hex) = %x', [XInt]);
Label5.Caption  := Format('XLongInt   = %d', [XLongInt]);
Label6.Caption  := Format('XChar      = %s', [XChar]);
Label7.Caption  := Format('XString    = %s', [XString]);
Label8.Caption  := Format('XSingle    = %f', [XSingle]);
Label9.Caption  := Format('XDouble    = %G', [XDouble]);
Label10.Caption := Format('XExtended  = %G', [XExtended]);
```

Running the program displays the following lines:

```
XInt (dec) = 123
XInt (hex) = 7B
XLongInt   = 12345678
XChar      = @
XString    = My dog has knees
XSingle    = 3.14
XDouble    = 9.8695877281
XExtended  = 9.51413
```

Format can also insert multiple values into strings. Enter as many format specifiers as you need, of any types, and supply in brackets that many arguments separated by commas. For example, Listing 7-4 contains sample code that you can insert into a Button's OnClick event handler. Also insert a Label object to display the formatted string result:

```
Pi=3.141593, Frac=0.141593, Int=3
```

Listing 7-4
Use this sample code in a Button's OnClick event handler to set a Label object's caption to a formatted string with multiple arguments.

```
procedure TForm1.Button1Click(Sender: TObject);
var
  R1, R2: Double;
  S: string;
begin
  R1 := Frac(Pi);
  R2 := Int(Pi);
  S := Format('Pi= %8.7G,  Frac=%8.6F,  Int=%G',
    [Pi, R1, R2]);
  Label1.Caption := S;
end;
```

USING THE HEADER COMPONENT

Delphi's Header component is useful for quick-and-dirty status panels. With this component, you need only a single object to construct subdivided panels. Users can resize a Header's sections by clicking and dragging, so this component is also useful for creating various types of programmable panels.

Insert a Header component into a form and insert one line per section into the Sections property, a TStrings object. Each line of text creates a new section in the Header panel. Click and drag a section's vertical line with the right mouse button to resize it.

TIP Use the *right* (secondary) mouse button to resize Header sections at design time. Use the *left* (primary) mouse button to resize Header sections at runtime.

The Header component has a few drawbacks over TPanel, which can generally produce better-looking status panels. Key differences between Header and TPanel components include the following:

- Header is not derived from TPanel (perhaps it should be); therefore, Header objects do not have the 3D graphics effects and beveled edges of TPanel objects.

- Text items are always left justified within Header sections.

- You can select a font for the entire Header, but you cannot select different fonts as you can for multiple TPanels.

- It is not possible to display raised blank spaces between Header sections as you can with multiple TPanels. Each section in a Header object immediately adjoins the section at left, with no extra space between items.

Despite these drawbacks, the Header component is useful for quick-and-dirty status panels. It also comes in handy for creating columnar displays. For example, insert a Header object into a form and align it with the top of the window. Enter these lines into Header1's Sections property (click its ellipsis button to open Delphi's string editor):

```
Item#
Description
Qty
Amt
Total
```

Insert five ListBox components into the form. Move and size them to appear directly under each column section in the Header.

TIP Header sections do not snap to Delphi's form grid. To size other components such as ListBoxes under each column, first size the ListBoxes, and then size the Header sections.

Make sure the Header1 object's AllowResize property is True, which permits users to size header sections at runtime. (For a standard status panel, you might want to set this property to False). Next, insert the code from Listing 7-5 into the Header1 object's OnSized event handler. This event is called after a click-and-drag operation that changes a header section size. Use the other event, OnSizing, to perform actions *during* a click-and-drag operation.

Listing 7-5

Insert this programming into a Header object's OnSized event handler to adjust ListBoxes to match the Header section widths.

```
procedure TForm1.Header1Sized(Sender: TObject;
  ASection, AWidth: Integer);
var
  C: TComponent;
  I, J, K: Integer;
begin
  K := 0;
  for I := 0 to Header1.Sections.Count - 1 do
  begin
    C := FindComponent('ListBox' + IntToStr(I + 1));
    if C <> nil then
    begin
      J := Header1.SectionWidth[I];
      TListBox(C).Width := J + 1;
      TListBox(C).Left := K;
      K := K + J;
    end;
  end;
end;
```

The programming in Listing 7-5 obtains the number of sections in a Header object by referring to the Count property in the Header's Sections. To determine the width of each section, the program refers to the SectionWidth property. For example, this sets J equal to the width of section number I:

```
J := Header1.SectionWidth[I];
```

The sample code also adjusts the Left property of each list box. To find each list box — named by default ListBox1, ListBox2, and so on — Listing 7-5 calls the Delphi FindComponent function. Use this function to search by name a form or other object's Components array. First, define a variable of the general-component type TComponent:

```
var
  C: TComponent;
```

Then, to find a component by name, use a statement such as this:

```
C := FindComponent('MyComponent');
```

After that statement, if C is not *nil,* it refers to the component named MyComponent. If C is nil, no object of the requested name exists. You'll usually follow calls to FindComponent with an *if* statement such as this:

```
if C <> nil then
  { ... perform action on C here }
```

Even better, use the Pascal *is* operator to confirm that C really is the type of object you think it should be:

```
if C is TListBox then
  { ... perform action on C here }
```

TIP When using *is* to test whether an object returned by FindComponent is a particular type, you do not also have to test whether the function result is nil. For example, if the expression "C is TListBox" is true, then C cannot be nil.

FindComponent returns a TComponent object, and you'll also usually have to use a type-cast expression to inform the compiler what type of component C *really* is. There are several ways to do this. You can use a type-cast expression of the component type (as in Listing 7-5) with C in parentheses. For example, this sets the Width value in the TListBox object referenced as C:

```
TListBox(C).Width := J + 1;
```

Or, you can use a *with* statement to tell Delphi to treat C as a particular type of component:

```
with C as TListBox do
begin
  Width := J + 1;
  ...
end;
```

Be careful when using FindComponent along with Pascal's *with* statement. Although you will usually want to search a form's Component array, other objects also have this array, and inside a *with* statement, you might end up searching another component list. Either don't call FindComponent inside a *with* statement, or use an expression such as MainForm.FindComponent to refer to the object with the Components array that you want to search.

Keyboard Status Panels

One of the classic elements of a well-groomed status panel is a set of keyboard toggle indicators. These typically show the settings of the Caps Lock, Num Lock, Scroll Lock, and Ins keys. The CapsLock application, which is shown in Figure 7-8, demonstrates the technique. Listing 7-6 shows the program's Main.Pas source code. There are several possible approaches for creating keyboard toggle indicators, but the one that I think looks the best shows dimmed text for keys in the off state and dark (normal) text for keys in the on state. However, accomplishing this with TPanel objects is not exactly straightforward, as I'll explain after the listing.

Figure 7-8
The CapsLock application displays the on/off states of the Caps Lock, Num Lock, Scroll Lock, and Ins keys. Normal text shows keys in the on state; dim text shows keys that are off.

Listing 7-6
Capslock\Main.Pas

```
unit Main;

interface

uses
  SysUtils, WinTypes, WinProcs, Messages, Classes, Graphics, Controls,
  Forms, Dialogs, ExtCtrls, StdCtrls, Buttons;

type
  TMainForm = class(TForm)
    StatusPanel: TPanel;
    CapsLockPanel: TPanel;
    NumLockPanel: TPanel;
    ScrollLockPanel: TPanel;
    InsPanel: TPanel;
    BitBtn1: TBitBtn;
    Label1: TLabel;
    Bevel1: TBevel;
    CapsLockLabel: TLabel;
    NumLockLabel: TLabel;
    ScrollLockLabel: TLabel;
    InsLabel: TLabel;
    procedure FormKeyDown(Sender: TObject; var Key: Word;
      Shift: TShiftState);
    procedure FormActivate(Sender: TObject);
  private
    { Private declarations }
  public
    { Public declarations }
    procedure UpdateKeyPanel;
  end;

var
  MainForm: TMainForm;

implementation

{$R *.DFM}

procedure TMainForm.UpdateKeyPanel;
begin
  CapsLockLabel.Enabled :=
    GetKeyState(VK_CAPITAL) and 1 = 1;
  NumLockLabel.Enabled :=
    GetKeyState(VK_NUMLOCK) and 1 = 1;
```

These five objects create the keyboard status panel.

Retrieves the state of any virtual key.

II

7

```
ScrollLockLabel.Enabled :=
    GetKeyState(VK_SCROLL)  and 1 = 1;
  InsLabel.Enabled :=
    GetKeyState(VK_INSERT)  and 1 = 1;
end;

procedure TMainForm.FormKeyDown(Sender: TObject; var Key: Word;
  Shift: TShiftState);
begin
  UpdateKeyPanel;
end;

procedure TMainForm.FormActivate(Sender: TObject);
begin
  UpdateKeyPanel;
end;


end.
```

Setting a Label's Enabled property False dims the Caption's setting Enabled True displays the Caption normally.

To create a keyboard toggle status panel, insert a TPanel object into a form and modify it as explained in this chapter. For example, set Height to 25 and select a 3D style. Align the panel with the window bottom. Next, insert subpanels into the main TPanel, and name these CapsLock-Panel, NumLockPanel, and so on. Delete all panel Captions.

Displaying dim text in TPanel objects (see Figure 7-8) is less than straightforward because this component does not dim its Caption text when TPanel's Enabled property is False. Because of this limitation, the CapsLock application inserts four Label objects into each subpanel. To display a dim label for a key that is off, the program sets the Label's Enabled property to False; to display a normal label for a key that is on, the program sets Enabled to True. The program does not assign text to the subpanel Captions.

Procedure UpdateKeyPanel shows how to obtain the current settings of the Caps Lock, Num Lock, Scroll Lock, and Ins keys. The procedure calls the Windows API function GetKeyState, to which you can pass any virtual key code. GetKeyState returns an integer value. If that value's least significant bit equals 1, the key is toggled on; otherwise, the key is off. A logical *and* expression examines this bit, resulting in a Boolean True or False value. Assigning that value to the Label object's Enabled property displays it in dim or normal style.

To properly show key values when the program starts and when the user presses one of the labeled keys, CapsLock creates two event handlers for the form — OnActivate and OnKeyDown. Each of these event handlers calls the UpdateKeyPanel procedure to update the status panel.

To detect changes to Caps Lock, Num Lock, Scroll Lock, and Ins keys in a form's OnKeyDown event handler, set the form's KeyPreview property to True.

Summary

- Use the Panel component to create toolbars and status panels. Typically, toolbars contain SpeedButton objects. Status panels display text.

- You can also use the Header component to create quick-and-dirty status panels, and to provide subdivided panels that users can resize by clicking and dragging.

- SpeedButtons can be spring-loaded (they pop back up when you release the mouse) or they can be sticky (they stay down when clicked).

- Group SpeedButton objects by setting their GroupIndex properties to the same nonzero, positive integer value. The SpeedButtons will then operate like a set of RadioButtons — only one button in the group may be down. Set AllowAllUp to True to permit all buttons in the group to be in the off state.

- Design floating toolbars by creating OnMouseDown, OnMouseMove, and OnMouseUp event handlers. Call the Windows SetCapture function to initiate a click-and-drag operation. Always pair every call to SetCapture with a call to ReleaseCapture.

- A status panel resembles a toolbar, but usually displays text instead of buttons. Subdivide a status panel by inserting Panel objects into a main Panel. Display text in panel subdivisions by assigning strings to the Caption property. Alternatively, insert Label objects into each subpanel and assign text to the Label Captions — you can also display dimmed text in status panels this way by setting a Label object's Enabled property to False.

- Use Delphi's Format function to create formatted strings. The function resembles the standard C and C++ function sprintf( ). Format is especially useful in creating strings for display in status panels, but it is a handy function for many other purposes as well.

- The Header component creates another kind of status panel with sections that users can resize by clicking and dragging. You can also use Header objects to create columnar displays.

- A classic status panel displays the settings of the Caps Lock, Num Lock, Scroll Lock, and Ins keys, as this chapter's CapsLock program demonstrates. Call the Windows GetKeyState function to obtain key-toggle settings.

Projects to Try

7-1: Create a toolbar that users can move to the window's top, bottom, right, or left borders. In addition to assigning a new value to the Panel's Align property, you'll have to adjust SpeedButton Left and Right properties to new relative positions within the toolbar Panel object boundaries.

7-2: Create a status panel that shows the date and time. (Hint: Refer to the Toolbar2 application's source code.) Test your application overnight to be sure it changes the date at midnight.

7-3: Design a floating color-selection toolbar, using the Toolbar3 application as a guide.

7-4: Experiment with runtime clicking and dragging of objects such as Buttons and SpeedButtons. Use programming similar to that in Toolbar3 to respond to OnMouseDown, OnMouseMove, and OnMouseUp events.

7-5: Write a test program with a status panel that displays an error message. Use the Format function to create a string from an integer error code. Add buttons or menu commands to the program to simulate various types of errors.

7-6: Insert the date and time into a Header component's sections. (Hint: Create date and time strings, and add them to the Sections property.)

7-7: Design a form template with the status panel from the CapsLock
sample application (refer back to Figure 7-8 and Listing 7-6).

Expert-User Tips

- Assign a value to the application object's HintPause property to alter
  the time delay for a hint box to appear. The default value is 800
  milliseconds. For example, to program a faster-appearing hint box,
  you can assign 250 (1/4 second) to Application.HintPause. You
  might do this in any event handler (use the form's OnCreate event
  to configure hints at startup).

- Hint boxes are yellow with black text, which resembles the original
  Post-It™ Notes. To change this color, you can assign a new TColor
  value to the application's HintColor property. For example, to create
  red hints, assign clRed to Application.HintColor. (Look up the TColor
  data type in Delphi's on-line help for more information.)

- When designing segmented status panels with multiple TPanel components, select a font for the main panel, and then set the Parent-
  Font property to True for each subpanel. Each subdivision will then
  use the main panel's font settings. This is easier than assigning font
  properties for each subpanel.

- You can use TPanel objects as platforms for displaying text anywhere
  in a form window — you don't have to restrict TPanels for use as
  toolbars and status panels. For example, Delphi's *Compiling* information dialog uses TPanels to display progress information during com-
  pilation. To see this window, choose the *Options|Environment*
  command, select the *Preferences* page tab to enable *Show compiler
  progress*, and compile a sample application.

- Insert a Panel into a form and set its Align property to alClient. This
  causes the Panel to completely fill the form window. Select values
  for BevelInner and BevelOuter, and try various BevelWidth and
  BorderWidth settings (25 and 10, for example). You can achieve
  some interesting window interiors by using a Panel as a window's
  background. (If components disappear, select the Panel and choose
  Edit|Send to Back.)

- Rather than use a glyph bitmap, you can use the SpeedButton Font property to display symbols. Set the button's Font to a TrueType font such as WingDings. The Caption still displays ASCII text characters. This works for any text item with a Font property.

- In a Header object, the Enabled property must be True for runtime resizing to work. Setting Enabled to False disables resizing, regardless of AutoResize's value.

- When using the Format function, a common mistake is forgetting to enter arguments in brackets. Remember that Format's Args parameter is an open array — in other words, a variable-length parameter list. For example, the expression [V1,V2,V3] passes to Args the variables V1, V2, and V3.

Coming Up

In the next chapter, you'll learn how to use Delphi's list components such as ListBox and ComboBox. You'll also investigate list-classes such as TList, TStrings, and TStringList.

8

Making Lists

*I*f there's one data structure that, sooner or later, every programmer uses, it's a *list*. It's not too surprising, then, to discover that one of the most useful Windows controls is the list box. With this control, and the related combo box, which adds a text-entry area to a list box, you can create string lists for just about any purpose. You can sort list-box data, and you can choose from several different types of list box and combo box styles — for example, to permit multiple selections, or to incrementally search a drop-down list based on partial entries.

Delphi also provides several related list-making classes, such as TList, TStrings, and TStringList. These are all useful weapons in the battle to create sophisticated user interfaces, and as you'll discover in this chapter, Delphi provides a rich assortment of tools for maintaining just about any imaginable type of list.

Components

- ComboBox — This standard Windows control combines a ListBox with an Edit object. Depending on the ComboBox object's style, users can choose from listed entries, which optionally appear in a drop-down box, or they can enter new data into the Edit control. Palette: Standard.

- ListBox — Use this general-purpose, standard Windows control to create lists of strings from which users can select entries using keyboard and mouse commands. As this chapter explains, ListBox objects provide a TStrings array named Items that provides easy access to ListBox data. Palette: Standard.

List Components

The two standard Windows components, ListBox and ComboBox, can probably handle the bulk of your program's list-selection requirements. As you'll learn in this section, Delphi enhances these standard Windows controls to provide easy access to listed data. For example, with simple statements, you can transfer ListBox and ComboBox strings to and from text files. This section's sample application — a To-Do List utility — also demonstrates how to transfer strings between two ListBox objects using one of Delphi's dialog-box templates.

LIST BOXES

The ListBox component provides a number of interesting properties that allow you to select among various styles. For example, ListBox objects normally have a dark outline border, but you can set BorderStyle to bsNone for a borderless list. (By the way, this configuration looks good with a ListBox inserted into a Bevel.) Assign a value to the Columns property to display listed items in more than one column. This value is zero by default — set it to 2 or more to create columnar lists.

There are many different ways to insert data into a ListBox object. At design time, click the ellipsis button for the Items property to open Delphi's *String list* editor, and enter your listed items. Or, you can copy text from another file into the editor. This method stores the listed strings in the program's .Exe code file and automatically inserts the strings into the ListBox object.

To insert strings into a ListBox at runtime, a program can call methods for the Items property of the TStrings class. Every ListBox object provides an Items object for easy access to listed data. For example, to prompt users for new strings and enter them into a ListBox, you can use programming such as this:

```
var
  S: string;
begin
  S := InputBox('Test Program', 'Enter a string', '');
  if Length(S) > 0 then
    ListBox1.Items.Add(S);
end;
```

Notice that you call Add for the Items object that ListBox1 owns. The ListBox itself does not have an Add method. You can simplify the preceding code by using a *with* statement:

```
with ListBox1.Items do
  Add(S);
```

To get strings out of a ListBox, use Items as an array. For example, define a string variable like this:

```
var
  S: string;
```

Next, assign any ListBox string to S by specifying an Item integer index with a statement such as:

```
S := ListBox1.Items[0];
```

Appearances are deceiving in this case because Items isn't an array. Actually, Items owns a Strings array that such statements use by default. The following statement is exactly equivalent to the preceding one:

```
S := ListBox1.Items.Strings[0];
```

Whatever method you use to index a ListBox's strings, limit the index to the range 0 to *Items.Count - 1*. Use a *for* loop, for example, to access all of a ListBox's strings:

```
for I := 0 to ListBox1.Items.Count - 1 do
begin
  S := ListBox1.Items[I];
  ShowMessage(S);  { Or do something else with S }
end;
```

For lengthy lists, you might want to supply data from a text file that users can prepare and edit with the Windows notepad. To load a text file's strings into a ListBox, call the LoadFromFile method for Items as in this example:

```
ListBox1.Items.LoadFromFile('C:\data\file.txt');
```

Call AddStrings to add multiple strings from one ListBox (or any other component with a TStrings property) to another. For example, this statement appends strings from ListBox2 to any strings already in ListBox1:

```
ListBox1.Items.AddStrings(ListBox2.Items);
```

To swap two listed items, call Exchange, as in this code, which swaps the first and last strings in a ListBox:

```
with ListBox1.Items do
  if Count >= 2 then Exchange(0, Count - 1);
```

To delete a string from a ListBox, call the Delete method, which requires the item's integer index. For example, this statement deletes the fourth item from ListBox1 (the first item's index is zero):

```
ListBox1.Items.Delete(3);
```

Rather than specify a literal index, to find the index of an item, call IndexOf, which returns –1 if the specified item doesn't exist:

```
Index := ListBox1.Items.IndexOf('Item to find');
  if Index >= 0 then { ... ok to use Index }
```

Call the Clear method to delete all items from a list:

```
ListBox1.Items.Clear;
```

SCROLLING IN LISTBOXES

Like a box of Cracker Jacks, ListBoxes come with a free surprise — if there are more lines to display than fit within the ListBox's space, a vertical scroll bar automatically appears. When the ListBox can display all items, the vertical scroll bar automatically disappears.

Two properties affect vertical scrolling. ItemHeight indicates the height in pixels of one text line. Set IntegralHeight to True to ensure that only full text lines appear in the ListBox's borders. Set IntegralHeight False to permit partial lines at the bottom of the ListBox.

When you select a Font for a ListBox, or for a form that contains a ListBox, Delphi automatically adjusts ItemHeight to a corresponding value. To override this automatic adjustment, you must set Style to lbOwnerDrawFixed or lbOwnerDrawVariable. For more information on creating owner-draw controls, see "Using the TStrings Class," later in this chapter.

ListBoxes can also display horizontal scroll bars. To enable horizontal scrolling, call the ListBox's inherited Perform method, which sends a message to the Windows ListBox control to which the ListBox component provides an object-oriented interface. The message to send in this case is LB_SETHORIZONTALEXTENT. Along with the message, pass a horizontal scrolling range in pixels, plus a third unused argument which is always zero. For example, this statement adds horizontal scroll bars to a ListBox, with a maximum scrolling range of 1000 pixels:

```
ListBox1.Perform(LB_SETHORIZONTALEXTENT, 1000, 0);
```

Instead of passing a literal range such as 1000, a better program would set the horizontal scrolling range to the width in pixels of the longest string. Listing 8-1 shows how to determine this value. The program calls TextWidth in the ListBox's Canvas (an object that gives you access to the Windows graphics device interface, or GDI). TextWidth returns the width in pixels of a string for the Canvas's current font. After the *for* loop executes, variable K equals the maximum string width in pixels, which the program passes to the ListBox using the LB_SETHORIZONTALEXTENT Windows message.

To keep horizontal scroll bar ranges in synch with a ListBox's data, perform the steps illustrated in Listing 8-1 after every addition and deletion, and after changing the ListBox's font.

Listing 8-1

Use this sample code to adjust ListBox horizontal scroll bar ranges to the width in pixels of the longest listed string.

```
var
  I, J, K: Integer;
begin
  with ListBox1 do
  begin
    K := 0;
    for I := 0 to Items.Count - 1 do
    begin
      J := Canvas.TextWidth(Items[I]);
      if J > K then K := J;
    end;
    Perform(LB_SETHORIZONTALEXTENT, K, 0);
  end;
end;
```

Horizontal scroll bars are not recommended for multicolumn ListBox objects. However, you may adjust column width by sending the ListBox object a LB_SETCOLUMNWIDTH message using a statement such as this:

```
ListBox1.Perform(LB_SETCOLUMNWIDTH, 100, 0);
```

FONT LISTS

The ListFont application demonstrates how to insert a list of system font names into a ListBox, and then use those names to display a string in each font style. Figure 8-1 shows the program's display. Run ListFont and select any font to display the sample text in the font's default style. Click the *Size* button to select a new point size. Listing 8-2 shows the program's source code.

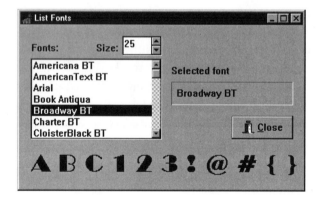

Figure 8-1
ListFont loads system font names into a ListBox object. Select any name to display a sample string in the font's default style. Click Size to select a new point size. Only TrueType fonts are scaleable to all sizes.

To insert a list of font names into a ListBox, the FontList program executes the following statement in the form's OnCreate event handler:

```
FontListBox.Items := Screen.Fonts;
```

To sort the font list alphabetically, set the ListBox's Sorted property to True.

Listing 8-2
Listfont\Main.Pas

```
unit Main;

interface

uses
  SysUtils, WinTypes, WinProcs, Messages, Classes, Graphics, Controls,
  Forms, Dialogs, StdCtrls, Spin, Buttons, ExtCtrls;

type
  TMainForm = class(TForm)
    FontListBox: TListBox;
    Label1: TLabel;
    SampleLabel: TLabel;
    SpinEdit1: TSpinEdit;
    Label3: TLabel;
    FontNameLabel: TLabel;
    Label2: TLabel;
    Bevel1: TBevel;
    CloseBitBtn: TBitBtn;
    procedure FormCreate(Sender: TObject);
    procedure FontListBoxDblClick(Sender: TObject);
    procedure FontListBoxKeyDown(Sender: TObject; var Key: Word;
      Shift: TShiftState);
    procedure SpinEdit1Change(Sender: TObject);
    procedure CloseBitBtnClick(Sender: TObject);
  private
    { Private declarations }
  public
    { Public declarations }
  end;

var
  MainForm: TMainForm;

implementation

{$R *.DFM}

procedure TMainForm.FormCreate(Sender: TObject);
begin
  FontListBox.Items := Screen.Fonts;
end;

procedure TMainForm.FontListBoxDblClick(Sender: TObject);
begin
  with FontListBox do
  if ItemIndex >= 0 then
  begin
    SampleLabel.Font.Name := FontListBox.Items[ItemIndex];
    FontNameLabel.Caption := SampleLabel.Font.Name;
  end;
end;
```

A string list of all available font names.

To change an object's font, assign its string name to Font.Name.

II

8

```
procedure TMainForm.FontListBoxKeyDown(Sender: TObject; var Key: Word;
  Shift: TShiftState);
begin
  if Key in [VK_RETURN, VK_SPACE] then
    FontListBoxDblClick(Sender);
end;
```
Simulates mouse double-click where user presses Enter or Space.

```
procedure TMainForm.SpinEdit1Change(Sender: TObject);
begin
  SampleLabel.Font.Size := SpinEdit1.Value;
end;
```
Assign new font size—display is automatically updated.

```
procedure TMainForm.CloseBitBtnClick(Sender: TObject);
begin
  Close;
end;

end.
```

FontList uses two techniques for selecting font names from the FontListBox object. In the ListBox's OnDblClick event handler, an *if* statement first checks whether the ListBox's ItemIndex property is greater than or equal to zero. If so, the user has selected an item from the ListBox and not simply double-clicked on hot air. The two subsequent statements assign the selected font's name from Items to the SampleLabel's Font.Name property. Simply assigning the Font property a new Name changes the font of the sample text displayed at the bottom of the window. Lastly, FontList assigns the font name to the Caption of another label, which displays the selected font inside an indented bevel just for looks.

In most cases, you'll also want users to be able to select ListBox items by pressing Enter, and possibly the spacebar. The ListFont demo enables these keys in the FontListBox's OnKeyDown event handler. The procedure checks whether Key is in the set of two values VK_RETURN and VK_SPACE, and if so, calls the FontListBoxDblClick handler. This simulates a double-click event when you press Enter or the spacebar.

Using Pascal's *in* operator and a set of values is often more convenient, and possibly more efficient, than multiple logical OR expressions. For example, rather than write something like this:

```
if (Key = VK_RETURN) or
   (Key = VK_SPACE ) or
   (Key = VK_F9    ) then {...}
```

you can test whether Key is *in* the set of three values with this statement:

```
if Key in [VK_RETURN, VK_SPACE, VK_F9] then {...}
```

SELECTING LISTED DATA

In some ListBoxes, you'll want users to be able to select only one item at a time. In others, you'll want to enable multiple selections. Single-item selection is easy — just use the default ListBox settings with property MultiSelect set to False. To enable multiple-item selection, set MultiSelect to True.

In addition to MultiSelect, set ExtendedSelect True or False depending on the type of multiple-item selection you want. When MultiSelect is False, ExtendedSelect has no effect (you can leave it set to its default True value). But when MultiSelect is True, ExtendedSelect configures multiple-item selection in one of two ways:

- *ExtendedSelect = True* — Users must press Ctrl and click the mouse to select multiple items. In addition, pressing Shift selects all items between the previously selected line and the one clicked. Pressing Ctrl+Shift and clicking does the same and retains any other individually selected items. Selecting a new item without pressing Ctrl or Shift unhighlights any previous selections, and clicking a selected item deselects it.

- *ExtendedSelect = False* — Users do not have to press any keys to select multiple items. Selecting a new item does not remove highlighting from previous selections.

You can assign these property values in the Object Inspector window or at runtime with statements like these:

```
ListBox1.MultiSelect := True;
ListBox1.ExtendedSelect := False;
```

With MultiSelect True and ExtendedSelect False, it is your responsibility to unhighlight selected items — when users press Esc, for example. A simple way to do this is by toggling the ExtendedSelect property on and off as Listing 8-3 demonstrates. Use this code in a ListBox's OnKeyDown event handler.

When MultiSelect is True, the SelCount property indicates the number of selected items. If there are no selected items, SelCount equals zero.

II

8

Listing 8-3

With ExtendedSelect False, use this OnKeyDown event handler to unhigh-light selected items in a ListBox when users press Esc.

```
procedure TForm1.ListBox1KeyDown(Sender: TObject; var Key: Word;
  Shift: TShiftState);
begin
  if Key = VK_ESCAPE then
  with ListBox1 do
  begin
    ExtendedSelect := True;
    ExtendedSelect := False;
  end;
end;
```

SelCount always equals –1 if MultiSelect is False, regardless of whether an item is selected. When MultiSelect is True, ItemIndex indicates the most recently clicked item, regardless of whether that item was selected or deselected. These anomalies can trip you up. For best results, do not use SelCount with single-entry ListBoxes, and do not use ItemIndex in multiple-entry ListBoxes.

Listing 8-4 suggests one way to obtain multiple selections from a ListBox. To try the technique, insert two ListBox objects into a form, and enter some strings into ListBox1's Items property. Set ListBox1's MultiSelect property True. Insert a Button into the form and use the listing for the Button's OnClick event handler. Run the program and click the button to transfer selected items from ListBox1 to ListBox2.

Listing 8-4

This Button OnClick event handler demonstrates how to obtain multiple selections from a ListBox. MultiSelect must be True for this code to work properly.

```
procedure TForm1.Button1Click(Sender: TObject);
var
  I: Integer;
begin
  ListBox2.Clear;
  for I := 0 to ListBox1.Items.Count - 1 do
    if ListBox1.Selected[I] then
      ListBox2.Items.Add(ListBox1.Items[I]);
end;
```

SELECTING LISTBOX ITEMS AT RUNTIME

It is sometimes useful to select ListBox items using program statements — for example, to restore a program window to a saved state, or to make preset selections from data sets. Clicking button A might automatically select items 3, 6, and 9; clicking button B would select items 2 and 7, and so forth.

To select items in a single-entry ListBox at runtime, assign a value to the ItemIndex property. For example, the following statement selects the sixth item (the first item's index is zero, so the sixth item's index equals five):

```
ListBox1.ItemIndex := 5;
```

However, that does not work when MultiSelect is True. In that case, to select items at runtime, assign True to entries in the Selected array. For example, the following two statements select the third and sixth items in ListBox1. Delphi automatically adjusts SelCount and ItemIndex to the proper values following each assignment:

```
ListBox1.Selected[2] := True;
ListBox1.Selected[5] := True;
```

Because the Selected array is inaccessible when MultiSelect is False, you might want to use an *if* statement such as the following to select the sixth item in ListBox1. This code works correctly for single-entry and multiple-entry ListBoxes:

```
with ListBox1 do
if MultiSelect then
  Selected[5] := True
else
  ItemIndex := 5;
```

USING LISTBOX DATA

As a practical example of using two ListBoxes and transferring data between them using Button objects, the ToDo application edits a simple list of projects to do. I used Delphi's *Dual list box* form template to create the program's window. I then modified the stock form for the ToDo program. Figure 8-2 shows ToDo's display. Later in this chapter, I'll explain some of ToDo's source code, which is too lengthy to print here.

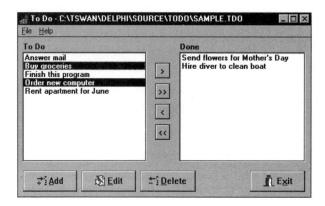

Figure 8-2
The ToDo application demonstrates how to use Delphi's Dual list box form template to transfer data between two ListBox objects.

The *Dual list box* form template provides most of the code needed to implement double ListBox transfers. To inspect this code, insert a new form into a project, and select *Dual list box* from the template gallery. Open the form's unit module to see how Delphi manages the two ListBoxes.

SORTED LIST BOXES

As I mentioned, creating a sorted ListBox is easy — just set the Sorted property to True. The ListBox automatically maintains sorted order for additions and deletions. However, if you *change* an item, the list may become unordered because Windows performs the sorting, not the Delphi component. For example, this statement assigns the string *Zebra* to ListBox1's first item:

```
ListBox1.Items[0] := 'Zebra';
```

To place the Zebra at the end of the corral where it probably belongs, simply toggle the Sorted property off and then back on. These statements force the ListBox to re-sort its data:

```
ListBox1.Sorted := False;
ListBox1.Sorted := True;
```

COMBO BOXES

ComboBoxes are great for creating selection lists with optional editing capabilities. The ComboBox component merges an input box (similar to Delphi's Edit component) with a ListBox. Users can select items from the list, and they can enter new data into the edit control's window. There are three basic ComboBox styles:

- *Simple (Style = csSimple)* — The ListBox is always visible. Users can select an item from the list, or they can enter a new item into the edit window.

- *Drop-Down (Style = csDropDown)* — The ListBox drops down when users click the down-arrow button next to the edit window — they can also press Alt+Down. As with the Simple style, users can select an item from the list, or they can enter a new item into the edit control. Incremental searching is also enabled for this style — type one or more characters and press the up- or down-arrow key to select the entry that most closely matches your input.

- *Drop-Down-List (Style = csDropDownList)* — As with the Drop-Down style, the list box drops into view on clicking the down-arrow button. With this style, the edit box is "read-only," and users must select a listed entry. However, users may type the first letter of an item to select it. For example, press the P key repeatedly to select all entries that begin with P.

 Unlike ListBox controls, ComboBoxes cannot display horizontal scroll bars. This is a limitation in Windows.

The Combos application illustrates the three ComboBox styles. Figure 8-3 shows the program's display. Listing 8-5 shows its source file.

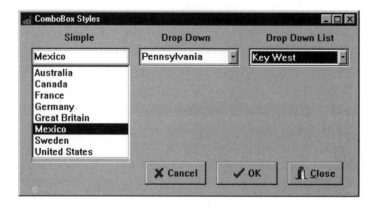

Figure 8-3
The Combos application illustrates the three ComboBox styles: Simple, Drop-Down, and Drop-Down-List.

Listing 8-5
Combos\Main.Pas

```
unit Main;

interface

uses
  SysUtils, WinTypes, WinProcs, Messages, Classes, Graphics, Controls,
  Forms, Dialogs, StdCtrls, Buttons;

type
  TMainForm = class(TForm)
    SimpleCB: TComboBox;
    DropDownCB: TComboBox;
    DropDownListCB: TComboBox;
    Label1: TLabel;
    Label2: TLabel;
    Label3: TLabel;
    CancelBitBtn: TBitBtn;
    OKBitBtn: TBitBtn;
    CloseBitBtn: TBitBtn;
    procedure CancelBitBtnClick(Sender: TObject);
    procedure OKBitBtnClick(Sender: TObject);
    procedure CloseBitBtnClick(Sender: TObject);
  private
    { Private declarations }
  public
    { Public declarations }
  end;
```

```
var
  MainForm: TMainForm;

implementation

{$R *.DFM}

procedure TMainForm.CancelBitBtnClick(Sender: TObject);
begin
  Close;
end;

procedure TMainForm.OKBitBtnClick(Sender: TObject);
var
  S1, S2, S3: string;
begin
  S1 := SimpleCB.Text;
  S2 := DropDownCB.Text;
  S3 := DropDownListCB.Text;
  ShowMessage('Your selections are: ' +
    S1 + ', ' + S2 + ', ' + S3);
end;

procedure TMainForm.CloseBitBtnClick(Sender: TObject);
begin
  OKBitBtn.Click;    { Simulate OK button click }
  Close;             { End program }
end;

end.
```

Get ComboBox entries from the Text field.

The Combos listing shows the correct way to obtain selections from a ComboBox object. In most cases, you should do this by referring to the object's Text property, which holds the text displayed in the edit control's window. You may use ListBox methods to obtain selections, for example, by referring to the Items array:

```
if ItemIndex >= 0 then
  S1 := SimpleCB.Items[ItemIndex];  { ??? }
```

However, this technique is questionable because it does not properly pick up user entries from the Text field. For best results, get selections from the Text property unless you need to perform actions on entries in the ListBox window. For example, this statement copies the selection from the SimpleCB ComboBox to a string variable S1:

```
S1 := SimpleCB.Text;
```

II

8

At design time, enter list items into a ComboBox's Items property. Enter or clear the Text property to change the string edit area, to which Delphi assigns the object's name by default.

ComboBoxes provide some other methods that you might find useful for designing your program's interface. Use the DroppedDown property to determine whether a ComboBox is hanging down:

```
if DropDownCB.DroppedDown then
   {... do something if ComboBox is open }
```

Assign True or False to DroppedDown to open and close the list portion of a ComboBox under program control. For example, insert a ComboBox object and a Button in a form, and use this statement in the Button's OnClick event handler to open and close the ComboBox list window:

```
with ComboBox1 do
   DroppedDown := not DroppedDown;
```

To select all text in a ComboBox's edit area, call the SelectAll method. This highlights the edit control's text — it does not select all listed items as the method's name seems to suggest. For example, you might use this statement in an OnKeyDown event handler to highlight the edit control's text when users press a certain key:

```
SimpleCB.SelectAll;
```

ComboBoxes are single-entry objects. Only ListBox components permit multiple selections.

Calling Clear erases all listed entries and any text in the edit window box from a ComboBox object. Use this statement to delete all text from a ComboBox:

```
ComboBox1.Clear;
```

If you want to delete only the text from the edit control, assign a null string to the ComboBox's Text property:

```
ComboBox1.Text := '';
```

You can also use the methods discussed earlier to make changes to listed items through the Items array. For example, this adds a new entry to a ComboBox's list box:

```
ComboBox1.Items.Add('Aardvark');
```

String and Other Lists

The ListBox and ComboBox objects are visual tools for creating selection lists in windows. Most programs also need internal list-making capabilities using objects not on Delphi's VCL palette. This section discusses three classes that you can use for managing string and other lists in your applications. In alphabetical order, the three classes are:

- *TList* — A general-purpose list-making class.
- *TStrings* — An abstract class that component properties use to manage lists of strings and other objects. TStrings objects do not allocate any memory for storage.
- *TStringList* — A class that applications can use to create lists of strings and objects. TStringList allocates memory for string storage.

 The preceding classes aren't strictly user-interface tools, but I want to introduce them here in Part II anyway because of their key importance in Delphi application development.

USING THE TLIST CLASS

Delphi uses the TList class as the basis for creating general-purpose lists. You can also use TList as a *container class* for storing objects of any types in lists. In most cases, to use TList, you'll need to create two of your own classes — one for the object items to store in the list, and one for the list itself. Create the item class in a unit module's implementation part as follows:

```
type
  TAnyItem = class
    Data: Integer;
    constructor Create(Data1: Integer);
  end;
```

As declared here, TAnyItem is a class data type that provides an integer variable named Data. This isn't practically useful, but demonstrates the basics for creating a list of TAnyItem objects. In addition to its Data member, the class has a constructor named Create for initializing objects of the class. *Always name the constructor Create.* Implement the constructor as you would any procedure, but use the keyword *constructor* in place of *procedure,* and preface the method name with TAnyItem and a period:

```
constructor TAnyItem.Create(Data1: Integer);
begin
  Data := Data1;
  inherited Create;
end;
```

The constructor saves the Data1 parameter in the object's Data variable, and then calls the inherited Create method in the ancestor class. Calling the inherited Create gives the ancestor class the opportunity to perform its own initializations, whatever they happen to be. (In object-oriented programming, we don't need to know all the gory details of an ancestor class's methods.) In this case, the ancestor is TObject, the granddaddy (or perhaps it's the grandmother) of all Delphi classes, even of those you create yourself.

NOTE ▶ Think of a class constructor as an initializer that prepares the internal elements of a new object. For each object of the class, the program must call the Create constructor to initialize the object.

You also need a class for the list. There's rarely any good reason to reinvent the wheel, so to take advantage of the methods that TList provides, derive the new class from TList. The new class *inherits* the properties and methods from TList. In other words, the new class is the same as TList plus whatever other capabilities you decide to add. To create the derived class, use this declaration in the unit's implementation:

```
type
  TAnyList = class(TList)
    destructor Destroy; override;
  end;
```

The TAnyList class overrides the Destroy destructor in the ancestor TList class. This is necessary because TList objects normally do not destroy the objects they contain. To add this capability to the derived class, implement the destructor, also in the unit's implementation, as follows:

```
destructor TAnyList.Destroy;
var
  I: Integer;
begin
  for I := 0 to Count - 1 do
    TAnyItem(Items[I]).Free;
  inherited Destroy;
end;
```

First, a *for* loop calls Free for all TAnyItem objects on the list. The TList class maintains a Count of items. The Items property contains pointers to (addresses of) objects in the list. To call a method such as Free requires a type-cast expression as shown, which in this example, informs the compiler that Items[I] is not just a pointer, but a TAnyItem object. Finally, the new destructor calls the inherited Destroy to give the TList class an opportunity to perform its own cleanups.

Armed with these basics, you can use TList to create lists of any kind of objects. The StrList sample program demonstrates the necessary steps. Figure 8-4 shows the program's display. Listing 8-6 gives the program's source code. Run the program, click *Add,* and enter a string. Repeat these steps several times to create a list of string objects in memory. Click *Update* to transfer the listed objects to the ListBox control. Click *Get* and enter a string to search the list. I'll explain more about the code after the listing.

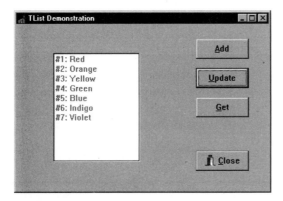

Figure 8-4

The StrList application demonstrates how to use Delphi's TList class to create lists of objects in memory.

Listing 8-6
Strlist\Main.Pas

```
unit Main;

interface

uses
  SysUtils, WinTypes, WinProcs, Messages, Classes, Graphics, Controls,
  Forms, Dialogs, StdCtrls, Buttons;

type
  TMainForm = class(TForm)
    AddButton: TButton;
    CloseBitBtn: TBitBtn;
    GetButton: TButton;
    ListBox1: TListBox;
    UpdateButton: TButton;
    procedure FormCreate(Sender: TObject);
    procedure FormDestroy(Sender: TObject);
    procedure AddButtonClick(Sender: TObject);
    procedure UpdateButtonClick(Sender: TObject);
    procedure GetButtonClick(Sender: TObject);
  private
    { Private declarations }
  public
    { Public declarations }
  end;

var
  MainForm: TMainForm;

implementation

{$R *.DFM}

type

{- New class of items to insert in a list }
  TStrItem = class
    S: string;
    I: Integer;
    constructor Create(S1: string; I1: Integer);
  end;

{- Derived class to hold TStrItem objects }
  TStrList = class(TList)
    destructor Destroy; override;
    function FindItem(S1: string): TStrItem;
  end;

var
  StrList: TStrList;        { List of TStrItems }
  ItemCount: Integer;       { Number of items inserted }
```

Declares a new class of string and Integer values.

Declares a class derived from TList to hold a list of TStrItem objects.

```
{- Create a new instance of TStrItem }
constructor TStrItem.Create(S1: String; I1: Integer);
begin
  S := S1;                  { Save string parameter }
  I := I1;                  { Save integer parameter }
  inherited Create;         { Call inherited Create }
end;

{- Destroy instance of TStrList }
destructor TStrList.Destroy;
var
  I: Integer;
begin
  for I := 0 to Count -1 do
    TStrItem(Items[I]).Free;  { Free all TStrItems }
  inherited Destroy;          { Call inherited destroy }
end;

{- Return object identified by S1 or nil for no match }
function TStrList.FindItem(S1: string): TStrItem;
var
  I: Integer;
  P: TStrItem;
begin
  for I := 0 to Count -1 do
  begin
    P := TStrItem(Items[I]);  { P refers to a TStrItem object }
    if Uppercase(P.S) = Uppercase(S1) then  { Match? }
    begin                { Found match }
      Result := P;   { Return P as function result }
      Exit;          { Exit function immediately }
    end;
  end;
  Result := nil;     { No match; return nil }
end;

{- TMainForm event handlers }

procedure TMainForm.FormCreate(Sender: TObject);
begin
  StrList := TStrList.Create;  { Create new StrList object }
  ItemCount := 0;              { Initialize insertion count }
end;

procedure TMainForm.FormDestroy(Sender: TObject);
begin
  StrList.Free;  { Also destroys listed items }
end;

{- Button event handlers }

procedure TMainForm.AddButtonClick(Sender: TObject);
var
  StrItem: TStrItem;   { New item to insert }
  S: string;           { User input string }
```

Use P to refer to each successive object in the TStrItem list.

Always call Create in reference to the class such as TStrList.

II

8

```
begin
  S := '';
  if InputQuery(Caption, 'Enter item', S) then     ──────▶  Prompt user for input.
  if Length(S) > 0 then
  begin
    Inc(ItemCount);
    StrItem := TStrItem.Create(S, ItemCount);
    StrList.Add(StrItem);
  end;
end;

procedure TMainForm.UpdateButtonClick(Sender: TObject);
var
  I: Integer;
  P: TStrItem;
begin
  ListBox1.Clear;                                  ──────▶  Erases ListBox1's entries.
  with StrList do
  for I := 0 to Count - 1 do
  begin
    P := TStrItem(StrList.Items[I]);
    ListBox1.Items.Add(Format('#%d: %s', [P.I, P.S]));
  end;
end;

procedure TMainForm.GetButtonClick(Sender: TObject);
var
  S: string;
  P: TStrItem;
begin
  UpdateButton.Click;                              ──────▶  To click a button under
  S := '';                                                  program control, call its
  if InputQuery(Caption, 'Enter item name', S) then         Click method.
  if Length(S) > 0 then
  begin
    P := StrList.FindItem(S);                      ──────▶  Returns a reference
    if P <> nil then                                        to an item or nil.
      ShowMessage(P.S + ', Number = ' + IntToStr(P.I))
    else
      ShowMessage('No such item');
  end;
end;

end.
```

StrList demonstrates how to create an *associative list,* which requires two classes. The first class, TStrItem, declares two data members — a string, S, and an integer value, I. The class also declares a Create constructor to initialize these variables. The second class, TStrList, which is derived from TList, declares two methods: a destructor and a function, FindItem, that searches a list for an object identified by a string argument.

To create the list object, the program defines a variable, StrList, of the TStrList class. If you prefer, these variables could also go into the form's class.

The TStrItem constructor assigns string and integer parameters to the class's S and I variables. This initializes new objects to be inserted into the list. Notice that the constructor calls the inherited Create even though TStrItem is a new class that is not derived from any other. This step isn't strictly necessary, but you should do it anyway because, in Delphi's Pascal, all classes are derived from the Adam-and-Eve ancestor TObject.

Because new classes are automatically derived from TObject, all Delphi classes and objects are related. Among other advantages, this means you can pass an object of *any* class type to a TObject parameter in a procedure or function.

TObject provides a default Create constructor and a default Destroy destructor, plus message dispatching code. If you purchased Delphi's run-time library source code, you can find TObject's Pascal declaration in the file System.Pas, located in the Source\Rtl\Sys path. TObject's methods are written in Assembly language in the files Clsf.Asm and Clsh.Asm. (You don't need the source code to use TObject, but if you do much programming with Delphi, you can learn a lot by browsing component methods.)

You do not have to explicitly derive classes from TObject, although you may if you wish. For example, the following two class declarations are equivalent:

```
type
  TNewClass1 = class
    {...}
  end;
  TNewClass2 = class(TObject)
    {...}
  end;
```

The TStrList destructor, Destroy, calls Free for each TStrItem object on the list. It then calls the inherited Destroy. You might use similar code in other methods — for example, one that clears objects from the list.

Function FindItem searches the list of objects for one that matches a string parameter. A *for* loop iterates through the list using TList's Count. To simplify the code, a statement assigns to P each listed object:

```
P := TStrItem(Items[I]);
```

P is a variable of the list-object class, TStrItem. Despite appearances, however, P is *not* a variable of that type. It is a *reference* to a TStrItem object. In Delphi, all class-object variables such as P are references — that is, they are pointers that refer to objects in memory. If you know other types of Pascal, the preceding code may appear to *copy* an entire TStrItem object to P, but that's not what happens in Delphi's Object Pascal. All that's assigned is the reference address of the TStrItem object in the list's Items array. *All class variables are references.*

Inside the *for* loop, an *if* statement compares the object's string (P.S) with the argument (S1) passed to FindItem. The statement uses Delphi's Uppercase function to compare the strings without regard for case. If the strings match, the program assigns P to the function's Result, and then exits the function immediately by calling Pascal's built-in Exit procedure. If there's no match, the final statement assigns *nil* to the function Result.

NOTE ▶ Although FindItem's declared result is TStrItem, the function actually returns a *reference* to a TStrItem object. This is just one additional benefit of Delphi's rule that all class-object variables are references. Consequently, Delphi permits assigning *nil* to FindItem's Result to indicate that it refers to no object.

StrList's OnCreate event handler for the program's form creates a new list by executing the following statement, which calls the TStrList Create method. An assignment statement constructs a TStrList object in memory, and it initializes the StrList variable to refer to that object:

```
StrList := TStrList.Create;
```

One of Delphi's cardinal rules is that you must free the objects you create. In this case, for example, the form's OnDestroy event handler frees the list object by calling the Free method, inherited from TList:

```
StrList.Free;
```

Because the TStrList destructor frees all listed objects, freeing the list properly disposes all memory allocated to the list and to its contained objects.

To add new objects to the list, AddButton's OnClick event prompts you to enter a string. These two statements create a new TStrItem object and add it to the list by calling TList's Add method:

```
StrItem := TStrItem.Create(S, ItemCount);
StrList.Add(StrItem);
```

When you click the *Update* button, its OnClick event handler transfers all listed object string and integer values to a ListBox component object. The expressions P.I and P.S refer to the data in each TStrItem object on the list. Similar expressions in GetButtonClick display object strings and integers after calling FindItem to search the list.

USING THE TSTRINGLIST CLASS

Delphi provides another class, TStringList, that uses a TList object to create string lists. TStringList is derived from TStrings, the class that components use for string-list properties. (I'll explain more about TStrings in the next section.) By using TStringList, you can create associative lists of strings and other objects, and you can assign those lists to a TStrings property in any Delphi component object.

One of the most common uses for TStringList objects is to read and write text files. Because TStringList uses Pascal strings, lines may be no longer than 255 characters, but this restriction shouldn't be a problem for most files. Listing 8-7 shows how to use TStringList to create a new text file. To try the code, create a project and insert two Button objects into the form. Also insert a Memo component. Enter the statements from Listing 8-7 into Button1's OnClick event handler.

Listing 8-7
This OnClick event handler demonstrates how to use TStringList to create a text file.

```
procedure TForm1.Button1Click(Sender: TObject);
var
  SL: TStringList;
begin
  SL := TStringList.Create;                              Create the list object.
  try
    SL.Add('This is the first line');
    SL.Add('This is the second line');
    SL.Add('This is THE END');
    SL.SaveToFile('anyname.txt');
  finally
    SL.Free;                              A finally-block frees SL even if an
  end;                                    exception occurs in the try-block.
end;
```

II

8

The sample program first creates a TStringList object named SL. It then adds some strings to the list, and calls SaveToFile to write them to a text file named ANYNAME.TXT. The procedure calls Free to delete the string list object from memory. *Always free the objects you create.* The *try-finally-end* statement block ensures that, even if any statement after *try* causes an exception, SL will be freed. See Chapter 18 for more information on exception handling.

Listing 8-8 demonstrates how to read a text file into a TStringList object. If you are creating the project, use this code for Button2's OnClick event handler. The procedure creates a TStringList object SL, and then calls LoadFromFile to read lines from ANYTEXT.TXT into the list object. An assignment copies this data to the Memo1 object's Lines property, an object of type TStrings.

Because TStringList is derived from TStrings, you can assign any TStringList object to a component object's TStrings property. You also can assign any TStrings property to a TStringList object.

Listing 8-8
This OnClick event handler demonstrates how to use a TStringList object to read a text file.

```
procedure TForm1.Button2Click(Sender: TObject);
var
  SL: TStringList;
begin
  SL := TStringList.Create;
  try
    SL.LoadFromFile('anyname.txt');
    Memo1.Lines := SL;
  finally
    SL.Free;
  end;
end;
```

Create objects outside of a try-block.

Use objects in a try-block.

Free objects in a finally-block.

Listing 8-8 demonstrates how to read a text file into an independent TStringList object, which you might want to do for a variety of list-handling purposes. However, you can more simply load a Memo component's Lines by calling its LoadFromFile method. This statement does all the work of Listing 8-8:

```
Memo1.Lines.LoadFromFile('anyname.txt');
```

Use AddStrings to attach multiple string lists to a TStringList object or a TStrings property. For example, if you have three TStringLists — T1, T2, and T3, you can insert them into a Memo object's Lines property with the following statements. The first assignment replaces Memo's text with strings from T1. The next two assignments append the other two lists:

```
with Memo1, Lines do
begin
  Lines := T1;
  AddStrings(T2);
  AddStrings(T3);
end;
```

TStringList is valuable not only for string lists, but for creating associations between strings and objects. The next section explains how to use this capability to display bitmaps in a ListBox control.

USING THE TSTRINGS CLASS

TStrings is an *abstract class,* which means that programs cannot create objects of this type. (Object-oriented gurus say that you cannot *instantiate* the class.) You may use TStrings only as a property of a component object. For example, you can store a list of strings and other objects in a ListBox's Items property, a TStrings object. To create your own list objects, use the TList and TStringList classes as described in the preceding sections.

Because TStringList is derived from TStrings, the information in this section applies to both classes. *Anything you can do with a TStrings property you can do with a TStringList object.*

The next program, GlyphLst, demonstrates how to use TStrings to create an associative array of strings and bitmaps. The demonstration displays all of Delphi's glyph bitmaps and their filenames in an owner-draw ListBox object. The term *owner-draw* means that the program, rather than Windows, takes over responsibility for drawing each ListBox item. Figure 8-5 shows GlyphLst's display. The program's source code is in Listing 8-9. I inserted comments into the code to explain the statements, which use some techniques not yet introduced.

If you did not install Delphi in the default directories on drive C:, modify the path name string in constant glyphPath, located just after the unit's *implementation* keyword.

Figure 8-5
GlyphLst displays an owner-draw ListBox of all the glyph bitmaps supplied with Delphi.

Listing 8-9
Glyphlst\Main.Pas

```
unit Main;

interface

uses
  SysUtils, WinTypes, WinProcs, Messages, Classes, Graphics, Controls,
  Forms, Dialogs, StdCtrls, Buttons, ExtCtrls;

type
  TMainForm = class(TForm)
    GlyphListBox: TListBox;
    BitBtn1: TBitBtn;
    PathLabel: TLabel;
    procedure FormCreate(Sender: TObject);
    procedure GlyphListBoxDrawItem(Control: TWinControl;
      Index: Integer; Rect: TRect; State: TOwnerDrawState);
    procedure FormClose(Sender: TObject; var Action: TCloseAction);
  private
    { Private declarations }
  public
    { Public declarations }
  end;

var
  MainForm: TMainForm;
```

```
implementation

{$R *.DFM}

const
  glyphPath = 'C:\Delphi\Images\Buttons';  { Change if necessary }

{- Load file names and bitmaps into GlyphList object }
procedure TMainForm.FormCreate(Sender: TObject);
var
  R: TSearchRec;      { Directory scan result record }
  K: Integer;         { while-loop control variable }
  Bitmap: TBitmap;    { Holds bitmaps. Do not Free! }
begin
Show;  { Make form visible while loading bitmaps }
  Screen.Cursor := crHourGlass;  { Show hourglass cursor }
  try
    PathLabel.Caption := glyphPath;  { Show path above ListBox }
    K := FindFirst(glyphPath + '\*.*', faAnyFile, R);  { Start scan }
    try
      while K = 0 do  { Scan directory for file names }
        begin
          if R.Name[1] <> '.' then  { Discard '.' and '..' paths }
          begin
            Bitmap := TBitmap.Create;  { Create object to hold bitmap }
            try  { Get bitmap and load from list }
              Bitmap.LoadFromFile(glyphPath + '\' + R.Name);
              GlyphListBox.Items.AddObject(R.Name, Bitmap);
            except
              Bitmap.Free;  { Executed if ANYTHING goes wrong }
              raise;        { Pass any exceptions up the call chain }
            end;
          end;
          K := FindNext(R);  { Continue directory scan }
        end;
    finally
      FindClose(R);
    end;
  finally
    Screen.Cursor := crDefault;  { Restore normal cursor }
  end;
end;

{- Draw bitmap and show file name in GlyphListBox entries }
procedure TMainForm.GlyphListBoxDrawItem(Control: TWinControl;
  Index: Integer; Rect: TRect; State: TOwnerDrawState);
var
  Bitmap: TBitmap;   { Reference to the bitmap }
  Offset: Integer;   { Separates image and text }
begin
  with (Control as TListBox).Canvas do
```

Modify this pathname for a nonstandard Delphi installtion.

Start directory scan.

This frees the bitmap if an exception occurs then reraises the exception for additional error handling.

Continue directory scan.
Restore normal cursor shape.

II

8

```
begin
  FillRect(Rect);                                          Erase the
  Bitmap := TBitmap(GlyphListBox.Items.Objects[Index]);    ListBox entry.
  if Bitmap <> nil then                                    Draw the
    begin { Draw bitmap and set offset for text }          bitmap.
      BrushCopy(Bounds(Rect.Left + 2, Rect.Top + 2, Bitmap.Width,
        Bitmap.Height), Bitmap, Bounds(0, 0, Bitmap.Width,
        Bitmap.Height), clRed);
      Offset := Bitmap.Width + 8;
    end;
  TextOut Rect.Left + Offset, Rect.Top, GlyphListbox.Items[Index]);
  end;
end;                                                       Display
                                                           associated
{- Delete the bitmap objects held in GlyphListBox }        string.
procedure TMainForm.FormClose(Sender: TObject;
  var Action: TCloseAction);
var
  I: Integer;
begin
  with GlyphListBox.Items do                               Free all created
    for I := 0 to Count -1 do                              objects before the
      TBitmap(Objects[I]).Free;                            program ends.
end;

end.
```

To create the GlyphLst project, insert a ListBox into a form and name it GlyphListBox. Then, follow these steps:

1. Select GlyphListBox and set its properties as follows: Integral-Height=True, ItemHeight=20, Style=lbOwnerDrawFixed. The Style setting tells the ListBox that the program will draw each item on request.

2. Create handlers for the form's OnCreate and OnClose events. Create a handler for the ListBox's OnDrawItem event, for which the program draws each ListBox item. Use the listing as a guide to writing the procedures.

3. Be sure to specify the correct path name in constant glyphPath. A more sophisticated program might use a menu and dialog to change directories — for simplicity, the demonstration uses a fixed path name.

Set a ListBox's Style to lbOwnerDrawVariable to display items of varying heights. Also create a handler for the OnMeasureItem event to specify each item's height in pixels. In the event handler, assign the correct value to the Height parameter for the listed item identified by the Index parameter. Owner-draw list boxes call OnMeasureItem only once when the window handle is created. If you don't implement OnMeasure, the object uses the ItemHeight property as the Height value of the OnMeasureItem event.

GlyphLst uses some interesting techniques that you'll find valuable in many situations. When the form is created, its OnCreate event handler first executes Show to make the form window visible. The procedure also displays an hourglass cursor. These finishing touches let users know that a lengthy operation is underway. Even on a fast 80486 or Pentium system, it may take several seconds to load the 162 bitmap files supplied with Delphi.

The procedure calls two Pascal functions to scan a directory for filenames. FindFirst begins the scan. To the function, pass a file specification including any path information, the constant faAnyFile to search all files, and the name of a TSearchRec variable, R. The function fills this record with the results of the search. R.Name, for example, provides the file's name as a Pascal string. If FindFirst returns zero, it was successful, and a *while* loop continues the scan. Call FindClose after all FindFirst and FindNext sequences. Pass the TSearchRec variable to FindNext to scan the next directory entry. When FindNext returns nonzero, the loop has reached the bottom of the directory's barrel.

The sample code uses exception handling in try-finally and try-except blocks to trap any file errors, and to ensure that all memory allocations to bitmaps are freed if any exceptions occur. Chapter 18 discusses Delphi exception handling in detail.

For each matching file, an *if* statement discards the "." and ".." pseudo files in DOS subdirectories. Three subsequent statements load the bitmap file and store it along with its name in the GlyphListBox object. Carefully examine these statements — they demonstrate the correct way to create an association in a ListBox component:

```
Bitmap := TBitmap.Create;  { Create object to hold bitmap }
Bitmap.LoadFromFile(glyphPath + '\' + R.Name); { Get bitmap }
GlyphListBox.Items.AddObject(R.Name, Bitmap);  { Add to list }
```

The first statement creates a bitmap object in memory. The second statement calls the LoadFromFile method for the Bitmap to read the bitmap file from disk. The expression R.Name, obtained from the directory scan, specifies the filename. The final statement adds the filename string and the Bitmap object to the GlyphListBox's Items property. Calling AddObject *associates* the string and the object in the list.

Objects are available through the ListBox's Objects array. Strings are available directly in Items, or in the Strings array. For example, after adding bitmaps and filenames to GlyphListBox, you can assign the first filename to a string variable S like this:

```
S := GlyphListBox.Items[0];
```

Similarly, you can refer to the list's bitmap objects. First, declare a variable of the object type:

```
var
  Bitmap: TBitmap;
```

Then, assign an object to Bitmap using a statement such as this:

```
Bitmap := TBitmap(GlyphListBox.Items.Objects[I]);
```

Notice that Objects is a property of Items. ListBoxes have a similar property, Strings, that you can use to access string data. Because Strings is the default property of Items, the following two statements compile to the same code:

```
S := GlyphListBox.Items[0];
S := GlyphListBox.Items.Strings[0];  { Same as preceding statement }
```

Use these concepts to access the listed filenames and bitmaps in GlyphListBox's OnDrawItem event handler. (See the procedure GlyphListBoxDrawItem in Listing 8-9.) The procedure uses some graphics methods not yet introduced. First, a *with* statement casts the Control parameter (of the general type TWinControl) to a TListBox object, and refers to its Canvas property. The program uses Canvas to draw objects in the visible ListBox.

If you are familiar with Windows programming, Canvas is Delphi's equivalent to a device context. Don't be concerned if you don't know what device contexts are — you'll learn about them, and more about Canvas, in Chapter 13.

FillRect clears the area where the bitmap is to be drawn. After that, the program assigns to Bitmap the object to be drawn from Items.Objects. The event receives the object's Index as a parameter, which tells the owner-draw procedure which item to draw.

BrushCopy copies the bitmap image into the ListBox, after which a local Offset variable separates the bitmap's filename from its image. Another Canvas method, TextOut, displays the filename.

Finally in the sample program, the form's OnClose event handler performs the critical task of disposing the bitmap objects. TStrings and TStringList objects dispose only strings automatically. If you add any objects to a list, you must free them as shown here.

Also examine the ToDo sample application on the book's CD-ROM. This program demonstrates other useful TStrings techniques. For example, Listing 8-10 shows the procedure that ToDo uses to move a selected item from one ListBox to another. Notice the TCustomListBox parameter. This class is TListBox's immediate ancestor. You could use TListBox as the parameter type, but using TCustomListBox ensures that the procedure works for any other objects of classes derived from TCustomListBox.

Listing 8-10

ToDo uses this procedure to move selected items from one ListBox to another.

```
procedure TMainForm.MoveSelected(List: TCustomListBox;
    Items: TStrings);
var
    I: Integer;
begin
    for I := List.Items.Count - 1 downto 0 do
        if List.Selected[I] then
        begin
            Items.AddObject(List.Items[I], List.Items.Objects[I]);
            List.Items.Delete(I);
        end;
    FileDirty := True;
end;
```

Scan list from bottom to top.

Add object to the Items TStrings parameter.

Delete the object from its original list.

The ToDo program calls MoveSelected using a statement such as the following, which transfers selected entries from the ListBox objects SrcList to DstList:

```
MoveSelected(DstList, SrcList.Items);
```

In MoveSelected (refer to the listing), parameter List is the destination ListBox; parameter Items is the source TStrings. A *for* loop scans List from bottom to top (note the use of Pascal's *downto* keyword). The scan must go in this direction because any deletions at item N alter the indexes of items N+1...

If a listed item is selected, AddObject copies the List's string and any associated object to parameter Items, of type TStrings. The procedure then deletes the original item. Calling Delete removes the string indicated by the passed index argument (I), and also sets Objects[I] to nil. Thus, one call to Delete removes a list's string and any associated object. However, it does not dispose of that object's memory — you *always* must do that by calling Free.

Summary

- Delphi's ListBox and ComboBox components are invaluable for adding selectable lists to application interfaces. You can select from a number of styles to create multiple-selection lists and to permit users to enter new data into a ComboBox's edit window.

- Delphi also provides the related list-making classes TList, TStrings, and TStringList. Use TList and TStringList to create independent list objects in memory. You cannot create TStrings objects — only components may use TStrings as a property's class type.

- All classes in Delphi are derived from TObject. This means that all class objects in Delphi applications are related.

- Because TStringList is derived from TStrings, anything you can do with a TStrings property (such as a ListBox's Items property) you can do with an independent TStringList object.

- An owner-draw ListBox control takes over responsibility for drawing individual items.

- You can use TStringList (or a TStrings component property) to create associative lists of strings and objects. This chapter's GlyphLst application demonstrates the technique by loading bitmaps and their file-names into a ListBox owner-draw control.

- A TStringList object or TStrings property provides access to string data through the Items property, or through the equivalent Items.Strings array. Associated object data is available through the Objects array.

- It is always your responsibility to free the objects you create. TList, TStringList, and TStrings automatically free only string data. If you insert other objects into a list, you must free those objects by calling Free.

Projects to Try

8-1: Write an application that uses a ListBox component to sort a text file.

8-2: Write code that reverses the order of entries in a ListBox or ComboBox object.

8-3: Write a procedure that loads a directory's filenames into a TStringList object.

8-4: Improve the GlyphList application by adding a *File* menu with commands for changing directories. Note: To prevent the program from attempting to load huge bitmaps into the ListBox, you might want to add code that rejects bitmap objects larger than a preset size.

8-5: *Advanced*. Create an owner-draw ListBox that displays sample strings in the fonts' styles. (Note: Some fonts are symbolic, and you'll have to display the font name separately from its sample string.)

8-6: *Advanced*. Use NewStr and DisposeStr, described next in "Expert-User Tips" to improve the StrList application. Use a PString pointer to address a dynamically allocated string in the TStrItem class. Add a destructor to that class and call DisposeStr to dispose of the allocated memory.

Expert-User Tips

- Lists require careful memory management. Use Pascal's MemAvail function to determine the total amount of available memory. The following statement sets a Label's Caption to show the total amount of available RAM:

```
Label1.Caption := IntToStr(MemAvail) + ' bytes';
```

- Use Pascal's MaxAvail function to determine the largest object that can be created in memory (equal to the total number of contiguously available bytes). For example, this sets a Label's Caption to show the largest free space in memory:

```
Label1.Caption := IntToStr(MaxAvail) + ' bytes';
```

- Even though MaxAvail may indicate that 10 megabytes are available, you may create objects no larger than 65,528 bytes. Call GetMem to allocate memory; call FreeMem to free it. For example, the following statements allocate and dispose a 1024-byte block of memory addressed by a Pointer P:

```
GetMem(P, 1024);
{ ... Use P here }
FreeMem(P, 1024);
```

- For lengthy string lists, conserve RAM by allocating only as much memory as needed for each string. To do this, call Pascal's NewStr function and DisposeStr procedure. For example, first declare a string S and a PString P:

```
var
  S: string;
  P: PString;
```

String S occupies 256 bytes (255 bytes for the characters and one byte that indicates the string's length). P is a pointer to a string of any length up to 255 characters. The following statements assign a string to S, then call NewStr to allocate the minimum amount of memory required to hold the actual string:

```
S := 'Original string';
P := NewStr(S);
```

P addresses a string that occupies only as much memory as needed to store *Original string*. Use P by dereferencing the pointer with Pascal's

∧ operator. For example, this copies the addressed string to a Label's Caption:

```
Label1.Caption := P^;
```

When you are finished using the addressed string, dispose of its allocated memory by calling DisposeStr:

```
DisposeStr(P);
```

- Look up more information on lb_ messages in Delphi's online Windows API help. Calling Perform to send a message — to enable horizontal scrollbars in list boxes, for example — is roughly but not exactly equivalent to calling the Windows SendMessage function. Perform calls the VCL WndProc (window procedure); SendMessage calls the procedure for the topmost window associated with a window handle.

- In complex applications, it might be convenient to create an array of TObject references to various components in a form. All classes derive from TObject, and therefore, an array of TObjects can refer to any Delphi object. For example, you can insert a set of component objects into a TObject array, and then use the array to perform operations on all objects. The ObjList application (see Listing 8-11) demonstrates the necessary techniques. The program's form window contains six CheckBox objects. Click the form's On/Off button to disable and enable the CheckBoxes. The program accomplishes this task by declaring a pointer to an array of TObjects, and then using GetMem to allocate memory for the number of CheckBoxes in the form. The form's OnCreate event handler assigns each CheckBox to the CheckBoxArray elements (remember, these are all *references*). The button's OnClick event handler uses a *for* loop to toggle each CheckBox object's Enabled property on and off. Finally, the form's OnDestroy event handler calls FreeMem to dispose of the allocated memory. Figure 8-6 shows the program's display.

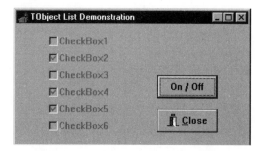

Figure 8-6

ObjList demonstrates how to create an array of TObject references for performing operations on sets of objects. For example, click the On/Off button to disable and enable the form's six CheckBoxes.

Listing 8-11

Objlist\Main.Pas

```pascal
unit Main;

interface

uses
  SysUtils, WinTypes, WinProcs, Messages, Classes, Graphics, Controls,
  Forms, Dialogs, StdCtrls, Buttons;

type
  TMainForm = class(TForm)
    CheckBox1: TCheckBox;
    CheckBox2: TCheckBox;
    CheckBox3: TCheckBox;
    CheckBox4: TCheckBox;
    CheckBox5: TCheckBox;
    CheckBox6: TCheckBox;
    OnOffButton: TButton;
    BitBtn1: TBitBtn;
    procedure FormCreate(Sender: TObject);
    procedure FormDestroy(Sender: TObject);
    procedure OnOffButtonClick(Sender: TObject);
  private
    { Private declarations }
  public
    { Public declarations }
  end;

var
  MainForm: TMainForm;
```

```
implementation

{$R *.DFM}

const
  numCheckBoxes = 6;

type
  PObjectArray = ^ObjectArray;
  TObjectArray = array[0..65520 div SizeOf(TObject)] of TObject;

var
  CheckBoxArray: PObjectArray;  { Pointer to array of CheckBox object }

procedure TMainForm.FormCreate(Sender: TObject);
begin
  GetMem(CheckBoxArray, numCheckBoxes * SizeOf(TObject));
  CheckBoxArray^[0] := CheckBox1;
  CheckBoxArray^[1] := CheckBox2;
  CheckBoxArray^[2] := CheckBox3;
  CheckBoxArray^[3] := CheckBox4;
  CheckBoxArray^[4] := CheckBox5;
  CheckBoxArray^[5] := CheckBox6;
end;

procedure TMainForm.FormDestroy(Sender: TObject);
begin
  FreeMem(CheckBoxArray, numCheckBoxes * SizeOf(TObject));
end;

procedure TMainForm.OnOffButtonClick(Sender: TObject);
var
  I: Integer;
begin
  for I := 0 to numCheckBoxes - 1 do
    with CheckBoxArray^[I] as TCheckBox do
      Enabled := not Enabled;
end;

end.
```

Literally "a pointer to a TObjectArray.

Allocate just enough memory to stores references (pointers) to the program's six checkboxes.

This for-loop shows how to use the object-reference array to perform an action on multiple component objects.

II

8

Coming Up

You'll find dozens more uses for string lists in Delphi's text-based components such as Memo, Notebook, and TabbedNotebook, which you will meet in the next chapter.

9

Working with Single-Line Strings

*I*n the old days of computing, we programmers were lucky if our terminals had upper- and lowercase letters plus a few standard punctuation symbols. Fortunately, we could select from a whole range of display colors — that is, as long as we chose green or orange. Today, with Windows and other graphical user interfaces, scaleable TrueType fonts and full-color monitors create limitless opportunities for interface designers, but programmers are faced with a completely new set of rules and regulations for working with character strings and other text objects.

In this chapter, you'll examine single-line strings and text components from two points of view — internal storage and external display. The old days of text-based terminals are gone for good, and creating a successful interface for a graphical operating system now demands attention to many new string storage and display techniques.

Components

- Edit — One of the simplest-looking controls in Windows, but also one of the most versatile, the Edit component can handle most single-line input tasks. The Edit object automatically supports cut, copy, and paste operations, and it comes with built-in keyboard, and mouse-handling features. Palette: Standard.

- Label — You have already used the Label component in previous chapters, but Labels have other uses that may not be obvious. For example, a Label can designate a hot key for other controls that don't support keyboard selection. Palette: Standard.

- MaskEdit — You might think of this component as an Edit box with brains. Use a MaskEdit component to create validated data-entry fields — for example, a telephone number input box that requires operators to enter digits in defined positions. Palette: Additional.

Character Strings

Delphi provides a healthy assortment of string operators, functions, and procedures. Before taking a look at string and text components, you need to thoroughly understand Delphi's two basic string formats as well as their operators and functions as the following section explains.

Pascal Strings vs. Null-Terminated Strings

A *String* is a fundamental data type built into Delphi's Object Pascal. An initial byte represents the number of characters in the string. Following this *length byte* are from 0 to 255 characters, for a maximum possible size of 256 bytes per string. Define a maximum-length string like this:

```
var
  S: String;
```

You can then assign a literal string to S:

```
S := 'Multimedia is hot!';
```

If you don't need 255 characters, you can save memory by specifying a smaller value in brackets. For example, this creates an 11-character string, which occupies 12 bytes of memory including the length byte:

```
var
  S: String[11];
```

Delphi stores literal and constant Pascal-type strings such as 'My string' in a unit's code segment. PChar literals and constant strings are stored in the data segment. Each unit has its own code segment, which can be up to 64K in length and contains the unit's code, constants, and literal strings.

You can also define a *null-terminated string,* which is simply an array of characters that ends with a byte equal to zero, known as the *null character.* There are three key differences between Pascal strings and null-terminated strings:

- Because a Pascal string represents its length using a byte, string variables can hold a maximum of 255 characters. ASCII strings may be as large as memory allows. With Delphi's 16-bit compiler, however, the maximum string size is 65,526 bytes including the null terminator. You have to call the StrAlloc function as explained in this chapter to allocate a string this large.

- You may index both types of strings as arrays of characters. Because Pascal strings begin with a length byte, refer to the first character in a Pascal string as S[1]. Refer to the first character in a null-terminated string as S[0].

- You may compare Pascal strings alphabetically using the usual logical operators: <, >, <=, >=, and =. You must call functions such as Str-Comp to compare null-terminated strings. The Pascal String is a native data type; null-terminated strings are simply arrays of characters that you can pass to and from various functions.

Define a null-terminated string as an array of Char. For example, this defines a 64-character string plus one byte reserved for the terminating null:

```
var
  S: array[0 .. 64] of Char;
```

Always try to use Pascal strings rather than null-terminated character arrays. Delphi's string functions are highly optimized, and you'll find them easier to use and generally more reliable — even if you are familiar with C and C++ null-terminated strings and string pointers. As a general rule, you'll need null-terminated strings only to pass arguments to Windows functions or if you must have strings larger than 255 characters. In that case, however, you may be able to use an array of strings, or a TStringList object, to store lengthy text data.

Each element of a Pascal or null-terminated string is a single byte of the type Char that represents the character's ASCII value. You can use Pascal's Chr function to assign ASCII values as characters to a string element:

```
S[3] := Chr(65);  { Assign ASCII 65 to S[3] }
```

You can also preface an ASCII value with a pound sign. The following statement is equivalent to the preceding one:

```
S[3] := #65;
```

Delphi defines the PChar data type as a pointer to a Char. Use this type to refer to null-terminated strings. For example, you may pass a null-terminated string to a function parameter of type PChar. As an example of this rule, insert this code into a form with two Label objects:

```
var
  S: String;
  P: array[0 .. 64] of Char;
begin
  S := 'Jumping Jack Flash';
  Label1.Caption := S;
  StrPCopy(P, 'Is a Gas, Gas, Gas');
  Label2.Caption := StrPas(P);
end;
```

The program assigns the literal string 'Jumping Jack Flash' to a String variable S, and then assigns that string to the first label's Caption property. (You could make the assignment directly, but I want to show the difference between the two kinds of strings.) The last two statements assign a literal string to the P array of Char by calling the StrPCopy function. Another function, StrPas, converts the null-terminated string P to a Pascal-String variable, which is assigned to the second label's Caption.

Experienced Delphi developers keep all of their strings in Pascal format, and use StrPCopy to convert strings temporarily to null-terminated strings for passing to Windows functions. This plan of action is usually cleaner than trying to maintain a mixture of different string types. Null-terminated string arrays are stored on either the stack or the program's data segment, and needlessly waste these precious resources.

Look up "String-handling Routines (Null-terminated)" in Delphi's online help for a list of functions you can use with PChar strings. Look up "String-handling Routines (Pascal-style)" for Pascal-String functions.

Dynamic Strings

When you define a string variable in a procedure, be aware that Pascal places the string on the system stack. For example, the following declarations consume a total of 1,024 bytes of stack space:

```
var
  S1, S2, S3, S4: String;  { ??? }
```

Declaring numerous strings this way is a highly questionable practice, and risks stack overflows. In a complex program with deeply nested levels of procedure calls, too many strings may evaporate the system stack faster than water in a desert.

Rather than create strings as variables in procedures and functions, it's more memory-efficient to define them as members of a class. For example, you can create string variables in a TForm class's private or public section using declarations such as:

```
TForm1 = class(TForm)
...
private
  S1, S2: String;
  ...
end;
```

Because Delphi constructs class objects in the Windows global heap — the pool of all free memory — the two strings S1 and S2 are allocated in the heap rather than on the relatively small, and more precious, system stack.

For even more efficient use of memory, declare PString variables for addressing strings dynamically allocated on the heap. For example, this defines a variable SP as a pointer to a string:

```
var
  SP: PString;
```

Allocate some memory to the pointer, and assign a literal string of characters with code such as this:

```
begin
  SP := NewStr('Place me on the heap');
```

Because SP is a pointer (that is, a memory address), you must *dereference* SP with Pascal's ^ operator to get to its addressed string. For example, the following statement assigns to a Label's Caption the string that SP addresses:

```
Label1.Caption := SP^;
```

After calling NewStr, you *must* dispose of the allocated memory at some point before the program ends. Do that by passing the string pointer to DisposeStr:

```
DisposeStr(SP);  { Dispose of memory allocated to SP }
```

Careful memory management is the key to success with dynamically allocated strings. After disposing a string's memory with DisposeStr, SP is freed for reuse; you may create another string with NewStr and assign the resulting address to SP. However, to reuse the same SP pointer after its initial NewStr allocation *without* having to call DisposeStr, use the AssignString function, which disposes and reallocates memory to a dynamic string before assigning it characters. The following code demonstrates how this function can eliminate many calls to DisposeStr. F represents any procedure or function with a String parameter:

```
var
  SP: PString;
begin
  SP := NewStr('The first string');        { First allocation to SP }
  F(SP^);                                    { Use the string }
  AssignString(SP, 'The second string');    { Reallocate, reassign }
  F(SP^);                                    { Use the string }
  AssignString(SP, 'The last string');      { Reallocate, reassign }
  F(SP^);                                    { Use the string }
  DisposeStr(SP);                            { Final disposal }
end;
```

Never perform operations that change the size of a dynamically allocated string. The number of characters in a dynamic string may vary up to the original defined length, but to alter the size of the string's allocated memory, you must dispose and reallocate the string. AssignString does this automatically, and is the safest method to use for this purpose.

You can also allocate memory for dynamic null-terminated strings. To do that, call StrAlloc. First, define a PChar variable to address the dynamic string:

```
var
  P: PChar;
```

Then, call StrAlloc to allocate memory to P. Allow one byte for the string's null terminator. For example, this statement creates a null-terminated string large enough to hold 64 characters plus a final null:

```
P := StrAlloc(65);
```

The largest value you can pass to StrAlloc is 65,526. The function returns a PChar pointer to the first location where you can store a character. Prior to that location, StrAlloc stores a hidden word equal to the size in bytes of the string object, which makes the actual amount of allocated memory two bytes larger than the requested size.

Call a function such as StrCopy to assign characters to the memory allocated for P:

```
StrCopy(P, 'Delphi is delectable');
```

Convert the null-terminated string that P addresses to a Pascal string S with a statement such as the following. The StrPas function accepts a PChar argument — you do not have to dereference the pointer:

```
S := StrPas(P);
```

Dispose of the memory allocated to P by calling StrDispose. Always match every call to StrAlloc with a call to StrDispose:

```
StrDispose(P);
```

Because StrAlloc stores the size of the string in memory, you should always dispose of dynamic null-terminated strings by calling StrDispose, which uses this size information to free the correct amount of memory.

STRING RESOURCES

If you have experience with other Windows development systems, you may be familiar with string table resources. A string table resource is a collection of strings, each from 1 to 255 characters long, that are stored in the program's .Exe code file.

String resources are supposed to permit developers to create language-independent versions of software that foreign-language translators can edit without having to recompile the code. In practice, however, language-independent programming is far more difficult than simply editing a few strings. But even so, you may find string table resources useful — especially when converting conventional Windows applications for Delphi. There's also a potential memory benefit to consider — string table resources efficiently use memory by keeping strings on disk until needed. Windows loads strings in blocks of 16 — in other words, if you load string number 3, Windows brings into memory strings indexed from 1 to 16.

A sample application, StrRes, demonstrates how to create and use string table resources. The program displays fictitious error messages when you click the *Live Dangerously* button. Figure 9-1 shows the program's display. Figure 9-2 shows one of the fictitious error messages. Each message comes from a string table resource defined in the Errmsg.Rc script (see Listing 9-1). Listing 9-2 gives the program's source code.

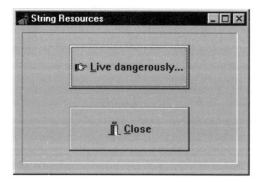

Figure 9-1

StrRes, which displays fictitious error messages, demonstrates how to use string table resources.

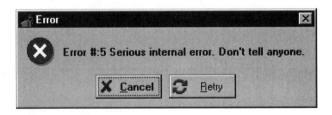

Figure 9-2

One of StrRes's fictitious error messages, each defined as an entry in a string table.

Listing 9-1

Strres\Errmsg.Rc

```
STRINGTABLE LOADONCALL MOVEABLE DISCARDABLE
BEGIN
  0,  "No error. Trust me."
  1,  "You can't be serious."
  2,  "Now you've done it."
  3,  "Your disk files are history."
  4,  "File not found. In fact, EVERYTHING is missing!"
  5,  "Serious internal error. Don't tell anyone."
  6,  "Feature unavailable. And you paid for this?"
END
```

A string table is a list of double-quoted literal strings prefaced with an integer index (refer to Listing 9-1). Despite the BEGIN and END keywords, the file is not a Pascal module — it's a Windows resource script. To use the table, you first have to compile the script. Go to a DOS prompt, and with Delphi's Bin directory on the path, enter this command to compile Errmsg.Rc and produce Errmsg.Res:

```
brc -r errmsg.rc
```

In the program module (refer to Listing 9-2), load the compiled resource file with a directive such as the following in the unit's implementation section. The command binds the string table resource into the program's compiled .Exe code file:

```
{$R Errmsg.Res}
```

Listing 9-2
Strres\Main.Pas

```
unit Main;

interface

uses
  SysUtils, WinTypes, WinProcs, Messages, Classes, Graphics, Controls,
  Forms, Dialogs, StdCtrls, Buttons, ExtCtrls;

type
  TMainForm = class(TForm)
    BitBtn1: TBitBtn;
    BitBtn2: TBitBtn;
    Bevel1: TBevel;
    procedure BitBtn1Click(Sender: TObject);
  private
    { Private declarations }
    function ErrorCancel(ErrNum: Word): Boolean;
  public
    { Public declarations }
  end;

var
  MainForm: TMainForm;

implementation

{$R *.DFM}
{$R Errmsg.Res}
```

Binds the resource file in the .Exe code file.

```
const
  maxErrorNumber = 6;

function TMainForm.ErrorCancel(ErrNum: Word): Boolean;
var
  ErrMsg: String;
  ErrStr: array[0 .. 63] of Char;
begin
  if LoadString(HInstance, ErrNum, ErrStr, 63) <= 0 then
    StrPCopy(ErrStr, 'Unknown problem');  { ErrStr := '...'; }
  ErrMsg := 'Error #:' + IntToStr(ErrNum) + ' ' + StrPas(ErrStr);
  ErrorCancel :=
    MessageDlg(ErrMsg, mtError, [mbRetry, mbCancel], 0) = mrCancel
end;
```

Call LoadString to read a string resource into a Char array.

This displays the sample error-message dialog.

```
procedure TMainForm.BitBtn1Click(Sender: TObject);
var
  ErrNum: Integer;
  Canceled: Boolean;
begin
```

```
    Canceled := False;
    repeat
      ErrNum := 1 + Random(maxErrorNumber);   { Simulate error }
      if ErrNum <> 0 then
        Canceled := ErrorCancel(ErrNum);
    until Canceled;
  end;

  end.
```

Returns are integer value at random from 0 to maxError-Number - 1.

Given these preparations, a program statement can load one of the strings into memory. Strings in string table resources are null-terminated character arrays, so you'll need an array of Char to hold the string. Windows limits string resource objects to 255 characters (256 bytes), but you can create smaller arrays if you are certain of your string lengths:

```
var
  AnyStr: array[0 .. 63] of Char;
```

Next, call LoadString and specify HInstance (the program's instance handle), the index of the string you want, the Char array, and the maximum number of characters the array can hold. For example, this loads the string indexed as 3 into AnyStr:

```
if LoadString(HInstance, 3, AnyStr, 63) > 0 then
  { ... do something with AnyStr }
```

If LoadString returns a value less than or equal to zero, Windows could not load the specified string. Otherwise, the character array contains the null-terminated string.

 For more information on using string table resources, look up STRINGTABLE in Delphi's online help, under the Windows API section.

Built-In Text Dialogs

Just in case you haven't discovered Delphi's string input and output dialogs, I'll mention them here. They are handy tools for displaying messages and prompting users for input. Try these — you'll find dozens of uses for these single-line text utilities.

DISPLAYING TEXT MESSAGES

Delphi provides five message dialogs, one of which is almost sure to meet your needs. Figures 9-3 through 9-7 show the five dialogs in order of complexity.

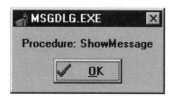

Figure 9-3
ShowMessage — Displays a string in a dialog box with an OK button.

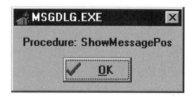

Figure 9-4
ShowMessagePos — Same as ShowMessage but with x- and y-coordinate parameters that specify the screen-relative location of the dialog box.

Figure 9-5
MessageBox — Encapsulates the Windows API MessageBox function. As shown here, under Windows 3.1, this function displays an old-style non-3D dialog that's as outdated as a hand-cranked telephone. For better-looking results, use one of the following two functions instead. Under Windows 95, MessageBox produces the same visual results as MessageDlg and Message-DlgPos. (All controls in Windows 95 have a 3D appearance.)

Figure 9-6

MessageDlg — Provides a wide variety of options for displaying messages and prompting for answers to questions. You can select an icon to display (for example, the information balloon shown here), and you can choose the types and number of buttons to offer.

Figure 9-7

MessageDlgPos — This is the same as MessageDlg but provides x- and y-coordinate parameters for positioning the dialog window anywhere on the Windows desktop.

ShowMessage and ShowMessagePos are procedures that display messages. They are suitable only for displaying static messages. MessageBox, MessageDlg, and MessageDlgPos are functions, and they return a value that indicates which button users clicked to close the dialog window. Use one of these functions to prompt users for answers to questions or to confirm choices — for example, "Are you *positively* sure you want to erase your hard drive?".

The MsgDlg application demonstrates the five types of message-display dialogs. Figure 9-8 shows the program's display. Listing 9-3 lists the program's source code.

II

9

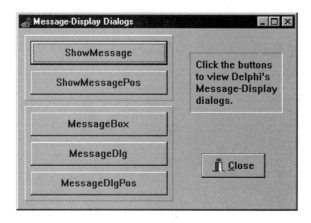

Figure 9-8

Run MsgDlg to experiment with the five types of message-display dialogs illustrated in Figures 9-3 through 9-7.

Listing 9-3

Msgdlg\Main.Pas

```
unit Main;

interface

uses
  SysUtils, WinTypes, WinProcs, Messages, Classes, Graphics, Controls,
  Forms, Dialogs, StdCtrls, ExtCtrls, Buttons;

type
  TMainForm = class(TForm)
    Button1: TButton;
    Button2: TButton;
    Button3: TButton;
    Button4: TButton;
    Button5: TButton;
    BitBtn1: TBitBtn;
    Label1: TLabel;
    Panel1: TPanel;
    Bevel1: TBevel;
    Panel2: TPanel;
    procedure Button1Click(Sender: TObject);
    procedure Button2Click(Sender: TObject);
    procedure Button3Click(Sender: TObject);
    procedure Button4Click(Sender: TObject);
    procedure Button5Click(Sender: TObject);
```

```
    private
      { Private declarations }
    public
      { Public declarations }
    end;

var
  MainForm: TMainForm;

implementation

{$R *.DFM}

procedure TMainForm.Button1Click(Sender: TObject);
begin
  ShowMessage('Procedure: ShowMessage');
end;
```

*Call these procedures
to display messages*

```
procedure TMainForm.Button2Click(Sender: TObject);
begin
  ShowMessagePos('Procedure: ShowMessagePos', 10, 20);
end;

procedure TMainForm.Button3Click(Sender: TObject);
var
  TheText, TheCaption: PChar;
begin
  TheText := StrAlloc(65);
  try
    TheCaption := StrAlloc(65);
    try
      StrPCopy(TheText, 'Function: MessageBox');
      StrPCopy(TheCaption, 'MessageBox Demonstration');
      if Application.MessageBox(TheText, TheCaption,
        MB_DEFBUTTON1 + MB_ICONEXCLAMATION + MB_OKCANCEL) = IDOK
        then ShowMessage('You selected OK')
        else ShowMessage('You selected Cancel');
    finally
      StrDispose(TheText);
    end;
  finally
    StrDispose(TheCaption);
  end;
end;
```

*As this procedure
shows, MessageBox is
relatively difficult to
use. Call the simpler
MessageDlg and
MessageDlgPos
functions instead.*

```
procedure TMainForm.Button4Click(Sender: TObject);
var
  W: Word;
  S: String[6];
begin
  W := MessageDlg('Function: MessageDlg',
    mtInformation, [mbYes, mbNo, mbIgnore], 0);
  case W of
```

*MessageDlg returns a
value that indicates
which button the
user clicked to close
the dialog window.*

*These parameters
select the dialog's
style and types of
buttons.*

II

9

```
      mrYes:    S := 'Yes';
      mrNo:     S := 'No';
      mrIgnore: S := 'Ignore';
    end;
    ShowMessage('You selected ' + S);
  end;

  procedure TMainForm.Button5Click(Sender: TObject);
  var
    W: Word;
    S: String[6];
    X, Y: Integer;
  begin
    X := 50; Y := 75;
    W := MessageDlgPos('Function: MessageDlgPos',
      mtWarning, mbAbortRetryIgnore, 0, X, Y);
    case W of
      mrAbort:  S := 'Abort';
      mrRetry:  S := 'Retry';
      mrIgnore: S := 'Ignore';
    end;
    ShowMessage('You selected ' + S);
  end;

  end.
```

MessageDLPos is the same as MessageDlg but lets you specify the dialog's position.

This parameter specifies context-sensitive help, but is unused here.

ShowMessage is easy to use. Just pass it any string or string variable to display a message. Remember that Delphi permits you to concatenate Pascal style strings with the plus operator — a fact that makes ShowMessage handy for displaying all sorts of values as well as for debugging errant variables. For example, to display the value of an Integer Count variable, use a statement such as this:

```
ShowMessage('Count = ' + IntToStr(Count));
```

ShowMessagePos is the same as ShowMessage but adds X and Y coordinate values, relative to the screen. To display the preceding message at the upper-left corner of the Windows desktop, use this statement:

```
ShowMessagePos('Count = ' + IntToStr(Count), 0, 0);
```

MessageBox is more complex to use. You need to pass it null-terminated strings plus a logical grouping of constants such as MB_OKCANCEL to select various options. (See the API on-line help for more information.) Function Button3Click in the sample listing shows how to use MessageBox, but I recommend that you instead use MessageDlg or MessageDlgPos, which are simpler in design and accept Pascal string arguments. Delphi defines MessageDlg as:

```
function MessageDlg(const Msg: string; AType: TMsgDlgType;
  AButtons: TMsgDlgButtons; HelpCtx: Longint): Word;
```

- *Msg* — Pass a literal, variable, or constant string to display in the dialog box.

- *AType* — Set this parameter to a constant such as mtWarning or mtError to select an appropriate icon and dialog caption.

- *AButtons* — Set this parameter to the *set* of buttons you want to display in the dialog. Surround the set with brackets. For example, pass the expression [mbYes, mbNo, mbCancel] to display Yes, No, and Cancel buttons. Delphi automatically adds appropriate glyphs to each button (they are BitBtn component objects). Alternatively, rather than define your own button set, pass a predefined set such as mbYesNoCancel, mbOkCancel, or myAbortRetryIgnore. These are already Pascal sets — don't surround them with brackets.

- *HelpCtx* — Set this parameter to zero unless you are defining a help context for the message box.

 Look up MessageDlg for more information on possible values you can pass to this function and to MessageDlgPos.

MessageDlg and MessageDlgPos return a value that indicates which button users clicked to close the dialog window. Because you determine which buttons the dialog displays, you have to check for only those buttons — you don't need to encode responses for every possible return value. A *case* statement is usually the cleanest construction. First, define a Word variable W and assign MessageDlg or MessageDlgPos to it with a statement such as this:

```
W := MessageDlg('Function: MessageDlg',
  mtInformation, [mbYes, mbNo, mbIgnore], 0);
```

Then, use a *case* statement to take an appropriate action based on which button the user selected:

```
case W of
  mrYes:    { action for Yes    };
  mrNo:     { action for No     };
  mrIgnore: { action for Ignore };
end;
```

MessageDlgPos is the same as MessageDlg but adds X and Y coordinate parameters for positioning the dialog on the Windows desktop. The coordinates are relative to the screen, but you can convert them to client-relative values to display dialogs within the program's window space. This makes for a friendlier interface because users tend to look for messages in specific locations relative to the application's window.

Listing 9-4 demonstrates how to use screen-relative coordinates to position items in windows. Define a TPoint variable P, set its X and Y members to 0, and call ClientToScreen, which returns a TPoint record with those values converted to equivalent screen coordinates. You can then call MessageDlgPos as shown (or call ShowMessagePos) to position the message box at the upper-left corner or another location of the application window's client area.

Listing 9-4

Use this code to position a message dialog within the application's window. The technique also applies to ShowMessagePos.

```
var
  W: Word;    { Result of MessageDlgPos }
  P: TPoint;  { Coordinate X, Y record }
begin
  P.X := 0;   { Assign client X value }
  P.Y := 0;   { Assign client Y value }
  P := ClientToScreen(P);  { Convert P to screen coordinates }
  W := MessageDlgPos('Function: MessageDlg',
    mtInformation, [mbYes, mbNo, mbIgnore], 0,
    P.X, P.Y);  { Pass converted X, Y to function }
end;
```

If you pass X and Y equal to –1 to ShowMessagePos or MessageDlgPos, the functions display their dialog windows at default locations selected by Windows.

PROMPTING FOR TEXT INPUT

Programming is a process of give and take. The preceding Message dialogs *give* users information. To *take* input from users, call the InputBox or InputQuery functions, which display the dialog shown in Figure 9-9. InputBox returns a string; InputQuery returns a Boolean True or False value, but the two functions are otherwise equivalent. Listing 9-5 demonstrates how to use InputBox and InputQuery. This isn't a complete program — to use the code, insert two Button objects into a form and copy the two procedures into OnClick event handlers for each Button.

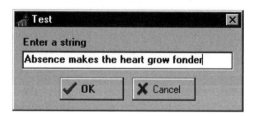

Figure 9-9

Call the InputBox or InputQuery functions to prompt users for single-line text strings. Both functions display the dialog shown here.

Listing 9-5

Copy these procedures to a program's unit as OnClick event handlers for two Button objects in a form, and run the program to experiment with the InputBox and InputQuery functions.

```
procedure TForm1.Button1Click(Sender: TObject);
var
  S: String;
begin
  S := InputBox('Test', 'Enter a string', '');
  if Length(S) > 0 then
    ShowMessage('You entered: ' + S);
end;

procedure TForm1.Button2Click(Sender: TObject);
var
  S: String;
begin
  S := '';
  if InputQuery('Test', 'Type QUIT to end', S) then
    if Uppercase(S) = 'QUIT' then
      Close;
end;
```

InputBox returns a string if the user clicks OK.

InputQuery returns True if the user clicks OK.

InputBox takes three string arguments: a caption, a prompt, and a default string value, which can be variable or constant. The sample listing passes a null string to InputBox for the default string, returned if users enter no changes. InputBox displays the default string highlighted in the dialog. The function also returns the default string if users click the Cancel button. If users click OK, InputBox returns the text entered in the dialog's Edit control. For example, use InputBox to prompt for a filename:

```
S := InputBox('Test', 'Enter filename', 'Readme.Txt');
ShowMessage('You entered: ' + S);
```

InputQuery is the same as InputBox, but it returns True if users click OK, or False if users click Cancel. InputQuery deposits user input into the default string, which must be a variable. The function is ideal for prompting users to enter strings such as filenames that default to known paths. For example, insert Button and Memo objects into a form, and then use the programming in Listing 9-6 to prompt for a filename, which defaults to C:\Delphi\Readme.Txt, and display the file's text in the Memo.

Listing 9-6

Insert Button and Memo objects into a form, and use this programming for the Button's OnClick event handler. The procedure calls InputQuery to prompt for a filename, which defaults to Delphi's Readme.Txt file.

```
procedure TForm1.Button1Click(Sender: TObject);
var
  Filename: String;
begin
  Filename := 'C:\Delphi\Readme.Txt';
  if InputQuery('Test', 'File?', Filename) then
    Memo1.Lines.LoadFromFile(Filename);
end;
```

Single-Line Text Components

Delphi offers three single-line text input and output components: Label, Edit, and MaskEdit. They are relatively simple to use, but the following sections describe some less obvious techniques that you'll find valuable.

LABELS

Labels are simply text objects that you can insert into forms and other container components such as a Panel. As you have discovered from this book's examples so far, Labels have numerous properties. You can set a Label's Font to alter its text style, you can display wrap-around text by setting WordWrap True, and you can change a Label's color with the Color property.

The Color property selects a Label's background color. Use the Font property to select a Label's foreground text color.

In most cases, Labels are noninteractive — they simply label another component, or they provide some on-screen information. One of the less obvious uses for a Label is to provide an accelerator hot key for another control that normally doesn't support keyboard selection. Follow these steps to try out this useful technique:

1. Insert three Edit objects and three Label objects into a form. Position each label to the immediate left of an Edit control.

2. Change Label1's Caption to &One. The ampersand designates a subsequent letter (O in this case) as the accelerator hot key.

3. Select Label1's FocusControl property, click the down arrow, and choose Edit1. When Label1 receives the input focus, it passes the focus to the indicated control.

4. Repeat steps 2 and 3 for the other two Labels. Set Label2's Caption to &Two, and Label3's to T&hree. Assign Label2's FocusControl to Edit2, and Label3's to Edit3.

5. Run the program and press Alt+O, Alt+T, and Alt+H to shift the focus to the labeled Edit boxes.

To center a label horizontally with an Edit or other associated control, first select the Edit control, press and hold the Shift key, and click the corresponding Label. Choose Delphi's *Edit|Align...* command, choose the *Vertical Centers* radio button, and press Enter or click OK. (Note: It appears from this test that Delphi mixes up Horizontal and Vertical Centers. In case this is changed in future releases, if the Label disappears, choose *Horizontal Centers.*)

II

9

EDIT BOXES

For general-purpose single-line input, you can't beat Delphi's Edit component. Following are some tips about selected Edit component properties:

- Set AutoSelect to True to highlight an Edit object's contents when the object receives the input focus.

- Set CharCase to ecNormal for normal entry. Set it to ecUpperCase or ecLowerCase to limit entry to upper- or lowercase.

- Set HideSelection False if you want highlighted text to remain selected when users shift the focus to another control. Set HideSelection to True for normal operation — selected text is unhighlighted when the focus leaves the Edit control.

- Set MaxLength to the maximum number of characters you want users to enter. Although you can set this property to zero for unlimited input length, in practice, there's never any good reason to use a value greater than 255, which is the maximum length of the Text property.

- The Edit component does not have a Caption property. Use a Label as explained in the preceding section to give Edit objects captions and hot-key accelerators. To display an object, insert characters into the Text property, or assign a string at runtime.

- To display text-screen DOS characters, set OEMConvert to True, and change Font to TrueType MS LineDraw. Set OEMConvert to False if you don't want ANSI characters converted (this is the normal setting for Windows).

OEMConvert must be False for Edit objects used to enter filenames. Edit components also provide numerous events. Some of the more useful of these are:

- *OnChange* — Called when the control's contents change in any way. If you enable this event, be aware that it will be called for *each* character entered into the control. To filter characters entered into an Edit control, you should instead use the OnKeyPress event.

- *OnClick* — Called when the user single-clicks the mouse in the Edit control. Note that this event handler is not called when the Edit control receives the focus by other means — when users press Tab, for example.

- *OnDblClick* — Called when the user double-clicks the mouse in the Edit control. The normal response for this event copies the Edit control's Text property to another object such as a ListBox.

- *OnEnter* — Called when the control receives the input focus — that is, when users select the control, tab to it, or click it with the mouse.

- *OnExit* — Called when the control loses the input focus — that is, when users shift the focus to another control.

- *OnKeyPress* — Called for every keypress. Generally, this event is the correct one to use for filtering keyboard input. For example, to prevent users from typing certain keys, if the event handler's Key parameter equals a target value, set Key to #0 to disable it.

The OnEnter and OnExit events are particularly useful for designing attractive interfaces. For example, you can use these events to color the focused Edit control, which can help draw the user's attention to the current field in a window with numerous input areas. First, declare a variable Old-Color of type TColor in the form class's *private* section, something like this:

```
TForm1 = class(TForm)
  Edit1: TEdit;
private
  OldColor: TColor;
...
public
...
end;
```

Next, create an OnEnter event handler for an Edit object. Assign the object's Color to the OldColor variable, and then select the color you want for the control's background. With this code, when users shift the focus to the control, its background changes to yellow:

```
procedure TForm1.Edit1Enter(Sender: TObject);
begin
  OldColor := Edit1.Color;
  Edit1.Color := clYellow;
end;
```

II

9

Also, create a handler for the Edit object's OnExit event. Assign the OldColor value to the object's Color property. When users shift the focus away from the control, the program restores its background to the saved color:

```
procedure TForm1.Edit1Exit(Sender: TObject);
begin
  Edit1.Color := OldColor;
end;
```

TELEPHONIC MNEMONICS

The TelName application on the CD-ROM demonstrates how to use Edit objects. This program uses Delphi to paint a pretty new face on some code I wrote for my *Dr. Dobb's* column, "Algorithm Alley", a few years back. The program solved one of my pet peeves — cutesy telephonic mnemonics in advertisements that read something like "To reach us by phone, just dial 1-800-CALL-US-NOW." It takes me forever and a day to look up the corresponding numbers on the telephone dial, so I wrote a program to convert the mnemonics to numbers. I also wrote the converse code that displays all possible permutations of any number. In my area, for example, the common exchange 293 can spell words such as AWE, AXE, and AYE, leading to some interesting mnemonics. (I have it in mind to request AWE-SOME for my next telephone number.)

To use TelName, enter a telephonic mnemonic in the *Telephone name* Edit control. Click the *Number* button to convert the name to its equivalent number. Or, enter a number in the *Telephone number* Edit control, and click *Names* to insert all possible mnemonic permutations into the window's list box. Note: On a telephone dial, digits 1 and 0 have no corresponding letters, and letters Q and Z have no corresponding digits.

Long telephone numbers in TelName produce numerous ListBox entries, which may cause Windows to run out of resources. The number of entries equals 3^n where *n* is the number of digits. Four digits produce 81 entries. Six digits produce 729 entries. For best results, type a maximum of three or four digits into the *Telephone number* Edit control before clicking *Names*. For example, to see what your telephone number spells, instead of entering all digits, enter the area code, exchange, and number separately.

Figure 9-10 shows TelName's display. Listing 9-7 shows the program's source code. For an explanation of how the algorithm works, and on permutations in general, see my article, "Algorithm Alley: Telephonic Mnemonics," *Dr. Dobb's Journal*, June 1993.

Figure 9-10

TelName converts telephonic mnemonics to equivalent telephone numbers, and can show all possible alphabetic permutations for any number. For best results, limit numbers to three or four digits before clicking Names.

Listing 9-7
TelName\Main.Pas

```
unit Main;

interface

uses
    SysUtils, WinTypes, WinProcs, Messages, Classes, Graphics, Controls,
    Forms, Dialogs, StdCtrls, Buttons, Mask;

type
  TMainForm = class(TForm)
    Label1: TLabel;
    Label2: TLabel;
    ListBox1: TListBox;
    CloseBitBtn: TBitBtn;
    NamesBitBtn: TBitBtn;
    NumberBitBtn: TBitBtn;
    NameEdit: TEdit;
```

```
    NumbEdit: TEdit;
    procedure FormCreate(Sender: TObject);
    procedure NumberBitBtnClick(Sender: TObject);
    procedure NamesBitBtnClick(Sender: TObject);
    procedure NumbEditKeyPress(Sender: TObject; var Key: Char);
    procedure NameEditKeyPress(Sender: TObject; var Key: Char);
  private
    { Private declarations }
    function TelNameToNum(TelName: String): String;
    procedure ListNames(TelNum: String);
  public
    { Public declarations }
  end;

var
  MainForm: TMainForm;

implementation

{$R *.DFM}

var
{- Array of telephone dialog letters }
  TelDial: array[0 .. 9] of String[3];

{- Return telephone digit that corresponds to C }
function DigitToLetter(C: Char): Char;
var
  I, J: Integer;
begin
  C := Upcase(C);
  for I := 0 to 9 do
    for J := 1 to 3 do
      if (C = TelDial[I][J]) then
      begin
        Result := Chr(I + Ord('0'));
        Exit;
      end;
  Result := C;   { Default }
end;

{- Return ordinal value of digit character C }
function ValueOfChar(C: Char): Integer;
begin
  Result := Ord(C) - Ord('0');
end;

{- Return number for a telephone alphabetic name }
function TMainForm.TelNameToNum(TelName: String): String;
var
  I: Integer;
```

```
begin
  Result := '';
  for I := 1 to Length(TelName) do
    Result := Result + DigitToLetter(TelName[I]);
end;

{- Insert all permutations of TelNum into ListBox1 }
procedure TMainForm.ListNames(TelNum: String);
var
  SP: PString;  { Pointer to dynamic string }

  {- Find N alphabetic permutations of digits in TelNum }
  procedure Permute(N: Integer);
  var
    I, Digit: Integer;
  begin
    Digit := ValueOfChar(TelNum[N]);
    for I := 1 to 3 do
    begin
      SP^[N] := TelDial[Digit][I];
      if (N = Length(TelNum)) then
        ListBox1.Items.Add(SP^)  }
      else
        Permute(N + 1);  { Call Permute recursively }
    end;
  end; { Permute }

begin
  if Length(TelNum) > 0 then
  begin
    SP := NewStr(TelNum);
    try                        { Create dynamic string }
      Permute(1);              { Start permutations }
    finally
      DisposeStr(SP);          { Dispose dynamic string }
    end;
  end;
end;

{- Initialize global variables }
procedure TMainForm.FormCreate(Sender: TObject);
begin
  TelDial[0] := '   ';  TelDial[1] := '   ';
  TelDial[2] := 'ABC';  TelDial[3] := 'DEF';
  TelDial[4] := 'GHI';  TelDial[5] := 'JKL';
  TelDial[6] := 'MNO';  TelDial[7] := 'PRS';
  TelDial[8] := 'TUV';  TelDial[9] := 'WXY';
end;

{- Do Number button click }
procedure TMainForm.NumberBitBtnClick(Sender: TObject);
```

Inserts letter into string.

Adds string to listbox.

Because this is in a finally block, the string is properly disposed even if permute causes an exception.

II

9

```
begin
  NumbEdit.Text := TelNameToNum(NameEdit.Text);
  NumbEdit.SetFocus;
end;

{- Do Names button click }
procedure TMainForm.NamesBitBtnClick(Sender: TObject);
begin
  ListBox1.Clear;
  ListNames(NumbEdit.Text);
  ListBox1.SetFocus;
end;

{- Click Names button for Enter key in Number Edit object }
procedure TMainForm.NumbEditKeyPress(Sender: TObject; var Key: Char);
begin
  if Key = #13 then
  begin
    NamesBitBtn.Click;
    Key := #0;
  end;
end;

{- Click Number button for Enter key in Name Edit object }
procedure TMainForm.NameEditKeyPress(Sender: TObject; var Key: Char);
begin
  if Key = #13 then
  begin
    NumberBitBtn.Click;
    Key := #0;
  end;
end;

end.
```

Clicking the Number button sets the focus to the NumbEdit control, so user can enter a number.

Likewise, clicking Names transfers the focus to the permuted list of telephone names.

Setting key to ASCII null disables the Enter key (#13).

Calling Click simulates a button Click event under program control.

Setting key to ASCII null disables the Enter key (#13).

TelName demonstrates some useful interface and string-handling techniques. Two labels provide accelerator hot keys for the Edit controls, using the methods discussed earlier. For example, the *Telephone name* label prefaces *n* in *name* with an ampersand, and the Label object's FocusControl property is set to NameEdit. With these property values, pressing Alt+N selects the labeled Edit object.

The program's Number and Names buttons demonstrate how to shift the focus to another control after a button's selection. This is useful for promoting a logical progression through a group of controls. For example, when you click the Number button, the program converts a telephonic mnemonic in the *Telephone name* Edit box to a number. Users will probably want to modify that number to list other possible spellings, so the Number button's OnClick event handler shifts the focus away from itself to the NumbEdit object. The following two statements handle the Number button's selection:

```
NumbEdit.Text := TelNameToNum(NameEdit.Text);
NumbEdit.SetFocus;
```

The first statement converts the NameEdit object's text — for example, *boat* — to an equivalent telephone number (2628). The second statement calls NumbEdit's SetFocus method to shift the focus to the next Edit object.

Clicking the Names button performs a similar task, using these three statements in the OnClick event handler:

```
ListBox1.Clear;
ListNames(NumbEdit.Text);
ListBox1.SetFocus;
```

First, the procedure clears the ListBox's current entries. It then calls ListNames, which permutes a telephone number into all possible alphabetic mnemonics. The last statement shifts the input focus to the ListBox so users can press arrow keys to view the listed results.

Providing efficient keyboard operations for graphical software is a black art that's not often practiced very well. In addition to permitting keyboard control over commands, a well-designed user interface uses methods such as SetFocus to minimize keypresses. Even though it's safe to say that most all Windows systems have a mouse input device, a finished application should be completely operable from the keyboard.

TelName takes two other measures to improve keyboard handling. When you press Enter in an Edit box, the input focus normally shifts to the next control in tab order. This offers an excellent opportunity for performing any needed processing on the Edit control's contents, thereby eliminating one button click. For example, run TelName and enter *boat* in the *Telephone name* Edit control. When you press Enter, the program shifts the focus to the *Telephone number* Edit area, and it converts *boat* to the equivalent number. Press Enter again to shift to the ListBox and insert all possible permutations of that number. When you try this, the effect seems obvious, but achieving a smooth keyboard interface often requires much thought and testing.

To reprogram the Enter key to accomplish these interactive tasks, TelName uses two OnKeyPress event handlers for the NumbEdit and NameEdit objects. In NumbEditKeyPress, for example, the program checks for a carriage return (the expression #13 represents an ASCII character with a value of 13). To process the information in the Edit window, the program simulates a button click with the statement:

```
NamesBitBtn.Click;
```

After that, the program throws out the carriage return because the button already shifts the focus to the next Edit window, and we don't want the current control to receive that character. To throw away the Enter keypress, simply set Key to ASCII null with this assignment:

```
Key := #0;
```

Notice also how procedure ListNames uses a dynamic string to conserve memory. The procedure declares a string parameter, TelNum, which occupies 256 bytes of RAM. An output string of that same length is needed to hold each successive permutation, but rather than declare another 256-byte string, the procedure declares a string pointer SP of type PString. The procedure prepares a dynamic copy of the TelNum parameter, calls the nested Permute procedure to find all alphabetic combinations of that number, and disposes the dynamic string with the following statements:

```
SP := NewStr(TelNum);   { Create dynamic string }
Permute(1);             { Start permutations }
DisposeStr(SP);         { Dispose dynamic string }
```

The memory savings in this small example are miniscule, but in complex programs with many strings, you can save a lot of RAM and reduce stack usage by dynamically creating string objects rather than declaring string variables in procedures and functions.

MASKED EDIT BOXES

The MaskEdit component provides a formatted Edit control that restricts users to entering required symbols at defined positions. A secondary string, called the EditMask, defines input rules. For example, a mask can define a formatted telephone number that requires users to enter a seven-digit phone number. Follow these steps to experiment with MaskEdit:

1. Insert a MaskEdit object from the *Additional* VCL palette into a form. Also enter an Edit object and Button object.

2. The MaskEdit component provides a property, EditMask, that defines the control's input format. You can assign a mask at design time by modifying this property. To do the same at runtime, double-click Button1 and enter this statement into its OnClick event handler:

```
MaskEdit1.EditMask := Edit1.Text;
MaskEdit1.SetFocus;
```

3. Run the program and enter **999\-9999;1;_** into the Edit1 object. Enter all punctuation as shown (note the final underscore). Click the button to copy that text to the MaskEdit object's EditMask property. The mask specifies a seven-digit telephone number (I'll explain more about the mask's format later).

4. Enter text into MaskEdit to experiment with your mask.

You can also test masks by clicking the ellipsis button for a MaskEdit object's EditMask property. This opens Delphi's *Input Mask Editor* dialog, which is shown in Figure 9-11. Select a sample mask, and enter test strings into the Test Input edit control. Load .Dem (Delphi Edit Mask) files by clicking the *Masks* button. Delphi provides several sample files with telephone number, date, time, and other formatting masks in a variety of languages. Listing 9-8 shows the text from Denmark.Dem, located in Delphi's Bin subdirectory.

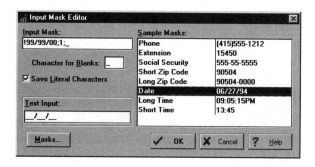

Figure 9-11

Delphi's Input Mask Editor dialog provides sample masks for a Mask-Edit component's EditMask property.

Listing 9-8

Denmark.Dem illustrates the format for an edit mask text file.

```
Phone | 48140001 | 00 09 99 99;1;_
Phone with Country | 48140001 | \+45 00 00 00 00;1;_
Social Security | 1234567890 | 000000\-0000;1;_
Zip Code | 3450 | 0000;1;_
Zip Code with Country | DK3450 | !>LL\-0000;1;_
Date | 260195 | 90\.90\.\1\900;1;_
Date (Windows) | 260195 | 90/90/00;1;_
Long Time | 210515 | !90:00:00;1;_
Short Time | 1345 | !90:00;1;_
```

TIP

For a table of script characters you can use to construct masks, search for EditMask in Delphi's on-line help.

An EditMask is a string of symbols that designate literal characters, input character sets, and control codes. A mask consists of three parts separated by semicolons:

- One or more characters that designate allowable input character sets.

- 1 to save literal characters in the input — hyphens in a telephone number, for example — or 0 not to save literal characters.

- The character to display for blanks in the MaskEdit window. This is usually an underscore or a blank.

A sample telephone EditMask string illustrates how to construct each part of a complete mask. Here's the mask:

```
!\(999\)000\-0000;1;_
```

At runtime, this mask causes the MaskEdit object to display the following input template:

```
(___)___-____
```

In the mask string, a leading exclamation point tells the control to discard trailing blanks from the resulting input. If you don't begin a mask with an exclamation point, trailing blanks are preserved. Type a back slash to designate a literal character — there are three in this example: the opening and closing parentheses around the number's three-digit area code, and the hyphen that separates the exchange and number. The control shows these characters in the edit window, and the text cursor automatically skips over them during typing.

A 9 in the mask indicates that users may enter a digit or nothing into this position. Use 0 to require a digit. Use capital A to permit alphanumeric entry; use capital C to require a character. See Delphi's on-line help for other mask symbols.

The second part of the edit mask (;1 in the preceding example) indicates whether to save literal characters in the resulting input. Enter ;0 to discard literals. With this option, the program receives a formatted telephone number such as (800)555-1212 as the string of digits 8005551212.

The third and final part of an edit mask designates the character to display for input positions in the mask template. Usually, you should specify an underscore or a blank, but you may use a different character if you wish. For example, change the preceding mask's trailing underscore to a period.

Periods and other punctuation characters in proportional fonts result in MaskEdit templates that occupy less space than the final input. For a better-looking template, when using a period as the input position character, select a monospace font such as Courier New for the MaskEdit control.

You may create your own .Dem files of mask templates for loading into Delphi's *Input Mask Editor* dialog. This is just a plain text file with the filename extension .Dem. Each line in the file consists of three parts: the mask's name, a sample input, and the edit mask string. For example, here's the Zip Code entry from Denmark.Dem:

```
Zip Code | 3450 | 0000;1;_
```

PASSWORD ENTRY

You can use an Edit or MaskEdit object to provide a password-entry box (this also applies to the database DBEdit component). Designate any character other than #0 in the PasswordChar property. For example, enter * or # in this property for a sample Edit object and run the program. Users can enter text into the control, but only the password character shows on screen.

Always give users the chance to confirm a password by typing it twice. One of the easiest methods for doing that is to insert two Edit or MaskEdit objects into a form. This form might be a dialog that a command displays, or that the program shows on start-up before allowing access to information. Create a handler for the form's OnCloseQuery event, and use programming similar to Listing 9-9 to compare the two Edit controls. The program allows the form to close only if the two passwords match.

Listing 9-9

Use two Edit objects and this OnCloseQuery event handler to prevent a form from closing unless the two password input controls match.

```
procedure TForm1.FormCloseQuery(Sender: TObject; var CanClose: Boolean);
begin
  if Edit1.Text <> Edit2.Text then
  begin
    ShowMessage('Password incorrect!');
    CanClose := False;                        This prevents the
    Edit1.SetFocus;                           form from closing.
  end;
end;
```

Alternatively, you can insert a Password Dialog form into an application. Follow these steps to try out this template:

1. Start a new project, and select *File | New Form* or click the *New form* speed button. Choose *Password Dialog* from the *Browse Gallery* dialog.

2. Insert a Button into the main form. Double-click the button and enter these statements into the Button object's OnClick event handler:

```
PasswordDlg.ShowModal;
ShowMessage(PasswordDlg.Password.Text);
```

3. Add Unit2 to Unit1's *uses* directive near the top of the Unit1 source code module.

4. Run the program and click the button. Enter a password in the dialog box. When you click OK, the program displays your entry in a ShowMessage dialog. Notice that the host program accesses the dialog's password text as the expression PasswordDlg.Password.Text. (Password is an Edit object that PasswordDlg owns.)

Summary

- Delphi's Label, Edit, and MaskEdit components can handle most of an application's single-line string requirements.

- Delphi supports two kinds of strings — Pascal-style and null-terminated. Pascal Strings are limited to 255 characters; null-terminated strings are simply arrays of Char bytes, and therefore, can be as large as memory allows, up to 65,526 characters.

- Try to use Pascal Strings for all of your string-handling needs. Pascal string procedures and functions are highly optimized, and because String is a built-in type, you can use strings in expressions. For example, to concatenate two or more strings, simply add them together with plus operators, as in the expression S1 + S2 + S3. You can also compare Pascal strings using the <, >, <=, >=, and = <>, operators. You must call functions such as StrComp to compare null-terminated strings.

- There are only two good reasons to use null-terminated strings: to pass one as a PChar pointer to a Windows API function, or to create strings that can hold more than 255 characters. Remember, however, you can use a TStringList object to store multiple strings — for example, to hold the lines from a text file. Hint: Call the TStringList object's LoadFromFile procedure.

- To conserve memory, allocate strings dynamically on the global heap. For Pascal-style strings, define a PString pointer, and call New-Str to create the string. Call DisposeStr to dispose of the allocated memory. For null-terminated strings, call StrAlloc to allocate memory to a PChar pointer. Call StrDispose to dispose of the allocated memory. Note the similarity in the two procedure names. Delphi won't let you use the wrong procedure, but if you can't get a StrDispose or DisposeStr statement to compile, you may have simply typed the wrong procedure name.

- To display messages, call ShowMessage or ShowMessagePos. To display messages and prompt users to click a button — for example, to request permission to delete a file — call MessageDlg or MessageDlgPos. You may also call the standard Windows

MessageBox function, but this produces an old-style window in Windows 3.1 that requires you to use null-terminated strings.

- To prompt users for single-line text entries, call InputBox or Input-Query. These functions can handle most single-line input needs, and they save you the time and effort of developing your own input dialogs with Edit components.

- As you probably know, you can use Label objects for labels and other static text items in forms. However, a Label object can also provide an accelerator hot key for another control such as Edit or MaskEdit that doesn't support Alt-key selection.

- For general-purpose single-line input needs, use the Edit object. This component has numerous properties and events that you can use to provide input areas. An Edit object is a virtual single-line text editor, and it automatically supports keyboard and mouse operations, including cut, copy, and paste.

- Try to make your applications operable with the keyboard and the mouse. For an example, run the TelName application, which demonstrates efficient keyboard interface techniques such as setting the focus on receiving a button click.

- Use a MaskEdit object to provide template-based Edit controls. Insert or select a mask for a MaskEdit object's EditMask property — for example, to require users to enter a telephone number or a date using a specific format.

- For password entry, assign a character to the PasswordChar property of an Edit or MaskEdit object (this also works for the database DB-Edit component). The objects display only that character for all input.

Projects to Try

9-1: Design a module that displays error messages using MessageDlg or MessageDlgPos.

9-2: Write a test program that lets users program accelerator hot keys for one or more Edit objects. You might include this code in a configuration utility or menu command.

9-3: Create MaskEdit objects for entering e-mail addresses for various services such as the Internet and CompuServe. Store your templates in a .Dem text file.

9-4: Write a general-purpose password entry dialog, or improve upon Delphi's Password Dialog template. Your template should provide the means for users to confirm a password by entering it twice.

9-5: Write ShowPChar and ShowPCharPos procedures that display null-terminated strings similar to ShowMessage and ShowMessagePos. If you need to use null-terminated strings, you will find these procedures useful for debugging. (And, just a word to the wise, if you use null-terminated strings, you *will* have some debugging to do.)

Expert-User Tips

- To conserve stack space, preface procedure and function string parameters with *const*. This tells Delphi that the procedure uses, but does not change, the string. Consequently, Delphi can pass the string by reference rather than copying the string's characters, which wastes stack space. For example, define a procedure like this to create a constant string parameter:

```
procedure MySubroutine(const S: String);
begin
end;
```

- Set Label's ShowAccelChar to False to disable the Label's capability to provide an accelerator key for other controls. You might want to do this, for example, to display ampersand characters in a Label's Caption. However, you can display an ampersand simply by typing two of them. The Label Caption &&Amp displays as &Amp.

- For limiting Edit control entry to upper- or lowercase, rather than write a keyboard filter for the control's OnKeyDown event, select a value for the CharCase property. You may set CharCase to ecLowerCase, ecNormal, or ecUpperCase.

II

9

- Label objects do not have window handles, and therefore, they consume less memory than Edit objects. To conserve memory, always use a Label rather than an Edit object for read-only text.

- MessageDlg and MessageDlgPos normally display glyph bitmaps on their buttons. If you don't want glyphs on buttons, insert the following statement in the main form's OnCreate event handler:

```
MsgDlgGlyphs := False;
```

- Set a Label object's Transparent property to True for displaying text labels on top of graphic images such as bitmaps.

- A Label is a nonwindowed control, and as such, it cannot appear on top of a windowed control such as a Button. If you cannot force a Label to appear on top of another component with the *Edit|Bring to Front* and *Edit|Send to Back* commands, you may be attempting the impossible. Try another approach to get the interface effect you want.

- The Edit component's Modified property, a Boolean True or False value, indicates whether any changes have been made to the control's contents since creating the Edit object or since setting Modified to False. After accepting input from an Edit object, set Modified to False. You can then inspect this property to determine whether the Edit object's contents have changed.

- You can access a MaskEdit object's text using two properties, EditText or Text. If the object's mask specifies that literal characters should be saved, EditText and Text have the identical content, and you can use either one to obtain the control's text. If the mask does not specify saving literal characters, EditText represents the text that users see in the MaskEdit window, and Text represents that same text minus its literal characters.

- To restrict MaskEdit entries to upper- or lowercase, set the CharCase property to ecLowerCase or ecUpperCase. To permit upper- and lowercase input, set CharCase to its default value, ecNormal. This may be simpler than specifying upper- and lowercase entry using mask symbols.

- When concatenating strings, keep in mind that every use of the plus operator consumes 256 bytes of stack space for temporary storage. Four plus operators will use up a minimum of 1,024 stack bytes. In many cases, you can use the Format function to reduce stack usage For example, to concatenate three strings A, B, and C, and assign the result to S, use a statement such as:

```
S := Format('%s%s%s', [A, B, C]);
```

Coming Up

You're just beginning to scratch the surface of Delphi's text input and output capabilities. In the next chapter, you investigate components for managing multiple-line text objects.

Working with Multiple-Line Text

*S*ooner or later, all programmers decide to write their own, personal text editors with features they've dreamed of using. Some of these ambitious souls actually manage to get a prototype up and running, but few ever finish the job. Designing even a simple text editor with minimal commands for inserting text, cutting and pasting lines, and reading and writing files is a tremendously painstaking chore. And, no, I never completed my own text editor, which remains in sorry state on a disk somewhere. I hope I never get the bright idea to finish it.

Fortunately, with Delphi's multiple-line text components, I'll never have to work on that code again. A single Memo object provides all the capabilities of the Windows Notepad editor. Just insert a Memo object into a form and wave your magic wand for an instant text editor.

In this chapter, you'll use the Memo and StringGrid components to build multiple-line text objects into your application's user interface. I'll also discuss related topics such as clipboard transfers and how to use the ScrollBar and ScrollBox components, which you'll almost always need when working with multiple-line text.

Components

- Memo — Practically a word processor in its own right, the Memo component adds Notepad-like capabilities to an application. This chapter's Readme text file viewer — which you can call from another application such as an installation utility — demonstrates how to use Memo objects. Palette: Standard.

- ScrollBar — This general-purpose component adds scroll bars to a form, or it can operate independently as a range-selection control. For example, in this chapter, you use a ScrollBar to create a color selection dialog. Palette: Standard.

- ScrollBox — You might call this one a container object with wheels. Use a ScrollBox to create scrollable objects, panels, text displays, options dialogs, and other complex interface elements that need scrolling capabilities. Palette: Additional.

- StringGrid — This highly capable component organizes string lists into a row-and-column format accessible as a two-dimensional array. With just this component, you have most of the interface elements needed to create tables and spreadsheets. This chapter's CharGrid application, which is similar to the Windows Character Map utility, demonstrates how to use StringGrid objects to create selectable speadsheets. Palette: Additional.

Thanks for the Memos

The Memo component encapsulates the standard Windows multiple-line Edit control. However, Memo is not just an old control in a new wrapper — it's a sophisticated multiline text editor that exemplifies the advantages of object-oriented programming. For example, the standard Edit control makes managing text buffers tedious and error prone. The Memo component bashes those barriers with intelligently designed methods for accessing multiline text in buffer or string-list formats.

READ-ONLY MEMOS

Read-only Memo objects are useful for informational displays. For example, see the Fancy application in Chapter 6. The program uses two Memo objects to display property values for various Panel 3D styles. Using a Memo object for read-only lists is a lot easier than creating multiple Labels.

To create a read-only Memo, set three properties to these values:

Property	Setting	Description
Enabled	False	Prevents users from selecting text in the Memo window.
TabStop	False	Prevents users from tabbing to the Memo object.
ReadOnly	True	Prevents users from making any changes or entering new text into the Memo's text.

After setting these values, assign text to the Memo object's Lines property. Click the ellipsis button to open Delphi's String list editor, and type or copy and paste your text.

The Memo component can hold up to 32K of text. Each line in a Memo object can be no longer than 1,024 characters, provided that the line's display width is no longer than 30,000 pixels. These are Windows limitations.

Delphi's on-line help incorrectly states that a Memo object can hold up to 255K of text. Technically, Memo's text buffer is limited to 32K, although the actual maximum depends on memory and other resources, and I have successfully pasted over 40K of text into a Memo object. For best results, however, limit text insertions to 32K.

TEXT FILE INPUT AND OUTPUT

The Memo component's Lines property is a TStrings object, and therefore, you can use the string-list techniques from Chapter 8 to read, write, and modify a Memo object's text. As long as your text object's lines are no longer than 255 characters each, you can access them using Lines. For example, this displays the first line in a Memo object:

```
ShowMessage(Memo1.Lines[0]);
```

Call the Lines LoadFromFile method to read a text file into a Memo object. Call SaveToFile to write a Memo object's contents to disk. With just these two procedures, you can construct your own Notepad-like editor.

II

10

As an example of text-file handling, the Readme application displays a read-only copy of a text file in a Memo component. When designing your program's interface, you might include Readme to display application notes rather than use the tired old method of calling Notepad, which permits users to inadvertently change your program's readme file. After the Readme listing, I'll also explain how to run the program from inside another Delphi application — for example, you might use the technique in a program installer. Figure 10-1 shows Readme's display. Listing 10-1 shows the source code.

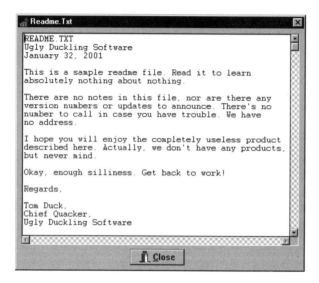

Figure 10-1

The Readme application demonstrates how to create a read-only text file viewer that another program — for example, an installation utility — can call to display application notes.

Listing 10-1
Readme\Main.Pas

```
unit Main;

interface

uses
  SysUtils, WinTypes, WinProcs, Messages, Classes, Graphics, Controls,
  Forms, Dialogs, StdCtrls, Buttons;
```

```
type
  TMainForm = class(TForm)
    Memo1: TMemo;
    BitBtn1: TBitBtn;
    procedure FormActivate(Sender: TObject);
  private
    { Private declarations }
  public
    { Public declarations }
  end;

var
  MainForm: TMainForm;

implementation

{$R *.DFM}

procedure TMainForm.FormActivate(Sender: TObject);
var
  FileName: string;
begin
  if ParamCount >= 1
    then FileName := ParamStr(1)
    else FileName := 'Readme.Txt';
  Memo1.Lines.LoadFromFile(FileName);
  Caption := FileName;
end;

end.
```

Returns a command line parameter entered by the user or by another program that runs this one.

Loads a text file with lines no greater than 255 characters each into a Memo object.

Readme's main form OnActivate event handler shows how to obtain a parameter passed from another process to an application. (Enter test parameters with *Run | Parameters*.) The global variable ParamCount equals the number of parameters, each of which is available through the ParamStr function, which returns a Pascal string. Pass the parameter's index to ParamStr. The parameter indexed by 0 equals the application's path name — display it in a Button's OnClick event handler with the statement:

```
ShowMessage(ParamStr(0));  { Show application pathname }
```

In Readme, if ParamCount is greater than or equal to 1, the program assigns a passed parameter to the FileName string; otherwise, it sets File-Name to the default file, Readme.Txt. A single statement loads that file's text into a Memo object:

```
Memo1.Lines.LoadFromFile(FileName);
```

After that, the program sets the form's Caption to the FileName string. When using Memo objects to display text files, use a Label, Caption, or other text object to display the path name so users know which file they are viewing.

Although ReadMe doesn't write to disk, you can do that easily by calling the SaveToFile procedure for a Memo object's Lines property. The procedure creates a new file, or it overwrites a file if one exists by that name. To guard against accidentally overwriting an existing file, call FileExists before calling SaveToFile, as in this sample code (assume FileName is a String variable):

```
FileName := 'C:\Anyfile.Txt';
if FileExists(FileName) then
  ShowMessage('File exists')
else
  Memo1.Lines.SaveToFile(FileName);
```

To pass parameters to programs, choose the *File|Run* command in the Program Manager or the File Manager, or inWindows 95, use the Start button's Run command. Enter C:\Path\Readme Filename.Txt to run Readme and pass it a parameter "Filename.Txt." When running programs inside Delphi, choose the *Run|Parameters* command, and enter one or more parameters to pass to the program the next time you compile and run it.

Although you can run Readme as a stand-alone application, I designed it to be called from another program such as an installation utility. To demonstrate this technique, which you can use to run any executable program, or a batch or PIF file, examine the Runme application located on the book's CD-ROM in the Readme directory. Load the program into Delphi, and press F9 to compile and run. Select the *Click Me* button to run the Readme application. Figure 10-2 shows Runme's display. Listing 10-2 lists the program's source code.

If Runme doesn't display the expected Readme.Txt file, follow these steps. Load the Readme.Prj file into Delphi and press Ctrl+F9 to compile. Then, load Runme.Prj and press F9. You should then be able to click *Click Me* to run the Readme demonstration.

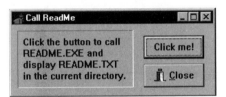

Figure 10-2

The Runme application, located in the Readme directory, demonstrates how an application can run another program. Select the Click Me button to run the Readme program (see Figure 10-1).

Listing 10-2

Readme\Test.Pas

```
unit Test;

interface

uses
   SysUtils, WinTypes, WinProcs, Messages, Classes, Graphics, Controls,
   Forms, Dialogs, ExtCtrls, StdCtrls, Buttons;

type
  TTestForm = class(TForm)
    ClickMeButton: TButton;
    Label1: TLabel;
    Bevel1: TBevel;
    BitBtn1: TBitBtn;
    procedure ClickMeButtonClick(Sender: TObject);
  private
    { Private declarations }
  public
    { Public declarations }
  end;

var
   TestForm: TTestForm;

implementation

{$R *.DFM}
```

II

10

```
procedure TTestForm.ClickMeButtonClick(Sender: TObject);
var
  K: Integer;  { Result of calling WinExec }
begin
  K := WinExec('Readme.Exe Readme.Txt', SW_SHOWNORMAL);
  if K < 32 then
    ShowMessage('Error running README.EXE');
end;

end.
```

Call WinExec to run a program from inside another program

The *Click Me* button's OnClick event handler demonstrates how to run a program from within another. Call the WinExec function with a string equal to the program's path name plus any parameters you want to pass to the program. Pass the constant SW_SHOWNORMAL to display the application's window normally. See the Windows ShowWindow function for other parameters you can use (SW_SHOWMINIMIZED, for example, to display the application as an icon on the Windows desktop).

If successful, WinExec returns an integer value greater than or equal to 32. Any value less than 32 indicates an error. (The return value is actually the instance handle of the target application, although this fact is of little practical value.) For example, add a Button to a form and use the following OnClick event handler to run the Windows Solitaire game. The procedure ignores any errors. Notice also that the path name passed to WinExec can specify only the program name — you don't have to include the .Exe code file extension:

```
procedure TForm1.Button1Click(Sender: TObject);
var
  K: Integer;
begin
  K := WinExec('C:\Windows\Sol', SW_SHOWMAXIMIZED);
end;
```

Open Delphi's online help, click the API button, and search for WinExec for more information about this function. Because this is a Windows function, its string parameter is declared as type PChar (pointer to a null-terminated character array). However, you can pass literal strings to PChar parameters as Runme's listing shows.

TEXT BUFFERS AND STRING LISTS

Naturally, you'll want to add, delete, insert, and modify text in your Memo objects. Successfully programming these and other tasks requires a good understanding of how Memo objects provide access to their text lines. You can access a Memo object's text using three methods:

- As the string value of the Text property, which does not appear in the Object Inspector and is available only at runtime. The maximum length of this property is 255 characters.

- As a list of strings in the Lines property, using the methods described in Chapter 9 for TStrings and TStringList objects. Each line may have from 0 to 255 characters.

- As an array of characters, addressed by a PChar pointer, by calling methods such as GetTextBuf and SetTextBuf.

Each technique provides access to the same text, but in different forms. Use the Text property for small Memo objects with text no longer than 255 characters. Use Lines for larger Memo objects. Use GetTextBuf, SetTextBuf, and other PChar pointer methods when you need to access text as a large block of characters, or when individual lines are longer than 255 characters.

To display a Memo object's text as a single string, use the Text property. For example, insert Memo and Button components into a form, and use this statement in the Button's OnClick event handler to display the Memo's text:

```
ShowMessage(Memo1.Text);
```

Paste some text into the Memo1 object's window and click the button. Notice that the Text property truncates Memo's contents to a maximum of 255 characters. You don't need to be concerned about storing too much text in this property — the property provides a *view* of Memo's contents as a Pascal string. That string simply cannot be larger than 255 characters.

For larger amounts of text, use the Lines property. Because this is an object of the TStrings type, you can transfer text between other objects that have TStrings properties. For example, use a statement such as this to copy a ListBox's Items to a Memo's Lines:

```
Memo1.Lines := ListBox1.Items;
```

You might use the reverse technique to permit users to enter ListBox items using Memo's text-editing features. Simply perform the assignment in the other direction, perhaps in a Button's OnClick event handler:

```
ListBox1.Items := Memo1.Lines;
```

To insert new text into a Memo object, you can assign strings to the Text property. But be careful with this method — it *replaces* the entire contents of the Memo, regardless of size:

```
Memo1.Text := 'I''d rather be sailing!';
```

Usually, it's just as well (if not better) to use the Lines property. Clear a Memo's contents by calling the Clear method like this:

```
Memo1.Lines.Clear;
```

However, because Lines is the default property of the Memo component, you may call Clear *without* referring to Lines. This statement is exactly equivalent to the preceding one:

```
Memo1.Clear;
```

Determine whether a Memo object is empty by inspecting the Count property of Lines:

```
if Memo1.Lines.Count = 0 then
  ShowMessage('You just clicked this button!')
else
  Memo1.Clear;
```

ACCESSING THE MEMO TEXT BUFFER

As I mentioned, in most cases, you can most easily access a Memo object's text through its string-list Lines object. However, if individual lines are longer than 255 characters, or if you need to perform operations directly on text buffers, you can access a Memo object's text as an array of Char bytes. For example, in some Windows text files, each string represents a paragraph that may be longer than 255 characters.

There are five methods for working with Memo text as arrays of Char — in other words, as null-terminated strings. The methods in the order I'll describe them are:

- *SetTextBuf* — Copies text into a Memo object. Equivalent to the Windows message wm_SetText.
- *SetSelTextBuf* — Replaces selected text in a Memo object with new text. Equivalent to the Windows message em_ReplaceSel.
- *GetTextLen* — Returns the number of characters in the Memo object's buffer. This value does not include the buffer's terminating null. Equivalent to the Windows message wm_GetTextLength.
- *GetTextBuf* — Copies a Memo object's text to a program Char array or PChar-addressed buffer. Equivalent to the Windows message wm_GetText.
- *GetSelTextBuf* — Copies selected text from a Memo object to a program Char array or PChar-addressed buffer. Equivalent to the Windows message em_GetSel followed by a string copy of selected text.

You may use these methods with arrays of Char bytes, or with PChar pointers. You may pass an array of Char to a PChar. For example, given these declarations:

```
var
  S: array[0 .. 128] of Char;
  P: PChar;
```

you can pass either S or P to any PChar parameter. These statements copy S and the string addressed by P to a Memo's text buffer (I assume you have initialized the strings somewhere else):

```
Memo1.SetTextBuf(S);  { Copy array S to Memo1 }
Memo1.SetTextBuf(P);  { Copy string at P to Memo1 }
```

In the following discussion, I'll use PChar pointers because these are more efficient, especially for large text buffers. However, the same techniques work with arrays of Char. Listing 10-3 shows how to use Set-TextBuf to copy a null-terminated string to a Memo object. (In case you want to try the code, it's in the form of an OnClick event handler for a Button object.) First, StrAlloc allocates memory for a 128-character string. Then, StrCopy copies literal text to the addressed memory. The expressions #13#10 insert new-line control codes at the ends of the first three lines. SetTextBuf copies the string into the Memo1 object. After that, StrDispose deletes the allocated memory.

Listing 10-3

This OnClick event handler demonstrates how to insert text into a Memo object by calling SetTextBuf.

```
procedure TForm1.Button1Click(Sender: TObject);
var
  P: PChar;
begin
  P := StrAlloc(128);
  try
    StrCopy(P,
      'Red skies at night,'#13#10 +
      ' Sailor''s delight;'#13#10 +
      'Red skies at morning,'#13#10 +
      ' Sailor take warning.');
    Memo1.SetTextBuf(P);
  finally
    StrDispose(P);
  end;
end;
```

Use a finally *block to ensure proper disposal of allocated memory even if an exception occurs in the preceding* trap *block.*

NOTE Memo objects (as well as Edit and other text components) manage their own string-buffer memory. For example, when you call SetText, Memo copies the string data into its own memory. It is still your responsibility to delete dynamic strings that you create, even after you assign them to a Memo object.

Call SetSelTextBuf to replace selected (that is, highlighted) text in a Memo object. For example, run a test program with the event handler in the preceding listing, and then insert another Button OnClick procedure with the code from Listing 10-4. Select some or all text in the Memo object, and click the second button to replace that text with the new jingle.

Listing 10-4
Use this OnClick event handler to replace selected text with new characters in a Memo by calling SetSelTextBuf.

```
procedure TForm1.Button2Click(Sender: TObject);
var
  P: PChar;
begin
  P := StrAlloc(128);
  try
    StrCopy(P,
      'How happy is the sailor''s life,'#13#10 +
      'From coast to coast to roam;'#13#10 +
      'In every port he finds a wife,'#13#10 +
      'In every land a home.');
    Memo1.SetSelTextBuf(P);
  finally
    StrDispose(P);
  end;
end;
```

Replaces selected text

If no text is selected in the Memo object, SetSelTextBuf inserts the new text at the current cursor position. To completely replace all of the text in a Memo, call the SelectAll method before calling SetSelTextBuf.

To copy the text from a Memo object into a Char array, call Get-TextBuf or GetSelTextBuf. Determine the required size of the buffer by calling GetTextLen, allocate that much memory plus one byte for a null-terminator, and call GetTextBuf to copy a Memo object's text into the allocated space. Call GetSelTextBuf to copy only selected text into the buffer.

Listing 10-5 demonstrates how to use GetTextLen and GetTextBuf. The procedure first determines Memo1's buffer length. If that length is greater than zero, the code calls StrAlloc, which allocates Len+1 bytes and assigns the memory's address to P. GetTextBuf copies Memo1's text to the allocated memory, after which a *for* loop exclusive-ORs each character in the buffer with hexadecimal FF. This encrypts the Memo object's text, which SetTextBuf copies back into the object. Finally, StrDispose deletes the allocated memory. Try this procedure and click the button to toggle text to and from its encrypted form.

II

10

Listing 10-5

Use this OnClick event handler to encrypt and decode a Memo object's text. The procedure copies Memo1's text to a dynamic buffer, encrypts each character with an exclusive-OR operation, and then copies the processed buffer back into the Memo object.

```
procedure TForm1.Button3Click(Sender: TObject);
var
  I, Len: Integer;
  P: PChar;
begin
  Len := Memo1.GetTextLen;
  if Len = 0 then
    ShowMessage('Text buffer is empty!')
  else begin
    P := StrAlloc(Len + 1);
    try
      Memo1.GetTextBuf(P, Len);
      for I := 0 to Len do
        P[I] := Chr(Ord(P[I]) xor $ff);
      Memo1.SetTextBuf(P);
    finally
      StrDispose(P);
    end;
  end;
end;
```

Allocates enough memory to hold the Memo's text plus one byte for a terminating null.

Encrypts each character using Pascal's exclusive or logical operator.

The listing demonstrates an important aspect of working with PChar pointers. Although a PChar variable is a pointer to a Char byte, Delphi treats the pointers as equivalent to arrays. For example, this statement assigns the letter A to the first character of a string buffer addressed by P:

```
P[0] := 'A';
```

In Listing 10-5, you can replace GetTextBuf with GetSelTextBuf to copy only selected text from a Memo object to your buffer. The two functions are otherwise the same. (If you try this, select all text *each time* before clicking the button, or the text will not be properly decoded.)

ENTER AND TAB KEYPRESSES

Depending on your interface needs for a Memo object, pressing Enter and Tab can have varying effects. For example, you might want users to enter multiple lines into a Memo window — in that case, you probably want an Enter keypress to begin a new line. If you don't want Enter to act that way, you can program the key to shift the focus to another control. You also can determine whether pressing Tab inserts a tab control code into a Memo's text, or shifts to the next control in tab order.

Set the WantReturns property to True to insert new lines into a Memo's text when users press Enter. Set WantReturns to False to send Enter keypresses to the form. However, this setting requires an appropriate setting for the form's KeyPreview property. Usually, if WantReturns is True, KeyPreview should be False so the control, not the form, receives the Enter keypress. If WantReturns is False, Keypreview should normally be True; otherwise, the form still does not receive the Enter keypress in its OnKeypress event handler.

Set WantTabs to True to insert tab control codes into a Memo's text when users press Tab. Set WantTabs to False to shift the focus to another control on receiving a Tab keypress. When WantTabs is True, a Memo object is like the Hotel California — you can check in by pressing Tab, but you can never press Tab to leave.

Pressing Ctrl+Enter always starts a new line in a Memo object, regardless of the value of WantReturns. Similarly, pressing Ctrl+Tab always inserts a tab control code regardless of the setting for WantTabs.

By sending a Memo object a Windows message, you can change the spacing of tab controls. Listing 10-6 demonstrates the technique with code that you can use in a form's OnCreate event handler. The TabStops typed-constant array has only one Integer value — in this case, set to 18. Because most fonts are proportional, Windows measures tab stops in dialog box units rather than in characters, as is common with text-only displays and monospace character sets. (The default tab setting is 32 dialog units.) The sample OnCreate event handler calls the Perform method (all components have it) to send Memo an em_SetTabStops message. The 1 parameter specifies that TabStops has only a single entry, which is repeated for all tabs. Look up the em_SetTabStops in Delphi's on-line API help for more information on setting tabs in text controls.

Listing 10-6 also demonstrates how to pass a variable to a message's LParam parameter by type-casting it to a Longint value. In this example, the @ sign specifies the *address* of the TabStops array. The full expression Longint(@TabStops) passes the array's address as a Longint, 32-bit, value.

Listing 10-6

Use this OnCreate event handler to set a Memo's tab stops in dialog box units.

```
procedure TForm1.FormCreate(Sender: TObject);
const
  TabStops: array[0 .. 0] of Integer = (18);
begin
  Memo1.Perform(em_SetTabStops, 1, Longint(@TabStops));
end;
```

Text and the Clipboard

Though of limited utility, the Windows clipboard is a popular way station for transmitting information to and from applications. Most Windows users quickly learn how to cut and copy text, even though they may not realize they are using the clipboard to perform these actions. Because the Edit, MaskEdit, and Memo components automatically support cut, copy, and paste, using these objects is all you need to do to provide clipboard services in your application.

 Database components TDBEdit, TDBMaskEdit, TDBImage, and TDB-Memo also support the clipboard methods described here.

To make the clipboard easier to use, especially for beginners who haven't yet mastered the subtleties of Windows keyboard commands, call the CopyToClipboard, CutToClipboard, and PasteFromClipboard methods in the Edit, MaskEdit, and Memo components. For example, to cut selected text from a Memo object to the clipboard, use this statement, perhaps in a Button's OnClick event handler, or in the procedure for a menu's *Edit|Cut* command:

```
Memo1.CutToClipboard;
```

The other procedures work similarly and require no parameters. The key to success is to realize that CopyToClipboard and CutToClipboard operate only on selected text. To copy all of a Memo's text to the clipboard, precede the operation with a call to SelectAll:

```
Memo1.SelectAll;
Memo1.CopyToClipboard;
```

 For more information on the Windows clipboard, see Chapter 16's discussion of data transfer techniques.

Scrolling Down the River

Several components provide automatic scrolling capabilities that require no programming. For example, the Memo component displays vertical and horizontal scroll bars as needed to provide access to text. Scrolling works exactly as expected — you don't need to worry about any magic settings.

For other scrolling tasks, you have two choices. You can insert a ScrollBar component into a form or you can use a ScrollBox object to provide a scrollable platform that can contain other objects. The next two sections explain how to scroll down the river with these two useful components.

SCROLLING WITH SCROLLBAR

The ScrollBar component creates a stand-alone scroll bar object that you can insert into a form or another container. Simply by writing one event handler, you can create code that responds to changes in the scroll bar's position. You can have as many ScrollBar objects as you need — they make useful interface devices for selecting values within low-to-high ranges. As an example of this concept, try the Test application in the ColorDlg directory on the CD-ROM. Run Test, and click the *Test* button to display the color-selection dialog shown in Figure 10-3. The source code for the Test application is shown in Listing 10-7.

II

10

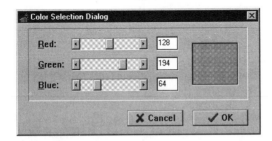

Figure 10-3

Run the Test application in the ColorDlg directory, and click the Test button to display the color-selection dialog shown here. The dialog demonstrates how to use ScrollBar objects as value selectors — in this case, to choose red, green, and blue values for a sample color, shown here as the gray box at right.

Listing 10-7
ColorDlg\ColorDlg.Pas

```pascal
unit Colordlg;

interface

uses
  SysUtils, WinTypes, WinProcs, Messages, Classes, Graphics, Controls,
  Forms, Dialogs, StdCtrls, Buttons, ExtCtrls;

type
  TColorDlgForm = class(TForm)
    RedSB: TScrollBar;
    GreenSB: TScrollBar;
    BlueSB: TScrollBar;
    RedLabel: TLabel;
    GreenLabel: TLabel;
    BlueLabel: TLabel;
    RedEdit: TEdit;
    GreenEdit: TEdit;
    BlueEdit: TEdit;
    ColorEdit: TEdit;
    OkBitBtn: TBitBtn;
    CancelBitBtn: TBitBtn;
    Bevel1: TBevel;
    procedure FormCreate(Sender: TObject);
    procedure SBChange(Sender: TObject);
    procedure EditChange(Sender: TObject);
    procedure FormActivate(Sender: TObject);
    procedure OkBitBtnClick(Sender: TObject);
    procedure CancelBitBtnClick(Sender: TObject);
  private
    RedPos, GreenPos, BluePos: Integer;  { For undo }
    EditControls: array[0 .. 2] of TEdit;
    ScrollBars: array[0 .. 2] of TScrollBar;
    procedure UpdateColor;
  public
    ColorResult: TColor;  { Selected color }
  end;

var
  ColorDlgForm: TColorDlgForm;

implementation

{$R *.DFM}

{- Update ColorResult using scrollbar positions }
procedure TColorDlgForm.UpdateColor;
begin
  ColorResult := RGB(
    RedSB.Position, GreenSB.Position, BlueSB.Position);
```

The Position property equals the scroll bar thumb box's relative position.

```
    ColorEdit.Color := ColorResult;  { Show color }
end;

{- Initialize TObject control arrays }
procedure TColorDlgForm.FormCreate(Sender: TObject);
begin
  EditControls[0] := RedEdit;
  EditControls[1] := GreenEdit;
  EditControls[2] := BlueEdit;
  ScrollBars[0] := RedSB;
  ScrollBars[1] := GreenSB;
  ScrollBars[2] := BlueSB;
end;

{- Update values in Edit boxes for ScrollBar changes }
procedure TColorDlgForm.SBChange(Sender: TObject);
begin
  with Sender as TScrollBar do
    EditControls[Tag].Text := IntToStr(Position);
  UpdateColor;
end;

{- Update scrollbar positions for Edit box changes }
procedure TColorDlgForm.EditChange(Sender: TObject);
begin
  with Sender as TEdit do
    ScrollBars[Tag].Position := StrToInt(Text);
end;

{- Save scrollbar positions for possible undo }
procedure TColorDlgForm.FormActivate(Sender: TObject);
begin
  RedPos := RedSB.Position;
  GreenPos := GreenSB.Position;
  BluePos := BlueSB.Position;
end;

{- Respond to OK button. Accept changes. }
procedure TColorDlgForm.OkBitBtnClick(Sender: TObject);
begin
  ModalResult := mrOk; { Close Window. Color in ColorResult. }
end;

{- Respond to Cancel button. Undo changes. }
procedure TColorDlgForm.CancelBitBtnClick(Sender: TObject);
begin
  RedSB.Position := RedPos;
  GreenSB.Position := GreenPos;
  BlueSB.Position := BluePos;
  ModalResult := mrCancel;
end;

end.
```

This program uses the Tag property to associate scroll bars with Edit objects.

Assignments to ModalResult are returned by the ShowModal method.

II
10

Table 10-1 lists some of the significant properties for the ColorDlg form's component objects, which demonstrate a few interesting interface techniques. Three labels designate Alt accelerator shortcut keys in their Caption properties, and set their FocusControl values to the appropriate Edit box. For example, run the program and press Alt+G to select the GreenEdit object.

Table 10-1

ColorDlg Form Component Properties

Component	Name	Property	Value
Form	ColorDlgForm	Caption	Color Selection Dialog
Label	RedLabel	Caption	&Red:
		FocusControl	RedEdit
Label	GreenLabel	Caption	&Green:
		FocusControl	GreenEdit
Label	BlueLabel	Caption	&Blue:
		FocusControl	BlueEdit
ScrollBar	RedSB	LargeChange	10
		Max	255
		Tag	0
ScrollBar	GreenSB	Tag	1
ScrollBar	BlueSB	Tag	2
Edit	RedEdit	Tag	0
Edit	GreenEdit	Tag	1
Edit	BlueEdit	Tag	2

Each of the three ScrollBars in the window has a LargeChange value of 10. This affects the amount of scrolling when users click inside the bar — in most cases, you should set LargeChange higher than Small-Change (usually equal to 1), which affects the amount of scrolling for the ScrollBar's arrow buttons. The ColorDlg ScrollBars also set their Max value to 255. Delphi's TColor data type represents colors as combinations of red, green, and blue (RGB), each in the range from 0 to 255.

Notice also from Table 10-1 that the ScrollBar and Edit components set their Tag values to 0, 1, and 2. The program uses these values to relate the components at runtime. To see how this works, examine the TColorDlgForm class in Listing 10-7. The private section defines these two arrays of objects:

```
EditControls: array[0 .. 2] of TEdit;
ScrollBars: array[0 .. 2] of TScrollBar;
```

The arrays provide handy means for accessing each of the form's Edit and ScrollBar objects. Remember, TEdit and TScrollBar variables are references, so these two arrays actually contain pointers to the objects, not the objects themselves. To initialize the arrays, the form's OnCreate event handler assigns objects to array positions, equal to the Object Tag values. For example, this statement assigns the first slot in EditControls to refer to the RedEdit component object:

```
EditControls[0] := RedEdit;
```

After preparing the component reference arrays, the program can use Tag values as indexes to access individual objects. For example, examine the SBChange procedure, which handles scroll bar OnChange events. Each ScrollBar object's OnChange event is set to this same handler. In the procedure, the Sender parameter passed to the procedure is the ScrollBar object that has changed. To update the associated Edit control so its integer value matches the ScrollBar's position, the procedure uses a *with* statement to treat Sender as a TScrollBar object, and then executes this statement:

```
EditControls[Tag].Text := IntToStr(Position);
```

IntToStr converts the ScrollBar's integer Position property to a string, and assigns the result to the Edit control's Text property, using the EditControls array and the Tag index to refer to the associated Edit control.

The EditChange procedure performs a similar task. When you enter a new value into an Edit window, the resulting OnChange event calls EditChange. The procedure uses a *with* statement to treat Sender as a TEdit object, and then executes this statement:

```
ScrollBars[Tag].Position := StrToInt(Text);
```

II

10

Function StrToInt converts the Edit control's Text property to an integer value, which the statement assigns to the ScrollBar's Position. This causes the thumb box in the scroll bar to move to a position that matches the Edit control. The ScrollBars array and the Tag property make it easy to select the ScrollBar associated with the Edit control that generated the OnChange event.

The two procedures, SBChange and EditChange, handle all OnChange events for the dialog's six ScrollBar and Edit objects. The procedures could handle practically any number of associated objects, and they demonstrate a useful technique for reducing code size. When you have numerous associated component objects in a window, consider using an array and a Tag index to refer to them in shared event handlers.

Procedure UpdateColor shows how to use ScrollBar Position values. In this case, the RGB function returns a LongInt value given three constituent bytes that represent red, green, and blue colors. The program assigns the resulting color to the ColorResult variable, declared in the TColorDlgForm class's public section.

UpdateColor also displays the current color selection using a cheap trick that is faster than the obvious graphics approach. In one version of the program, I had used a Shape component object to display the sample color, but due to the way Windows works, each color change caused Shape to erase itself to white, which produced an annoying flash between color assignments. To solve the problem, I used an Edit component, set Enabled and TabStop to False, and set ReadOnly to True. You can't select or enter text into the resulting Edit object. Procedure UpdateColor assigns ColorResult to the Edit object's Color property, which doesn't erase itself between updates. When you need a simple colored box, try an Edit component instead of Shape.

ColorDlg implements an undo feature, which all dialogs that have Cancel buttons need. In this case, the form's OnActivate event handler saves the current ScrollBar Position value in three class variables — RedPos, GreenPos, and BluePos. If the user clicks *Close* to end the dialog, the button's OnClick event handler assigns the saved values back to the ScrollBar Position properties.

At first glance, those assignments might not seem enough to completely undo all changes to the dialog. What's not obvious is that *assigning new values to the ScrollBar generates OnChange events*. Thus, the three assignments in the CancelBitBtnClick handler cause three calls to

SBChange, which resets the Edit controls and updates the sample color window. Trace these events by pressing F8 and F7 to run the Test program, or set breakpoints at strategic spots, and verify the sequence that occurs when you click *Cancel*.

To use the color selection dialog, add ColorDlg.Pas to any project and insert ColorDlg to the main form's *uses* directive. Call the Show-Modal function to display the dialog window:

```
ColorDlgForm.ShowModal;
```

ShowModal returns a value that indicates which button the user clicked to end the dialog. You can inspect this value and take appropriate action. For example, rather than call ShowModal as in the preceding line, use this slightly more complex code:

```
with ColorDlgForm do
if ShowModal = mrOk then
  ShowMessage(Format('Color value = $%-.6x', [ColorResult]));
```

If ShowModal returns mrOk, ShowMessage displays the ColorResult value from ColorDlgForm, using Format to insert the value in hexadecimal into the message dialog. The funny-looking text, "%-.6x", formats ColorResult as a left-justified (-) hexadecimal (x) value in six columns padded to the left with zeros (.6).

 Forms and other components use the TControlScrollBar class as a property for horizontal and vertical scroll bars. This class has the same properties and methods as the TScrollBar class, which you can use as independent objects in a form.

SCROLLING WITH SCROLLBOX

A ScrollBox is a kind of Panel that can scroll up, down, left, and right. The ScrollBox component is a *container* that can hold other objects such as buttons, labels, Edit input boxes, radio buttons — even other Scroll-Box panels. When you're thirsty for a general-utility scrolling platform, a ScrollBox is bound to hit the spot.

Creating ScrollBox objects is easy. Just insert one into a form, and size it or set Align to alClient to have the panel completely fill the window's client area. This is a good setting for creating scrollable dialog boxes and data-entry forms with too many controls to fit comfortably in a single window. Scrolling is automatic, and scroll bars appear as needed to provide users with access to controls beyond the window's borders.

Design your ScrollBox objects in their fully open capacity. For example, you might maximize the form window, and insert all controls where you want them. After designing the window, shrink the design form back to its final size.

ScrollBoxes are also useful for scaling windows for different display resolutions. For example, you can design a full-screen entry form for 1024-by-768 displays that still works correctly on laptops with 640-by-480 resolutions. On a laptop, users have to scroll the window to reach all controls.

Edit, button, and other controls that can receive the input focus automatically scroll into view. Try inserting a dozen Edit objects into a ScrollBox. Run the program, and press Tab. As the input focus changes, the current Edit box automatically scrolls into view.

Sometimes, you may need to display a specific control. For example, users might select a program command or click a button. You can call the object's SetFocus method, or you can call the ScrollBox's ScrollInView procedure. For example, to ensure that Edit7 is in view, execute a statement such as this:

```
ScrollBox1.ScrollInView(Edit7);
```

COMPONENTS AND CONTROLS

As you become more familiar with containers such as the ScrollBox component, you will discover the need to access components in various ways. Although all component objects are available by name, such as Label2 or Edit9, it's not always convenient to refer to objects individually. In a form or ScrollBox (or a Panel) with dozens of buttons, it's just plain silly, not to mention inefficient, to write code such as this:

```
Button1.Enabled := False;
Button2.Enabled := False;
...
Button38.Enabled := False;
```

Containers such as forms and ScrollBoxes provide the Components array, which you can use to access all of a parent's owned objects.

ComponentCount equals the number of those components. You can use these properties to write loops such as this:

```
for I := 0 to ComponentCount -1 do
  Components[I].Enabled := False;
```

Containers also provide similar array and count properties, Controls and ControlIndex. However, these properties provide access only to components that are also child windows of their parents. The Components and ComponentCount properties provide access to owned component objects. The Controls array lists the window relationships among component objects. The Components array lists the object relationships. These are not always the same. For example, a ScrollBox owns its components as child window controls. The form that owns the ScrollBox owns those same objects as components.

These concepts are not purely academic — you can use them to your advantage in writing code that affects groups of objects. To better understand the difference between the Controls and Components arrays, run the ContComp (Controls and Components) application on the CD-ROM. The sample program lists components and controls in four list boxes for a ScrollBox and for the main window form. Figure 10-4 shows the program's display. Listing 10-8 gives the program's source code, which includes two procedures that you can use to investigate the control and component relationships of your application's forms. The code provides valuable insights that will help you to fine-tune your program's code. I'll explain more about this after the listing.

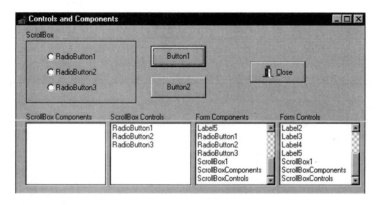

Figure 10-4

ContComp displays the control and component relationships of its own objects for a ScrollBox, which contains three RadioButton controls, and the form window.

Listing 10-8
ContComp\Main.Pas

```
unit Main;

interface

uses
  SysUtils, WinTypes, WinProcs, Messages, Classes, Graphics, Controls,
  Forms, Dialogs, StdCtrls, Buttons;

type
  TMainForm = class(TForm)
    ScrollBox1: TScrollBox;
    Label1: TLabel;
    RadioButton1: TRadioButton;
    RadioButton2: TRadioButton;
    RadioButton3: TRadioButton;
    Button1: TButton;
    Button2: TButton;
    ScrollBoxComponents: TListBox;
    ScrollBoxControls: TListBox;
    FormComponents: TListBox;
    FormControls: TListBox;
    Label2: TLabel;
    Label3: TLabel;
    Label4: TLabel;
    Label5: TLabel;
    CloseBitBtn: TBitBtn;
    procedure FormCreate(Sender: TObject);
  private
    { Private declarations }
  public
    { Public declarations }
  end;

var
  MainForm: TMainForm;

implementation

{$R *.DFM}

procedure ListControls(ListBox: TListBox; Control: TWinControl);
var
  I: Integer;
begin
  with Control do
  for I := 0 to ControlCount - 1 do
    ListBox.Items.Add(Controls[I].Name);
end;
```

Accesses the form's controls.

```
procedure ListComponents(ListBox: TListBox; Component: TComponent);
var
  I: Integer;
begin
  with Component do
  for I := 0 to ComponentCount - 1 do
    ListBox.Items.Add(Components[I].Name);
end;
```
Access the forms
components.

```
procedure TMainForm.FormCreate(Sender: TObject);
begin
  ListControls(ScrollBoxControls, ScrollBox1);
  ListComponents(ScrollBoxComponents, ScrollBox1);
  ListControls(FormControls, MainForm);
  ListComponents(FormComponents, MainForm);
end;

end.
```

To investigate control and component relationships in your own applications, copy the ListControls and ListComponents procedures into any unit module. You probably won't want to include the code in the final application, so I didn't bother making them members of a class. In any event handler (the sample program uses the form's OnCreate procedure), call the two procedures to insert owned controls and components into ListBoxes. Pass a ListBox and a component object as arguments. You may pass any TComponent-derived object to ListComponents and any TWinControl-derived object to ListControls. However, the object components must provide Controls and Components arrays.

Getting back to ScrollBoxes, as Figure 10-4 shows, ScrollBox1 does not own the three RadioButton component objects. However, the objects are child windows of the ScrollBox. From this information, you can write an efficient procedure to perform operations on all of the ScrollBox's controls. For example, add a third Button to the program and use the OnClick event handler in Listing 10-9 to disable each RadioButton.

Refer once again to Figure 10-4 (or run the ContComp program) and examine the FormComponents and FormControls lists. The form owns all of the component objects in this program, despite the fact that the three RadioButtons are inside the ScrollBox. However, a control as a child window may have only one parent; therefore, the form's Controls array does not list the RadioButtons.

II

10

Listing 10-9

Try this OnClick event handler for a third Button in the ContComp program to disable the ScrollBox's RadioButtons. The code accesses each button through the ScrollBox's Controls array.

```
procedure TMainForm.Button3Click(Sender: TObject);
var
  I: Integer;
begin
  with ScrollBox1 do
  for I := 0 to ControlCount - 1 do
    Controls[I].Enabled := False;
end;
```

An object's ComponentIndex property equals that object's index in its owner's Components array. Likewise, an object's ControlIndex equals the object's index in its owner's Controls array. If T is a Label object owned by a form, and if K equals T.ComponentIndex, then TheForm.Components[K] refers to T. Similarly, if T is a control that is a child window of a form, TheForm.Controls[K] refers to T. If you spend some time investigating these relationships, you'll discover many opportunities for efficiently accessing component objects through the Controls and Components arrays.

String Grids

Finally in this chapter is an example of what has to be one of Delphi's most versatile components, the StringGrid. Practically a full-blown spreadsheet, StringGrid organizes string and other object data into a row-and-column table layout. The CharGrid application on the CD-ROM demonstrates how to use StringGrid. As shown in Figure 10-5, the program displays a StringGrid that shows all the symbols in any Windows font. Select a font from the *Font* ComboBox. Double-click any character in the grid to add it to the *To Copy* Edit window. Or, you can also click the *Select* button. Click the *Copy* button to copy the chosen characters to the clipboard. You can then switch to another application and paste the characters into any text input field. Listing 10-10 shows CharGrid's source code.

Use CharGrid to insert hard-to-type characters such as copyright ©
and trademark ® symbols into Pascal strings.

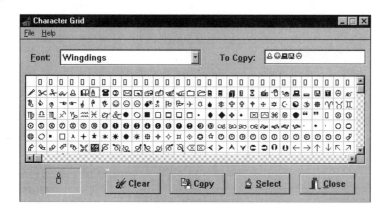

Figure 10-5
The CharGrid application demonstrates how to use Delphi's StringGrid component. The program displays all of the characters for any Windows font (it works similarly to the CharMap utility supplied with Windows).

Listing 10-10
CharGrid\Main.Pas

```
unit Main;

interface

uses
  SysUtils, WinTypes, WinProcs, Messages, Classes, Graphics, Controls,
  Forms, Dialogs, Grids, StdCtrls, Buttons, ExtCtrls, Menus, About;

type
  TMainForm = class(TForm)
    StringGrid1: TStringGrid;
    FontCB: TComboBox;
    FontLabel: TLabel;
    CloseBitBtn: TBitBtn;
    CopyEdit: TEdit;
    CopyLabel: TLabel;
    SelectBitBtn: TBitBtn;
    ClipBitBtn: TBitBtn;
    CharLabel: TLabel;
    Bevel1: TBevel;
```

II

10

```
      ClearBitBtn: TBitBtn;
      MainMenu1: TMainMenu;
      FileMenu: TMenuItem;
      FileExit: TMenuItem;
      HelpMenu: TMenuItem;
      HelpAbout: TMenuItem;
      procedure FormCreate(Sender: TObject);
      procedure FontCBChange(Sender: TObject);
      procedure FontCBKeyDown(Sender: TObject; var Key: Word;
        Shift: TShiftState);
      procedure StringGrid1DblClick(Sender: TObject);
      procedure StringGrid1KeyDown(Sender: TObject; var Key: Word;
        Shift: TShiftState);
      procedure StringGrid1SelectCell(Sender: TObject; Col, Row: Longint;
        var CanSelect: Boolean);
      procedure FileExitClick(Sender: TObject);
      procedure HelpAboutClick(Sender: TObject);
      procedure SelectBitBtnClick(Sender: TObject);
      procedure ClipBitBtnClick(Sender: TObject);
      procedure ClearBitBtnClick(Sender: TObject);
    private
      { Private declarations }
    public
      { Public declarations }
    end;

var
  MainForm: TMainForm;

implementation

{$R *.DFM}

{- Initialize controls }
procedure TMainForm.FormCreate(Sender: TObject);
var
  Ascii, IRow, ICol: Integer;
begin
{- Initialize FontCB ComboBox with font names }
  FontCB.Items := Screen.Fonts;
{- Show current StringGrid font in FontCB's edit box }
  FontCB.ItemIndex :=
    FontCB.Items.IndexOf(StringGrid1.Font.Name);
{- Insert characters into grid }
  Ascii := 0;
  with StringGrid1 do
  for IRow := 0 to RowCount do
    for ICol := 0 to ColCount do
    begin
      Cells[ICol, IRow] := Chr(Ascii);
      Inc(Ascii);
    end;
{- Assign sample character and font }
```

Rather than use a font-selection dialog, it's often easier to present users with a ComboBox or List-Box of font names.

```
  with StringGrid1 do
    CharLabel.Caption := Cells[Row, Col];
  CharLabel.Font.Name := StringGrid1.Font.Name;
end;

{- Change grid, edit box, and sample to selected font }
procedure TMainForm.FontCBChange(Sender: TObject);
begin
  StringGrid1.Font.Name := FontCB.Text;
  CopyEdit.Text := '';  { Optional: Erase current entries }
  CopyEdit.Font := StringGrid1.Font;
  CharLabel.Font.Name := StringGrid1.Font.Name;
end;
```

Represents the user's selected font name.

```
{- Close FontCB drop-down list on pressing Enter or Esc }
procedure TMainForm.FontCBKeyDown(Sender: TObject; var Key: Word;
  Shift: TShiftState);
begin
  if Key in [vk_Return, vk_Escape] then
  begin
    FontCB.DroppedDown := False;
    Key := 0;
  end;
end;
```

Cancels the keypress.

```
{- Grid double-click event handler }
procedure TMainForm.StringGrid1DblClick(Sender: TObject);
begin
  with CopyEdit, StringGrid1 do
    Text := Text + Cells[Col, Row];
end;

{- Select character on pressing Enter or Space }
procedure TMainForm.StringGrid1KeyDown(Sender: TObject; var Key: Word;
  Shift: TShiftState);
begin
  if Key in [vk_Return, vk_Space] then
    StringGrid1DblClick(Sender);  { Same as double-clicking grid }
end;

{- Show selected character }
procedure TMainForm.StringGrid1SelectCell(Sender: TObject; Col,
  Row: Longint; var CanSelect: Boolean);
begin
  CharLabel.Caption := StringGrid1.Cells[Col, Row];
end;

{- File|Exit menu command }
procedure TMainForm.FileExitClick(Sender: TObject);
begin
  Close;
end;

{- Help|About menu command }
```

```
procedure TMainForm.HelpAboutClick(Sender: TObject);
begin
  AboutForm.ShowModal;
end;

{- Select button click handler }
procedure TMainForm.SelectBitBtnClick(Sender: TObject);
begin
  StringGrid1DblClick(Sender);  { Same as double-clicking grid }
end;

{- Copy selected characters to clipboard }
procedure TMainForm.ClipBitBtnClick(Sender: TObject);
begin
  with CopyEdit do
  begin
    if SelLength = 0 then
      SelectAll;         { Select all text if none selected }
    CopyToClipboard;   { Copy selected text to clipboard }
  end;
end;

{- Clear text in copy-to edit box }
procedure TMainForm.ClearBitBtnClick(Sender: TObject);
begin
  CopyEdit.Text := '';
end;

end.
```

If not text is selected, SelectAll before copy to Clipboard.

The StringGrid component operates like a two-dimensional ListBox. The RowCount property specifies the number of rows; ColCount specifies the number of columns. On the simplest level, you can use these values to access a grid's string data through the Cells two-dimensional array. For example, the sample form's OnCreate event handler assigns all possible ASCII values to the program's StringGrid1 object with these statements (Ascii, IRow, and ICol are Integer variables):

```
Ascii := 0;
with StringGrid1 do
for IRow := 0 to RowCount do
  for ICol := 0 to ColCount do
  begin
    Cells[ICol, IRow] := Chr(Ascii);
    Inc(Ascii);
  end;
```

You can also access a grid's strings through the Rows and Cols arrays, which are single-dimensional string arrays. Each element of Rows and Cols is a TStrings string-list object. To load a row's data from a disk file, for example, you can use a statement such as:

```
with StringGrid1 do
Rows[0].LoadFromFile('C:\YourFile.Txt');
```

Or, you might load multiple rows with code such as this:

```
with StringGrid1 do
for I := 0 to RowCount do
  Rows[I].LoadFromFile('C:\YourFile.Txt');
```

When making numerous additions to a string grid's rows and columns this way (and in general when adding strings to TStrings and TStringList objects), surround lengthy processes with BeginUpdate and EndUpdate to reduce display chatter. For example, the preceding example might be smoother when coded as follows:

```
with StringGrid1 do
for I := 0 to RowCount do
with Rows[I] do
begin
  BeginUpdate;
  Rows[I].LoadFromFile('C:\YourFile.Txt');
  EndUpdate;
end;
```

Most StringGrid capabilities are the same as for TStrings, which you've already examined in depth, so I won't discuss StringGrid further here. However, the sample program demonstrates an unrelated but useful technique for ComboBox drop-down lists that you might find helpful. In the FontCB object's OnKeyDown event handler, if the passed Key parameter is vk_Return or vk_Escape, the procedure sets the ComboBox's DroppedDown property False. It then sets Key to zero. Run the program, open the Font list, and press Enter or Esc to close the list window. This small touch helps make CharGrid's keyboard interface friendlier.

The StringGrid's OnKeyDown event handler shows how to program keys for a StringGrid object. Here, if Key equals vk_Return or vk_Space, the procedure calls StringGrid1DblClick, which simulates the double-clicking of a grid cell. For this technique to work, you must install a handler for the grid's OnDblClick event.

TIP

In general, I find it easiest to program mouse events first (such as OnClick and OnDblClick), and then to add keyboard operations, I simply call the mouse handlers from OnKeyDown or OnKeyPress procedures.

Summary

- The Memo and StringGrid components provide multiple-line text-handling objects. Memo is like having the Windows Notepad utility in a component. StringGrid is practically a full-blown spreadsheet that organizes string lists in a row-and-column format.

- A Memo can hold up to 32K of text, which is accessible in three ways: as the string Text property, as a string list in the Lines property, or as an array of Char by calling methods such as GetTextBuf and SetTextBuf.

- Text components such as Memo and Edit provide automatic clipboard cut, copy, and paste transfers. However, you can call CopyToClipboard, CutToClipboard, and PasteFromClipboard in Edit, MaskEdit, and Memo components to perform clipboard transfers under program control.

- Call WinExec to run other applications such as this chapter's Readme text file lister. Use Delphi's ParamCount variable and ParamStr function to access parameters such as filenames passed to applications.

- Use a ScrollBar component as a range-selection object. Use a Scroll-Box object to provide a scrollable Panel-like surface that can hold other controls.

- In a container object such as a form or a ScrollBox, the Components array lists all components owned by a parent object. The Controls array lists all components that are child windows of their parent. These arrays do not necessarily list the same components. Use the programming in this chapter's ContComp application to investigate the component and control relationships among objects. Understanding these relationships can help you to write efficient code — for example, a loop that disables all child controls in a ScrollBox without affecting other objects on the form.

- A StringGrid provides a row-and-column format for storing string and other object data. Use the two-dimensional Cells array to access individual cells. Use the Rows and Cols single-dimensional arrays to access a grid's data as string lists.

Projects to Try

10-1: Use WinExec to construct a control-panel application that displays application icons. Users should be able to click an icon to run programs. You might provide this program along with products composed of multiple utilities.

10-2: Write a replacement for the Windows Notepad that's more suitable for listing program source code. Your program should use a monospace font (or it should have a Font command to select fonts). Elsewhere in this book, you'll learn about search and replace commands as well as printing, which you'll want to add to your ultimate text editor. However, this project is still a useful exercise in using the Memo component.

10-3: Write code to copy selected text to and from multiple Memo objects.

10-4: Write a program that sorts a Memo object's strings. (Hint: You might use a ListBox, or you can write code that implements a sorting algorithm.)

10-5: Write a program that encrypts and decrypts text files. Add password protection to the program.

10-6: Add individual color samples for red, green, and blue to the ColorDlg dialog.

Expert-User Tips

- The Windows API WinExec function returns immediately — it does not pause the current application to run another, as some programmers mistakenly assume. After application A calls WinExec to run application B, it is perfectly safe to close application A while B remains running. A and B are independent coprocesses — it is immaterial which one started the other.

- StringGrid normally fixes its first row and column in place because you most likely will display headers in these cells. If you don't need headers (as in the CharGrid application), release the entire grid by setting FixedCols and FixedRows to zero.

- A form's OnActivate event is called when the form receives the input focus due to the user switching back to the form from another one in the same application. The OnActivate event is not equivalent to the Windows wm_Activate message.

- StringGrid's VisibleColCount and VisibleRowCount indicate how many nonfixed columns and rows are visible in a grid. The Row and Col variables indicate the cell that has the current input focus.

- To enable cell editing in StringGrid objects, set the Options. GoEditing subproperty to True. If you want users to be able to press Tab to move from cell to cell, set Options. GoTab True.

- To enable row and column resizing by clicking and dragging the mouse, set a StringGrid's Options. GoRowSizing and Options. GoColSizing subproperties to True. To enable clicking and dragging rows and columns to new positions, set Options. GoRowMoving and Options. GoColMoving to True.

- When a component is created, it inserts itself into its owner's Components list. Ownership means that the child components will be destroyed when their owner is destroyed. A *Parent* determines a display context. Without a Parent, a control would be invisible. All components that you create at design time are owned by a form.

Coming Up

Dealing with disk files, filenames, directories, and related matters is a major part of most software development projects. In the next chapter, you'll learn about Delphi's directory navigation and related file components.

CHAPTER 11

Navigating Directories and Files

*E*ffective directory and file management is essential in any file-based application. Even the simplest utility probably needs to read and write option settings in a Windows initialization (.Ini) file, and it's the rare program that doesn't need at least one of the file-handling techniques described in this chapter.

Delphi provides four directory and file components that you can use to construct file-selection and directory-navigation dialogs. In this chapter, you'll use these components to build a file-selection dialog and program that can run any executable program. You'll also learn how to use the TIniFile object to read and write .Ini files. For a practical example of .Ini file handling, this chapter explains the inner workings of a moderately complex utility program, SysColor, a system-colorizer that can alter on-screen colors such as button shadows and window title bars. The program reads and writes color settings in a Windows .Ini file.

Components

- DirectoryListBox — Displays, and permits users to change, the current directory and subdirectories. In most cases, you'll relate a DirectoryListBox object with a FileListBox to display files as users browse a disk's directory tree. Palette: System.

- DriveComboBox — Shows and permits selecting all drives connected with the system. You will normally relate a DriveComboBox with a DirectoryListBox so users can switch to another drive and browse its directories. Palette: System.

- FileListBox — Displays files in the current directory. A FileListBox object can display all files or those matching one or more wildcard filters, such as *.Pas and *.Txt. You will normally relate a FileListBox with an Edit control to provide users with a means to enter and edit filenames. Palette: System.

- FilterComboBox — Lists wildcard filters which users can select to limit the types of files that a related FileListBox displays. Palette: System.

Creating a Directory Dialog

Delphi's four directory and file components provide an Erector set of tools you can use to build file-selection dialogs. In this section, you'll meet each component, and then you'll use them to construct a file-selection dialog that you can put to work in your application's *File|Open, File|Save*, and other file-handling commands.

NOTE ▶ As you probably realize, Delphi also provides OpenDialog and SaveDialog components on the Dialogs palette (see Chapter 12). Use the following techniques when you need to customize these standard dialog boxes — for example, to add a wildcard filter editor, as one of this chapter's projects suggests.

DIRECTORYLISTBOX

Figure 11-1 shows the custom dialog box you'll create later in this section. In the dialog, the DirectoryListBox object displays a directory tree outline. Users can double-click and use the keyboard to select directories in this window.

You can use a DirectoryListBox alone in a window, but you'll usually also want to display files in selected directories. To do that, assign the name of a FileListBox object to the DirectoryListBox's FileList property. This is easiest to do in the Object Inspector window, but you may make the assignment at runtime with code such as the following. Insert DirectoryListBox and FileListBox objects into a form, and then insert this statement into the form's OnCreate event handler:

```
DirectoryListBox1.FileList := FileListBox1;
```

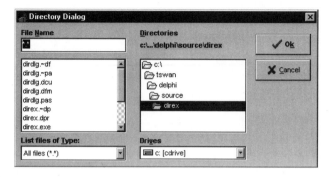

Figure 11-1

The custom dialog box in this chapter uses Delphi's four directory and file components: DirectoryListBox, DriveComboBox, FileListBox, and FilterComboBox.

Delphi shows the current directory and file lists at design time, but you must run the program to select new directories and files, and to scroll the windows.

To show the currently selected path as a string, insert a Label object into the form (usually, it should go above the DirectoryListBox). Assign the Label's name to the DirectoryListBox's DirLabel property. Or, to make the association at runtime, insert this statement into the form's OnCreate event handler:

```
DirectoryListBox1.DirLabel := Label1;
```

The DirectoryListBox component assigns directory paths, including the current drive letter, to the Label's Caption. To display deeply nested paths, the component replaces the root directories with an ellipsis. This keeps the Label relatively short (about 24 characters maximum, or approximately the width of an unmodified DirectoryListBox object). For example, DirectoryListBox displays this path:

```
C:\Delphi\Demos\Doc\FormDll
```

as the shortened Caption:

```
C:\...\Doc\FormDll
```

The Drive property gives the currently selected drive letter. For example, this sets a char C to the drive letter:

```
C := DirectoryListBox1.Drive;
```

Use the Directory property to determine the currently selected path.
To display full path names that are not shortened with an ellipsis, do
not assign a Label object name to the DirLabel property. Instead, insert a
Label into the form, and in the DirectoryListBox's OnChange event handler, assign the object's Directory string to the Label's Caption.

DRIVECOMBOBOX

Unless you need to permit access only to a specific drive, you'll probably
want to insert a DriveComboBox object and relate it to a DirectoryListBox.
If you are following along, insert a DriveComboBox object into the form
(usually, it goes below the DirectoryListBox). Assign a DirectoryListBox's
name to the DriveComboBox's DirList property, or use this statement in
the form's OnCreate event handler:

```
DriveComboBox1.DirList := DirectoryListBox1;
```

When users select a different drive, the DirectoryListBox automatically
updates its tree. If you also associated a FileListBox with the DirectoryList-
Box, the file list is also updated.

The full list of available drives is available through the DriveCombo-
Box's Items property, an object of type TStrings. You can assign this list
to any other TStrings property, or to a TStringList variable. For example,
to display all available drives, insert a ListBox into the form, and add this
statement to the form's OnCreate event handler:

```
ListBox1.Items := DriveComboBox1.Items;
```

FILELISTBOX

As you can probably guess, a FileListBox displays filenames in the current directory. Most often, a DirectoryListBox is associated with a FileList-
Box. This way, the list automatically changes when users browse through
directories.

You will usually also add two more components: an Edit control and
a FilterComboBox. If you are following along, insert the Edit control

now (the next section explains how to use FilterComboBox). Usually, the control goes above the FileListBox. Assign the Edit object's Name to the FileListBox's FileEdit property, or insert this statement into the form's OnCreate event handler:

```
FileListBox1.FileEdit := Edit1;
```

When you run the program, the Edit control initially shows the filter *.*, which selects all files. As users select filenames, the FileListBox inserts them into the Edit window. Users can also type entries and filters into the control.

To create a read-only Edit control that users cannot modify, but that still displays the current file selection, set the Edit object's ReadOnly property to True. To also prevent users from tabbing to the control and highlighting its text, set Enabled False. (Delphi's on-line help incorrectly suggests setting Visible to False, which causes the Edit control to disappear — probably not the effect you want.)

Obtain the selected file in a FileListBox's FileName property. This string includes the current drive letter and path. For example, to select files by double-clicking, create a handler for the FileListBox's OnDblClick event, and insert this statement:

```
ShowMessage(FileListBox1.FileName);
```

Run the program and double-click filenames to display them in the ShowMessage window. To also select files by pressing Enter, create a handler for the FileListBox's OnKeyPress handler, and insert this code to call the double-click procedure if Key equals a carriage-return control code:

```
if Key = #13 then
  FileListBox1DblClick(Sender);
```

If you don't need the full path name in a FileListBox's FileName string, pass it to one of Delphi's File-Management functions: ExtractFile-Ext, ExtractFileName, and ExtractFilePath. To try these functions, insert three Labels into the form (if you are following along, Delphi names them Label2, Label3, and Label4). Assign pieces of selected file paths with this code in the FileListBox's OnDblClick event handler:

```
with FileListBox1 do
begin
  Label2.Caption := ExtractFileExt(FileName);
  Label3.Caption := ExtractFileName(FileName);
  Label4.Caption := ExtractFilePath(FileName);
end;
```

Users can select multiple files in a FileListBox if its MultiSelect property is True. With this setting, users can hightlight multiple filenames by pressing the Shift and Ctrl keys while clicking the mouse pointer. If you choose this option, you'll need to write code and insert an OK button to provide the selection list to the application.

An Edit control associated with a File ListBox in its FileEdit property displays the most recently selected filename when MultiSelect is True. Instead of an Edit object, however, you might want to insert a ListBox into the form for displaying selected filename strings.

Listing 11-1 shows how to create a list of multiple filename selections. If you are following along, insert another ListBox into the form (Delphi names it ListBox2), and insert a BitBtn with its Kind property set to bkOk. Insert the programming in Listing 11-1 into the BitBtn's OnClick event handler.

Listing 11-1

This OnClick event handler demonstrates how to create a list of multiple selections in a FileListBox object.

```
procedure TForm1.BitBtn1Click(Sender: TObject);
var
  I: Integer;
begin
  ListBox2.Clear;
  if FileListBox1.SelCount > 0 then
  for I := 0 to FileListBox1.Items.Count - 1 do
    if FileListBox1.Selected[I] then
      ListBox2.Items.Add(FileListBox1.Items[I]);
end;
```

If SelCount is greater than 0, the user has selected at least one filename. The *for* loop uses the Count property in Items to determine how many *total* filenames the FileListBox displays. For each item *N*, if Selected[N] is True, the program adds that item to ListBox2's Items stringlist. Replace the ListBox in Listing 11-1 with a TStringList object if you need a list of filename selections not related to a component such as a ListBox.

You can improve the efficiency of the code in Listing 11-1 by using a *with* statement, but I prefaced properties with the object name to make it clear what the statements are doing. To make this change, replace the statements after the call to ListBox2's Clear method with the following:

```
with FileListBox1, Items do
if SelCount > 0 then
for I := 0 to Count - 1 do
  if Selected[I] then
    ListBox2.Items.Add(Items[I]);
```

FILTERCOMBOBOX

Use a FilterComboBox to provide a selectable list of wildcard filters such as *.Pas and *.Ini. If you are following along, insert a FilterComboBox object into the form (usually, it goes under a FileListBox). To automatically update the current file list when users select a filter, assign the name of the FileListBox object to the FilterComboBox's FileList property. Or, insert this statement into the form's OnCreate event handler:

```
FilterComboBox1.FileList := FileListBox1;
```

Open Delphi's Filter editor by clicking the ellipsis next to the Filter-ComboBox's Filter property. Enter filters into the editor in this format:

All files (*.*)	| *.*
Text files (*.Txt)	| *.Txt
Pascal files (*.Pas)	| *.Pas

The strings in the left column appear in the FilterComboBox. The strings in the right column are the actual filters passed to the FileListBox. If that object has an associated Edit control, selecting a new filter also inserts it into the Edit window.

Unfortunately, because the Filter property of the FilterComboBox is a string, all filters combined may have only up to 255 characters. This is usually more than enough room for most filters, but I wish Delphi had defined Filter as a TStrings property.

PUTTING THE DIRECTORY DIALOG TOGETHER

If you have been following along, your form looks something like the jumbled dialog in Figure 11-2. In this section, you'll clean up the mess with a better-looking file-selection dialog you can use for many file- and directory-handling chores. Listing 11-2 shows DirDlg's source code (you can find it on the CD-ROM in the DirEx directory). There's not a lot of code in this module — most of the dialog's operations are automatic and result from associating the file and directory objects.

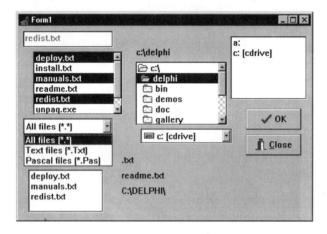

Figure 11-2

The result of the preceding sections showing Delphi's file and directory components. The DirEx application (refer back to Figure 11-1) cleans up this mess with a customizable file-selection dialog.

A test program in the DirEx directory shows how to use the DirDlg dialog. The form's ShowModal function returns the value of ModalResult, which an application can inspect to find out which button users clicked to close the dialog's window. For example, Listing 11-3, extracted from the DirEx test program, displays a selected filename in a ShowMessage dialog if ShowModal returns mrOk. To make that happen, the dialog's OK and Cancel buttons set their ModalResult properties to mrOk and mrCancel respectively. You can also assign values to ModalResult at runtime with a statement such as:

```
ModalResult := mrOk;
```

Listing 11-2

The DirDlg module in the DirEx subdirectory. Most of the file-selection dialog's capabilities are the result of associating file and directory objects.

```
unit Dirdlg;

interface

uses
  SysUtils, WinTypes, WinProcs, Messages, Classes, Graphics, Controls,
  Forms, Dialogs, StdCtrls, Buttons, FileCtrl;

type
  TDirDlgForm = class(TForm)
    FileListBox: TFileListBox;
    DirectoryListBox: TDirectoryListBox;
    DriveComboBox: TDriveComboBox;
    FilterComboBox: TFilterComboBox;
    FileNameEdit: TEdit;
    FileNameLabel: TLabel;
    DirectoriesLabel: TLabel;
    DirLabel: TLabel;
    ListFilesLabel: TLabel;
    DrivesLabel: TLabel;
    OkBitBtn: TBitBtn;
    CancelBitBtn: TBitBtn;
    procedure FileListBoxDblClick(Sender: TObject);
  private
    { Private declarations }
  public
    { Public declarations }
  end;

var
  DirDlgForm: TDirDlgForm;

implementation

{$R *.DFM}

procedure TDirDlgForm.FileListBoxDblClick(Sender: TObject);
begin
  OkBitBtn.Click;
end;

end.
```

Simulates clicking the OK button when user double-clicks a filename.

Listing 11-3

This code, extracted from the DirEx test program, calls ShowModal to display the file-selection dialog (refer back to Figure 11-1). If ShowModal returns mrOk, the procedure displays the selected filename in a ShowMessage dialog.

```
procedure TMainForm.TestBitBtnClick(Sender: TObject);
begin
  with DirDlgForm do
  if ShowModal = mrOk then
    ShowMessage('Selected file = ' + FileNameEdit.Text);
end;
```

Developing Directory-Based Utilities

As you build forms such as the file-selection dialog in the preceding section, you'll want to use them in other applications. To organize your application's source code, it's usually best to create a separate directory for each program module. One or more programs can use these modules simply by adding them to the project.

As an example of this concept, and to show how to use the file-selection dialog in a practical utility, DirExec duplicates the File Manager's capability to run any executable code file. The program can also open any file in the Windows registration database. For example, DirExec opens the Notepad editor to display a text file ending in .Txt.

Try creating this application yourself — it will give you some experience using Delphi's Project Manager to set up multiple module development projects. Create a directory for your program, and start a new project. View the Project Manager, and click the *Add* button. Change to the DirEx directory, and choose the DirDlg.Pas file. This adds the DirDlg module to the program's project. You must also add the module's unit name to the host program's *uses* directive. You can then add buttons or commands to the project to open the dialog for selecting filenames. Use Listing 11-4 as a guide. After the listing, I'll explain how the program runs applications and opens registered files. Figure 11-3 shows the program's display.

Figure 11-3

The DirExec application demonstrates how to use this chapter's file-selection dialog to run other programs and to open registered files such as, for example, text files in the Windows Notepad.

Listing 11-4

DirExec\Main.Pas

```
unit Main;

interface

uses
  SysUtils, WinTypes, WinProcs, Messages, Classes, Graphics, Controls,
  Forms, Dialogs, StdCtrls, Buttons, ShellAPI, DirDlg;

type
  TMainForm = class(TForm)
    RunBitBtn: TBitBtn;
    BitBtn2: TBitBtn;
    procedure RunBitBtnClick(Sender: TObject);
  private
    { Private declarations }
  public
    { Public declarations }
  end;

var
  MainForm: TMainForm;

implementation

{$R *.DFM}

function ExecuteFile(const pFileName, pParams, pDir: String;
  ShowCmd: Integer): THandle;
var
  FileName, Params, Dir: array[0..79] of Char;
```

After adding a module to a project, insert its unit name in the program's uses directive.

Copy this function to any project to give it the ability to run other applications and to open registered document files

II

11

```
begin
  Result := ShellExecute(Application.MainForm.Handle, nil,
    StrPCopy(FileName, pFileName), StrPCopy(Params, pParams),
    StrPCopy(Dir, pDir), ShowCmd);
end;

procedure TMainForm.RunBitBtnClick(Sender: TObject);
begin
  with DirDlgForm do
  if ShowModal = mrOk then
  if ExecuteFile(FileNameEdit.Text, '', DirectoryListBox.Directory,
  SW_SHOW) <= 32 then
    MessageDlg('Unable to open file or program', mtError, [mbOk], 0)
  else
    Application.Minimize;
end;

end.
```

This Windows function runs a code file or opens a document.

Optional: Minimizes this application when running another.

In the preceding chapter, you learned how to use WinExec to run other programs. Windows 3.1 and later versions support a newer function, ShellExecute, that is more capable than WinExec and can open any registered file — for example, those with names ending in .Txt and .Bmp.

The DirExec example (refer to Listing 11-4) includes a function, ExecuteFile, that you can cut and paste into any application. The function calls ShellExecute with six parameters: the current application's window handle (found in the Handle property in the Application's MainForm), *nil* for an optional operation (specify 'Print' here to print a file rather than open it), and three null-terminated strings. Because ShellExecute is a Windows API function, you cannot feed it Pascal strings. The three strings represent the filename, any parameters, and the directory path.

To use ShellExecute, add ShellAPI to the module's *uses* directive.

ShellExecute returns the instance handle of the opened application. If valid, this value is greater than 32, a fact that the test program's *Run* button OnClick event handler uses to display an error message with MessageDlg. Notice the call to Application.Minimize near the end of the listing. This step is optional, but moves the program window out of the way of the selected application.

Search Delphi's on-line help under "File-management routines" for a grab bag of useful file-handling procedures and functions.

Drag-and-Drop Files

Any program that can display a text file should enable drag-and-drop services so users can drag filenames from the Windows File Manager and drop them into the application's Memo or other component object. Delphi doesn't provide drag-and-drop files directly, but you can add this feature with only a little extra effort.

The first step is to inform Windows that your program's window can accept drag-and-drop files. Do that in the form's OnCreate event handler by adding this statement:

```
DragAcceptFiles(Handle, True);
```

Also, insert the ShellAPI unit into the module's *uses* directive. ShellAPI declares DragAcceptFiles as:

```
procedure DragAcceptFiles(Wnd: HWnd; Accept: Bool);
```

- *Wnd* — A handle to the current window, the one to which filenames can be dragged and dropped. Usually, you should pass the Handle property of the form that accepts the file drop.

- *Accept* — Set this parameter to True to inform Windows that this window will accept dragged-and-dropped filenames. Set this parameter to False to disengage dragging and dropping. Microsoft recommends doing this before the program ends — in Delphi applications, you can disable dragging and dropping in a form's OnDestroy event handler.

For any window that calls DragAcceptFiles, when you drag a filename from the Windows File Manager to that window and release the mouse button, Windows sends the window a wm_DropFiles message. Along with the message is the file's name. To receive this message, insert a message handler into a *protected* section of your form's class. (The declaration can go anywhere in the class, but is usually in a private or protected section.) For example, add the following lines between the *private* and *public* declarations in a form's class declaration:

```
protected
  procedure WMDropFiles(var Msg: TMessage);
    message wm_DropFiles;
```

II

11

NOTE

Protected procedures are in a kind of never-never land between private and public declarations. Only class methods, and methods in derived classes, can access protected methods. This differs from *private* declarations, which are accessible *only* to members of the class, but not to any derived classes. Any statement can access a class's *public* declarations — they are like the laundry hanging between buildings. Protected items are in the hallway — you have to be in the building to get at them. Private declarations are in your own room. As long as you keep the door locked, nobody can touch them but you.

Implement the WMDropFiles method to perform an action when users drop a filename into the window. The procedure should have the general format shown in Listing 11-5.

Listing 11-5

Implement the WMDropFiles method using code like this. The comment indicates where you can perform an action with a dropped filename.

```
{- Handle wm_DropFiles message }
procedure TMainForm.WMDropFiles(var Msg: TMessage);
var
  Filename: array[0 .. 256] of Char;
begin
  DragQueryFile(
    THandle(Msg.WParam),
    0,
    Filename,
    SizeOf(Filename));
  { ... Perform action with dropped filename }
  DragFinish(THandle(Msg.WParam));
end;
```

In WMDropFiles, a null-terminated string, FileName, holds the dropped filename. You can make this string longer if necessary, but 256 characters should be enough for even the most deeply nested path names, and for long filenames under Windows NT and Windows 95. Call DragQueryFile to obtain the dropped information. ShellAPI defines this function as:

```
function DragQueryFile(Drop: THandle; FileIndex: Word;
  FileName: PChar; cb: Word): Word;
```

- *Drop* — A handle to an internal structure that contains information about dragged-and-dropped filenames. Usually, you should pass to Drop the Msg.WParam field from the wm_DropFiles message cast to a THandle object.

- *FileIndex* — Set this parameter to $FFFF (equal to –1 in hexadecimal) to request the number of dropped filenames. Pass a value from zero to the number of dropped filenames minus one to copy the names to the FileName parameter.

- *Filename* — An array of Char large enough to hold a complete path name, usually at least 256 bytes. Insert a null-terminated string into the array, or pass *nil* to request the number of dropped files. Pass *nil* also to request the size of a specific filename in bytes.

- *cb* — the size of the Filename buffer in bytes.

If you pass –1 to the FileIndex parameter, DragQueryFile returns the number of dropped files. Declare a Word variable to hold the function result:

```
var
   NumFiles: Word;
```

Next, call DragQueryFile to determine the number of filenames dropped into the window:

```
NumFiles := DragQueryFile(
   THandle(Msg.WParam),.
   $FFFF,
   nil,
   0);
```

Although the Windows API on-line help tells you to pass –1 to the FileIndex parameter, because this is an unsigned Word, Object Pascal doesn't permit you to use negative values here. (Pascal's type checking is stronger than C, which does permit assigning negative values to unsigned integer objects.) Simply use $FFFF, which equals –1 in hexadecimal, to satisfy the compiler's requirements.

In many cases, you'll need to accept only a single filename. As a practical example, the DropFile application on the CD-ROM demonstrates how to program a Memo object to accept drag-and-drop filenames. Run

II

11

DropFile and drag any text filename from the Windows File Manager into the program's Memo window, which reads the file from disk and displays its lines. Figure 11-4 shows the program's display. Listing 11-6 shows the program's source code.

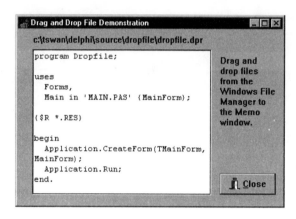

Figure 11-4

The DropFile program demonstrates drag-and-drop filename handling. The illustration shows the program's DropFile.Dpr project file, which I dragged to the Memo object's window from the Windows File Manager.

Listing 11-6
DropFile\Main.Pas

```
unit Main;

interface

uses
  SysUtils, WinTypes, WinProcs, Messages, Classes, Graphics,
  Controls, Forms, Dialogs, StdCtrls, Buttons, ShellAPI;

type
  TMainForm = class(TForm)
    Memo1: TMemo;
    BitBtn1: TBitBtn;
    Label1: TLabel;
    FileNameLabel: TLabel;
    procedure FormCreate(Sender: TObject);
    procedure FormDestroy(Sender: TObject);
```

```
  private
    { Private declarations }
  protected
    procedure WMDropFiles(var Msg: TMessage);
      message wm_DropFiles;
  public
    { Public declarations }
  end;

var
  MainForm: TMainForm;

implementation

{$R *.DFM}

{- Handle wm_DropFiles message }
procedure TMainForm.WMDropFiles(var Msg: TMessage);
var
  Filename: array[0 .. 256] of Char;
begin
  DragQueryFile(
    THandle(Msg.WParam),
    0,
    Filename,
    SizeOf(Filename));
  with FileNameLabel do
  begin
    Caption := LowerCase(StrPas(FileName));
    Memo1.Lines.LoadfromFile(Caption);
  end;
  DragFinish(THandle(Msg.WParam));
end;

{- Tell Windows this window can accept drag-and-drop files }
procedure TMainForm.FormCreate(Sender: TObject);
begin
  DragAcceptFiles(Handle, True);
end;

{- Disable drag-and-drop files (recommended) }
procedure TMainForm.FormDestroy(Sender: TObject);
begin
  DragAcceptFiles(Handle, False);
end;

end.
```

Declare a Windows-message handler for WM_DropFiles

Get the dropped filename.

Use the filename to read the file into a Memo object.

Enable drag-and-drop.

Disable drag-and-drop.

II

11

To enable drag-and-drop filenames, the DropFile form's OnCreate event handler calls DragAcceptFiles. To cancel dragging and dropping, the OnDestroy procedure calls the same function, but passes False to the second parameter.

The TMainForm class declares a WMDropFiles message handler. When Windows issues a wm_DropFiles message to the window, parameter Msg contains the passed information. The procedure's implementation uses this information in a call to DragQueryFile to obtain the dropped filename. Because this name is a null-terminated string, the program passes it to StrPas to convert the text to a Pascal string, assigned to the FileNameLabel's Caption and passed to the Memo1 object's LoadFromFile method. I added a call to LowerCase to convert the filename to lowercase, which is easier on the eyes (at least on *my* eyes).

One problem with the foregoing techniques is that they don't work when dragging filenames onto a minimized application's icon. The reason is that Delphi's main form window is not visible when the program is minimized. To implement dragging and dropping for this condition, you have to add code for the application's window handle. This is the window that shows the minimized icon — it is not the same window used by the form.

Follow these steps to add minimized-icon dragging and dropping to the DropFiles application. Add a second call to DragAcceptFiles in the form's OnCreate event handler. The statement tells Windows that the Application's window can accept drag-and-drop files:

```
DragAcceptFiles(Application.Handle, True);
```

To disable dragging and dropping for this window, add a similar statement to the form's OnDestroy event handler, but pass False to the second DragAcceptFiles parameter:

```
DragAcceptFiles(Application.Handle, False);
```

The Application object does not handle messages in the same way as a form class. The messages arrive in a raw state, just as they are passed around by Windows, and you need a special procedure to handle them. Declare the procedure as follows (its name is unimportant) in the form class's *protected* section. For example, add this declaration below the one for WMDropFiles:

```
procedure AppOnMsg(var Msg: TMsg; var Handled: Boolean);
```

Parameter Msg is of type TMsg, which is undocumented in Delphi's on-line help. WinTypes.Pas in the runtime library defines the record as:

```
TMsg = record
  hwnd: HWnd;
  message: Word;
  wParam: Word;
  lParam: LongInt;
  time: Longint;
  pt: TPoint;
end;
```

It is in this form that messages arrive in Application. In this case, we are interested in only one message, wm_DropFiles. In addition, we want to recognize that message only when the application is minimized. Listing 11-7 shows how to write the handler.

Listing 11-7
Insert this message handler into DropFiles to enable drag-and-drop files for the application's minimized icon.

```
procedure TMainForm.AppOnMsg(var Msg: TMsg; var Handled: Boolean);
var
  Filename: array[0 .. 256] of Char;
begin
  with Application do
  if (Msg.Message = wm_DropFiles) and IsIconic(Handle) then
  begin
    DragQueryFile(THandle(Msg.WParam),
      0, Filename, SizeOf(Filename));
    with FileNameLabel do
    begin
      Caption := LowerCase(StrPas(FileName));
      Memo1.Lines.LoadfromFile(Caption);
    end;
    DragFinish(THandle(Msg.WParam));
  end;
end;
```

Delphi's text editor has a minor bug that incorrectly highlights Message (a nonreserved Pascal directive) in the expression Msg.Message. Because the editor does not perform full syntax parsing, it incorrectly highlights Message when used as an identifier. This is a minor problem, but I wanted to point out that the highlighted Message you see on screen in this case is not a reserved word.

The AppOnMsg procedure inspects Message.Msg for a wm_DropFiles message. If the application is also minimized (IsIconic returns True), the procedure calls DragQueryFile to obtain the filename and load its text into the sample program's Memo object.

There's one final step in making all of this code work properly. You have to assign the message handler (AppOnMsg in this example) to the Application's OnMessage event handler. To ensure that the program receives all intended messages, perform this step as early as possible — in the form's OnCreate event handler, for example. Create a handler for DropFile's OnCreate event, and insert this statement:

```
Application.OnMessage := AppOnMsg;
```

You can now run DropFile and minimize its window on the Windows desktop. Drag a text filename from the File Manager and drop it on the icon. When you open DropFile's window, you'll see the file's text in the Memo object.

Reading and Writing .Ini Files

Delphi's TIniFile class simplifies the tedious chore of reading and writing Windows initialization files identified by the .Ini extension. The TIniFile class is not a component, and it does not appear on Delphi's VCL palette. For this reason, you have to create and free TIniFile objects, and call their methods, completely under program control.

In most programs, you'll need two procedures to read and write .Ini file settings. For example, you can store options and other settings, which experienced users can modify by loading the .Ini file into a text editor. To create or update the file, first create a TIniFile object. Declare it like this:

```
var
   IniFile: TIniFile;
```

Then, in the procedure's body, create the IniFile object by calling TIniFile's Create method:

```
IniFile := TIniFile.Create('YourProg.Ini');
```

When you are done using the IniFile object, free it with this statement:

```
IniFile.Free;
```

If you don't include drive and path name information in the filename string, the .Ini file is created in the Windows directory. This is usually best, but some programmers create .Ini files in the application's home directory. Wherever you locate the file, after creating the IniFile object, call its methods to read and write initialization settings. Each setting must be in a bracketed section, followed by one or more values. For example, here are the first three lines from the SysColor.Ini file, created by the SysColor application described later in this section:

```
[SysColor]
Scroll Bar=12632256
Background=4210688
```

There are two ways to read .Ini file settings into a TStrings or TStringList object. Define the object:

```
var
  StringList: TStringList;
```

Create the string list and call ReadSectionValues for the IniFile object to load the list with the initialization file's settings. For example, use statements such as these:

```
StringList := TStringList.Create;
IniFile.ReadSectionValues('SysColor', StringList);
```

The first statement creates the string list. The second calls ReadSection-Values, passing the section name [SysColor] *without* brackets as a string and the StringList object. Each item in the string list includes the item's name, an equal sign, and a value, with no spaces around the equal sign. Alternatively, to load only the item names, call ReadSection like this:

```
IniFile.ReadSection('SysColor', StringList);
```

IniFile also provides methods to read and write individual values. For example, SysColor writes a CheckBox setting with the statement:

```
IniFile.WriteBool('Options', 'Save settings',
  SaveCheckBox.Checked);
```

■■
11

The first argument, 'Options', specifies the section into which the item is to go. The second argument is the name of this item, and the final argument is its value. If Checked is True, the resulting .Ini file lines look like this:

```
[Options]
Save settings=1
```

To read a setting, call one of the IniFile class's Read methods. For example, SysColor loads the *Save settings* CheckBox value with the statement:

```
SaveCheckBox.Checked :=
  IniFile.ReadBool('Options', 'Save settings', False);
```

The other read and write methods — ReadInteger, ReadString, WriteInteger, and WriteString — work similarly, but read and write values of the indicated types.

After reading .Ini file settings into a string list, you'll want to locate specific settings. Do that by indexing the Values array of the target string list. For example, if T is a TStringList object loaded by an IniFile object's ReadSectionValues method, then Values[S] equals the string value of the item identified as S. You can assign that value to a string:

```
S := T.Values['Button color'];
```

But, you'll probably want to convert it to an integer or other binary value for use in the program. Do that by calling a conversion function such as StrToImt:

```
K := StrToInt(T.Values['Button color']);
```

THE SYSCOLOR UTILITY

A full-length program, SysColor, puts the foregoing concepts into action. The program's source code is a bit long to list completely here, so I'll present portions of it at a time. Explanations of each portion follow the listings. Of course the complete source is on the CD-ROM, in the SysColor directory. Figure 11-5 shows the program's display. See the sidebar, "How to Use Syscolor," for instructions.

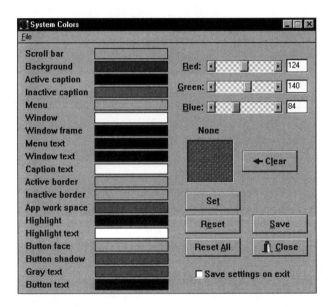

Figure 11-5

SysColor displays and lets you select 19 Windows system colors, such as the windows background color, and active or inactive window title color.

Using the Windows File Manager or the Explorer, drag and drop SysColor.Exe to the StartUp window in the Program Manager, or to the *Programs|StartUp* folder in Windows 95. This will automatically load your saved color settings the next time you start Windows. You can leave SysColor running or quit the application without affecting color settings.

Listing 11-8 shows SysColor's interface section. The numbered Label and Shape components display the labeled color rectangles in the window. (Chapter 13 introduces Shape and other graphics techniques.)

II

11

How to Use SysColor

The labeled color rectangles show current color settings. Click any color box to select it and transfer its color to the large sample box, initially labeled *None*. The box shows the selected color and its name. Click *Clear* to disassociate the sample box with any selected color (this is useful for testing color values without affecting a labeled setting).

Use the *Red, Green,* and *Blue* scroll bars to adjust color values, or you can enter integers from 0 to 255 in the three Edit controls to the right of the scroll bars. The large sample box shows the new color. If you selected a labeled color rectangle, it also shows this color as you change it.

Click the *Set* button to transfer the labeled colors to Windows. For example, change Active caption to fire-truck red and click *Set*. You'll see the active window caption change to a red background that will surely help wake you up in the morning.

Click the *Reset* button to return the labeled colors to their original settings when you started the program. Follow this by clicking *Set* if you want to restore the Windows system colors to their original values.

Click the *Reset all* button to reset labeled colors to their start-up values as well as restore the Windows system colors. This button performs the same actions as clicking *Reset* followed by *Set*.

Click the *Save* button to save the current color selections in SysColor.Ini, located in the Windows directory. The next time you run SysColor, it displays the saved values in the labeled color rectangles. If you don't want to use saved colors, simply delete SysColor.Ini and rerun the program, which will display the current Windows color values.

Click the *Close* button to end the program (or you can choose the *FileIExit* command). If the *Save settings on exit* check box is enabled, the program updates SysColor.Ini when you quit. Disable the check box if you don't want to automatically save your color selections.

Listing 11-8
SysColor\Main.Pas (interface section).

```
unit Main;

interface

uses
    SysUtils, WinTypes, WinProcs, Messages, Classes, Graphics, Controls,
    Forms, Dialogs, StdCtrls, Buttons, ExtCtrls,
    AboutDlg, IniFiles, Menus;
```

```
const
  maxColors = 19;              { Number of Windows system colors }
  redMask = $000000FF;         { Red value extraction mask }
  greenMask = $0000FF00;       { Green value extraction mask }
  blueMask = $00FF0000;        { Blue value extraction mask }
  iniFileName = 'SysColor.Ini'; { Located in Windows directory }

type
  TMainForm = class(TForm)
    BlueEdit: TEdit;
    BlueLabel: TLabel;
    BlueSB: TScrollBar;
    ClearBitBtn: TBitBtn;
    CloseBitBtn: TBitBtn;
    ColorEdit: TEdit;
    ColorLabel: TLabel;
    FileAbout: TMenuItem;
    FileExit: TMenuItem;
    FileMenu: TMenuItem;
    GreenEdit: TEdit;
    GreenLabel: TLabel;
    GreenSB: TScrollBar;
    Label1: TLabel;
    Label2: TLabel;
    Label3: TLabel;
    Label4: TLabel;
    Label5: TLabel;
    Label6: TLabel;
    Label7: TLabel;
    Label8: TLabel;
    Label9: TLabel;
    Label10: TLabel;
    Label11: TLabel;
    Label12: TLabel;
    Label13: TLabel;
    Label14: TLabel;
    Label15: TLabel;
    Label16: TLabel;
    Label17: TLabel;
    Label18: TLabel;
    Label19: TLabel;
    MainMenu1: TMainMenu;
    N1: TMenuItem;
    RedEdit: TEdit;
    RedLabel: TLabel;
    RedSB: TScrollBar;
    ResetAllBitBtn: TBitBtn;
    ResetBitBtn: TBitBtn;
    SaveBitBtn: TBitBtn;
    SaveCheckBox: TCheckBox;
    SetBitBtn: TBitBtn;
    Shape1: TShape;
    Shape2: TShape;
```

Numbered Label objects go with their like-numbered Shapes.

II

11

```
        Shape3:  TShape;
        Shape4:  TShape;
        Shape5:  TShape;
        Shape6:  TShape;
        Shape7:  TShape;
        Shape8:  TShape;
        Shape9:  TShape;
        Shape10: TShape;
        Shape11: TShape;
        Shape12: TShape;
        Shape13: TShape;
        Shape14: TShape;
        Shape15: TShape;
        Shape16: TShape;
        Shape17: TShape;
        Shape18: TShape;
        Shape19: TShape;
        procedure ClearBitBtnClick(Sender: TObject);
        procedure EditChange(Sender: TObject);
        procedure FileAboutClick(Sender: TObject);
        procedure FileExitClick(Sender: TObject);
        procedure FormClose(Sender: TObject; var Action: TCloseAction);
        procedure FormCreate(Sender: TObject);
        procedure FormDestroy(Sender: TObject);
        procedure ResetAllBitBtnClick(Sender: TObject);
        procedure ResetBitBtnClick(Sender: TObject);
        procedure SaveBitBtnClick(Sender: TObject);
        procedure SaveCheckBoxClick(Sender: TObject);
        procedure SBChange(Sender: TObject);
        procedure SetBitBtnClick(Sender: TObject);
        procedure ShapeMouseDown(Sender: TObject; Button: TMouseButton;
          Shift: TShiftState; X, Y: Integer);
      private
        IniFile: TIniFile;                                      For reading and
        IniItemList: TStringList;                               writing color set-
        EditControls: array[0 .. 2] of TEdit;                   tings in the Sys-
        ScrollBars: array[0 .. 2] of TScrollBar;                Color.Ini file.
        Shapes: array[0 .. maxColors - 1] of TShape;
        CurrentShape: TShape;
        procedure UpdateColor;
        procedure InitSysColorArray;
        procedure ChangeSystemColors;
        procedure SetScrollBars(C: TColor);
        procedure LoadSettings;
        procedure SaveSettings;
      public
        { Public declarations }
      end;

    var
      MainForm: TMainForm;

    implementation

    {$R *.DFM}
```

The program defines a few constants near the top of the listing. maxColors equals the number of Windows system colors. redMask, greenMask, and blueMask are 32-bit, unsigned hexadecimal integers used to extract individual color values from TColor objects. For example, the expression *C and greenMask* isolates a TColor's green color value. iniFileName is the name of the program's initialization file. Because the name does not include a drive letter or any path information, its location is the Windows directory.

The TMainForm class declares numerous objects that construct the window's interface. Each Label object's number matches the corresponding Shape (for example, Label7 goes with Shape7). This relationship is not arbitrary, and as I'll explain in a moment, when you have a lot of related components, you can take advantage of Delphi's automatic object naming conventions to write code for related objects. Most of the other objects and event handlers are self explanatory, so I'll explain only the elements I added to TMainForm's *private* section. There are five private data members:

- *IniFile* — This object is constructed in the form's OnCreate event handler and destroyed in OnDestroy. IniFile provides access to the Syscolor.Ini file for various procedures. The object opens and closes that file as needed to read and write its settings, so it's more efficient to declare the object in the form's class than it is to declare TIniFile objects in individual procedures.

- *IniItemList* — This is a string list of identifiers for the SysColor.Ini file, which stores color settings as 32-bit decimal integers. For example, the IniItemList entry for the SysColor.Ini setting *Background=4210688* is the string '*Background*'. I find that it's helpful to keep the item labels in a separate string list, which I'll explain more about later in this chapter.

- *EditControls* — This is an easy-access array to the three Edit windows next to the scroll bars. (Chapter 9's ColorDlg application also uses this array.)

- *ScrollBars* — This is also an easy-access array to the three ScrollBar objects. (Chapter 9's ColorDlg application uses this array, too.)

- *Shapes* — This array contains references to the 19 Shape objects that display Windows system colors. Using an array simplifies the code — for example, rather than write 19 event handlers, the program can use the array to refer to color rectangle *n* with the expression *Shapes[n]*. As SysColors demonstrates, object-reference arrays can help streamline code, and you'll find them valuable in many situations.

- *CurrentShape* — This is a reference to the currently selected color rectangle. When equal to *nil*, there is no selection. Alternatively, I could have used an integer index into the Shapes array to indicate the current color, perhaps with –1 representing no selection. However, because all Delphi objects are references (that is, they are address values), it is often best to define variables such as CurrentShape that refer to the actual target object. For example, the program can assign *Shapes[n]* to *CurrentShape*, and then use the CurrentShape reference to perform actions on the selected object.

In addition to its data members, SysColor defines six private procedures in the TMainForm class. Following are brief introductions to each procedure. Complete descriptions of how they work follow their implementations.

- *UpdateColor* — This procedure sets the large color sample box, an Edit object named ColorEdit, to the color that the three ScrollBars represent. The procedure also sets the CurrentShape's color if one is selected. In addition, UpdateColor saves the current color in a global SysColorArray array.

- *InitSysColorArray* — This procedure initializes the global SysColorArray, which stores the current Windows system colors along with the currently modified color set. The array makes it easy for the program to reset colors to their start-up values. The program also uses the SysColorArray to update the SysColor.Ini file.

- *ChangeSystemColors* — This procedure transfers to Windows the current color selections. For each color, all active applications receive a wm_SysColorChange message that indicates the application should update its windows, buttons, and other affected items. Delphi applications automatically perform these updates — you don't have to write code to support wm_SysColorChange messages.

- *SetScrollBars* — This procedure sets the three ScrollBars' Position properties to values that match a color passed as an argument.

- *LoadSettings* — This procedure reads the SysColor.Ini file, if it exists.

- *SaveSettings* —This procedure creates or updates the SysColor.Ini file's color settings.

Listing 11-9 shows SysColor's global declarations and initialization procedures. Explanations follow the listing.

Listing 11-9
SysColor\Main.Pas (globals and initializations).

```
type
{- Holds current system colors }
  SysColorRec = record
    OriginalColor: TColor;   { Color on starting program }
    CurrentColor: TColor;    { New color selected by user }
  end;

var
{- Array of SysColorRec values }
  SysColorArray: array[0 .. maxColors - 1 ] of SysColorRec;

{- Update sample colors from scrollbar positions }
procedure TMainForm.UpdateColor;
begin
{- Update color edit box (the large sample window) }
  ColorEdit.Color :=
    RGB(RedSB.Position, GreenSB.Position, BlueSB.Position);
{- Update labeled Shape color box and SysColorArray }
  if CurrentShape <> nil then with CurrentShape do
  begin
    Brush.Color := ColorEdit.Color;
    SysColorArray[Tag - 1].CurrentColor := Brush.Color;
  end;
end;

{- Load system colors into the SysColor array }
procedure TMainForm.InitSysColorArray;
var
  I: Integer;
begin
  for I := 0 to maxColors - 1 do with SysColorArray[I] do
  begin
    OriginalColor := GetSysColor(I);
    CurrentColor := OriginalColor;
    Shapes[I].Brush.Color := OriginalColor;
  end;
end;

{- Change system colors to values in SysColorArray }
procedure TMainForm.ChangeSystemColors;
```

Call this Windows function to get a system color setting.

```
var
  I: Integer;
  InxArray: Array[0 .. maxColors - 1] of Integer;
  ClrArray: Array[0 .. maxColors - 1] of TColor;
begin
  for I := 0 to maxColors -1 do
  begin
    InxArray[I] := I;
    ClrArray[I] := SysColorArray[I].CurrentColor;
  end;
  SetSysColors(maxColors, InxArray[0], ClrArray[0]);
end;
```

The SysColorRec data type declares a record of two TColor values. OriginalColor is the color value obtained from Windows at start-up. CurrentColor is the color value shown in a labeled color rectangle. The SysColorArray holds 19 SysColorRec records, one for each Windows system color.

Procedure UpdateColor calls the Windows RGB function to combine the three ScrollBar Position properties into a TColor-compatible LongInt 32-bit integer. Assigning this value to the ColorEdit object's Color property updates the large color sample below the scroll bars.

If the user has selected a labeled color (CurrentShape is not equal to nil), UpdateColor also assigns the new color to the CurrentShape's Brush.Color subproperty, and saves the color in the SysColorArray. Notice that the Shape's Tag equals its index in SysColorArray.

Procedure InitSysColorArray shows how to obtain the current color settings from Windows. A *for* loop calls the API GetSysColor function with an argument I equal to the color's index. The loop saves each color in SysColorArray, and displays it by updating the Shape's Brush.Color subproperty. This is a good example of how useful object-reference arrays such as Shapes can be.

Procedure ChangeSystemColors transfers the 19 color values to Windows by calling the API function SetSysColors. This function requires three arguments: the number of colors, an array of color-index integers, and an array of the 32-bit color values. The statement that calls SetSysColors passes the addresses of the two arrays, InxArray and ClrArray, by indexing their first elements.

Look up SetSysColors in Delphi's online API reference. The two arrays are declared as untyped *var* parameters. To give an array's address to such a parameter, pass its first element as procedure ChangeSystemColors demonstrates.

Listing 11-10 shows three form-maintenance event handlers, which are responsible for initializing SysColor's objects and for performing clean-up chores when the program ends. Explanations follow the listing.

Listing 11-10
SysColor\Main.Pas (form-maintenance event handlers).

```
{- Initialize TObject control arrays }
procedure TMainForm.FormCreate(Sender: TObject);
var
  I: Integer;
begin
{- Construct IniFile object instance }
  IniFile := TIniFile.Create(iniFileName);
{- Miscellaneous initializations }
  CurrentShape := nil;  { No selected labeled color shape }
{- Assign object references to easy-access arrays }
  EditControls[0] := RedEdit;
  EditControls[1] := GreenEdit;
  EditControls[2] := BlueEdit;
  ScrollBars[0] := RedSB;
  ScrollBars[1] := GreenSB;
  ScrollBars[2] := BlueSB;
{- Assign Shape color box object references to Shapes array }
  for I := 0 to maxColors -1 do
    Shapes[I] := TShape(FindComponent('Shape' + IntToStr(I + 1)));
{- Create item list from Labels for Ini file read/write }
  IniItemList := TStringList.Create;
  with IniItemList do
  for I := 0 to maxColors -1 do
    Add(TLabel(FindComponent('Label' + IntToStr(I + 1))).Caption);
{- Load current colors and possible Ini file settings }
  InitSysColorArray;  { Initialize SysColor array }
  LoadSettings;       { Load SysColor.Ini settings if present }
end;

{- Save settings if SaveCheckBox selected }
procedure TMainForm.FormClose(Sender: TObject;
  var Action: TCloseAction);
begin
  if SaveCheckBox.Checked then
    SaveSettings;  { Save settings in SysColor.Ini }
end;

{- Last chance to clean up }
procedure TMainForm.FormDestroy(Sender: TObject);
begin
  IniItemList.Free;
  IniFile.Free;
end;
```

Returns a reference to a component object by name such as Label7.

II

11

Procedure FormCreate handles the form's OnCreate event. The procedure initializes variables, and calls methods to bring the display to life. The first *for* loop shows a useful technique for setting up an object-reference array. Let's look at it closely:

```
for I := 0 to maxColors -1 do
  Shapes[I] := TShape(FindComponent('Shape' + IntToStr(I + 1)));
```

The goal is to assign to Shapes a reference to each of the Shape objects, each representing one labeled color rectangle in the window. Function FindComponent returns a reference to the object of the name passed as a string. To refer to Shape1, Shape2, ..., Shape19, the program uses IntToString to convert the *for* loop's control variable plus one to a string, which is attached to *Shape*. To complete the assignment, the program casts FindComponent's return value to a TShape object. You'll find many uses for FindComponent, especially when building arrays of object references such as Shapes.

A similar *for* loop in the same procedure creates the list of identifiers for the SysColor.Ini file. After creating IniItemList, a TStringList object, the loop inserts the program's Labels as the .Ini file's settings. Here again, FindComponent returns the object references to Label1, Label2, ..., Label19. The program casts the function's return value to a TLabel object, and inserts into IniItemList that object's Caption field. Finally, FormCreate calls InitSysColorArray to obtain the current Windows color settings. After this, LoadSettings reads SysColor.Ini, if it exists.

Procedure FormClose handles the form's OnClose event. The procedure calls SaveSettings to update or create SysColor.Ini if you enabled the *Save settings on exit* CheckBox. Procedure FormDestroy handles the OnDestroy event. This is the last chance the program has to clean up before going to that big bit bucket in the sky. Typically, as demonstrated here, this event is a good opportunity to free memory allocated to objects. In this case, the program frees the IniItemList string list object that the form's OnCreate event handler created.

Listing 11-11 shows how SysColor handles events for ScrollBar, Edit, and Shape objects. Together, these procedures select and change the window's color rectangles. Explanations follow the listing.

Listing 11-11

SysColor\Main.Pas (Scrollbar, Edit, and Shape event handlers).

```
{- Set scrollbar positions to match color C }
procedure TMainForm.SetScrollBars(C: TColor);
begin
{- The following assignments also update Edit boxes }
  RedSB.Position   := C and redMask;
  GreenSB.Position := (C and greenMask) shr 8;
  BlueSB.Position  := (C and blueMask) shr 16;
end;

{- Update values in Edit boxes for ScrollBar changes }
procedure TMainForm.SBChange(Sender: TObject);
begin
  with Sender as TScrollBar do
    EditControls[Tag].Text := IntToStr(Position);
  UpdateColor;
end;

{- Update scrollbar positions for Edit box changes }
procedure TMainForm.EditChange(Sender: TObject);
begin
  with Sender as TEdit do
    ScrollBars[Tag].Position := StrToInt(Text);
end;

{- Select color shape on mouse down event }
procedure TMainForm.ShapeMouseDown(Sender: TObject;
  Button: TMouseButton; Shift: TShiftState; X, Y: Integer);
var
  P: TLabel;    { Pointer to matching TLabel object }
begin
  CurrentShape := TShape(Sender);  { Save clicked Shape }
  P := TLabel(FindComponent('Label' + IntToStr(CurrentShape.Tag)));
  if P <> nil then
    ColorLabel.Caption := P.Caption;  { Show color name }
  SetScrollBars(CurrentShape.Brush.Color);  { Synch scroll bars }
end;
```

Use these expressions to extract the Red, Green, and Blue byte values from.

11

Procedure SetScrollBars updates the three ScrollBar Position properties to match the red, green, and blue subvalues in TColor parameter C. Assigning values to Position moves the ScrollBar's thumb box (also called a scroll box) to a relative position within the control's range. Three logical *and* expressions use the redMask, greenMask, and blueMask constants to isolate subvalues in color C. The *shr* (shift right) operators move the isolated values to the least significant positions in the resulting integers, which are assigned to Position.

Chapter 9 explains how procedures SBChange and EditChange handle OnChange events for the ScrollBar and Edit objects. The objects' Tag values equal their indexed positions in the object-reference arrays Edit-Controls and ScrollBars. With these arrays, the Scrollbar and Edit controls can share the same event handlers, and cooperate so that, if you enter a value into an Edit window, the ScrollBar's thumb box follows along. Likewise, moving the thumb box updates the Edit window's value.

Procedure ShapeMouseDown handles clicking of a labeled color rectangle. Because Shape components are not selectable Windows controls, they don't have OnClick events. However, you can recognize mouse clicks for these and other nonwindow objects by creating an OnMouse-Down event handler such as ShapeMouseDown.

The procedure first assigns to CurrentShape a reference to the selected Shape, passed to the procedure in parameter Sender. The program next calls FindComponent to locate Label$n$, where n equals the Shape's Tag value. Using Tags with FindComponent this way is an efficient means for forming relationships among objects, and for taking advantage of Delphi's naming conventions. Normally, you should name objects according to their purposes, but in this case, it's easier to work with the 38 Labels and Shapes using their default names, Label1, Label2, ..., Label 19, Shape1, Shape2, ..., Shape 19.

The final SysColor code fragment in Listing 11-12 shows how the program creates, reads, and updates the SysColor.Ini file. Explanations follow the listing.

Procedure LoadSettings reads SysColor.Ini, if the file exists. Studying this code line by line will provide insights you can use in your own initialization-file-handling routines. For holding the file's settings, LoadSettings creates a TStringList object, IniValueList. The program then calls ReadSectionValues for the IniFile object. The *'SysColor'* argument indicates the section in the .Ini file to read, in this case, section *[SysColor]*. Each element in the resulting IniValueList object is a string in the form:

```
Identifier=Value
```

Listing 11-12

SysColor\Main.Pas (SysColor.Ini file procedures)

```
{- Load colors and options from SysColor.Ini if present }
procedure TMainForm.LoadSettings;
var
  IniValueList: TStringList;
  I: Integer;
begin
  IniValueList := TStringList.Create;
  try
  {- [SysColor] settings }
    IniFile.ReadSectionValues('SysColor', IniValueList);
    for I := 0 to IniValueList.Count - 1 do
    with SysColorArray[I] do
    begin
      CurrentColor := StrToInt(
        IniValueList.Values[IniItemList[I]]);
      OriginalColor := CurrentColor;
    end;
  {- [Options] settings }
    SaveCheckBox.Checked :=
      IniFile.ReadBool('Options', 'Save settings', False);
  finally
    IniValueList.Free;
  end;
  ChangeSystemColors;
  InitSysColorArray;
end;

{- Create or update SysColor.Ini color settings only }
procedure TMainForm.SaveSettings;
var
I: Integer;
begin
{- [SysColor] settings }
  for I := 0 to IniItemList.Count - 1 do
    IniFile.WriteString('SysColor', IniItemList[I],
      IntToStr(SysColorArray[I].CurrentColor));
end;

{- Write check box setting to SysColor.Ini }
procedure TMainForm.SaveCheckBoxClick(Sender: TObject);
begin
  IniFile.WriteBool('Options', 'Save settings',
    SaveCheckBox.Checked);
end;
```

Reads Syscolon settings into a TString List object.

Use a try-finally block to ensure disposal of the TString List object.

Reads an individual Boolean value.

This writes color values to Syscolor.Ini.

This writes SaveCheck-Box as a Boolean True or False value to Syscolor.ini.

II

11

To obtain the Value portion of each setting, use the Values array in the IniValueList string-list object. LoadSettings uses this technique to assign color values to the SysColorarray. Examine this assignment carefully:

```
CurrentColor := StrToInt(
  IniValueList.Values[IniItemList[I]]);
```

The expression IniItemList[I] refers to one of the identifier labels created back in the form's OnCreate event handler (see procedure Form-Create and the statements starting from *with IniItemList...*). These strings represent the *Identifier* portion of the setting *Identifier=Value*. Use the *Identifier* string as an index in the Values array to obtain that setting's *Value*. This is also a string, so to assign it to CurrentColor, the program calls StrToInt.

LoadSettings uses another .Ini file technique to read the *Save settings on exit* CheckBox. Call ReadBool for the IniFile object, passing the section header ('Options'), the setting identifier ('Save settings'), and a default value. If the setting exists, ReadBool returns it. If not, it returns the default value, assigned here to SaveCheckBox's Checked property. Call the similar ReadInteger and ReadString functions to read integer and string values.

After loading the .Ini file's settings, LoadSetting frees the IniValueList object. The procedure calls ChangeSystemColors to transfer the loaded colors to Windows. The final call to InitSysColorArray reinitializes the array by obtaining those saved colors back from Windows. This ensures that the values in the array are the ones actually used — they may differ in some cases due to the way Windows selects closely-matching colors depending on the display driver's capabilities.

Procedure SaveSettings is simpler than LoadSettings. A *for* loop calls the IniFile's WriteString method to write the current color settings. To WriteString, pass the .Ini file's section header ('SysColor'), the *Identifier* portion of each setting (InitItemList[I]), and a string representing the *Value* portion. Here, IntToStr converts the CurrentColor value from the SysColorArray. When done writing all colors, SaveSettings frees the IniFile object.

Notice that SaveSettings does *not* save the SaveCheckBox's Checked property. When I tried to do exactly that in an earlier version, I realized that saving this CheckBox created a Catch-22 situation. You could check the box, which saved it to the .Ini file, but if you unchecked it, the file was not updated, causing the box to be set again from the old file the next time SysColor started.

The solution is to update SaveCheckBox's value *every time the CheckBox changes*. Procedure SaveCheckBoxClick handles this task for the control's OnClick event. The procedure calls WriteBool to save the current setting (which has already changed by the time the OnClick event handler is called). This points out a good rule of thumb in using .Ini files for saving program options — you may need to update individual elements if their values affect whether the .Ini file is updated.

Listing 11-13 shows a sample SysColor.Ini file. Refer to this listing while you investigate SysColor's.Ini file-handling routines.

Listing 11-13
Sample SysColor.Ini file.

```
[SysColor]
Scroll Bar=12632256
Background=4210688
Active caption=8755968
Inactive caption=8421440
Menu=12632256
Window=16777215
Window frame=0
Menu text=0
Window text=0
Caption text=16777215
Active border=4227072
Inactive border=8421440
App work space=12632256
Highlight=32768
Highlight text=16777215
Button face=12632256
Button shadow=8421504
Gray text=8421504
Button text=0

[Options]
Save settings=0
```

NOTE ▶ The rest of SysColor's listing, which you can find on the CD-ROM, provides event handlers for the window's buttons and CheckBox. These handlers, which have obvious purposes, merely call other procedures in the program, so I won't list or discuss them here. I added comments to the listing, however, in case you want to investigate the program further.

II

11

Summary

- Use the DirectoryListBox, DriveComboBox, FileListBox, and Filter-ComboBox components to construct custom file-selection dialogs. By associating these objects, you enable them to work together so that, for example, when users change directories in a DirectoryListBox, the associated FileListBox automatically updates its contents.

- Add ShellAPI to a module's *uses* directive, and call ShellExecute to run programs or load registered files. For example, you can display a text file in the Windows Notepad utility simply by opening a .Txt file with ShellExecute.

- Delphi components do not recognize drag-and-drop filenames, but you can easily add this capability by writing a procedure that responds to the wm_DropFiles message. To enable drag-and-drop files, call DragAcceptFiles in the form's OnCreate event handler.

- When you minimize an application, its main form is hidden. For this reason, implementing drag-and-drop files for a program minimized as an icon requires the Application object to respond to the wm_Drop-Files message. To program a response for that or for any other Windows message, assign a message handler to the Application's OnMessage property. You must perform this assignment at runtime.

- Initialization files store options, settings, and other values. Use the TIniFile class to construct an object for which you can call methods such as ReadSectionValues, ReadBool, and WriteString to read and write .Ini file settings.

- This chapter's SysColor utility demonstrates practical .Ini file-handling methods. The program also illustrates numerous application interface techniques and Pascal programming concepts.

Projects to Try

11-1: Write a general-purpose .Ini file editor.

11-2: Add a section to the SysColor.Ini file that saves the program's window position. Runnning SysColor should move the window back to its last-known position.

11-3: Write your own wildcard filter editor, similar to Delphi's, and add it to this chapter's customizable directory dialog. Write the user's filters to an initialization (.Ini) file.

11-4: Write a file utility that can change file attributes such as the Archive and Readonly settings. Use the FileGetAttr and FileSetAttr functions in Delphi's file-management routines (search for them on-line).

11-5: *Advanced.* This chapter introduces many of the techniques needed to create a custom File Manager utility. There's always a good market for programs of this nature that enhance standard Windows tools. As an advanced project, consider writing your own File Manager (Windows 3.1) or Explorer (Windows 95) utility.

11-6: *Advanced.* SysColor updates all Windows system colors, even if the color values haven't changed. This results in lots of messages whizzing among application event buffers. Write a more efficient version that updates only the minimum number of colors when users click the Set button.

Expert-User Tips

- Use the file and directory components described in this chapter only when you need a custom file-selection dialog. The next chapter explains how to use Delphi's OpenDialog and SaveDialog components, which are usually more than adequate for file and directory interface objects.

- If you store .Ini files in specific paths, be sure to give users the option of selecting an alternate location. In most cases, it's best to store .Ini files in the Windows directory, but this is not a requirement. To store .Ini files in the program's installed directory, use function ParamStr(0) to obtain the application's path.

- Call DiskFree to determine the amount of available disk space, which you might want to add to this chapter's file-selection dialog. Examine other file and directory functions by searching Delphi's on-line help for "File-management routines."

II

11

- Don't go hog-wild with this chapter's message-handling techniques. Before writing a message handler for an application or form, thoroughly investigate whether the capability you need already exists as an event handler.

- In C, a statement may assign signed values such as –1 to unsigned WORD parameters. Pascal type-checking rules do not permit this practice, but the work-around is easy. For example, to pass –1 to a Windows API function WORD parameter, use the hexadecimal equivalent constant $FFFF.

- Remember always to free the objects you create. When creating global dynamic objects such as TStringLists, create them in the form's OnCreate event handler. Call Free for each created object in the form's OnDestroy handler.

- Never create new sections in the standard Windows initialization file, Win.Ini, — an unfortunately common practice among in far too many applications. Unless you are writing system software, you should also avoid writing values to System.Ini.

Coming Up

The next chapter covers Delphi's dialog components, and reveals tips for writing your own modal and modeless dialog operations.

12 Communicating with Dialog Boxes

*I*n Windows, a dialog box is technically a window of a particular style that lacks minimize and maximize buttons, and usually contains check boxes, radio buttons, and other interactive controls. In Delphi, however, any form can have dialog box characteristics, and the dividing lines between an application's dialogs and its other windows blur in the light of the modern graphical user interface.

You might think of a dialog box, as I mean it here, as a program's voice and ears. It gives users a way to select options and enter input. It can post messages, ask questions, and receive responses. In this chapter, you'll learn about Delphi's common-dialog components, as well as the Notebook, TabbedNotebook, and TabSet components, which are tremendously useful in creating multipage dialog boxes and other kinds of windows.

Components

- ColorDialog — This component encapsulates the Windows common color dialog. Use it for a general-purpose color-selection tool. Palette: Dialogs.

- FindDialog — This component encapsulates the Windows common find dialog. Use it to perform data searches. Palette: Dialogs.

- FontDialog — This component encapsulates the Windows font-selection dialog. Use it to permit users to choose text fonts, and to set the foreground color for displayed text. Palette: Dialogs.

- Notebook — This component provides a multipage container that you can use with a TabSet object to provide tabbed toolbars and other interactive control sets. Palette: Additional.

- OpenDialog — This component encapsulates the Windows common file-open dialog. Use it to select files and browse directories, typically in response to a *File|Open* command. Palette: Dialogs.

- ReplaceDialog — This component encapsulates the Windows common replace dialog. Use it to perform search-and-replace operations. Palette: Dialogs.

- SaveDialog — This component encapsulates the Windows common file-save dialog. Use it to enter or select filenames, and to browse directories, typically in response to a *File|Save as* command. Palette: Dialogs.

- TabbedNotebook — This component provides a multipage panel-like object that resembles a stack of file folders with labeled tabs on the top edge. Users can select TabbedNotebook pages by clicking tab labels, which makes this component especially suitable for complex options dialogs with too many controls to fit comfortably in a single window. Palette: Additional.

- TabSet — This component provides a toolbar of selectable tabs, which you can use in conjunction with other components to provide them with a page-turning capability. This chapter's TabEdit application demonstrates how to use a TabSet object to create a multipage text editor. Palette: Additional.

 Common dialogs are so named because Windows provides them in the dynamic link library CommDlg.Dll. The ColorDialog, FindDialog, FontDialog, OpenDialog, ReplaceDialog, and SaveDialog components provide object-oriented wrappers for the corresponding Windows dialogs. The other components in this chapter are unique to Delphi.

Dialog Modes

Applications use dialogs in one of two ways: as modal windows that retain the input focus until closing, or as modeless windows that permit users to switch away from them. For example, an options dialog is typically a modal window that users must close before continuing to use the application. However, a search-and-replace dialog is typically modeless so that users can start a search, switch to an edit window, and then continue searching.

MODAL DIALOGS

Call a form's ShowModal method to display a modal dialog. Users must close the dialog window before the program continues. For example, if MyDialog is a form, a menu command or button OnClick event handler might bring up the dialog window with the statement:

```
MyDialog.ShowModal;
```

Usually, the dialog's *Close, Cancel,* or other form-closing buttons assign a value to ModalResult, which ShowModal returns. To determine whether users clicked the dialog's *OK* button, use a statement such as the following to examine ShowModal's return value:

```
if MyDialog.ShowModal = mrOk then
  { ... take action if user clicked OK button }
```

In the dialog modules, assign to ModalResult the value you want ShowModal to return. Either set the button's ModalResult property to mrOk (standard Button and BitBtn components do this for you automatically), or in the form's *OK* button OnClick event handler, use a statement such as:

```
ModalResult := mrOk;
```

MODELESS DIALOGS

As Windows defines it, a modeless dialog is a child window that doesn't capture the input focus, and that permits users to run the application normally while the dialog box is on display. In Delphi, however, a modeless dialog is simply any form window that the program selectively makes visible. To display a form as a modeless dialog, call the Show method:

```
MyDialog.Show;
```

Calling Show sets the form's Visible property to True and calls BringToFront to display the dialog box on top of other potentially obscuring windows. To hide the dialog window, set Visible to False:

```
MyDialog.Visible := False;
```

To determine whether a modeless dialog is active, inspect its Visible property.

Common Dialogs

Four common dialog components — FontDialog, ColorDialog, Open-Dialog, and SaveDialog — provide font, color, and filename selection windows. The TabEdit application on the CD-ROM demonstrates how to use these components. TabEdit's source code is too long to list in full here, so I'll present the listings in relatively small snippets. Of course, all of the program's source code is on the CD-ROM. Figure 12-1 shows TabEdit's display.

Figure 12-1

TabEdit provides a multipage text editor, similar to Delphi's unit module editor. Because TabEdit's source code is lengthy, listings in this chapter show only relatively small snippets. Load TabEdit's project file into Delphi to inspect the entire program.

FONT AND COLOR DIALOGS

As Listing 12-1 shows, the FontDialog and ColorDialog components are effortless to use. Insert these objects into a form, and call their Execute methods to display them as modal dialogs. If Execute returns True, the user clicked *OK* to close the dialog window, and you can copy or use the FontDialog's Font property or the ColorDialog's Color property to obtain the user's selection.

Listing 12-1
The FontDialog and ColorDialog components are easy to use.

```
procedure TMainForm.OptionsFontClick(Sender: TObject);
begin
  if FontDialog1 Execute then
    Memo1.Font := FontDialog1.Font;
end;

procedure TMainForm.OptionsBackgroundClick(Sender: TObject);
begin
  if ColorDialog1 Execute then
    Memo1.Color := ColorDialog1.Color;
end;
```

Call Execute to bring up common font and color-selection dialogs.

The ColorDialog component offers three options, which you can program using the Object Inspector or by assigning True or False to three properties at runtime:

- *cdFullOpen* — When this option is False, a dialog provides a color selection grid from which users can pick colors. When cdfullOpen is True, the color dialog shows its full selection palette complete with red, green, blue, and other color-value controls. On relatively slow computers, it can take several seconds for Windows to construct the full dialog, so don't use this option if you know your application will run on slow systems. Users can still open the full dialog by clicking the *Define custom colors* button.

- *cdPreventFullOpen* — Set to True to prevent users from opening the full color-selection dialog (the *Define custom colors* button is permanently disabled). You might use this option to limit colors to a pre-defined set.

II

12

- *cdShowHelp* — Set to True to display a Help button. Set to False if your program doesn't implement on-line help. If your program has on-line help, set cdShowHelp to True and assign an appropriate value to the dialog's HelpContext property.

The FontDialog component offers many more options, some of which are obvious — fdTrueTypeOnly, for example, and fdFixed-PitchOnly. Following are some tips about less-obvious options:

- *fdAnsiOnly* — Set to True to display only fonts that implement the Windows character set. For example, when fdAnsiOnly is True, the font dialog does not list the WingDings symbol font.

- *fdEffects* — Set to False to disable strikeout, underline, and color options. You should always disable these features if your program doesn't use them. Unfortunately, however, it's not possible to enable and disable the three options selectively (a Windows limitation). This is an all-or-nothing option.

- *fdNoFaceSel* — Normally, the dialog displays the current font in the edit portion of the font-list combo box. Set fdNoFaceSel to True if you want the edit control to be blank when the dialog appears.

- *fdNoSimulations* — Set to True to prevent listing GDI-simulated fonts. (This switch has little practical benefit, and on my systems, appears to produce the same font lists.)

- *fdNoSizeSel, fdNoStyleSel* — These switches determine whether size and style options are initially selected (highlighted). If you want users to select a new font, but you don't want to display the current font's characteristics, set these two options and fdNoFaceSel to True.

- *fdWysiwyg* — Set to True to list only fonts that are available to both the printer and the screen. When fdWysiwyg is False, users can select fonts that may not print as displayed. If the affected text appears only on screen and is never printed, set this option to False.

- *fdLimitSize* — Set to True only when also specifying MinFontSize and MaxFontSize property values to limit size choices to a specific range.

OPEN AND SAVE DIALOGS

As a text editor, TabEdit is a useful program in its own right, but it also serves as a template for any file-handling program. The first step is to write two procedures — one to read a file from disk, and the other to create or write file data. I usually write these procedures separately rather than code file input and output in menu-command event handlers. This makes the program's file procedures available to any routines that need them. Listing 12-2 shows TabEdit's LoadFile and SaveFile procedures, which are explained after the listing.

Listing 12-2
TabEdit's file input and output procedures.

```
{- Read file from disk }
procedure TMainForm.LoadFile(const Path: String);
begin
  with Pages[TabSet1.TabIndex] do
  try
    Memo1.Lines.LoadFromFile(Path);
    Dirty := False;
    Page.Clear;
    SetFilename(Path);
  except
    MessageDlg('Error reading file', mtError, [mbOk], 0);
  end;
end;

{- Write current file to disk }
procedure TMainForm.SaveFile(Index: Integer);
begin
  with TabSet1, Pages[Index] do
  begin
    try
      Memo1.Lines.SaveToFile(Filename);
      Dirty := False;
    except
      MessageDlg('Error writing file', mtError, [mbOk], 0);
    end;
  end;
end;
```

II

12

LoadFile and SaveFile use Pascal exceptions to *try* statements that might fail. In case of errors, an *except* statement block displays a message dialog. Chapter 18 explains more about exception handling, but it's very easy to use. Just put all statements that might generate exceptions — for example, SaveToFile, in a *try* block. Insert the procedure's error response in the *except* block, and finish with an *end* keyword.

Listing 12-3 shows TabEdit's *File*-menu event handlers. The procedures use the OpenDialog and SaveDialog components, and call the procedures in Listing 12-2. Use this listing as a guide to adding *Open, Save,* and *Save as* commands to your own applications.

Listing 12-3
TabEdit's File-menu event handlers.

```
{- File|Open command }
procedure TMainForm.FileOpenClick(Sender: TObject);
begin
  with Pages[TabSet1.TabIndex] do
  begin
    if Dirty then FileSaveClick(Sender);
    if {still} Dirty then Exit;  { File not saved }
    if FileOpenDialog.Execute then
      LoadFile(FileOpenDialog.Filename);
  end;
end;


{- File|Close command }
procedure TMainForm.FileCloseClick(Sender: TObject);
var
  W: Word;
begin
  with TabSet1, Pages[TabIndex] do
  begin
    if Dirty then
    begin
      W := MessageDlg('Save changes to ' + Tabs[TabIndex] + '?',
      mtWarning, [mbYes, mbNo, mbCancel], 0);
      case W of
        mrYes: FileSaveClick(Sender);
        mrNo: Dirty := False;
        mrCancel: Exit;
      end;
    end;
    if {still} Dirty then Exit;  { File not saved }
    Page.Clear;
    Memo1.Clear;
    Filename := untitledName;
    Tabs[TabIndex] := Filename;
  end;
end;
```

The Dirty flag indicates whether any changes were made to the file.

Setting Dirty to false throws out changes.

```
{- File|Save command }
procedure TMainForm.FileSaveClick(Sender: TObject);
begin
  with TabSet1, Pages[TabIndex] do
  if Filename = untitledName then
    FileSaveAsClick(Sender)
  else
    SaveFile(TabIndex);
end;
```

Default to File|Save
as *command for*
unnamed files.

```
{- File|Save As command }
procedure TMainForm.FileSaveAsClick(Sender: TObject);
begin
  with TabSet1, Pages[TabIndex] do
  if FileSaveDialog.Execute then
  begin
    SetFilename(FileSaveDialog.Filename);
    SaveFile(TabIndex);
  end;
end;
```

FileOpenClick saves the current file if Dirty is True, which indicates the user made changes to the file. After this chore, the procedure displays a FileOpenDialog by calling its Execute method. If the method returns True, then LoadFile attempts to read the dialog's selected Filename.

FileCloseClick prompts users to save any changes and closes the current file. FileSaveClick defaults to FileSaveAsClick if the current file is not named; otherwise, the procedure calls SaveFile to attempt to write the current file to disk. Neither of these procedures uses any dialog components.

FileSaveAsClick calls Execute for the FileSaveDialog object. If the method returns True, then the users selected a new filename (or gave permission to overwrite an existing file), and the program calls SaveFile to write the current file to disk. The SetFilename statement assigns the file's name to the page tab label.

FILTERS AND MULTIPLE FILE TYPES

In a program that opens different types of files, it's often best to limit the SaveDialog's filters to the same types of files as the one most recently opened. For example, if users open a text file, the SaveDialog might display only .Txt files. If users open a bitmap, the SaveDialog would display

.Bmp files. This reminds users of the types of files they are opening and saving. If you instead program the same filters in both the OpenDialog and SaveDialog dialogs, users might imagine they can convert between file types simply by altering the extension (for example, by saving a .Txt file as a .Bmp file). Unless your application can perform such conversions, it's best not to imply that it can.

To reprogram the SaveDialog Filter, use the following statement after executing an OpenDialog object. When users next attempt to save the file, the SaveDialog will display only files with the same extension. For example, if you open a .Bmp file, the resulting string assigned to the SaveDialog object's Filter property is *Files *.Bmp|(*.bmp)*:

```
SaveDialog1.Filter :=
  'Files (*'
  + ExtractFileExt(OpenDialog1.FileName)
  + ')|*'
  + ExtractFileExt(OpenDialog1.FileName);
```

CREATING A HISTORY LIST

OpenDialog and SaveDialog components have a TStrings proptery, HistoryList, that you can use to save recently selected filenames. This creates a history of filenames from which users can select the files they worked with earlier. You might even save the history list in a disk file for restoring the next time the application is started.

Creating a history list requires three steps:

1. Insert an OpenDialog or SaveDialog component object into a form.
2. Change the OpenDialog or SaveDialog FileEditStyle property to fsComboBox.
3. Add selected filenames to the OpenDialog or SaveDialog HistoryList property.

To complete step 3, in the OnClick command or button event handler that opens or saves a file, execute the dialog and add a selected filename to the history list with code such as this:

```
with OpenDialog1 do
if Execute then
begin
  { Open file here }
  FileName := Lowercase(FileName);
  HistoryList.Add(FileName);
end;
```

You can do the same with a SaveDialog object. When the user next opens the dialog, the most recently selected files appear in the combo-box edit window. (Try the preceding code in a button's OnClick event handler to see the effect. Be sure to set the dialog's FileEditStyle property to fsComboBox, or the history list will not appear.)

To limit the number of filenames in the HistoryList, declare a constant in the module:

```
const
  maxHistoryList = 6;
```

Then, use the following programming to insert filenames into the HistoryList. The most recently selected files appear at the top of the list; older files scroll off the bottom when the list reaches its maximum size:

```
with OpenDialog1 do
if Execute then
begin
  { Open file here }
  FileName := Lowercase(FileName);
  with HistoryList do
  begin
    if Count = maxHistoryList then
      Delete(Count - 1);
    HistoryList.Insert(0, FileName);
  end;
end;
```

You might also want to include a command or option to erase the history list. To do that, use statements such as these:

```
OpenDialog1.HistoryList.Clear;
SaveDialog1.HistoryList.Clear;
```

II

12

Paged Dialogs

Even with today's high-resolution monitors, available space on screen is as rare as an empty lot in Manhattan. To get some additional real estate for controls and other objects, you can create multipage windows and dialog boxes. This can also help organize controls into categories that users select by choosing labeled tabs. The following sections suggest ways to create multipage windows with the TabSet, Notebook, and TabbedNotebook components.

TabSet

Figure 12-2 shows a TabSet object in a test window. To create the figure, I clicked the Tabs property's ellipsis, and entered seven labels, Tab1, Tab2, ..., Tab7. However, because there's only enough room for six of the seven labels, the component displays horizontal arrow buttons that users can click to scroll the TabSet left and right.

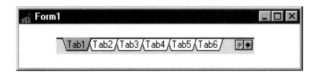

Figure 12-2
TabSet displays horizontal arrow buttons so users can scroll the tabs left and right if there isn't enough room for all tabs.

The TabEdit application uses a TabSet object, aligned to the bottom of the window, to create the illusion of a multiple-page Memo object. Actually, the program has only one Memo. To store multiple files in memory, the program uses a global Pages array of TPageRec records. Each TPageRec record contains a TStringList object (Page). When you select a tab to turn the page, the program assigns the selected string list to the Memo object.

Listing 12-4 shows the program's TabSet event handlers. In most cases, you need to respond to only two events — one generated *before* a Tab change and one generated *after*. The reason there are two events is to give your program the opportunity to detach the current page when a tab is about to change, and then attach a new page after the change. The meaning of a *page* depends entirely on your application — the TabSet component merely gives you a controlled means for creating the multipage illusion.

Listing 12-4

TabSet's two event handlers from the TabEdit application.

```
{- A tab is changing. Save Memo's text in a TStringList object }
procedure TMainForm.TabSet1Change(Sender: TObject; NewTab: Integer;
  var AllowChange: Boolean);
begin
  with TabSet1, Pages[TabIndex] do
  begin
    Page.Clear;
    Page.Assign(Memo1.Lines);
  end;
end;

{- A tab has changed. Assign a TStringList object to Memo }
procedure TMainForm.TabSet1Click(Sender: TObject);
begin
  with TabSet1 do
    Memo1.Lines.Assign(Pages[TabIndex].Page);
end;
```

Procedure TabSet1Change first clears the current TStringList Page object. Next, the procedure calls Assign for Page, passing the Memo's Lines property (an object of type TStrings). This saves the Memo object's current contents in Page before the TabSet changes.

After the change, the TabSet1Click method again calls Assign. This time, however, the assignment goes in the opposite direction — from the Page TStringList indexed by TabIndex to Memo1's Lines TStrings list. Now, the Memo object displays the new page of text associated with the selected tab.

Apparently for legal reasons, which I'm told involve Borland's efforts to protect its patent rights, Delphi's runtime library source code does not include the TabSet and TabbedNotebook components. To obtain the source code for these components, write to Borland's Legal Department and request the Tabs.Pas, Tabs.Doc, and Tabnotbk.Pas files.

II

12

NOTEBOOK

The Notebook component provides a multipage container that you'll most often use in conjunction with a TabSet object. For a practical demonstration of the technique, try the Palette application on the CD-ROM. With just two event handlers, the program creates a tabbed toolbar, similar to Delphi's VCL palette. Figure 12-3 shows Palette's display. Click a page tab to change to another page of SpeedButtons. Select any SpeedButton to show its caption in the large Label. Listing 12-5 shows the program's source code.

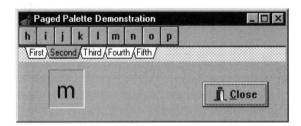

Figure 12-3
The Palette application demonstrates how to create a tabbed toolbar, similar to Delphi's VCL palette.

 To conserve space in this chapter, I deleted most of the 36 Speed-Button object declarations from the TMainForm class.

Listing 12-5
Palette\Main.Pas

```
unit Main;

interface

uses
  SysUtils, WinTypes, WinProcs, Messages, Classes, Graphics, Controls,
  Forms, Dialogs, Buttons, ExtCtrls, Tabs, StdCtrls;

type
  TMainForm = class(TForm)
    TabSet1: TTabSet;
    Notebook1: TNotebook;
    SpeedButton1: TSpeedButton;
    SpeedButton2: TSpeedButton;
```

```
{ ... }
    SpeedButton36: TSpeedButton;
    BitBtn1: TBitBtn;
    Label1: TLabel;
    Bevel1: TBevel;
    procedure TabSet1Click(Sender: TObject);
    procedure SpeedButton1Click(Sender: TObject);
  private
    { Private declarations }
  public
    { Public declarations }
  end;

var
  MainForm: TMainForm;

implementation

{$R *.DFM}

procedure TMainForm.TabSet1Click(Sender: TObject);
begin
  with TabSet1 do
    NoteBook1.ActivePage := Tabs[TabIndex];
end;

procedure TMainForm.SpeedButton1Click(Sender: TObject);
begin
  with Sender as TSpeedButton do
    Label1.Caption := Caption;
end;

end.
```

Changes a NoteBook's active page to match a selected.

Follow these steps to recreate the Palette program and construct a tabbed toolbar using the Notebook component:

1. Insert a Notebook component into a form, and set its Align property to alTop. Change the Notebook's Height to 25.

2. Insert a TabSet component into the form. Set its Align property to alTop. This places the TabSet object directly beneath the Notebook.

3. Select TabSet1's Tabs property, and click the ellipsis button to run Delphi's *String list editor*. Enter labels for the toolbar's tabs, one label per line. (To recreate the example program, enter *First, Second, Third, Fourth,* and *Fifth.*)

II

12

4. Select Notebook1's Pages property, and click the ellipsis button to open Delphi's *Notebook editor.* Click the *Edit* button to modify the default page name to *First.* Then, click the *Add* button to add pages for the remaining tab labels. When associating a Notebook with a TabSet using the technique described here, each Notebook page should have a matching TabSet label.

5. The Notebook's ActivePage property equals the string name of the pages you entered in the preceding step. Change ActivePage to *First.* Insert SpeedButton objects into Notebook1 (click the mouse inside the Notebook1 object, and then drag each SpeedButton to its final position).

6. Repeat step 5 for the other Notebook pages. Change ActivePage to *Second, Third, ... Fifth,* and insert a few Speedbuttons into each page. You can label your SpeedButtons as I did in the demonstration, or assign them glyph bitmaps. Insert a Label object and select a large font size to show the selected button's caption.

7. When you are done preparing each Notebook page, set ActivePage to *First* and the TabSet's PageIndex property to 0. Create an OnClick event handler for all SpeedButton objects. Also, create an OnClick handler for TabSet1. Insert the statements in the listing. To turn the page on the toolbar, the TabSet1 handler assigns the tabbed label to Notebook1's ActivePage. The SpeedButton OnClick handler displays the selected button's caption.

To create a tabbed toolbar at the bottom of a window, reverse steps 1 and 2 and set Align for both objects to alBottom.

TABBEDNOTEBOOK

The primary difference between a TabbedNotebook and a pair of Notebook and TabSet objects is appearance. Use a TabbedNotebook to create multipage dialogs that look like file folders with selectable tabs along the top. Use the Notebook and TabSet components when you need more control over object positions, and when you want the flexibility of programming page-turning operations using separate components.

A TabbedNotebook is particularly useful for creating categorical options dialogs — for example, with printing options on one page, color setups on another, and general-purpose options on still another page. By dividing controls into categories, you can program an Options command that opens a single window, which users will probably find less confusing than multiple commands in an Options menu.

To use a TabbedNotebook object, insert it into a form. Usually, you'll want to set the object's Align property to alClient so the TabbedNotebook completely fills the window, but of course, that's up to you. Select the Pages property to create each labeled page using the same Notebook editor mentioned in the preceding section. On each page, insert the controls that you need (CheckBoxes, RadioButtons, and other objects).

At runtime, there are two ways to display a specific page. Usually, you won't need to do that because users can select the pages they want. However, to display a page by number, assign a value to PageIndex. The first index is zero, so 2 represents the third page:

```
TabbedNotebook1.PageIndex := 2;  {Display page 3}
```

Alternatively, to display a page by its labeled name, assign a string to ActivePage:

```
TabbedNotebook1.ActivePage := 'General options';
```

For a cleaner window in a complex options dialog with many pages, assign a value to TabsPerRow. For example, if your dialog has 12 pages, set TabsPerRow to 4 to stack folders in three rows of four. As shown in Figure 12-4, the result is visually pleasing and lends a well-organized appearance to an otherwise overwhelmingly complex dialog window.

Delphi automatically adjusts TabsPerRow so that all labels fit comfortably on their tabs. For this reason, you should assign a new value to TabsPerRow *after* creating all TabbedNotebook pages.

To change the default system font for tab labels, select a different font for the TabFont property. The Font property affects the font for control objects inserted into a TabbedNotebook. The two fonts may be different. For example, you can use italic text for tab labels and normal text for controls on the tabbed pages.

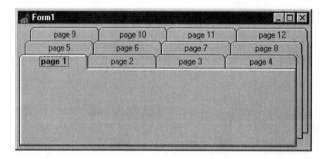

Figure 12-4

Assign a value to TabsPerRow to stack TabbedNotebook pages in rows and columns.

Component objects may belong to the form even when they appear to reside inside a TabbedNotebook. For example, insert a *Close* button into the form and drag it over the TabbedNotebook. The button appears on top of the notebook page, but it still belongs to the form. Because of its relationship to its parent object, the button remains visible for all notebook pages. This works even when the TabbedNotebook completely fills the form's client area.

After setting a TabbedNotebook's Align property to alClient, it is difficult to insert objects into the form, but here's an easy solution. Temporarily set Align to alNone. Select the Button or BitBtn (or other component you want to insert) in the VCL palette, and then maximize the form window. Click the mouse pointer in the form background to insert your object, and drag the resulting button onto any TabbedNotebook page (it doesn't matter which one). Shrink the window back to normal size, and set the TabbedNotebook's Align property back to alClient. When you run the program, the button will remain visible regardless of which page is active.

Alternatively, hold down the Shift key when you click on the form to drop the component. Shift-clicking drops the object into the *parent* of the target container (usually the form) rather than the container itself.

One common use for a TabbedNotebook is to hold Memo objects, one per page. Insert the Memos into the TabbedNotebook pages, and set the Memo Align properties to alClient. Because the TabbedNotebook owns the Memos, they fill the page but do not obscure the tabbed labels. This is a quick-and-dirty method for creating a multipage text editor, but you'll have to carefully program the module to perform operations on only the current page. For example, to copy text to the clipboard, inspect PageIndex to determine which Memo object to use:

```
case TabbedNotebook1.PageIndex of
  0: Memo1.CopyToClipboard;
  1: Memo2.CopyToClipboard;
  2: Memo3.CopyToClipboard;
end;
```

This works, but it is not the most elegant solution. Listing 12-6 shows a more general approach that works regardless of how many pages the TabbedNotebook object has. The program assigns to variable P, of type TComponent, the result of FindComponent, which searches for Memo objects using PageIndex to create the object names (Memo1, Memo2, ..., MemoN). If the search succeeds, the program calls CopyToClipboard for the located Memo on the current page. You might use similar code in an *Edit|Copy* menu command or as a button's OnClick event handler.

Listing 12-6

To copy selected Memo object text to the clipboard, use FindComponent to locate the Memo on the current TabbedNotebook page, and then call CopyToClipboard for that Memo.

```
procedure TForm1.Copytoclipboard1Click(Sender: TObject);
var
  P: TComponent;
begin
  P := FindComponent('Memo' +
    IntToStr(TabbedNotebook1.PageIndex + 1));
  if P <> nil then
    TMemo(P).CopyToClipboard;
end;
```

Call FindComponent to obtain a reference to a named object.

Usa a type-cast to tell Delphi what type of object P refers to.

Selecting a component with the Object Inspector's drop-down list automatically turns to the Notebook or TabbedNotebook page that contains the object.

II

12

INSERTING PAGES AT RUNTIME

The AddPage application on the CD-ROM shows how to add new pages to a TabbedNotebook object at runtime. The program also demonstrates how to insert a control into a page — again, entirely under program control. Listing 12-7 shows the program's source code. Run AddPage and click the *Add page* button to insert new pages into the TabbedNotebook. Click *Add control* to insert a ListBox into the current page.

Listing 12-7
AddPage\Main.Pas

```
unit Main;

interface

uses
   SysUtils, WinTypes, WinProcs, Messages, Classes, Graphics, Controls,
   Forms, Dialogs, Buttons, StdCtrls, TabNotBk;

type
   TMainForm = class(TForm)
     TabbedNotebook1: TTabbedNotebook;
     AddPageButton: TButton;
     CloseBitBtn: TBitBtn;
     AddControlButton: TButton;
     procedure AddPageButtonClick(Sender: TObject);
     procedure AddControlButtonClick(Sender: TObject);
   private
     { Private declarations }
   public
     { Public declarations }
   end;

var
   MainForm: TMainForm;

implementation

{$R *.DFM}

{- Insert new page into TabbedNotebook }
procedure TMainForm.AddPageButtonClick(Sender: TObject);
begin
   with TabbedNotebook1 do
     Pages.Add(Format('Page %d',[Pages.Count-1]));
end;

{- Insert new control into current page }
procedure TMainForm.AddControlButtonClick(Sender: TObject);
var
   L: TListBox;
   P: TWinControl;
```

Adds a page to a TabbedNotebook object.

```
begin
  L := TListBox Create(Self);                              Create the
  with TabbedNotebook1 do                                  control-object
  begin                                                    to insert.
    P := Pages.Objects[PageIndex] as TWinControl;
    L.Parent := P;
    L.SetBounds(10, 10, 100, 100);
{- Insert page tab label into edit control for demonstration.
   You don't have to perform this step. }
    L.Items.Add(TTabPage(P).Caption);                      Always remember
  end;                                                     to specify the
end;                                                       object's parent.

end.
```

Procedure AddPageButtonClick shows how to add a page to a Tabbed-Notebook object. Simply add a string to the Pages property. The procedure calls Format to create string labels such as *Page 1, Page 2, ..., Page N.*

Procedure AddControlButtonClick shows how to add a new control object to the TabbedNotebook's current page. First, Create constructs the new control. Then, P is set to refer to the page, using the Objects array in the TabbedNotebook's Pages string list. The program assigns the page reference P as the control's parent, and then calls SetBounds to define the control's width, height, and position. (Other types of control objects require different kinds of initializations.) Finally, just to display something in the new control, the Add method adds the current page tab label to the newly inserted ListBox. You don't have to perform this final step.

Searching with Dialogs

Delphi's FindDialog and ReplaceDialog components are as easy to use as peanut butter. The sticky part, however, is writing find-and-replace code that works in conjunction with these modeless dialog boxes. After the following brief introductions, a sample application provides a shell that you can use for implementing *Find* and *Replace* commands.

FIND DIALOG

The FindDialog component offers two methods and one event. To display the dialog window shown in Figure 12-5 and start a search, call the Execute method. Call CloseDialog to hide the dialog. To perform the actual search, write a handler for the OnFind event, generated when users click the *Find Next* button.

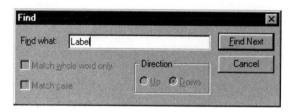

Figure 12-5
The FindDialog component displays this modeless dialog.

To obtain the text that users enter into the *Find what* edit control, use the FindDialog object's FindText property. You can also select various Options — for example, to hide or disable the *Match case* check box.

FIND AND REPLACE DIALOG

As shown in Figure 12-6, the ReplaceDialog component is an expanded version of FindDialog, with a second edit control for entering replacement text. To FindDialog's members, ReplaceDialog adds another property, ReplaceText, which contains the text users enter into the *Replace with* edit window. Call Execute to display a Replace-Dialog object. Call CloseDialog to hide the dialog window.

ReplaceDialog recognizes two events. Create an OnFind event handler to search for text items. Create an OnReplace event handler to perform the actual replacement. There are a few tricks to writing this code, as I'll explain next.

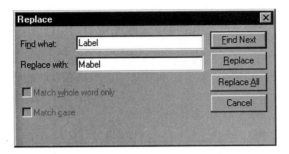

Figure 12-6
The ReplaceDialog component displays this modeless dialog.

PROGRAMMING FIND AND REPLACE COMMANDS

Unfortunately, programming *Find* and *Replace* commands is a lot more difficult than inserting a couple of components into a form. To simplify the job, follow the plan outlined in the FindRepl application on the CD-ROM. Figure 12-7 shows the program's display. It lists some object names (cut from the SysColor utility) in a ListBox. Click the *Find* button to find items in the ListBox. Click *Replace* to replace items or partial items. Listing 12-8 shows how the program performs these operations.

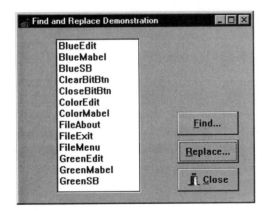

Figure 12-7
The FindRepl application outlines the programming needed for an application's Find and Replace commands.

II

12

Listing 12-8
FindRepl\Main.Pas

```
unit Main;

interface

uses
  SysUtils, WinTypes, WinProcs, Messages, Classes, Graphics, Controls,
  Forms, Dialogs, StdCtrls, Buttons;

type
  TMainForm = class(TForm)
    ListBox1: TListBox;
    FindDialog: TFindDialog;
    FindBitBtn: TBitBtn;
    CloseBitBtn: TBitBtn;
    ReplaceBitBtn: TBitBtn;
    ReplaceDialog: TReplaceDialog;
    procedure FindBitBtnClick(Sender: TObject);
    procedure FindDialogFind(Sender: TObject);
    procedure ReplaceBitBtnClick(Sender: TObject);
    procedure ReplaceDialogFind(Sender: TObject);
    procedure ReplaceDialogReplace(Sender: TObject);
  private
    FindIndex, FoundPos, FoundLen: Integer;
    FoundItem: Boolean;
  public
  end;

var
  MainForm: TMainForm;

implementation

{$R *.DFM}

{- Begin a FindDialog operation }
procedure TMainForm.FindBitBtnClick(Sender: TObject);
begin
  FindDialog.Execute;
  FindIndex := 0;
  ListBox1.ItemIndex := -1;
end;

{- Continue a FindDialog operation }
procedure TMainForm.FindDialogFind(Sender: TObject);
var
  S: String;
```

Because the dialog is modeless, the program does not pause here.

```
begin
  while FindIndex < ListBox1.Items.Count do
  begin
    S := ListBox1.Items[FindIndex];
    Inc(FindIndex);
    if Pos(FindDialog.FindText, S) <> 0 then
    begin
      ListBox1.ItemIndex := FindIndex - 1;
      Exit;
    end;
  end;
  ShowMessage('No more matches!');
  FindDialog.CloseDialog;
end;
```

You must perform the actual searching, for example, by calling Pos to compare strings.

Closes the modeless dialog.

```
{- Start a ReplaceDialog operation }
procedure TMainForm.ReplaceBitBtnClick(Sender: TObject);
begin
  ReplaceDialog.Execute;
  FindIndex := 0;
  ListBox1.ItemIndex := - 1;
  FoundItem := False;
end;


{- Continue a ReplaceDialog operation }
procedure TMainForm.ReplaceDialogFind(Sender: TObject);
var
  S: String;
begin
  while FindIndex < ListBox1.Items.Count do
  begin
    S := ListBox1.Items[FindIndex];
    Inc(FindIndex);
    FoundPos := Pos(ReplaceDialog.FindText, S);
    if FoundPos <> 0 then
    begin
      ListBox1.ItemIndex := FindIndex - 1;
      FoundLen := Length(ReplaceDialog.FindText);
      FoundItem := True;
      Exit;
    end;
  end;
  ShowMessage('No more matches!');
  ReplaceDialog.CloseDialog;
end;


{- Perform replacement for a ReplaceDialog operation }
procedure TMainForm.ReplaceDialogReplace(Sender: TObject);
var
  S: String;
```

```
begin
  if frReplaceAll in ReplaceDialog.Options then
    ShowMessage('Replace All not implemented')
  else if not FoundItem then
    ShowMessage('Click Find to begin/continue search')
  else begin
    S := ListBox1.Items[FindIndex - 1];
    Delete(S, FoundPos, FoundLen);
    Insert(ReplaceDialog.ReplaceText, S, FoundPos);
    ListBox1.Items[FindIndex - 1] := S;
    FoundItem := False;
  end;
end;

end.
```

Programming a *Find* command is the easiest of the two tasks. First, insert an event handler for a command or button that begins a search. Call the FindDialog's Execute method, and prepare global variables used to continue searching. For example, FindRepl starts a search with these statements:

```
FindDialog.Execute;
FindIndex := 0;
ListBox1.ItemIndex := -1;
```

The first line brings up the modeless dialog. The second initializes a global variable used to indicate the ListBox line most recently searched. The last line sets ItemIndex in the ListBox object to –1 so no lines are initially highlighted.

When you start searching by clicking the dialog's *Find next* button, the FindDialogFind event handler performs the actual search using the global FindIndex to determine which ListBox item to examine. Function Pos examines whether the FindText property is found in the target string S, copied from the ListBox's Items. If Pos is nonzero, a match was found, and the assignment to ItemIndex highlights the matching item.

Notice that the event handler Exits after finding a match. This does not close the dialog—it merely returns control to the program so users can perform other actions. However, if the global FindIndex equals the count of items, the program calls ShowMessage to tell users the search is over. CloseDialog then hides the FindDialog window.

Writing the code for a *Replace* command is more difficult. Start the search as for *Find,* but initialize any global variables you need for making replacements. (See ReplaceBitBtnClick in the listing.) You'll need a Boolean flag such as FoundItem to indicate that an item was found. Initialize this variable to False at the start of the search. Here's how the sample program responds to clicking the *Replace* button:

```
ReplaceDialog.Execute;
FindIndex := 0;
ListBox1.ItemIndex := -1;
FoundItem := False;
```

The first line calls Execute to display the modeless dialog box. The second line assigns zero to FindIndex, which represents the ListBox line being searched. The third line assigns –1 to the ListBox's ItemIndex property so no lines are initially highlighted. The final line initializes the global Boolean flag, FoundItem, to False.

To finish the *Replace* command, you'll need two event handlers. The first (ReplaceDialogFind in the listing) is similar to the FindDialog's event handler. On finding a matching item, initialize global variables you need for performing a replacement. Set the FoundItem flag to True so that the second event handler can determine that it was called as the result of a matching search.

In that handler (see ReplaceDialogReplace), if FoundItem is True, the procedure executes its replacement statements. As the listing shows, you can also detect whether users clicked the *Replace all* button by testing whether constant frReplaceAll is in the dialog's Options set. Of course, the actual replacement code will be unique to your program, but Delphi can't do *everything* (can it?).

Summary

- A dialog box is a program's voice and ears. In Delphi, any form window can have dialog characteristics for prompting users, displaying messages, and presenting options.

II

12

- Delphi encapsulates common Windows dialogs in the ColorDialog, FindDialog, FontDialog, OpenDialog, ReplaceDialog, and SaveDialog components. This chapter also discuses the related TabSet, Notebook, and TabbedNotebook components, which are handy for creating multi-page dialog box windows.

- Dialogs can be modal (capture and retain the input focus) or mode-less (capture, but do not retain the input focus). Call a form's Show-Modal method to display a modal dialog. Call Show to display a modeless dialog window. To display common Windows dialogs, call their component Execute methods.

- You will normally use the TabSet and Notebook components together to create the illusion of a tabbed panel. This chapter's TabEdit multi-page text editor demonstrates this useful interface technique.

- You can also use TabSet and Notebook components to create tabbed toolbars, similar to Delphi's VCL palette. This chapter's Palette application explains the technique.

- The primary difference between a pair of TabSet and Notebook objects, and the TabbedNotebook component, is appearance. Tabbed-Notebooks look like stacked file folders with labeled tabs along the top. The TabbedNotebook component is especially suitable for creating multipage options dialogs.

- Writing *Find* and *Replace* commands is no simple task. Delphi's FindDialog and ReplaceDialog components provide standard tools for creating find and replace modeless dialogs, but it's up to you to supply the actual search-and-replace programming. This chapter's FindRepl application outlines the fundamental steps.

- Delphi's TextDemo demonstration (see file Search.Pas in the Demos\Textdemo directory) contains a general-purpose text search routine that you can extract for Find and Replace operations.

Projects to Try

12-1: Write a telephone dialer dialog. The window should look like a touch-tone phone. Return a phone number through ShowModal if users click the Dial button.

12-2: Add a ColorDialog component and command to the SysColor utility from the preceding chapter.

12-3: *Advanced.* Implement *Find* and *Replace* commands for a TStringList object.

12-4: *Advanced.* Use Notebook and TabSet components to create a multi-page Options dialog. This takes a little more effort than using a TabbedNotebook as suggested in this chapter, but gives you extra flexibility. For example, you can place TabSets where you like, and if space is limited, you can take advantage of the TabSet component's capability to scroll tab labels horizontally.

Expert-User Tips

■ ShowModal returns an integer value. To return other types of objects from a modal dialog, add a function to the form's class to return the data you need. For example, declare a String function in the form class's public section:

```
TYourForm = class(TForm)
...
public
  function GetStringResult: String;
end;
```

Implement the function to return the result of the dialog such as an Edit control's Text property:

```
function TYourForm.GetStringResult: String;
begin
  with Edit1 do
  if Length(Text) = 0 then
    Result := 'Default string'
  else
    Result := Text;
end;
```

Call ShowModal to display the dialog form window and then call the "get result" function immediately after:

```
if YourForm.ShowModal = mrOk then
  S := YourForm.GetStringResult;
```

II

12

- Modeless dialogs that are on display during lengthy operations may not react promptly enough to user input. This is a Windows limitation that you can usually work around inside loops by calling ProcessMessages for the global Application object. For example, write time-intensive loops like this:

```
while Flag do
begin
  PerformOperation;
  Application.ProcessMessages;
  Flag := ContinueOperation;
end;
```

- If you are familiar with Borland Pascal, you may have written code to transfer dialog information to and from application variables. In Delphi, declare variables in the dialog form's class, and either provide functions to return those variables, or access them directly through the class's public section. For example, follow these steps to demonstrate how to access a dialog's controls:

1. Insert a Button into a form (module Unit1). Select Delphi's *New form* SpeedButton or command and choose the Standard dialog box with buttons along the right border.
2. Insert a CheckBox into the second form (module Unit2).
3. Add Unit 2 to Unit1's *uses* declaration. This permits the Button object's event handlers, and other code in the main form, to access the second module's public items.
4. Implement the Button's OnClick event handler in module Unit1 as follows. As the statements illustrate, you can directly access the Checked property in the dialog's CheckBox1 object. The dialog object itself stores its control values, and therefore, Borland Pascal's transfer mechanism isn't needed in Delphi applications.

```
with BtnRightDlg do
if ShowModal = mrOk then
  if CheckBox1.Checked then
    ShowMessage('Checkbox is enabled')
  else
    ShowMessage('Checkbox is disabled');
```

- If you receive a GPF (general protection fault) immediately on running an application, the cause is often a reference to a method in a form that does not yet exist. For example, in a program with a dialog box, you cannot call YourDialog.AnyMethod in the main form's OnCreate event handler because YourDialog is not yet initialized. To repair the problem, move the statement to the form's OnActivate event handler, and use a Boolean flag to indicate whether the dialog has been initialized. Alternatively, instead of writing code to initialize dialog form properties at runtime, use the Object Inspector to program property values.

- Each page in a TabbedNotebook component is a TTabPage object. Refer to these objects through the Objects and Pages properties. For example, the following procedure displays the Caption of the first page tab in a TabbedNotebook object:

```
procedure TForm1.Button1Click(Sender: TObject);
var
  P: TTabPage;  { Reference to a TabbedNotebook page }
begin
  with TabbedNotebook1 do
    P := TTabPage(Pages.Objects[0]);  { P refers to page 1 }
    ShowMessage(P.Caption);  { Display page tab label }
end;
```

- To prevent users from selecting a specific page in a TabbedNotebook object, create a handler for the OnChange event, which has two parameters in addition to Sender: NewTab, representing the tab index that the user clicked; and AllowChange, which you can set to indicate whether that page is selectable. For example, in the TabbedNotebook object's OnChange handler, use this statement to disable the third page (the first page index equals zero):

```
if NewTab = 2 then
  AllowChange := False;
```

II

12

Coming Up

This chapter concludes Part II's investigation into user-interface construction techniques using Delphi components. In Part III, you'll consider the other side of the development coin—the internal tasks that your application performs.

III The Application

*M*ost applications fall into, or they use major elements from, the categories described in the chapters in Part 3. Before reading these chapters, you should be comfortable with Delphi's commands and windows, and you should fully understand the techniques of programming component properties and events as explained in Part 2.

In the following chapters, you'll learn how to create a wide variety of applications that use advanced-level components for graphics, printer output, multiple document interfaces (MDI), clipboard data transfers, dynamic data exchange (DDE), object linking and embedding (OLE), and database management.

Part 3 Chapters

Developing Graphics Applications

*R*egardless of your artistic skills (mine never progressed much beyond crayons and chalk), with the help of Delphi's Canvas property, you can draw and paint any shape you can imagine. In addition, Delphi's graphics components, data types, procedures, and functions greatly simplify programming tasks such as working with bitmaps, and reading and writing metafiles.

In this chapter, I'll introduce Delphi's graphics components and techniques, and I'll explain how to use the extensive Canvas property that many components provide for a general-purpose drawing surface. I'll also cover related graphics topics such as graphics file handling, off-screen bitmaps, and drag-and-drop objects.

Components

- Image — Use this component to import bitmaps, icons, and metafiles into a form. An Image object is a wrapper that contains a graphical figure in its Picture property. Palette: Additional.

- Shape — Use this component to create geometrical shapes such as filled and unfilled ellipses and rectangles. Choose the shape you want by setting a Shape object's Shape property (the property and component have the same name). Palette: Additional.

- PaintBox — Use this component to add drawing and painting capabilities to components such as Panel that don't have a Canvas property. You can also use a PaintBox object to restrict drawing to one or more rectangular areas in a form window. Palette: System.

Introducing the Canvas

All graphics operations take place on the Canvas property, which many components provide. For example, the form has a Canvas property, as do TBitmap, TComboBox, TListBox, TPaintBox, and other components. The Canvas property embodies the Windows graphics device interface (GDI), and it provides a device-independent surface for drawing graphical objects in windows. (The next chapter covers printing of graphics and text.)

For those who are familiar with Windows programming, Delphi's Canvas is an object-oriented encapsulation of a handle to a device context (HDC). To create graphics on a device, methods in the TCanvas class call Windows GDI functions.

DRAWING WITH THE CANVAS

The Canvas property is a comprehensive, object-oriented wrapper for the Windows GDI. The Canvas, which is always ready to use, is an object in its own right, and its TCanvas class provides dozens of properties, methods, and events. Generally, you'll use a Canvas property in two ways:

- To configure graphical output by assigning colors, patterns, fonts, and other values to Canvas properties and subproperties.

- To produce visual shapes by calling graphical methods, some of which also provide supporting services such as determining the display pixel width of a string.

The Canvas property is not available at design time in the Object Inspector window. To use the Canvas, you must write statements that assign values to Canvas properties and that call Canvas methods. For example, to draw a blue rectangle filled with yellow diagonal hatches in the form window, insert these statements into a form's OnPaint event handler:

```
with Canvas do
begin
  Pen.Color := clBlue;
  Brush.Color := clYellow;
  Brush.Style := bsDiagCross;
  Rectangle(10, 10, 100, 100);
end;
```

See the next chapter for information about displaying and printing text with the Canvas text output methods.

DRAWING WITH SHAPES

Rather than call Canvas methods to draw shapes at runtime, you can insert a Shape object into a form. The end results are visually the same, but the Shape component gives you the means to arrange graphics objects at design time by clicking and dragging, and by assigning property values. For example, insert a Shape object from the Additional palette into the form from the preceding section, or use a fresh form. Select a Shape property value such as stRoundRect, or insert this statement into the form's OnCreate or another event handler:

```
Shape1.Shape := stRoundRect;
```

To change a Shape's color and pattern at design time, use the Object Inspector to assign values to its Brush and Pen subproperties. The Brush affects the shape's interior. The Pen affects the shape's outline. Try different settings, or assign values at runtime with statements such as the following in the form's OnCreate or another event handler:

```
with Shape1 do
begin
  Shape := stRoundRect;
  Brush.Color := clLime;
  Brush.Style := bsCross;
  Pen.Color := clNavy;
  Pen.Width := 3;
end;
```

 Because many components have a Canvas property, if graphics do not appear as expected, the cause may be a *with* statement that refers to an object's Canvas when you meant to use the form's property. Either don't use *with*, or use statements such as MainForm.Canvas.

CANVAS PROPERTIES

The Canvas property provides eight subproperties for configuring graphics. You can assign values to these properties only at runtime, usually in a form's OnCreate or OnPaint event handler. Following are brief descriptions of each property:

- *Brush* — Provides the fill color and pattern for circle, rectangle, and polygon interiors, and also the background color for text. Has no effect on lines and text foreground color. Assign values to the Brush's Color and Style subproperties.

- *ClipRect* — Clips graphics to within this rectangle's boundaries. Usually equal in size to the window's client area. You can assign new values to its Left, Top, Right, and Bottom Integer subvalues to clip graphical output to another region. (Hint: See the PaintBox component for an easier method.)

- *CopyMode* — Determines how to combine bits when calling a Canvas's CopyRect method, which you can use to copy one object's Canvas into another. For example, set CopyMode to cmNotSource-Copy to invert pixels before copying them to another Canvas.

- *Font* — Assign subproperties to select font styles for text that you will draw by calling the Canvas's TextOut and TextRect methods. This Font object is not related to the form's Font property — initialize Canvas.Font properties before drawing text.

- *Handle* — For calling GDI methods that require a handle to a device context, pass Canvas.Handle to an HDC parameter. This makes it possible to call GDI functions that Canvas does not encapsulate.

- *Pen* — Affects lines and outlines. Assign values to the Pen's Color, Style, Mode, and Width subproperties.

- *PenPos* — Gives the internal pen's location (PenPos.X, PenPos.Y) that determines where the next graphical output will appear. Although Delphi permits assigning new values to PenPos, you should instead call the Canvas's MoveTo method to change the pen's internal location.

- *Pixels* — Provides a two-dimensional array to the Canvas's individual pixels. Each element of the array is a TColor value. For example, the expression Pixels[0,0] (use square brackets) returns the color of the pixel at coordinate (0,0). If you really like to do graphics the hard way, you may also color individual pixels by assigning new color values to this array.

 The Pixels property is a *pseudo* array; it is not a bitmap. The TCanvas class translates references and assignments to Pixels[X,Y] into GDI Get-Pixel and SetPixel function calls. For this reason, using Pixels is one of the most inefficient methods available for creating graphics. Use Pixels only when you absolutely must have access to individual pixel colors.

CANVAS METHODS AND EVENTS

The Canvas property provides numerous methods that can help tame the madness every programmer experiences sooner or later with the Windows GDI. There are several shape-producing methods, such as Arc, Ellipse, FloodFill, Polygon, Rectangle, and RoundRect, that correspond directly with GDI functions of the same names. After you become familiar with the general technique for calling Canvas methods, you'll find them easy to use. For example, to draw an ellipse, insert statements such as these into an OnPaint event handler:

```
Canvas.Pen.Color := clMaroon;
Canvas.Brush.Color := clYellow;
Canvas.Ellipse(10, 20, 100, 100);
```

 Assign values to Canvas properties before each use of the Canvas in an OnPaint event handler. For example, to draw a blue line, assign clBlue to the Canvas's Pen.Color subproperty, and then call the MoveTo and LineTo methods. You cannot preconfigure Canvas properties in a form's OnCreate event handler because OnPaint receives a device context from Windows, and this context is provided to your program via Canvas. Thus the Canvas in OnPaint will not contain any property values you assign outside of the event handler.

The less obvious methods you can call for a Canvas property include the following:

- *CopyRect* — Copies all or a portion of one Canvas to another. Set the CopyMode property to determine how pixels are combined in the final result. Look up CopyMode in Delphi's online help for settings you can use.

- *Draw* — Draws an object of the TGraphic class, which is the immediate ancestor of the TIcon, TBitmap, and TMetafile classes. You may pass any icon, bitmap, or metafile object to Draw.

- *DrawFocusRect* — Draws a rectangle using exclusive-OR logic. Call a second time with identical arguments to erase the rectangle. Use this method to draw drag-and-drop outlines.

- *FrameRect* — Draws an unfilled rectangle using the current Pen, but ignoring the Canvas's brush. Use FrameRect rather than Rectangle when you want a plain outline without having to set Brush properties.

- *StretchDraw* — Same as Draw, but stretches or shrinks an icon, bitmap, or metafile to fit within a defined rectangle.

The Canvas property also recognizes two events that might be useful in special circumstances. In most applications, you won't need to provide handlers for them — just be aware of them in case you need their special services. The two events are:

- *OnChange* — Called after a Canvas property value has been changed.

- *OnChanging* — Called immediately before a Canvas property will change.

Because the Canvas property is not available at design time, you can't use the Object Inspector to create handlers for these two events. To use them, declare procedures in the form's class:

```
TForm1 = class(TForm)
  procedure MyOnChange(Sender: TObject);
  procedure MyOnChanging(Sender: TObject);
...
end;
```

Assign the procedure names to OnChange and OnChanging in the form's OnCreate event handler:

```
Canvas.OnChange := MyOnChange;
Canvas.OnChanging := MyOnChanging;
```

Implement the procedures to perform whatever actions you need. For example, write an OnChange event handler as follows (OnChanging is similar in design):

```
procedure TForm1.MyOnChange(Sender: TObject);
begin
  SavedPenColor := Canvas.Pen.Color;
end;
```

 Delphi's smart project manager will delete the preceding declarations if the event handlers contain no statements or comments. *When creating multiple event handlers, don't compile the program until after inserting at least one statement or comment into each handler's procedure.*

Drawing and Painting

Windows applications *draw* individual shapes such as lines and filled rectangles. They *paint* graphical objects to maintain the illusion of over-lapping windows on a desktop. A program may have to draw a shape only once, but it must always be ready to paint that shape if, for example, the user hides and then uncovers the application window.

A simple test demonstrates the difference between drawing and painting. Insert a Button object into a form. Create an OnClick event handler for the Button with the programming from Listing 13-1. Run the program and click the button to outline the button with a rounded red rectangle. Hide and uncover the window, and the rectangle disappears.

Quit the test program and return to Delphi. Insert an OnPaint event handler for the form, and copy the statements and *var* declaration into that procedure. Delete the OnClick event handler. Now when you run the program, it outlines the Button from the start, and the outline does not disappear when you hide and uncover the window.

Listing 13-1

Use this OnClick event handler to demonstrate drawing and painting.

```
procedure TForm1.Button1Click(Sender: TObject);
var
  X1, Y1, X2, Y2: Integer;
begin
  Canvas.Pen.Color := clRed;
  Canvas.Pen.Width := 2;
  with Button1 do
  begin
    X1 := Left - 3; Y1 := Top - 3;
    X2 := Left + Width + 4; Y2 := Top + Height + 4;
    Canvas.RoundRect(X1, Y1, X2, Y2, 4, 4);
  end;
end;
```

It's usually easiest to delete a handler by removing its declarations and statements, leaving a bare *begin* and *end* block. Don't delete the entire procedure. For example, to remove the Button's OnClick event handler, reduce the procedure in Listing 13-1 to:

```
procedure TForm1.Button1Click(Sender: TObject);
begin
end;
```

When you next save the source code file, Delphi's smart project manager deletes the procedure declaration and body along with any references to that procedure in object events.

In most cases, you can simply insert drawing statements into a form or a PaintBox OnPaint event handler. If you draw objects in other procedures, however, you must also provide code to recreate those objects in an OnPaint event. If you don't do that, your graphics will vanish like smoke in the breeze when users cover and uncover the application's window.

Call the form's Invalidate method to inform Windows that the form (or control) needs to be repainted. Call the form's Update method to repaint immediately. For example, suppose your program has an OnPaint event handler that draws some graphics based on global variables. If those variables change, don't draw the new shape — instead, insert these statements to repaint the graphics by forcing an OnPaint event to occur:

```
MainForm.Invalidate;
MainForm.Update;    { optional }
```

Never do that inside an OnPaint event handler. The purpose of these statements is to cause an OnPaint event to occur — executing them inside OnPaint will cause the program to endlessly repaint itself. Invalidate tells Windows that the object needs painting. Windows will issue a wm_Paint message to the object when no other messages are pending. Update, which is optional, tells Windows to issue the wm_Paint message immediately.

THE PAINTBOX COMPONENT

Insert a PaintBox object into a form or another container such as a Panel to give it graphics capabilities. All coordinates are relative to the container. For example, insert a Panel into a form, and stretch it a bit to make room for the PaintBox object. Select the PaintBox component from the System palette, and click the mouse pointer inside the Panel. To reposition the combined object, simply drag the Panel — you don't have to also select the PaintBox.

You have just given a Panel new graphics capabilities. You might use this technique to draw shapes, bitmaps, and other graphics in a tool-bar or a status line. For example, to draw a navy blue box inside the Panel, insert the following statements into PaintBox1's OnPaint event handler. (Be sure to create a handler for the PaintBox object, *not* for the form.) Here's the entire procedure for reference:

```
procedure TForm1.PaintBox1Paint(Sender: TObject);
begin
  with PaintBox1.Canvas do
  begin
    Pen.Color := clNavy;
    Rectangle(0, 0, 100, 100);
  end;
end;
```

You can also use a PaintBox object to restrict drawing to a specific rectangle in a form or other container. To compartmentalize a form or container into multiple sections, you may insert as many PaintBoxes as you need.

USING PENS AND BRUSHES

Every Canvas has Pen and Brush properties. The Pen specifies the color and style of lines, and also the outlines for shapes such as ellipses and rectangles. The Brush specifies shape interior colors and patterns. Pens have four significant properties:

- *Color* — Affects line and outline, but not shape interior colors. Assign to Pen.Color any TColor value or constant such as clRed or clLime. To match desktop colors, assign a constant such as clWindow or clWindowText.

- *Mode* — Determines the logical method for drawing lines and outlines. Assign to Pen.Mode a constant such as pmBlack (always black) or pmNotCopy (inverse of Pen color). Use pmXor so you can redraw a line to erase it and restore its former background.

- *Style* — Selects a solid, dashed, or dotted line style. For example, assign to Pen.Style a constant such as psSolid or psDashDot. In 16-bit Windows, lines with widths greater than 1 pixel are always solid. Windows 95 allows you to set the style of thick and thin lines.

- *Width* — Specifies the width in pixels of lines and outlines. In 16-bit Windows, this property must equal 1 (the default) to use a Pen Style other than psSolid.

TIP

For a complete list of Color, Mode, and Style constants, view those properties for the TPen class in Delphi's on-line help. Or, if you have Delphi's runtime library source code, browse the Graphics.Pas file.

Brushes have three significant properties:

- *Bitmap* — Assign a TBitmap object with a dimension up to 8-by-8 pixels. The brush will replicate the Bitmap (like wallpaper) to fill interior shapes.

- *Color* — Same as Pen.

- *Style* — Specifies a pattern to use for painting interior shapes. For example, assign to Brush.Style a constant such as bsCross or bsFDiagonal. Use bsSolid when assigning a Bitmap. To draw an outline shape with the background showing through, set Style to bsClear. For a complete list of Style constants, look up the Style property for the TBrush class in Delphi's on-line help.

NOTE Pens and Brushes have methods such as Create and Free that are common to many components. Pens and Brushes also have an OnChange event handler that you can use to notify the program of any changes to Pen and Brush properties, although using this event is rarely necessary.

The PolyFlow application on the CD-ROM is one of my oldest Pascal standard test programs. PolyFlow is a good example of drawing versus painting; it also shows how to use a Timer object to create graphics animations. Figure 13-1 shows PolyFlow's display. Listing 13-2 lists the program's source code.

Figure 13-1
Polyflow, an old standard with a new Delphi interface, demonstrates drawing versus painting, and it shows how to use a Timer object to create graphics animations.

Listing 13-2
PolyFlow\Main.Pas

```
unit Main;

interface

uses
  SysUtils, WinTypes, WinProcs, Messages, Classes, Graphics, Controls,
  Forms, Dialogs, Menus, ExtCtrls;
```

```
const
  maxIndex = 100;      { Maximum number of lines visible }
  dx1: Integer = 4;    { "Delta" values for controlling }
  dy1: Integer = 10;   {   the animation's personality.  }
  dx2: Integer = 3;
  dy2: Integer = 9;

type
  LineRec = record        { Line ends and color }
    X1, Y1, X2, Y2 : Integer;
    Color: TColor;
  end;

type
  TMainForm = class(TForm)
    MainMenu1: TMainMenu;
    Demo1: TMenuItem;
    Exit1: TMenuItem;
    Timer1: TTimer;
    procedure Exit1Click(Sender: TObject);
    procedure FormCreate(Sender: TObject);
    procedure Timer1Timer(Sender: TObject);
    procedure FormPaint(Sender: TObject);
    procedure FormResize(Sender: TObject);
  protected
    procedure CreateParams(var Params: TCreateParams); override;
  private
    LineArray: array[0 .. maxIndex - 1] of LineRec;
    Index: Integer;      { Index for LineArray }
    Erasing: Boolean;    { True if erasing old lines }
    function Sign(N: Integer): Integer;
    procedure InitLineArray;
    procedure MakeNewLine(R: TRect; Index: Integer);
    procedure DrawLine(Index: Integer);
  public
    { Public declarations }
  end;

var
  MainForm: TMainForm;

implementation

{$R *.DFM}

procedure TMainForm.CreateParams(var Params: TCreateParams);
begin
  inherited CreateParams(params);
  with Params.WindowClass do
  {- Repaint the window automatically when resized }
    Style := Style or cs_HRedraw or cs_VRedraw;
end;
```

Use override to replace an inherited virtual method.

Call the inherited method.

Add new statements in the replacement method.

```
{- Return -1 if n < 0 or +1 if n >= 0 }
function TMainForm.Sign(N: Integer): Integer;
begin
  if N < 0 then Sign :=  -1 else Sign := 1;
end;

{- Erase LineArray and set X1 to -1 as "no line" flag }
procedure TMainForm.InitLineArray;
var
  I: Integer;
begin
  Index := 0;
  Erasing := False;
  FillChar(LineArray, SizeOf(LineArray), 0);
  for I := 0 to maxIndex - 1 do
    LineArray[I].X1 := - 1;
end;

{- Create new line, direction, and color }
procedure TMainForm.MakeNewLine(R: TRect; Index: Integer);
  procedure NewCoord(var C, Change: Integer; Max: Integer;
    var Color: TColor);
  var
    Temp: Integer;
  begin
    Temp := C + Change;
    if (Temp < 0) or (Temp > Max) then
    begin
      Change := Sign(-Change) * (3 + Random(12));
      repeat
        Color := RGB(Random(256), Random(256), Random(256));
        Color := GetNearestColor(Canvas.Handle, Color)
      until Color <> GetBkColor(Canvas.Handle);
    end else
      C := Temp;
  end;
begin
  with LineArray[Index] do
  begin
    NewCoord(X1, dx1, R.Right, Color);
    NewCoord(Y1, dy1, R.Bottom, Color);
    NewCoord(X2, dx2, R.Right, Color);
    NewCoord(Y2, dy2, R.Bottom, Color)
  end
end;

{- Draw or erase a line identified by Index }
procedure TMainForm.DrawLine(Index: Integer);
begin
  with Canvas, LineArray[Index] do
  begin
    Pen.Color := Color;
    MoveTo(X1, Y1);
    LineTo(X2, Y2);
  end;
end;
```

```
{- Draw some lines at each timer interval }
procedure TMainForm.Timer1Timer(Sender: TObject);
var
  R: TRect;
  I, OldIndex: Integer;
begin
  R := GetClientRect;
  for I := 1 to 10 do   { 10 = number of lines }
  begin
    OldIndex := Index;
    Inc(Index);
    if Index = maxIndex - 1 then
    begin
      Index := 0;       { Wrap Index around to start }
      Erasing := True;  { True until window size changes }
    end;
    if Erasing then
      DrawLine(Index);  { Erase old line }
    LineArray[Index] := LineArray[OldIndex];
    MakeNewLine(R, Index);
    DrawLine(Index);    { Draw new line }
  end;
end;
```

Drawing multiple lines in the Timer event makes the program fast at a low timer interval.

```
{- Paint or repaint screen using data in LineArray }
procedure TMainForm.FormPaint(Sender: TObject);
var
  I: Integer;
begin
  with Canvas do
    for I := 0 to maxIndex - 1 do
      if LineArray[I].X1 >= 0 then { Draw non-flagged lines }
        DrawLine(I);
end;
```

This procedure paints the window's invalid region using saved line coordinates and colors.

```
{- Start new lines when window size changes }
procedure TMainForm.FormResize(Sender: TObject);
begin
  InitLineArray;    { Erase LineArray and reset globals }
end;
```

Most graphics programs require reinitializing when the window's size changes.

```
{- Initialize globals and LineArray }
procedure TMainForm.FormCreate(Sender: TObject);
begin
  with Canvas.Pen do
  begin
    Style := psSolid;
    Width := 1;
    Mode := pmXor;
  end;
  Randomize;
  InitLineArray;
end;
```

Use pmXor drawing mode so redrawing a line erases it.

```
{- End program }
procedure TMainForm.Exit1Click(Sender: TObject);
begin
  Close;
end;

end.
```

PolyFlow's OnTimer event handler (see procedure Timer1Timer) draws 10 lines of the animation. It could draw only one line, but this would slow the effect unacceptably. The form's OnPaint event handler redraws the entire window so that, when you hide it and then uncover it, the program restores the animation's current state. This is a typical Windows graphics technique — parts of the program draw shapes and store their parameters (see LineArray in the listing). To maintain the window, an OnPaint event handler uses those parameters to repaint the program's graphics.

Try running PolyFlow, and cover a portion of its window. Notice that the Timer events continue running. In addition to creating animations, you can use this same technique to program other background processes, but be careful not to lock up the system by executing lengthy operations in a Timer event.

Graphics Programming Techniques

All Delphi applications use the Graphics unit, which provides classes such as TPen, TBrush, TFont, TCanvas, and related declarations. This section covers some other classes and advanced graphics techniques such as bitmaps, graphics files, and how to create drag-and-drop objects.

GRAPHICS CLASS RELATIONSHIPS

When you first begin to design your graphical program, you may be unsure whether to use the Image or Shape components or an object of the TPicture class. To decide on the best course for your program, first understand the relationships among the following classes:

- *TCanvas* — As mentioned, this class provides a painting surface on which you can draw and paint graphics by calling methods and assigning property values. You never create a stand-alone TCanvas object — you will always use this class as the Canvas property of another object such as a PaintBox or a form.

- *TGraphic* — This class is the immediate ancestor for the TBitmap, TIcon, and TMetafile classes. You never create a stand-alone TGraphic object. Instead, you use this class as a parameter data type or as a component property. You may assign a bitmap, icon, or metafile object to any TGraphic parameter, variable, or property.

- *TPicture* — This class creates a container that holds a TGraphic object, which can be a bitmap, an icon, or a metafile. TPicture's file-handling methods determine an image's type from its filename extension, which simplifies graphics file handling. You'll find the TPicture class used as the Picture property in other objects such as the Image component, and as a parameter data type. You can also create a stand-alone TPicture object — for example, to provide a container for a bitmap loaded from a disk file.

- *TGraphicsObject* — This class is the immediate ancestor for the TFont, TPen, and TBrush classes. Use TGraphicsObject as a procedure or function parameter data type so you can pass fonts, pens, or brushes as arguments to subroutines. You never create a stand-alone object of the TGraphicsObject class.

- *TGraphicControl* — This component class is the ancestor for the graphical component classes TSpeedButton, TTabButton (used by the TabbedNotebook component), TShape, TPaintBox, TImage, TBevel, and TCustomLabel (the immediate ancestor to TLabel). The TGraphicControl class provides a Canvas, which, for example, a SpeedButton uses to display its glyph bitmap. You will probably not need TGraphicControl in application development. It is valuable mostly for writing visual components that do not have associated window handles, and therefore take less memory than components that serve as interfaces for standard Windows elements such as buttons and check boxes. The Controls unit (not Graphics) declares TGraphicControl.

DRAWING WITH COMPONENTS

To draw graphics, you may call Canvas methods and you may insert one of the following two components into a form or another container:

- *Image* — This component contains a Picture (TPicture class) object, which contains a Graphic property (TGraphic class). Because the TGraphic class is the ancestor to TBitmap, TIcon, and TMetafile, an Image component object can hold and display a bitmap, icon, or metafile referenced as Image.Picture.Graphic.

- *Shape* — This component draws an image by calling Canvas methods. Use a Shape to draw and paint lines, rectangles, circles, and other objects.

The important difference between these two components is that an Image object *contains* a graphical image; a Shape object *draws and paints* a figure using an inherited Canvas. Use Image and Shape components to create graphics at design time. Use Canvas to draw and paint at runtime.

To store graphical objects in memory, create an object of the TPicture class. You can also construct individual TBitmap, TIcon, and TMetafile objects, but it is often best to create a TPicture object that contains a bitmap, icon, or metafile image. For example, try the Button OnClick event handler in Listing 13-3, which loads and displays a bitmap file entirely at runtime without using graphics components.

Listing 13-3

Try this Button OnClick event handler to load and display a bitmap file entirely under program control.

```
procedure TForm1.BitBtn1Click(Sender: TObject);
var
  P: TPicture;                                        Create the object.
begin
  P := TPicture.Create;
  try
    P.LoadFromFile('C:\Windows\Winlogo.Bmp');         Use the object
    Canvas.Draw(0, 0, P.Graphic);                     in a try block.
  finally
    P.Free;
  end;
end;                       Free the object in a finally block.
```

Listing 13-3 demonstrates some key graphics techniques. Variable P is a TPicture object, constructed by calling TPicture.Create as the procedure's first statement. To ensure proper disposal of the resulting object, all statements that use P are inside a *try* block, and a *finally* block calls P.Free.

Inside the *try* block, TPicture's LoadFromFile method reads a bitmap file (change the filename if you want). To display the image, the program calls the Canvas's Draw method, which Delphi defines as follows:

```
procedure Draw(X, Y: Integer; Graphic: Tgraphic);
```

- *X, Y* — Client-area coordinates relative to the object that provides the Canvas. Set these values to zero to display the image in the Canvas's upper left corner.

- *Graphic* — Pass a TBitmap, TIcon, or TMetaFile object to this parameter. Or, as the listing demonstrates, when using a TPicture object, pass its Graphic property.

Alternatively, you can insert an Image component into a form and use its Picture property to load and display a bitmap. The following programming performs the identical tasks as in Listing 13-3:

```
with Image1 do
  Picture.LoadFromFile('C:\Windows\Winlogo.Bmp');
```

The difference between the techniques is purely a design choice. If it is more convenient to use a component, the preceding code is the simplest approach, and it doesn't require you to construct and free objects or call a Canvas's Draw method. If you need to construct and use objects at runtime, use the technique in Listing 13-3. However, TPicture does not use a window handle; TImage does. This makes TPicture the more memory-efficient choice.

METAFILE, BITMAP, AND ICON FILES

Using the preceding information, you can construct an image file viewer that can display a metafile (.Wmf), icon (.Ico), or bitmap (.Bmp) file, and copy any of those files to another directory. Figure 13-2 shows MetaMore's display opened to a Windows metafile supplied with Microsoft Office. The program, which is shown in Listing 13-4, can also read, display, and copy bitmap and icon files.

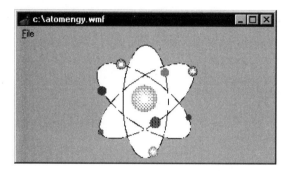

Figure 13-2

MetaMore can display any metafile, bitmap, or icon file.

Listing 13-4

MetaMore\Main.Pas

```
unit Main;

interface

uses
    SysUtils, WinTypes, WinProcs, Messages, Classes, Graphics, Controls,
    Forms, Dialogs, Menus, ExtCtrls;

type
    TMainForm = class(TForm)
        Image1: TImage;
        MainMenu1: TMainMenu;
        FileMenu: TMenuItem;
        FileOpen: TMenuItem;
        N1: TMenuItem;
        FileExit: TMenuItem;
        OpenDialog1: TOpenDialog;
        SaveDialog1: TSaveDialog;
        FileSaveAs: TMenuItem;
        procedure FileOpenClick(Sender: TObject);
        procedure FileSaveAsClick(Sender: TObject);
        procedure FileExitClick(Sender: TObject);
```

```
    private
      { Private declarations }
    public
      { Public declarations }
    end;

var
  MainForm: TMainForm;

implementation

{$R *.DFM}

procedure TMainForm.FileOpenClick(Sender: TObject);
begin
  with OpenDialog1 do
  begin
    if Execute then
      Image1.Picture.LoadFromFile(Filename);
    Caption := Lowercase(Filename);
  end;
end;

procedure TMainForm.FileSaveAsClick(Sender: TObject);
begin
  with SaveDialog1 do
  begin
    Filename := Caption;
    if Execute then
      Image1.Picture.SaveToFile(Filename);
    Caption := Lowercase(Filename);
  end;
end;

procedure TMainForm.FileExitClick(Sender: TObject);
begin
  Close;
end;

end.
```

Loads a metafile, icon, or bitmap file based on the filename extension.

NOTE MetaMore cannot translate file types. For example, if you load a bitmap, you must save it as a bitmap.

MetaMore uses an Image component object, which is often the simplest approach. Alternatively, you could construct a Picture object as Listing 13-3 demonstrates. Or, you can create an object for a specific type of image file. For example, Listing 13-5 shows a Button OnClick event handler that creates a TMetaFile object and loads and displays a Windows metafile.

Listing 13-5

Try this Button OnClick event handler to construct a TMetaFile object and load and display a Windows metafile.

```
procedure TForm1.Button1Click(Sender: TObject);
var
  MetaFile: TMetaFile;                              Use a MetaFile object if you
begin                                               don't want to insert an Image
  MetaFile := TMetaFile.Create;                     component into the form.
  try
    MetaFile.LoadFromFile('C:\msoffice\clipart\anchor.wmf');
    Canvas.Draw(0, 0, MetaFile);
  finally
    MetaFile.Free;                                  Always free the
  end;                                              object you create.
end;
```

As with the TPicture class, this technique takes more programming than using an Image component, but uses less memory and fewer Windows resources. First, create the TMetaFile object by calling the class's Create method. Use the resulting object in a *try* block, and free it in *finally*. This ensures proper disposal in case an exception occurs.

To load a metafile, call the MetaFile object's LoadFromFile method (change the filename if necessary). Call the Canvas's Draw method to display the MetaFile. You can pass MetaFile to Draw because the TMetaFile class is a TGraphic descendent.

You can use the same programming in Listing 13-5 to load and display bitmap and icon files. Simply replace TMetaFile with TBitmap or TIcon, and load a file of the appropriate type. Use TPicture (see Listing 13-3) to load metafile, icon, and bitmap files based on the filename extension.

Instead of Draw, call StretchDraw to resize an image to fit within a defined rectangle. For example, to fill the window's client area with the MetaFile image, replace the Canvas.Draw statement in Listing 13-5 with this line:

```
Canvas.StretchDraw(ClientRect, MetaFile);
```

Delphi defines StretchDraw as:

```
procedure StretchDraw(const Rect: TRect; Graphic: Tgraphic);
```

- *Rect* — Defines a rectangular area for displaying an image. Assign values to this record's Left, Top, Right, and Bottom integers; or if more convenient, you can assign TPoint records to Rect's TopLeft and BottomRight members.

- *Graphic* — Any TBitmap, TIcon, or TMetaFile object. StretchDraw resizes the image to fit within Rect's defined area.

BITMAP RESOURCES

Unlike in conventional Windows programming, you won't use many resource objects in Delphi applications. One exception to this rule is a bitmap that you want to include with your application. You could distribute a separate bitmap file and use a TPicture or TBitmap object to load and display it. Or, you can create the bitmap as a resource (.Res) using Delphi's Image Editor on the *Tools* menu.

After creating the resource file with a bitmap (let's assume you named it YOURBITS), bind the resource into the compiled .Exe code file by inserting this directive in the module's implementation:

```
{$R Yourbits.Res}
```

Use the programming in Listing 13-6 to create a bitmap object, and call the Windows API function LoadBitmap to obtain a handle to the bitmap resource. Assign LoadBitmap's return value to a TBitmap object's Handle property. The string YOURBITS is the resource name that you assigned in the Image Editor. (The Yourbits.Res file could be named something else — it doesn't have to be the same as the name of the resource it contains.) Call the Draw or StretchDraw (commented out) methods as shown in the sample listing.

OFFSCREEN BITMAPS

The TBitmap class provides a Canvas property that you can use to draw offscreen. Simply construct a TBitmap object, and call methods in its Canvas property to draw on a virtual canvas that remains hidden from view. You can then display the resulting graphics all at once by calling methods such as Draw, StretchDraw, CopyRect, and BrushCopy for a form or Paint-Box's Canvas. This technique is important in animations, as well as for hiding the details of a complex image's formation until the figure is complete.

Listing 13-6

This Button OnClick event handler demonstrates how to load and display a bitmap resource bound into the program's compiled .Exe code file by Delphi's Image Editor.

```
procedure TForm1.BitBtn1Click(Sender: TObject);
var
  YourBits: TBitmap;
begin
  YourBits := TBitmap.Create;
  try
    YourBits.Handle := LoadBitmap(HInstance, 'YOURBITS');
    Canvas.Draw(0, 0, YourBits);
(*    Canvas.StretchDraw(ClientRect, YourBits); *)
  finally
    YourBits.Free;
  end;
end;
```

Delete these comment symbols and the preceding statement to view the difference between Draw ansd StretchDraw.

Listing 13-7 demonstrates the basic techniques required to draw in an offscreen bitmap. To try the code, use the listing as a Button's OnClick event handler. The program draws a rectangle and ellipse offscreen, and then displays the resulting image by calling CopyRect.

In Listing 13-7, the Source and Dest TRect records specify the size of the offscreen bitmap, as well as the location to which the image is copied onto the form. Create the bitmap object by calling TBitmap.Create. Assign Width and Height values to create a bitmap of the size you need.

To draw offscreen, call methods such as Rectangle and Ellipse, and assign values to Pen and Brush properties and subproperties. *Be sure to call methods and make assignments for the bitmap's Canvas.* When you are done creating your image, call a form or PaintBox Canvas method such as CopyRect to bring the offscreen image into view.

Calling TBitmap.Create creates a memory device context, which consumes Windows resources and time. In this example of a simple button click, the end result is quick enough, but in a fast loop or a performance-critical OnPaint event handler, for the best speed, create the bitmap object in the form's OnCreate handler and destroy it in OnDestroy.

Listing 13-7

This Button OnClick event handler demonstrates how to draw into an offscreen bitmap.

```
procedure TForm1.BitBtn1Click(Sender: TObject);
var
  OffScreen: TBitmap;
  Dest, Source: TRect;
begin
  Source := Rect(0, 0, 255, 255);
  Dest := Rect(10, 10, 265, 265);
  OffScreen := TBitmap.Create;
  try
    OffScreen.Width := Source.Right + 1;
    OffScreen.Height := Source.Bottom + 1;
    with OffScreen.Canvas do
    begin
      Pen.Color := clRed;
      Brush.Color := clAppWorkSpace;
      Rectangle(0, 0, 255, 255);
      Ellipse(63, 63, 127, 127);
    end;
    Canvas.CopyRect(Dest, OffScreen.Canvas, Source);
  finally
    OffScreen.Free;
  end;
end;
```

Be careful to use the bitmap's Canvas when drawing off-screen.

Call CopyRect to display the offscreen image.

When using *with* statements, be especially careful that you draw into the intended Canvas. To draw offscreen, call methods for a TBitmap object's Canvas. Copy the offscreen image by calling a method for a form or PaintBox's Canvas.

DRAG-AND-DROP OBJECTS

When you design a Delphi application, you click and drag component objects around in a form window. But how can you do the same for graphics shapes in your own applications? The answer requires a bit of programming which is not difficult to understand, but does require careful attention to detail, especially in mouse coordinate handling.

For an example of drag-and-drop graphics, try the DragMe application on the CD-ROM. As shown in Figure 13-3, the program displays three shapes: a yellow rounded rectangle, a red circle, and a blue square. Each figure is a Shape component object. Run the program and click and drag the objects around the application window. Listing 13-8 shows the steps needed to create this useful illusion, which you can put to work to make draggable any shape you can draw.

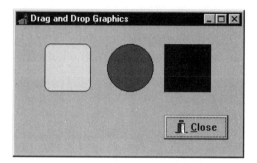

Figure 13-3
The DragMe application displays three Shape objects, which you can click and drag to move around the program's window.

DragMe declares five variables in the module's form class. Dragging is True during a drag-and-drop operation. XOffset and YOffset are the pixel coordinates of the mouse cursor relative to the Shape that is being dragged. These values make it possible to "pick up" the shape by clicking the mouse anywhere inside its borders. FocusRect is a TRect record with Left, Top, Right, and Bottom values that define the outline rectangle you see while clicking and dragging a shape. PS is a *pointer to a shape,* which the program uses to refer to the shape that is being dragged around.

Three event handlers implement dragging and dropping for any Shape object. When you click the mouse pointer inside a Shape, procedure ShapeMouseDown begins a drag-and-drop operation. First, the program sets the Dragging flag to True. It then saves the mouse X- and Y-coordinate values in XOffset and YOffset. This marks the mouse location relative to the shape's upper-left corner. The program also saves the Sender parameter, type-cast to a TShape object, in PS for future reference to the shape being dragged. Using PS, the program assigns values to FocusRect for drawing the dotted outline during dragging with this statement:

```
Canvas.DrawFocusRect(FocusRect);  { Draw outline }
```

Listing 13-8
DragMe\Main.Pas

```
unit Main;

interface

uses
  SysUtils, WinTypes, WinProcs, Messages, Classes, Graphics, Controls,
  Forms, Dialogs, ExtCtrls, StdCtrls, Buttons;

type
  TMainForm = class(TForm)
    Shape1: TShape;
    Shape2: TShape;
    Shape3: TShape;
    BitBtn1: TBitBtn;
    procedure ShapeMouseDown(Sender: TObject; Button: TMouseButton;
      Shift: TShiftState; X, Y: Integer);
    procedure ShapeMouseMove(Sender: TObject; Shift: TShiftState;
      X, Y: Integer);
    procedure ShapeMouseUp(Sender: TObject; Button: TMouseButton;
      Shift: TShiftState; X, Y: Integer);
    procedure FormCreate(Sender: TObject);
  private
    Dragging: Boolean;          { Drag operation in progress flag }
    XOffset, YOffset: Integer;  { Offsets from shape upper left }
    FocusRect: TRect;           { Dotted outline while dragging }
    PS: TShape;                 { Reference to shape dragging }
  public
    { Public declarations }
  end;

var
  MainForm: TMainForm;

implementation

{$R *.DFM}

procedure TMainForm.ShapeMouseDown(Sender: TObject;
  Button: TMouseButton; Shift: TShiftState; X, Y: Integer);
begin
  Dragging := True;            { Set dragging flag true }
  XOffset := X;                { Keep offsets from shape upper left }
  YOffset := Y;
  PS := Sender as TShape;      { Assign reference to shape }
  with PS do                   { Create outline rectangle }
    FocusRect := Rect(Left, Top, Left + Width, Top + Height);
  Canvas.DrawFocusRect(FocusRect);  { Draw outline }
end;
```

Set Dragging True in the MouseDown event so the MouseMore event can detect that a dragging operation is in effect.

```
procedure TMainForm.ShapeMouseMove(Sender: TObject;
  Shift: TShiftState; X, Y: Integer);
begin
  if Dragging then  { Move outline only if dragging }
  begin
    Canvas.DrawFocusRect(FocusRect);  { Erase outline }
    with FocusRect do
    begin  { Move outline rectangle }
      Left := (PS.Left + X) - XOffset;
      Top := (PS.Top + Y) - YOffset;
      Right := PS.Width + Left;
      Bottom := PS.Height + Top;
    end;
    Canvas.DrawFocusRect(FocusRect);
  end;
end;
```

Erase the all shape outline.

Draw the new outline at the mouse location.

```
procedure TMainForm.ShapeMouseUp(Sender: TObject;
  Button: TMouseButton; Shift: TShiftState; X, Y: Integer);
begin
  if Dragging then  { Move shape only if dragging }
  begin
    Canvas.DrawFocusRect(FocusRect);
    Dragging := False;
    with Sender as TShape do
    begin  { Move shape to new location }
      Left := (Left + X) - XOffset;
      Top := (Top + Y) - YOffset;
    end;
  end;
end;
```

Erase the final outline when user releases the mouse button.

Reset the flag to cancel the dragging operation.

```
procedure TMainForm.FormCreate(Sender: TObject);
begin
  Dragging := False;
end;

end.
```

DragFocusRect draws a dotted rectangular outline using exclusive-OR logic. Calling DragFocusRect twice for the same TRect record erases the outline. When you move the mouse, if Dragging is True, the OnMouse-Move event handler, ShapeMouseMove, calls DragFocusRect to erase the rectangle in its old position. The procedure then assigns new values to FocusRect's Left, Top, Right, and Bottom members. When reading this code, keep in mind that the X and Y mouse coordinate parameters are relative to the shape being dragged, not to the window or the screen. Thus, the new FocusRect position equals the shape's location (which hasn't changed) plus X and Y, minus the offsets from the shape's upper left to the location where you clicked the mouse. Calling DrawFocusRect with these new values moves the outline as you drag the mouse.

When you release the mouse button, the third and final event handler, ShapeMouseUp, moves the shape to its new location. (Checking whether Dragging is true in this case is probably unnecessary because an OnMouseUp event can't occur without a prior OnMouseDown event, but it's always best to be careful.) Once again, the program calls DrawFocus-Rect, this time to erase the final outline. After setting the Dragging flag to False, it's a simple matter to move the shape by assigning new values to its Left and Top properties, completing the illusion of the shape hopping to the last-known position of the focus rectangle.

Remember that objects can share event handlers. For example, to add a new draggable shape to DragMe, simply insert a Shape object and set its OnMouseDown, OnMouseMove, and OnMouseUp events to the module's existing event handlers.

Summary

- Various components provide a Canvas property that you can use to paint graphics. Canvas is an object of the TCanvas class, which encapsulates the Windows graphics device interface (GDI) and the concept of a handle to a device context.

- To configure graphical output, assign values to the Canvas Pen and Brush properties. To draw shapes, call methods in Canvas such as Rectangle and Ellipse.

- Applications draw individual shapes such as lines and rectangles. They paint graphical objects in response to an OnPaint event in order to maintain the illusion of overlapping windows on a desktop. This chapter's PolyFlow application demonstrates the differences between drawing and painting.

- Use the PaintBox component to provide a Canvas and add graphics capabilities to objects such as the Panel component. You can also use one or more PaintBox objects to restrict graphical output to a defined rectangular region in a form.

- TGraphic is the ancestor class for TBitmap, TIcon, and TMetafile. The TPicture class contains a TGraphic object. Your program may create TPicture objects to store graphical images in memory. Or, you can insert an Image component into a form, and use its Picture property for this same purpose.

- The TPicture class's file-handling methods, LoadFromFile and SaveToFile, determine the type of graphics image from the filename extension. A TPicture object can therefore read and write metafile, bitmap, and icon image files.

- Call the Canvas Draw or StretchDraw methods to draw any TGraphic object (a metafile, bitmap, or icon). Use Draw to draw graphics in their defined sizes. Use StretchDraw to resize images to fit within a defined rectangle.

- The TBitmap class provides a Canvas property that you can use to draw complex images offscreen. Call a form or PaintBox's CopyRect or BrushCopy methods to draw the finished offscreen image.

- Create drag-and-drop Shape objects by implementing OnMouse-Down, OnMouseMove, and OnMouseUp event handlers, as this chapter's DragMe application demonstrates.

Projects to Try

13-1: Try inserting Image, Shape, and PaintBox objects into a Panel to create a graphical toolbar. You might use these objects along with the usual SpeedButtons and sub-Panels to dress up an application's toolbars and status lines.

13-2: Write an application that displays Delphi's Calendar.Bmp file located in the directory C:\Delphi\Images\Backgrnd. Add drag-and-drop icons that users can move into a day square — for example, to indicate a birthday or an appointment.

13-3: Write a utility program that displays all icon files in the C:\Delphi\Images\Icons directory.

13-4: Write a program that displays a bitmap file upside down. (Hint: Use an offscreen bitmap.)

13-5: *Advanced*. Develop animation procedures that display bitmaps stored in a TStringList's Objects array. (Hint: See Chapter 8's description of owner-draw controls and the Glyphlst project on the CD-ROM.)

Expert-User Tips

- If your graphical output doesn't appear as expected, make sure you have assigned a color value to the Canvas's Pen.Color property. If your image still doesn't appear, be sure you are drawing to the correct Canvas. Beware of *with* statements, which might cause statements to refer to the Canvas property in an object such as a bitmap instead of the intended form or PaintBox.

- Because of changes in the Windows 95 desktop, drawing on an icon — for example, to animate a minimized application — is no longer recommended. However, you can do this for Windows 3.1 applications by assigning a TIcon object to the Application.Icon property. The TIcon class is derived from TGraphic — use TIcon in the same way you use a TBitmap object.

- To delete an image such as a large bitmap associated with an Image component object, pass *nil* to the Picture property's Assign method. For example, the following statement clears any image data for Image1, which you might do to conserve memory:

```
Image1.Picture.Assign(nil);
```

- Calling a form's Update method after Invalidate is optional. However, you should always call Invalidate before calling Update. Calling Update alone does nothing. Calling Invalidate (and optionally Update) also generates an OnPaint event for any PaintBox objects in a form.

- Don't call Update too frequently, or you might cause your program to become sluggish. Windows consolidates multiple calls to Invalidate, and will issue a single wm_Paint message when all's quiet on the message front. Usually, this results in cleaner displays with as little flicker as possible. Use Update strictly to force an immediate screen update — prior to a lengthy calculation, for example, that might overly delay the next OnPaint event.

- Assignments to a TBitmap object's Height and Width properties cause the bitmap to be copied in memory. You may change a TBitmap object's dimensions at any time, but if you make an image smaller, any pixels outside of the new dimensions are permanently lost.

Coming Up

In a graphical user interface, printing and displaying graphics are intimately related subjects. The next chapter covers Delphi's text output and printing capabilities.

14 Developing Printer Applications

*F*or printing text and graphics, many development systems require you to use archaic Windows "escape" commands that can make writing even simple printing modules as pleasant as a toothache. Fortunately, Delphi's printer-related components, procedures, and functions take the hard out of hard copy. It's about time somebody made printer application development this painless.

In this chapter, I'll explain how to display printer setup dialogs, and how to use Delphi's Printers unit to print text and graphics. I'll also suggest a technique for creating a print-preview command — a feature that all printer applications should provide so users can inspect output on screen rather than waste a small forest in discarded test pages.

Components

- PrintDialog — Use this component to prompt users at the start of a print job. The component encapsulates a standard Windows dialog that prompts users for pages to print, and provides access to printer setup options. Palette: Dialogs.

- PrinterSetupDialog — Use this component to display one or more setup dialogs provided by installed printer drivers. You should always include this dialog in printer applications to give users a method for configuring printers, or for selecting among multiple printer devices and output ports. Palette: Dialogs.

- TPrinter — This component is not on the VCL palette, but is defined as a class in the Printers unit. Among its other members, the TPrinter class provides a Canvas property that gives you a WYSIWYG drawing surface for printing text and graphics. Palette: none.

Plain-Text Printing

There are two ways to print text in Delphi applications. In this section, I'll explain the simplest method — using Pascal's Write and Writeln (pronounced write-line) procedures along with a Text output file. That's not a disk file, but a *file* in the general programming sense as a destination for a stream of data. When you have only text to print, these are the techniques to use.

The following Write and Writeln techniques print text using True-Type and other graphics fonts, which you can style in bold or italic if you wish. Even though these techniques are strictly for printing text, the methods do not use the printer's native character set unless you have installed a generic text-only printer driver.

THE PRINTER UNIT

To every module that needs printing capabilities, add the Printers unit to the module's *uses* declaration. For example, start a new project and modify the main unit's *uses* declaration like this:

```
uses
   SysUtils, WinTypes, WinProcs, Messages, Classes, Graphics, Controls,
   Forms, Dialogs, Printers;
```

The Printers unit provides a Printer object of the TPrinter component class. All printer output commands go through this object, which also provides useful information such as the pixels width and height of a page.

This may be obvious, but the Printers unit is plural; its Printer object is singular. If you have trouble getting started printing, make sure you didn't mix up the words.

A bit later in this section, I'll describe each TPrinter class member. But first, let's take a look at a simple print job that demonstrates how to use the Printers unit and its Printer object. Connect your printer, turn it on, and follow these steps:

1. Add Printers to the main unit's *uses* declaration.

2. Insert a Button object into the form, and double-click the object to create an OnClick event handler.

3. Use the programming in Listing 14-1 as the OnClick procedure. The code demonstrates rudimentary text-printing techniques.

4. Run the program and click the button to print the following string at the top of the page:

Hello printer!

Listing 14-1
This Button OnClick event handler demonstrates rudimentary text-printing techniques.

```
procedure TForm1.Button1Click(Sender: TObject);
var
  FPrn: System.Text;
begin
  AssignPrn(FPrn);
  Rewrite(FPrn);
  try
    Writeln(FPrn, 'Hello printer!');
  finally
    CloseFile(FPrn);
  end;
end;
```

Initialize the Text file

Use the Text file in a try block

Close the Text file in a finally block

To provide a destination file to which the program sends text output, define FPrn (you can name it something else) of type System.Text. Perform two steps to attach this file variable to Pascal's output procedures, and to open it for business:

```
AssignPrn(FPrn);   { Attach file for output }
Rewrite(FPrn);     { Open the file }
```

The Printers unit provides AssignPrn to assign an output file and to provide an output buffer in memory. Rewrite is a standard Pascal procedure that opens a text file. After those two steps, you can call Writeln to print strings. (Those who know Pascal but develop exclusively for Windows may be unfamiliar with Write and Writeln, so I'll briefly review them here.) Calling Writeln prints a string and starts a new line. To handle any possible exceptions, use FPrn inside a *try* block:

```
try
  Writeln(FPrn, 'Plain text is plain and simple!');
  { ... insert other output statements here }
```

Close the printer, which finishes the print job and ejects any partially completed page, by calling CloseFile. For safety, insert this statement in a *finally* block, which is guaranteed execution even if printing failed:

```
finally
  CloseFile(FPrn);
```

You can also print multiple values, integers, floating-point variables, and other simple-data-type objects:

```
Writeln(FPrn, 'Number of components = ', ComponentCount);
```

Use Write to print text and not start a new line. For example, the following lines are equivalent to the single preceding statement:

```
Write(FPrn, 'Number of components = ');
Write(FPrn, ComponentCount);
Writeln(FPrn);  { Start new line }
```

 Attempting to pass to Read or Readln a printer output file that was assigned with AssignPrn generates a runtime error exception. You cannot read data from a printer output device.

CONTROL CODES AND FONTS

Write and Writeln respond to four control codes, which you can use to send commands to the printer:

Control Code	Command
#9	Tab
#10	New Line
#13	Carriage Return
^L	New Page

You can embed these ASCII values in strings, or print them with Write statements such as these:

```
Write(FPrn, #9);   { Tab }
Write(FPrn, #13);  { Flush output buffer }
Write(FPrn, #10);  { Flush and start new line }
Write(FPrn, ^L);   { Flush and start new page }
```

Write and Writeln expand tabs to eight times the average character width in pixels of the current font. When printing with a proportional font, this means you cannot use tabs to align non-numerical columns with Write and Writeln. In most proportional fonts, however, digits are monospace in size, so you might be able to use tab control codes to align purely numerical columns.

The Printer object provides a Canvas property that, among other talents, determines the printer's font, which defaults to System in 10 points. You can change the printer's font by assigning its name to the Canvas's Font.Name property. For example, use these statements to select the TrueType Courier New font in 9 points for subsequent Write and Writeln statements:

```
with Printer.Canvas do
begin
  Font.Name := 'Courier New';
  Font.Size := 9;
end;
```

Always call AssignPrn and Rewrite before changing Font property values in the Printer's Canvas.

The selected font affects character pixel height and width, and therefore changes the number of lines per page (more on this later). You may use any installed font, but TrueType fonts are usually best for printing because the Windows GDI can render characters for any graphics print driver, even if it does not directly support TrueType.

You should also be able to use the Write and Writeln techniques described here to print on text-only printers such as those old hammer-head clunkers. (I kept my ancient NEC thimble printer on the floor, and it still shook the room so badly I feared head crashes every time I printed a listing.) If you must support a text-only printer, use the Control Panel to install the Windows *Generic / Text Only* driver and give it a whirl. There's no guarantee this will work, however, and for best results you should specify that a graphics printer is required for your printing applications.

PRINTER STATISTICS

The PrnInfo application shown in Figure 14-1 prints statistics about your printer's capabilities and the current font. The program also demonstrates how to determine the number of lines per page, which might be useful in some applications. Listing 14-2 shows the source code for PrnInfo.

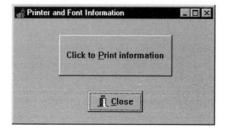

Figure 14-1
Click PrnInfo's large button for a printed report about your printer's resolution, driver, lines per page, and average characters per line.

Turn on your printer, and click the large button. Here's what PrnInfo printed for my system:

```
Device = Canon BJ-200e on LPT1:
Font = System
Font Size = 10 points
PageHeight = 3736 pixels
PageWidth = 2880 pixels
Extent.Cx = 7168 pixels
Extent.Cy = 60 pixels
Lines per page = 59
Chars per line = 90
```

Listing 14-2
PrnInfo\Main.Pas

```
unit Main;

interface

uses
  SysUtils, WinTypes, WinProcs, Messages, Classes, Graphics, Controls,
  Forms, Dialogs, Printers, StdCtrls, Buttons;

type
  TMainForm = class(TForm)
    PrintButton: TButton;
    CloseBitBtn: TBitBtn;
    procedure PrintButtonClick(Sender: TObject);
  private
    { Private declarations }
  public
    { Public declarations }
  end;

var
  MainForm: TMainForm;

implementation

{$R *.DFM}

procedure TMainForm.PrintButtonClick(Sender: TObject);
var
  FPrn: System.Text;
  Extent: TSize;
  Metrics: TTextMetric;
  I, LinesPerPage, CharsPerLine, AverageWidth: Integer;
  S : String;
begin
  AssignPrn(FPrn);
  Rewrite(FPrn);
{- Fill test string with ASCII values 32 to 255 }
  try
    S[0] := Chr(224);     { Tricky way to set string length }
    for I := 32 to 255 do     { Fill string with test characters }
      S[I - 31] := Chr(I);
    with Printer, Canvas do
    begin
      {- Determine number of lines per page }
      GetTextExtentPoint(Handle, @S[1], Length(S), Extent);
      LinesPerPage := PageHeight div (Extent.Cy + 2);
      if PageHeight mod Extent.Cy <> 0 then
        Dec(LinesPerPage);
```

Insert Printers into the module's uses statement.

Use this record structure to obtain printer statistics.

This forces the string length to 224 characters for the subsequent loop, but you shouldn't use this method except for special cases such as this one.

These statements calculate the number of lines per page

III

14

```
    {- Determine average number of characters per line }
    GetTextMetrics(Handle, Metrics);
    AverageWidth := Metrics.tmAveCharWidth;
    CharsPerLine := PageWidth div AverageWidth;
    {- Print the report }
    Writeln(FPrn, 'Device = ', Printers[PrinterIndex]);
    Writeln(FPrn, 'Font = ', Font.Name);
    Writeln(FPrn, 'Font Size = ', Font.Size, ' points');
    Writeln(FPrn, 'PageHeight = ', PageHeight, ' pixels');
    Writeln(FPrn, 'PageWidth = ', PageWidth, ' pixels');
    Writeln(FPrn, 'Extent.Cx = ', Extent.Cx, ' pixels');
    Writeln(FPrn, 'Extent.Cy = ', Extent.Cy, ' pixels');
    Writeln(FPrn, 'Lines per page = ', LinesPerPage);
    Writeln(FPrn, 'Chars per line = ', CharsPerLine);
  end;
finally
  CloseFile(FPrn);
  end;
end;

end.
```

Call Get Text Metrics to fill the TTextMetric structure with printer statistics.

Always remember to close the output file when you're done using it.

Extent.Cx equals the number of horizontal pixels that would be required to print the program's test string. (PrnInfo does not print this string, which is used only to prepare the report.) Extent.Cy equals the height in pixels of the test string. The number of lines per page is accurate only if you print all lines on the page with the same font. The number of characters per line is approximate for proportional fonts.

To display statistics about a different font, add statements such as the following immediately above the call to GetTextExtentPoint:

```
Font.Name := 'Courier New';
Font.Size := 24;
```

PrnInfo demonstrates how to call Windows API functions that require a handle to a printer device context. Simply pass the Handle property of the Printer's Canvas to this parameter. For example, this calls GetTextExtentPoint:

```
GetTextExtentPoint(Handle, @S[1], Length(S), Extent);
```

To satisfy the function's PChar parameter, the statement passes the address of the test string's first character (@S[1]). A similar statement calls another API function, GetTextMetrics:

```
GetTextMetrics(Handle, Metrics);
```

Use these techniques, and PrnInfo's reported values, only with the Write and Writeln text-printing methods described here. As I'll explain later in this chapter, other text-printing techniques give you better control over results.

PRINTING STRING LISTS

To print a TStrings or TStringList object's text lines, use Writeln as described in this section. Add Printers to the module's *uses* directive, and insert this code to print a string list:

```
var
  FPrn: TextFile;
  I: Integer;
begin
  AssignPrn(FPrn);
  Rewrite(FPrn);
  try
    for I := 0 to Memo1.Lines.Count - 1 do
      Writeln(FPrn, Memo1.Lines[I]);
  finally
    CloseFile(FPrn);
  end;
end;
```

You can use this code to print any TStrings component property — for example, the Lines property in a Memo object, or Items in a ListBox.

PRINTER DIALOGS

Menu commands for printing vary among applications, but most use at least one of the following, by tradition on the *File* menu. The four standard menu commands are:

- *File|Page Setup...* — Optional. Displays an application dialog that configures headers, page numbers, margins, and any other miscellaneous settings that you need. There aren't any standard methods for implementing this command except that it should permit users to configure whatever items are unique to your application's printing features.

- *File|Print Preview* — Optional. Displays simulated printout pages in a window. There aren't any standard ways to implement this command, but later in this chapter I'll suggest a technique that should work for most applications.

- *File|Print Setup...* — Displays the current printer driver's setup dialog, which typically includes an Options button that opens additional dialog boxes. This command should never print anything.

- *File|Print...* — Displays a print configuration dialog for users to enter the number of copies they want and a range of page numbers. If the user clicks the dialog's OK button, the program should begin printing immediately. This command's dialog box includes a *Setup* button that displays the same setup dialog as the *File|Print Setup* command.

The first two commands are optional. *File|Print Setup* and *File|Print* are standard, although you can get away with only *File|Print* in a pinch, since this command permits access to the driver's setup dialog. However, most applications should implement at least the *File|Print Setup* and *File|Print* commands. The Lister application on the CD-ROM — and shown in Figure 14-2 and Listing 14-3 — demonstrates how to use Delphi's PrinterSetupDialog and PrintDialog components in writing a program's *File|Print* and *File|Print Setup* commands. The Lister program can print any .Pas, .Txt, or other text file. To demonstrate printing numerical data as well as text, Lister prefaces lines with line numbers. Printed text uses the Courier New font in 10 points.

To implement the *File|Print Setup* command, insert a PrinterSetup-Dialog component object into the form. The object is represented by an icon, which does not appear at runtime. In a Button or menu command OnClick event handler, insert the statement:

```
PrinterSetupDialog1.Execute;
```

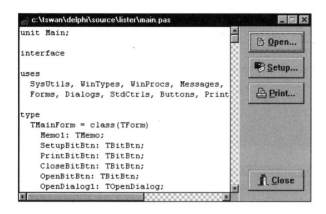

Figure 14-2

The Lister application prints any text file and demonstrates how to implement File | Print Setup and File | Print commands.

Listing 14-3

Lister\Main.Pas

```
unit Main;

interface

uses
  SysUtils, WinTypes, WinProcs, Messages, Classes, Graphics, Controls,
  Forms, Dialogs, StdCtrls, Buttons, Printers;

type
  TMainForm = class(TForm)
    Memo1: TMemo;
    SetupBitBtn: TBitBtn;
    PrintBitBtn: TBitBtn;
    CloseBitBtn: TBitBtn;
    OpenBitBtn: TBitBtn;
    OpenDialog1: TOpenDialog;
    PrintDialog1: TPrintDialog;
    PrinterSetupDialog1: TPrinterSetupDialog;
    procedure OpenBitBtnClick(Sender: TObject);
    procedure SetupBitBtnClick(Sender: TObject);
    procedure PrintBitBtnClick(Sender: TObject);
  private
    { Private declarations }
  public
    { Public declarations }
  end;
```

Add Printers to uses statement

```
var
  MainForm: TMainForm;

implementation

{$R *.DFM}

procedure TMainForm.OpenBitBtnClick(Sender: TObject);
begin
  with OpenDialog1 do
  if Execute then
  begin
    Memo1.Lines.LoadFromFile(FileName);
    Caption := Lowercase(FileName);
  end;
end;

procedure TMainForm.SetupBitBtnClick(Sender: TObject);
begin
  PrinterSetupDialog1.Execute;
end;

procedure TMainForm.PrintBitBtnClick(Sender: TObject);
var
  FPrn: System.Text;    { Printer output text file }
  I: Integer;           { Memo1.Lines index }
  LCol: Integer;        { Line number column width }
begin
  if PrintDialog1.Execute then
  begin
    AssignPrn(FPrn);  { Direct Write/Writeln to FPrn }
    Rewrite(FPrn);    { Open printer output file }
    try
      Printer.Canvas.Font := Memo1.Font;  { Use Memo's font }
      with Memo1, Lines do
      begin { Set line number column width for file size:     }
        if Count < 10 then LCol := 1       { 0 .. 9 lines      }
        else if Count < 100 then LCol := 2  { 10 .. 99 lines    }
        else if Count < 1000 then LCol := 3 { 100 .. 999 lines  }
        else LCol := 4;                     { You must be kidding }
        for I := 0 to Count - 1 do
        begin
          Write(FPrn, I + 1:LCol, ': ');  { Print line number }
          Writeln(FPrn, Lines[I]);        { Print line }
        end;
      end;
    finally
      CloseFile(FPrn);  { Close printer output file }
    end;
  end;
end;

end.
```

This displays the printer driver's setup dialog.

This displays the Print dialog that users can use to start a print job

Alternatively, you can perform another action if users close the setup dialog by selecting its *OK* button, although this is rarely necessary:

```
if PrinterSetupDialog1.Execute then
  { ... take action if user selected OK }
```

Implement a *File| Print* command similarly, but insert a PrintDialog component object (this also has no runtime appearance). Listing 14-4 shows the general layout of the command's OnClick event handler. Inside the *try* block, insert Write and Writeln statements as the Lister application's PrintBitBtnClick procedure demonstrates.

Listing 14-4
Implement a File|Print command using code such as this.

```
if PrintDialog1.Execute then
begin
  AssignPrn(FPrn);
  Rewrite(FPrn);
  try
    { ... Write text to FPrn }
  finally
    CloseFile(FPrn);
  end;
end;
```

In most cases, you'll want to use the same font for printing as you do for displaying text on screen. When using a component such as Memo for displaying text, simply assign the object's Font to the Printer's Canvas with a statement such as the following, but be sure to open the output file beforehand:

```
Printer.Canvas.Font := Memo1.Font;
```

It's up to you to use any information supplied in the PrintDialog object. After calling Execute, use the Copies, FromPage, ToPage, and other property values in your print loop:

```
with PrintDialog1 do
for Copy := 1 to Copies do
  for Page := FromPage to ToPage do
    { ... Print pages here }
```

The TPrinter Class

Before getting to the next section, which explains how to print graphics and WYSIWYG text, scan the following explanations of TPrinter's properties and methods. You'll need a good understanding of these items when your printing needs extend beyond Delphi's Write and Writeln procedures.

 Refer to all properties and events mentioned in this section through the Printer object. For example, the expression Printer.Canvas accesses the Printer's Canvas object. To use these properties and methods, add *Printers* to your application module's *uses* directive.

TPRINTER PROPERTIES

- *Aborted* — Becomes True if user aborts printing, for example, by closing the Print Manager. Inspect this Boolean variable in your print loop to determine whether TPrinter's Abort method has been called, in which case you should end the loop immediately *without* calling EndDoc.

- *Canvas* — To print graphics and WYSIWYG text, assign values to the Canvas's Pen, Brush, and other properties, and call its methods, exactly as you do for displaying graphics.

- *Fonts* — A TStrings list of all fonts that the current printer supports. You may always print using TrueType fonts because the GDI can render TrueType characters even for older printer drivers that do not support TrueType.

- *Handle* — Pass this value to any Windows API function that requires a handle to a device context (HDC) — for example, GetText Metrics.

- *Orientation* — One of two values: poPortrait or poLandscape. You can assign these values before printing, or you can inspect them to determine page parameters.

- *PageHeight* — Height of one printer page in pixels. This value can vary widely among printers.

- *PageNumber* — Current page number. The meaning of a *page* is up to your application. The Printer object increments PageNumber every time you call the NewPage method, and for plain-text printing, also when Writeln starts a new page.

- *PageWidth* — Width of one printer page in pixels. This value can vary widely among printers.

- *PrinterIndex* — Index of the current printer name in the Printers string list.

- *Printers* — A TStrings string list of installed printers. The expression Printer.Printers[PrinterIndex] gives the name of the current printer.

- *Printing* — True while printing is in progress.

- *Title* — A string, which you may assign, that identifies the print task in the Print Manager or a network task header.

TPRINTER METHODS

- *Abort* — You may call abort to terminate a print job in progress. For example, you can display a modeless dialog box before your application enters its print loop. Use a global flag to indicate whether the user clicked the dialog's *Abort* button, and if so, call Printer.Abort and exit the printer-output loop. (Do *not* also call EndDoc.) Calling Abort sets the Printer.Aborted flag to True.

- *BeginDoc* — Call this before beginning a new print job. You do not have to call BeginDoc when using the Write and Writeln plain-text techniques described at the beginning of this chapter.

- *EndDoc* — Call this after finishing the print job. EndDoc flushes the output buffer and ejects the final page if necessary. Do *not* call EndDoc when using the Write and Writeln plain-text techniques. Also, do *not* call EndDoc after terminating a print job by calling Printer.Abort.

- *NewPage* — Call this procedure at any time to start a new page. The meaning and contents of a page are up to you and your program to provide. NewPage merely flushes the output buffer and ejects the current page.

 Never construct an object of the TPrinter class. The Printers unit provides a Printer object of this class data type ready to use.

Graphics Printing

The text-printing techniques described in the preceding section represent a reasonable compromise between ease-of-use and results. When you need more control over output parameters — to more accurately position text on the page, for example, or to handle tabs for proportional fonts — you can use the following methods. In this section, I'll explain how to print forms, graphics, WYSIWYG text, and bitmaps. This section's font sampler application, FontSamp, also suggests a general-purpose technique for previewing printed output on screen.

PRINTING FORMS

You might want to include a command that prints a snapshot of a form's onscreen appearance. This is easy to do — just call the form's Print method. You do not have to call any TPrinter methods, and you do not have to add Printers to the module's *uses* declaration.

To print a form, insert a PrintDialog object and implement a Button or menu command's OnClick event handler with a statement such as this:

```
if PrintDialog1.Execute then
    Print;
```

To print a specific form by name, use this statement:

```
AboutBox.Print;
```

Internally, the form component's Print method copies the current window's client area to an offscreen bitmap. The Print method then prints this bitmap by calling the Windows API StretchDIBits function. Assign one of three values to the form's PrintScale property to determine how the output is scaled. You can do this at runtime or in the Object Inspector. The three PrintScale choices are:

- *poNone* — No scaling. The size of the printed form depends on the printer's resolution. Using this option to print forms on laser printers results in tiny windows that are cute but unreadable (at least I can't see them). You'll rarely have use for this option.

- *poPrintToFit* — Scale to page size. The printed form fills the page in at least one direction (typically horizontally). This option is the most wasteful of printer ink, but when you want a form to fill the page, this is the right option to use.

- *poProportional* — Scale using printer's pixels-per-inch property. This results in the best-looking output, which at normal viewing distance, looks similar in size to the form's onscreen appearance. That's not to suggest the sizes match exactly; the printed output is simply a good compromise between readability and space.

PRINTING GRAPHICS OBJECTS

The techniques for printing graphics and WYSIWYG text — that is, text printed *as* graphics objects — requires different techniques than printing plain-text with Write and Writeln statements. You use the same Printers unit and Printer object, but you call methods in the TPrinter class to begin and end a print job. You have to define the meaning of a page for your application, and you have to draw every output object. This takes more work, but provides the utmost control over results.

Listing 14-5 demonstrates the basic steps required to print the contents of an Image component. You don't have to use the component, but it's useful for this demonstration.

There are three basic steps:

1. Call the Printer's BeginDoc procedure to begin printing.

2. Call methods for the Printer's Canvas. For example, call Draw to print a TGraphic object (a bitmap, an icon, or metafile), or you can call methods such as Ellipse and Rectangle. Whatever you deposit on the Printer's Canvas will end up on the printed page, within the limits of your printer's capabilities. For better error control, perform these steps inside a *try* block.

3. Call EndDoc when you are finished printing. For better error control, call EndDoc in a *finally* block.

To try the procedure in Listing 14-5, insert an Image component and a Button into a form. The size of the Image object is unimportant. Use the Image object's Picture property to load any bitmap file. Insert the programming from the listing into the Button's OnClick event handler, run the program, and click the button to print the bitmap.

The code in Listing 14-5 works, but as you know if you ran the suggested test, unless you also scale your images according to the printer's resolution, the results may be too small to be readable. This is especially true of laser printers, which provide far greater resolution than current display screens. (Don't you wish you could buy a high-speed CRT with 300 dots-per-inch resolution?)

To scale images, call the Windows API GetDeviceCaps (that's Caps for *capabilities*) and request the logPixelsX and logPixelsY values for the Printer object's device context handle. This obtains the logical pixels per inch for the device, which when divided by the form's PixelsPerInch property, scales the image to an appropriate size.

Listing 14-5
Follow this general plan to print graphics.

```
procedure TForm1.Print1Click(Sender: TObject);
begin
  Printer.BeginDoc;
  try
    Printer.Canvas.Draw(0, 0, Image.Picture.Graphic);
  finally
    Printer.EndDoc;
  end;
end;
```

The *actual* number of pixels per inch for a specific device may differ from its *logical* values for many reasons, one of which is that Windows displays text on screen larger than real-life so small point sizes are readable on low-resolution displays.

Listing 14-6 improves on the procedure in Listing 14-5 by scaling the printed image according to the printer's resolution. Replace the test program's OnClick event handler with this listing, rerun, and print. The image size should now be closer to its onscreen appearance. (Again, that's not to say the display and printed sizes match; only that they appear similar at normal viewing distances.)

The procedure in Listing 14-6 initializes two integer variables, ScaleX and ScaleY, to values equal to the printer's logical pixels per inch obtained by GetDeviceCaps divided by the form's PixelsPerInch property. There's only one such property because VGA display modes are square, and the number of pixels per inch should be the same vertically and horizontally. The same fact is not necessarily true for all output devices, however, which is why GetDeviceCaps provides values for X- and Y-axes.

Listing 14-6
Use this code to scale an image according to the printer's resolution.

```
procedure TForm1.Button1Click(Sender: TObject);
var
  ScaleX, ScaleY: Integer;
  R: TRect;
begin
  Printer.BeginDoc;
  with Printer do
  try
    ScaleX := GetDeviceCaps(Handle, logPixelsX) div PixelsPerInch;
    ScaleY := GetDeviceCaps(Handle, logPixelsY) div PixelsPerInch;
    R := Rect(0, 0, Image1.Picture.Width * ScaleX,
      Image1.Picture.Height * ScaleY);
    Canvas.StretchDraw(R, Image1.Picture.Graphic);
  finally
    EndDoc;
  end;
end;
```

After setting ScaleX and ScaleY, the procedure creates a TRect record, R, of the output's dimensions. Multiplying the Image object's Picture.Width and Picture.Height by the scaling factors adjusts the rectangle to a comfortable fit. Finally, StretchDraw draws the bitmap by referring to the Picture's Graphic property.

Printing actually begins when the program calls EndDoc or New-Page. Drawing to the Printer's Canvas property does not produce any output.

PRINTING BITMAPS, ICONS, AND METAFILES

You don't have to use an Image component to print graphics. You can use the same technique in Listing 14-6 to print bitmaps, icons, and metafiles. Construct a TPicture object (see the preceding chapter for instructions), and pass its Graphic property to the Printer Canvas's Draw or StretchDraw methods. Listing 14-7 shows how to scale and print the Winlogo.Bmp file entirely under program control.

Listing 14-7
Use this code to print any bitmap, icon, or metafile.

```
procedure TForm1.Button1Click(Sender: TObject);
var
  P: TPicture;
  ScaleX, ScaleY: Integer;
  R: TRect;
begin
  P := TPicture.Create;
  try
    P.LoadFromFile('C:\Windows\Winlogo.Bmp');
    Printer.BeginDoc;
    with Printer do
    try
      ScaleX := GetDeviceCaps(Handle, logPixelsX) div PixelsPerInch;
      ScaleY := GetDeviceCaps(Handle, logPixelsY) div PixelsPerInch;
      R := Rect(0, 0, P.Width * ScaleX, P.Height * ScaleY);
      Canvas.StretchDraw(R, P.Graphic);
    finally
      Printer.EndDoc;
    end;
  finally
    P.Free;
  end;
end;
```

Rather than use an Image component, create a TPicture object.

Pass the TPicture object's Graphic property to the Printer's Canvas. This prints the bitmap.

End the print job and free the TPicture object.

Listings 14-6 and 14-7 produce the same results. Which technique to use depends on whether you want to use an Image component or construct a TPicture object under program control. Displaying the Image object is probably easier, so if you can't decide, use the method in Listing 14-6. However, Listing 14-7 is more efficient in its use of memory because the bitmap object exists only within the scope of the event handler.

NOTE

Delphi's Manuals.Txt file suggests another method for printing bitmaps that requires allocating and freeing memory, and calling the Windows API functions GetDIBSizes, GetDIB, and StretchDIBits. I can't see any good reason to go to all that trouble when it's so much easier to pass a TGraphic object to the Printer Canvas Draw or StretchDraw methods, which hide all the Windows API function calls. After all, that's what objects are supposed to do, right?

PRINTING GRAPHICS SHAPES

To display and print graphics shapes, write a procedure that draws graphics and text to a Canvas passed as an argument. Call your procedure to print on the Printer object's Canvas. Call the same procedure in a form's OnPaint event handler to display graphics. The trick is to scale the printed image so it comes out a reasonable size. On the CD-ROM, the PrintGr application demonstrates how to display and print graphics shapes and text. Figure 14-3 shows PrintGr's display — nothing fancy, but adequate for the demonstration. Listing 14-8 lists the program's source code. Run the program, and select the *File|Print* command to print.

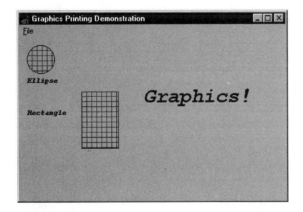

Figure 14-3
PrintGr demonstrates one way to display and print graphics shapes and text.

Listing 14-8

PrintGr\Main.Pas

```pascal
unit Main;

interface

uses
  SysUtils, WinTypes, WinProcs, Messages, Classes, Graphics, Controls,
  Forms, Dialogs, Menus, Printers;

type
  TMainForm = class(TForm)
    MainMenu1: TMainMenu;
    File1: TMenuItem;
    Print1: TMenuItem;
    N1: TMenuItem;
    Exit1: TMenuItem;
    PrintDialog1: TPrintDialog;
    procedure Print1Click(Sender: TObject);
    procedure FormPaint(Sender: TObject);
    procedure Exit1Click(Sender: TObject);
  private
    procedure PaintGraphics(C: TCanvas; ScaleX, ScaleY: Integer);
  public
    { Public declarations }
  end;

var
  MainForm: TMainForm;

implementation

{$R *.DFM}

procedure TMainForm.PaintGraphics(C: TCanvas;
  ScaleX, ScaleY: Integer);
var
  R: TRect;
  P: TPoint;

  function ScalePoint(X, Y: Integer): TPoint;
  begin
    Result := Point(X * ScaleX, Y * ScaleY);
  end;

  function ScaleRect(L, T, R, B: Integer): TRect;
  begin
    Result := Rect(L * ScaleX, T * ScaleY, R * ScaleX, B * ScaleY);
  end;
```

Pass the form's Canvas to draw onscreen; pass the Printer's Canvas to print.

These functions scale coordinates and rectangles to the printer's resolution.

```
begin
  with C do
  begin
    Pen.Color := clBlue;
    Brush.Color := clRed;
    Brush.Style := bsCross;
    Font.Name := 'Courier New';
    Font.Size := 8;
    Font.Style := [fsBold, fsItalic];
    R := ScaleRect(12, 12, 57, 57);
    Ellipse(R.Left, R.Top, R.Right, R.Bottom);
    R := ScaleRect(100, 85, 160, 174);
    Rectangle(R.Left, R.Top, R.Right, R.Bottom);
    P := ScalePoint(12, 60);
    TextOut(P.X, P.Y, 'Ellipse');
    P := ScalePoint(12, 110);
    TextOut(P.X, P.Y, 'Rectangle');
    Font.Size := 24;
    Font.Style := [fsBold, fsItalic];
    P := ScalePoint(200, 75);
    TextOut(P.X, P.Y, 'Graphics!');
  end;
end;

procedure TMainForm.Print1Click(Sender: TObject);
var
  ScaleX, ScaleY: Integer;
begin
  if PrintDialog1.Execute then
  Printer.BeginDoc;
  try
    ScaleX := GetDeviceCaps(Printer.Canvas.Handle,
      logPixelsX) div PixelsPerInch;
    ScaleY := GetDeviceCaps(Printer.Canvas.Handle,
      logPixelsY) div PixelsPerInch;
    PaintGraphics(Printer.Canvas, ScaleX, ScaleY);
  finally
    Printer.EndDoc;
  end;
end;

procedure TMainForm.FormPaint(Sender: TObject);
begin
  PaintGraphics(Canvas, 1, 1);
end;

procedure TMainForm.Exit1Click(Sender: TObject);
begin
  Close;
end;

end.
```

Assign Pen, Brush, and Font properties to the Canvas before drawing and printing.

This procedure prints the window's graphics

Perform scaling

This procedure paints graphics in the form window. Note that both printing and painting call PaintGraphics, which handles the actual output

The program calls procedure PaintGraphics to display and print its shapes and text. The procedure declares three parameters: a TCanvas, and two Integers, ScaleX and ScaleY, for scaling coordinates.

Two functions perform the scaling. ScalePoint multiplies X and Y by the scaling factors, and returns a TPoint record. ScaleRect does the same but returns a TRect record. PaintGraphics shows how to use these functions. For example, to paint an ellipse, the program executes these statements:

```
R := ScaleRect(12, 12, 57, 57);
Ellipse(R.Left, R.Top, R.Right, R.Bottom);
```

Calling ScaleRect adjusts the coordinates to account for the greater resolution of most printers. This isn't the only way to perform scaling — the next section demonstrates another technique.

CREATING A PRINT-PREVIEW COMMAND

Although the term *WYSIWYG* has come to define hard-copy *quality*, to a programmer, producing WYSIWYG output is largely a matter of relative positioning. Unless the display and printer resolutions match exactly, it's not possible to produce the same onscreen and printed graphics, but with careful programming and scaleable TrueType fonts, the results are good enough for most applications.

The final program in this chapter demonstrates WYSIWYG output, and reveals a few more printing techniques, such as multiple-page printing and how to implement a print-preview window. The program, FontSamp, displays a list of fonts. Select one or more font names, or click the *Select all* button to choose all fonts, and then click *Print* to print sampler pages of each selected font in a variety of sizes and styles. Click *Preview* to view sampler pages before printing. Figure 14-4 shows the program's main display. Figure 14-5 shows the preview window. Load the FontSamp project into Delphi and view the Project Manager to inspect the program's modules.

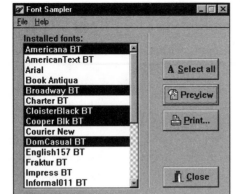

Figure 14-4

FontSamp's main display. Select one or more font names from the list box. Click Print to print samples of each font. Click Preview to view sample pages before printing.

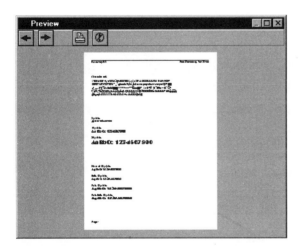

Figure 14-5

FontSamp's print-preview window showing the TrueType font Broadway BT.

FontSamp's print-preview window displays TrueType fonts such as Arial more accurately than bitmapped fonts such as Courier. Maximize the print-preview window for best results.

Delphi's TBitmap class simplifies the steps needed to create a print-preview window. FontSamp creates a TBitmap object with its width and height set to the same ratio as an 8-1/2 by 11-inch page. To preview printed output, the program draws onto the bitmap's Canvas. To print, the program draws onto the Printer's Canvas. The result is a true visual representation of the program's printed output.

Almost.

In practice, it's difficult at best to match printed output exactly in a small bitmap. Non-TrueType fonts are particularly ornery, and don't resize well. One plan that seems to work, but doesn't require months of coding, is to code all coordinates as floating-point values that represent inches. (You could use metric measurements just as well.) This plan keeps the program neat and simple. For example, to print text at mid page, assuming an 11-inch vertical dimension, you select a Y-coordinate of 6.5 inches. All you need are some simple functions to convert inches to pixels based on the Canvas's logical resolution.

Three modules in FontSamp fulfill this plan: Main, Preview, and DrawPage. Listing 14-9 shows the Main module's *Preview* and *Print* button OnClick event handlers.

Listing 14-9

FontSamp\Main.Pas Preview and Print button OnClick event handlers.

```
procedure TMainForm.PreviewBitBtnClick(Sender: TObject);
begin
  if PreviewForm.ShowModal = mrOk then
    PrintBitBtn.Click;  { User selected preview's print button }
end;

{- This is the procedure that prints the pages }
procedure TMainForm.PrintBitBtnClick(Sender: TObject);
var
  PpiX, PpiY, Page, FirstPage, LastPage: Integer;

  {- Initialize PrintDialog1 object}
  procedure InitPrintDialog;
  begin
    with PrintDialog1 do
    begin
      MinPage := 1;
      MaxPage := FontListBox.SelCount;
      FromPage := MinPage;
      ToPage := MaxPage;
    end;
  end;
```

This value is set by the Print button's OnClick event handler.

Initialize the PrintDialog objects fields before displaying the dialog.

```
{- Initialize printing variables }
procedure InitParameters;
begin
{- Do our own scaling based on Page width and height. This
seems to be more reliable than GetDeviceCaps. }
  PpiX := Trunc(Printer.PageWidth / 8.5);
  PpiY := Trunc(Printer.PageHeight / 11.0);
{- Set FirstPage and LastPage }
  if PrintDialog1.PrintRange = prAllPages then
  begin
    FirstPage := 1;
    LastPage := FontListBox.SelCount;
  end else
  begin
    FirstPage := PrintDialog1.FromPage;
    LastPage := PrintDialog1.ToPage;
  end;
end;

begin
  InitPrintDialog;
  if PrintDialog1.Execute then
  begin
    Printer.BeginDoc;
    try
      InitParameters;
      for Page := FirstPage to LastPage do
      begin
        DrawOnePage(Printer.Canvas, FontListBox, Page,
          Printer.PageWidth, Printer.PageHeight, False,
          PpiX, PpiY);
        Printer.NewPage;
      end;
    finally
      Printer.EndDoc;
    end;
  end;

end;
```

Trunc returns the integer (unrounded) portion of a floating-point value

Set up FirstPage and LastPage variables for the upcoming printer output for-loop.

Call NewPage to eject each page after printing.

The *Preview* button's OnClick event handler displays the Preview window by calling ShowModal. If that function returns mrOk, the user clicked the preview's *Print* speed button. To print, the procedure calls the *Print* button's Click method.

The *Print* button's OnClick event handler calls two local procedures to initialize the print dialog and other parameters. Set the PrintDialog1 object's MinPage and MaxPage properties to the page range. In this case, there's one font sampler per page, so the maximum page number equals

FontListBox.SelCount. Set FromPage and ToPage to these same values so they appear in the print dialog's edit windows.

To initialize printing, procedure InitParameters prepares variables PpiX and PpiY equal to the number of logical pixels per inch for the assumed page size of 8-1/2 by 11 inches. Doing the calculations this way seems more accurate than calling GetDeviceCaps. The procedure inspects the PrintDialog1 object's PrintRange property. If this equals the constant prAllPages, the user clicked the dialog's *All* radio button; otherwise, the user may have modified the page range and you can get these values from ToPage and FromPage as shown.

Following these initializations, the program is ready for printing. A *for* loop handles this by calling a procedure, DrawOnePage (in the DrawPage module) with various arguments. The most important argument is the first: Printer.Canvas, which directs output to the printer. Printer.PageWidth and Printer.PageHeight give DrawOnePage the output's boundaries for a single page. Calling Printer.NewPage ejects each page after drawing.

The Preview module in Listing 14-10 also calls DrawOnePage to simulate printed pages. This module is relatively short, so I'll list it in full here.

Listing 14-10
FontSamp\Preview.Pas

```
unit Preview;

interface

uses
  SysUtils, WinTypes, WinProcs, Messages, Classes, Graphics, Controls,
  Forms, Dialogs, StdCtrls, Buttons, ExtCtrls, DrawPage;

type
  TPreviewForm = class(TForm)
    ToolBar: TPanel;
    LeftPageSB: TSpeedButton;
    RightPageSB: TSpeedButton;
    PrintSB: TSpeedButton;
    CloseSB: TSpeedButton;
    procedure FormCreate(Sender: TObject);
    procedure FormResize(Sender: TObject);
    procedure FormPaint(Sender: TObject);
    procedure FormDestroy(Sender: TObject);
    procedure CloseSBClick(Sender: TObject);
    procedure PrintSBClick(Sender: TObject);
```

```
        procedure FormActivate(Sender: TObject);
        procedure LeftPageSBClick(Sender: TObject);
        procedure RightPageSBClick(Sender: TObject);
      private
        PreBits: TBitmap;          { Preview bitmap with canvas }
        PpiX, PpiY: Integer;       { Logical pixels per inch }
        Page: Integer;             { One font sampler per page }
        procedure InitGlobals;     { Initialize global variables }
      public
        FontListBox: TListBox;     { Reference to form's ListBox }
      end;

var
  PreviewForm: TPreviewForm;

implementation

uses Main;

{$R *.DFM}

const
  border = 10;        { Top and bottom preview bitmap borders }

{- Create form and a bitmap to represent the preview page }
procedure TPreviewForm.FormCreate(Sender: TObject);
begin
  FontListBox := nil;
  PreBits := TBitmap.Create;
end;

{- Initialize global variables and window size }
procedure TPreviewForm.InitGlobals;
begin
  PreBits.Width := ClientWidth div 2;      { Bitmap width = 1/2 client width }
  PreBits.Height := Round(1.3 * PreBits.Width);  { 1.3 = 8-1/2 x 11 ratio }
  PpiX := Round(PreBits.Width / 8.5);      { Logical pixels per inch }
  PpiY := Round(PreBits.Height / 11.0);    { Logical pixels per inch }
  if WindowState <> wsMaximized then       { Adjust window bottom }
    ClientHeight := ToolBar.Height + PreBits.Height + border * 2;
end;

{- Tip: OnResize is called before OnActivate, but
only if the form is NOT maximized, in which case FormResize
is never called. Don't use OnResize as your only
display initializer—also initialize in OnActivate. }
procedure TPreviewForm.FormResize(Sender: TObject);
begin
  InitGlobals;
  DrawOnePage(PreBits.Canvas, FontListBox, Page,   { Redraw page }
    PreBits.Width, Height, True, PpiX, PpiY);
  Invalidate;
end;
```

Add this statement to a module's implementation so statements can refer to the main form's component objects.

Tells Windows to issue a wm-Paint message to the form window.

```
{- Because the program does its own scaling, we can call Draw
instead of StretchDraw as some previewers do. This keeps the
display fast and keeps the text looking as WYSIWYG as possible. }
procedure TPreviewForm.FormPaint(Sender: TObject);
begin
  Canvas.Draw(ClientWidth div 4, ToolBar.Height + border, PreBits);
end;
```

Draw is faster than StretchDraw — always call Draw if possible.

```
procedure TPreviewForm.FormDestroy(Sender: TObject);
begin
  PreBits.Free;
end;


procedure TPreviewForm.CloseSBClick(Sender: TObject);
begin
  ModalResult := mrCancel;
end;


procedure TPreviewForm.PrintSBClick(Sender: TObject);
begin
  ModalResult := mrOk;
end;
```

Returns mrOK via the preview form's ShowModal function. See top of Listing 14-9.

```
{- This procedure prepares the FontListBox, and it draws
the first page (or a blank if no font is selected). The
procedure also enables and disables the toolbar SpeedButtons }
procedure TPreviewForm.FormActivate(Sender: TObject);
begin
{- If you don't assign a ListBox to PreviewForm.FontListBox, this
statement picks up the ListBox from the parent form. }
  if FontListBox = nil then
    FontListBox := MainForm.FontListBox;
{- Draw first page }
  Page := 1;
  InitGlobals;
  DrawOnePage(PreBits.Canvas, FontListBox, Page,
    PreBits.Width, Height, True, PpiX, PpiY);
{- Enable / disable speed buttons in toolbar }
  with FontListBox do
  begin
    LeftPageSB.Enabled := SelCount > 1;
    RightPageSB.Enabled := SelCount > 1;
    PrintSB.Enabled := SelCount > 0;
  end;
end;
```

Sets FontListBox to refer to the MainForm's object — this does not copy the object.

Set Enabled True if SelCount is greater than the specified values.

```
{- Display previous page }
procedure TPreviewForm.LeftPageSBClick(Sender: TObject);
begin
  if Page > 1 then
  begin
    Dec(Page);
    DrawOnePage(PreBits.Canvas, FontListBox, Page,
      PreBits.Width, Height, True, PpiX, PpiY);
    Invalidate;
  end;
end;

{- Display next page }
procedure TPreviewForm.RightPageSBClick(Sender: TObject);
begin
  if Page < FontListBox.SelCount then
  begin
    Inc(Page);
    DrawOnePage(PreBits.Canvas, FontListBox, Page,
      PreBits.Width, Height, True, PpiX, PpiY);
    Invalidate;
  end;
end;

end.
```

These procedures demonstrate how to implement multipage previews.

Invalidate the window to redraw it.

The Preview module declares several variables private to the TPreviewForm class. PreBits, a TBitmap object, represents one page of the preview. PpiX and PpiY are the logical pixels per inch of this bitmap. Page is the page number. FontListBox is a reference to the parent form's FontListBox. Procedure InitGlobals initializes these variables.

The Preview form creates the PreBits bitmap in an OnCreate event handler. Procedure InitGlobals shows how to perform some necessary calculations for the simulated output page. Assigning values to PreBits.Width and PreBits.Height sizes the bitmap relative to the Preview form window, but in the ratio of the 8-1/2 by 11-inch page size. The program sets PpiX and PpiY to the logical pixels per inch for this same page size — this is *not* equal to the pixels per inch of the screen or the form window, but of the bitmap that simulates the output page. Finally, unless the window is maximized, the program assigns an adjusted value to the form's ClientHeight property. This moves the window bottom so the Preview bitmap page is always completely visible. Try resizing the Preview window and watch how the window bottom seeks its own level.

Skip down to the OnPaint event handler, FormPaint. To display a preview page, the program passes the PreBits bitmap to the Canvas's Draw method. This keeps the output very fast. Alternatively, a print-preview command could form a bitmap in real size and then use StretchDraw to display that bitmap in a window. This is easier to program, but gives poor results.

Because the program uses Draw, it has to redraw each page when:

- The Preview window first appears;
- When the window changes size;
- When the user requests a different page.

The OnResize event handler, FormResize, initializes global variables according to the current window size, and calls DrawOnePage to form the preview output. To draw on the offscreen bitmap, the program passes PreBits.Canvas to DrawOnePage. It then calls Invalidate, which causes Windows to issue a wm_Paint message to the window. This leads to an OnPaint event, which as you've seen, draws the bitmap by calling the Canvas.Draw method (the one in the *form's* Canvas, not the bitmap's).

When the Preview form is first activated, its OnActivate event handler initializes some values such as the FontListBox reference and the Page number. It then calls DrawOnePage to form the first output page. It is not necessary to call Invalidate to force an OnPaint event, which occurs automatically after OnActivate. The OnActivate handler also enables and disables the Preview window's SpeedButtons depending on the number of selected fonts (FontListBox.SelCount).

The FormActivate procedure assigns FontListBox to the MainForm's FontListBox. This assignment does not create a second list box. Use *nil* as shown here as a flag to indicate whether a reference such as FontList-Box has been initialized. For example, you could insert two or more ListBox objects with different font sets in them, and assign references to them to PreviewForm.FontListBox. Or, you can let the module detect that FontListBox is *nil,* in which case it picks up the parent's FontListBox by default. (FontListBox is initialized to *nil* in the form's OnCreate event handler.) This is a good example of defensive programming — the module works correctly regardless of whether another module initializes the public FontListBox variable.

Finally, in the Preview module are the OnClick event handlers for the toolbar's previous- and next-page SpeedButtons. The procedures simply increment or decrement the Page variable, and call DrawOnePage to form the bitmap. As I explained, calling Invalidate forces an OnPaint event to occur, which draws the new bitmap on the Preview form's Canvas.

As you may have surmised by now, DrawOnePage is the glue that holds this program's graphical output together. Listing 14-11 shows the module, DrawPage, that implements this procedure.

Listing 14-11
FontSamp\DrawPage.Pas

```
unit Drawpage;

interface

uses SysUtils, Graphics, StdCtrls;

{- Call DrawOnePage to form each sampler page either during
printing or for previewing with an offscreen bitmap. }

procedure DrawOnePage(
    Canvas: TCanvas;        { Printer or TBitmap Canvas for preview }
    FontListBox: TListBox;  { List of fonts with multiple selections }
    Page,                   { Page number (FontList selection index) }
    PageWidth,              { Unscaled page width in pixels }
    PageHeight: Integer;    { Unscaled page height in pixels }
    Previewing: Boolean;    { True if previewing; else printing }
    PpiX, PpiY: Integer     { Pixels per inch on X- and Y- axes }
);

implementation

uses Main;

var
    C: TCanvas;
    PointSize: Integer; { Relative font size for all text }
    FontName, HeaderName: String[40];
    PixelsPerInchX, PixelsPerInchY: Integer;
    Preview: Boolean;

{- Return selected font at index }
function SelectedFont(ListBox: TListBox; Index: Integer): String;
var
    I: Integer;
```

```
begin
  with ListBox do
  for I := 0 to Items.Count - 1 do
  if Selected[I] then
  begin
    Dec(Index);
    if Index <= 0 then
    begin
      Result := Items[I];
      Exit;
    end;
  end;
  Result := 'System';
end;
```

This is just to ensure that Result is set to a value in the unlikely event that the preceding if-statement fails.

```
{- Assign font name, style, and size to Canvas font }
procedure SetFont(const Name: String; Style: TFontStyles;
  Size: Integer);
begin
{- Adjust point size for preview page's logical pixels per
inch relative to the form's actual pixels per inch. This allows
the program to draw into the bitmap with TextOut, and then
display the bitmap in real size with Canvas.Draw. Some print
previewers use StretchDraw, which produces relatively poor results.}
  if Preview then
    Size := Round(Size * (PixelsPerInchY / MainForm.PixelsPerInch));
{- Assign parameters to Canvas C Font property }
  C.Font.Name := Name;
  C.Font.Style := Style;
  C.Font.Size := Size;
end;

{- Return pixel width of Name in inches }
function InchWidth(const Name: String): Double;
begin
  Result := C.TextWidth(Name);
  Result := Result / PixelsPerInchX;
end;

{- Return pixel height of Name in inches }
function InchHeight(const Name: String): Double;
begin
  Result := C.TextHeight(Name);
  Result := Result / PixelsPerInchY;
end;
```

Scale the integer value from TextWidth to a floating point Double Value returned by the InchWidth function.

```
{- Write string S at inch coordinates X and Y }
procedure TextAtInch(X, Y: Double; const S: String);
var
  Px, Py: Integer;
```

```
begin
  Px := Round(X * PixelsPerInchX);
  Py := Round(Y * PixelsPerInchY);
  C.TextOut(Px, Py, S);
end;
```

Call TextOut to display or print a string.

```
{- Draw a line at inch coordinates X1, Y1, X2, Y2 }
procedure LineAtInch(X1, Y1, X2, Y2: Double);
var
  Px1, Py1, Px2, Py2: Integer;
begin
  Px1 := Round(X1 * PixelsPerInchX);
  Py1 := Round(Y1 * PixelsPerInchY);
  Px2 := Round(X2 * PixelsPerInchX);
  Py2 := Round(Y2 * PixelsPerInchY);
  C.MoveTo(Px1, Py1);
  C.LineTo(Px2, Py2);
end;

{- Draw header at top of page }
procedure DrawHeader(const Name: String);
var
  S: String[24];
begin
  SetFont(HeaderName, [fsBold], 12);
  TextAtInch(0.5, 0.5, Name);
  SetFont(HeaderName, [fsItalic], 12);
  S := 'Font Sampler by Tom Swan';
  TextAtInch(8.0 - InchWidth(S), 0.5, S);
  LineAtInch(0.5, 0.5, 8.0, 0.5);
end;

{- Draw footer at bottom of page }
procedure DrawFooter(Page: Integer);
begin
  SetFont(HeaderName, [], 12);
  TextAtInch(0.5, 10.5, 'Page ' + IntToStr(Page));
end;
```

Use an empty set to specify no formatting — that is, no bold or italic styles.

```
{- Draw sample character set (ASCII 32-255) }
procedure DrawCharacterSet;
var
  H: Double;
  procedure DrawOneLine(J, K: Integer);
  var
    I: Integer;
    S: String;
  begin
    S := '';
    for I := J to K do
      S := S + Chr(I);
    TextAtInch(0.5, H, S);
    H := H + InchHeight('M');
  end;
```

```
begin
  SetFont(HeaderName, [fsBold], 12);
  TextAtInch(0.5, 1.4, 'Character set:');
  SetFont(FontName, [], 10);
  H := 1.5 + InchHeight('M');
  DrawOneLine(32, 80);
  DrawOneLine(81, 129);
  DrawOneLine(130, 178);
  DrawOneLine(179, 227);
  DrawOneLIne(228, 256);
end;

{- Draw sample text in 8, 14, and 24 point sizes }
procedure DrawPointSamples;
var
  H, M: Double;
  procedure DrawOneSample(Pts: Integer);
  begin
    SetFont(HeaderName, [fsBold], 12);
    TextAtInch(0.5, H, IntToStr(Pts) + ' points:');
    M := InchHeight('M');
    H := H + M;
    SetFont(FontName, [], Pts);
    TextAtInch(0.5, H, 'AaBbCc 1234567890');
    H := H + M * 2;
  end;
begin
  H := 4.0;
  DrawOneSample(8);
  DrawOneSample(14);
  DrawOneSample(24);
end;

{- Draw normal, italic, bold, and bold-italic samples }
procedure DrawNormBoldItal;
var
  H, M: Double;
  procedure DrawOneLine(const S: String; Style: TFontStyles);
  begin
    SetFont(HeaderName, [fsBold], 12);
    TextAtInch(0.5, H, S);
    M := InchHeight('M');
    H := H + M;
    SetFont(FontName, Style, 12);
    TextAtInch(0.5, H, 'AaBbCc 1234567890');
    H := H + M * 2;
  end;
begin
  H := 7.0;
  DrawOneLine('Normal 12 points:', []);
  DrawOneLine('Italic 12 points:', [fsItalic]);
  DrawOneLine('Bold 12 points:', [fsBold]);
  DrawOneLine('Bold Italic 12 points:', [fsBold, fsItalic]);
end;
```

```
{- Printing and preview code calls this procedure to draw
each page. See declaration at top of file for descriptions
of the parameters. }
procedure DrawOnePage(Canvas: TCanvas; FontListBox: TListBox;
  Page, PageWidth, PageHeight: Integer; Previewing: Boolean;
  PpiX, PpiY: Integer);
begin
{- Save some parameters in global variables for easy access }
  C := Canvas;
  C.Pen.Color := clBlack;
  PixelsPerInchX := PpiX;
  PixelsPerInchY := PpiY;
  Preview := Previewing;
{- Draw the font samples on the Canvas (Printer or Preview) }
  with Canvas do
  begin
    FillRect(ClipRect);     { Erase page }
    if (FontListBox = nil) or (FontListBox.SelCount < 1) then
      Exit;  { Display / print blank page if no font selected }
    FontName := SelectedFont(FontListBox, Page);
    HeaderName := 'Arial';
    DrawHeader(FontName);   { These statements draw the }
    DrawFooter(Page);       { header, footer, and font samples }
    DrawCharacterSet;
    DrawPointSamples;
    DrawNormBoldItal;
  end;
end;

end.
```

It's totally up to you to decide how to implement your program's drawing procedures, but I usually consign them to a separate module. In addition to making the program easier to maintain, separating graphics statements has helped me to port several programs to multiple operating systems which tend to have very different drawing commands. The Draw-Page module has only a single public procedure, DrawOnePage, which as you've seen, FontSamp calls to print and preview sampler pages.

In your own applications, design the preview and drawing modules before implementing the program's printing commands. This saves paper and forces you to think carefully about how you will scale output for different resolutions. Because I followed this plan in writing FontSamp, its printing commands worked the first time I tried them. (Okay, maybe it was the third time, but anyway, the printing commands seemed easier to construct because I had already solved the hard problems in the Preview and DrawPage modules.)

I won't explain all of the DrawPage module's code, which does not contain any printing statements. However, the importance of the module is that it draws on a Canvas, regardless of its type. Therefore, the program can pass to DrawOnePage the Printer's Canvas to print, or the PreBits bitmap's Canvas to draw preview pages offscreen.

Programming would be nice and neat if the preceding statement were always 100% true. In practice, however, achieving WYSIWYG output is not so simple, and I needed a flag, Previewing, to determine whether the module was printing or previewing. Procedure SetFont uses this flag to reduce font point size when previewing, which is necessary because text would normally be rendered for the *window's* scale, not the simulated bitmap page's. To get around this problem, the program could draw fonts in their real sizes and call StretchDraw to paint the resulting bitmap. But, as I mentioned, the results are poor and they display slowly.

Summary

- Use the PrintDialog and PrinterSetupDialog components to prompt users to print, and to provide access to installed printer device driver setups.

- The TPrinter component, which is not on the VCL palette, provides printing capabilities. Add Printers to your program's *uses* directive. You can then assign values to the global Printer object's properties, and call methods such as Printer.BeginDoc and Printer.NewPage. You never create an object of the TPrinter class. Instead, use the Printer object provided by the Printers unit.

- There are two ways to print: For plain text printing, use a Text file along with Pascal's Write and Writeln procedures. For graphics and WYSIWYG text printing, use the Printer object's Canvas. Call Begin-Doc to start a print job. Draw on the Canvas as you do to display graphics in a window. Call NewPage to eject a page. Call EndDoc to end printing.

- To print a form, call its Print method, which paints the form's client area on an offscreen bitmap. The method uses the Printer object's BeginDoc and EndDoc techniques to print the resulting bitmap.

- Create a print-preview command by separating graphics output statements in a module, or a procedure such as DrawOnePage in the FontSamp application. To print, pass the Printer's Canvas to the procedure. To draw simulated preview pages, pass a TBitmap's Canvas and draw the bitmap using the form's Canvas.Draw method (not the bitmap's).

Projects to Try

14-1: Improve the Lister demonstration by adding a menu command for selecting a font, style, and size, and for making line numbers optional. You might also implement a *File|Page Setup* command to configure headers, page numbers, and so on. Simply print these items as you do other text using Write and Writeln. (Hint: Use the method demonstrated by the PrnInfo application to calculate the number of lines per page.)

14-2: Changing fonts in PrnInfo causes the program to print its report in that same font, which can cause problems — for example, if you select a large point size or a symbolic font. Revise this *feature* (well, maybe it's a bug) by writing a procedure that returns printer statistics for any font, style, and point size, and then use your procedure to print the report in a standard font.

14-3: Write a utility to determine the number of lines per page for every installed font. Print a report of this information.

14-4: Design a printer diagnostic program that prints a test pattern. This program is useful for checking edge sharpness, text appearance, line straightness, and other useful information.

14-5: *Advanced.* Design and implement a Delphi project documenter that prints all .Pas files in the current directory as well as the .Dpr project file. Also print icons and bitmap files.

Expert-User Tips

- If text does not print in the expected size, make sure your code calls Print.BeginDoc before changing the Printer Canvas Font and its subproperties.

- You must eventually call CloseFile for a System.Text variable passed to AssignPrn. Attempting to assign a second output file without closing a currently assigned file will raise an exception.

- When printing plain text, watch for the Printer object's PageNumber property to change after each call to Writeln. When PageNumber advances, a new page has been started. Rather than calculate the number of lines per page as this chapter suggests, you can use this technique to write a header line at the top of each new page.

- Allow a small border in printed output. Many printers lose sharpness at the extreme ranges as represented by the Printer object's Page-Height and PageWidth properties.

- Assign a string to the Printer object's Title property to identify a print job in the Windows Print Manager and on network page headers.

- To create an abort printing dialog, use a separate form and call its Show method to display it. Have the form set a global variable True as a flag that indicates the user clicked an Abort button. Check for this flag inside your program's printer output loop, and if the flag is True, call the Printer.Abort method to cancel printing. You do not also have to call EndDoc in that case.

- To detect whether a print job was aborted (for example, by a print loop calling Printer.Abort), inspect the read-only Printer.Aborted flag.

Coming Up

The multiple document interface, or MDI, has been one of Windows' controversial features among programmers since day one. MDI isn't appropriate for all programs, but is useful for creating multiple-page windows using a standard interface, as explained in the next chapter.

CHAPTER 15

Developing MDI Applications

Windows developers enjoy a love/hate relationship with the MDI, or multiple document interface. In fact, most programmers love to hate it. But the MDI isn't as poorly conceived as many claim. When you need a framework for managing multiple documents, with one data block per window, the MDI offers a standard interface that's easy to use and, with Delphi's help, mostly straightforward to program.

This chapter explains how to use Delphi forms to construct MDI main and child windows. I'll also explain related topics, such as how to create a Window menu, how to subclass a form, how to add window titles to a menu, and how to merge child- and main-window menus.

Components

- TForm — This component, which is the same as the one you have used in single-document interface (SDI) applications, is not on the VCL palette. MDI applications use objects of the TForm class for main and child windows. Set the main window's FormStyle property to fsMDI-Form; for child windows, set this property to fsMDIChild, and follow instructions in this chapter to construct child windows at runtime — in response to a *File|Open* command, for example Palette: none.

- MainMenu — Every MDI application's main form window must have a MainMenu component object, introduced in Chapter 5. Most MDI MainMenu objects have *File* and *Window* menu items, although you are free to name your menus as you want. MDI child windows may also have MainMenu objects for merging into the main window menu. Palette: Standard.

Pronounce MDI as "M," "D," "I," to avoid confusing it with MIDI, the musical instrument device interface. MDI and MIDI are unrelated.

Fundamentals of MDI Programming

There are three basic parts of every MDI application:

- The MDI main-window form
- One or more document MDI child-window forms
- The MDI main menu

Unlike in conventional Windows programming, a Delphi form object takes the place of the standard MDI frame and client windows. Classically, the *frame window* is the visible one; the *client window* is a kind of silent partner that handles global operations, creates child windows, and performs message services. In Delphi applications, the frame and client windows still exist, but you'll rarely use them. For all practical purposes, you can treat the frame and the client as one window, represented to your program as the main-window form.

Document child windows are also forms, but unlike windows such as an About box dialog that you insert into a module, MDI child windows cannot stray out of their backyard. They are restricted to appearing inside the main window's client area, and when you minimize a child window, its icon displays inside the main window, not on the Windows desktop.

Except for these differences, MDI main and child windows are similar to single-window application forms. In MDI applications, you can insert toolbars, status lines, component objects and graphics, and use all other Delphi programming techniques. Typically, however, the MDI is most advantageous in applications that work with multiple documents.

The MDI is often considered a file-handling system, but an application's child windows do not have to be associated with disk files. You can also use the MDI to construct multiwindow applications of other kinds. The term *document* in this chapter means any information that can be displayed in a window, not necessarily data in a disk file.

MDI MAIN-WINDOW FORM

Follow these steps to create the main window for an MDI application:

1. Start a new project. If this brings up Delphi's *Browse Gallery* dialog, select *Blank project*.
2. Assign a Name such as MainForm to the form.
3. Set the FormStyle property to fsMDIForm.
4. Save the project in a new directory. Name the unit module Main.Pas; name the project as you like (use the name MDITest if you are following along).

Only the main-window form may have its FormStyle set to fsMDI-Form, and there can be only one such window per application. To ensure that the window's form object is automatically created, select *Options | Project,* and verify that MainForm is shown in the *Main form* list box and is listed under *Auto-create forms.*

This is all you need to do to create an MDI application's main window. You can now proceed to the next section to create your program's child windows and menu.

To try the techniques in this chapter, when you start a new project, if you see Delphi's Browse Gallery dialog, select *Blank project* under the *Templates* page tab. Do *not* select *MDI Application,* which prepares a new project with default menus, a child window form, and event handlers. Later in this chapter, I'll explain how to use the gallery template to begin MDI applications. If you don't see the Browse Gallery dialog when you begin a new application, choose *Options | Environment* to enable the *Gallery* check box, *Use on New Project.*

MDI CHILD-WINDOW FORM

Every MDI application also needs at least one child-window form and unit. Follow these steps to add an MDI child window to the MDI application you created in the preceding section:

III

15

1. Choose *File | New Form,* or click the *New form* SpeedButton. If this brings up Delphi's *Browse Gallery* dialog, select *Blank form.*

2. Change the new form's Name property to ChildForm.

3. Set FormStyle to fsMDIChild.

4. Select *Options | Project* to open the *Project Options* dialog. Highlight the ChildForm object, and click the single-line right-arrow button to move the object from the *Auto-create forms* list to the *Available forms* list. If you don't perform these steps, a child window will be created automatically when the program starts. There is nothing technically wrong with this, but the result may confuse users who expect to open and create child windows using commands such as *File | New* and *File | Open.* Most MDI applications create their child windows under program control.

5. Save the project. When prompted, name the unit module Child.Pas. You can now insert programming to construct child windows in response to commands such as *File | New* and *File | Open.* The next section explains how.

Among other files in the MDI project directory are the following three Pascal modules:

- *Child.Pas* — The child-window form's unit module. This module contains programming specific to the type of document or other information provided by the child window. A child window may also have a menu, which is merged into the main form's menu.

- *Main.Pas* — The main-window form's unit module. Insert event handlers for any objects in the main-window form, as well as for menu items. Typically, at least one event handler in this module should create instances of the program's child windows. For details on writing this code, see "Child Windows" and "Creating Child Window Instances" later in this chapter.

- *MDITest.Dpr* — The program's project file.

 MDI application child windows do not all have to be of the same types. If your application needs different types of child windows, simply add as many additional forms as you need by repeating steps 1–5.

Be sure to set FormStyle to fsMDIChild. For more information on creating multiple types of child window forms, see "Different-Type Child Windows" in this chapter.

MDI MAIN MENU

The third and final required item in every MDI application is a main menu object. At least one command in this menu creates child-window form objects. Follow these steps to create this menu:

1. Insert a MainMenu component object into the Main form. (Be sure to select the Main, not the Child, form.) Double-click the MainMenu object to open Delphi's Menu Designer.

2. Create a File menu, and change its Name property to FileMenu. Insert commands such as *File | New, File | Open,* and *File | Save.* The section, "Creating Child Window Instances" in this chapter describes how to construct child-window objects for these and other menu commands.

3. Create a *Window* menu, and change its Name property to Window-Menu. Insert commands such as *Cascade, Tile,* and *Arrange all.* To learn how to write event handlers for these and other *Window* menu commands, see the section "Window Menu Commands" in this chapter.

4. Close the Menu Designer or shove it aside, select the Main module form, and set its WindowMenu property to WindowMenu. This setting causes the application to list the titles of open child windows — you don't have to write any code to make this happen.

Of course, the exact menu commands in your application depend on your program's needs. At the very minimum, however, an MDI application should have commands to create and open document child windows, and a menu usually named *Window* for listing the titles of open windows.

You may assign to WindowMenu only a top-level menu — in other words, a TMenuItem object that represents a menu item in the main window's menu bar. Do not assign a menu command object to this property.

Child-window forms may also have MainMenu objects. When users activate an instance of the child window, its menu commands automatically merge into the main form's menu according to the menu items' GroupIndex property. See "Merging Menus" in this chapter for instructions on merging MDI menus.

ACCESSING CHILD WINDOWS

Three form properties provide access to child windows — you'll find numerous examples of each property throughout this chapter. The three properties are:

- *ActiveMDIChild* — A reference to the currently active child window. If there are no children, ActiveMDIChild is *nil*. This property is a reference to a TForm object, and therefore, you'll often need to cast ActiveMDIChild to the child window's class.
- *MDIChildCount* — The integer count of child windows that the MDI parent window owns. If there are no children, MDIChildCount is zero.
- *MDIChildren* — An array of TForm object references to all child windows owned by the MDI parent window. The expression MDIChildren[0] references the first child window in the array; the expression MDIChildren[MCIChildCount – 1] references the last child window.

If ActiveMDIChild is *nil,* or if MDIChildCount equals zero, there are no child windows. In such cases, the program should not refer to the MDIChildren array, although doing so does not necessarily generate an exception. Specifically, the expression MDIChildren[0] is *nil* when MDIChildCount equals zero.

Child Windows

A child window in an MDI application operates much like the main window in a single-window application. Child windows can have component objects such as Memos and Buttons. Typically, a child window displays a document — for example, a text file, for example, or a bitmap. Users can open multiple child windows, arrange them in cascaded or tiled order, and minimize them to icons. Child windows may have toolbars and status lines, but traditionally, these kinds of objects usually appear in the main window.

Selecting a child window can also optionally merge commands into the application's main menu. This technique is especially useful when you are using multiple types of child windows, each with its own command requirements. The following section discusses these child-window programming techniques, and lists an MDI application shell that you can use to begin new programs.

SAME-TYPE CHILD WINDOWS

The MDIDemo application on the CD-ROM demonstrates how to create same-type MDI child windows. The program shows how to program common menu commands such as *File | New, File | Open, Window | Cascade* and *Window | Tile.* Figure 15-1 shows the program's display with a few sample windows open.

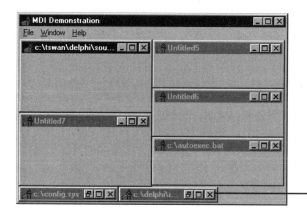

Minimized child windows under Windows 95.

Figure 15-1
The MDIDemo application demonstrates same-type child-window programming. Windows 95 shows minimized child windows by stacking their window headers along the main window's bottom border. This replaces the window icons displayed under Windows 3.1.

Listing 15-1 shows the MDIDemo application's Child.Pas module. In this demonstration, the child window displays no real data, so the module is simplistic. However, it shows the bare-minimum procedures a child window typically provides.

Listing 15-1
MDIDemo\Child.Pas

```pascal
unit Child;

interface

uses
  SysUtils, WinTypes, WinProcs, Messages, Classes, Graphics, Controls,
  Forms, Dialogs;

type
  TChildForm = class(TForm)
    procedure FormClose(Sender: TObject; var Action: TCloseAction);
  private
  {- Private declarations }
  public
  {- Public declarations }
    procedure LoadData(const FileName: String); virtual;
    procedure SaveData(const FileName: String); virtual;
  end;

var
  ChildForm: TChildForm;

implementation

{$R *.DFM}

procedure TChildForm.FormClose(Sender: TObject;
  var Action: TCloseAction);
begin
  Action := caFree;
end;

procedure TChildForm.LoadData(const FileName: String);
begin
  ShowMessage('LoadData from ' + FileName);
  Caption := LowerCase(FileName);
end;

procedure TChildForm.SaveData(const FileName: String);
begin
  ShowMessage('SaveData to ' + FileName);
  Caption := LowerCase(FileName);
end;

end.
```

These methods are virtual so another class can inherit and override them.

Disposes of the child window when it closes.

The child-window module can provide procedures to load and save document data. Procedures such as LoadData and SaveData are declared as public members of the TChildForm class. You make them public so the main module's *Open* and *Save* commands can call them.

The sample listing also declares LoadData and SaveData *virtual*. As a result, another module can inherit the TChildForm class and *override* the procedures. For example, you can add another child-window form to the program, and base the form's class on TChildForm rather than the usual TForm. You can then write LoadData and SaveData procedures for reading and writing the module's specific data. Inheriting a class is often called *subclassing a form,* a technique I'll demonstrate later in this chapter.

You should always provide an OnClose event handler for each type of child window. Set the Action parameter to caFree so the application disposes of the child window object when you close its window. If you don't set Action to caFree, closing the window minimizes it in the main window's client area.

In addition to OnClose, you may also want to write an OnClose-Query event handler to warn users when they close a window with unsaved data. In the procedure, set CanClose to False to prevent the window from closing; set CanClose to True if the window may close. See "Closing a Window" in Chapter 3 for more information about OnClose and OnCloseQuery events. MDI application main windows are not permitted to close, and thus the application will not end — unless all child windows can close.

MDIDemo's sample LoadData and SaveData procedures do not read or write any real files, so feel free to play with the program's *Open, Save,* and *Save as* commands. To confirm that the program calls the procedures at the proper times, ShowMessage displays a dialog with the current filename. Typically, when child windows display file documents, the LoadData and SaveData procedures should also assign the current filename to the child form's Caption.

You can easily modify MDIDemo to read and write real data. For example, insert a Memo object into the Child module's form. Set the Memo's Align property to alClient, select an appropriate font, delete "Memo1" from the Lines property, and set ScrollBars to ssBoth. In place of the ShowMessage statements from Listing 15-1, insert the following commands to read and write text files. You have just constructed an MDI text editor!

III

15

```
{- Replace ShowMessage statement in LoadData with: }
Memo1.Lines.LoadFromFile(FileName);

{- Replace ShowMessage statement in SaveData with: }
Memo1.Lines.SaveToFile(FileName);
```

Long path names can look messy in window Captions, and you may want to use the ExtractFileName function to assign to child window title bars filenames without the drive and path information. To do this, add SysUtils to the module's *uses* statement, and declare a String variable in the TChildForm class. Assign the full filename to the string variable for use in input and output statements, and assign to the window's Caption property the result of function ExtractFileName from the SysUtils unit. Look up "file-management routines" in Delphi's on-line help for more information on this and other file functions.

CREATING CHILD WINDOW INSTANCES

Listing 15-2 shows MDIDemo's TMainForm class declaration and the File menu's OnClick event handlers. This portion of the listing demonstrates how to create new instances of the TChildForm class.

Because MDIDemo's main module is lengthy, I'll present it in pieces. To inspect the full listing, load the MDIDemo project into Delphi.

The CreateChild procedure, declared privately to the TMainForm class, creates instances of the TChildForm class. Privately declared items are accessible only from methods in the class. This helps ensure that other modules do not indiscriminately call procedures and functions that perform critical services. The CreateChild procedure also shows how to create a form object at runtime. To do that, declare a variable of the class type:

```
var
   Child: TChildForm;
```

Next, in the procedure body, call the class's Create method with Application as an argument. Assign the resulting object to the variable:

```
Child := TChildForm.Create(Application);
```

Listing 15-2

MDIDemo's File menu OnClick event handlers.

```
unit Main;

interface

uses
  SysUtils, WinTypes, WinProcs, Messages, Classes, Graphics, Controls,
  Forms, Dialogs, Menus, Child, About;

type
  TMainForm = class(TForm)
    MainMenu1: TMainMenu;
    FileMenu: TMenuItem;
    FileOpen: TMenuItem;
    FileSave: TMenuItem;
    FileSaveAs: TMenuItem;
    FileNew: TMenuItem;
    N1: TMenuItem;
    FileExit: TMenuItem;
    WindowMenu: TMenuItem;
    WindowCascade: TMenuItem;
    WindowTile: TMenuItem;
    WindowArrangeIcons: TMenuItem;
    N2: TMenuItem;
    WindowCloseAll: TMenuItem;
    WindowMinimizeAll: TMenuItem;
    HelpMenu: TMenuItem;
    HelpAbout: TMenuItem;
    OpenDialog: TOpenDialog;
    FileClose: TMenuItem;
    N3: TMenuItem;
    SaveDialog: TSaveDialog;
    procedure FileNewClick(Sender: TObject);
    procedure FileOpenClick(Sender: TObject);
    procedure FileCloseClick(Sender: TObject);
    procedure FileSaveClick(Sender: TObject);
    procedure FileSaveAsClick(Sender: TObject);
    procedure FileExitClick(Sender: TObject);
    procedure WindowCascadeClick(Sender: TObject);
    procedure WindowTileClick(Sender: TObject);
    procedure WindowArrangeIconsClick(Sender: TObject);
    procedure WindowMinimizeAllClick(Sender: TObject);
    procedure WindowCloseAllClick(Sender: TObject);
    procedure HelpAboutClick(Sender: TObject);
    procedure FileMenuClick(Sender: TObject);
    procedure WindowMenuClick(Sender: TObject);
  private
  {- Private declarations }
    procedure CreateChild(const Name: string);
  public
  {- Public declarations }
  end;
```

Add the Child unit to the Main Module's uses statements so the program can construct child-window objects.

III

15

```
var
  MainForm: TMainForm;

implementation

{$R *.DFM}

const
  maxChildren = 10;  { Optional: No maximum required }

procedure TMainForm.CreateChild(const Name: String);
var
  Child: TChildForm;
begin
  Child := TChildForm.Create(Application);
  Child.Caption := Name;
end;
```

These statements declare and create a new child window object of the TChild-Form class, declared in the Child unit.

```
procedure TMainForm.FileNewClick(Sender: TObject);
begin
  CreateChild('Untitled' + IntToStr(MDIChildCount + 1));
end;


procedure TMainForm.FileOpenClick(Sender: TObject);
begin
  if OpenDialog.Execute then
  begin
    CreateChild(Lowercase(OpenDialog.FileName));
    with ActiveMDIChild as TChildForm do
      LoadData(OpenDialog.FileName);
  end;
end;


procedure TMainForm.FileCloseClick(Sender: TObject);
begin
  if ActiveMDIChild <> nil then
    ActiveMDIChild.Close;
end;
```

If not nil, ActiveMDIChild refers to the current child window object.

```
procedure TMainForm.FileSaveClick(Sender: TObject);
begin
  if Pos('Untitled', ActiveMDIChild.Caption) = 1 then
    FileSaveAsClick(Sender)
  else with ActiveMDIChild as TChildForm do
    SaveData(Caption);
end;
```

```
procedure TMainForm.FileSaveAsClick(Sender: TObject);
var
  FExt: String[4];
begin
  with SaveDialog do
  begin
    FileName := ActiveMDIChild.Caption;
    FExt := ExtractFileExt(FileName);
    if Length(FExt) = 0 then
      FExt := '.*';
    Filter := 'Files (*' + FExt + ')|*' + FExt;
    if Execute then
    with ActiveMDIChild as TChildForm do
      SaveData(FileName);
  end;
end;

procedure TMainForm.FileExitClick(Sender: TObject);
begin
  Close;
end;
```

A window caption is a handy place to store a filename.

NOTE The reason for passing Application, and not MainForm, to Create is because Application represents the MDI's frame window, which is the *real* window that owns the child window. MainForm is a kind of stepparent.

The program's *File|New* event handler, procedure FileNewClick, calls CreateChild. The *File|Open* handler does the same, but also calls the Child.Pas module's LoadData public procedure. However, these are only suggested techniques for constructing child windows and loading data from files; and you are free to code the modules as you want.

Use the MainForm object's ActiveMDIChild property to perform operations on the current child window. This property equals *nil* if there are no child windows, and you should always check for this condition before using the property. For example, the sample program's *File|Close* event handler, procedure FileCloseClick, closes the active child window with the statement:

```
if ActiveMDIChild <> nil then
  ActiveMDIChild.Close;
```

Never use an unrestricted statement such as the following, which will generate an exception if there are no child windows. This happens because the statement may attempt to call a method (Close) for a *nil* reference:

```
ActiveMDIChild.Close;  { ??? }
```

III

15

TIP

As I suggested, the child module should perform its own data-save verification in OnClose and OnCloseQuery event handlers. The window will not actually close unless the child object verifies that it *can* close — an example of sound object-oriented programming.

MainForm's FileSaveClick and FileSaveAsClick procedures call the SaveData procedure for the active child-window object. If the window caption is *Untitled*, FileSaveClick defaults to FileSaveAsClick; otherwise, the code calls SaveData with the current filename, picked up from the window caption. FileSaveAsClick uses the technique suggested in Chapter 12 to limit SaveDialog files to those with the same extension as the current window's.

Finally in this portion of the listing, the MainForm's *File|Exit* event handler, procedure FileExitClick, simply calls Close. It can do this because the parent object will attempt to close and free all of its child windows. However, the application will end only if all children can close.

WINDOW MENU COMMANDS

Most MDI applications provide a Window menu, which performs operations on child windows such as cascading, tiling, and arranging icons in the main window's client area. Listing 15-3 shows MDIDemo's Window menu OnClick event handlers, and also demonstrates how to write custom window commands such as *Close all,* which Delphi doesn't provide.

Listing 15-3
MDIDemo's Window menu OnClick event handlers.

```
procedure TMainForm.WindowCascadeClick(Sender: TObject);
begin
  Cascade;
end;

procedure TMainForm.WindowTileClick(Sender: TObject);
begin
  Tile;
end;

procedure TMainForm.WindowArrangeIconsClick(Sender: TObject);
begin
  ArrangeIcons;
end;
```

```
procedure TMainForm.WindowMinimizeAllClick(Sender: TObject);
var
  I: Integer;
begin
  for I := MDIChildCount - 1 downto 0 do
    MDIChildren[I].WindowState := wsMinimized;
end;

procedure TMainForm.WindowCloseAllClick(Sender: TObject);
var
  I: Integer;
begin
  for I := 0 to MDIChildCount - 1 do
    MDIChildren[I].Close;
end;
```

The first three procedures implement the standard Window menu commands, *Cascade, Tile,* and *Arrange icons.* Because these are so common, the TForm class provides the necessary code in its Cascade, Tile, and ArrangeIcons methods. Simply call these methods in response to the appropriate menu commands. You may also call these methods at other times — for example, in response to a toolbar SpeedButton's OnClick event.

Two other standard commands you can add to the Window menu are *Next* and *Previous.* Simply call the main form's Next and Previous methods. However, you may want to disable these commands if there's only one window using statements such as the following in the Window menu's OnClick event handler (assume WindowNext and WindowPrevious are TMenuItem objects):

```
WindowNext.Enabled := MDIChildCount > 1;
WindowPrevious.Enabled := WindowNext.Enabled;
```

In addition to standard Window menu commands, you can write new commands to perform operations on all child windows. For example, MDIDemo implements a *Window|Minimize all* command with this *for* loop:

```
for I := MDIChildCount - 1 downto 0 do
  MDIChildren[I].WindowState := wsMinimized;
```

To make the icons come out in a sensible order, the *for* loop counts down from the last child window to the first. Use the main-window form's MDIChildren array to access each child window. The array's elements are of type TForm, so unless you are using an inherited method or property such as WindowState as shown here, you'll need to use a type-cast expression to call methods and use properties in your child-window class. For example, the following calls a fictitious YourMethod procedure for the first child window:

```
if MDIChildCount > 0 then
  TChildForm(MDIChildren[0]).YourMethod;
```

Alternatively, use a *with* statement such as this:

```
if MDIChildCount > 0 then
with MDIChildren[0] as TChildForm do
  YourMethod;
```

A properly designed MDI application should always check whether there's at least one child-window object before performing actions through the MDIChildren array. Either check whether MDIChildCount is greater than zero, or test whether ActiveMDIChild is not *nil*.

Although not all MDI applications provide a *Window|Close all* command, maybe they should. I tend to open lots of windows as I work on various projects, and it's helpful to have a method for shutting down all windows without having to close them one by one. MDIDemo performs this action in procedure WindowCloseAllClick, which executes the following *for* loop to close the windows in first-to-last order:

```
for I := MDIChildCount - 1 downto 0 do
  MDIChildren[I].Close;
```

Internally, MDIChildren is implemented as a TList object, and therefore, it is permissible to perform operations such as the preceding that affect the number of child windows.

Miscellaneous MDI Commands

Listing 15-4 shows the remainder of MDIDemo's Main.Pas source code module.

Listing 15-4

MDIDemo's miscellaneous procedures.

```
procedure TMainForm.HelpAboutClick(Sender: TObject);
begin
  AboutForm.ShowModal;
end;

procedure TMainForm.FileMenuClick(Sender: TObject);
begin
  FileNew.Enabled := MDIChildCount < maxChildren;
  FileOpen.Enabled := FileNew.Enabled;
  FileClose.Enabled := MDIChildCount > 0;
  FileSave.Enabled := FileClose.Enabled;
  FileSaveAs.Enabled := FileClose.Enabled;
end;

procedure TMainForm.WindowMenuClick(Sender: TObject);
var
  I: Integer;
begin
  with WindowMenu do
  for I := 0 to Count - 1 do
    with Items[I] as TMenuItem do
      Enabled := MDIChildCount > 0;
end;

end.
```

The HelpAboutClick procedure displays the program's About box dialog, which isn't shown here. Procedures FileMenuClick and Window-MenuClick are the OnClick event handlers for the FileMenu and Window-Menu objects. The program calls these procedures when users open the menus. The procedures enable and disable commands based on program conditions. For example, *File\New* is disabled when MDIChildCount equals maxChildren, which effectively limits the number of child windows that users can open. All Window menu commands are disabled when there are no child windows. If you add Next and Previous commands as suggested, you should enable them separately if MDIChildCount is greater than one.

You don't have to limit the number of child windows. I included this feature in MDIDemo just to show the programming. MDI applications may have as many child windows as memory and other resources allow.

DIFFERENT-TYPE CHILD WINDOWS

An MDI application's child windows may be of different types. For each type of child window, simply add a new form to the project, and add programming to the main module to construct window instances. For example, try the following steps to add to MDIDemo a child window that can display bitmap files.

NOTE ▶ To follow along and preserve the original program, copy the following files from the MDIDemo directory to a blank directory: About.Dfm, About.Pas, Child.Dfm, Child.Pas, Main.Dfm, Main.Pas, Mdidemo.Dpr.

Open the Mdidemo project file in the new directory, and then perform the following steps:

1. Add another module to MDIDemo by selecting *File/New Form* or clicking the *New Form* SpeedButton. Choose *Blank form* from the *Browse Gallery* dialog.

2. Set the new form's Name property to ChildBmpForm. Set FormStyle to fsMDIChild. Choose *Options|Project* to move ChildBmpForm from the list of *Auto-create forms* to the list of *Available forms.*

3. Save the project, and when prompted, name the unit module Childbmp.Pas.

4. Select the ChildBmp form, and create a handler for its OnClose event. Assign caFree to Action. (Use Listing 15-1 as a guide.) This frees the form object when you close the child window. If you don't perform this step, closing the window minimizes it in the main window's client area.

5. Insert an Image component object from the Additional palette to the ChildBmp form. Set the Image1 object's Align property to alClient and its Stretch property to True.

6. In the ChildBmp unit, add Child into the *uses* statement and change the TChildBmpForm's base class from TForm to TChildForm. This causes TChildBmpForm to inherit the properties and methods from TChildForm, a technique often called *subclassing a form.* TChildBmpForm's class declaration should look like this:

```
TChildBmpForm = class(TChildForm)
```

7. Add LoadData and SaveData procedures to the TChildBmpForm class. Designate the procedures with the *override* directive, which tells Delphi to replace the virtual methods inherited from TChild-Form. Listing 15-5 shows the completed source code. Use the listing as a guide to constructing your module.

8. Finally, reprogram the main module to construct instances of the bitmap child class. Add ChildBmp to the Main module's *uses* statement, and rewrite the CreateChild procedure as shown in Listing 15-6. Press F9 to compile and run the modified program. Open a bitmap file. (If you added a Memo object to the Child module as suggested, you can also open text files.) The program constructs the proper type of window based on the filename extension.

Listings 15-5 and 15-6 are not on the CD-ROM. Follow the preceding steps to create the new child-window module, and use the listings printed here as guides to programming MDIDemo's ChildBmp and Main modules.

Listing 15-5

The completed ChildBmp module source code. This listing is not on the CD-ROM — use it as a guide to adding a bitmap child-window module to the MDIDemo application.

```
unit Childbmp;

interface

uses
  SysUtils, WinTypes, WinProcs, Messages, Classes, Graphics, Controls,
  Forms, Dialogs, Child, ExtCtrls;

type
  TChildBmpForm = class(TChildForm)
    Image1: TImage;
    procedure FormClose(Sender: TObject; var Action: TCloseAction);
  private
  {- Private declarations }
  public
  {- Public declarations }
    procedure LoadData(const FileName: String); override;
    procedure SaveData(const FileName: String); override;
  end;
```

Use override directives to replace inherited virtual methods.

```
var
  ChildBmpForm: TChildBmpForm;

implementation

{$R *.DFM}

procedure TChildBmpForm.FormClose(Sender: TObject;
  var Action: TCloseAction);
begin
  Action := caFree;
end;

procedure TChildBmpForm.LoadData(const FileName: String);
begin
  Image1.Picture.LoadFromFile(FileName);
  Caption := LowerCase(FileName);
end;

procedure TChildBmpForm.SaveData(const FileName: String);
begin
  Image1.Picture.SaveToFile(FileName);
  Caption := LowerCase(FileName);
end;

end.
```

The replacemeht methods load and save graphics files.

Listing 15-6

The Main module's reprogrammed CreateChild procedure for the modified MDIDemo application. Also add ChildBmp to the module's uses statement. This listing is not on the CD-ROM.

```
procedure TMainForm.CreateChild(const Name: String);
var
  Child: TChildForm;
  FExt: String[4];
begin
  FExt := ExtractFileExt(Name);
  if FExt = '.bmp' then
    Child := TChildBmpForm.Create(Application)
  else
    Child := TChildForm.Create(Application);
  Child.Caption := Name;
end;
```

In the new CreateChild procedure, if the file extension is .Bmp, the program constructs a TChildBmpForm child window; otherwise, it constructs a TChildForm object. Because LoadData and SaveData are virtual procedures (refer to Listings 15-1 and 15-5), the type of child window object determines what type of data is loaded.

To better understand the value of using virtual methods in subclassed forms, see the Main module's FileOpenClick procedure in Listing 15-2. If the child window is a TChildForm object, the procedure calls the original LoadData procedure. If the window is a TChildBmpForm object, the procedure calls the overridden method. These calls are directed not by explicit code in the program, but by the *types* of child-window objects referenced by ActiveMDIChild. This is sound object-oriented programming — the child-window objects determine the kind of data that is appropriate to load and save.

Because of the program's object-oriented design, it's relatively easy to add other types of child windows. Simply create and program a new form module as you did TChildBmpForm. Derive the new form class from TChildForm, and write LoadData and SaveData procedures. Modify CreateChild in the Main module to construct instances of your new class, and you're done.

MERGING MENUS

Especially in MDI applications with multiple types of child windows, you may want to modify menu commands, or even add menus, depending on which type of child window is active. This is easy to do, but requires attention to some details that may not be obvious.

In the parent window — the one with FormStyle set to fsMDIForm — the MainMenu object should contain global commands that apply generally to all child windows. For example, the parent window's menu normally provides a *Window* menu with *Cascade, Tile,* and other commands that affect all windows, regardless of type. The main window's menu should also have commands such as *File | New, File | Open,* and *File | Close* that open and close child windows.

In each child window that requires unique commands, or that needs to change menu items based on various conditions, you can insert another MainMenu object. I like to name these objects according to the module — ChildFormMenu or ChildBmpFormMenu, for example. Insert commands into these MainMenu objects for merging with the parent window's menu.

Menu merging in MDI applications is automatic for any child window that has a MainMenu object. For this reason, you should set all MainMenu objects' AutoMerge properties to False. Technically speaking, only the parent window's AutoMerge property *must* be False. Child window Main-Menu AutoMerge values are ignored, but set them all False anyway.

NOTE See Chapter 5 for instructions on merging menus in nonMDI applications. Only nonMDI applications use the AutoMerge property.

Next, assign GroupIndex values to specific menu items. These values determine where to insert menus and whether to replace a menu item or add new commands. When merging, the application uses GroupIndex values according to the following rules:

- Menu items with the same GroupIndex values are replaced. For example, if a MainMenu item has a GroupIndex of 10, any menu items in a child window's MainMenu with that same GroupIndex replace the parent items.

- Menu items with unique GroupIndex values are inserted. Assign higher values to insert menu items in the child window to the right of lower-valued items in the parent. Assign lower values to insert menu items to the left of parent items.

In addition to merging menus, you can also call TMenuItem methods to enable and disable menu items, to insert or change commands, and to perform other menu tricks. For example, a child-window can add a check mark to an *Options|Save* command with a statement such as this:

```
MainForm.OptionsSave.Checked := True;
```

The trick here is gaining access to the MainForm object from inside the child module. Do that by adding Main (or another unit name) to a *uses* clause in the child module. To prevent a circular reference, you must do this in the child's implementation, not in the *uses* clause in the interface part. Because the Main module's *uses* already refers to the child module; referring back to Main in the child causes the circular reference, which Object Pascal does not allow. In the child module, locate the *implementation* keyword and form-loading directive, and add a *uses* clause as shown here. You can then access menu items in the MainForm object:

```
implementation
{$R *.DFM}
uses Main;
```

Circular unit references occur when two modules — call them Chicken and Egg — refer to each other in their interface sections' *uses* statements. Object Pascal does not permit this because of the possibility that module Chicken will use a declaration from module Egg, which might require a declaration from module Chicken. To resolve the Chicken-and-Egg paradox, add the secondary module to a *uses* statement in the primary module's interface section; add the primary module to a *uses* statement in the secondary module's implementation section. Unit *interfaces* may not circularly refer to each other, but their *implementations* may do so without restriction.

Other MDI Techniques

Following are some other MDI techniques you might find useful.

CLIENT AND FRAME WINDOWS

It may be necessary at times to gain access to the MDI application's client and frame windows. You probably won't need to use these techniques unless you call Windows API functions that require window handles. Delphi's TForm class should provide adequate services for most MDI applications.

Use the ClientHandle property in the main form object to refer to the client window. In classic MDI programming, this window provides global operations — such as message handling — that apply to all child windows.

The ClientHandle value, of type HWnd (window handle), is valid only in forms with FormStyle set to fsMDIForm.

You can refer to the frame window by using the main form's Handle property. This value always references the window handle of the form in both MDI and nonMDI applications. In a form with FormStyle equal to fsMDIForm, the Handle property refers to the MDI frame window.

USING THE **MDI** APPLICATION TEMPLATE

For rapid programming of MDI prototypes, select *MDI Application* from the *Browse Gallery* dialog's *Templates* page tab when you begin a new project. If you don't see this dialog, select *Options|Environment,* and enable the *Gallery* check box, *Use on New Project.*

Create a fresh directory to hold the files this option generates. When the template prompts you, change to the fresh directory. Delphi will then construct an MDI application with a status panel, a toolbar, and a menu with *File, Edit, Window,* and *Help* items. Figure 15-2 shows the resulting form window.

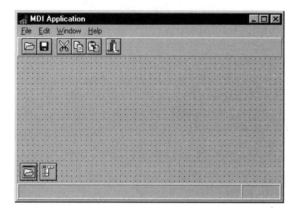

Figure 15-2
The MDI Application template creates a form with a status panel, a toolbar, and a main menu.

The following notes will help you get started using the MDI Application template:

- The ChildWin.Pas module declares the TMDIChild class. You might add LoadData and SaveData procedures to this class, or you can read and write data in the Main module. If there's only one type of child window in your application, you can add the programming to Main; otherwise, make each window class responsible for its own input and output, and base additional window classes on TMDIChild.

- By default, the Application is named MDIApp. To rename it, select *File|Save Project as,* and enter a new file name. Save and compile the project. You can then delete all Mdiapp.* files from the project directory.

- The Main.Pas module declares the TMainForm class. Hint: Review the class declarations in this module for various object names. Some names, such as Edit1 are defaults; others, such as SaveBtn, are named according to use. The template's naming conventions are not the same as the applications in this book. You may change them, but if you do so, you must change them *every* place they occur. It is not enough, for example, to change an object's Name property — you must also globally search and replace that object name in any statements that refer to it. Delphi automatically updates only object name *declarations;* it does not search for and replace object names used in statements.

- Select *View|Project Manager* and highlight ChildWin to open the child window's unit and form. You can then insert any objects you want into the child-window, create a merged menu, and write code for child window commands.

- In the Main module, add data-loading statements to procedure FileOpenItemClick. As I mentioned, you can read files directly, or you might call a LoadData procedure for the ActiveMDIChild window.

- Insert a SaveDialog object into the main form, and write code to save data in the FileSaveItemClick and FileSaveAsItemClick procedures. Or, you might call a SaveData procedure that you add to the child window class.

- Optionally program Cut, Copy, and Paste commands by calling clipboard procedures. For example, you can insert a Memo object into the ChildWin form, and call the object's CutToClipboard method. See Chapter 16 for more information on clipboard programming.

- Insert an OnCloseQuery event handler into the ChildWin module. Set CanClose to False to prevent users from closing windows without saving changes.

Summary

- MDI applications use Delphi's TForm component, which is not on the VCL palette, to construct main and child windows. The main window takes the place of the frame and client windows used in classic Windows programming.

- Every MDI application has three basic parts: a main-window form, one or more document child-window forms, and a main menu. Use the main form's WindowMenu property to designate a top-level menu item for listing window titles.

- Set the main form's FormStyle property to fsMDIForm. There can be only one such form per application. In all child windows, set Form-Style to fsMDIChild. You may create as many types of child windows as your application needs.

- To construct a child window at runtime, call the window class's Create method. Pass Application to Create's parent-object parameter.

- Every child window should implement OnClose and OnCloseQuery event handlers. Use these events to warn users about unsaved data when they attempt to close windows.

- The main form's ActiveMDIChild property refers to the current child window. If this property is *nil,* there are no child windows. Always check whether ActiveMDIChild is *nil* before using this property to call methods and assign property values.

- The main form's MDIChildCount property equals the number of child windows. If MDIChildCount is zero, there are no child windows.

- The MDIChildren array provides indexed access to all child windows owned by the application.

- Child-window MainMenu objects automatically merge with the main form's MainMenu. Use the GroupIndex property to control merging.

- The main form's Handle refers to the MDI application's frame window. The ClientHandle property refers to the client window. Most MDI applications do not need to use these properties.

- Use the MDI Application project template to rapidly create MDI projects with default menus, a toolbar, and a status line.

Projects to Try

15-1: Add a metafile child window to MDIDemo.

15-2: Write a file-view application that works with a variety of file types.

15-3: Design a *File|Save all* command that calls a virtual SaveData procedure in a child-window class.

15-4: *Advanced.* Add a *Window|Restore* command to the MDIDemo application. The command should restore child windows to their former positions and sizes following a *Tile, Cascade,* or *Minimize all* command. *Remember to use object-oriented programming.* Child window objects should be able to restore *themselves* to a saved position and size. Don't burden the parent; put your kids to work.

15-5: Write an MDI text editor using the MDI Application template. The results don't have to be fancy, but the exercise will help you understand various template conventions.

15-6: *Advanced.* Convert MDIDemo into an improved MDI Application template. Insert virtual methods such as LoadData and SaveData in the TChildForm class. Don't create objects of that class; instead, subclass new forms based on TChildForm, and write LoadData and SaveData replacement procedures to read and write specific types of files. Ideally, to program a new application, you will simply add a new child-window form, write LoadData and SaveData procedures, and construct child instances in the main module.

Expert-User Tips

- Only one window in an MDI application may have its FormStyle set to fsMDIForm. This window must be the application's main window, selected with *Options|Project.*

- If creating a child window causes a GPF (general protection fault), the form's FormStyle property is probably not set correctly. All child-window forms must have their FormStyle property set to fsMDIChild. The program's main window must have its FormStyle set to fsMDIForm, and only one window per application may have that setting.

- If you don't want a child window to automatically appear when you run the application, choose *Project|Options* and move the child window to the list of *Available forms*. However, there is nothing technically wrong with having the application automatically create the first child window. For example, an MDI text editor could offer users a blank window at startup. The application could create additional child windows as explained in this chapter — only the first window is automatically constructed.

- If closing an MDI application's child-window causes it to minimize to an icon (or a title bar in Windows 95), make sure the child-window module has an OnClose event handler that sets Action to caFree. If you don't assign this value to Action, the application will not free the child window object when the window closes. This is not an error, however, and it can be a useful design technique. For example, the Windows 3.1 Program Manager minimizes its program group windows when you close them and when you click their minimize buttons.

- When constructing forms and other objects at runtime (such as the TChildForm objects in this chapter), remember to assign the constructed object instance into the instance variable — don't call the Create method using the uninitialized instance variable. For example, this is a typical error:

```
var
  Child: TChildForm;
begin
  Child.Create(Application);
  ...
```

The faulty statement literally attempts to have the child give birth to itself, which, fortunately for the world's population, even real children cannot do. The statement will always cause a general protection fault (GPF) because Child has not been initialized, and calling an uninitialized object's methods is a programming error (though not a compiling error). Use the following code to call the *class* Create method, and assign the resulting object to the Child reference:

```
var
  Child: TChildForm;
begin
  Child := TChildForm.Create(Application);
```

- You are not required to save references to child-window objects. Merely creating a child instance with Application as the parent constructs the child window. The parent is responsible for maintaining and freeing the resulting objects. As a demonstration of this principle, you can shorten the CreateChild procedure in MDIDemo's Main module to the following. However, this makes it more difficult to perform operations on newborn children such as assigning Caption strings:

```
procedure TMainForm.CreateChild(const Name: String);
begin
  TChildForm.Create(Application);
end;
```

- In MDI applications with multiple types of child windows, name the unit modules ChildXXX.Pas, where XXX is the document filename extension. For example, use Childtxt.Pas for .Txt files or Childbmp.Pas for .Bmp files. Of course, you can name the modules as you want, but this is a useful convention for identifying modules by their file types.

- Menu merging is automatic in MDI applications. Set all MainMenu AutoMerge properties to False. The parent MDI window's AutoMege property *must* be False. Use the AutoMerge property to perform menu merging only in non MDI applications.

- Avoid dropping components into the MDI main form. Lightweight controls like TLabel won't be drawn at all, and normal window handle controls (like TButton) might not work correctly when dropped into the client area of an MDI main form. This is due to quirks in the Windows MDI interface. Top- or bottom-aligned TPanels, however, are acceptable. Insert other control objects into child-window forms.

Coming Up

Transferring data from one application to another is one of the murkiest subjects in Windows programming. The next chapter will help you wade through the swamplands of clipboard, DDE, and OLE data transfer techniques.

Developing Data Transfer, DDE, and OLE Applications

*S*haring data among applications is like making a horse drink water. You can lead your code to a multitasking environment, but it will take some extra coaxing to make it share information with other programs.

Windows provides three basic methods for sharing data: the clipboard, dynamic data exchange (DDE), and object linking and embedding (OLE). Which method to use depends on your application's needs and the type of data you have to share. In this chapter, I'll explain how to use the clipboard to transfer text and graphics, how to use DDE to establish links with programs such as Microsoft Excel and Word, and how to link and embed OLE objects in Delphi applications.

Components

- DdeClientConv — A DDE client application (an application that receives data from a DDE server) uses this component to establish a link, called a conversation, with the server. Every client application has at least one of these objects. Palette: System.

- DdeClientItem — In addition to a DdeClientConv object, a DDE client application uses one or more DdeClientItem objects as containers that receive data from the server. Every client application has at least one of these objects for each DdeClientConv object. Palette: System.

- DdeServerConv — A DDE server application (an application that sends data to a DDE client) can use this component to originate a DDE conversation. Most server applications use at least one of these objects, but it is possible to originate a conversation without the DdeServerConv component. Palette: System.

- DdeServerItem — A DDE server application uses one or more of these objects to send data to the client. The DdeServerItem object may or may not be associated with a DdeServerConv object, but it usually is. Palette: System.

- OleContainer — Use this object to construct an OLE container application that can hold objects from OLE servers. For example, using OleContainer, your application documents can combine Excel spreadsheets, Word documents, and Visio Express drawings. Users can edit data in these objects directly from your application. Palette: System.

Clipboard Transfers

As most Windows users know, an *Edit* menu's *Cut, Copy,* and *Paste* commands transfer data to and from the Windows clipboard. The most common use for these commands is probably for shuffling text between applications, or even within the same program.

Delphi's Edit, MaskEdit, and Memo components (as well as the database components TDBEdit, TDBImage, and TDBMemo) support single-statement clipboard transfers. Call methods CutToClipboard, CopyToClipboard, and PasteToClipboard to transfer object data. For example, to cut selected text from a Memo component, use the statement:

```
Memo1.CutToClipboard;
```

The other two procedures are equally simple to use:

```
Memo1.CopyToClipboard;
Memo1.PasteFromClipboard;
```

For text-based components, only *selected* text is copied or cut to the clipboard. To copy or cut all of an object's text, call Memo1.SelectAll before performing the clipboard operation.

The TClipboard Class

To cut, copy, and paste other kinds of data, use the TClipboard class in the Clipbrd unit (note the abbreviated spelling). Because TClipboard is not a component on the VCL palette, to use the class, you must add the unit's name to the module's *uses* clause:

```
uses
    SysUtils, WinTypes, WinProcs, Messages, Classes, Graphics,
    Controls, Forms, Dialogs, Clipbrd;
```

TCLIPBOARD PROPERTIES

The TClipboard class provides the following properties:

- *AsText* — Use this string property to copy and paste text to and from the clipboard. To copy a string to the clipboard, simply assign a Pascal string to AsText. To receive a string, use AsText in a statement. Because AsText is a Pascal String, its length is limited to 255 characters. To read and write lengthier clipboard text, use the SetTextBuf and GetTextBuf TClipboard methods. If the clipboard has text, the following expression is true:

```
Clipboard.HasFormat(cf_Text)
```

- F*ormatCount* — This integer property equals the number of elements in the Formats array. Valid array index expressions range from *Formats[0]* to *Formats[FormatCount −1]*.

- *Formats* — An array of Word values that represent the clipboard's registered data types, or *formats*. The FormatCount property equals the number of elements in the Formats array. Table 16-1 lists standard clipboard format constants from WinTypes.Pas.

ADDITIONAL FORMATS

The Clipbrd unit registers two additional clipboard formats from the standards listed in Table 16-1. The unit does this by executing these statements in any program that uses Clipbrd:

```
cf_Picture := RegisterClipboardFormat('Delphi Picture');
cf_Component := RegisterClipboardFormat('Delphi Component');
```

III

16

Table 16-1

Clipboard Formats from WinTypes.Pas.

Constant	Format Value
cf_Text	1
cf_Bitmap	2
cf_MetaFilePict	3
cf_SYLK	4
cf_DIF	5
cf_TIFF	6
cf_OEMText	7
cf_DIB	8
cf_Palette	9
cf_PenData	10
cf_RIFF	11
cf_Wave	12

Use the cf_Picture and cf_Component variables along with the Clipboard's HasFormat function to determine if the clipboard currently contains a TGraphics picture (an icon, a bitmap, or a metafile) or a component object.

This is an example of registering a custom clipboard format, which you can do in your own applications. For example, use these techniques to register a special structure's format to transfer data of that type to other applications using the clipboard.

TCLIPBOARD METHODS

Call methods in the TClipboard class to cut, copy, and paste data, and also to perform miscellaneous clipboard operations. The Clipbrd unit provides a Clipboard object that's ready to use — you do not have to construct an object of the TClipboard class. Simply add Clipbrd to the module's *uses* directive, and call methods using statements such as:

```
if Clipboard.HasFormat(cf_Bitmap) then
  { ... copy bitmap from clipboard }
```

Following are brief descriptions of key TClipboard methods:

- *Assign* — To copy graphics to the clipboard, pass to Assign any TGraphic, TBitmap, TPicture, or TMetafile object or object property.

- *Clear* — Clears any data in the clipboard. You don't usually have to call this method because assigning new information to the clipboard performs an automatic Clear.

- *Close* — Closes the clipboard following a call to Open. Each Open statement should have a corresponding Close. You don't have to call Open and Close unless you access the clipboard by calling Windows API functions. Methods in the Clipboard object open and close the clipboard automatically as needed.

- *GetAsHandle* — Returns a Windows handle to clipboard data. Use this only if you need to call Windows API functions that require handles, or when converting conventionally written programs to Delphi. Most applications don't need to use this function.

- *GetComponent* — Retrieves a Delphi component object from the clipboard. For more information on using GetComponent and Set-Component see, "Component Objects and the Clipboard," in this chapter.

- *GetTextBuf* — Apparently undocumented, this function retrieves text from the clipboard as a null-terminated buffer. Use this function only when text lengths exceed 255 characters; otherwise, you can more simply use the AsText property to retrieve clipboard text. See "Text and the Clipboard" in this chapter for more information on using GetTextBuf and SetTextBuf.

- *HasFormat* — Returns True if the clipboard has data in the format specified by a Word argument passed to HasFormat. See Table 16-1 for standard constant values to use with this function. Always call HasFormat before copying information from the clipboard into an application object or other variable.

- *Open* — You need to open the clipboard only if you call Windows API functions to access the clipboard. All methods in the Clipboard object open the clipboard automatically as needed. Calling Open temporarily prevents other tasks from using the clipboard. Each call to Open should have a corresponding call to Close.

III

16

- *SetAsHandle* — Assigns data to the clipboard using a Windows handle. See GetAsHandle.

- *SetComponent* — Assigns a component object to the clipboard. See GetComponent.

- *SetTextBuf* — Assigns null-terminated text data to the clipboard. Use this function only with strings longer than 255 characters. To copy Pascal strings to the clipboard, assign them to the Clipboard's AsText property.

TEXT AND THE CLIPBOARD

Text-based components such as Memo and Edit support clipboard transfers with methods. Use the methods described in this section for other kinds of text such as string variables and large character buffers.

Call SetTextBuf to copy large text buffers to the clipboard. For example, if Buffer is a PChar pointer to a null-terminated string buffer, this statement copies the text to the clipboard:

```
Clipboard.SetTextBuf(Buffer);
```

To retrieve text from the clipboard, allocate memory for a buffer, and call the Clipboard's GetTextBuf function, which returns the number of characters copied:

```
Buffer := StrAlloc(1024);
Len := Clipboard.GetTextBuf(Buffer, 1024);
```

Unfortunately, GetTextBuf requires you to determine in advance the size of the text buffer, but the Clipbrd unit provides no method for determining that size. Follow these steps to try an alternate technique that works around this problem and shows another way to copy and paste clipboard text.

The following steps use a Memo component for convenience in demonstrating how to read and write null-terminated clipboard text buffers. You can more easily perform these operations for a Memo object by calling the CopyToClipboard, CutToClipboard, and PasteFromClipboard methods.

1. Start a new project, and add Clipbrd to the main form's *uses* directive.

2. Insert a Memo object into the form, and set the Memo's ScrollBars to ssBoth. Insert two Buttons, and change their Captions to Copy and Paste.

3. Double-click the Copy button to create a handler for its OnClick event. Insert the code from Listing 16-1 into the procedure.

4. Double-click the Paste button to create a handler for its OnClick event. Insert the code from Listing 16-2 into the procedure.

5. Run the test program and use the Windows Notepad utility to open a text file. Select all lines, and choose *Edit | Copy* to transfer the text to the clipboard. Switch back to the test program, and click the Paste button to copy the clipboard text to the Memo object. Select a portion of the text, and click Copy to copy the highlighted characters to the clipboard. Switch back to the Notepad, and choose *Edit | Paste* to confirm that the test program copied the selected text.

Listing 16-1

This OnClick event handler demonstrates how to use the Clipboard's Set-TextBuf method to copy a null-terminated string buffer to the clipboard.

```
{- Copy null-terminated text buffer to clipboard }
procedure TForm1.Button1Click(Sender: TObject);
var
  P: PChar;  { Pointer to character buffer }
begin
  with Memo1 do
  begin
    if SelLength = 0 then    { If no text selected, }
      SelectAll;             { select all lines of Memo1. }
    if SelLength = 0 then    { If still no text selected, }
      Exit;                  { Memo1 is empty—exit now. }
    P := StrAlloc(SelLength + 1); { Allocate char buffer }
    try
      GetTextBuf(P, SelLength + 1);  { Copy Memo1 text to buffer }
      Clipboard.SetTextBuf(P);  { Copy text buffer to clipboard }
    finally
      StrDispose(P);  { Dispose of character buffer }
    end;
  end;
end;
```

This step is optional but recommended.

Listing 16-2

This OnClick event handler demonstrates an alternative to the Clipboard's Get-TextBuf method, which requires you to determine the buffer size in advance.

```
{- Copy null-terminated text buffer from clipboard }
procedure TForm1.Button2Click(Sender: TObject);
var
  Data: THandle;
  DataPtr: PChar;
  P: PChar;
begin
  Clipboard.Open;
  try
    Data := GetClipboardData(cf_Text);
    if Data = 0 then Exit;
    DataPtr := GlobalLock(Data);
    try
      P := StrNew(DataPtr);
      Memo1.SetTextBuf(P);
    finally
      GlobalUnlock(Data);
      StrDispose(P);
    end;
  finally
    Clipboard.Close;
  end;
end;
```

Open the Clipboard and use it in a try block.

Close the Clipboard in a finally block to guard against any exceptions.

Listing 16-1 checks that the Memo1 object has some selected text — if not, the procedure calls SelectAll. This step is optional, but makes it easy to copy all of a document to the clipboard without requiring users to select every character. StrAlloc prepares a buffer into which Get-TextBuf copies the Memo1 object's text. The program then calls the Clipboard's SetTextBuf to copy that buffer to the Windows clipboard.

When performing memory allocations, it's always wise to insert subsequent statements into *try-finally* blocks. As Listing 16-1 demonstrates, the memory allocated to P is disposed by StrDispose regardless of whether any statement in the *try* block raises an exception.

Listing 16-2 works around the Clipboard's lack of a method for determining how much text the clipboard holds. Instead of calling Get-TextBuf to retrieve text from the clipboard, the procedure calls Windows API functions to obtain that data in raw, binary form via the Windows API function, GetClipboardData. The procedure's inner *try* block calls StrNew to allocate memory to a PChar pointer P, and then copy the clipboard data block as a null-terminated string to that memory. For demonstration only, the procedure passes the string to the Memo component.

When using the clipboard transfer method in Listing 16-2, you must call Open and Close as shown because the procedure bypasses the Clipboard object's methods.

GRAPHICS AND THE CLIPBOARD

Use the Clipboard's Assign method to cut, copy, and paste TGraphics. To demonstrate the technique, insert two Image objects and a Button into a form. Double-click the Button and type the following statements in the object's OnClick event handler. (You would normally perform these operations in separate places in the program, or in separate applications. For the demonstration, however, we'll perform both transfers at once.)

```
Clipboard.Assign(Image1.Picture);  { Copy to clipboard }
{... elsewhere or in another module }
if Clipboard.HasFormat(cf_Picture) then
  Image2.Picture.Assign(Clipboard);  { Copy from clipboard }
```

Select Image1 and use its Picture property to load an icon, a bitmap, or a Windows metafile. Run the program, and click the button to transfer the image from Image1 to Image2 via the Windows clipboard.

The first statement calls the Clipboard's Assign method to copy a TGraphics property (Image1.Picture) to the clipboard. The second statement calls the TGraphics object's Assign method, passing Clipboard as an argument. You may use Clipboard this way to receive graphics data. However, you should probably test whether the clipboard has data in the correct format. For example, to receive a bitmap image copied to the clipboard by another application such as the Windows Paint utility, use code such as:

```
if Clipboard.HasFormat(cf_Bitmap) then
  Image2.Picture.Bitmap.Assign(Clipboard)
else
  Image2.Picture.Bitmap.Assign(nil);
```

Using the Picture property allows the object to work with icon, bitmap, and metafile data. Calling Assign for a TBitmap object is more restrictive, but either technique is acceptable.

COMPONENT OBJECTS AND THE CLIPBOARD

Call the Clipboard's SetComponent method to copy any visual component object to the clipboard. Call the Clipboard's GetComponent method, in either the same or in another application, to paste a visual component object from the clipboard.

Internally, SetComponent and GetComponent use a memory stream to copy components to and from memory. To retrieve a component, in addition to calling GetComponent you have to register the component's class with Delphi's memory-streaming system. An example of component clipboard transfers will explain the basic techniques. Follow these steps:

1. Insert a Button and a ScrollBar (the object to be copied) into a form.

2. Create an OnClick event handler for the Button, and insert this statement to copy the ScrollBar object to the clipboard when you click the Button:

```
Clipboard.SetComponent(ScrollBar1);
```

3. Run the application and click the button. Then quit to get back to Delphi. Save the application.

4. Start a new project, and insert a Button object into the form. Create an OnClick event handler for the Button with the following statement:

```
if Clipboard.HasFormat(cf_Component) then
  Clipboard.GetComponent(Self, Self);
```

5. Move to the final *end* in the unit module, and insert the following initialization statement. The unit should end (including the final end with period) as shown here:

```
initialization
  RegisterClasses([TScrollBar]);
end.
```

6. Run the second application, and click the button to copy the Scroll-Bar object from the clipboard and paste it into the form. (If this doesn't work, you may have copied something else to the clipboard. In this case, rerun the first application, and then run the second.)

The Clipboard's GetComponent function requires two arguments that represent the pasted object's owner and parent. Although these are often the same, they might not be when you are pasting components into a container such as a GroupBox. In that case, the form is usually the owner and the GroupBox is the parent of the pasted object, and you might use code such as:

```
if Clipboard.HasFormat(cf_Component) then
  Clipboard.GetComponent(Self, GroupBox1);
```

TIP

In the preceding fragments, I assume the statements are in an event handler for the form or an object in that form, in which case, *Self* refers to the form object.

By the way, the preceding examples introduce a new keyword added to Delphi's Object Pascal. To perform initializations for any unit module one time when the application begins, insert statements between the keyword *initialization* and the final *end* and a period. This replaces the old style *begin-end* initialization section in units, which Delphi still supports. In new units, use the new format as shown here:

```
unit AnyUnit;
...
initialization { same as begin }
  { Statements to perform when application begins. }
end.
```

You may use *begin* or *initialization*, but the latter helps the compiler to locate mismatched pairs of *begin* and *end* keywords elsewhere in the module.

Dynamic Data Exchange (DDE)

The Windows clipboard works well enough, but it's as primitive as a cork bulletin board on which users cut, copy, and paste information by tacking up notes and tearing off phone-number tabs. Like a bulletin board, the clipboard requires its participants to voluntarily transfer information.

The Windows Dynamic Data Exchange (DDE) protocols work more like a modern bulletin board accessed over a network via modems. To

III

16

transfer data, two applications, known as the client and the server, start a *conversation* through which data may flow. After the applications establish a conversation, DDE transfers can occur automatically, or one application can request data from the other.

A DDE conversation takes two to tango. The data sender is called the *server application*. The data receiver is called the *client application*. If you find these terms confusing, just remember that the server *serves* data to *clients*. However, a DDE conversation is a two-way street, and during a conversation, data can flow in either direction, blurring the distinction between client and server.

DDE is suitable for dynamically updating information among multiple applications. For example, with DDE, you can write a program that automatically updates a graphic image as users enter data into a spreadsheet. Or, you might use DDE to construct multiple applications that share information.

DDE can help prevent destruction of data by inexperienced users. For example, you can write a client application to display the results of spreadsheet calculations. However, users cannot use the client application to modify the original spreadsheet formulas.

UNDERSTANDING DELPHI'S DDE COMPONENTS

Use Delphi's four DDE components — DdeClientConv, DdeClientItem, DdeServerConv, and DdeServerItem — to construct client and server applications that can communicate using DDE. *Conv* stands for *conversation,* which represents the established link between two DDE-aware tasks. You can start a DDE conversation when you design the application, or you can link a client and a server at runtime.

The DdeClientConv component operates something like a modem that receives a call from another computer. A client conversation object "picks up the phone" to establish a link with the remote system that originated the call. Most DDE applications need only one DdeClientConv object, although you may use multiple objects to establish more than one communication path.

The DdeClientItem component represents the data that comes in through the modem over the conversation path. An application that receives multiple types of data might have many DdeClientItem objects associated with the same DdeClientConv. However, a client application typically needs only one DdeClientConv and one associated DdeClient-Item object.

In the server application — in other words, the data sender — use a DdeServerConv object to initiate a conversation. You'll normally need only one DdeServerConv object per application, but you may use several to establish multiple conversations. Insert one or more DdeServerItem objects to represent the data to send to clients. Most DDE server applications need only one DdeServerConv and one associated DdeServerItem object.

To send and receive DDE information in the same application, insert DdeServer and DdeClient objects into the project's form window.

DDE CONVERSATION TERMS

Three terms define a DDE conversation and the data items that flow between two or more applications. These terms are:

- *Service* — Identifies the server, usually by its executable filename minus the .Exe extension. In some cases, however, a DDE Service is a different identifier. In a Delphi client application, the Service is always the server's filename minus .Exe.

- *Topic* — Identifies a unit of data such as a filename, or a window caption. There are no set rules about what a Topic means. In Delphi applications, however, a Topic is either the server application's main window caption, or the name of a DdeServerItem object in the server.

- *Item* — Identifies an element of text data sent by a server to a client application. The text may be any practical length, but most DDE transfers are small enough to fit in a Pascal string, which can hold up to 255 characters. For larger blocks of text, Delphi's DDE components represent Items as TStrings string-lists.

ESTABLISHING CLIENT/SERVER CONVERSATIONS

As an example of using DDE, in this section you'll construct simple client and server applications that transfer text between two Edit control objects. Typing data in the server's Edit window automatically updates

III
16

the client's Edit object. Typing in the client's Edit window does not update the server, an example of a typical one-way DDE conversation.

NOTE ▶ Listings of the programming in this and the next few sections are in the Dde1 subdirectory on the CD-ROM.

Unless you already have the server application (Excel, for example), it's usually best to develop the server before writing the client. At a minimum, a server application requires a DdeServerItem object and some data to send to clients. Follow these steps to create a simple server that sends an Edit object's text to a client application. I'll use default component object names, which will help clarify the relationships among the DDE objects.

1. Create a blank directory to hold the project files. Start a new project, and name the form ServerForm. Set the form's Caption to Server1.

2. Save the project in the blank directory. Name the unit module Server.Pas and the project Server1.Dpr.

3. Insert a DdeServerItem object from the System VCL palette into the form. The server sends data through this object. Also, insert Edit, Button, and BitBtn objects. Set Button1's Caption to *Edit Copy*. Change BitBtn1's Kind property to bkClose. Arrange and resize the form window to resemble Figure 16-1.

4. Create a handler for the Edit1 object's OnChange event. Insert the statement from Listing 16-3, procedure Edit1Change, to assign the Edit1 object's Text property to DdeServerItem1's Text. When Edit1's text changes, this sends the text to any client applications that have established a link with the server.

5. Create a handler for the Button1 object's OnClick event. Insert the statement from Listing 16-3, procedure Button1Click, to call DdeServerItem1's CopyToClipboard method. This informs client applications of the server's Service and Topic names. You'll use this information in writing the client application.

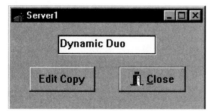

Figure 16-1

Server1's form window. Enter text into the Edit object to automatically update the Client1 application's Edit window. Instructions for constructing the Client1 project follow the Server.Pas listing.

III

16

Listing 16-3

Dde1\Server.Pas

```
unit Server;

interface

uses
  SysUtils, WinTypes, WinProcs, Messages, Classes, Graphics, Controls,
  Forms, Dialogs, StdCtrls, DdeMan, Buttons;

type
  TServerForm = class(TForm)
    DdeServerItem1: TDdeServerItem;
    Edit1: TEdit;
    Button1: TButton;
    BitBtn1: TBitBtn;
    procedure Edit1Change(Sender: TObject);
    procedure Button1Click(Sender: TObject);
  private
    { Private declarations }
  public
    { Public declarations }
  end;

var
  ServerForm: TServerForm;

implementation

{$R *.DFM}

procedure TServerForm.Edit1Change(Sender: TObject);
begin
  DdeServerItem1.Text := Edit1.Text;
end;
```

This sends a text string to a Dde client.

```
procedure TServerForm.Button1Click(Sender: TObject);
begin
  DdeServerItem1.CopyToClipboard;
end;

end.
```

I've been known to talk to myself, but my conversations tend to be more interesting when I chatter with at least one other person. Likewise, every Server application needs one or more clients to engage in a conversation and transmit data. Follow these steps to construct a client application to obtain text items from the server created in the preceding paragraphs. *In step 2, be sure to save the project files in the same directory as the server.*

1. Start a new project. Name the form ClientForm, and change its Caption to Client1.

2. Save the project in the directory that holds the Server1 project. Name the unit module Client.Pas and the project Client1.Dpr.

3. Insert a DdeClientConv object from the System VCL palette into the form. Also, insert a DdeClientItem object. Unlike servers, client applications need conversation and item objects to establish a conversation with a server and to receive data items. To provide a place for displaying received data, insert a standard Edit object into the form. Also, insert a BitBtn and change its Kind property to bkClose. Make the client form resemble Figure 16-2. You might want to move the form down so it doesn't exactly overlap the server window.

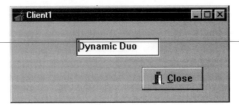

Figure 16-2
Client1's form window. Text entered into the Server1 Edit control (see Figure 16-1) is automatically reflected in Client1. However, text entered into Client1 does not update the Server — this is a typical DDE feature that can help prevent the destruction of original data provided by a server application.

4. Select the DdeClientItem1 object (the icon without the arrows), and set its DdeConv property to DdeClientConv1. This establishes the relationship between the conversation and the item object, and it tells DdeClientItem1 from where to receive its data.

5. Use the Windows 3.1 File Manager or the Windows 95 Explorer to run the Server1 application. Click the *Edit Copy* button to copy the server's Service and Topic names to the clipboard. You may leave Server1 running for the rest of these steps.

6. Return to Delphi. Select the DdeClientConv1 object (the icon with the arrows), and click the ellipsis button next to the DdeService or DdeTopic properties (it doesn't matter which one). Click the resulting *DDE Info* dialog's *Paste Link* button. You should see the strings *SERVER1* and *Server1* in the two edit windows. If not, switch to Server1, click *Edit Copy,* and then *immediately* switch back to Delphi and try again. If you know a server's Service and Topic strings, you can enter them into the dialog, but this will attempt to execute the server, and the two strings must be valid or Delphi will reject them. Click OK to close the *DDE Info* dialog.

7. Create a handler for the form's OnCreate event, and insert the programming from Listing 16-4 to assign the name of the server's DdeServerItem1 object to the DdeItem property in the client's DdeClientItem1 object. The client has now specified the Service (SERVER1), Topic (Server1), and Item (DdeServerItem1) strings that a DDE conversation requires. You can specify the Service and Topic at design time, but you will normally assign the Item at runtime because, if the DdeClientConv object's ConnectMode property is set to ddeAutomatic (the default value), the DdeServerItem1 and Text properties in the DdeClientItem1 object are subject to change via the established link. *Because of DDE's interactive nature, this fact is true even at design time.*

8. Finally, create a handler for the DdeClientItem1 object's OnChange event, which occurs when new information comes in from the server. Insert the statement from Listing 16-4 to assign the DdeClientItem1 object's Text (representing the received data) to the Edit1 object's Text property.

III

16

9. Save the project. Press F9 to compile and run Client1. If Server1 is not already running, this also starts the server. Make both the Client1 and Server1 windows visible. Enter text into Server1's Edit1 window — you should see your typing in the Client1 Edit1 object. However, text entered into Client1 is not reflected back to the server.

If you experience difficulties establishing a DDE conversation, either quit Delphi or start a new project and run the client and server applications using the Program Manager, the File Manager, the Windows 95 Explorer, or the Task Bar. For unknown reasons, running a client application in Delphi's Debug mode does not always establish a conversation correctly with the server. Also try running the server *before* starting the client, which might be necessary if the server's executable file is not in a system-PATH directory.

Listing 16-4
Dde1\Client.Pas

```
unit Client;

interface

uses
  SysUtils, WinTypes, WinProcs, Messages, Classes, Graphics, Controls,
  Forms, Dialogs, DdeMan, StdCtrls, Buttons;

type
  TClientForm = class(TForm)
    DdeClientItem1: TDdeClientItem;
    DdeClientConv1: TDdeClientConv;
    Edit1: TEdit;
    BitBtn1: TBitBtn;
    procedure FormCreate(Sender: TObject);
    procedure DdeClientItem1Change(Sender: TObject);
  private
    { Private declarations }
  public
    { Public declarations }
  end;

var
  ClientForm: TClientForm;

implementation

{$R *.DFM}
```

```
procedure TClientForm.FormCreate(Sender: TObject);
begin
  DdeClientItem1.DdeItem := 'DdeServerItem1';
end;

procedure TClientForm.DdeClientItem1Change(Sender: TObject);
begin
  Edit1.Text := DdeClientItem1.Text;
end;

end.
```

This receives a text string sent by the server.

Establishing Conversations at Runtime

The preceding section demonstrated how to establish a DDE conversation by specifying Service and Topic strings in the Object Inspector. You can also start a DDE conversation at runtime, which may sometimes be more convenient, especially if your program gabs with many servers over multiple conversation paths.

Establishing a DDE conversation at runtime is entirely the client application's job. You write the server application no differently than in the preceding demonstration. The client initializes the DDE Service and Topic names, and specifies the name of a data item to receive from the server. Because the program performs these jobs in code, it also has to call one or two methods to link to a server.

For example, you can convert the preceding Client1 application to initialize a conversation at runtime by deleting the DdeService and DdeTopic strings from the DdeClientConv1 object. Optionally set ConnectMode to ddeManual, and then modify the form's OnCreate event handler to match Listing 16-5. (The listing is from a modified client application in directory Dde2 on the CD-ROM.)

The modified OnCreate event handler calls SetLink for the DdeClientConv1 object. The two strings initialize the DdeService and DdeTopic properties respectively — never simply assign strings to these properties; always call SetLink to initialize them. SetLink returns True if it was able to link to the specified server. Also, assign an item name to the DdeItem property in the DdeClientItem1 object. Finally, if the DdeClientConv1's ConnectMode is ddeManual, call OpenLink to begin the conversation. If ConnectMode is ddeAutomatic, SetLink calls OpenLink automatically.

III

16

Listing 16-5

This modified OnCreate event handler shows how to establish a DDE conversation at runtime.

```
procedure TClientForm.FormCreate(Sender: TObject);
begin
  if DdeClientConv1.SetLink('SERVER2', 'Server2') then
  begin
    DdeClientItem1.DdeItem := 'DdeServerItem1';
    if DdeClientConv1.ConnectMode = ddeManual then
      DdeClientConv1.OpenLink;
  end;
end;
```

To determine the Service and the Topic of a DDE server application, run the application, select some data, and choose *Edit | Copy*. (Try this with Microsoft Excel.) Switch to Delphi, insert a DdeClientConv object into a form, click the ellipsis button next to the DdeService property, and click *Paste Link* in the *DDE Info* dialog. This should display the Service and Topic strings that the server pasted to the Windows clipboard. However, this technique does not tell you the names of data items, which you'll need to complete the client application. Consult the server's documentation, or contact the software vendor, but be prepared to put on your gumshoes and do some detective work to determine the server's item names. Item names typically specify data addresses, offsets, or other locations. For example, a spreadsheet application's items are usually cell ranges; a database's items might be record field names.

RECEIVING DATA FROM A DDE SERVER

A DDE client application receives data from a server through a DdeClientItem object. Implement the object's OnChange event handler to respond to new data that comes in from the server. For example, the OnChange event handler in Listing 16-4 assigns the Text property from the DdeClientItem1 object to an Edit object's Text.

For longer blocks of text data, use the DdeClientItem's Lines property, an object of the TStrings type. For example, to receive a multiline text item over a DDE conversation, use code such as the following, which assigns the received text to a Memo object's Lines property:

```
with ddeClientItem1 do
  Memo1.Lines := ddeClientItem1.Lines;
```

Most DDE applications receive data automatically through a Dde-ClientItem's OnChange event. However, a client application can also request specific data from a server — a specified cell in a spreadsheet, for example. To request a specific item of data, call the DdeClientConv object's RequestData function, which returns a PChar pointer to a null-terminated string. For example, this code fragment requests the DdeServerItem1 item and assigns the resulting null-terminated string to a Label object's caption. Always call StrDispose to dispose of the memory that RequestData allocates to incoming data.

```
var
  P: PChar;
begin
  P := DdeClientConv.RequestData('DdeServerItem1');
  if P <> nil then
  try
    Label1.Caption := StrPas(P);
  finally
    StrDispose(P);
  end;
end;
```

Sending Data to a DDE Server

Sending data to a DDE client is usually a simple matter of assigning strings to a DdeServerItem object's Text or Lines properties. This automatically sends the data to any clients with which the server is holding a conversation. Alternatively, a client application can reverse roles and send data to a server. To do that, call methods PokeData (for up to 255 characters) or PokeDataLines (large text blocks) for the client's Dde-ClientConv object. Each function returns True if successful. Pass two string arguments to PokeData: the name of the DdeServerItem to which you want to send data, and the text to send.

```
with DdeClientConv1 do
  if not PokeData('DdeServerItem1', 'I''d rather go sailing') then
    ShowMessage('Poke failed');
```

Use PokeDataLines the same way, but pass a TStrings object or a TStringList object as the second argument. Poking works only if the server voluntarily accepts poked data. In Delphi applications, you must also create a handler for the DdeServerItem's OnPokeData event, triggered when a client attempts to poke data to the cooperating server. In the event handler, the poked data is available through the DdeServerItem's Text or Lines properties.

DDE MACROS

If a server supports macros, a client application can send macro commands to perform operations in the server. For example, a Delphi DDE client application can use this technique to send and execute a macro for a Microsoft Word document.

In pure Delphi applications, the meaning of a macro is up to you to define. If your server does support macros, however, you can use components to send and receive macro commands. To do this, the server's DdeServerConv object implements a handler for an OnExecuteMacro event. When this event occurs, your server should execute the macro commands in the DdeServerItem Lines property. (Although you could also use the Text property, you'll usually use Lines, because a macro is probably composed of multiple lines.)

On the client side of the coin, call ExecuteMacro or ExecuteMacroLines for a DdeClientConv object. You'll normally use ExecuteMacroLines to send a multiline macro command to a server for execution. If that command is in a TStringList object named Macro, use this code to send it to the server:

```
with DdeClientConv1 do
  if not ExecuteMacroLines(Macro, True) then
    ShowMessage('Macro failed');
```

ExecuteMacro and ExecuteMacroLines return True if successful. The first argument to ExecuteMacro is a PChar pointer to a string; it's a TStrings or TStringList object for ExecuteMacroLines. The second argument is True if you want the program to wait for the server to execute the macro; set the second argument to False to let the client continue while the server does whatever it does with the posted macro.

DDE EXAMPLE PROGRAM

As a final demonstration of DDE conversations, the CD-ROM's DdeColor directory contains two applications, CServer and CClient, that send and receive color information via a DDE conversation. Figure 16-3 shows CServer's display. Figure 16-4 shows CClient's window.

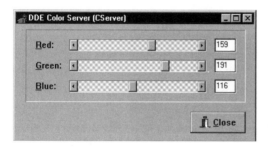

Figure 16-3
CServer's display. This server application sends color information to any client applications that establish a DDE conversation with CServer.

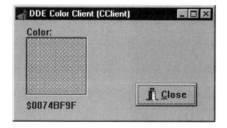

Figure 16-4
CClient's display. This client application starts a conversation with the server, and automatically receives color information over the link.

To compile the programs, switch to the DdeColor directory, and load CServer's project file into Delphi. Press Ctrl+F9 to compile but not run the program. Do the same for CClient's project. Quit Delphi or start a new project, and then run CClient.Exe using the Program Manager or the Windows 95 Explorer. This also starts CServer, unless it's already running (minimize other windows if the program's window does not become visible). Use the server's scroll bars to update the sample color in the client application.

The example server has three scroll bars that you can adjust to create a color value composed of red, green, and blue byte values from 0 to 255. The server makes the selected color available to any client applications that establish a conversation with the server. The example client automatically receives the server's color values, which the program samples in a disabled Edit object. A Label object displays the color's value in hexadecimal. Colors that match Delphi's standards, such as cl_White and cl_Fuschia, are displayed by name.

A significant difference in the CServer application is the use of a DdeServerConv object to initiate a conversation. Use this object to specify a DDE Topic that is not equal to the server's window caption. In CServer, for example, the DdeServerConv object is named ColorServer. The corresponding DdeServerItem object specifies ColorServer in its ServerConv property — this tells the server item how to send data over a conversation. In the CClient application, the DdeTopic property of the DdeClientConv1 object is also set to ColorServer.

Listing 16-6 shows how the CClient application receives from the server a text item that represents a color value in hexadecimal. Safely converting this text to a binary color however, requires careful programming.

Received text may be zero length, in which case the OnChange event handler for the DdeClientItem1 object sets a string variable to the default *$0*. (Preface hexadecimal string values with a dollar sign.) Otherwise, the program assigns the incoming Text to string S. This string may have trailing blanks, which can cause the StringToColor function to generate an exception. A while loop therefore removes any trailing blanks. Notice that the program calls System.Delete to access Pascal's string-Delete procedure, because Delete is also a method in numerous Delphi components.

Some servers may send control codes in their text data. Set the Format-Chars property to True for the client application's DdeClientConv object. This strips backspace (#8), tab (#9), line feed (#10), and carriage return (#13) control codes from received text.

Listing 16-6

It can take careful programming to·use text data received from a server application. This fragment is from the CClient application in the DdeColor directory on the CD-ROM.

```
procedure TMainForm.DdeClientItem1Change(Sender: TObject);
var
  S: String;
  C: TColor;
begin
  with DdeClientItem1 do
  begin
    if Length(Text) = 0 then
      S := '$0'   { Default string }
    else
      S := Text;  { String from server }
    try
      while S[Length(S)] = asciiBlank do    { Delete trailing blanks }
        System.Delete(S, Length(S), 1);     { from string. }
      C := StringToColor(S);                { Convert to color }
      ColorValueLabel.Caption := S;         { Assign to label }
      Edit1.Color := C;                     { Show color }
    except
      ShowMessage('Bad color format from server');
    end;
  end;
end;
```

Precede hexadecimal values with a dollar sign.

To call Delphi's string Delete procedure, preface it with system.

III

16

Object Linking and Embedding (OLE)

The most sophisticated data-sharing technique available in Windows is known as *object linking and embedding,* or OLE. The key advantage that OLE offers is a shift from an application-oriented view of computing to one that centers on documents. Computer users work with data, and placing the emphasis on documents *as objects* is more natural for many users. With OLE, users can also combine information in unforeseen ways. For example, a word processor document can contain graphical images created by software unknown to the word processor's author. OLE makes it possible for users, not just software designers, to create new types of documents that are not limited to a single application-specific format.

As with DDE, OLE requires two cooperating applications — a client and a server. The client application is known as an *OLE container.* The server provides commands for editing specific types of data. The container receives objects from an OLE server, either directly, by way of the Windows clipboard, or by dragging and dropping files from the Windows File Manager or the Windows 95 Explorer. For example, as an OLE server, an audio-waveform editor could provide commands for creating sound documents that an OLE container could store along with text that describes the sound. The container provides generic commands for creating new sound-and-text documents, but the OLE servers provide the commands for creating, editing, and viewing or playing the individual pieces of data.

Delphi's OLEContainer component simplifies the task of writing an OLE container application. At this time, Delphi does not provide components specifically for implementing servers. It's possible to write OLE servers in Delphi, but you must call Windows API functions to do so, and you'll need to study C and C++ OLE references to accomplish this difficult task. In this section, I'll explain how to use OLEContainer to create a container application.

WRITING AN **OLE** CONTAINER APPLICATION

Currently, there are two versions of OLE that affect how objects are created and edited. Under OLE 1.0, all editing takes place in the originating server. Under OLE 2.0, editing may take place inside the container application, or the server may take over that duty in its own windows. Delphi supports the newest release of OLE, version 2.02. (However, in this chapter, I'll refer to this version as 2.0.) To provide for OLE 2.0 in-place editing, a Delphi application should contain:

- One OleContainer for each OLE object in the container
- A MainMenu object
- A Toolbar Panel (optional)
- A Status line Panel (optional)

With these items, the server can insert its own menus, toolbar SpeedButtons, and status messages into the container. For example, when editing an embedded or linked Word 6.0 object in a container, Word's menus augment the container's menus. Users see the familar word-processor's commands, but they are still running the container — they don't have to explicitly switch to or run the server.

NOTE For a server to use a container's toolbar, it's Align property must equal either alBottom, alLeft, alRight, or alTop, and Locked must be False. Also, the container should probably use the MDI interface to manage the main window's client area and to provide child windows for document editing.

To create an OLE container, insert an instance of the OleContainer component into a form. The resulting object looks like a Panel with an indented surface. In it, you can insert an OLE object, displayed as an icon or in its full likeness. Try these steps to write a bare-bones OLE container application that demonstrates the fundamentals of working with OLE objects:

1. Insert an OleContainer object from the System VCL palette into a form.

2. Insert a MainMenu object from the Standard palette. Double-click the menu icon, and enter two menus: *File* and *Edit*. Set the *Edit* menu's GroupIndex property to 1. In the *File* menu, insert an *Exit* command. In *Edit*, insert the command *Insert object...*

3. Quit the Menu Designer, and select *File | Exit* from the form's menu bar. Enter Close; into the command event handler. Select *Edit | Insert object*, and enter the programming from Listing 16-7.

Listing 16-7
This procedure demonstrates the required steps for inserting an OLE object into an OleContainer component.

```
procedure TForm1.Insertobject1Click(Sender: TObject);
var
  P: Pointer;
begin
  if InsertOLEObjectDlg(Form1, 0, P) then
  begin
    OleContainer1.PInitInfo := P;
    ReleaseOleInitInfo(P);
  end;
end;
```

The InsertObject1Click procedure declares a Pointer variable, P, to which the InsertOLEObjectDlg function allocates and initializes memory for an OLE object information record. To the dialog function, pass the name of the form that contains the OleContainer component, a help context index (0 here because the sample program does not have on-line help), and the Pointer P. The function displays the *Insert Object* dialog in Figure 16-5, from which users can select the type of object to create. If InsertOLEObjectDlg returns True, the user closed the dialog by selecting OK, and the program should initialize the OleContainer to contain the new object. To do that, assign pointer P to the OleContainer's PInitInfo property, which copies the object information into the OleContainer. After this step, call ReleaseOleInitInfo to free the memory allocated to the pointer by the *Insert Object* dialog function.

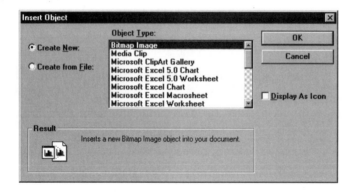

Figure 16-5

Call the global InsertOLEObjectDlg function to display this dialog from which users can select the type of OLE object to create.

InsertOLEObjectDlg and ReleaseOleInitInfo are global functions; they are not members of the OleContainer class.

To display messages in the container's status panel, the server application sends a message to the container, which triggers the OleContainer component's event, OnStatusLineEvent. The server doesn't display the message — that's still your application's job. The event receives a Pascal string parameter named Msg with the server's text, which you may use in any way you want. For example, to display a server message in a Status Panel, assign it to the Panel object's Caption with a statement such as:

```
StatusPanel.Caption := Msg;
```

LINKING AND EMBEDDING

When users insert an OLE object into a container application, they can choose whether to link or embed the object. This is entirely the user's choice, and has little bearing on the container, except when it comes to saving objects in the application's document file (of course, the nature of this file depends on your application).

Choose the *Insert Object* dialog's *Create New* radio button to create a new object of the selected type. (Refer back to Figure 16-5.) This option creates an embedded object, which the container application owns. Choose the dialog's *Create from File* radio button to forge a link to an OLE server application's document. The server owns this document, not the container.

Generally, you should create linked objects for very large documents or for those that must be shared by numerous applications. For example, a worksheet that contains frequently updated information, and that various OLE containers refer to for printing reports and displaying graphics, should be linked to the container. You should embed only relatively small documents or when you need unique copies of objects in one or more containers. For example, a clip art picture that users might edit should probably be embedded in the container to preserve the original drawing.

You may embed an OLE object into a container application at design time by assigning values to the OleContainer component's Obj-Class, ObjDoc, and ObjItem properties. (These are roughly equivalent to DDE's Service, Topic, and Item elements.) Select the ellipsis button for either ObjClass or ObjDoc to open the *Insert Object* dialog, and select the object you want to embed or link. Or, you can paste an OLE object from the clipboard into ObjItem. Be warned, however, that embedding an OLE object at design time inserts the object's bytes into the compiled .Exe code file, which may cause it to grow to elephantine proportions. To reduce code file size, you can link objects at design time, or you can link or embed them at runtime. If the container application permits users to edit embedded objects, you should *not* embed them at design time because no standard methods exist for updating objects stored in .Exe code files.

The following notes will help you decide whether linking or embedding is appropriate for your application. Create a linked object . . .

- to have the server application create and store the object in a file or in memory,
- if multiple container applications need to share the same object, especially if that object undergoes frequent updates,
- if you want the document to be stored in a server-native file format so that users can edit the file using the server or the container.

Create an embedded object . . .

- if you want the container application to store the object in its own data files,
- if you want a unique copy of an object in each container that contains it,
- if you want users to be able to edit the embedded object only by using the container application.

To read and write embedded objects in disk files, call the LoadFrom-File and SaveToFile methods in the OleContainer component. You can override these methods in a form class to read and write embedded objects along with your application's other data using Object Pascal file streams (see Chapter 20).

OLE MENU MERGING

To support OLE 2.0 in-place editing, the container application's Main-Menu object assigns standard values to top-level menu item GroupIndex properties. When users edit an object, the OLE 2.0 server replaces the container's menus with a subset of its own commands. The server replaces menus with equal GroupIndexes; it inserts menus to the left of menus with higher GroupIndexes. The server also provides *Update* and *Exit to Container* or similar commands, usually in the *File* menu, for saving new or modified objects back to the container application.

Table 16-2 lists suggested top-level menus and commands for an OLE container application. Set the top-level menu item's GroupIndex to the values in the table to enable OLE 2.0 server menu merging. For example, set the Edit menu's GroupIndex to 1 so the server can replace this menu with its own commands.

Table 16-2

Suggested OLE 2.0 container application menus and GroupIndex property values.

Menu	Suggested commands	GroupIndex
File	New, Open, Exit	0
Edit	Insert object, Paste special, Object (set Enabled to false)	1
Object	Deactivate	2
View	none	3
Window	Cascade, Tile, Arrange icons	4
Help	none	5

You do not have to set every menu item's GroupIndex value. Assign values only to top-level menu items.

Assign the name of your application's *Object* menu, with a GroupIndex value of 2, to the form's ObjectMenuItem property. In a single-document application, assign this property for the main form. In an MDI application, assign the property in your program's child window form. By making this assignment, the OleContainer object in the form automatically makes object-editing commands available for selected objects.

Use GroupIndex values other than those in Table 16-2 to prevent OLE 2.0 server applications from replacing your application menus. For example, if you assign a value of 9 to all top-level menu GroupIndex properties, the server's menu items will be added to your application's menu commands. To reduce the potential for confusion (two *Edit* menus, for example), if you employ this trick, your application should not use any of the menu names listed in the table.

OLE AND THE CLIPBOARD

You should add a *Paste Special* command to your application's *Edit* menu so users can paste OLE objects from the Windows clipboard. Not all OLE server applications can copy objects to the clipboard, but this command will enable users to paste objects for those that do. You need a *Paste Special* command to separate it from your application's normal *Edit | Paste* operation.

To implement a *Paste Special* command, declare the following array and Word variables in the unit's implementation section. Or, you can insert these items into a form class, in which case you don't need the *var* keyword:

```
var { Declare in unit or form class }
  Formats: array[0 .. 1] of BOleFormat;
  FEmbedClipFmt: Word;
  FLinkClipFmt: Word;
```

The BOleFormat record contains fields needed for pasting objects from the clipboard. (Delphi's on-line and printed documentation list these fields, but you don't need to pay attention to them.) The other two variables identify registered clipboard formats for embedded and linked objects. Initialize these items by adding the statements in Listing 16-8 to the main form's OnCreate event handler. The final statement also enables drag-and-drop objects, discussed in the next section.

Listing 16-8
Initialize OLE clipboard and drag-and-drop objects by adding these statements to the form's OnCreate event handler.

```
FEmbedClipFmt := RegisterClipboardFormat('Embedded Object');
FLinkClipFmt := RegisterClipboardFormat('Link Source');
Formats[0].fmtId := FEmbedClipFmt;
Formats[0].fmtMedium := BOLEMediumCalc(FEmbedClipFmt);
Formats[0].fmtIsLinkable := False;
StrPCopy(Formats[0].fmtName, '%s');
StrPCopy(Formats[0].fmtResultName, '%s');
Formats[1].fmtId := FLinkClipFmt;
Formats[1].fmtMedium := BOLEMediumCalc(FLinkClipFmt);
Formats[1].fmtIsLinkable := True;
StrPCopy(Formats[1].fmtName, '%s');
StrPCopy(Formats[1].fmtResultName, '%s');
RegisterFormAsOleDropTarget(Self, Formats);
```

After making these preparations, implement the *Paste Special* command using the programming in Listing 16-9. Procedure PasteSpecialClick calls two global functions, PasteSpecialEnabled and PasteSpecialDlg, both of which return True if successful. The second function displays the Paste Special dialog window shown in Figure 16-6, which is similar to the Insert Object dialog but provides access to an OLE object on the clipboard. Users can choose to paste the object by embedding or linking it into the container.

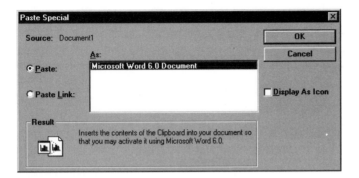

Figure 16-6

PasteSpecialDlg displays the Paste Special dialog, from which users can embed or link objects copied by an OLE server to the Windows clipboard.

Listing 16-9

Implement a Paste | Special command with this programming.

```
procedure TForm1.PasteSpecialClick(Sender: TObject);
var
  ClipFmt: Word;
  DataH: THandle;
  P: Pointer;
begin
  if PasteSpecialEnabled(Self, Formats) then
  if PasteSpecialDlg(Self, Formats, 0,
  ClipFmt, DataH, P) then
  begin
    OLEContainer1.PInitInfo := P;
    ReleaseOLEInitInfo(P);
  end;
end;
```

DRAG-AND-DROP OBJECTS

Use the programming in Listing 16-10 to implement drag-and-drop objects for a form's OnDragDrop event. The event handler receives a Source TObject parameter. Test whether Source is a TOLEDropNotify object, and if so, assign that object's PInitInfo property to the OleContainer's PInitInfo. This plops the dropped object into the container with hardly a splash.

Listing 16-10

Drop a dragged OLE object into a container with this programming.

```
procedure TForm1.FormDragDrop(Sender, Source: TObject;
  X, Y: Integer);
begin
  if Source is TOLEDropNotify then
  with Source as TOLEDropNotify do
    OLEContainer1.PInitInfo := PInitInfo;
end;
```

Summary

- The Windows clipboard, though primitive, is the easiest method for sharing data among applications. The clipboard requires the voluntary cooperation of two applications (or two processes in the same application).

- Dynamic Data Exchange, or DDE, offers a more sophisticated method for sharing text data. To use DDE, a client and a server application establish a conversation through which data can flow. Data normally flows from the server to the client, but the applications can reverse their roles and pass data in the other direction.

- Object Linking and Embedding, or OLE, shifts the focus from the application to the document, which many users find more natural. Also, with OLE, users can build new document types in ways not foreseen by application designers.

- An OLE container application links or embeds objects. An OLE server application provides editing and other commands for specific kinds of objects. Use Delphi's OleContainer component to construct OLE container applications.

Projects to Try

16-1: Write your own Clipboard viewer that supports standard formats as well as TPicture and TComponent objects.

16-2: Write a DDE server application that creates a letter in Microsoft Word or another word processor. Your program might offer several different types of business and personal letter formats.

16-3: Write a DDE client application that prints labels or names and addresses entered into a Microsoft Excel or other spreadsheet application.

16-4: *Advanced.* Write a read-only OLE container application that links two or more documents from OLE server applications on your system — a worksheet and a word-processor document, for example.

Expert-User Tips

- In programs that paste large objects such as bitmaps to the clipboard, you may want to give users the chance to clear the clipboard before the program ends. This can help conserve memory. For example, insert a prompt such as *Clear large bitmap on clipboard?* into a main form's OnClose event handler, and call *Clipboard.Clear* if the user answers Yes.

- Although DDE can transfer only text data, that text may represent numeric values, filenames, or structures of bytes represented as hexadecimal strings. It may take some creative programming to use DDE to transfer binary objects, but if you can figure out how to represent your data as text, DDE can carry the information.

- When communicating with servers that do not use their filenames as the Service, in the client application's DdeClientConv object, set DdeService to the identifier obtained from the server's documentation. Set ServiceApplication to the server's filename. The client can then start the server if ConnectMode, also in the DdeClientConv object, is set to ddeAutomatic.

- To add scroll bars to OLE objects, insert an instance of the OleContainer component into a ScrollBox. To make the scroll bars visible, set the Range subproperties of VertScrollBar and HorzScrollBar to values greater than the ScrollBox's Width and Height, respectively.

III

16

- To prevent editing of an OLE object, set the OleContainer's Auto-Activate property to aaManual. With this setting, the application must set the Active property to True to enable editing.

- To distribute an OLE container application, you must also provide and install file BOLE16D.DLL, Borland's OLE 2.02 support library. Your program's installation utility should copy this file to the Windows\System directory. Your installer should also verify that Microsoft's OLE libraries are installed in Windows\System. See Deploy.Txt in your Delphi installation directory for a list of the required files.

Coming Up

Every computer needs a good database system, and as you'll discover in the next chapter, Delphi offers database development tools that are as good as they come.

Developing
Database
Applications

*D*elphi is truly a one-stop shop for Windows programming, but as this chapter explains, Delphi is also a database developer's dream come true. With Delphi, you can create, edit, and write software for just about all types of desktop databases such as dBASE, Paradox, and ODBC systems such as Microsoft Access. You can also develop sophisticated client/server applications for remote data servers operating on the smallest PC network up to the largest of mainframes. I believe in never saying never, but I'll say it anyway — with Delphi, it's likely you will *never* need another database management system.

In this chapter, I'll explain how to get started with Delphi's database components and how you can use them to create and use databases in a variety of formats. After you master a few basics, you'll learn how to perform searches with SQL (structured query language) and how to create relational database applications based on the master-detail table model.

Delphi's Desktop edition, which includes the Borland Database Engine (BDE), provides a complete set of programming tools for many popular desktop database systems such as dBase and Paradox. Delphi's Client/Server edition includes all of these features, and it provides access to remote database servers such as Oracle, Sybase, Microsoft SQL Server, and Informix. You may use either edition with this chapter.

Components

- BatchMove — Performs operations on records and tables, such as updating all records that match a specified argument. Palette: Data Access.

- Database — Provides additional database services such as server log-ins and local aliases. Palette: Data Access.

- DataSource — Connects dataset components such as Table and Query with data-aware components such as DBEdit and DBMemo. Every database application needs at least one DataSource object. Palette: Data Access.

- DBCheckBox — A data-aware CheckBox component. Palette: Data Controls.

- DBComboBox — A data-aware ComboBox component. Palette: Data Controls.

- DBEdit — A data-aware Edit single-line text entry component. Palette: Data Controls.

- DBGrid — A data-aware text-only Grid component. Palette: Data Controls.

- DBImage — A data-aware graphical Image component. Palette: Data Controls.

- DBListBox — A data-aware ListBox component. Palette: Data Controls.

- DBLookupCombo — A data-aware ComboBox component with the ability to search a lookup table. Palette: Data Controls.

- DBLookupList — A data-aware ListBox component with the ability to search a lookup table. Palette: Data Controls.

- DBMemo — A data-aware Memo multiline text-entry component. Palette: Data Controls.

- DBNavigator — A sophisticated database browsing and editing tool. This component is to database programming what a remote control is to a video recorder. Users click DBNavigator buttons to move through database records, insert new records, delete records, and perform other navigational operations. Palette: Data Controls.

- DBRadioGroup — A data-aware RadioGroup component. Palette: Data Controls.

- DBText — A data-aware read-only text component for displaying database information that you don't want users to be able to edit. (Note: Use the standard Label component, not DBText, to label input fields on data-entry screens.) Palette: Data Controls.

- Query — Issues SQL statements to the BDE or to a SQL server. Palette: Data Access.

- Report — Provides access to Borland's extensive database report generator, ReportSmith, included with Delphi. Palette: Data Access.

- StoredProc — Enables applications to execute stored procedures on a database server. Unless you are developing client/server database applications, you probably won't need to use this component. Typical stored procedures include commands for obtaining information on locked processes and the log-on IDs of database users. However, the exact procedures available depend on the server. Palette: Data Access.

- Table — Gives applications access to databases through the BDE. This component is usually associated with a DataSource object, which connects the Table with data-aware controls. Most database applications have at least one Table object. Palette: Data Access.

 Data-aware controls resemble their data-blind cousins, but can use information from databases. For example, a DBListBox is similar to a plain ListBox, but it can obtain its information from a database Table through a DataSource object.

Database Development

Delphi's database components put an object-oriented face on database application development. Even more important, database components *standardize* access to databases in a variety of formats. This means your applications can access data in dBASE files, Paradox tables, Microsoft Access and other Open Database Connectivity (ODBC) systems, or if you have the Client/Server edition, through remote SQL servers. Best of all, you can use all other Delphi components, interface techniques, and Object Pascal programming in your database applications.

PROGRAMMING THE DATABASE FORM

You can develop database applications using the same tools and techniques described throughout this book. A database application differs from other Windows software only in its ability to read and write information in database tables. In terms of the program's user interface, you develop the application's form as you do any other window.

However, a typical database form may require numerous edit controls, labels, and grids, as well as components that provide the necessary links to database tables. It can be tedious to program all of these objects individually, and to get a leg up on new database applications, you can instead use the *Database Form Expert* command located on Delphi's *Help* menu. (Why this command isn't on the *Tools* menu is the eighth wonder of the world — not really, but the command doesn't have anything to do with Delphi's on-line help.) The Expert is an interactive tool for constructing database forms. In a nutshell, you answer various prompts and select options that the Expert offers. When you're done, the Expert creates a brand-new form complete with all database components in their proper places. You can move these components and make other modifications to the final form, but in many cases, the end results require little polishing.

NOTE ▶   I tend to prefer programming from scratch — it's the only way I can be sure I know exactly what my code is doing. But I can't think of a single reason *not* to use the Database Form Expert. Even if you are as wary of application generators as I am, you'll want to give the Expert a chance to prove its value. It gets my vote.

Follow these steps to create a database form for a table in a sample database supplied with Delphi (or you can use another database table if you have one):

1. Start a new project. (Choose Blank from the *Gallery* dialog if it appears.)

2. Select *Database Form Expert* on the *Help* menu. The Expert presents several dialog-box pages, with options for creating a variety of forms. On the first page, choose *Create a simple form* and *Create a form using TTable* objects. These are the default settings.

3. Click the Next button to move to the next page. (Click Prev if necessary to return to previous pages.) Select a table by opening the ComboBox labeled *Drive or Alias name*. Select DBDEMOS or another database if available on your system.

4. In the *Table name* list, you should now see the names of tables that make up the DBDEMOS database. Choose animals.dbf (or another table) and move to the next page.

5. The Expert now lists the fields available in the selected table. Click the double-arrow button to move all fields to the *Selected* list, or you can Shift- and Ctrl-click individual fields and use the single-arrow buttons. Drag and drop, or click the up and down arrows, to arrange your selected fields in any order, and then move to the next page.

6. Choose a layout option: *Horizontal* for side-by-side data entry controls, *Vertical* to place each control under the preceding one, or *Grid* to create a spreadsheet-like appearance for viewing and editing multiple records, one per row. If you are following along, choose *Grid*, and then move to the next page.

7. The final Expert page has only one check box, *Generate a main form*. Make sure this box is selected, and click the Create button, which as its lightning bolt glyph suggests, generates the new database form in a flash.

On the final Database Form Expert page, if you disable the *Generate a main form* check box, you have to insert programming to display the generated form — by calling ShowModal, for example. With the check box selected, the new form is designated as the program's main one, and you may use the Project Manager to delete the new project's old main form, which is blank and serves no purpose.

You can now press F9 to compile and run the database application. Figure 17-1 shows the program's window. At top is a DBNavigator object with buttons for browsing records, adding new rows, deleting records, and so on. Feel free to use these controls, but be aware that *any changes you make are immediately stored in the database*. For example, change the Area for Angel Fish from Computer Aquariums to Florida Keys (I like computers, but I'd rather watch real fish). Quit, and rerun the program to verify that your editing stuck.

One problem you may notice is that bitmap data fields do not display as graphics, but are instead identified as Blobs (Binary Large Objects). This occurs because the DBGrid component, used if you selected the Expert's grid layout, doesn't know how to display graphics. We'll fix this problem later by inserting a DBImage control into a project. The Expert doesn't do this automatically.

TIP

Although DBNavigator is easy to program, some users may find its complexity intimidating at first. The component comes with built-in help hints, which you can enable by setting the ShowHint property to True. This enables default hints, which you can change if necessary by editing the Hints property.

NAME	SIZE	WEIGHT	AREA	BMP	
Angel Fish	2	2	Computer Aquariums	(Blob)	
Boa	10	8	South America	(Blob)	
Critters	30	20	Screen Savers	(Blob)	
House Cat	10	5	New Orleans	(Blob)	
Ocelot	40	35	Africa and Asia	(Blob)	

Figure 17-1

A sample database application created by the helpful Database Form Expert for the DBDEMOS database and the Animals table.

DBNavigator is a powerful control, and you should be careful not to delete records or make any drastic changes, which become permanent when you move the highlighted field to another row or record. Before doing that, however, you can undo any editing by selecting the X button. Clicking the checkmark button *posts* the current record to the database. The plus and minus buttons add and delete records. The circular arrow refreshes the data by reloading from the table. The other buttons browse through the table's records.

TABLES, DATABASES, AND ALIASES

Before creating databases and writing applications to access database information, it's important that you understand three related terms as used in database programming and by the BDE. These are:

- Table — This is an individual, *flat-file* data source, which you can think of as having rows (records) and columns (fields). One field in the table is the primary key on which the information in the flat file is indexed. Tables may also be indexed on secondary keys. A table is often called a *dataset*.

- Database — This is a collection of one or more tables (usually at least two). When one table refers to another through a key value in a specified field, the result is known as a *relational database.*

- Alias — This is a name registered with the BDE that hides actual drives and pathnames that locate database files. Always use aliases to refer to databases; never hard code file and path names in your applications. By using aliases, you can move your database files to other locations — or transfer them to a network — and all of your applications will work without modification.

CREATING A NEW DATABASE

Although it's possible to use Delphi to write an application that can create new databases, Borland's crack programmers have already done that job for you in the Database Desktop. Use this utility to construct new database tables, modify the fields in existing databases, view database information, and create aliases for data sources.

To create a new database, the first step is defining a place to store your information, and assigning an alias that refers to this location. The exact names are up to you, but on my system, I used the Windows File Manager to create a directory, C:\Database. I then created subdirectories such as C:\Database\Names and C:\Database\Inventry. Follow these steps to create an alias to a database in the path C:\Database\Wines (create this path if you want to follow along):

1. Start the Database Desktop from either the Windows Program Manager, the Windows 95 Explorer or Task Bar, or Delphi's *Tools* menu. Choose *File|Aliases*. Alternatively, you may use the BDE Config utility — run it and choose the Aliases page.

2. Click the *New* button to create a new alias. Enter the alias name — it can be any string, but is usually the same as the directory or network file in which the database is located. For example, enter WINES as an alias for a database you might use for keeping track of a wine cellar's inventory.

III

17

3. Set Driver Type to STANDARD (the default value) unless you are creating a client/server database, in which case you may select INTRBASE. (On a minimum Delphi installation, only STANDARD is available.) Click *OK* to close the dialog window.

4. Click the Browse button, and pull down the Driver (or alias) Combo-Box control. Choose C: (or another path), and then select DATABASE followed by WINES in the path list box. If you are running the BDE Config utility, you have to enter the PATH manually.

5. Click the OK button to close the browser, and then click *Keep New* to save the WINES alias. Click OK and answer Yes when prompted whether to save the public aliases in IDAPI.CFG. You can now refer to the WINES alias in Delphi applications rather than hard code drive and path names to this database. If you are running BDE Config, select *File | Save,* and then exit.

After registering the WINES alias and creating a place to store the files, follow these steps to create a flat-file database for a simple wine-cellar inventory:

1. Start the Database Desktop.

2. Select *File | New* and choose the *Table* submenu command. You'll see a list of available database formats. Select Paradox 5.0 for Windows, the default. (When creating a new database, Paradox is probably the best choice, although you may choose one of the offered dBASE or Intrbase formats if you prefer.)

3. You now see the main entry screen for inserting and editing fields. Enter field names, types (press the space bar for a list), a size for alphabetic fields, and an asterisk (you can type any character) to indicate a primary key field on which the database is indexed. Table 17-1 lists some sample fields. (This is only a demonstration, and a real wine-cellar database would have many more fields.)

4. After entering your fields, click Save as, and choose an alias for refering to the new database. You can select an existing alias that you created earlier, or you can click the Aliases button and create a new alias. If you neglected to create a directory path to hold the database files, do that before clicking the Aliases button.

Table 17-1
Sample Wine-Cellar Database Fields.

Field name	Type	Size	Key
Name	Alpha	32	*
Number	Number		
Source	Alpha	32	
Vintage	Date		
Purchased	Date		

Database Components

After creating a new database or choosing an existing one for which you have registered an alias, you are ready to write a Delphi application to access the database's information. As mentioned, the easiest method for doing this is to use the Database Form Expert on Delphi's Help menu. As explained next, however, you may construct database applications from scratch by inserting component objects into a form.

You may store your applications in the same paths that hold database tables, but because Delphi generates numerous files that you don't need to keep, it's probably best to create separate directories for databases and their applications.

DATA ACCESS COMPONENTS

The components on the Data Access palette provide access to databases and objects in your application forms. Use these components as gateways to database information. In most cases, you will need instances of the two components, Table and DataSource. The other components perform lookups (Query), generate reports via the ReportSmith program (Report), and perform global operations such as updating all fields in matching records (BatchMove). You probably won't need the StoredProc component unless you are developing client/server databases.

The first component to use is Table, which creates a bridge between an application and a database alias as shown in Figure 17-2. In addition to a Table, you'll need a DataSource object, which links data-aware controls to the database. The DataSource object feeds data to and from other objects and the Table. The Table object handles the actual transactions for the database. All of this takes place courtesy of the BDE, which performs the real work of reading and writing data in whatever format you have selected. The data-aware controls might be additionally linked to create interactive data-entry screens. For example, linking a DBNavigator object to a DataSource, which is connected to a Table, creates a browsing toolbar that you can use to view, edit, insert, and delete records displayed in DBEdit and other control windows. Until you get used to which objects link to others, all of this may seem overly complex. However, after you create one or two sample applications, you'll find that data-entry screens fit together as easily as a child's building blocks.

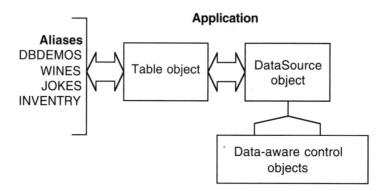

Figure 17-2

A Table object forms a bridge between the application and a database, identified by a registered alias. A DataSource object links the Table with data-aware controls such as DBEdit and DBNavigator.

Follow these steps to create Table, DataSource, and data-aware control objects for entering and viewing information in the sample wine-cellar database (you can also use these instructions with any other database on your system):

1. Start a new blank-form project.

2. Insert Table and DataSource objects into the form. These are displayed as icons that do not appear at runtime. I'll use Delphi's default Names for all objects in this demonstration, but in your own programs, you may want to assign descriptive Name properties to the objects. (I strongly suggest using the words Table and Source in these names, which will remind you of their purposes — MasterTable and NamesSource, for example.)

3. Select the Table1 object, and drop down the list of aliases in the DatabaseName property. Select WINES or another listed name.

4. Remember that a database may be composed of one or more tables. Even though our sample wine-cellar database has only one dataset table, in addition to a DatabaseName alias, you also have to specify a TableName. Select that property, and choose Wines.Db or another table name. *Remember: All Table objects must specify a DatabaseName and a TableName.*

5. Next, select the DataSource1 object. Link it to Table1 by selecting that object from the DataSet property's drop-down list. With this step, you have completed the bare-minimum requirements for connecting an application to a database, and you can now insert data-aware controls in the form for viewing and editing database information. *Remember: All DataSource objects must be linked through the DataSet property to a Table object.*

6. One component you will almost always use is DBNavigator. Select that component from the Data Controls palette, and insert it into the form at a convenient location, somewhere near the top border. Specify the DataSource1 object for the DBNavigator's DataSource property. This tells the data-aware control where its data comes from. *Remember: All data-aware controls must be linked via the DataSource property to a DataSource object.*

7. To provide a platform for viewing and editing database information, insert a DBGrid object into the form. Specify DataSource1 as the DBGrid1 object's DataSource property. Resize and position the controls and the window as you want.

III

17

8. Now get ready for some magic. Select the Table1 object, and double-click the Active property to change its value to True. *This opens the database inside the developing application.* You see the database table's field names in the DBGrid object, and if the table has any information, you see that as well. This is an active control, and the database is open at this time. It's convenient to have live data available when designing database applications, but you may set Active to False to close the table. In that case, insert the following assignment into the form's OnCreate event handler (or another procedure) to open the database and table:

```
Table1.Open;  ( Open database and table )
```

9. Perhaps a DBGrid isn't the best control for editing this database, so quit the application and return to Delphi. Select and delete the DBGrid1 object. Then, insert DBEdit controls, one per table field. For each DBEdit object, set its DataSource property to DataSource1. Because this control accesses an individual cell in a record, you also have to specify the object's DataField property. For example, set DataField to Name. Also, insert standard Label component objects to identify the DBEdit windows. You don't *have* to label the edit controls, but you should usually do so.

Memorize the fact that a DataSource object's icon is the one with the arrows, which represent the links between a Table and the application's data-aware controls (see Figure 17-2).

DATA CONTROLS COMPONENTS

When designing data-entry forms, you will of course have to decide which fields you want to display in which positions. There are two basic choices: use a DBGrid for a row-and-column display, or use individual controls such as DBText, DBEdit, and DBMemo for selected fields. DBGrid displays all available fields in their physical order. It's up to you which individual fields to display with other data-aware controls.

Many times, however, you'll want to limit the fields that a DBGrid displays, or you may want to change their column order. In addition, you may want to create *calculated fields,* which might execute a formula using the values in other cells. You can carry out these tasks by modifying the *virtual fields* that the Table component provides from the dataset's *physical fields.* A virtual field could display a portion or modified version of a physical field — for example, a person's last name or the full spelling of a state abbreviation.

Using the wine database from the preceding section — or you can use the Database Form Expert to create a sample application for any dataset table — double-click the Table1 object in the form. As shown in Figure 17-3, this displays the component's Fields editor which initially lists the dataset's physical field names.

Figure 17-3
Double-click a Table object to display the Fields editor, which you can use to create calculated fields.

The changes you make with the Fields editor do not modify the physical dataset. Use the *Add* button to reinstate any fields you deleted. (Try this: Click *Clear all,* and answer Yes to the prompt that asks if you want to delete all field components. Then, click *Add* and *OK* to add the fields back again.) Each field is declared in the form as a component of a dataset field type — TStringField, TFloatField, TDateField, and others. Using the Fields editor reprograms these object declarations.

Each field in a Table dataset becomes an object in the form's class. Use the Object Inspector to modify the properties of these objects the same way you program values for other component objects. For example, if you are following along, select the Table1Name object in the

Object Inspector's drop down list, and change the object's ReadOnly property to True. Users will then be unable to make changes to values in this field.

The Fields editor programs the number, the names, and the types of data fields that a Table component makes available to a DataSource object. It is still your responsibility to perform the actual calculations, or to insert values into any virtual fields that you add. Adding a field using the Fields editor does *not* create a new column in the dataset table — use the Database Desktop to make changes to a table's *physical* information. Use the Fields editor to make changes that reshape that information for use in the application.

For example, given a dataset with two Date fields, you might want to display the number of days between them. It would be pointless to store this information in the database because it will potentially change every day for every record. This is a perfect example of the kind of field that the application should calculate. Follow these steps:

1. Reinsert a DBGrid object if necessary into the sample application, and set its DataSource property to DataSource1. Set Table1's Active property to True to display the sample database in the grid. Repeat the instructions in the preceding section if you experience trouble or if you didn't save the project.

2. Double-click the Table object to open the Fields editor, and delete all fields from the wine database except Name, Vintage, and Purchased. (You may use a different database for these steps — any dataset with two date fields will do.)

3. Click *Define* to open the *Define Field* dialog, which creates a *virtual* field — it doesn't modify the physical table. Enter a Name such as Days for the new field, which must differ from other field names. As shown in Figure 17-4, you'll see the component object name (Table1Days) in the second edit window. This is the name of the object as it will be declared in the form's class — you can modify the automatically generated name at this time, or you can use the Object Inspector later on to change the object's Name property.

4. Select a *Field type* for this new virtual field. In this example, Integer-Field is appropriate. This option designates the data type, such as TStringField and TIntegerField, for declaring the object in the form class. (Each field becomes a component object in the form.)

5. Be sure the Calculated check box is checkmarked, and then click OK to add the new field to the Table1 object. You can then close the Fields editor, or shove its window aside. Notice that the DBGrid object now displays a new column labeled Days. (Drag the vertical bar to the right of the Name column to shorten this field and make the other columns visible.) Also examine the form's class declaration, which now includes an object declaration for the new virtual field:

```
Table1Days: TIntegerField;
```

6. It's up to you to provide the programming that calculates the new field's value. Do that by selecting the Table1Days object using the Object Inspector's drop-down list. (You cannot select this component in the form because dataset fields have no visual representation.) Double-click the Table1Days object's OnGetText event, and enter the programming in Listing 17-1.

7. Press F9 to run the program and display the calculated fields.

Figure 17-4
Enter virtual and calculated fields by clicking the Fields editor's Define button to display this dialog.

Listing 17-1

Enter this programming into the Table1Days OnGetText event handler to create a calculated field value listing the number of days between two date fields.

```
procedure TForm1.Table1DaysGetText(Sender: TField; var Text: OpenString;
  DisplayText: Boolean);
begin
  Text := FloatToStr(
    Table1Purchased.Value - Table1Vintage.Value);
end;
```

Data-aware controls trigger the OnGetText event to obtain a field's information. Assign to the Text parameter the data you want to display. In Listing 17-1, the program calculates the number of days between the two date objects by referencing their Value fields. The type of Value depends on the object — in this case, for TDateField objects, Value is a floating-point data type. (Look up Value in Delphi's on-line help for its other types.) The program simply subtracts the two date field Values, and assigns the result *as text* to the Text parameter. This displays the number of days between the two dates in the DBGrid's calculated field.

Calculated fields that generate exceptions may create an endless loop of error messages. If you can't seem to get rid of the errors — which is common because closing the error dialog attempts to redisplay the window, which recalculates the faulty field, which generates another exception — switch over to Delphi, select *Options|Environment,* and enable the *Break on exception* check box. Because you are running the program in the Delphi debugger, setting this option works even for an executing application. This should halt the endless errors and return you to Delphi. You may also have to select *Program Reset* in the *Run* menu. Don't reboot until you try these recovery steps. Eventually, however, you still may have to reboot to reclaim any memory blocks lost by resetting. Note that this option works *only* when you run an application from inside Delphi.

BLOBS

Gone are the days when databases were composed of nothing but boring, uppercase text. Well, maybe those days aren't entirely gone, but they are certainly on the run. Let's take a look at how you can create graphical databases with Delphi and the BDE's capability to access Blobs. In case you've forgotten, that stands for Binary Large Objects.

Figure 17-5 shows the Fishy application's display. Listing 17-2 shows the program's source code. To compile and run the program, you must have installed Delphi's demo files, specifically the ones in the Delphi\Demos\Data path. There should be a DBDEMOS alias registered for this database. If you can't get the Fishy application to work, the trouble is probably in the installation (reinstall Delphi to fix it) or the database alias registration (use Database Desktop or BDE Config to fix it).

Figure 17-5

The Fishy application demonstrates Delphi's capability to read and write Blob fields in databases. In this case, the Blob is the bitmap image shown at right in the program's window.

There's not much to the Fishy application's listing. To create the program, I used the Database Form Expert, opened the DBDEMOS alias, and selected the Animals.Dbf file. After the Expert created the form, I shuffled the components around and I added a DBImage object to display the bitmap Blob field, labeled BMP in the Animals dataset table. If you try this, set the DBImage object's DataSource property to DataSource1, and set DataField to BMP.

Just for show, the Fishy demonstration implements an OnDblClick event for the DBImage1 object. I used the code shown at the end of the listing to determine how large to make the final Blob window (200 by 160 in this case). Double-click the image to see these values. In a more extensive application, you might implement this same event to load a bitmap image, or to run a bitmap editor for creating and modifying bitmap images stored in databases.

Listing 17-2

Fishy\Main.Pas

```
unit Main;

interface

uses
  SysUtils, WinTypes, WinProcs, Messages, Classes, Graphics, Controls,
  StdCtrls, Forms, DBCtrls, DB, DBTables, Mask, ExtCtrls, Dialogs, Grids,
  DBGrids, Buttons;

type
  TMainForm = class(TForm)
    ScrollBox: TScrollBox;
    DBNavigator: TDBNavigator;
    Panel1: TPanel;
    DataSource1: TDataSource;
    Panel2: TPanel;
    Table1: TTable;
    DBImage1: TDBImage;
    DBGrid1: TDBGrid;
    Table1NAME: TStringField;
    Table1AREA: TStringField;
    Table1BMP: TBlobField;
    BitBtn1: TBitBtn;
    procedure FormCreate(Sender: TObject);
    procedure DBImage1DblClick(Sender: TObject);
  private
    { private declarations }
  public
    { public declarations }
  end;

var
  MainForm: TMainForm;

implementation

{$R *.DFM}

{- Open the Table1 dataset }
procedure TMainForm.FormCreate(Sender: TObject);
begin
  Table1.Open;
end;

{- Respond to double-click in Blob image }
procedure TMainForm.DBImage1DblClick(Sender: TObject);
begin
  with DBImage1.Picture do
  ShowMessage('W=' + IntToStr(Width) +
    ' H=' + IntToStr(Height));
end;

end.
```

This double-click event handler displays the database blob's width and height.

Structured Query Language

The Structured Query Language, or SQL, is an industry-standard data access and manipulation language. The American National Standards Institute (ANSI) developed the first SQL standard in 1986, and the current standard is ANSI SQL 1989. Because it has no control structures, SQL is not a programming language. Instead, SQL defines commands such as SELECT, JOIN, and UPDATE for performing operations on database tables. SQL is archaic and difficult to use, but almost all databases support at least a subset of the language, so you'll benefit from knowing how to use it. Because Delphi and the BDE perform most database services, you'll probably need to learn only one SQL command: SELECT.

 Some pronounce SQL as "sequel"; others say "S, Q, L." Many more use other terms that I wouldn't *dare* repeat here.

BDE supports a subset of the SQL standard for Paradox and dBase databases. With these formats, you may use the SQL commands SELECT, INSERT, UPDATE, and DELETE. Other servers provide varying SQL support, and for these you may use all recognized SQL commands in Delphi applications.

THE QUERY COMPONENT

Database applications use a Query component to issue SQL statements to a database. You need one Query object for each database to which you post SQL commands. In Delphi applications, you'll mostly use Query objects to perform searches based on arguments such as "all persons with brown eyes who were born on Tuesday and belong to a bowling league" or other earth-shaking criteria.

An instance of the Query component resembles a Table object. The Query component provides a gateway to a database through a registered alias. In addition to a Query component, you'll need a DataSource object to link Queries with data-aware controls. The controls typically show the results of SQL commands.

III
17

BUILDING AN SQL EDITOR

The SQLPlay application on the CD-ROM provides a starting place for building an Editor to issue SQL commands to a selected database. The program also demonstrates how to interrogate the BDE for all database aliases and table names. Figure 17-6 shows the program's main window after performing a search using SQL's SELECT command.

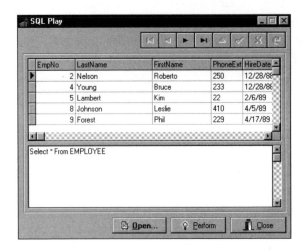

Figure 17-6
The SQLPlay application provides the basic elements of an SQL editor.

Figure 17-7 shows the dialog box opened by clicking the *Open* button. Use this dialog to select a database and table, and then click *OK* to return to the program's main window. Enter SQL commands into the Memo box below the DBGrid object that shows database information. Click *Perform* to execute your commands. For example, open the DBDEMOS database and the Employee table. Then, edit the Memo window's command to the following lines, which search for all Employees with last names equal to Johnson. Click Perform or press Alt+P to issue the SQL command for the database table:

```
Select * From Employee
  where Lastname="Johnson"
```

Figure 17-7
Click SQLPlay's Open button and select a database alias and table from this dialog's combo box controls.

Listing 17-3 shows SQLPlay's dialog module, Open.Pas. This unit demonstrates how to obtain all registered database aliases and their dataset table names.

Listing 17-3
SQLPlay\Open.Pas

```
unit Open;

interface

uses WinTypes, WinProcs, Classes, Graphics, Forms, Controls, Buttons,
  StdCtrls, ExtCtrls, Db;

type
  TOpenForm = class(TForm)
    OKBtn: TBitBtn;
    CancelBtn: TBitBtn;
    Bevel1: TBevel;
    ComboBox1: TComboBox;
    Label1: TLabel;
    Bevel2: TBevel;
    Label2: TLabel;
    ComboBox2: TComboBox;
    procedure FormActivate(Sender: TObject);
    procedure ComboBox1Change(Sender: TObject);
  private
    { Private declarations }
  public
    { Public declarations }
  end;

var
  OpenForm: TOpenForm;
```

III

17

```
implementation

{$R *.DFM}

procedure TOpenForm.FormActivate(Sender: TObject);
begin
  Session.GetAliasNames(ComboBox1.Items);
end;

procedure TOpenForm.ComboBox1Change(Sender: TObject);
begin
  Session.GetTableNames(ComboBox1.Text, '*.*',
    False, False, ComboBox2.Items);
  ComboBox2.ItemIndex := 0;
end;

end.
```

On the form's activation (see procedure FormActivate), the dialog box unit calls GetAliasNames to obtain a string list of database aliases from the BDE. This method — and several others — are provided by the TSession class. To use this object, add Db to the module's uses clause, and call TSession methods in reference to the Session object, which Delphi creates automatically. GetAliasNames clears and inserts alias names into a TStrings property or a TStringList object. Here, the program uses the method to initialize ComboBox1's Items.

After the user selects a database, the ComboBox1Change procedure — triggered when the control's edit window changes — calls another TSession method, GetTableNames. This procedure requires five arguments. TSession declares GetTableNames as:

```
procedure GetTableNames(const DatabaseName, Pattern: string;
  Extensions, SystemTables: Boolean; List: Tstrings);
```

- *DatabaseName* — This is the name of a database or alias such as DBDEMOS.

- *Pattern* — Set this to a filename filter such as *.Db to restrict table names to matching files.

- *Extensions* — Set to True if you want the returned names to include filename extensions. This parameter is meaningful only for desktop database applications.

- *SystemTables* — Set to True to obtain system tables as well as to use datasets from a remote server. This parameter is meaningful only for client/server database applications.

- *List* — Pass any TStrings property or TStringList object to this parameter. GetTableNames clears the list and inserts dataset table names into the list. The sample application uses this parameter to initialize ComboBox2's Items. Setting that object's ItemIndex to zero also displays the first listed entry in the combo box's edit window.

Listing 17-4 shows SQLPlay's main module, which performs the SQL commands. I'll also explain after the listing how the main form's component objects cooperate to show the results of a database search in the DBGrid object (you can use the same methods for any data-aware controls).

Listing 17-4
SQLPlay\Main.Pas

III

17

```
unit Main;

interface

uses
  SysUtils, WinTypes, WinProcs, Messages, Classes, Graphics, Controls,
  Forms, Dialogs, StdCtrls, Buttons, ExtCtrls, Grids, DBGrids, DBCtrls, DB,
  DBTables, Open;

type
  TMainForm = class(TForm)
    DataSource1: TDataSource;
    DBNavigator1: TDBNavigator;
    DBGrid1: TDBGrid;
    Memo1: TMemo;
    Bevel1: TBevel;
    PerformBitBtn: TBitBtn;
    CloseBitBtn: TBitBtn;
    OpenBitBtn: TBitBtn;
    Query1: TQuery;
    procedure OpenBitBtnClick(Sender: TObject);
    procedure PerformBitBtnClick(Sender: TObject);
  private
    { Private declarations }
  public
    { Public declarations }
  end;

var
  MainForm: TMainForm;
```

```
implementation

{$R *.DFM}

procedure TMainForm.OpenBitBtnClick(Sender: TObject);
begin
  if OpenForm.ShowModal = mrOk then
  begin
    Query1.Close;
    try
      Query1.DatabaseName := OpenForm.ComboBox1.Text;
      Query1.SQL.Clear;
      Query1.SQL.Add('SELECT * From ' +
        OpenForm.ComboBox2.Text);
      Memo1.Lines := Query1.SQL;
      Query1.Open;
      Memo1.SetFocus;
      PerformBitBtn.Enabled := True;
    except;
      ShowMessage('Unable to open database');
    end;
  end;
end;

procedure TMainForm.PerformBitBtnClick(Sender: TObject);
begin
  Query1.Close;
  try
    Query1.SQL := Memo1.Lines;
    Query1.Open;
  except
    ShowMessage('Invalid query');
  end;
end;

end.
```

Close the Query object in case it is open.

Add a SELECT command

Open Query object to issue a SELECT command

Procedure OpenBitBtnClick displays OpenForm's window by calling ShowModal. If the user ends the dialog by clicking OK, the program closes the Query1 object to prepare for opening a new database. Query objects operate like Tables, but they can also execute SQL statements. This takes a few setup statements. First, the program assigns Database-Name from the dialog's ComboBox1 edit window. Then, two statements clear the current SQL string list in the Query object, and call Add to insert a statement such as:

```
SELECT * From Animals
```

The SQL SELECT command searches a dataset such as Animals for matching entries. The asterisk selects all columns (or fields) of the Animals table. Because there is no WHERE clause to restrict the selection of rows, all rows (or records) in the Animals table will be included in the result set. To allow you to edit the SQL commands, the program assigns Query1's SQL property to a Memo object. The program then calls Open for Query1, which issues the SQL statement to the dataset.

 Calling Open for a Query object issues *only* the SELECT SQL command. For other SQL commands such as INSERT and DELETE, call the ExecSQL method.

The PerformBitBtnClick procedure executes the SQL commands that you enter into the Memo window. First, the program closes the Query1 object. Always close Queries and Tables before making significant changes to their properties. Assign a TStrings or TStringList object to the SQL property, and then Open the database to issue the command, which in this example must be SELECT.

To experiment with SQLPlay, run the program and open the DBDEMOS database. Select the HOLDINGS dataset table. Click OK to get back to the program's main window, and click inside the Memo pad. Edit the default SQL statement to the following, and press Alt+P to perform the command, which searches the dataset for all holdings in which shares are greater than 1000:

```
SELECT * From HOLDINGS
 WHERE shares >10000
```

You can continue to refine a search. For example, add another restriction after the preceding two lines to display shares greater than 1000 *and* having a purchase price more than $50:

```
and pur_Price>50
```

 After opening a database with SQLPlay's Open button, you may choose another dataset table without reopening the dialog. For example, replace all lines in the Memo window with *SELECT * From Animals,* and press Alt+P to open the Animals table and display all of its records.

Master-Detail Databases

Most databases are *relational,* which simply means they have two or more tables that are related by field values. For example, a Customer table might have a unique ID field used in the Purchases table to identify each purchase that a specific customer has made. This setup is called a *one-to-many relationship.* Individual records are uniquely identified by a key (the ID field) in the *master* table (Customer). One or more related records are linked to customers in the *detail* table (Purchases).

UNDERSTANDING THE MASTER-DETAIL MODEL

Delphi comes with several useful examples of master-detail database tables. For a sample, run the SQLPlay application from the preceding section, and open the DBDEMOS database alias. Select the MASTER table, and click OK to return to the main window. The DBGrid object lists various stocks, each uniquely identified by a primary key named SYMBOL.

Now, enter this SQL statement into the Memo window:

```
SELECT * From HOLDINGS
  WHERE SYMBOL="SMC"
```

Press Alt+P to perform the statement and select all HOLDINGS with the symbol SMC. The master table has only one such entry; the detail table may have several records, one for each purchase of this particular stock.

PROGRAMMING MASTER-DETAIL APPLICATIONS

The MasterSource and MasterFields properties of the Table component define master-detail relationships in Delphi database applications. Use these properties as follows:

- *MasterSource* — For the detail Table object, assign the name of a DataSource component object linked to a master Table. Leave this property blank in the master Table object.

- *MasterFields* — Also for the detail Table object, assign a string with one or more field names to this property, which defines the field (column) over which two tables are connected or *joined*.

You may specify multiple fields separated by semicolons in the Master-Field's string. Here are some sample assignments that show the allowable formats:

```
DetailTable.MasterFields := 'Symbol';
DetailTable.MasterFields := 'Symbol;Exchange';
```

Contrary to some accounts, you don't have to specify MasterFields in the master table. Assign a string to this property only in the detail Table object. In addition, specify the detail table's IndexFieldNames or Index-Name properties. Always use IndexName when possible because it produces faster lookups. Specify IndexFieldNames when no index exists for the joined field.

For an example of how to create a master-detail database application, run the Master program on the CD-ROM. This program uses the Master and Holdings tables from the DBDEMOS database supplied with Delphi. Figure 17-8 shows the program's display. Click the DBNavigator buttons to browse the Master table and display entries from Holdings with matching Symbol fields. Listing 17-5 shows the only significant programming in this application: the form's OnCreate event handler, which opens the two database Table objects. Components and their properties take care of all other aspects of this program's operation — a powerful demonstration of Delphi's visual programming capabilities.

Listing 17-5
Master\Main.Pas (OnCreate event handler)

```
procedure TMainForm.FormCreate(Sender: TObject);
begin
  MasterTable.Open;
  DetailTable.Open;
end;
```

Table 17-2 shows significant property values for the Master program's Table and DataSource objects. In general, every master-detail relationship needs two pairs of these objects related by the properties shown in the table. The table also shows a sample data-aware control (EditSYMBOL) linked to MasterSource, and the DetailDBGrid object linked to Detail-Source. These items represent the minimum required elements of a master-detail database application. (By the way, I used the Database Form Expert to begin this application, which I modified by renaming components, inserting the DBGrid object, and making minor adjustments to the display.)

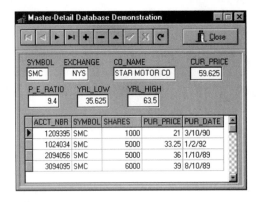

Figure 17-8

The Master application demonstrates master-detail databases. Click the DBNavigator buttons to view stocks from the Master table and show any holdings of those stocks in the DBGrid from the detail Holdings table.

Table 17-2

The Master Application's Table and DataSource Properties

Component	Name	Property	Value
Table	MasterTable	DatabaseName	DBDEMOS
		TableName	master.dbf
DataSource	MasterSource	DataSet	MasterTable
Table	DetailTable	DatabaseName	DBDEMOS
		IndexName	SYMBOL
		MasterFields	SYMBOL
		MasterSource	MasterSource
		TableName	holdings.dbf
DataSource	DetailSource	DataSet	DetailTable
DBEdit	EditSymbol	DataField	SYMBOL
		DataSource	MasterSource
DBGrid	DetailDBGrid	DataSource	DetailSource

Summary

- Delphi's database components fall into two categories: Data Access components provide gateways and links between the application and databases; Data Controls components include data-aware controls and other objects for displaying and editing data fields, and for navigating through database records.

- Delphi's Desktop and Client/Server editions include the Borland Database Engine (BDE), which provides a complete set of programming tools for many popular database systems including dBASE, Paradox, and ODBC systems such as Microsoft Access and B-Trieve. Delphi's Client/Server edition includes all of the Desktop edition's features plus it provides access to remote database servers such as Oracle, Sybase, Microsoft SQL Server, Interbase, and Informix.

- For a head start on creating a new database application, use the *Database Form Expert* command located on Delphi's *Help* menu. The Expert creates a form with Data Access and Data Controls components that you can modify after generating the form.

- A *table* is one dataset, conceptually a row-and-column collection of data cells. Rows are equivalent to records; columns are equivalent to fields. A *database* is a collection of one or more tables. An *alias* is a name that hides drive, network, and path, and filename information for actual database directories and files. Always use aliases to refer to databases; that way, your applications will work without recompilation if you move the database files to other directories, or if you install them over a network after you test your code.

- Most database applications need a Table and a DataSource object. A Table provides a gateway to a database table (best referenced with an alias). A DataSource object links a Table with one or more Data Controls objects.

- Use the Database Desktop to create and modify database tables. You can also view and edit database information using this extensive program, which serves as a front end to the BDE.

III

17

- BDE supports a subset of standard SQL commands (SELECT, INSERT, UPDATE, and Delete) for Paradox and dBASE. You may use the full language with other servers depending on their SQL support.

- The Query component executes SQL statements. Because Delphi's database components offer much of what SQL can do, you'll probably need to use only the SQL SELECT command — to perform searches, for example, and to restrict datasets to records that match various arguments.

- A master-detail database application joins two database tables using a common field such as a customer number or a stock market trading symbol. The master-detail model requires two pairs of related Table and DataSource objects.

Projects to Try

17-1: Write a single-table name-and-address database application. Or think up some other simple application. Use the Database Form Expert to create a suitable viewer and editor.

17-2: Expand your name-and-address database to include a unique identifying number for each record. Program additional tables and develop master-detail relationships. For example, rather than store important dates such as birthdays and anniversaries directly in the master records, create a Dates detail table linked to the master names. With this setup, any name can have a potentially unlimited number of important dates. You'll save disk space as well by not reserving space in records for which you don't need to record dates.

17-3: Use this chapter's SQLPlay application to explore other datasets in Delphi's supplied DBDEMOS database. Experiment with SQL Select commands to search for records with specified field values.

17-4: Try other Database Form Expert options. For example, you can use the Expert to create master-detail relationships, and to insert Query objects for performing searches.

Expert-User Tips

- Consider using DDE to share data among multiple database applications. This will be more efficient (and is certainly more user friendly) than writing data to temporary disk files, which is a common practice. See Chapter 16 in this book for instructions on establishing DDE conversations.

- Although mentioned a few times in this chapter, the advice bears repeating — always register alias names using the Database Desktop or the BDE Config utility; never hard code database drive and path-name information in your applications.

- The Database Form Expert creates a secondary form for a fresh application. To use this form as the program's main window, click the Project Manager's *Options* button, and specify the form under *Main form.* You can then use the Project Manager to delete the project's blank form.

- The ODBC driver for Access 2.0 is designed for use with Microsoft Office. To create Access database applications with Delphi, you must acquire the full ODBC Desktop Driver. The driver is available from Microsoft, and on the ODBC SDK, which includes drivers for Access, Btrieve, dBASE, Excel, Fox, Paradox, and Text databases.

- To distribute a database application, you need to supply your program's .Exe code file (plus any supporting data files), and the Borland Database Engine. All necessary files are in the Redist subdirectory located on the Delphi CD-ROM. Full installation programs are also provided. Create individual diskettes by copying the Disk1, Disk2, ..., Diskn directories in Bdeinst (BDE only), Rptinst (ReportSmith report generator), and Sqlinst (SQL server). Instruct your users to run the Setup.Exe program on Disk1 for each of the three sets. You'll need a total of nine diskettes to distribute the full BDE, ReportSmith, and SQL server files. If you distribute your application on a CD-ROM, simply copy the directories to your disk image. You do not need to distribute ReportSmith and SQL server unless your application uses these tools.

III

17

Coming Up

In the next and final part of the book, you take a look at advanced topics in Delphi and Object Pascal programming, including exceptions, component construction, and such subjects as writing DLLs, using Delph's command-line tools, writing application-level event handlers, and more.

IV

Advanced Techniques

*A*fter creating an application's interface and programming its content, many programmers ship the beast out the door and never look back. But the most successful developers take the time to add finishing touches using advanced Delphi techniques that can turn a merely good application into a great piece of software.

The chapters in Part 4 explain how to handle errors gracefully with exceptions, how to construct custom components, and how to hone your Delphi skills with dynamic link libraries (DLLs), file streams, application-wide event handlers, runtime-type information, plus other advanced tips and techniques.

Part 4 Chapters

18 Handling Exceptions

*D*ealing with errors is one of the dirty necessities of a software developer's life. There's no getting around this duty — if your applications fail due to an error condition, your software will be as popular as a fur coat in the tropics during a heat wave. A *robust* application handles all possible conditions that might cause the program to halt or to produce incorrect results.

Such conditions are called *exceptions,* and handling them is the subject of this chapter. Object Pascal provides a highly sophisticated exception-handling mechanism, and every Delphi application has a default exception handler that displays an error message and prevents the program from halting unexpectedly if an exception occurs. By incorporating additional exception handling, you can further tailor your application's responses to unexpected conditions and, when trouble brews, perform essential cleanup chores such as freeing allocated memory, saving critical data, and closing files.

Introducing Exceptions

Experienced developers incorporate error handling into their projects during the development cycle. Object Pascal's exception handling is an object-oriented technique that minimizes the hassle of writing this code. Exceptions facilitate developing code and its error-handling together, and as you will learn in this chapter, exception handlers tend not to get in the way of the program's algorithms the way other techniques do. If you have wished for better error control methods than deeply nested *if* statements, Boolean flags, and special function return values, exception handling is right up your alley.

WHERE DO EXCEPTIONS ORIGINATE?

Exceptions can arise from a number of different sources. For example, your program can generate exceptions for abnormal conditions. Delphi components can generate exceptions for a variety of events such as assigning an out-of-range value to a property, or attempting to index a nonexisting array element.

Runtime library procedures and functions can also produce exceptions. Executing a math expression that performs an illegal operation such as dividing by zero guarantees an exception. Other examples of exception-producing operations include referencing a *nil* pointer, allocating more memory than the largest available free block, and executing an illegal typecast expression.

Potentially, then, *every* statement in a program may lead to an exception. However, some statements are relatively safe, and a large part of your task in writing robust code will be deciding which statements need protection and which ones can do no harm. This chapter's examples explore typical cases that will help you make these decisions for your own programs.

However, this doesn't mean you have to write statements to handle every possible exception. Delphi's global exception handler, which is added to every application, automatically handles exceptions by displaying a dialog box with a description of the problem and the location of the faulty statement. This default response is adequate for test programs and examples such as most of those in this book, but you'll need to write exception handlers to deal with your program's unique requirements.

Some of the types of operations that can raise exceptions involve the following:

- File handling
- Memory allocations
- Windows resources
- Objects and forms you create at runtime
- Hardware and operating system conflicts

Exceptional Keywords

Object Pascal provides several keywords specifically for creating and handling exceptions. These keywords are *try, except, on-do-else, finally, raise,* and *at.* You'll meet all of them in this chapter. Don't try to use these words for other purposes.

Earlier Borland and Turbo Pascal compilers do not recognize Object Pascal's exception keywords. Exception handling is new to Delphi's Object Pascal compiler.

A Few Good Terms

In the preceding paragraphs, I've loosely used a few new terms such as *exception* and *handler* without explaining their meanings. Following are more formal definitions of these and other terms and phrases that you'll need to know before using exceptions in your applications:

- *Exception* — An unusual or unexpected condition that interrupts the normal flow of a program.

- *Raising an exception* — The notification of an unusual or unexpected condition. Component methods, runtime library subroutines, expressions, hardware faults — even assigning a value to a component property — can potentially raise exceptions. Your application also can raise an exception on detecting a condition that requires special handling. Use the *raise* keyword to raise an exception.

- *Exception handler* — Code that resolves the condition that raised an exception. This code should restore the system to a stable condition so the program may continue to run normally.

- *Exception instance* — An object of a class usually derived from the Exception class defined in the SysUtils unit. The exception instance typically contains information that describes the nature of an exceptional condition. Raising an exception allocates memory for an exception instance. Handling the exception automatically frees the allocated memory.

- *Runtime error address* — The address of the statement that raised an exception. Raising an exception automatically records this address, but you may use the *at* keyword in a *raise* statement to designate a different address value — for example, to point to the location of a critical variable. The runtime error address is available to exception handlers through the global ErrorAddr variable. Delphi's default exception handler displays this address in an error message dialog box.

- *Try block* — One or more statements preceded by the key word *try* for which you want to handle exceptions those statements might raise or for which you want to free a resource such as a memory allocation.

- *Except block* — One or more statements that handle exceptions raised by statements in a preceding *try* block. *Except* blocks begin with the keyword *except*, and may optionally contain *on-do-else* clauses. The *except* block must immediately follow a *try* block.

- *Finally block* — One or more statements that must execute to free allocated memory, close files, or perform other critical tasks in the event of an exception raised by statements in a preceding *try* block. *Finally* blocks begin with the keyword *finally* and they must immediately follow a *try* block. *Finally* blocks do not handle exceptions — only *except* blocks can do that.

- *Protected-statement block* — One or more statements that have specific handlers for any exceptions those statements might raise. A protected block is composed of a pair of *try* and *except* blocks.

- *Protected-resource block* — One or more statements that have specific deallocation handlers for any exceptions the use of a resource might raise. Examples of resources include memory allocations, Windows resources, and files. A protected-resource block is composed of a pair of *try* and *finally* blocks.

- *Robust application* — A program that uses protected-statement and protected-resource blocks to handle all possible error conditions that might occur, and to safely deallocate resources. A robust application takes only time; it leaves no footprints.

PROTECTED-STATEMENT BLOCKS

The *try-except* block is your basic tool for handling exceptions. Listing 18-1 shows a schematic for creating a protected-statement block. Notice that the block ends with the key-word *end* and a semicolon. Comments indicate the types of statements you may insert in various positions.

Listing 18-1
A schematic for creating a protected-statement block.

```
{- Unprotected statements }
try
  {- Protected statements that may raise an exception}
except
  {- Statements to handle any raised exceptions }
end;
```

Try a real-life example to learn how to use the schematic in Listing 18-1 and create a protected block. Start a blank project, and insert a Button object into the form. Double-click the button, and use Listing 18-2 as a guide to writing an OnClick procedure using a protected-statement block.

Close WinSpector if it is running. Also, select *Options | Environment* and disable the *Break on exception* checkbox. See "Environmental Considerations" in this chapter for advice on using these options for debugging a program's exception handling. While learning how to use exceptions, however, it's best to disable these extra exception-reporting devices.

Listing 18-2
This OnClick Button event handler demonstrates how to create a protected-statement block using try *and* except.

```
procedure TForm1.Button1Click(Sender: TObject);
var
  I, J, K: Integer;
begin
  I := 0;
  J := 10;
  try
    K := J div I;
  except
    ShowMessage('Divide error!');
  end;
end;
```

Because I=0, this statement raises an exception.

The procedure in Listing 18-2 performs the mathematical equivalent of eating peas with a knife. The expression *J div I* attempts to divide 10 by zero, which causes the Object Pascal runtime library to raise an exception. However, because the expression is in a *try* block, the procedure handles the exception by displaying a message. The ShowMessage statement in the *except* block executes only if one or more statements in the preceding *try* block fail. The program exercises total control over any exceptional conditions — if the program enters the *except* block, K's value is undefined. Of course, this is only a simplistic example, but in deeply nested, complex code, such knowledge is priceless.

To demonstrate what happens when unprotected statements raise exceptions, delete *try, except,* and the first *end* from Listing 18-2, and rerun the program. Click the button to view the dialog box that the application's default exception handler displays, shown in Figure 18-1. This experiment shows that even if you don't use protected blocks, all exceptions are eventually handled. The default response to those exceptions may be inadequate for a commercial-grade application, but at least the program doesn't explode in a puff of smoke. A default response is better than none.

When an exception occurs in a *try* block, excecution immediately jumps to the first statement in the *except* block. Other statements in the *try* block do not execute after the one that raised the exception. Consider the protected block in Listing 18-3 (assume all variables are integers). If any of the division expressions fail *for any reason,* execution immediately jumps to ShowMessage, after which the procedure continues normally following the protected block's *end.* For example, if the second division fails, the third statement in the *try* block does not execute.

Figure 18-1
A Delphi application's default exception handler displays this dialog box for any unhandled exceptions.

Listing 18-3

If any one of the three division statements raises an exception, execution immediately jumps to ShowMessage (assume all variables are integers).

```
try
  K := J div I;
  R := Q div K;
  S := T div R;
except
  ShowMessage('Divide Error');
end;
```

Listing 18-3 demonstrates one of the key advantages of exception handling — the elimination of repetitive error checks following individual, related statements. It's useful to compare the non-exception error-handling equivalent, of which there are countless variations. Listing 18-4 shows a typical messy case. *Don't ever write code like this.*

The following three points answer some typical questions about how protected blocks affect program flow:

- If a statement in an *except* block handles an exception, the procedure or function continues normally after the protected block's end.

- If no statement handles an exception, *the current procedure or function immediately exits,* and the exception passes up through the call chain until it finds a suitable handler.

- Unhandled exceptions eventually reach the application's default exception handler, which displays the dialog box in Figure 18-1. The default exception handler is a catchall for any exceptions for which you do not provide a handler. You do not have to write a default exception handler — Delphi automatically attaches it to every compiled application. Later in this chapter, I'll explain how to replace the default handler with your own code, which is rarely necessary, but might be useful in advanced projects.

Listing 18-4

With exception handling, you'll never need to write messy code like this.

```
if I = 0 then
  ShowMessage('Divide error')
else begin
  K := J div I;
  if K = 0 then
    ShowMessage('Divide error')
  else begin
    R := Q div K;
    if R = 0 then
      ShowMessage('Divide error')
    else
      S := T div R;
  end;
end;
```

PROTECTED-RESOURCE BLOCKS

Displaying error messages is only one aspect of exception handling. A robust application must also restore stability when disaster strikes. For example, if a disk error occurs or if the system runs low on gas, the application must free any allocated memory blocks that might needlessly occupy space until the user reboots. A robust program gracefully recovers from errors by closing open files, deallocating Windows resources, and doing all that's possible to restore order in the midst of chaos.

Use the *try* and *finally* keywords to create protected-resource blocks. Listing 18-5 shows the basic schematic, which closely resembles a protected-statement block. In fact, the only difference is the word *finally* in place of *except*. However, despite an apparent similarity, protected-resource blocks differ greatly in operation from protected-statement blocks.

Listing 18-5

A schematic for creating a protected-resource block.

```
{- Allocate memory or other resource}
try
  {- Statements that may raise an exception }
finally
  {- Free the resource}
end;
```

Statements in the *finally* block always execute, regardless of whether any statements in the *try* block raise an exception. Typically, the statements in the *finally* block free memory, close files, and perform other must-do operations that restore stability to the system when an exception occurs.

Statements outside a *try* block that raise an exception immediately cause the procedure or function to exit, skipping the *finally* block. To guarantee execution of the *finally* block, place in the *try* block all statements that might raise an exception and leave an allocated resource dangling.

A common confusion with protected-resource blocks is where to place a statement that allocates a resource. Even though this may raise an exception (for example, if a memory allocation fails due to a shortage of RAM), the allocation statement does not belong in the *try* block. The purpose of a *finally* block is to deallocate a resource, and you don't want to deallocate something that wasn't allocated in the first place. Therefore, you should place the allocating statement before the *try* block. Inside that block, insert any statements that might raise an exception, causing the procedure or function to exit and leaving the allocated resource dangling somewhere in memory until the user reboots.

A simple example explains how to use protected-resource blocks to guard against dangling resources, which can eventually choke the RAM out of your system. Disappearing icons, text that strangely reverts to the System font, and a general sluggishness are the symptoms of a *resource leak,* usually caused by dangling memory and other resource allocations. Start a new project, insert a Button object into the form, double-click the Button to create an OnClick event handler, and fill in the procedure using Listing 18-6 as a guide.

Listing 18-6

This OnClick Button event handler demonstrates how to create a protected-resource block using try *and* finally.

```
procedure TForm1.Button1Click(Sender: TObject);
var
  I, J, K: Integer;
  P: Pointer;
begin
  I := 0;
  J := 10;
  GetMem(P, 4098);
  try
    K := J div I;
  finally
    FreeMem(P, 4098);
    ShowMessage('Memory was freed');
  end;
end;
```

These statements always execute even if a statement in the Try block raises an exception.

Listing 18-6 resembles the protected-statement block, but adds a memory allocation statement that calls GetMem to reserve 4,098 bytes of RAM. Notice that this statement (as well as the obviously harmless integer variable assignments) are placed outside the *try* block. Inside *try* is the potentially faulty division expression. If that division were not inside *try*, and if the statement's execution raised an exception, the procedure would immediately end, leaving the allocated memory block lost in space.

The *finally* block guards against this possibility by calling FreeMem regardless of whether the division raises an exception. (Assign 2 to I and rerun to prove this.) The ShowMessage statement is just for demonstration — in practice, *finally* blocks usually carry out their services in silence.

A *finally* block does not handle exceptions — only an *except* block can do that. A *finally* block merely guarantees execution of statements regardless of whether any statements in the preceding *try* block raise an exception. When you run the sample code in Listing 18-6, the default exception handler displays an error message dialog. Read on for instructions for handling exceptions *and* protecting against dangling resources.

Nested try-except and try-finally Blocks

If you are just getting started with exception handling, you may wonder how you can handle exceptions *and* protect resource allocations. These are entirely separate operations, and you cannot merge *try-except* and *try-finally* blocks. There is no such animal as a *try-except-finally* block in Delphi's Object Pascal.

However, you can nest a *try-except* block inside a *try-finally* block to handle exceptions and to prevent dangling resources. Listing 18-7 shows the basic schematic for accomplishing this additional level of protection.

Before going hog wild nesting *try-except* and *try-finally* blocks, consider carefully what the program in Listing 18-7 accomplishes. *You may not need this additional complexity.* As mentioned earlier in this chapter, if an exception is handled, the program proceeds normally after the protected-statement block's *end*. In this case, because the example *except* block handles all possible exceptions, the *try-finally* block is superfluous, and you can instead use this code:

```
{- Allocate resource }
try
  {- Statements that might raise exceptions }
except
  {- Statements that handle ALL exceptions }
end;
{- Free the resource }
```

Listing 18-7

A schematic for creating nested protected-statement and protected-resource blocks.

```
{- Allocate resource }
try
  try
    {- Statements that might raise exceptions }
  except
    {- Statements that handle exceptions }
  end;
finally
  {- Free the resource }
end;
```

In practice, you won't trap all exceptions this way. Later in the chapter, I'll explain how to trap only specific exceptions, which you'll normally want to do rather than subvert the default exception handlers entirely.

You need the nested layout in Listing 18-7 only when the *except* block handles a *specific* type of exception, in which case, other types of exceptions might cause the procedure to end prematurely. In such cases, you must nest the *try-except* block inside the *try-finally* block to clean up any allocated resources. Later in this chapter, I'll explain how to handle specific types of exceptions using *on-do* statements. For now, Listing 18-8 shows a runnable example of the schematic in Listing 18-7. Listing 18-9 shows this same code with the nested *try-except* block banished to a callable function, which is somewhat less efficient, but eliminates the nesting that some developers find confusing. Try this code as you did before by inserting Buttons into a form and creating OnClick event handlers.

Listing 18-8

This Button OnClick event handler demonstrates how to nest a try-except block inside a try-finally block to handle exceptions and to prevent dangling resources. In practice, you need to use this design only when handling specific types of exceptions in the except block, which might cause the procedure to end prematurely for other unhandled exceptions.

```
procedure TForm1.Button1Click(Sender: TObject);
var
  I, J, K: Integer;
  P: Pointer;
begin
  I := 0;
  J := 10;
  GetMem(P, 4098);
  try
    try
      K := J div I;
    except
      ShowMessage('Divide error');
    end;
  finally
    FreeMem(P, 4098);
    ShowMessage('Memory was freed');
  end;
end;
```

Listing 18-9

This function and OnClick event handler is operationally identical to the code in Listing 18-8, but it places the nested try-except block inside a callable function, GetInt. The result is a cleaner program at the expense of an additional function call. Here again, you need to use this technique only if the except block handles specific types of exceptions. In this sort of code, because the except block is now in a separate function that you may some-day modify to handle only specific exceptions (or none at all), the OnClick event handler should use try-finally for safety.

```
function GetInt: Integer;
var
  I, J: Integer;
begin
  I := 0;
  J := 10;
  try
    Result := J div I;
```

```
    except
      ShowMessage('Divide error');
    end;
end;

procedure TForm1.Button1Click(Sender: TObject);
var
  K: Integer;
  P: Pointer;
begin
  GetMem(P, 4098);
  try
    K := GetInt;
  finally
    FreeMem(P, 4098);
    ShowMessage('Memory was freed');
  end;
end;
```

TIP

Listing 18-9 demonstrates how exception handling *decouples* a program's normal statements from its error-handling logic. For example, delete *try, except,* and the first *end* from the GetInt function, and rerun the program. The Button's OnClick event handler still frees the allocated memory even though the function no longer handles the exception raised by the faulty division. If the OnClick event handler did not use *try-finally,* GetInt's exception would cause the OnClick procedure to end, leaving the allocated memory dangling.

Handling and Raising Exceptions

The preceding sections introduce most of the exception-handling techniques you'll need to write robust Delphi applications. In this part, you'll go beyond the basics to learn how to handle specific types of exceptions, and how to raise and reraise exceptions of your own. First, however, you need to consider some environmental options that affect how your development system responds to exceptions.

ENVIRONMENTAL CONSIDERATIONS

Use the WinSpector utility to augment how your development system responds to serious exceptions, especially a dreaded general protection fault, or GPF. Delphi's exception handling responds to GPFs, even those arising from serious system difficulties, as well as less dangerous application errors. But WinSpector provides additional reporting on GPFs that you may find useful.

Because I use a number of development systems, I usually run Win-Spector all the time in the background. When writing Delphi code, however, I close WinSpector unless I experience serious trouble. WinSpector seems to slow an application's response to exceptions, and besides, Delphi's exception handling already provides all the error-handling logic I need. (Considering some of the software messes I've gotten myself in, that's saying a lot!)

The second environmental consideration when developing applications — and especially for debugging exception handlers — is whether to have Delphi halt a program when an exception occurs. To enable this feature, choose the *Options/Environment* command, and switch on the *Break on exception* check box.

Try running a test program (containing Listing 18-2's event handler, for example) with this option on and off. When selected, the option displays a full report of any exceptions, and the program halts at the statement that caused the problem. Figure 18-2 shows the resulting dialog box that Delphi displays. It's important to understand that Delphi itself, not the application's default exception handler, displays this dialog window. You must run your program inside Delphi (in other words, in debug mode) to see it.

If you are following along, read the dialog's information, and click the OK button. Delphi highlights the statement that raised the exception. The program is still running, but is paused at the offending statement. Press F9 to continue running, or press F8 or F7 to single-step the program starting at this location. *You must run and exit the program before you can continue to develop the code.*

To follow along, press F9. You will see yet another error message dialog — in this case, the one that the application's default exception handler displays. If your code handles the exception, you'll see that response. The multitude of dialogs may be confusing, but after you understand the different levels of exception handling that are taking place, you'll find the information invaluable in chasing down bugs — especially any errors in your own exception handlers.

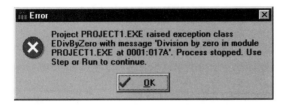

Figure 18-2

Turn on the Environment option, Break on exception, *to halt the program and display a dialog box similar to this one, which provides detailed information about the exception. Delphi, not the application's default exception handler, displays this dialog. To see it, you must run your program in Delphi's debug mode.*

If you enable the *Break on exception* check box, run the compiled application from the Windows File Manager or the Windows 95 Explorer to test how the finished program responds to errors outside of Delphi. Run your code inside Delphi with the option enabled for information on exceptions *in addition* to any exception handling your application provides.

THE EXCEPTION INSTANCE

As mentioned, an exception is an event or condition that interrupts the normal flow of a program. Physically, however, an exception is an *object* of a class, usually derived from the Exception class defined in the SysUtils unit. This object is called the *exception instance*.

Raising an exception creates an exception instance. If a statement in the *except* part of a protected-statement block handles the exception, the program automatically destroys the exception instance. If no statement handles the exception, the application passes the exception instance upwards in the call chain until finding a suitable handler, or until reaching the default exception handler.

The *only* safe way to destroy an exception instance is to handle the exception. Handling an exception destroys the exception instance automatically. In the following sections, you'll learn how to reference exception instances. *Never write code to free or destroy these objects.* Attempting to free an exception instance will cause a fatal application error.

HANDLING SPECIFIC EXCEPTIONS

The exception instance identifies what type of exception occurred. Delphi provides numerous classes, all derived from Exception, that describe the nature of specific problems. You may use this information to refine your program's response to exceptions, and you may write exception handlers that are triggered by specific kinds of problems. To accomplish these tasks, use an *on-do* statement inside an *except* block.

The *on-do* statement performs two services: it identifies a specific kind of exception, and it can provide a reference to the exception instance. Typically, the exception instance provides information about what kind of problem occurred. Your program can use this information to resolve the problem and to display helpful notes to users.

The Except1 sample application on the CD ROM demonstrates how to use *on-do* to reference an exception instance. Figure 18-3 shows the program's window and the dialog displayed when you click the button. This forces an exception to occur by attempting to assign illegal values to the window's two scrollbar controls. Listing 18-10 shows the Button object's OnClick event handler.

The program calls SetParams for the two scrollbars, but it mistakenly reverses the Min and Max arguments. The ScrollBar component specifies that Min must be less than or equal to Max, and the first call to SetParams raises an exception.

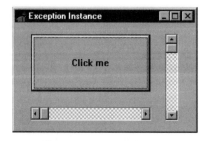

Figure 18-3
Clicking Except1's button forces an exception and displays the dialog box shown here.

Listing 18-10

Except1\Main.Pas (Button1 object's OnClick event handler)

```
procedure TMainForm.Button1Click(Sender: TObject);
begin
  try
    ScrollBar1.SetParams(0, 500, 0);
    ScrollBar2.SetParams(0, 500, 0);
  except
    on E: Exception do
      ShowMessage(E.Message);
  end;
end;
```

This provides a reference to the exception object.

In the *except* block, an *on-do* statement declares a variable E of the Exception class. (You can use any name, but E is convenient.) This statement does not create a new Exception instance; it simply creates a reference (E) to the exception instance that describes the problem. The program uses E's Message string property to display a meaningful message in a dialog box.

You can also use *on-do* to trap specific types of exceptions. For example, you might want to handle divide-by-zero exceptions, but allow another handler higher in the call chain to handle other exception types. In that case, specify the exception class you need in an *on-do* statement. For example, Listing 18-11 shows the same code from Listing 18-2, but this time, specifically handles only the exception EDivByZero.

Listing 18-11

This OnClick Button event handler demonstrates how to create a protected-statement block using try and except for a specific type of exception.

```
procedure TForm1.Button1Click(Sender: TObject);
var
  I, J, K: Integer;
begin
  I := 0;
  J := 10;
  try
    K := J div I;
  except
    on E: EDivByZero do
      ShowMessage(E.Message);
  end;
end;
```

It is usually best to handle specific exceptions rather than blindly handle them all.

Table 18-1 lists all exception classes defined in the SysUtils unit. They are all derived, not necessarily directly, from the Exception class. Use them as Listing 18-11 demonstrates — replace EDivByZero with any exception class listed in the table. You can also use these classes for pure identification purposes without creating a reference to the exception instance. For example, replace the *on-do* statement in the listing with the following:

```
on EDivByZero do
  ShowMessage('Divide error');
```

The first line compares the exception instance's class with EDivByZero, and if the object is of that class, calls ShowMessage. Exceptions of other types travel upwards through the call chain. Use this programming if you don't need to refer to the exception instance.

The *except* block may respond to more than one type of exception. For instance, the following handles three types of exception objects; others continue up the chain until they find a handler:

```
on EDivByZero do
  ...;
on EInOutError do
  ...;
on EOutOfMemory do
  ...;
```

In case you jumped ahead to this section, be sure to read the earlier advice under "Protected-Resource Blocks" and "Nested *try-except* and *try-finally* Blocks." When you use *on-do* to handle specific exception classes, the presence of other types of unhandled exceptions will cause the current procedure or function to exit immediately. In such cases, use a *try-finally* block to free allocated memory, close files, and perform other must-do operations.

RAISING A NEW EXCEPTION

Use the *raise* keyword to raise a new exception. Following *raise,* create an exception instance of the Exception or any derived class. Assuming the program has a Boolean variable ErrorFlag that, if True, indicates a problem, the program can raise an exception with code such as this:

```
if ErrorFlag then
  raise Exception.Create('Error');
```

Table 18-11

Exception Classes Defined in the SysUtils Unit.

Exception class	Description
EAbort	Silent exception raised by calling Abort.
EBreakpoint	Breakpoint reached in code. For Delphi's internal use only.
EConvertError	Conversion error — for example, string to an integer.
EDivByZero	Integer attempt to divide by zero.
EFault	Base class for hardware faults. Never used directly as an exception object.
EGPFault	General protection fault.
EInOutError	File input/output error.
EIntError	Base class for integer math exceptions. Never used directly as an exception object.
EIntOverFlow	Integer overflow.
EInvalidCast	Invalid type-cast expression.
EInvalidOp	Invalid floating-point math operation.
EInvalidOpCode	Invalid op code (commonly caused by attempting to run data as code, perhaps due to a bad pointer).
EInvalidPointer	Invalid pointer — for example, attempting to use a nil pointer.
EMathError	Base class for floating-point math exceptions. Never used directly as an exception object.
EOutOfMemory	Unable to fulfill requested memory allocation.
EOverflow	Floating-point overflow (value too large).
EPageFault	Hardware memory page fault.
EProcessorException	Processor-generated exception.
ERangeError	Value out of range.
ESingleStep	Program operating in single-step mode. For Delphi's internal use only.
EStackFault	System stack overflow or underflow. Because Windows does not permit an application to continue after a stack error, trapping this exception has no practical benefit. Stack errors are always fatal.
EUnderflow	Floating-point math underflow (value too small).
EZeroDivide	Floating-point attempt to divide by zero.

In place of Exception, you may use any of the classes from Table 18-1. You can also raise exceptions of your own classes, but more on that later.

The results of this code are identical in every way to exceptions raised by components, math expressions, hardware faults, or any other source. You can write exception handlers for the exceptions your code raises, or you can let the application's default exception handlers catch them.

NOTE ▶ Raising an exception immediately searches for the nearest exception handler in the procedure or function that calls *raise*. If the procedure or function itself has no handlers, *raise* effectively exits the subroutine.

For a demonstration of raising exceptions, run the Except2 demonstration on the CD-ROM and enter a value from 0 to 99 in the Edit window. Figure 18-4 shows the program's display. Click the *I'm done* button to end the program. Enter an out-of-range value to force an exception that prevents the program from closing. Listing 18-12 shows the button's OnClick event handler.

In the Button object's OnClick event handler, StrToInt converts the Edit1 object's Text property to an integer value, and assigns that value to N. The subsequent *if* statement raises an exception if N is not within the range of 0 to 99. Following the *raise* keyword, the program creates an exception instance of the ERangeError class. In this program, the default exception handler receives the ERangeError object and displays the message in a dialog box.

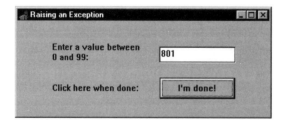
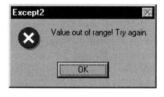

Figure 18-4

Entering an out-of-range value in the Except2's Edit window raises an exception that prevents the program from closing.

Less obvious is the fact that the sample event handler might fail due to another type of exception: a *conversion error* raised by calling StrToInt. Run the program again and enter 3.14159 or your name into the Edit window, and then click the button. This time you see a different message because the exception raised by StrToInt causes the event handler to exit immediately, which skips the rest of the procedure's code.

IV

18

Listing 18-12

Except2\Main.Pas (Button OnClick event handler)

```
procedure TMainForm.Button1Click(Sender: TObject);
var
  N: Integer;
begin
  N := StrToInt(Edit1.Text);
  if (N < 0) or (N > 99) then
    raise ERangeError.Create('Value out of range! Try again')
  else begin
    ShowMessage('Success! Click Ok to end program');
    Close;
  end;
end;
```

Raises a range-error exception

A better version of this event handler uses a *try-except* block to handle this situation, and to give users a chance to correct bad input, no matter what the cause. You may also have noticed that you have to press Tab or click the mouse to get back to the Edit window after closing the error message dialog. With exceptions, we can do better. Listing 18-13 shows the final OnClick event handler extracted from the Except3 project on the CD-ROM.

Listing 18-13

Except3\Main.Pas (Button OnClick event handler).

```
procedure TMainForm.Button1Click(Sender: TObject);
var
  N: Integer;
begin
  try
    N := StrToInt(Edit1.Text);
    if (N < 0) or (N > 99) then
      raise ERangeError.Create('Value out of range! Try again')
    else begin
      ShowMessage('Success! Click Ok to end program');
      Close;
    end;
  except
    on E: Exception do
    begin
      ShowMessage(E.Message + ' Try again.');
      Edit1.SetFocus;
    end;
  end;
end;
```

TIP

You will rarely handle exceptions in the same procedures that raise them, but there's no restriction on doing so.

The new procedure adds a *try-except* block to handle any exceptions, *including the one raised in the procedure.* Any input errors display an error message to which the program tacks on a friendly encouragement to *try again.* In addition, SetFocus highlights the Edit1 object's input window so users can simply enter another value. With exceptions, this program is not only robust, its interface is also easier to use.

This new code is beginning to get a little long in the tooth — or anyway, on the page — but let's do one more version. Listing 18-14 calls a local, nested function, GetInteger, that returns Edit1's Text property as a numeric value. The result is much cleaner.

Listing 18-14

The final, final improved OnClick event handler. (You'll find a copy of this code in the Except3 directory in file Main2.Pas.)

```
procedure TMainForm.Button1Click(Sender: TObject);
var
  N: Integer;

  function GetInteger: Integer;
  begin
    Result := StrToInt(Edit1.Text);
    if (Result < 0) or (Result > 99) then
      raise ERangeError.Create('Value out of range!')
    else begin
      ShowMessage('Success! Click Ok to end program');
      Close;
    end;
  end;

begin
  try
    N := GetInteger;
  except
    on E: Exception do
    begin
      ShowMessage(E.Message + ' Try again.');
      Edit1.SetFocus;
    end;
  end;
end;
```

Try to keep your procedures and functions short — you'll find this will improve your understanding of the program and help you to keep its error-handling logic from becoming unwieldy.

RERAISING AN EXCEPTION

As you develop your application, you will write numerous procedures and functions that provide exception handlers, and you will often want to add new capabilities to this existing code. For example, you might have a program that closes a file in the event of a disk error. Another module might need to handle that same exception for its own purposes. Rather than close the file in two different places — a poor programming practice that complicates future maintenance — the secondary exception handler can *reraise* the exception. This keeps the exception alive so that, after the secondary handler performs its actions, the exception object travels up the call chain to reach other handlers that watch for it.

If you are familiar with object-oriented programming, you might think of reraising an exception as a kind of runtime subclassing. An exception handler can augment other handlers by trapping specific types of exceptions, performing some action, and then reraising the exception to keep it alive for additional handling. This is similar to the way a method in a derived class calls an inherited method to augment what that code does.

To handle an exception and not destroy the exception instance, use the *raise* keyword alone with no argument. Do this for all types of exceptions by using code such as the following (*Statement* represents one or more statements that might raise an exception):

```
try
  Statement;
except
  ShowMessage('OOPs!');
  raise;  { Reraise the exception }
end;
```

If Statement raises an exception, execution jumps to ShowMessage. After that, the use of *raise* with no argument reraises the exception. Running this code would display two messages: the first by ShowMessage, and the second by the application's default exception handler.

To reraise a specific type of exception, use the same code, but insert *raise* into an *on-do* statement as follows:

```
try
  Statement;
except
  on E: EOverflow do
  begin
    ShowMessage('OOPs!');
    raise; { Reraise specific exception }
  end;
end;
```

Reraising an exception immediately exits the procedure or function that calls *raise*.

Creating Exception Classes

When you need to raise an exception, you can choose one of the Exception classes in SysUtils (see Table 18-1) or you can create your own classes. You may derive your class from Exception, or you can create a fresh class of your own design.

Derive your exception class from Exception if you want the application's default handler to trap any unhandled exceptions of your class. Create a fresh class of your own design if you do not want the default handler to recognize your exceptions. Be forewarned, however, that any unhandled exceptions of such a class will cause a fatal application error.

DERIVED EXCEPTION CLASSES

The simplest method is to define a new class type based on Exception. For example, insert the following type declaration into a unit's interface (it can go in the implementation, but you'll probably want to make the class available to other modules so they can create and handle exceptions of the new class):

```
type
  TCustomException = class(Exception);
```

The new class simply provides a unique class name for identifying a specific type of problem — the class doesn't need a body. With this declaration, you can raise exceptions of the TCustomException class. For example, insert this statement into a Button's OnClick event handler:

```
raise TCustomException.Create('Custom exception');
```

An exception handler can then trap TCustomException objects, but allow all other types of exceptions to pass to their handlers. Try these methods by starting a blank project and inserting the preceding *type* declaration into a unit's interface or implementation section. Insert the *raise* statement into a Button object's OnClick event handler, run the program, and click the button to see how the program handles the custom exception.

If you want, you may add methods and variables to your exception class, just as you can to any other class. For example, you might want to save the coordinate values of the mouse to indicate its pointer location for an error related to mouse movements. Insert the *type* declaration and class constructor from Listing 18-15 into the unit.

Listing 18-15
A custom exception class may declare variables and methods as in this example, which records coordinate values.

```
type
   TMouseException = class(Exception)
     X, Y: Integer;
     constructor Create(const Msg: string; XX, YY: Integer);
   end;

constructor TMouseException.Create(const Msg: string;
   XX, YY: Integer);
begin
   X := XX;
   Y := YY;
   Message := Msg;  { Inherited from Exception }
end;
```

This declares a new exception derived from the Exception class.

The class must implement a Create constructor.

Because TMouseException is derived from Exception, it inherits that class's properties and methods, including the string Message. To its inherited items, TMouseException adds X and Y integers for recording a coordinate location. To use the custom exception class, perhaps in an

OnMouseDown event handler, raise an exception of the TMouseException class, passing a string and a pair of coordinate values:

```
raise TMouseException.Create('Custom exception', X, Y);
```

Elsewhere, use a protected-statement block as follows to trap EMouseException errors and display the message along with the values of X and Y. The code leaves undisturbed any other exceptions that might arise:

```
try
  {- Statement that might raise a TMouseException exception }
except
  on E: TMouseException do
    ShowMessage(E.Message + #13#10 +
      'X=' + IntToStr(E.X) + ', Y=' + IntToStr(E.Y));
end;
```

NONDERIVED EXCEPTION CLASSES

You can also create entirely new exception classes that are not based on Exception. The simplest case is a class that has no body. Because it is a base class, however, its declaration must end with *end;*. For example, insert this *type* declaration into a unit:

```
type
  TBareException = class
  end;
```

Then, in a Button's OnClick event handler, insert the following statement to *raise* an exception of the TBareException class:

```
raise TBareException.Create;
```

TIP Because all classes derive from TObject, even a spanking new base class comes with Create and Free methods already built in.

Run the program and click the button to display a system-error dialog. If you use this technique, you should handle all instances of your exception class, and you might want to install your own default exception handler. The class could have additional variables and methods — it's up to you what to put into an exception class.

TIP

For best results in your program's error handling, derive your exception classes from SysUtil's Exception. Don't create nonderived exception classes unless you have compelling reasons for doing so.

THE EXCEPTION BASE CLASS

By basing your exception classes on Exception, your classes inherit a wealth of members. For example, the Exception base class provides a number of methods for constructing exception objects in different ways. All of these constructors are named Create, and they all have the singular purpose of creating an error message string out of different sorts of arguments. You may call these constructors to create exception instances of your derived classes, or you may call them for Exception objects or for any of the derived classes in Table 18-1. I'll run through Exception's constructors briefly here — one of them is sure to suit your needs.

The simplest Create is the one you've already seen. Pass a string variable or constant as an error message:

```
raise Exception.Create('Trouble in Paradise');
```

Call CreateFmt and pass a string with formatting commands plus a set of values to insert in the string. (For help with these techniques, see "Using the Format Function" in Chapter 7, and look up *Format* in Delphi's online help.) For example, this statement raises an exception with an error message that displays two integer values:

```
raise Exception.CreateFmt('Error: X=%d Y=%d', [X, Y]);
```

The SysUtils unit installs a string table resource that contains various standard error messages you can use in raising exceptions. Call CreateRes and pass a string-table ID as an argument — in this case, to notify users that their disk is crammed full of junk (whose isn't?):

```
raise Exception.CreateRes(SDiskFull);
```

Table 18-2 lists other string-table resource identifiers you can pass to CreateRes, most of which have obvious meanings. Use these strings whenever possible; they help save memory.

Table 18-2

The SysUtils unit defines these string-table resource identifiers in the resource script file SysUtils.Rc. Pass a constant such as SAccessDenied to Exception CreateRes and similar constructors.

Resource ID	String
SInvalidInteger	"'%s' is not a valid integer value"
SInvalidFloat	"'%s' is not a valid floating point value"
SInvalidDate	"'%s' is not a valid date"
SInvalidTime	"'%s' is not a valid time"
SInvalidDateTime	"'%s' is not a valid date and time"
STimeEncodeError	"Invalid argument to time encode"
SDateEncodeError	"Invalid argument to date encode"
SOutOfMemory	"Out of memory"
SInOutError	"I/O error %d"
SFileNotFound	"File not found"
SInvalidFilename	"Invalid filename"
STooManyOpenFiles	"Too many open files"
SAccessDenied	"File access denied"
SInvalidDrive	"Invalid drive"
SEndOfFile	"Read beyond end of file"
SDiskFull	"Disk full"
SInvalidInput	"Invalid numeric input"
SDivByZero	"Division by zero"
SRangeError	"Range check error"
SIntOverflow	"Integer overflow"
SInvalidOp	"Invalid floating point operation"
SZeroDivide	"Floating point division by zero"
SOverflow	"Floating point overflow"
SUnderflow	"Floating point underflow"
SInvalidPointer	"Invalid pointer operation"
SInvalidCast	"Invalid class typecast"
SGPFault	"General protection fault"
SStackFault	"Stack fault"
SPageFault	"Page fault"
SInvalidOpCode	"Invalid opcode"
SBreakpoint	"Breakpoint interrupt"
SSingleStep	"Single-step interrupt"
SOperationAborted	"Operation aborted"
SModuleException	"%s in module %s at %p"

Resource ID	String
SAddressException	"%s at %p"
SException	"Exception %s in\x0Amodule %s at %p.\x0A%s%s\x0A"
SExceptTitle	"Application Error"
SInvalidFormat	"Format '%s' invalid or incompatible with argument"
SArgumentMissing	"No argument for format '%s'"

The remaining Exception constructors are variations on the preceding themes. Following are examples of them all. CreateResFmt loads a string-table resource with an embedded %s string-formatting command (notice that you must pass a *string* set to this constructor). CreateHelp adds a help-context identifier (it's up to your exception handler to use it). CreateFmtHelp combines a formatting string with a help-context identifier. CreateResHelp combines a string-table resource with a help-context identifier. CreateResFmtHelp puts the whole ball of wax together with a resource string containing formatting codes such as %s or %d and a help-context identifier.

```
raise Exception.CreateResFmt(SInvalidInteger, [IntToStr(N)]);
raise Exception.CreateHelp('Whoops, sorry', 123);
raise Exception.CreateFmtHelp('Error N=%d', [N], 123);
raise Exception.CreateResHelp(SFileNotFound, 123);
raise Exception.CreateResFmtHelp(SInvalidInteger, [S], 123);
```

Using Other Exceptional Techniques

The following sections discuss advanced exception techniques that are useful in special circumstances.

SILENT EXCEPTIONS

A silent exception is one that has no apparent effect on a program. However, it is very useful in aborting deeply nested processes. The silent exception instance is an object of the EAbort class, which is derived from Exception. Delphi's default exception handler is programmed not to display any error messages when it receives an EAbort exception. Instead, the default handler merely destroys the exception instance and returns control to the program.

Call the Abort procedure to raise an exception of the EAbort class. For example, a *while* loop that inspects a NormalCondition Boolean flag could also inspect another flag, SpecialConditionFlag, and abort the loop by calling Abort (I made up the flag names — they represent any kind of conditions your program needs to monitor):

```
while NormalCondition do
begin
  if SpecialConditionFlag = False then
    Abort;
end;
```

Calling Abort is equivalent to raising an EAbort exception, which you may do the hard way in order to pass a string message along with the object (because the exception is normally silent, however, the program never displays this string):

```
raise EAbort.Create('Operation aborted');
```

The importance of this technique is that it produces no onscreen effect. The loop ends silently by raising an exception of the EAbort class, which the default exception handler receives and returns normal control to the program. However, if your program includes an exception handler, that handler may respond to EAbort just as it does for any other exceptions. If you do *not* want to recognize silent exceptions (so that they remain silent), use the following *try-except* block, which handles the exception but calls ShowMessage only if the exception is not of the EAbort class.

```
try
  {- Statements that may call Abort }
except
  on E: Exception do
    if not (E is EAbort) then
      ShowMessage(E.Message);
  raise;
end;
```

EXCEPTIONS AND RUNTIME ERROR ADDRESSES

As you have probably noticed, the default exception handler built into your applications and Delphi's *Break on exception* dialog display the address of the statement that raised an exception. You may use this address by referring to the global ErrorAddr variable in an exception handler. For example, this displays ErrorAddress if an exception occurs:

```
try
  {- Statements that might raise exceptions }
except
  E: TAnyException do
  ShowMessage('Address = ' +
    IntToStr(Seg(ErrorAddr)) + ':' +
    IntToStr(Ofs(ErrorAddr)));
end;
```

REPLACING THE DEFAULT EXCEPTION HANDLER

For truly advanced work, you can get out the pick and shovel and excavate a custom default exception handler that operates on the Application object level. This technique provides access to all unhandled exceptions, which can be useful for debugging the application's exception-handling capabilities as well as replacing the default handler's dialog box with a more descriptive display.

Even if you don't need to write a default exception handler for your application, you'll want to try the technique in this section. Being able to trap unhandled exceptions on the application level is potentially valuable for debugging your program's error handling. The sample application in this section uses this method to maintain a list of all unhandled exceptions during the course of the program.

The TApplication component provides a procedure, HandleException, that processes any unhandled exceptions that arise during a program's execution. You should not attempt to override this method. Instead, to augment the default handler, you may provide a procedure for the Application object's OnException event. The HandleException method calls the OnException procedure, if one is assigned, instead of displaying a default error message.

Figure 18-5 shows the ExList application's display. Run this program and click the three Exception buttons to generate three types of exceptions. After you close the resulting default dialog box, the program adds the exception error messages to the form's ListBox. Clicking Exception1 raises a divide-by-zero exception. Clicking Exception2 raises a file-not-found exception. Clicking Exception3 converts all listed strings to uppercase — but the programming contains an intentional bug that raises an index-out-of-bounds exception. Listing 18-16 shows the program's source code.

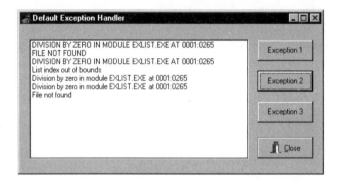

Figure 18-5

The ExList application on the CD-ROM demonstrates how to write a default exception handler. All unhandled exceptions pass through the new handler, which in this program adds the error messages to a ListBox component. This provides a complete tracking of unhandled exceptions in the application.

Listing 18-16
ExList\Main.Pas

```
unit Main;

interface

uses
  SysUtils, WinTypes, WinProcs, Messages, Classes, Graphics, Controls,
  Forms, Dialogs, Buttons, StdCtrls;

type
  TMainForm = class(TForm)
    ListBox1: TListBox;
```

```
    Button1: TButton;
    Button2: TButton;
    Button3: TButton;
    BitBtn1: TBitBtn;
    procedure FormCreate(Sender: TObject);
    procedure Button1Click(Sender: TObject);
    procedure Button2Click(Sender: TObject);
    procedure Button3Click(Sender: TObject);
  private
    procedure NewOnException(Sender: TObject; E: Exception);
    { Private declarations }
  public
    { Public declarations }
  end;

var
  MainForm: TMainForm;

implementation

{$R *.DFM}

procedure TMainForm.NewOnException(Sender: TObject; E: Exception);
begin
  Application.ShowException(E);
  ListBox1.Items.Add(E.Message);
end;

procedure TMainForm.FormCreate(Sender: TObject);
begin
  Application.OnException := NewOnException;
end;

{- Raise a divide-by-zero exception }
procedure TMainForm.Button1Click(Sender: TObject);
var
  I, J, K: Integer;
begin
  I := 0;
  J := 10;
  K := J div I;   { Divide by zero! }
end;

{- Raise a file-not-found exception }
procedure TMainForm.Button2Click(Sender: TObject);
var
  T: TextFile;
begin
  AssignFile(T, 'XXXX.$$$');
  Reset(T);  { Open a non-existent file! }
  try
    { You would normally use T here }
```

1. Declare the OnException event handler.

2. Implement the OnException event handler.

3. Assign the event handler to Application.OnException.

```
     finally
       CloseFile(T);   { For safety's sake }
     end;
   end;

   {- Raise an index-out-of-bounds exception }
   procedure TMainForm.Button3Click(Sender: TObject);
   var
     I: Integer;
   begin
     with ListBox1.Items do
     for I := 0 to Count do   { Should be Count 1! }
       Strings[I] := Uppercase(Strings[I]);
   end;

   end.
```

It takes a bit more work to assign an Application event handler than it does to create one, say, for a Button object's OnClick event. This is because the Application object is not accessible to Delphi's Object Inspector. To create the OnException event handler therefore requires three steps, numbered in comments in the listing. The steps are:

1. Declare the OnException event handler in the form's class. It must have the parameters shown here, although the procedure name is up to you.

2. Implement the OnException event handler. Remember to preface its name with the form class name and a period.

3. Assign the event handler to Application.OnException. The Application object's HandleException method checks whether the program has assigned a procedure to OnException. If so, HandleException calls the procedure for any unhandled exceptions it receives.

A custom OnException event handler receives only exceptions derived from the Exception class except for EAbort exceptions, which remain silent.

You may perform whatever actions you want in the OnException handler. In the sample program (see step 2), the first statement calls the Applicaton's ShowException method. This is what the default handler already does. In addition, the program uses the Add method for the List-Box1's Items string list to keep a copy of each error message. Notice that the event handler receives the exception object as parameter E. (This object is destroyed elsewhere; you don't have to free it.)

You may silence the default event handler by deleting the call to Application.ShowException. Don't do this indiscriminately, however, as it could hide a serious defect in your code. Your OnException event handler probably should display some kind of message on receiving unhandled exceptions.

Summary

- Experienced developers incorporate error-handling code into their programs as they write them. Delphi's exception-handling mechanisms make this relatively easy to do.

- Exceptions can arise from a number of sources. Components, mathematical expressions, file input/output operations, memory shortages, and other events can raise exceptions. You can also raise an exception to notify your application of a problem.

- Protected-statement blocks use the *try-except* keywords to handle exceptions that statements in the *try* part might raise.

- Protected-resource blocks use the *try-finally* keywords to execute must-do code such as freeing allocated memory even if an exception occurs for a statement in the *try* block.

- An exception is an object of a class, usually derived from Exception, that describes the nature of an exception. Raising an exception creates this object. Handling the exception destroys it. You must never explicitly free an exception instance.

- Use *on-do* statements in an *except* block to handle specific types of exceptions. When using this technique, remember that any unhandled exceptions of types not mentioned in *on-do* statements will cause the current procedure or function to exit after the *except* block. Use *try-finally* blocks to clean up any resource allocations in such cases.

- To raise an exception, call *raise* with a newly created exception instance. To reraise an exception after handling it in an *except* block, call *raise* with no arguments.

- You may create your own exception classes, either from scratch, or by deriving them from Exception. In most cases, you should derive your exception classes from Exception because Delphi's default exception handlers recognize only exceptions of these types.

- The Exception class provides a number of Create constructors for creating error messages from strings, values, and string-table resources.

- Call Abort to raise a silent exception of the EAbort class. The default exception handlers do not display an error-message dialog for EAbort exceptions.

- Augment the default exception handler by declaring, implementing, and assigning an OnException event handler in your program's TForm derived class. See the ExList application on the CD-ROM for instructions. Use this technique to debug your program's unhandled exceptions, or to replace the default error-message dialog.

Projects to Try

18-1: Rewrite Listing 18-13 to call a function that converts Edit1's Text property to an integer value. This will demonstrate how, with exceptions, you can make major modifications to a program and remain confident of its error-handling logic.

18-2: Replace the default Application exception handler with your own version that displays a more helpful dialog box. For example, your dialog might include a *Help* button that users can click for information about specific types of exceptions.

18-3: Convert the ExList application into a module that you can incorporate into any application for debugging unhandled exceptions. Add a command to your module to save the list of exception messages in a text file.

Expert-User Tips

- One way to think of exceptions is to consider them as a means for returning multiple types of objects from procedures and functions.

You aren't *required* to use exceptions for error handling. You could raise exceptions to pass objects around and use *try-except* blocks to catch those objects. I don't recommend that you go overboard using exceptions this way, but it is helpful to understand that using them for error control is voluntary. The meaning of exception objects, especially those of your own classes, is up to you to define.

- The default HandleException method in TApplication sends the Windows message wm_CancelMode to release the mouse if it had been captured at the time the exception occurred.

- When constructing hierarchies of exception classes, carefully place any *on-do* statements that refer to your classes to handle most-derived exception objects first. Consider the following code, which is similar to other examples in the chapter:

```
try
  K := J div I;
except
  on E: EDivByZero do
    ShowMessage('Divide error');
  on E: Exception do
    ShowMessage('Other error');
end;
```

This code uses two *on-do* statements (you can have as many as you need in an *except* block). The first statement traps EDivByZero exceptions, perhaps to do something special with those types of errors. The second traps all other exceptions. It would be a mistake to reverse the *on-do* statements because if the ancestor-class exceptions are trapped first, they would include EDivByZero exceptions (which are derived from Exception) and the special Divide error code would never be executed.

- There are two default exception handlers in a Delphi application: one is provided by the VCL and it protects every window procedure through which message traffic passes. This handler traps unhandled exceptions, displays an error message, and continues executing the program. The other default exception handler is in the RTL (runtime library), provided by the SysUtils unit. This handler is below the VCL default handler, so it's unlikely that you'll ever see it in action. When this handler traps an exception, it displays a detailed message (with exception address information for debugging), and then terminates the application. These exceptions are not recoverable.

Coming Up

The next chapter presents tips and fundamental techniques for readers interested in writing custom components.

Constructing Custom Components

A s you acquire new Delphi skills, you may begin to wonder how components actually work. Or, perhaps you have a great idea for an hyperactive confabulator that would make a *super* visual component. Most Delphi developers will never need to build a custom component, but if you are interested in this advanced subject, this chapter will help you get started in component design.

In the following sections, you'll learn about the parts of a component and how they interact with Delphi's development environment. You'll create, test, and install new components into the Visual Component Library (VCL), and you'll take a look at several key component construction techniques. After reading this chapter, you'll be prepared to go beyond the basics in component design, a subject that could easily fill a book of this size.

Introducing Components

A component is an Object Pascal class that conforms to certain rules and regulations. You can build a component from an existing one, and you can construct a component from scratch. Most often, however, you'll base your components on those that come with Delphi. For example, if you want to add some spice to button objects, you can base a new component on Delphi's TButton class and stir in whatever new ingredients you like.

The following are some of the reasons you may want to construct custom components. These are not hard-and-fast rules — they are merely suggestions that may help you decide whether you need to construct a custom component:

- You need to modify an existing component for a special purpose — for example, you need an Image component that can load a bitmap from a hardware device your company is developing. By basing your component on Image, all of that component's properties, methods, and events are available to your enhanced design. You may derive new components from TButton, TListBox, or any other component class.

- You want to create a Delphi component interface for a Windows control that you own. Usually, you'll derive this kind of component from TWinControl, which provides basic properties, methods, and events common to all Windows controls.

- You want to create an entirely new component out of thin air. This will take some effort, but you can save yourself a lot of time by basing the component on TCustomControl, which provides a GDI Canvas along with properties, methods, and events common to all components.

- Your application has special graphics requirements, and you want to construct a component that provides these capabilities. You will base most graphics components on the TGraphicControl class. A sample module in this chapter uses this method to create a BarChart component that displays (you guessed it) a bar chart from a set of data points managed by a string list.

- You want to create a nonvisual component — one that does not appear on the component palette. You've met a few instances of nonvisual components — the TClipboard class, for example. These are relatively rare, but they take advantage of component construction techniques, such as published properties, that can contribute greatly to a program's reliability and ease of maintenance.

COMPONENT AUTHORS AND COMPONENT USERS

Throughout this book so far, you have been a component user. By the time you finish this chapter, you will also be a component author. Component users create multiple objects from components at design time by inserting them into a form window, and at runtime, by calling their Create methods. Component authors create new component classes from which users may create one or more objects at design time and at runtime.

Another difference between component users and component authors concerns access to a component's elements. As a component user, you have only restricted rights of access to a component's innards. For example, you can assign values only to published properties, and you can create events only for those actions the component makes available in the Object Inspector window.

As a component author, you have no such restrictions. *You* decide which properties to publish and how to create the actions your components need. All of your component's elements are available to your program, and you can gain access to protected elements in existing components that are hands-off for users. In return for this freedom, you accept a greater responsibility for writing robust code. Errors on the component level tend to have more serious consequences than application errors.

Creating your own components:

- Provides access to restricted parts of components.

- Makes it possible to add and modify existing component properties, methods, and events.

- Requires a good working knowledge of Object Pascal, object-oriented programming, and exception handling.

Aim to make your components safe to use, even by rank beginners. If a component requires a certain item, it should provide a default value in case users don't supply one. Never assume that users will know how to deploy your components correctly. Ideally, users should be able to do *anything* with a component without causing serious harm.

A FEW GOOD TERMS

Following are definitions of terms that you'll need to know for constructing custom components. The glossary conforms to the use of these terms in other published information about Delphi, but I've tried to be more rigorous here (and throughout the book) on subtle meanings of related words such as object and class, or declaration and definition. These and other hair-splitting distinctions are much more important to component authors than to users.

- *Declaration* — A statement of an a item's name, type, and parameters.

- *Definition* — The creation or implementation of a declared item.

- *Class* — The declaration of a new type that encapsulates data and code for operating on that data. Conceptually, a class resembles a simple data type such as Object Pascal's Integer type. Class names traditionally begin with T (TButton, for example).

- *Instance* — The definition in memory of a class variable. A program may define as many instances of a class as it needs. Conceptually, an instance is similar to a variable of a simple data type such as Integer. For example, you may define as many Integer variables as your program needs, but there is only one Integer "class."

- *Component* — A class derived directly or indirectly from TComponent with special access paths to its data, published properties, and other features that conform to Delphi's requirements for a visual or non-visual component. You declare and implement components in Object Pascal units.

- *Object* — Same as instance. In past versions of Borland Pascal, an object was what a class is in Delphi, leading to much confusion in currently published books and manuals. In this book, I use the word *object* strictly to mean an instance of a class.

- *Access specifier* — One of the keywords *private, protected, public,* or *published* that divide a class declaration into sections. Program statements have varying degrees of access rights to declarations, based on their access specifiers. Private declarations are for use only in the unit that declares the class; protected declarations are also available to derived classes; public declarations are available to all users; and published declarations are properties that define access rules for class data and that appear in the Object Inspector window.

- *Field* — A variable declared in a class.

- *Method* — A procedure or function declared in a class.

- *Method implementation* — The body of a method, including any variables and statements that perform the method's actions.

- *Property* — A published field that typically specifies methods for reading and writing the field's value; also, a published event handler such as OnClick.

- *Event* — A pointer to a user-supplied procedure for specific objects. Contrast this to a method, which performs the identical operations for all objects of the method's class. An event property allows an object to *delegate* actions to another object, which can potentially perform widely varying operations for the same type of event. For example, two Buttons could respond differently to an OnClick event, but the TButton's Hide method works the same for all Button objects.

- *Unit* — A Pascal module stored and compiled separately from other modules. A unit may contain one or more components. However, you may install only entire units, including all of their components, on the component palette. To install individual components, they must be in separate units.

- *Interface part* — Publicly shareable declarations and definitions in a unit; preceded by the *interface* keyword.

- *Implementation part* — Private nonshareable declarations and definitions in a unit; preceded by the *implementation* keyword.

- *Initialization part* — Statements executed when the module is loaded into memory; preceded by the *initialization* keyword and terminated by *end* and a period.

- *Visual component* — A component with a runtime visual representation. Some components such as the TClipboard class are nonvisual, but they are still components in every other way. Visual components may or may not appear on the palette. For example, TForm is a visual component, but is not available on the palette.

IV
19

NOTE
You probably realize this by now, but for those who skipped ahead to this chapter, in this book I refer to components on the component palette by their hint-text names — Button, ListBox, and others. Those components' classes are named TButton and TListBox. When prefaced with a capital T, a name refers to a class declaration; without the T, it refers to the component as used in Delphi's form designer.

COMPONENT CLASS HIERARCHY

Most new components are based on existing component classes. A *derived* component inherits all of the properties, methods, and events from its *ancestor* component. To master component construction, you will need to become intimately familiar with Delphi's component library and the methods it provides to derived components. Figure 19-1 shows the hierarchy of the classes that typically serve as ancestor components. Use this figure to explore the properties, methods, and events that your derived components inherit. *Try never to reinvent capabilities that you can inherit from another component class.*

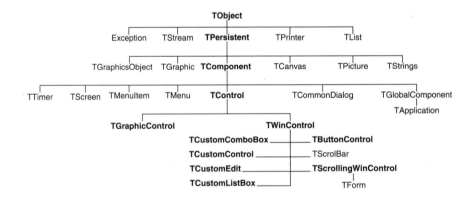

Figure 19-1
Delphi component class hierarchy.

TIP
To become an expert component author, you will eventually need to purchase a copy of Delphi's runtime library source files (you don't need them for this chapter). The source files include all of the programming for the visual component library, and you will learn numerous tricks and

techniques by browsing through the files. Contact Borland for ordering details. You get the runtime library source files with Delphi's Client/Server edition, and in Borland's. Delphi RAD Pack (Rapid Application Development Package). The RAD Pack also includes Visual Solutions Pack, an updated version of Turbo Debugger for Windows that recognizes Object Pascal language extensions, Resource Workshop, and a new Resource Expert for converting dialogs and menus in resource scripts into Delphi forms. The Visual Solutions Pack also includes several extensive VBX custom controls that you can install and use as Delphi components.

Developing a Component

In the following sections, you will construct two components that demonstrate component programming and the process of installing a finished component into Delphi's component palette. These steps are all reversible, so don't hesitate to play.

First, you'll create a simple component just to demonstrate some of the required steps. After that, you'll construct a more complex component that demonstrates more about properties, methods, and events, plus techniques for registration, debugging, and installation.

FIRST STEPS

Components require different programming techniques than applications. You program components in unit modules with Delphi's text editor — you don't use forms, projects, or the Object Inspector window. You may type a component's unit module from scratch, but it's easier to use the Component Expert to create a shell that you can fill in. Follow these steps to use the Expert to create a new component that adds a *bleep* to the standard Button object:

1. Select *File | Close Project* if enabled.
2. Select *File | New Component* to run Delphi's Component Expert.
3. Enter the *Class Name* TDing.
4. Tab to *Ancestor type*, and select TButton from the drop-down list.

5. *Palette Page* should read Samples.

6. Click the Component Expert dialog's *OK* button.

7. Save the resulting unit as Ding.Pas.

These steps create a component template ready for you to fill in with whatever programming you want. In addition to the component's unit module, you need a 24-by-24 pixel, 16-color bitmap to represent the component on the component palette. Store the bitmap in a component resource file (.Dcr) using the Image Editor. The bitmap resource name must be the same as the class name (TDing in this case).

NOTE ⮞ If you don't care to create your own files, copy the two files Ding.Dcr and Ding.Pas from the CD-ROM's Ding directory to your hard disk before continuing. These two files — a resource file with a bitmap, and a unit with the component class — are the bare minimum required files for a custom component. Choose *File | Open File,* not *File | Open Project,* to open the Ding.Pas file.

Listing 19-1 shows the finished Ding.Pas file. If you are entering this file from scratch, use the listing as a guide to filling in the shell you created with the preceding steps.

The finished program adds only a few lines to the Expert's component template. To provide a bell sound when users click the button, I declared procedure Click in the TDing class with an *override* directive:

```
procedure Click; override;
```

The TButton class on which TDing is based provides a Click procedure along with numerous other properties and methods. The override declaration tells the compiler that the new component will replace the inherited Click with its own programming. In addition to declaring the method, you also have to implement it by writing the procedure's body. In this example, the replacement Click method executes two commands:

```
MessageBeep(0);
inherited Click;
```

The first line sounds a tone by calling the Windows API Message-Beep function. The second line calls the inherited Click procedure to perform TButton's actions, which include executing the OnClick event handler if one is assigned.

Listing 19-1
Ding\Ding.Pas

```
unit Ding;

interface

uses
  SysUtils, WinTypes, WinProcs, Messages, Classes, Graphics, Controls,
  Forms, Dialogs, StdCtrls;

type
  TDing = class(TButton)
  private
    { Private declarations }
  protected
    { Protected declarations }
  public
    { Public declarations }
    procedure Click; override;
  published
    { Published declarations }
  end;

procedure Register;

implementation

procedure Register;
begin
  RegisterComponents('Samples', [TDing]);
end;

procedure TDing.Click;
begin
  MessageBeep(0);
  inherited Click;
end;

end.
```

Overrides the Click procedure inherited from TButton.

Called only where installing the component on the pallette — this procedure is deleted from applications that use the component.

TIP   When overriding a method, you will almost always call the inherited method. This is how you build new capabilities into a component while retaining what its methods already do. You are not required to call an inherited method, but if you don't, your program may skip an important initialization buried somewhere in an ancestor class. For safety, always call the inherited method in replacement procedures and functions unless you have an excellent reason for not doing so.

Notice that the Ding.Pas module includes a Register procedure that is not a member of the TDing class. Delphi calls this procedure as part of its component palette installation process. Follow these steps to install the new component (afterward, I'll explain how to delete the component, so don't be nervous about trying this):

1. Save the module using *File | Save File* (Ctrl+S), or click the *Save file* SpeedButton.

2. Select *Options | Install Components*. In the resulting dialog, click the Add button, and then click *Browse* to locate the Ding.Pas file. When you return to the *Install Components* dialog, check that *Installed units* lists the Ding component, and that its directory is added to the *Search path*.

3. Click OK to compile Ding.Pas and link it in Complib.Dcl, Delphi's component DLL.

4. After Delphi's wheels stop spinning, click the Samples page tab in the component palette. You should see the DNG (Ding) component icon. That's all it takes to compile and install a component into Delphi!

You don't have to open a component's .Pas file in Delphi's editor in order to compile and install it in the component palette.

You'll also want to test the new component. To do that, start a new project and insert a DNG object into the form. Press F9 to compile and run. Click the button, and you should hear a chime or beep. The new button is identical in every way to a Button object, but clicking it now produces a sound. This demonstrates the power of object-oriented programming. With only a few strokes, you added a new capability to an existing component class.

Follow these steps to remove the Ding component or another from the component palette. Select *Options | Install Components,* and highlight the Ding unit in the lefthand ListBox. This lists the component classes in the unit — there's only one in this case, TDing. Click the *Remove* button to remove the unit from the list. If you make a mistake, click *Revert*. Click *OK* to recompile Complib.Dpr and remove the Ding component from the component palette. You may add and remove components using these techniques as often as you wish.

PROPERTIES, METHODS, AND EVENTS

Writing custom components involves programming three main elements that are present in every component class: properties, methods, and events. In this and the next several sections, you will develop, test, and install a more extensive component that uses all three of these elements. The finished result, BarChart, displays a bar chart from a set of data points managed by a string list. Figure 19-2 shows a sample of the component in use.

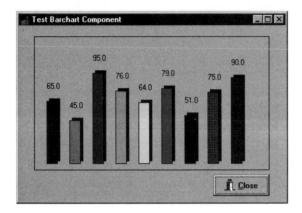

Figure 19-2
An example of the BarChart component that you'll develop, test, and install into Delphi.

Try out the BarChart component to become familiar with it — this will help you to understand its programming. First, you must install the BarChart component into the component palette. Copy the BarChart directory from the CD-ROM, and then follow these steps:

1. Select *Options | Install* Components.
2. Click *Add*.
3. Click *Browse* and locate Barchart.Pas.
4. Click *OK*.

If you already have a BarChart component, temporarily delete it from the palette. Or, you can rename all of this book's BarChart files to some other name, and globally search and replace all occurrences of *BarChart*

in the Barchart.Pas file. You will also have to rename the TBarChart icon in the .Dcr resource file. Use the Image Editor to make this change.

Start a new project, and select the Samples page tab in the component palette. You should see the new BarChart component. For a demonstration, load the sample Bartest project in the Barchart directory, compile, and run. Get back to Delphi, select the BarChart object, and modify the data points in its Data string list. Each point must be a floating-point number, or BarChart will display an error message *and erase the Data*. (Set a data point to XYZ to see this effect.) As you add and delete data points, you see the results in the form window. This demonstrates that a component object is alive at design time as well as at runtime.

If you tried to open the Bartest project before installing the BarChart component, you received an error message from Delphi. This is because you must install all components used by a project before you can open it. After compiling a project, you may remove and add components from the palette without affecting .Exe code files you have already compiled. However, you cannot compile, open, or view a project unless all of its components are available to Delphi.

Listing 19-2 shows the interface section of the Barchart.Pas unit, including the TBarChart class declaration.

The Barchart unit uses several other unit modules, all of which were selected by the Component Expert. You may use other units as well, but because you are not programming a form, Delphi can't automatically add unit names to *uses* as it does for applications. If you call a function or procedure, or if you attempt to construct an object of a class, and you receive an *Unknown identifier* error, look up the identifier's type in Delphi's on-line help and add the item's unit to the *uses* directive.

TBarChart (the derived class) inherits the properties, methods, and events from TGraphicControl (the ancestor class). As you can see from Figure 19-1, the ancestor class is derived from four other classes: TControl, TComponent, TPersistent, and TObject. Therefore, TBarChart inherits all of the properties, methods, and events from those classes. As they used to say to me at the airline counter before I learned how to travel light, "That's a lot of baggage!" But don't fret that this needlessly bloats your new class. Because numerous components are also derived from these same classes, all the inherited methods and events are probably hanging around somewhere in your application anyway. Inheriting them just means the new class gains access to them — *inheriting* is not the same as *copying*.

Listing 19-2
Barchart\Barchart.Pas interface

```
unit Barchart;

interface

uses
  SysUtils, WinTypes, WinProcs, Messages, Classes, Graphics, Controls,
  Forms, Dialogs;

type
  TBarChart = class(TGraphicControl)
  private
    FPen: TPen;
    FBrush: TBrush;
    FData: TStrings;
    FLabels: Boolean;
    XBase, YBase: Integer;
    XIncrement, YIncrement: Integer;
    procedure SetPen(Value: TPen);
    procedure SetBrush(Value: TBrush);
    procedure SetData(Value: TStrings);
    procedure SetLabels(Value: Boolean);
    function YData(N: Integer): Integer;
  protected
    procedure Paint; override;
  public
    constructor Create(AOwner: TComponent); override;
    destructor Destroy; override;
  published
    procedure StyleChanged(Sender: TObject);
    property Pen: TPen read FPen write SetPen;
    property Brush: TBrush read FBrush write SetBrush;
    property Data: TStrings read FData write SetData;
    property Labels: Boolean read FLabels write SetLabels;
    property DragCursor;
    property DragMode;
    property Enabled;
    property ParentShowHint;
    property ShowHint;
    property Visible;
    property OnDragDrop;
    property OnDragOver;
    property OnEndDrag;
    property OnMouseDown;
    property OnMouseMove;
    property OnMouseUp;
  end;

procedure Register;
```

Derive the new class from TGraphic Control and from its ancestor classes as shown in Figure 19-1.

Private declarations are available only in the unit that declares the class.

Most components override their inherited constructor and destructor methods.

Declare Register in the unit's interface so Delphi can install the component on the palette.

IV

19

The TBarChart class begins with several private declarations. All fields and methods following *private* are strictly for use by the unit that declares the class. No other unit anywhere — component or application — may refer to any of the class's private declarations. This is an example of *data hiding*, which experienced programmers realize is one of the keys to successful software development. Bugs are often caused by the indiscriminate use of data, and hiding sensitive items (such as the BarChart's FData string list) guarantees that if any bugs show up with this field, the trouble must be in this module, because *only* this module can refer to FData. Data hiding also frees the developer to modify a class's code without worry that changes will affect other modules.

However, the TBarChart class needs to make the FData string list available so that component users can supply new data for bar chart objects. The class does this by *publishing* the field, which specifies access methods that control how users read and write sensitive data — but more on this later. First, I want to explain TBarChart's other private parts.

Private data fields that are to be published are traditionally prefaced with the letter F. Though not required, this convention will help you keep track of private and published names. For example, FData's published property name is Data. *In component programming, you must be able to distinguish between a field's private and published names.*

The TBarChart class declares fields FPen, FBrush, FData, and FLabels. Try these properties in the sample program. For example, double-click the Brush property in the Object Inspector window, and change its Color subvalue. Also, toggle the Labels property from True to False to erase the data point labels above the bars.

TBarChart also declares a few miscellaneous variables just for convenience. By declaring these variables after the private access specifier, you can be sure that no other module can affect TBarChart objects *except* through the access methods that the class specifically provides.

In addition to fields, the class's private section also declares five methods: four procedures and one function. The "Set" procedures assign values to their respective fields. SetPen assigns a value to FPen, SetBrush assigns a value to FBrush, and so on. In a moment, you'll learn how published properties use these methods to write their associated field values. The YData function returns an integer coordinate for a data point indexed by N.

Here again, all of these methods are private to the class. This means that *only* statements in this unit may call them. No other modules may call SetPen or SetLabels. This restricts the use of the component, and helps prevent bugs. However, because the properties are public, assignments to them using the Object Inspector do call SetPen and SetLabels.

In a class's private, protected, and public sections, field declarations must precede method and property declarations.

Following its private section, the TBarChart class declares a replacement procedure, Paint, in a *protected* section. TBarChart inherits Paint from its ancestor class, and to replace that method, it must end the declaration with the *override* directive. Methods and fields declared in a protected section are one cut above those in a private section. The unit may use these elements, as may any classes derived from TBarChart.

However, the component's users cannot directly call the protected Paint. This provides a measure of safety because Paint is called in response to the window receiving a wm_Paint message. The new class replaces Paint so it can draw a bar chart, but it would be a mistake for applications to call this procedure directly. You may declare fields, methods, and properties in a class's protected section.

The TBarChart class declares two other methods: a constructor Create, and a destructor Destroy. Both are inherited, and both need an *override* directive. They are declared in the class's public section so that users may call them. If you didn't put Create in the public section, programs would have no way to construct TBarChart objects. You may declare fields, methods, and properties in a public section. Any statement anywhere in the application that uses TBarChart may call public methods, and read and write any public data fields.

Finally in the TBarChart class is a lengthy section preceded by the access specifier *published*. In this section are the names of properties that you want Delphi to make available in the Object Inspector window for objects of the class. Any methods declared here are public (StyleChanged, for example), but you'll normally publish only the names of data fields and events.

Some of TBarChart's published properties are new; others are inherited from an ancestor class. For example, the *Visible* property is available in all visual components. If you don't want the component's users to be able to change Visible's value, don't publish it. It's up to you to decide which properties to publish, but you'll generally publish most inherited ones, especially those such as Enabled and Visible that users will expect to find in the Object Inspector.

Properties that are new to TBarChart use a different type of property declaration that specifies an access path to data. For example, look closely at the Pen property's published declaration:

```
property Pen: TPen read FPen write SetPen;
```

A colon follows the property name Pen, after which an expression states the property's data type (TPen), and its read and write access methods. Object Pascal statements can directly assign TPen values, so the read access method is simply the FPen data field's name. The write method, however, is a private method in the class, SetPen. *This means that all assignments to the Pen property actually call SetPen.*

The other properties use similar programming. By publishing them and providing read and write access methods, you carefully control the use of the component's data. TBarChart is only a relatively simple example, but in a more complex situation, this control is invaluable. For example, you might program a Set method to prevent users from assigning illegal or out-of-range values to variables.

There are other ways to publish properties. If you provide only a read method, the property is effectively read-only. You may also create a write-only property for restricting sensitive fields such as a password or an encryption key, but such uses are rare. A property statement may also have additional commands for default values and specifying whether the property is to be stored in a form file. These techniques go beyond this chapter's introduction, but you can read about them in Delphi's on-line help and the *Component Writer's Guide.*

The final line of the Barchart unit's interface declares a procedure that all component units must have for installation onto the palette. The Component Expert inserts this declaration for you, but if you write a component from scratch, you must remember to enter the line:

```
procedure Register;
```

Delphi calls Register when you install the component on the palette. A unit that lacks a Register procedure cannot be installed. Register is called only when the component is linked into the palette. A program must never call Register, which the Delphi linker will remove from applications that use the component module.

COMPONENT CLASS REGISTRATION

Listing 19-3 shows the Barchart unit's Register implementation. The procedure calls RegisterComponents, which requires two arguments: a component palette page name, and a set of component classes in the unit. Surround one or more class names with square brackets to create the set argument.

Listing 19-3
Barchart Unit's Register procedure implementation

```
{- Delphi calls this to install component onto the palette }
procedure Register;
begin
  RegisterComponents('Samples', [TBarChart]);
end;
```

If your unit has multiple component classes, insert them into the component name set, separated by commas. For example, in a unit with three classes, you might call RegisterComponents like this:

```
RegisterComponents('VBX', [THisCtrl, THerCtrl, TItsCtrl]);
```

Or, you may call RegisterComponents multiple times. These statements are operationally the same as the preceding single statement, but are slightly easier to edit in case you have to change how many components the unit registers. Also use this form to install components on different palette pages (you still have to bracket the component names):

```
RegisterComponents('VBX', [THisCtrl]);
RegisterComponents('VBX', [THerCtrl]);
RegisterComponents('Samples', [THisCtrl]);
```

You don't have to register *every* class in a unit; only those that you want to install on the component palette. A unit may also provide procedures, functions, variables, classes, and nonvisual components that don't need to be selected from the palette at design time.

COMPONENT INITIALIZATION

A component's Create constructor initializes objects of the component class. Every component must have a Create constructor. If your component has nothing to initialize, you don't need to override the Create constructor that you inherit from an ancestor class, but it's the rare component that doesn't have to perform *some* initializations.

Likewise, most every component needs a Destroy destructor to free any resources allocated to component objects. For example, if you create an object or allocate some memory in the component's constructor, you must insert a corresponding deallocation statement in the destructor. Failing to do this is sure to cause an eventual loss of memory (the so-called *memory leak* error). Listing 19-4 shows TBarChart's constructor and destructor implementations.

Listing 19-4

TBarChart's constructor and destructor implementations.

```
{- Create component instance at runtime AND design time }
constructor TBarChart.Create(AOwner: TComponent);
begin
  inherited Create(AOwner);
  Width := 65;
  Height := 65;
  FPen := TPen.Create;
  FPen.OnChange := StyleChanged;
  FBrush := TBrush.Create;
  FBrush.OnChange := StyleChanged;
  FData := TStringList.Create;
  FLabels := True;
end;

{- Destroy component instance at runtime AND design time }
destructor TBarChart.Destroy;
begin
  FPen.Free;
  FBrush.Free;
  FData.Free;
  inherited Destroy;
end;
```

Call the inherited constructor, usually before statements that perform new actions.

Free any resources allocated in the constructor.

Call the inherited destructor, usually as the last step.

Create should always call its inherited constructor, usually as the first step. Unlike inherited methods, you must call the inherited Create constructor. *Never skip this step, or the object will not be initialized!* After call-ing the inherited Create, the constructor assigns values to the Width and Height properties, inherited from the ancestor class. These values deter-mine the initial appearance of the object when users insert it into a form.

Next, the constructor creates the FPen, FBrush, and FData fields, which are all objects of Delphi classes. This is a good example of how a component unit may access the class's private declarations. In addition to creating the fields, the program assigns a procedure, StyleChanged, to the FPen and FBrush OnChange event. Using the Object Inspector to assign values to those fields calls StyleChanged, which invalidates the window (try it with a sample project). Due to this code, when users change the Brush property's color, for example, the effect is immediate.

As a last step, the component specifies a default value for the Boolean field, FLabels. The published property statement in the class declaration may specify this *same* value to prevent writing this field to the form file if the property value matches. Because the constructor will assign this value, there's no reason to waste space writing the default value to the form file. To do this, change the property's declaration to:

```
property Labels: Boolean read FLabels write SetLabels default True;
```

As I mentioned, the class destructor must free any allocated resources. TBarChart's destructor, Destroy, does this by calling Free for the FPen, FBrush, and FData fields that the constructor created. As a last step, the destructor calls its inherited Destroy. Components must do this so that any ancestor class allocations are also freed. *Never skip this step.*

Any exceptions that occur in the constructor will leave the object partially initialized. You should program destructors to allow for this possibility — for example, by checking whether pointers are initialized before freeing memory allocated to them.

A component's class constructor is called not only at runtime, but also when the user inserts a component object into a form. Likewise, if the user deletes the object or closes the form or the project, the program calls the component's destructor. Other methods may be called as well — for example, to make assignments to properties. *Component objects are alive at runtime and during application development.*

VISUAL COMPONENT PAINTING

To make their grand appearances on Delphi's stage, visual components override an inherited Paint method. The method calls Canvas functions, sets pen and brush colors, and does whatever is necessary to draw the component object.

Delphi takes care of providing handles, clicking and dragging, resizing, and other design-time features. All you need to do is decide how you want your component objects to look. Listing 19-5 shows the implementation of TBarChart's Paint method along with supporting constants and the YData function, which converts data points to Y- coordinate values for drawing the chart's bars.

Listing 19-5
TBarChart's Paint method implementation and supporting players.

```
const
{- Fixed constants }
  numClrs = 16;              { Number of colors in colorArray }
  spaceAtBottom = 10;        { Reserved pixels below chart }
  spaceAtLeft = 20;          { Reserved pixels at left of chart }
  spaceAtTop = 40;           { Reserved pixels above chart }
  spaceAtRight = 20;         { Reserved pixels at right of chart }
  yScaleMax = 100.0;         { Maximum Y scale value }
  yScaleIncrement = 10.0;    { Increment for Y scale markers }
{- Typed constants }
  spaceVertical: Integer = spaceAtTop + spaceAtBottom;
  spaceHorizontal: Integer = spaceAtLeft + spaceAtRight;
  yScale: Integer = Trunc(yScaleMax / yScaleIncrement);
{- Array of colors used to draw topmost bars }
  colorArray: array[0 .. numClrs - 1] of TColor = (
    $0000000, $0FFFFFF, $0FF0000, $000FF00,
    $00000FF, $0FFFF00, $000FFFF, $0FF00FF,
    $0880000, $0008800, $0000088, $0888800,
    $0008888, $0880088, $0448844, $0884488
  );

{- Return Y-coordinate for data point N }
function TBarChart.YData(N: Integer): Integer;
var
  F: Double;
begin
  F := (StrToFloat(FData[N]) / yScaleIncrement) * yIncrement;
  Result := YBase - Round(F);
end;
```

```
{- Paint component shape at runtime AND design time }
procedure TBarChart.Paint;
var
  XMax, YMax: Integer;
  Width1, WidthD2: Integer;
  I, X1, Y1, X2, Y2: Integer;
begin
  with Canvas do
  begin
  {- Erase background }
    Pen.Color := FPen.Color;
    Brush.Color := FBrush.Color;
    X1 := Pen.Width div 2;
    Y1 := X1;
    XMax := Width - Pen.Width + 1;
    YMax := Height - Pen.Width + 1;
    Rectangle(X1, Y1, X1 + XMax, Y1 + YMax);
    if FData.Count = 0 then Exit;
  {- Initialize variables }
    try
      XIncrement := (XMax - spaceHorizontal) div FData.Count;
      YIncrement := (YMax - spaceVertical) div yScale;
      Width1 := XIncrement div 2;
      WidthD2 := Width1 div 2;
      XBase := spaceAtLeft + WidthD2;
      YBase := YMax - spaceAtBottom;
      Canvas.Font := Self.Font;
    {- Draw barchart }
      for I := 0 to FData.Count - 1 do
      begin
        X1 := spaceAtLeft + (XIncrement * I);
        Y1 := YData(I);
        X2 := X1 + Width1;
        Y2 := YBase;
        if FLabels then
        begin
          Brush.Color := FBrush.Color;
          TextOut(X1, Y1 - 30, FData.Strings[I]);
        end;
        Brush.Color := clBlack;
        Rectangle(X1 + 4, Y1 - 4, X2 + 4, Y2 - 4);
        Brush.Color := colorArray[(I + 2) mod numClrs];
        Rectangle(X1, Y1, X2, Y2);
      end;
    except
      ShowMessage('Error in data point ' + IntToStr(I));
      FData.Clear;
      Invalidate;
    end;
  end;
end;
```

This gives the component a visual appearance at design time and at run time.

IV

19

Paint calls Windows GDI functions through the services of the Canvas object inherited from TGraphicControl. To draw the BarChart's window — what the user initially sees when inserting a BarChart object into a form — Paint assigns the Canvas Pen and Brush colors using the data field FPen and FBrush, which the user can program in the Object Inspector. After preparing a few variables, Paint calls Rectangle and, like magic, a white box appears in the form. *This is all you need to do to give components their design-time appearance.*

Of course, your component probably needs to do more than display a simple box. The rest of TBarChart's Paint method draws the bars and text labels (if FLabels is True). There are two important concerns in this part of the program. One, if FData.Count is zero, there are no data points in the Data property's string list. Paint exits in this case to prevent a divide-by-zero error. The second concern is exception handling, which Paint provides by inserting its math and drawing commands in a *try* block.

Despite this level of protection, any exceptions that occur in a Paint method will cause an endless loop — an anomaly that TBarChart works around in its *except* block. If an error occurs in the *try* block, Delphi will display a dialog box, which when closed, causes the underlying window to become invalid, which causes Windows to issue another wm_Paint, which reenters the Paint method, which generates another exception, and so on until the cows come home. (They never did when this happened to me — maybe we don't have any cows around here.)

For this reason, TBarChart handles any exceptions by displaying an error message, clearing the FData string list, and invalidating the window. Try this by inserting some bad data such as XYZ or another string into the Data property. You'll receive an error message that tells you the faulty data point index (the first index is zero as it is for all string lists), and the object clears.

Rather than clear Data, which is probably not the best response, the program might display a message or a symbol of some kind *inside the object,* or it could set a flag that the program could inspect. You might want to experiment with these alternative responses in the *except* block.

COMPONENT PROPERTY ACCESS METHODS

Listing 19-6 shows the rest of TBarChart's programming. These procedures implement the property access methods for the FPen, FBrush, FData, and FLabels fields.

Listing 19-6
TBarChart's property access method implementations.

```
{- Local event handler redraws shape when necessary }
procedure TBarChart.StyleChanged(Sender: TObject);
begin
  Invalidate;
end;

{- Assign new brush data to FBrush field }
procedure TBarChart.SetBrush(Value: TBrush);
begin
  FBrush.Assign(Value);
end;

{- Assign new pen data to FPen field }
procedure TBarChart.SetPen(Value: TPen);
begin
  FPen.Assign(Value);
end;

{- Assign new string list to FData field }
procedure TBarChart.SetData(Value: TStrings);
begin
  FData.Assign(Value);
  Invalidate;
end;

{- Assign new Boolean value to FLabels field }
procedure TBarChart.SetLabels(Value: Boolean);
begin
  if FLabels <> Value then  { Exit if no change needed }
  begin
    FLabels := Value;  { Assign to FLabels, NOT Labels ! }
    Invalidate;  { Redraw component to add/remove labels }
  end;
end;

end.
```

Issues a WM-Paint message for any changes to the object's FBrush, FPen, and FData fields.

These access methods write values for published properties to the class's private FBrush, FPen, and FData fields.

IV

19

The StyleChanged procedure calls Invalidate so that Windows issues a wm_Paint message for the object's window. This eventually leads to a call to Paint, which erases and redraws the bar chart image. The program doesn't call StyleChanged; it assigns the procedure to the TPen and TBrush OnChange event. Any changes to the Pen and Brush properties therefore redraw the object.

Procedures SetBrush, SetPen, and SetData operate similarly. They each receive a parameter of their field type, which they pass to the field's Assign method. You can be sure that Assign does whatever is necessary to dispose of any existing resources before accepting the new data. For example, assigning a new Pen disposes of the Windows pen resource (if there is one) referenced by the FPen field.

Notice that SetData, which assigns the Data string list property, calls Invalidate to redraw the window. This is because the TStrings class does not provide an OnChange event; if it did, you could assign StyleChanged as for the Pen and Brush properties.

In a property access method, checking whether a value is the same as the new value can help prevent annoying flicker, especially for complex visual components such as BarChart. If SetLabels assigned the new value and called Invalidate, the object would flutter every time users highlighted the Labels property in the Object Inspector.

SetLabels assigns a user value to the FLabel's Boolean switch. This procedure demonstrates a common design for property access methods. Conventionally, the method first checks whether the Value is the same as the object's field. If so, there is nothing to do, and the procedure exits. Otherwise, the program assigns Value to the FLabels field, and invalidates the window to redraw it and remove or insert the data point labels.

Never assign values to *properties* in a property access method. Assign values *only* to data fields, usually declared in the class's private section. Ignoring this rule can cause a stack overflow, and may shut down Delphi and possibly Windows. In the example listing, SetLabels is the access method that the program calls for assignments to the Labels property. If SetLabels were to assign a value to Labels, the program would call SetLabels recursively until the stack blows. Be very careful when writing property access methods to assign values only to actual data fields in the class.

Understanding Component Design

The remainder of this chapter provides tips that you'll find useful in understanding component design techniques. As I mentioned, component construction could easily fill a book of this size, so the following is necessarily incomplete. However, I've tried to touch on subjects that are of key interest to component authors, and that will suggest topics to search for in other sources.

CUSTOM COMPONENTS

In the VCL, you'll come across components with the word Custom in their names. For example, TCustomEdit is derived from TWinControl in the StdCtrls unit using the declaration:

```
TCustomEdit = class(TWinControl)
...
end;
```

Immediately following, you'll find this declaration for the TEdit component, the one that applications use:

```
TEdit = class(TCustomEdit)
...
end;
```

The reason for having two classes instead of just TEdit is to provide you with a raw edit-control class with no published properties (actually, there is one, TabStop, which gets a default value of True). Components with Custom in their names publish no (or only essential) properties.

If you derive your components from TEdit, all of its published properties become published in the derived class. If you instead derive your class from TCustomEdit, which provides the actual programming for TEdit, you decide which properties to publish.

COMPONENT DEBUGGING

Debugging and testing components is complicated by the fact that you are using the very development system into which you want to install the component. Delphi can compile only projects — to compile components, you must install them on the component palette. When that's not convenient, you can take one of two approaches:

- Develop your component as an application, and then convert it to a component. I created the TBarChart component using this method.
- Include a component unit in a test project, and construct objects of the component's class in a procedure or function. You'll have to run the program to view the component, but this method will help you to debug your code before installing the component on the palette.

To experiment with the second technique — which is essential for writing complex components — remove the BarChart component from the component palette and copy the Barchart.Pas file to a fresh directory. You don't need the Barchart.Dcr resource file, because Delphi uses this file only to install the component's palette icon. Follow these steps to create a test program that creates a BarChart object entirely under program control:

1. Start a blank project. Name the form MainForm, and set its Caption to *Test BarChart Component*. Save the project in the directory that contains the copy of Barchart.Pas. Name the unit Main.Pas and the project BarTest.Prj.
2. Add BarChart to the Main unit's *uses* directive.
3. Because the BarChart component is not on the component palette, you have to declare objects of the class manually. Do that by typing object declarations into the form's class — just as Delphi does automatically for finished components. For example, enter the following declaration in the TMainForm class's public section:

```
BarChart1: TBarChart;
```

4. Create a handler for the form's OnCreate event (or you may use any event handler — a Button's OnClick, for example). Create the component instances you need. This takes a minimum of two steps: (1)

Call Create to construct the object, and (2) Assign a parent object to the object's Parent field. Usually, you can use Self as arguments in both tasks. Self refers to the form object (because this is a method of the form's class), and you'll probably want to have the form own the object (step 1) and serve as its parent (step 2). For example, use these statements to create a BarChart object:

```
BarChart1 := TBarChart.Create(Self);
BarChart1.Parent := Self;
```

5. You'll also have to initialize other fields such as Left, Right, Width, and Height, which determine the object's position and size. In addition, you need to add statements to assign any required data — the BarChart object's Data string list, for example. Listing 19-7 shows the finished unit, stored as Main2.Pas in the Barchart directory.

Listing 19-7

Barchart\Main2.Pas. This file demonstrates how to construct an object at runtime for a component not on the component palette. Use this file to create a test project for the BarChart component class.

```
unit Main;

interface

uses
  SysUtils, WinTypes, WinProcs, Messages, Classes, Graphics, Controls,
  Forms, Dialogs, BarChart;

type
  TMainForm = class(TForm)
    procedure FormCreate(Sender: TObject);
  private
    { Private declarations }
  public
    BarChart1: TBarChart;
    { Public declarations }
  end;

var
  MainForm: TMainForm;

implementation

{$R *.DFM}
```

Declare the object in the form's public section.

```
procedure TMainForm.FormCreate(Sender: TObject);
begin
  BarChart1 := TBarChart.Create(Self);
  BarChart1.Parent := Self;
  with BarChart1 do
  begin
    Left := 20;
    Top := 20;
    Width := 375;
    Height := 200;
    Data.Add('65.0');
    Data.Add('45.0');
    Data.Add('95.0');
    Data.Add('76.0');
    Data.Add('51.0');
    Data.Add('90.0');
  end;
end;

end.
```

Create the object and assign the form (referenced here by self) as its parent.

Initialize other object properties as needed.

Do not insert data fields or method declarations in the default published section of a form class (the section immediately following the class declaration up to the first access specifier, usually *private*. If you modify the default published section, you will receive an error message because this is where Delphi declares objects and event handlers. Consider a class's default published section *hands off* for your own declarations.

CLASS PROPERTIES

A property may be any data type except a file. However, a property cannot be a Pascal array, because properties are not real fields and access to them is controlled by read and write methods. You may, however, create array-like properties that call methods to read and write their elements. (For more information, see "Array Properties" in this chapter.) Except for these restrictions, a property may publish any kind of field.

 Events are actually data fields of the TNotifyEvent or a similar type. An event is a *pointer* to a user-supplied method. However, an event is not itself a method, and therefore, publishing an event actually publishes a data field (the pointer), not code.

Properties appear to the component user as fields, but they are actually encapsulated methods for reading and writing other data fields, which are normally private to the component class. Properties may also be calculated. For example, you can write a property access method that computes a property value from other data fields. However, be careful not to introduce too many dependencies among calculated properties, or the order in which they are initialized will become critical, a fact that can complicate future maintainence.

Publishing properties makes available runtime type information about the class that Delphi uses in several ways. For example, the Object Inspector uses runtime type information to display and edit property values, which are stored in a .Dfm form file. After compiling this chapter's BarTest project, open the Main.Dfm file to view how Delphi stores properties. Listing 19-8 shows a sample file. I deleted some lines to keep the listing short — use Delphi to open the file to inspect the whole shebang.

Listing 19-8

Barchart\Main.Dfm form file for the BarTest project.

```
object MainForm: TMainForm
  Left = 200
  Top = 95
  Width = 435
  Height = 300
  ...
  object BarChart1: TBarChart
    Left = 24
    Top = 16
    Width = 377
    Height = 209
    Hint = 'BarChart component'
    Brush.Color = clSilver
    Data.Strings = (
      '65.0'
      '45.0'
    ...
      '90.0')
    Labels = True
    ParentShowHint = False
    ShowHint = True
  end
end
```

Delphi stores property values entered with the ObjectInspector in a .Dfm form file.

That looks like Pascal, but it isn't. A form file contains property values as entered into the Object Inspector window. Delphi loads the property values *after* it calls the component's constructor, which gets first crack at initializing property values.

There's one more way to initialize property values. After calling the component's constructor and loading property values from the form file (or its image bound into the compiled .Exe code file), Delphi calls a virtual Loaded method that you can override. Place this declaration in the component class's protected section:

```
procedure Loaded; override;
```

Implement the procedure to perform any additional initializations for the object. These initializations take priority over any values assigned in the constructor or from the form file (in other words, by the Object Inspector). Users can still set properties using the Object Inspector, but when they run the program, Loaded will again be called, so don't replace any values that you want users to be able to program.

Loaded is useful for providing default values for properties that users may decide to leave blank or that don't have form-file values. The Loaded function is also a good place to adjust a fixed-size component's dimensions. For example, the DBNavigator component uses this technique to initialize default hint strings if the user doesn't enter any into the Hints field; it also makes minor adjustments to the object's size and position.

Always call the inherited Loaded method in your replacement procedure, or you may skip an important initialization required by an ancestor class. Loaded is also the only chance you get to access any associated objects (siblings, child objects, or linked objects) during the loading process. For example, a data-aware component cannot use its Data-Source property until Loaded is called.

ARRAY PROPERTIES

Properties may not be Pascal arrays, but you can create an array property that is used just like an array. Array properties are especially valuable for creating advanced data structures such as associative and sparse arrays. Like all properties, an array property provides access methods for reading and writing data. The property's class can choose any method for the actual data storage. For example, this is how the TStrings property provides access to string data using array indexing, but internally, links strings efficiently into a list.

Array properties may also use any kind of data type for indexes. You can create an array indexed on floating-point values or strings. Common Pascal arrays may use only ordinal indexes such as integers, characters, and enumerated constants.

Listing 19-9 is a Crt application that demonstrates how to program array properties. You may use the same technique in a component, but as this program illustrates, you can also publish array properties as protected members of any class.

Listing 19-9
Daynames\Crtapp.Pas

```pascal
program CrtApp;

uses SysUtils, WinCrt;

type

  TDayNames = class
  private
    function GetName(N: Integer): String;
  protected
    property DayStr[N: Integer]: String read GetName; default;
  end;

function TDayNames.GetName(N: Integer): String;
begin
  if (N < 0) or (N > 6) then
    raise ERangeError.Create('Array index out of range');
  case N of
    0: Result := 'Sunday';
    1: Result := 'Monday';
    2: Result := 'Tuesday';
    3: Result := 'Wednesday';
    4: Result := 'Thursday';
    5: Result := 'Friday';
    6: Result := 'Saturday';
  end;
end;

var
  DayNames: TDayNames;
  I: Integer;
```

Declares are array-like property that calls GetName.

This makes DayStr the class's default property.

```
begin
  DayNames := TDayNames.Create;
  try
    Writeln('Default property (DayNames[I])');
    for I := 0 to 6 do
      Writeln(DayNames[I]);
    Writeln;
    Writeln('Named property (DayNames.DayStr[I])');
    for I := 6 downto 0 do
      Writeln(DayNames.DayStr[I]);
  finally
    DayNames.Free;
  end;
end.
```

To create a Crt application, select *Options|Environment* and enable the *Use on new project* checkbox. Create a new project and select *CRT Application* from the project gallery. The resulting program provides a text-like screen in a window that's useful for quick and dirty tests like this one.

The example program creates a small class, TDayNames, that provides the days of the week as a pseudo string array. The class declares a private function, GetName, that's used as the pseudo array's read-access method. The class's protected section declares that access method as a property DayStr, followed by square brackets containing an integer argument. This argument could be any data type, even a string. Following the closing bracket are a colon, the data type of the array elements, and the read-access method, GetName.

Ending the property declaration with *default* sets this property as the class's default. This means users of class objects can treat the object as though it were the property. Only one property of any class may be the default. For example, the program's first *for* loop uses the DayNames object as though it were an array:

```
for I := 0 to 6 do
  Writeln(DayNames[I]);
```

You can also refer to the property as a field in the object:

```
for I := 6 downto 0 do
  Writeln(DayNames.DayStr[I]);
```

The TStrings class uses this same method to provide access to its strings using an expression such as Items[I] or Items.Strings[I], which are the same because Strings is the default property of TStrings.

When the program uses an expression such as DayNames[I], the compiler generates a call to the designated read-access method, in this example, function GetName. In the listing, GetName first checks whether the index is in range — if not, it raises an ERangeError exception. Insert this statement into the main program's *try* block to test the exception:

```
Writeln(DayNames[7]);  { ??? }
```

Function GetNames uses a *case* statement to return a day-name string for the index values 0 to 6. Because the sample class is read-only, it does not provide a write-access method, but this is equally easy to do. Declare the write-access method, which must have an index value parameter (it can be any type, but is Integer here), as follows:

```
procedure SetName(N: Integer; const S: String);
```

Next, add *write SetName* to the property declaration:

```
property DayStr[N: Integer]: String read GetName write SetName; default;
```

Implement procedure SetName to store its passed string at the specified index. For example, you might insert the string into a list and record the index value in an object. The read-access method would then search the list for this index and return the associated string — an example of an associative, sparse array. Only entered strings are stored on the list; unused index positions occupy no space.

Noncomponent classes such as TDayNames may not publish properties, but can declare them in a protected or public section as demonstrated here. This is a useful technique for controlling access to data fields.

Summary

- Writing your own components is no simple task, but offers advanced programmers additional tools and capabilities not available to application developers. You can base new components on any supplied with Delphi, or you can construct entirely new ones.

- A component is a special class declaration and unit that conform to Delphi's requirements for visual components. Use the Component Expert to create a shell unit that you can fill in. The shell includes a Register procedure, which is required to install the component on the component palette. Register is removed from application code.

- Components publish properties to provide access methods for reading and writing class data fields. Users can view and edit published properties that have write-access methods in the Object Inspector window.

- Components require constructor and destructor methods. Visual components implement a Paint method to create their on-screen appearance, both in the form at design time, and in the running program.

- For debugging components, create them under program control rather than install them on the component palette. This makes it possible to use Delphi's debugger to single-step the component's programming, and to insert breakpoints and inspect variables.

- Properties may be any data types except files and Pascal arrays. You may create an array property that calls read and write access methods, but that is used as an array. Use this technique to create associative and sparse array data structures.

Projects to Try

19-1: Create a Date and Time component that you can insert into a form. Add an alarm feature that rings a bell or pops up a message. You might use a string list data field to enter alarm dates and times.

19-2: Add a Font property to the TBarChart component. Initialize the Font to the form's font (see the Paint method's assignment to Canvas.Font for a hint on how to do that).

19-3: Improve TBarChart's exception handling. Rather than delete data points if an exception occurs, try one of the other suggested responses. For example, you might display a bomb symbol instead of a dialog box, or you might test individual data points for validity in some other way.

19-4 Create a bitmapped version of the RadioButton component with a custom symbol (a diamond, for example) in place of the usual black dot.

19-5: *Advanced.* Create an animated icon component that displays a sequence of bitmaps. You might use the component to display animations during lengthy file, printing, and other operations.

19-6 *Advanced.* Add an array property to the TBarChart class that publishes the unit's currently static color array. This array provides 16 color values for drawing successive bars. (Colors repeat if there are more than 16 bars.) Improve the BarChart component by making it possible for users to edit these color values.

IV
19

Expert-User Tips

- You can provide online help for your components. When users select your component and press F1, Delphi initiates an on-line help search indexed on the keyword *class_<name>*, where *<name>* is your component's class name. For more information, see the on-line help topic *Merging Your Help into Delphi.*

- Removing a component from the component palette does not affect any compiled applications that use that component. However, the component must be installed before you can load any project that uses it.

- To create a property that is available only at runtime, but is not visible in the Object Inspector window, place the property declaration in the class's public section, but don't publish it. (Actually, it's not possible to declare a public, published property, which would create conflicting access paths to the associated field. A property can be public or it can be published; it can never be both.)

- Delphi can compile only projects. To compile a unit under development, *use* it in a test project. Delphi compiles modified data component units as necessary when you install them.

- Properties may be in a class's protected, public, or published sections. You may declare properties in a class's private section, but it is pointless to do so because the class's unit already has full access to all private data fields. The purpose of a property is to provide controlled access to private and protected data.

- The Object Inspector automatically sorts property names alphabetically. You may declare properties in any order in the class. This has no effect on their order in the Object Inspector.

- However, the order of calculated properties may be important. Delphi loads property values from a form file in their declared order. Because each assignment calls the property's write-access method if it has one, any dependencies might be affected by which property Delphi loads first. Insert a comment after any properties that must be loaded before others so you don't accidentally rearrange their orders incorrectly. (You'll find a few instances of dependent properties in the runtime library source files.)

- Properties may be any data type except files, but there are additional restrictions on what kinds of properties a class can publish. You can't publish Pascal arrays, for example, nor can you publish read-only or write-only properties because the Object Inspector must be able to read and write them. Published properties may also not use Pascal's Real or Extended data types. For floating-point properties, use Single, Double, or Comp.

Coming Up

Everybody loves a bargain, and I hope that you'll find something of exceptional value in the next chapter, which collects tips, tricks, and techniques for sharpening your Delphi programming skills.

20 Honing your Delphi Skills

I'm always on the prowl for wild new ideas, and as I wrote this book, I collected several hot tips and tricks for this final chapter. There's absolutely no order or theme to the following grab bag, but you're sure to find numerous hints and suggestions that will help sharpen your Delphi programming skills.

Topics in this chapter include: CRT applications, command-line tools, reducing code file size, a few useful functions, tips on creating and using online help, how to create and use dynamic link libraries, how to insert forms and other components into a DLL, how to use runtime type information, application event handlers, file streams, useful DOS batch files, and other tidbits.

CRT Applications

Have you tried writing a CRT application? This is simply a text-only program that doesn't require a form and doesn't use components. A CRT application is the economy model — it costs you little in time and effort, but it gets you where you're going in a hurry.

Use CRT applications to test Object Pascal programming methods, to experiment with algorithms, and to run plain-text examples from Pascal tutorials. To create a CRT application, select *Options|Environment* and enable the *Gallery* check box, *Use on new project*. Close the *Environment Options* dialog, and start a new project. Select *CRT Application* from the *Gallery* dialog.

Next, specify a directory in which Delphi should save the shell file, Crtapp.Pas. Modify the shell as you wish, and press F9 to compile and run. This creates Crtapp.Exe, which you can also run using the Windows File Manager or Program Managers, or the Windows 95 Explorer. Crtapp.Exe is a *Windows,* not a DOS program that displays output in a text-only window. For example, enter the programming from Listing 20-1 for a handy utility that you can use to discover values for various key combinations. Run the program and press any key (but not function keys). Press Ctrl+C to quit, followed by Alt+F4 to close the inactive output window.

Listing 20-1

Keytest\Keytest.Pas. A sample CRT application that you can use to discover keypress values. Press Ctrl+C to quit.

```
program KeyTest;
uses WinCrt;
var
 Ch : char;
begin
  Writeln('Keyboard tester');
  Writeln('To quit, press Ctrl+C,');
  Writeln('or close the window');
  Writeln;
  repeat
    Ch := ReadKey;
    Writeln(Ord(Ch):4);
  until False;
end.
```

Use Write, Writeln, Read, and Readln for input and output in CRT applications. For example, define a string variable, and try this short program to prompt users for input and then display the response:

```
var
  S: String;
begin
  Write('What''s your name? ');
  Readln(S);
  Writeln('Your name is ', S);
end.
```

A CRT application is a project, but it doesn't have a .Dpr project file. Even though a CRT application has only a single Crtapp.Pas file, choose *File|Project save* to save it. Select *File|Project open* to open a Crtapp.Pas file. If you open the file with *File|Open file,* you can view and modify its text, but you can't compile it. You may rename a Crtapp.Pas file if you want, but the *program* identifier on the first line must match the filename or Delphi will display an error message when you reopen the project. For this reason, it's best to use *File|Save Project As* to rename a CRT application project.

Command-Line Tools

Delphi comes with DOS command-line tools that you can use to build Windows applications. The results are the same as with the integrated environment, but the command-line tools permit development on DOS-only systems. You can also select esoteric compiler options and produce linker map files for use during debugging.

The first step in using Delphi's command-line tools is to get to a DOS prompt. You can either quit Windows or open a DOS prompt window. Check if Delphi's Bin (binaries) directory is on the system path (type PATH). If not, enter and run the Delpath.Bat batch file in Listing 20-2.

Listing 20-2
Delpath.Bat

```
@echo off
rem
rem delpath.bat -- Configure PATH for Delphi command line
rem
set path=%path%;c:\delphi\bin
echo Configured for Delphi command line
path
```

With the Bin directory on the path, change to any Delphi project directory. For example, copy the Polyflow application from the CD-ROM to your hard disk, and enter a command such as:

```
cd \demos\polyflow
```

To compile the application, run the Dcc (Delphi Command-line Compiler) from the DOS prompt. This runs the Borland Pascal compiler, version 8.0. The compiler looks for. Pas files by default, so the first attempt fails:

```
C:\DEMOS\POLYFLOW>dcc polyflow
Delphi Compiler   Version 8.0   Copyright (c) 1983,95 Borland International
Error 15: File not found (POLYFLOW.PAS).
```

To compile a project, you have to supply the .Dpr extension. However, the second try also fails with an out-of-memory error:

```
C:\DEMOS\POLYFLOW>dcc polyflow.dpr
Delphi Compiler   Version 8.0   Copyright (c) 1983,95 Borland International
POLYFLOW.DPR(12)
Error 1: Out of memory.
```

Delphi projects require lots of linker memory. Because Dcc is a protected mode DOS application, you can give it more memory by adjusting the XMS (eXtended Memory System) setting in your default PIF file using the Windows PIF Editor. Alternatively, you can specify the -l option to create a temporary link buffer on disk. Adding this option successfully creates Polyflow.Exe:

```
C:\DEMOS\POLYFLOW>dcc -l polyflow.dpr
Delphi Compiler   Version 8.0   Copyright (c) 1983,95 Borland International
POLYFLOW.DPR(12)
12 lines, 1.1 seconds, 131442 bytes code, 3644 bytes data.
```

You can now run the program. If you have Windows 95 or Windows NT, simply type Polyflow; if you are running Windows 3.1 or Windows for Workgroups 3.11, you must use the File Manager or the Program Manager to run the compiled program.

Reducing Code File Size

A compiled Delphi application code file includes *everything* required to run the program. If you are a Visual Basic programmer, you may raise your eyebrows when you see the large code files that Delphi creates, but there's a good reason for these large files. As you probably know, VB programs require the Visual Basic runtime library (VBRun300.Dll, for example) to be installed in Windows\System. Running a VB program opens and uses the subroutines in this library.

However, VB programs are not compiled to native processor code. They are translated to *pseudocode* (P-Code). VBRun interprets P-Code and issues the actual instructions that run a VB program. This additional layer of processing is the reason that VB applications run more slowly than Delphi programs or those produced with a C or C++ development system.

Delphi code files are true, native code executables, and they include all runtime library subroutines that the application uses. There's no getting around the fact that fast native code files are necessarily larger than relatively slow P-Code files. You can't have your cake and eat it too, and you can't have the benefits of native code without larger code files.

You can, however, strip out debugging information that Delphi adds to executable files. Use the *Options* menu *Project* and *Environment* commands and disable all debugging checkboxes. Recompile to create a code file without debugging information.

You can also run the W8Loss.Exe utility to put your code files on a diet. (Whoever came up with "W8Loss" deserves a *Cute Filename Award*.) W8Loss consolidates duplicate segment fixup records, rearranges information in the .Exe code file, and performs other space-saving reorganizations. For example, using W8Loss from DOS, I was able to reduce Polyflow.Exe's code file by 38,456 bytes:

```
C:\DEMOS\POLYFLOW>dir *.exe
POLYFLOW EXE      195,328 07-12-95  11:46a

C:\DEMOS\POLYFLOW>w8loss polyflow
W8LOSS version 1.0 (c) Copyright 1993-95 Borland International
Processing polyflow.exe...

C:\DEMOS\POLYFLOW>dir *.exe
POLYFLOW EXE      156,872 07-12-95  11:46a
```

Delphi's smart linker includes only referenced procedures and functions in the final code file. It strips unused procedures and functions from the .Exe image. However, because components have more relatives than a royal family, most applications will include nearly all of the core VCL code from the Classes, Controls, Graphics, and Forms units. Small applications will therefore produce seemingly out-of-proportion code files, but as you add new programming to those applications, they will grow at a slower rate. In other words, a Delphi application that doubles in source-code size will likely *not* double in code-file size.

IV

20

Useful Functions

Every programmer has a library of subroutines that have proven their value over the years. Following are some useful additions you can make to your library.

CALLBACK FUNCTIONS

A callback function is a subroutine in your program that Windows calls. A typical use for a callback function is to enumerate a list of items such as the titles and handles for all windows, or the names of available fonts. You may specify a class method as a callback function, or you can write a stand-alone callback. The following examples demonstrate both techniques.

Start a blank project, and insert a ListBox object into the form. Enlarge the ListBox to fill most of the default form window. Add this declaration to the TForm1 class's private section:

```
function EnumWinProc(Handle: HWnd): Boolean; Export;
```

The EnumWinProc function receives a window handle, and it returns True to continue enumerating windows, or False to stop. The Export directive tells the compiler that Windows will call this function. Implement the function by typing the lines from Listing 20-3 into the unit's implementation.

Listing 20-3
A callback function that inserts a window title into a ListBox.

```
function TMainForm.EnumWinProc(Handle: HWnd): Boolean;
var
  Sz: array[0 .. 132] of Char;
begin
  Result := True;
  if GetWindowText(Handle, Sz, Sizeof(Sz)) <> 0 then
    ListBox1.Items.Add(StrPas(Sz));
end;
```

Finally, create an OnCreate event handle for the form, and insert the following statement to enumerate all windows. Run the program to fill the ListBox with the titles of all open windows.

```
EnumWindows(@TForm1.EnumWinProc, Longint(Self));
```

The first argument to EnumWindows (a Windows API function) is the address of the callback function. The @ sign returns the address of an item, in this case, function EnumWinProc in the TForm1 class. The second argument passes the address of the current object (the Form1 object in this example) to the callback function. This second argument is the essential trick for using a method as a callback — all methods receive an undeclared Self pointer to the object for which they are called. Passing Self, cast to a Longint value, to EnumWindows provides the object's Self address to the callback function.

NOTE ▶ Load and run the EnumWin project on the CD-ROM for an example of this technique.

You can also write a stand-alone callback function, but this takes additional steps to create a *procedure instance,* which you pass to Windows. Listing 20-4 demonstrates the technique. Load the Enumfon project, and run it to fill a ListBox with the names of available fonts.

The program implements the callback function EnumFontsProc in the unit's implementation. It is not a class member, and therefore, the program does not need to declare it in the unit's interface. The callback function receives parameters that describe the system's fonts — here, we are only interested in the font names. The function also receives a 32-bit Pointer, named Data, that the program is free to use for any purposes. Here, we use it as a TStrings reference to insert font names into a string list. Returning 1 as the function result tells Windows to continue enumerating fonts until exhausting the supply.

The form's OnCreate event handler demonstrates the correct way to call a Windows enumeration function such as EnumFonts. First, call MakeProcInstance to create a procedure instance handle for the callback function. Pass the function address and the program's instance handle, and save the result in a TFarProc variable.

It is essential that the program free any procedure instances it creates, and you should always use a *try-finally* protected-resource block to ensure that FreeProcInstance is called even if the program raises an exception. In the *try* block, call the enumeration function — EnumFonts in the

IV

20

demonstration. The final argument passes a ListBox object's Items property as a Pointer — the callback function receives this pointer in its Data parameter.

Listing 20-4

Enumfon\Main.Pas. This program demonstrates how to enumerate font names using a stand-alone callback function.

```pascal
unit Main;

interface

uses
  SysUtils, WinTypes, WinProcs, Messages, Classes, Graphics, Controls,
  Forms, Dialogs, StdCtrls, Buttons;

type
  TMainForm = class(TForm)
    ListBox1: TListBox;
    Label1: TLabel;
    BitBtn1: TBitBtn;
    procedure FormCreate(Sender: TObject);
  private
    { Private declarations }
  public
    { Public declarations }
  end;

var
  MainForm: TMainForm;

implementation

{$R *.DFM}

function EnumFontsProc(var LogFont: TLogFont;
  var TextMetric: TTextMetric; FontType: Integer;
  Data: Pointer): Integer; export;
begin
  with TStrings(Data) do
    Add(StrPas(LogFont.lfFaceName));
  Result := 1;
end;

procedure TMainForm.FormCreate(Sender: TObject);
var
  Proc: TFarProc;
begin
  Proc := MakeProcInstance(@EnumFontsProc, HInstance);
  try
    EnumFonts(Canvas.Handle, nil, Proc, Pointer(ListBox1.Items));
  finally
    FreeProcInstance(Proc);
  end;
end;

end.
```

This is the callback function, which Windows calls.

Create a procedure instance for the callback function.

DATE AND TIME FUNCTIONS

Object Pascal's System unit, which all applications use, defines the TDateTime data type as equivalent to Float. There are a baker's dozen plus an extra helping of procedures and functions that use TDateTime for just about any date and time operation you could possibly need.

The integer part of a TDateTime variable equals the number of days that have passed since January 1, 0001. TDateTime stores the time as the variable's fractional part, equal to the *proportion* of the day starting from midnight that has passed. For example, 0.75 represents 6:00 pm — three fourths of the day past midnight. (Impress your family tonight; announce that it's past 0.95 hours and time for bed.)

Use Object Pascal's Trunc function to extract the day part of a TDateTime value. Given two TDateTime variables Date1 and Date2, the following statement assigns to an integer N the number of days between the two dates. It doesn't matter which date you specify first:

```
N := abs(Trunc(Date1) - Trunc(Date2));
```

IV
20

A POWERFUL FUNCTION

Object Pascal lacks a function that can raise a floating-point base value to a floating-point exponent, but scientific applications often need this capability. Listing 20-5 presents the missing Power function. Copy the constant, exception class type, and function to any module, and call Power as the program's Test procedure demonstrates.

I've published versions of Power elsewhere, but I included a new version of it here to demonstrate how math functions should use exception handling. It is illegal to raise a negative base to a fractional exponent or to raise zero to a nonzero exponent less than one. The Power function here raises an EPower exception in both instances. Run the program to demonstrate how the Test procedure deals with these kinds of errors.

The Power function raises an exception of the EPower class, derived from the general-purpose EMathError class, which is derived from Exception. To use the Power function, add the SysUtils unit to the program's *uses* directive (Delphi applications automatically do this, but CRT applications don't). To raise an exception, Power executes this statement:

```
raise EPower.CreateFmt(sFmt, [Base, Exponent])
```

The CreateFmt function, inherited from Exception, takes two arguments: a string with embedded formatting commands, and a set of values. When an exception occurs, EPower's Message field contains a string that shows the values that caused the error:

```
Error in Power function. Base=-7.20 Exp=3.50
```

Listing 20-5

Power\Crtapp.Pas. This program contains function Power, which can raise a floating-point base to a floating-point exponent. Choose File | Open Project to open the Ctrapp.Pas file.

```
program CrtApp;

uses WinCrt, SysUtils;

const
  sFmt = 'Error in Power function. Base=%f Exp=%f';

type
{- Declare exception class }
  EPower = class(EMathError);

{- Return Base raised to Exponent }
function Power(Base, Exponent: Double): Double;
  function F(B, E: Double): Double;
  begin
    Result := Exp(E * Ln(B));
  end;
begin
  if Base = 0.0 then
    if Exponent = 0.0 then
      Result := 1.0
    else if Exponent < 1.0 then
      raise EPower.CreateFmt(sFmt, [Base, Exponent])
    else
      Result := 0.0
  else if Base > 0.0 then
    Result := F(Base, Exponent)
  else if Frac(Exponent) = 0.0 then
    if Odd(Trunc(Exponent)) then
      Result := -F(-Base, Exponent)
```

The exception class performs no actions, so it can be a pure declaration without any class members.

This raises an exception of the EPower class.

```
    else
      Result :=  F(-Base, Exponent)
  else raise EPower.CreateFmt(sFmt, [Base, Exponent]);
end; { Power }

{- Test procedure }
procedure Test(Base, Exponent: Double);
begin
  try
    Writeln(Base:8:3, ' ^ ', Exponent:8:3, ' = ',
      Power(Base, Exponent));
  except
    on E: EPower do
      Writeln(E.Message);
  end;
end;

begin
  test(  7,     3   );
  test(  7,    -3   );
  test( -7,     3   );
  test( -7,    -3   );
  test(  7,     3.5 );
  test(  7,    -3.5 );
  test(  7.2,   3   );
  test(  7.2,  -3   );
  test( -7.2,   3   );
  test( -7.2,  -3   );
  test(  7.2,   3.5 );
  test(  7.2,  -3.5 );
{- These four tests produce expected exceptions }
  test( -7,     3.5 );
  test( -7,    -3.5 );
  test( -7.2,   3.5 );
  test( -7.2,  -3.5 );
end.
```

Trap any exceptions raised by calling Power. Other exceptions continue up the call chain until handled in the program or by a default exception handler.

IV

20

Runtime Type Information

A compiler obviously can determine from the program's source code the types of objects it creates. But for objects created at runtime, the source code may not be available, and objects must contain runtime type information that describes what they are. This is a controversial subject in object-oriented programming, and there are currently few if any standards on the best format to use for runtime object identification.

RTTI declarations are in the Typinfo.Int file located in Delphi's Doc directory. Borland states in the file that RTTI declarations will change in future Delphi releases.

As an example of how to use the Typinfo unit, the CD-ROM contains Inidata.Pas, written by this book's technical reviewer, Danny Thorpe, a Quality Assurance Engineer for Borland. Danny's unit uses object RTTI to write object property values in Windows initialization (.Ini) files. Using this nifty unit, you can write all of a dialog box's checkbox, edit window, radio button, and other controls to a .Ini file, and easily read those values back. Here are some notes from Danny that describe his unit:

RTTI allows developers to write code that works with objects in a generic manner by figuring out at runtime exactly what attributes an object has. Compiled code is often referred to as early bound because all linkage and access decisions are made at compile time. RTTI allows you to create code that is late bound, which means linkage and access is determined at runtime.

The IniData unit can write user data contained in any form. The purpose of the unit is to load and store only the user data that a component contains. The unit is built on some assumptions that are unrealted to RTTI— such as the fact that a component has only one important property containing user data, and that this property is a simple one (not a list or class, for example). If you want to store everything in a form, simply write it to a stream. IniData is for more precision work. — Tech ed.

For a demonstration of how to use Inidata.Pas, load the Options project on the CD-ROM into Delphi. Run the program, and select its options on the sample dialog box's three TabbedNotebook pages. Click the Save button to save the options to Test.Ini in the Windows directory. Quit and rerun to load the options from disk. Here's a sample Test.Ini file that I created:

```
[TMainForm]
CheckBox1=cbUnchecked
CheckBox2=cbGrayed
CheckBox3=cbChecked
RadioButton1=False
RadioButton2=False
RadioButton3=True
Edit1=Foundations of
Edit2=Delphi Development
```

The .Ini file's section header equals the form's class name. Each item is a named component object, with a value equal to one component property. (You can save only one object property.) Figure 20-1 shows Option's window. The project's Main.Pas file in Listing 20-6 shows how to use the Inidata unit.

The sample program's OnCreate event handler registers component classes and one property to read and write in the .Ini file. For example, to register the TRadioButton component, FormCreate executes the statement:

```
RegisterINIDataProp('TRadioButton', 'Checked');
```

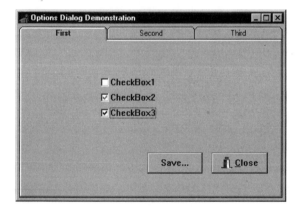

Figure 20-1

The Options application demonstrates how to use the Inidata unit to read and write object properties in .Ini files.

Listing 20-6

Options\Main.Pas. This program demonstrates how to use the Inidata.Pas unit, which is also in the Options directory.

```
unit Main;

interface

uses
   SysUtils, WinTypes, WinProcs, Messages, Classes, Graphics, Controls,
   Forms, Dialogs, Inidata, StdCtrls, Buttons, TabNotBk, IniFiles;
```

Add these units to the program's uses statement.

```
type
  TMainForm = class(TForm)
    TabbedNotebook1: TTabbedNotebook;
    CheckBox1: TCheckBox;
    CheckBox2: TCheckBox;
    CheckBox3: TCheckBox;
    RadioButton1: TRadioButton;
    RadioButton2: TRadioButton;
    RadioButton3: TRadioButton;
    Edit1: TEdit;
    Edit2: TEdit;
    BitBtn1: TBitBtn;
    BitBtn2: TBitBtn;
    procedure FormCreate(Sender: TObject);
    procedure BitBtn1Click(Sender: TObject);
  private
    procedure LoadOptions;
    procedure SaveOptions;
  public
    { Public declarations }
  end;

var
  MainForm: TMainForm;

implementation

{$R *.DFM}

procedure TMainForm.LoadOptions;
var
  IniFile: TIniFile;
begin
  IniFile := TIniFile.Create('test.ini');
  try
    LoadDataFromINI(MainForm, IniFile);
  finally
    IniFile.Free;
  end;
end;

procedure TMainForm.SaveOptions;
var
  IniFile: TIniFile;
begin
  IniFile := TIniFile.Create('test.ini');
  try
    SaveDataToINI(MainForm, IniFile);
  finally
    IniFile.Free;
  end;
end;
```

This loads component property values from the .Ini file.

This saves component property values to the .Ini file.

```
procedure TMainForm.FormCreate(Sender: TObject);
begin
  RegisterINIDataProp('TCheckBox', 'State');
  RegisterINIDataProp('TRadioButton', 'Checked');
  RegisterINIDataProp('TEdit', 'Text');
  LoadOptions;
end;

procedure TMainForm.BitBtn1Click(Sender: TObject);
begin
  SaveOptions;
end;

end.
```

Register the component properties (one per component) to read and write in .Ini files.

Because TCheckBox components can have three states, you have to register the State, not the Checked, property. You can also register the Edit component using these statements:

```
RegisterINIDataProp('TRadioButton', 'Checked');
RegisterINIDataProp('TEdit', 'Text');
```

Examine the LoadOptions and SaveOptions procedures for examples of how to read and write object properties to the .Ini file. LoadOptions creates a TIniFile object, and calls LoadDataFromINI in the Inidata unit to read saved properties into MainForm's objects. SaveOptions similarly calls SaveDataToINI to create or update the .Ini file.

On-line Help

Creating a Windows on-line help file by hand is to documentation what assembly language is to programming. The steps are tedious, the process is error prone, and the results are likely to make you long for the good old days when users didn't *expect* software to be helpful.

Before stepping out on the on-line help limb, I urge you to search for a help file generator that can construct Windows .Hlp files more or less automatically. I can't recommend a specific program because I haven't used them extensively. However, they generally provide an input system for entering context-sensitive search strings, index values, keywords, footnotes, titles, and text. A compiler of sorts reads this information and spits out the .Hlp file.

For masochists in the audience who are determined to write online help files the hard way, open the file Cwh.Hlp in Delphi's Bin directory. This additional Windows help file, "Creating Windows Help," which is not installed in the Delphi Program Manager window, contains a complete tutorial on building on-line help files. You'll need a rich-text-format editor (such as Word 6), the Microsoft help compiler (Hc.Exe, supplied with Delphi), a spreadsheet or database for keeping track of context-sensitive indexes, IDs, and keywords, and a case of good strong drink. The Cwh.Hlp file explains in detail how to create rich-text-format files, how to use the HotSpot editor to create hyperlinked graphics images in help files, and how to create context-sensitive help indexes.

After creating the .Hlp file, assign the filename to the Application object's HelpFile property. You have to do this at runtime (in a form's OnCreate event handler, for example). Enter a statement such as this:

```
Application.HelpFile := 'HelpMe.Hlp';
```

To provide specific help for objects in a form, assign help context index values in the range –MaxLongInt to MaxLongInt. For example, using the Object Inspector, assign 1003 to a Button object's HelpContext property. You can assign help context values at runtime, but you'll normally do that when you design the form.

There are no easy ways to dynamically update help context values, and you must keep account of the values that you assign. Good help generators do this automatically, but when creating on-line help manually, you'll need a spreadsheet or a database to record topics, context-sensitive strings, context index values, and keywords.

To open the help file to a specific topic, call the HelpContext method for the Application object. For example, use a statement such as:

```
Application.HelpContext(Button1.HelpContext);
```

Alternatively, to jump to a subject indexed by a context-sensitive string, call HelpJump like this:

```
Application.HelpJump('Subject');
```

HelpJump returns a Boolean True or False value, depending on whether the Application has a help file assigned. You might display an error message if HelpJump returns False:

```
if not Application.HelpJump('Subject') then
   ShowMessage('Unable to open help file');
```

TIP Your application must have at least one HelpContext value equal to the help file's *Contents* page index. If you don't assign a nonzero value to at least the main form's HelpContext property, the user will not be able to press F1 to bring up context-sensitive on-line help.

Try these steps to create a small application that displays context-sensitive, on-line help using the Helpex.Hlp example help file in Delphi's Bin directory:

1. Start a blank project.

2. Select the form, and assign the value 1 to its HelpContext property.

3. Create an OnCreate event handler for the form, and insert the following statement to assign the help filename. Adjust the drive and path names as necessary:

```
Application.HelpFile := 'C:\Delphi\Bin\Helpex.Hlp';
```

4. Insert a Button object into the form. Leave its HelpContext property set to 0, the default value. This causes the Button to inherit the form's context-sensitive help index.

5. Double-click Button1 and enter the following HelpJump statement between *begin* and *end*:

```
Application.HelpJump('x_topic2');
```

6. Run the program. Press F1 to open the help file and display the page indexed by the form's HelpContext property (*x_topic1*). Click Button1 to display the page indexed by the context-sensitive string, *x_topic2*.

7. End the program and return to Delphi. Change Button1's Help Context property to 2, and rerun. Now when you press F1, the *x_topic2* screen appears because the button has the input focus and its HelpContext value overrides the form's.

TIP Pressing F1 executes Application.HelpContext(N) where *N* equals the focused object's HelpContext property. If that value is 0, Delphi uses the parent object's HelpContext (usually the form's).

Dynamic Link Libraries

A dynamic link library, or DLL, is a kind of dynamic subroutine package that resides in a separate code file, and that applications (and other tasks) can share. Most of Windows is distributed among .DLL files, custom control libraries are often supplied as DLLs, and you can develop other kinds of libraries with functions to share among multiple applications.

Using Delphi, you can write and use your own DLLs, and you can call functions in DLLs developed with other systems. You can place component objects into forms, and stuff the window into a DLL. Other applications, even those not developed with Delphi, can use the DLL — it's a complete package wrapped into a shareable code file library. However, an existing DLL's external functions compiled with C or C++ may or may not be compatible with Object Pascal functions, so before looking at DLL construction, read the next section for a technique that you may have to use to call a DLL's exported code.

CALLING FOREIGN FUNCTIONS

Functions compiled with a Microsoft C (MSC) or compatible compiler are not directly compatible with Object Pascal functions. There's an easy way around the trouble, however, that sacrifices nothing in efficiency. To call a C function, you need to provide an extra parameter that accounts for the way MSC-style functions return values. An example will explain the problem and its solution.

Suppose you have a DLL with a function that returns a double floating-point value. The function's C module declares it as:

```
double far PASCAL Flotsom(double X, double Y)
```

You might imagine that you can declare a Pascal function of the same name with two Double parameters and a Double return result. That won't work, however, because some C compilers return floating-point function results by storing values via a pointer; Object Pascal functions return floating-point results on the stack, as do Borland C++ functions. To declare the equivalent Pascal function for a foreign C compiler, use a statement such as:

```
procedure Flotsom(X, Y: Double; Offset: Word); far; external 'FLOAT';
```

This assumes the Flotsom function is in a dynamic link library named FLOAT.DLL. In Pascal, the function becomes a procedure with an extra Word parameter, Offset. This is the stack-based offset address where you want the function to stuff its return value. To use the function, declare some Double variables:

```
var
  Result, X, Y: Double;
```

Then, call Flotsom with X and Y, plus the stack-based offset address (courtesy of Pascal's Ofs function) of the Result variable:

```
X := 3.14159;
Y := 9.51413;
Flotsom(X, Y, Ofs(Result));
```

CREATING A DLL

As a Delphi project, a DLL is a *library* with exported procedures and functions that other applications can call. Except for its exported subroutines, everything else inside a DLL is locked up as tight as an armored car. One of the key jobs in creating a new DLL, then, is deciding how to provide access to its contents.

One of the controversial questions that speeds around the information highway is whether a DLL can construct a form and other component objects. The answer is, Yes absolutely! In fact, this is one of the primary reasons for writing a Delphi DLL. You may place a form and any Delphi components into a DLL. Any program written in any other Windows development system can load the DLL to display the form. This is a great way (in fact, it's the only reliable method) for combining Delphi's capabilities with other systems such as C, C++, and Visual Basic.

When creating a new DLL, first test the form and its components as a common Delphi application. Create, write, and test this project as you do any other. As an example, the ColorDll application on the CD-ROM creates the foreground and background color grid dialog in Figure 20-2. The entire dialog is in a separate DLL that other applications, regardless of their source, can use.

NOTE ►
All of the following files are on the CD in the Colordll directory. Copy the directory to your hard drive, and then open the Colorlib project in Delphi. Press Ctrl+F9 to compile the DLL.

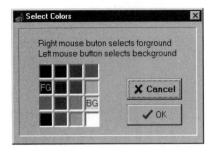

Figure 20-2
The Colorlib DLL displays this color selection dialog, using a ColorGrid component object. This demonstrates that a Delphi DLL may have form objects and any other component instances that you can use in applications.

To write the program, I first developed the color dialog as a common Delphi application. When I was satisfied, I modified the source code files as follows. You can use these steps to convert any Delphi project into a DLL:

1. Name the form unit something like ClrForm and the project ColorLib, or whatever you want to call the final DLL. Save the project as you normally do.

2. Declare a procedure or function in the form unit's interface section — not in the form's class. Users of the DLL call this subroutine to gain access to the library. You may declare as many access routines as your DLL needs. For example, Clrform.Pas declares function FBGetColors as follows. So that other languages may call the function, declare only Windows data types (WordBool, for example, rather than Pascal's Boolean). Follow the declaration with the keyword *export*, which tells the compiler to make this function available to the DLL's users.

```
function FBGetColors(var FColor, BColor: TColor): WordBool; export;
```

3. Implement the access procedure or function. Listing 20-7 shows the final result for the sample color selection dialog. I'll explain this part of the program after these steps.

4. After you are finished writing the form unit, convert the application project into a DLL. To do this, select the *View|Project Source* command to open the .Dpr project file. Switch to that page in the unit text editor, and make the following changes.

5. Change *program* to *library*.

6. Delete *Forms* from the *uses* directive. (Projects need this unit for calling Application methods. DLLs are not applications, and their project files don't need the Forms unit. However, the DLL's other units may reference Forms — a DLL is not restricted from using Forms.)

7. Between the {$R} resource directive and the final line of the project's *uses* directive, add the word *exports*, followed by the name of the unit's access procedure or function — FBGetColors in this example. You may insert one or more subroutine names here.

8. Delete all statements between *begin* and *end*, leaving the initialization code block empty. Listing 20-8 shows the final result for the ColorLib project.

9. Press Ctrl+F9 to compile and create the .Dll code file. You cannot run a DLL, so if you press F9 by mistake, you receive an error message. This still compiles the DLL, however, and does no harm.

In the DLL's unit, Clrform.Pas, the access function FBColors shows how a DLL creates a form object. The function returns WordBool (Windows' Boolean data type) to indicate whether the user closed the dialog by clicking Ok (True) or Cancel (False). First, the function initializes its return value to False. Next, it constructs a ColorForm object by calling the TColorForm class's Create method. Because you converted the application into a DLL, it no longer creates its form automatically, and the function has to do this under program control.

Always use a *try-finally* block as Clrform.Pas demonstrates to guarantee that, even if an exception occurs, the form object will be deleted.

Inside the *try* block, the program calls ColorForm's ShowModal method, which returns the value assigned to ModalResult by the dialog's Ok and Cancel Button OnClick event handlers. If ShowModal returns

IV

20

mrOk, the program assigns the ColorGrid object's foreground and background colors to the access function's variable parameters. This passes the dialog's information back to the host program. To indicate success, the program assigns True to the function result.

Listing 20-7

Colordll\Clrform.Pas. The Colorlib DLL uses this unit to display the color dialog window in Figure 20-2.

```
unit Clrform;

interface

uses
  SysUtils, WinTypes, WinProcs, Messages, Classes, Graphics, Controls,
  Forms, Dialogs, StdCtrls, Buttons, ColorGrd, ExtCtrls;

type
  TColorForm = class(TForm)
    ColorGrid: TColorGrid;
    Label1: TLabel;
    Label2: TLabel;
    CancelBitBtn: TBitBtn;
    OkBitBtn: TBitBtn;
    Bevel1: TBevel;
    procedure CancelBitBtnClick(Sender: TObject);
    procedure OkBitBtnClick(Sender: TObject);
  private
    { Private declarations }
  public
    { Public declarations }
  end;

var
  ColorForm: TColorForm;

function FBGetColors(var FColor, BColor: TColor): WordBool; export;

implementation

{$R *.DFM}

{- Exit dialog via Cancel button }
procedure TColorForm.CancelBitBtnClick(Sender: TObject);
begin
  ModalResult := mrCancel;
end;
```

Use Windows data types so C, C++, and other programming languages can use the CLL.

Declare the DLL's access method in the unit's interface.

```
{- Exit dialog via Ok button }
procedure TColorForm.OkBitBtnClick(Sender: TObject);
begin
  ModalResult := mrOk;
end;

{- Get foreground and background colors }
function FBGetColors(var FColor, BColor: TColor): WordBool;
begin
  Result := False;
  ColorForm := TColorForm.Create(Application);
  try
    if ColorForm.ShowModal = mrOk then
    with ColorForm do
    begin
      FColor := ColorGrid.ForegroundColor;
      BColor := ColorGrid.BackgroundColor;
      Result := True;
    end;
  finally
    ColorForm.Free;
  end;
end;

end.
```

Listing 20-8

Colordll\Colorlib.Dpr. To convert an application project to a DLL, modify its .Dpr file as illustrated here.

```
library Colorlib;                                    Declare DLLs using library keyword.

uses
  Clrform in 'CLRFORM.PAS' {ColorForm};

exports
  FBGetColors;                                       Export the DLLs access method(s).

{$R *.RES}

begin
end.
```

The *finally* block calls ColorForm's Free method to destroy the form object and all of its components. This returns system memory to its state at the beginning of the function. You must be especially careful in a DLL to create and free objects properly, or you can easily introduce a memory leak (which makes the floor all sticky and is a real mess to clean up).

For safety, exported routines in a DLL should be wrapped in an unqualified *try-except* block. This will prevent any exceptions escaping from the DLL's scope, which is dangerous because exception handling is language-oriented under 16-bit windows. (Ideally, exception handling would be coordinated by the operating system. This is not the case for 16-bit Windows.) One way to handle critical errors is for the DLL exception handler to call a function supplied by the program that uses the DLL. This callback function could raise an application exception, which can report the problem. This solution keeps any exceptions within their respective domains — DLL exceptions stay in the DLL; application exceptions stay in the application.

Delphi DLLs that use forms and other components will contain most if not all of the VCL's binary code. DLLs may also contain Turbo Debugger for Windows debugging information. Reduce their file sizes by switching off debugging using the Options menu and recompiling. You can also reorganize the library file with the W8Loss.Exe utility. For example, running Colorlib.Dll through W8Loss reduced its file size from 228,352 bytes down to 181,968 bytes.

USING A DLL

If you are following along, you now have Colorlib.Dll in a directory. Next, you'll create a sample application that calls the DLL's access function to display a color selection dialog. Just for fun, the sample application colors its background and text using the returned color values.

You may create the application yourself, or load the sample Testdll project from a copy of the CD-ROM's Colordll directory.

Listing 20-9 shows the Testdll.Pas source code, which demonstrates how a Delphi application loads and uses a DLL.

Listing 20-9

Colordll\Testdll.Pas. This program demonstrates how to load and use the Colorlib DLL from the preceding section.

```pascal
unit Main;

interface

uses
  SysUtils, WinTypes, WinProcs, Messages, Classes, Graphics, Controls,
  Forms, Dialogs, StdCtrls;

type
  TMainForm = class(TForm)
    Button1: TButton;
    Memo1: TMemo;
    procedure Button1Click(Sender: TObject);
  private
    { Private declarations }
  public
    { Public declarations }
  end;

var
  MainForm: TMainForm;

implementation

{$R *.DFM}

{- Declare external function in the Colorlib.Dll }
function FBGetColors(var FColor, BColor: TColor): WordBool; far;
  external 'Colorlib';

{- Activate color dialog in the Colorlib.Dll }
procedure TMainForm.Button1Click(Sender: TObject);
var
  FColor, BColor: TColor;
begin
  FColor := Font.Color;     { Form's text color }
  BColor := Color;          { Window background color }
  if FBGetColors(FColor, BColor) then  { Call DLL ! }
  begin
    Color := BColor;           { Assign window color }
    Font.Color := FColor;   { Assign text color }
  end;
end;

end.
```

Applications declare the DLL's access method(s) using this format.

Calls the DLL access Method, which displays a Delphi form and its component objects.

IV

20

In the host application (the one that uses the DLL), declare the same access procedure or function that the DLL's unit declares. As Testdll.Pas shows, however, use a slightly different form as Testdll.Pas shows. Declare the function far (32-bit pointer), which is required because the declaration must go in the unit's implementation, and implementation subroutines are usually near (16-bit pointer). Also declare the function *external,* followed by the string name of the DLL (minus the .DLL extension if that's what it is). This tells the compiler that the program will *import* the function, which as you recall, the DLL *exports*.

The final step is the easiest. Simply call the access function as the sample program's OnClick button event handler demonstrates. The DLL opens the dialog form window, and fully controls all component objects and whatnot. If the function returns True, the program uses the selected color values passed back via the two TColor variable parameters.

FASTEST DLL CREATION

Follow these steps for the fastest way in the west to create a DLL — it's probably the fastest way in the north, south, and east as well:

1. Start a new project, and select *CRT Application* from the *Gallery* dialog. Choose a directory when prompted for the generated .Pas and other project files.

2. Select *File│Save as,* and rename the project anything you like (MyLib to follow along).

3. In the unit's source code, change *program* to *library*.

4. Press Ctrl+F9 to compile. This produces MyLib.DLL, which is merely an empty shell, but is ready for filling with procedures and functions.

The preceding steps are a kind of ad hoc DLL Expert that you can use to create new dynamic link library projects when you don't want to include a form window in the final result.

Application and Message Event Handlers

The TApplication class provides a number of events for which you can write handlers. Because the Application object is not visible in the form, and TApplication is not available on the VCL palette, you have to use a different technique to create these handlers. Perform these steps:

- Declare the handler in the form class's private or public section (usually private). Do not declare handlers above the private keyword where Delphi automatically generates component object declarations and methods.

- Implement the handler by writing a procedure. Preface the procedure name with the form's class name. In general, use the same format that Delphi uses when it creates event handlers for objects that you select using the Object Inspector window's Events page tab.

- Assign the handler to an Application event property: OnActivate, OnDeactivate, OnException, OnHelp, OnHint, OnIdle, or OnMessage.

TApplication Event Handlers

Follow these steps for an example of assigning Application event handlers. The sample program demonstrates a highly useful technique that you can use to perform background processing *without* using a Timer object:

1. Create a blank project. Insert a Label and a Memo object into the form.

2 Add the following two declarations to the TForm1 class's private section. X is an integer (initialized to zero automatically when the form is created) that the AppOnIdle event handler will increment and display in the Label's Caption. The event handler must have the parameters and general form shown here, but you can name it as you like — search specific events for the required formats of their handler procedures:

```
X: Integer;
procedure AppOnIdle(Sender: TObject; var Done: Boolean);
```

3. Implement the AppOnIdle procedure by inserting the following lines into the unit's implementation section. Notice that the form's class name precedes the procedure name separated by a period. The event handler increments the private X variable and displays it by converting X to a string and assigning the result to the Label's Caption.

```
procedure TForm1.AppOnIdle(Sender: TObject; var Done: Boolean);
begin
  Inc(X);
  Label1.Caption := IntToStr(X);
end;
```

4. To connect the event handler with TApplication's OnIdle event, assign the handler's procedure name to the event. You may do this at any place in the program, but you'll most often do it in a form's OnCreate event handler. Select the form and double-click its OnCreate event value to create this handler, and insert the following assignment statement:

```
Application.OnIdle := AppOnIdle;
```

5. Run the program, which continually updates the Label, even while you enter text into the Memo window.

Trap a Windows message by creating a handler for Application.OnMessage. This can help you fine-tune the application's responses to various messages, or provide services for messages not normally recognized. Declare an OnMessage event handler as follows:

```
procedure AppOnMessage(var Msg: TMsg; var Handled: Boolean);
```

- *Msg* — A record of type TMsg that contains the window handle, the message value, parameters, the time the message was posted, and cursor coordinates. These values depend on the specific message received.

- *Handled* — If your OnMessage event handler handles a message, set this parameter to True. If you don't handle a message, or if you want to retain its default actions, set Handled to False.

DEFAULT MESSAGE HANDLER

Another way to handle Windows messages is by writing a method indexed to a specific message constant. For example, you can use this technique to *subclass* a menu item's response to a command selection. The program's form can watch for the command message, perform some additional processing when it comes down the line, and pass the message on to perform its usual activity.

Try the following steps to subclass a File menu's Exit command, and display a message with Yes and No buttons that users can click to end the program or abort the command's selection:

1. Start a blank project. Insert a Menu object, and enter a *File* menu with an *Exit* command.

2. Select the *File | Exit* command in the form, and enter Close; into the command's event handler.

3. Run the program, and select *File | Exit* to test that this closes the program.

4. You will now subclass the exit command's event handler by trapping its wm_Command Windows message, issued when you select the command. Insert the following message handler declaration into the TForm1 class's public section. The procedure traditionally has the same name as the message, minus the underscore in the constant of the same name. The procedure receives a TWMCommand variable containing information about this type of Windows message:

```
procedure WMCommand(var Message: TWMCommand); message wm_Command;
```

5. Implement WMCommand as follows.

```
procedure TForm1.WMCommand(var Message: TWMCommand);
begin
  if Message.ItemId = Exit1.Command then
  begin
    if MessageDlg('Quit program?', mtConfirmation,
      [mbYes, mbNo], 0) = mrNo then
    begin
      Message.Result := 1;    { Message was handled }
      Exit;                   { Exit without calling inherited }
    end;
  end;
  inherited WMCommand(Message); { Call inherited method }
  Message.Result := 1;   { Indicate message was handled }
end;
```

6. Run the program, and select *File| Exit.* If you answer *Yes,* the program ends; if you answer *No,* the program continues. There are other ways to provide this kind of prompt, but the importance of the technique demonstrated here is that the form class intercepts a Windows message to provide additional programming, or to replace that message's actions.

The WMCommand message event handler inspects the ItemId field in the Message record. This field equals the command value, automatically assigned to TMenuItem.Command properties when you design a Menu object. Use the object's property to find this value as demonstrated here for Exit1.Command.

Set the Message parameter's Result field to 0 to indicate that a message was not handled. Set Result to 1 if you handle a message. In this case, Result's value doesn't matter because the inherited procedure probably sets it, but I included the assignments anyway.

You can use the technique described here to override *any* message handler in a class. Look up the declaration in the unit's interface file (Forms.Int, for example), and copy the declaration to your form class. Implement the procedure — remember to preface its name with the class name and a period. Include an *inherited* statement to retain default processing; don't call *inherited* if you want to completely replace a message's response with your own programming.

OVERRIDING WINPROC

There's yet another way to get to the messages that whiz around Windows and its myriad tasks. You can override the low-level window procedure, WinProc, which performs message handling for forms. Do that by declaring the following procedure in the form class's protected or public section:

```
procedure WndProc(Var Message: TMessage); override;
```

The NonClien application on the CD-ROM demonstrates how to trap messages by overriding (subclassing) a form's window procedure. Listing 20-10 shows the program's source code. The program intercepts left and right mouse button double-clicks in the window's title bar, part of the window's *"nonclient"* area. Delphi normally ignores nonclient messages — which are named wm_NC . . . — but you can trap these messages by overriding the form's window procedure as shown here.

To override the form's window procedure, declare WndProc (it must be named that) as shown either in the form class's protected or public section. WndProc receives a single parameter of type TMessage that describes the message's content. Insert an *override* directive at the end of the declaration.

Listing 20-10
Nonclien\Main.Pas

```
unit Main;

interface

uses
  SysUtils, WinTypes, WinProcs, Messages, Classes, Graphics, Controls,
  Forms, Dialogs, StdCtrls;

type
  TMainForm = class(TForm)
    Label1: TLabel;
  private
    { Private declarations }
  public
    procedure WndProc(Var Message: TMessage); override;
    { Public declarations }
  end;

var
  MainForm: TMainForm;

implementation

{$R *.DFM}

procedure TMainForm.WndProc(var Message: TMessage);
begin
  with Message do
  case Msg of
    wm_NCLButtonDblClk:
      ShowMessage('Nonclient left button click');
    wm_NCRButtonDblClk:
      ShowMessage('Nonclient right button click');
  end;
  inherited WndProc(Message);
end;

end.
```

Declare WndProc in the class's protected or public section.

Implement WndProc to tap into the form or other class's message handling.

Call the inherited method to process other messages.

IV

20

Implement the overridden window procedure by examining the Msg field in the Message variable. Msg equals a Windows message constant. Most often, you'll use a *case* statement as in the sample listing to compare Msg with one or more Windows messages — in this case, the two nonclient double-click messages. Call the inherited WndProc to process other messages, or you may set Message.Result to nonzero and call Exit to indicate that you have handled a message. However, you should pass most messages onto the inherited method for default processing.

To anticipate a question from the lowest-of-the-low systems programmers out there, yes it is possible to tap into the message stream even earlier than WinProc — that is, *before* the messages get to the form. If you scan the public Delphi archives, you may come across a method for doing this which attaches a window procedure to the Application's Handle using SetWindowLong. If so, ignore that advice — there's an easier way. Simply create an Application.OnMessage event handler to obtain messages at their point of arrival into the *real* application window. The TApplication class's ProcessMessages function — the so-called *message loop* in a Delphi application — triggers the OnMessage event for all messages *except* wm_Quit. Application.OnMessage processes only messages that are posted to the application's message queue for any window in that application. A component's WndProc method will handle all messages delivered to that component's window handle via PostMessage *and* SendMessage.

File Streams

Delphi includes an object-oriented file-streaming system that you can use to read and write data, components, and other objects in disk files. Listing 20-11 demonstrates how to use the TStream and TFileStream classes to write a Button object to a disk file, and then read it back. The application also demonstrates how to create a component object entirely under program control. Run the program. Click Create to create a button and display it on the form. Click Write to stream the button to a disk file named Test.Stm (you can name the file anything you like, and the filename doesn't have to end with .Stm). Clicking Write destroys the button object and removes it from the window. Click Read to read the object back from the file stream.

The unit defines a TButton object, B, to be streamed to and from a disk file. To identify on screen whether the button came from the program or the stream, two event handlers BOnClick1 and BOnClick2 display different messages using the ShowMessage procedure. Procedure EnableButtons enables and disables the Create, Write, and Read buttons to suggest a correct order of operation. This prevents, for example, creating or reading more than one Button object at a time, which this simple demonstration is not designed to do.

Listing 20-11
Compstrm\Main.Pas

```
unit Main;

interface

uses
  SysUtils, WinTypes, WinProcs, Messages, Classes, Graphics, Controls,
  Forms, Dialogs, Buttons, StdCtrls;

type
  TMainForm = class(TForm)
    CreateButton: TButton;
    WriteButton: TButton;
    ReadButton: TButton;
    CloseBitBtn: TBitBtn;
    procedure FormCreate(Sender: TObject);
    procedure CreateButtonClick(Sender: TObject);
    procedure WriteButtonClick(Sender: TObject);
    procedure ReadButtonClick(Sender: TObject);
    procedure FormDestroy(Sender: TObject);
  private
    { Private declarations }
    procedure EnableButtons;
    procedure BOnClick1(Sender: TObject);
    procedure BOnClick2(Sender: TObject);
  public
    { Public declarations }
  end;

var
  MainForm: TMainForm;

implementation

{$R *.DFM}

const
  fileName = 'Test.Stm';  { The stream's filename }
```

IV

20

```
var
  B: TButton;  { Object to be streamed to and from disk }

{- OnClick event handler before writing Button to stream }
procedure TMainForm.BOnClick1(Sender: TObject);
begin
  ShowMessage('Thanks. I needed that!');
end;

{- OnClick event handler after reading Button from stream }
procedure TMainForm.BOnClick2(Sender: TObject);
begin
  ShowMessage('Hello. It''s nice to be back!');
end;

{- Enable and disable buttons depending on whether the Button
object and Test.Strm file exist }
procedure TMainForm.EnableButtons;
begin
  CreateButton.Enabled := False;  { Disable all buttons }
  WriteButton.Enabled := False;
  ReadButton.Enabled := False;
  if B <> nil then
    WriteButton.Enabled := True    { Allow write if B exists }
  else begin
    CreateButton.Enabled := True;  { Allow create if B doesn't exist}
    if FileExists(fileName) then
      ReadButton.Enabled := True   { Allow read if file exists }
  end;
end;

{- Initialize other buttons to control clicking order }
procedure TMainForm.FormCreate(Sender: TObject);
begin
  EnableButtons;
end;

{- Create Button object entirely under program control }
procedure TMainForm.CreateButtonClick(Sender: TObject);
begin
  B := TButton.Create(Self);        { Create the Button object }
  B.Parent := Self;                 { Assign parent object }
  B.Left := 240;                    { Assign left position }
  B.Top := 72;                      { Assign top position }
  B.Caption := 'Click me!';         { Assign label }
  B.OnClick := BOnClick1;           { Assign first event handler }
  EnableButtons;                    { Update operation order }
end;
```

```
{- Write Button object to file stream, and then destroy it }
procedure TMainForm.WriteButtonClick(Sender: TObject);
var
  Stream: TStream;
begin
{- Create a new disk file stream }
  Stream := TFileStream.Create(fileName, fmCreate);
  try
    Stream.WriteComponent(B);          { Write Button object }
    B.Free;                            { Destroy Button object }
    B := nil; { Prevent form's OnDestroy from Freeing again }
    EnableButtons;                     { Update operation order }
  finally
    Stream.Free;   { Destroy the file stream object }
  end;
end;
```

Declare the file stream.

Use this argument to create a new file for a stream.

Write the component to the stream.

Free the stream, and close the file, in a finally block.

```
{- Read Button object from stream }
procedure TMainForm.ReadButtonClick(Sender: TObject);
var
  Stream: TStream;
begin
{- Create stream object in read-only mode }
  Stream := TFileStream.Create(fileName, fmOpenRead);
  try
    B := TButton(Stream.ReadComponent(nil));  { Read & Create B }
    B.Parent := Self;                { Always assign parent! }
    B.OnClick := BOnClick2;          { Assign second event handler }
    EnableButtons;                   { Update operation order }
  finally
    Stream.Free; { Destroy the file stream object }
  end;
end;
```

```
{- Destroy button if user closes app before completing test }
procedure TMainForm.FormDestroy(Sender: TObject);
begin
  if B <> nil then B.Free;
end;

{- Register the TButton class with Delphi stream system }
begin
  RegisterClass(TButton);
end.
```

Register the component classes for which you will read and write objects in file streams.

The CreateButtonClick event handler creates a new button object by calling the TButton class's Create constructor and assigning the resulting object reference to B. To make the object visible, it must have a Parent, which in this case is the main form (referenced by Self in a form class's method such as this one). Most objects also need Left and Top values to position them — you may also set the object's Width and Height, but these and other properties have default values. So the button does something when you click it, the procedure assigns BOnClick1 to the button object's OnClick event.

The WriteButtonClick procedure demonstrates how to create a new disk file stream. Do that by calling TFileStream's Create constructor with two arguments, a filename and a mode constant such as fmCreate, and save the resulting object reference in a TStream or TFileStream variable. Table 20-1 lists other mode constants you can pass to TFileStream.Create.

Table 20-1

TFileStream.Create Mode Constants

Constant	Effect
fmOpenRead	Open file for reading
fmOpenWrite	Open file for writing
fmOpenReadWrite	Open file for reading and writing
fmShareExclusive	Open file for application's exclusive use
fmShareDenyWrite	Prevent other applications from writing to file
fmShareDenyRead	Prevent other applications from reading from file
fmShareDenyNone	Allow other applications to read and write file
fmCreate	Create a new file and open for writing

Use logical *or* expressions to combine file mode constants. Share.Exe must be installed to use file-sharing modes. For example, the following expression opens a file for reading and writing, but prevents other applications from writing to the file as long as it remains open:

```
fmOpenReadWrite or fmOpenDenyWrite
```

Call TStream's WriteComponent method to write a component object to the stream. You may write as many components as you need, and they may be of the same or of different types. After writing the Button object, the sample application destroys it and sets its reference B to *nil*. If you close the application, this prevents the form's OnDestroy event handler from freeing the same object again, which would cause a general protection fault (GPF).

The WriteButtonClick procedure uses a *try-finally* block to ensure that the Stream object is freed even if an exception occurs — due to a write-protected disk error, for example. Always use *try-finally* this way in your procedures and functions that create TFileStream objects.

Procedure ReadButtonClick reads the streamed object from disk. Again, the first step calls TFileStream's Create constructor, but this time using the fmOpenRead mode. This statement reads the object from the file stream and assigns it to B:

```
B := TButton(Stream.ReadComponent(nil));
```

Call the TStream ReadComponent method to read one component from the file stream. Pass a component reference to ReadComponent to read an object into an existing one, or pass *nil* as in this example to have ReadComponent construct an entirely new object. ReadComponent returns type TComponent, so you have to use a type cast to assign the result to a specific type of component reference such as B.

 After reading an object from a stream, be sure to give it a Parent — this information is not saved in the stream because a different form or the same one at a different location in memory might own the object. You will also have to reassign any event handlers. As a general rule, any specific address information (event handlers, references to other objects, and the Parent property) are not streamed because this information is likely to be different on reading the objects.

Before an application can read and write component objects in file streams, it has to *register* their classes with Delphi's file-streaming mechanism. You may do this in the form's OnCreate event handler, but to ensure that the job is carried out as early as possible, add a *begin* keyword above the unit's *end*. In between, insert calls to RegisterClass for each class for which this module will stream objects. Register *classes,* not objects.

 For more information on Delphi's streaming system, open the *Component Writer's Guide* in the Windows help file, Cwg.Hlp, located in Delphi's Bin directory. Search for the TFileStream class.

Still More Tips

I found the following tidbits floating around in my notes along with some DOS batch files that I have found useful while using and learning about Delphi. Maybe you will too.

FOCUS CHANGES

Never perform any actions that cause a focus change in an event handler that is itself involved in a focus change. For example, attempting to display a message dialog in an OnExit event for an Edit component can cause the program to lose the capability to tab to other controls.

To experiment with this problem, place some Edit objects into a form, and call ShowMessage for one object's OnExit event. Run the program and tab from control to control. After you close the message dialog, you'll have trouble shifting the focus to other controls — giving the dialog box the focus interferes with the process of giving the next control the focus, which is what OnExit was doing when you interrupted it. For example, pressing Tab after closing the dialog probably does not move the focus to the next Edit window as expected. This problem isn't going to blow up your programs, but if you seem to have trouble tabbing among controls in a window, this is the likely cause.

EVENT HANDLER ORDER

Delphi applications call these events in this order when first creating a form: OnCreate, OnShow, OnPaint, OnActivate, OnResize, and OnPaint once more. Just thought you'd like to know.

MINIMIZED APPLICATIONS

Delphi 1.0 has a known bug, which isn't serious, but prevents applications from starting as minimized icons, or as buttons on the Windows 95 task bar. Delphi applications ignore the Run minimized setting in the Windows 3.1 Program Manager or the Hidden check box in the Windows 95 task bar options.

You can easily fix this problem, which will probably be repaired in a future Delphi release. Until then, to display the window properly, insert this statement in the form's OnCreate event handler:

```
ShowWindow(Handle, CmdShow);
```

MULTIPLE PROGRAM INSTANCES

As you probably know, you can run multiple instances of some Windows programs, but others restrict you to running them only once. The traditional response when users attempt to rerun a single-instance program is to find that program's window and make it active. You can easily construct a Delphi application to do this by modifying the project file. Follow these steps to try out the technique:

1. Start a blank project. You'll want to save its files on disk so you can run the compiled .Exe code file from the File Manager or the Windows 95 Explorer. Create a directory for the project.

2. Select *View|Project Source* to open the program's project file. The project is actually the program's main Pascal program.

3. Add the Dialogs and WinProcs units to the project file's *uses* directive.

4. Modify the project's statements between *begin* and *end* using Listing 20-12 as a guide.

5. Save the project to establish its directory, and press Ctrl+F9 to compile. Run the .Exe code file using the File Manager or the Explorer. Without closing the window, run it again — this time you see a message that the program is already running. Close the message dialog to switch automatically back to the first program instance.

Listing 20-12

Use this listing as a guide to modifying a project to prevent it from running multiple times.

```
program Project1;

uses
  Forms,
  Dialogs,
  WinProcs,
  Unit1 in 'UNIT1.PAS' {Form1};

{$R *.RES}

begin
  if HPrevInst = 0 then
  begin
    Application.CreateForm(TForm1, Form1);
    Application.Run;
  end else
  begin
    ShowMessage('Application is already running');
    SetFocus(FindWindow('TForm1', nil));
  end;
end.
```

If true, this is the first program instance; otherwise, the program is already running.

Bring up the first program instance.

The modified project inspects HPrevInst (handle to previous instance), which if equal to zero indicates that this is the first time the program has been executed. Running the application sets HPrevInst to the application's instance handle, so on a second invocation, the handle will be nonzero. In that case, the project's *else* statements display a message and call the Windows API SetFocus function to switch to the first instance. FindWindow locates that instance's window handle by searching for the window class name, which is the same as the form's class. The second argument is always nil.

To switch silently to the first program instance, delete the ShowMessage statement.

SOME USEFUL DOS BATCH FILES

Do you still type commands at the DOS prompt as often as I do? I'm a die-hard Windows fan, but there are times when I know how to get a job done in a text-only window, and nothing else will do as well. I'm also always writing batch files to perform various operations in a DOS window. Following are some that I've found especially useful with Delphi.

Listing 20-13 shows the Clean.Bat file from the CD-ROM. Run this program to erase all but the essential files in a Delphi project. Listing 20-14 is part of the Cleanall.Bat file that you can run to delete wasteful files after you compile this book's example programs. To use these programs, copy them to the directory that contains your project subdirectories. Run Cleanall to clean all directories. Or, run Clean to clean individual ones like this:

```
Clean Polyflow
```

Listing 20-13
Clean.Bat

```
@echo off
rem
rem CLEAN.BAT
rem Delete files created by Delphi
rem Called by CLEANALL.BAT
rem Input %1==subdirectory where clean.bat is stored
rem
rem ex. call clean Polyflow
rem
if "%1"=="" goto ERROR
if exist %1\NUL goto CONTINUE
goto ERROR
:CONTINUE
cd %1
echo Cleaning %1
rem
rem Add new files to delete here:
rem
if exist *.bak del *.bak
if exist *.~* del *.~*
if exist *.dsk del *.dsk
if exist *.dsm del *.dsm
if exist *.dcu del *.dcu
REM if exist *.exe del *.exe
rem
rem Go back to directory that has clean.bat
rem
:REPEAT
cd ..
if exist clean.bat goto END
goto REPEAT
:ERROR
echo.
echo Error cleaning: %1
echo No such directory
pause
:END
```

Delete REM to erase .Exe code files. If you make this change, use the program only to clean Delphi project directories!

Listing 20-14

Cleanall.Bat (partial listing—full program on disk)

```
@echo off
rem
rem cleanall.bat -- call clean.bat for all source directories
rem
echo working...
if exist *.bak del *.bak
call clean aboutex
call clean addpage
call clean barchart
call clean bitview
call clean bitview2
...
echo done
:END
```

For safety, I commented out the instruction in Clean.bat that erases .Exe code files. If you enable this line, be extremely careful not to erase other applications on your hard drive. You should *not* install Clean or Cleanall in a global Path directory. Also, you may want to keep .Opt, .Res, and .Dsk files depending on whether you wish to retain options settings, resources, and the desktop configuration for your projects.

Friends kid me that there's not enough sex in my books, but I'll get the last laugh yet. Listing 20-15 shows one of my favorite batch files, Sex.Bat — short for "Search Delphi EXamples." You need the Grep.Com utility from Delphi's Bin directory on the current PATH. Enter a command such as *Sex TButton* to locate all .Pas files among Delphi's demos that use that component. Similar batch files for database examples (Sexdb.Bat) and for this book's applications (Sexts.Bat) are in the Batch directory on the CD-ROM. Unless you installed Delphi in the default directory C:\Delphi, you'll have to modify the path names in these files.

Finally, Listing 20-16 shows the batch file that I probably used more than any other program while writing this book. You need to have the VCL runtime library source files to use it, and you need to place the Grep.Com utility in a PATH directory. Change the drive and Delphi installation path name if necessary. Enter a command such as *VCL TCustomListBox* to locate all files that use that component. I probably run this one a hundred times daily.

Listing 20-15
Sex.Bat (who says there's no sex in my books?)

```
@echo off
rem
rem - sex.bat -- Search Delphi EXamples using Grep utility
rem              -         --
rem
if "%1" == "" goto END
grep -lid "%1" c:\delphi\demos\*.pas
rem
rem doc subdirectory
rem
grep -lid "%1" c:\delphi\demos\doc\*.pas
:END
```

Listing 20-16
Vcl.Bat. Use this batch file to search Delphi's VCL runtime library source files (available in the Client/Server edition or by separate purchase from Borland)

```
@echo off
rem
rem vcl.bat -- Change to and search Delphi's vcl directory
rem
c:
cd\delphi\source\vcl
if "%1"=="" goto LISTFILES
grep -li "%1" *.pas
goto END
:LISTFILES
dir /w
:END
```

IV
20

GET READY FOR 32 BITS

With the introduction of Windows 95, 32-bit programs will soon be the norm. As you read these words, Borland is readying a 32-bit version of Delphi for release in the near future. What will this mean to application developers?

Probably not much at first. Delphi 16-bit applications will operate unchanged, and will continue to enjoy full support under Windows 95 and Windows NT. By writing 16-bit code, you tap into the huge Windows 3.1 market of more than 30 million systems. It will take time, perhaps years, before all of these Windows users make the leap from version 3.1 to Windows 95. Most will eventually jump in, but meanwhile, there's no reason for developers to suffer 32-bit anxiety attacks. You can do a lot with a 16-bit development system, and that fact will not soon change.

Following are some of the new features you may receive in Delphi's 32-bit version. Changes are more than likely going to occur on low levels that do not concern applications. As with any new product, however, you can expect new features and commands. Speaking of low-level concerns, Delphi uses a mixed memory model that resembles C's large model. In this model:

- Class methods are far addresses.
- A unit's interface procedures are also far.
- A unit's private implementation procedures can be near (they are far if compiled with the {$F+} option).
- All pointers are far, including object references.
- Global variables are ds-based and near.
- Procedure parameters and local variables are ss-based and near.
- Explicitly declared Far procedures are far.
- Virtual method tables are far (they were near in Borland Pascal).

Few of the preceding points need to change for 32-bit programming, because most pointers and references are already far. However, here's a peek at some of the key differences and new features in the coming 32-bit Delphi:

- Memory allocations as big as the largest available block, potentially multiple megabytes in size.
- Huge arrays indexed by 32-bit integers.
- A new 32-bit Integer type.
- Virtually unlimited stack space with on-demand stack expansion (the default virtual stack size will be one megabyte).

- A gaggle and a half of new 32-bit Windows operating system services such as multithreading, asynchronous file input and output, memory mapped files, and many more goodies.

- A built-in 32-bit assembler, which will require careful examination and possible revision of any 16-bit assembly language instructions and addressing modes.

- The elimination of low-level code that manipulates pointer selectors and offsets.

- Incompatibility with Windows hooks and other low-level devices. You'll have to revise this and other low-level 16-bit code due to 32-bit Windows' strict process address-space separation.

- Incompatibility with existing VBX controls, which are inherently 16-bit in nature, and will probably not work under 32-bit Windows. The same will not be true of Delphi components, which will share 16- and 32-bit source-code compatibility. (Of course, any specific 32-bit features will require 32-bit Windows.)

- Full support of Windows 95 common controls including TreeView outlines, image lists, tab controls, rich-text-format (RTF) editing, and others.

- Unlimited size multiline edit controls under Windows NT. Multiline edit controls under Windows 95 will be limited to 64K as they are under Windows 3.1. This is an operating system limitation that is unrelated to Delphi's multiline edit components.

- New resource formats that require script files to be recompiled. You will not be able to link 16-bit .Res files into 32-bit code files, so don't discard those resource scripts! When creating resources outside of Delphi (using Resource Workshop, for example), *always create the .Rc script and compile it to create the binary .Res image. Never edit a .Res file directly!*

IV

20

Final Note

This is the last chapter in the book, but it's not the end of the line. In fact, your experiences (and mine) with Delphi are just beginning. Delphi's popularity has zoomed skyward since I began writing *Foundations of Delphi Development*. Software developers worldwide are adopting Delphi at a tremendous pace as more and more discover the value of visual, object-oriented programming that really works.

If you have read through most of this book, you now have a firm foundation in Delphi development techniques. I hope you have enjoyed the journey. Now it's your turn. Dig through the on-line help and the printed references. Learn to teach yourself new topics by writing short test programs. Order the VCL source code library, and browse the files for hints on component construction. Join an electronic Delphi forum (you can find me from time to time on Borland's Compuserve forums). Write favorable letters about the author to the publisher. And above all, have fun. Good luck!

How to Use the CD

*T*he accompanying CD contains the entire Foundations of Delphi Development in easy-to-use hypertext form. It also contains copies of all the source code used in the book.

Installation Instructions

1. Put the CD in your CD drive.
2. From Windows Program Manager (or File Manager) select *File| Run*.
3. Enter d:SETUP (where d is the drive letter of your CD drive).

This creates a program group "IDG Books" and the Foundations of Delphi Development icon. Double-click on the icon to start the program.

Project Source Code

All Delphi project files are stored in named subdirectories under the D:\Source main directory, where D: is your CD's drive letter. For example, D:\Source\Calc32 contains the files for the Calc32 demonstration project.

To use a sample project, copy all files from a CD directory to a new blank directory on your hard drive. For example, to use the Calc32 demonstration, create a directory such as C:\Projects\Calc32 and copy to it all files from D:\Source\Calc32. Open the project file (Calc32.Dpr if you are following along) using Delphi's *File|Open Project* command. Press F9 to compile and run. Some projects require special handling. See the text in the book for details.

For easier use, copy all project files from the CD to your hard drive. To do that, first create a blank directory such as C:\Projects. Change to C:\Projects, and run the DOS XCopy utility to copy all directories and files. For example, enter these commands at a DOS prompt:

```
c:
md \Projects
cd \Projects
xcopy d:\source *.* /s
```

You'll need about 17MB of available space to hold all project directories. You'll need additional free space to compile the projects. To conserve disk space, after compiling one or more projects, run the Cleanall.Bat batch file from a DOS prompt. This will delete files that Delphi creates and restore the directories to their original installed configurations. To clean an individual directory, run the Clean.Bat program. For example, enter *Clean Calc32*.

 Clean.bat deletes .Exe and other files. Run Clean.Bat and Cleanall.Bat only in the C:\Projects directory that holds this book's project directories.

Viewer Documentation

The viewer used for this CD is the Microsoft Multimedia Viewer, which is used in many multimedia products, such as Microsoft Bookshelf. On the viewer's toolbar are the following buttons. To select an option, click on the appropriate button or press the underlined letter.

Contents	Move to the contents page.
Index	Display a list of key words and phrases.
Go Back	Return to the previously viewed page.
History	Display a list of the most recently viewed pages and select one to return to.

Search   Perform a full-text search for any word or phrase used in the text.

<<   View the previous page.

>>   View the next page.

Text References

Within the text, certain words and phrases are highlighted in red or blue.

A red highlight means there is a glossary definition for the term. When you click on the term, a pop-up window appears that contains the definition. When you click anywhere else or press Escape, the pop-up window disappears. (You may also use the tab keys to select a highlighted term and press Enter to display the reference.)

A blue highlight is a reference to another page in the document. When you click on a reference to a figure, table, or listing, a new window opens that contains the figure, table, or listing. When you click on a reference to a chapter or sidebar, the screen changes to the first page of the chapter or sidebar.

Search

When you select the Search button, a dialog box appears. Using this dialog box, you may search all of the book, or selected sections, for any word or phrase. To search the entire book, simply type the word or phrase in the Search by Word box and press Enter or click OK. To search only specific sections, select the parts to search in the Topic Groups box.

You can do more complex searches by using the keywords AND, OR, NEAR, and NOT to narrow the search; click the Hints button for some samples.

To limit the search to the topics selected on a previous search, select the Options button and check List of Previous Topics Found.

To limit the search to topic titles only, select the Options button and check Topic Titles Only.

Search Results

When a search has completed, the Search Results dialog box is displayed. You can use this dialog box to review all the "finds" of your search. All topics containing the searched text are listed. You can scroll through this list to look for likely areas to view.

Click the Go To button to display the topic. The Search Results dialog box stays open on top of the document so you can move easily from place to place within the list, reviewing all references to the searched text. In the document, the text found is highlighted wherever it appears.

The Previous Match and Next Match buttons move within a topic, stopping at each highlighted find.

The To Search button returns to the Search dialog box.

The Cancel button closes the Search Results box, leaving the current topic on display.

Index

The Index box provides a list of all indexed key words and phrases. Type the first character or characters of a word or phrase and the list will move to the first entry that matches the characters entered. Click OK to select a key word.

If only one topic contains a reference for the key word selected, that topic will be displayed immediately. If more than one topic is referenced, a dialog box listing all related topics is displayed. Select the topic desired and click OK. Click To Index to return to the index list, or click Cancel to close the dialog.

B Bonus Programs and Files

*T*he CD contains several free bonus shareware and public domain files, projects, and demonstrations stored in named subdirectories under D:\Bonus where D: is your CD's drive letter. To use the bonus programs, copy them to blank directories on your hard drive. Or, you can run sample .Exe code files directly from the CD. *Please respect the rights of Shareware authors by registering the programs that you use.* You may freely use programs marked *Freeware.* Following are brief descriptions of the free bonus files on the CD.

Some bonus directories contain a Readme file. Open this file using the Windows Notepad or Write utilities for more information and any special instructions.

Animate

Author: Dave Baldwin

This program demonstrates clever techniques for creating graphics animations. Run Animate.Exe for several samples that rival the Saturday morning cartoons. Unpack Bitmaps.Zip, Demosrc.Zip, and Inststuf.Zip using Pkunzip or a similar dearchiving tool for the demonstration source files and more information about the program. *Freeware.*

This package may be copied and distributed freely providing that it is not modified, no fee is charged, and it is not made part of a package for which a charge is made. If you upload this package to other bulletin boards, the author would appreciate it if you would try to keep the upload current.

Please report all bugs, suggestions, and problems to:

Dave Baldwin,
CompuServe ID: 76327,53.
22 Fox Den Rd., (Summer)
Hollis, NH 03049
(603) 465-7857
144 13th St. East, (Winter)
Tierra Verde, FL 33715
(813) 867-3030

Consol

Author: Danny Thorpe

Use Danny's cool Consol module to create text-output windows that are far superior to those produced by standard CRT applications. Consol supports color text and fonts. Run Termdemo.Exe for a sample display. To use Consol in your own programs, install the Console.Pas unit on Delphi's component palette. Follow instructions in Readme.Txt. *Freeware.*

Ctdemo

Author: Gamesman, Inc.

This program demonstrates several interesting VBX controls suitable for use as Delphi components. The actual package, which you can order from the company, includes source code for Visual Basic, dBase for Windows, and Delphi. Open Readme.Wri in the Windows Write utility for more information. *Shareware.*

New Ordering Information

This product is currently shipping. It sells for a suggested list price of $90.00 plus shipping. There is a $5.00 cost for shipping (Canada & U.S.A.), $10.00 foreign, or $20.00 for Fed Ex. You can order through the following manner.

1. Register the product through Compuserve via SWREG #3852. The bill for the product will then be placed into your Compuserve bill. (No Fed Ex available this manner)

2. Order using VISA (sorry, no M.C. yet). Call 1-800-670-8045.

3. Send a check directly to the following address.

Gamesman Inc.
1161 McMillan Avenue
Winnipeg Manitoba Canada
R3M 0T7
Tel : (204) 475-7903
Fax : (204) 284-3307
CSID : 75201,3524

If you do have any additional questions, please feel free to call and ask for Craig Gluck. He will be happy to be of any assistance.

Dbqcdemo

Author: Ron Stevenson

This demonstration package includes an enhanced DBLookupCombo component that you can fill with SQL queries. Run the Dbqcdemo.Exe program for a demonstration, which requires Delphi's database files to be installed under the alias DBDEMOS. *Shareware.*

The shareware version of this component is limited to 25 items in the Combo's dropdown list. For $20 (U.S.), you'll receive the unlimited version with full source code. The company accepts MasterCard and Visa. The component will be sent to you by CompuServe email. You will be notified as planned enhancements become available.

Created by Ron Stevenson
CompuServe ID 75342,2651

Applications Method, Inc.
Partners in Information Technology
6300 Southcenter Boulevard
Seattle, WA 98188
(206) 244-2400

Reminder

Author: David M. Swan

My brother donated this practical database application, which displays reminders about birthdays and other important dates. Before running Rem.Exe, use Database Desktop to define the alias *Remind* for the directory where you copied Reminder's files. You might want to drag Rem.Exe into your Startup folder to post reminders every time you turn on your computer. Now maybe I'll remember to send my brother a birthday card. Thanks Dave. I can take a hint. *Freeware*.

Vclref

Author: Borland International

This 1072-page document contains Borland's complete reference to the entire Visual Component Library. To use this reference, you must first install Acrobat Reader 2.0 furnished with Delphi. If you didn't already install Acrobat, insert the Delphi CD and run Install.Exe located in the Manuals directory. After installing, run Acrobat Reader and open the Vclref.Pdf file to view the VCL reference. You may copy Vclref.Pdf to your hard drive (you'll need about 5.2MB available space), or you may open the file directly from this book's CD. *Freeware*.

IDG Books Worldwide License Agreement

Important — read carefully before opening the software packet. This is a legal agreement between you (either an individual or an entity) and IDG Books Worldwide, Inc. (IDG). By opening the accompanying sealed packet containing the software disc, you acknowledge that you have read and accept the following IDG License Agreement. If you do not agree and do not want to be bound by the terms of this Agreement, promptly return the book and the unopened software packet(s) to the place you obtained them for a full refund.

1. **License.** This License Agreement (Agreement) permits you to use one copy of the enclosed Software program(s) on a single computer. The Software is in "use" on a computer when it is loaded into temporary memory (i.e., RAM) or installed into permanent memory (e.g., hard disk, CD-ROM, or other storage device) of that computer.

2. **Copyright.** The entire contents of this disc and the compilation of the Software are copyrighted and protected by both United States copyright laws and international treaty provisions. You may only (a) make one copy of the Software for backup or archival purposes, or (b) transfer the Software to a single hard disk, provided that you keep the original for backup or archival purposes. The individual programs on the disc are copyrighted by the authors of each program respectively. Each program has its own use permissions and limitations. To use each program, you must follow the individual requirements and restrictions detailed for each in Appendix A and B of this book. Do not use a program if you do not want to follow its Licensing Agreement. None of the material on this disc or listed in this Book may ever be distributed, in original or modified form, for commercial purposes.

3. **Other Restrictions.** You may not rent or lease the Software. You may transfer the Software and user documentation on a permanent basis provided you retain no copies and the recipient agrees to the terms of this Agreement. You may not reverse engineer, decompile, or disassemble the Software except to the extent that the foregoing restriction is expressly prohibited by applicable

law. If the Software is an update or has been updated, any transfer must include the most recent update and all prior versions. Each shareware program has its own use permissions and limitations. These limitations are contained in the individual license agreements that are on the software discs. The restrictions include a requirement that after using the program for a period of time specified in its text, the user must pay a registration fee or discontinue use. By opening the package which contains the software disc, you will be agreeing to abide by the licenses and restrictions for these programs. Do not open the software package unless you agree to be bound by the license agreements.

4. **Limited Warranty.** IDG Warrants that the Software and disc are free from defects in materials and workmanship for a period of sixty (60) days from the date of purchase of this Book. If IDG receives notification within the warranty period of defects in material or workmanship, IDG will replace the defective disc. IDG's entire liability and your exclusive remedy shall be limited to replacement of the Software, which is returned to IDG with a copy of your receipt. This Limited Warranty is void if failure of the Software has resulted from accident, abuse, or misapplication. Any replacement Software will be warranted for the remainder of the original warranty period or thirty (30) days, whichever is longer.

5. **No Other Warranties.** To the maximum extent permitted by applicable law, IDG and the author disclaim all other warranties, express or implied, including but not limited to implied warranties of merchantability and fitness for a particular purpose, with respect to the Software, the programs, the source code contained therein and/or the techniques described in this Book. This limited warranty gives you specific legal rights. You may have others which vary from state/jurisdiction to state/jurisdiction.

6. **No Liability For Consequential Damages.** To the extent permitted by applicable law, in no event shall IDG or the author be liable for any damages whatsoever (including without limitation, damages for loss of business profits, business interruption, loss of business information, or any other pecuniary loss) arising out of the use of or inability to use the Book or the Software, even if IDG has been advised of the possibility of such damages. Because some states/jurisdictions do not allow the exclusion or limitation of liability for consequential or incidental damages, the above limitation may not apply to you.

7. **U.S.Government Restricted Rights.** Use, duplication, or disclosure of the Software by the U.S. Government is subject to restrictions stated in paragraph (c) (1) (ii) of the Rights in Technical Data and Computer Software clause of DFARS 252.227-7013, and in subparagraphs (a) through (d) of the Commercial Computer—Restricted Rights clause at FAR 52.227-19, and in similar clauses in the NASA FAR supplement, when applicable.

Index

● B ●

● F ●

● **H** ●

• P •

• S •

Introducing the Foundations™ Series
For Working Programmers...

IDG BOOKS WORLDWIDE

Books in the *Foundations* series are designed to complement the way professional programmers work. Written only by seasoned software developers and trainers who understand programming, *Foundations* books help lighten workloads and provide solutions to development problems.

Foundations™ of Visual C++ Programming for Windows 95

by Paul Yao & Joseph Yao

Here is the organized guide for working programmers who want to master Visual C++. Includes tips on tools, internals, design issues, avoiding common mistakes, testing problems, and working sample code from the book. Bonus includes a hypertext version of the book, plus all the source code.

EXPERT AUTHOR PROFILE
Paul Yao (Bellevue, WA) is president of The Paul Yao Company. He is a contributing editor to *Microsoft Systems Journal* and has been a regular instructor of Windows programming since 1986. Joseph Yao (Fairfax, VA) is a principal software engineer at Hadron, Inc., and a C++ expert.

ISBN: 1-56884-321-6
$39.99 USA/$54.99 Canada
includes one CD-ROM

Foundations™ of Visual Basic "X" Programming

by Doug Hergert

This book lays the foundations of Visual Basic programming for working programmers. Comprehensive stand-alone tutorial chapters make programming a snap. Includes working sample code from the book and Visual Basic shareware.

EXPERT AUTHOR PROFILE
Doug Hergert (San Francisco, CA) has been writing about computers since 1981 and two of his past books have been bestsellers. He is also the author of IDG's *QBasic Programming For Dummies.*®

ISBN: 1-56884-320-8
$39.99 USA/$54.99 Canada
includes one CD-ROM

> Available: October 1995; subject to software availability

Foundations™ of Delphi Programming

by Tom Swan

Now working programmers can find a complete guide to Delphi. This book shows programmers how to produce programs as powerful and efficient as ones written in C and C++, and offers a comprehensive overview of Delphi and rapid application development. Bonus CD includes a handy, hypertext version of the book!

EXPERT AUTHOR PROFILE
Tom Swan (Key West, FL) is an internationally acclaimed author. He has written more than 30 computer books including IDG's bestselling *Type & Learn™ C*. Swan is also a former columnist for *PC Techniques* and has written for *Dr. Dobb's Journal* and *PC World*.

ISBN: 1-56884-347-X
$39.99 US/$54.99 Canada
includes one CD-ROM

> Available: September 1995

Foundations™ of World Wide Web Programming with HTML and CGI

by Ed Tittel, Mark Gaither, Sebastian Hassinger, & Mike Erwin

This book guides working programmers to create cutting-edge World Wide Web documents using Hypertext Markup Language (HTML) and advanced scripting techniques. Knowing how to produce and post Web pages is one of the most marketable skills around and the *Foundations™* series will give programmers an extra advantage! Extra CD includes valuable Net programming tools.

EXPERT AUTHOR PROFILE
Ed Tittel (Austin, TX) is the author of ten computer books, including IDG's *HTML For Dummies®*. Mark Gaither (Cedar Park, TX) is a software engineer at HaL Software Systems. Sebastian Hassinger (Austin, TX) is an Internet consultant and an expert in CGI programming. Mike Erwin (Austin, TX) is an expert on Internet connectivity.

ISBN: 1-56884-703-3
$39.99 US/$54.99 Canada
includes one CD-ROM

FOR MORE INFORMATION OR TO PLACE AN ORDER CALL 1.800.762.2974

For volume discounts & special orders please call Tony Real, Special Sales, at 415.655.3048

Order Center: **(800) 762-2974** *(8 a.m.–6 p.m., EST, weekdays)*

Quantity	ISBN	Title	Price	Total

Shipping & Handling Charges

	Description	First book	Each additional book	Total
Domestic	Normal	$4.50	$1.50	$
	Two Day Air	$8.50	$2.50	$
	Overnight	$18.00	$3.00	$
International	Surface	$8.00	$8.00	$
	Airmail	$16.00	$16.00	$
	DHL Air	$17.00	$17.00	$

*For large quantities call for shipping & handling charges.
**Prices are subject to change without notice.

Ship to:

Name _____

Company _____

Address _____

City/State/Zip _____

Daytime Phone _____

Payment: ☐ Check to IDG Books (US Funds Only)

☐ VISA   ☐ MasterCard   ☐ American Express

Card # _____ Expires _____

Signature _____

Subtotal _____

CA residents add
applicable sales tax _____

IN, MA, and MD
residents add
5% sales tax _____

IL residents add
6.25% sales tax _____

RI residents add
7% sales tax _____

TX residents add
8.25% sales tax _____

Shipping _____

Total _____

Please send this order form to:
IDG Books Worldwide
7260 Shadeland Station, Suite 100
Indianapolis, IN 46256

Allow up to 3 weeks for delivery.
Thank you!

IDG BOOKS WORLDWIDE REGISTRATION CARD

RETURN THIS REGISTRATION CARD FOR FREE CATALOG

Title of this book: Foundations of Delphi Development for Windows 95

My overall rating of this book: ☐ Very good [1] ☐ Good [2] ☐ Satisfactory [3] ☐ Fair [4] ☐ Poor [5]

How I first heard about this book:

☐ Found in bookstore; name: [6]

☐ Advertisement: [8]

☐ Word of mouth; heard about book from friend, co-worker, etc.: [10]

☐ Book review: [7]

☐ Catalog: [9]

☐ Other: [11]

What I liked most about this book:

What I would change, add, delete, etc., in future editions of this book:

Other comments:

Number of computer books I purchase in a year: ☐ 1 [12] ☐ 2-5 [13] ☐ 6-10 [14] ☐ More than 10 [15]

I would characterize my computer skills as: ☐ Beginner [16] ☐ Intermediate [17] ☐ Advanced [18] ☐ Professional [19]

I use ☐ DOS [20] ☐ Windows [21] ☐ OS/2 [22] ☐ Unix [23] ☐ Macintosh [24] ☐ Other: [25]_____
(please specify)

I would be interested in new books on the following subjects:
(please check all that apply, and use the spaces provided to identify specific software)

☐ Word processing: [26]

☐ Data bases: [28]

☐ File Utilities: [30]

☐ Networking: [32]

☐ Other: [34]

☐ Spreadsheets: [27]

☐ Desktop publishing: [29]

☐ Money management: [31]

☐ Programming languages: [33]

I use a PC at (please check all that apply): ☐ home [35] ☐ work [36] ☐ school [37] ☐ other: [38] _____

The disks I prefer to use are ☐ 5.25 [39] ☐ 3.5 [40] ☐ other: [41]_____

I have a CD ROM: ☐ yes [42] ☐ no [43]

I plan to buy or upgrade computer hardware this year: ☐ yes [44] ☐ no [45]

I plan to buy or upgrade computer software this year: ☐ yes [46] ☐ no [47]

Name: _____ Business title: [48] _____ Type of Business: [49] _____

Address (☐ home [50] ☐ work [51] /Company name: _____)

Street/Suite# _____

City [52] /State [53] /Zipcode [54]: _____ Country [55] _____

☐ **I liked this book!** You may quote me by name in future
IDG Books Worldwide promotional materials.

My daytime phone number is _____

IDG BOOKS

THE WORLD OF
COMPUTER
KNOWLEDGE

 # YES!

Please keep me informed about IDG's World of Computer Knowledge.
Send me the latest IDG Books catalog.

NO POSTAGE
NECESSARY
IF MAILED
IN THE
UNITED STATES

BUSINESS REPLY MAIL
FIRST CLASS MAIL   PERMIT NO. 2605   FOSTER CITY, CALIFORNIA

IDG Books Worldwide
919 E Hillsdale Blvd, STE 400
Foster City, CA 94404-9691